create™

AF861315

Course	Advanced Accounting
Course Number	**ACIS 4114**
	Bowe Hansen
	VIRGINIA TECH
	ACCOUNTING & INFORMATION SYS

create™

http://create.mheducation.com

ISBN-10: 1307012647 ISBN-13: 9781307012644

Contents

Credits

CHAPTER

12 Investments

OVERVIEW

In this chapter, you will learn about various approaches we use to account for investments that companies make in the debt and equity securities of other companies. An investing company always has the option to account for these investments at fair value, with changes in fair values reported in the income statement. However, depending on the nature of a *debt* investment, investors use accounting approaches that either ignore most fair value changes (*held-to-maturity* investments) or that include fair value changes only in other comprehensive income (*available-for-sale* investments) until the debt investment is sold. For an *equity* investment, when an investor owns enough stock to "significantly influence" an investee but does not control it, the investor uses the *equity method* of accounting, which ignores fair value changes but includes a portion of the investee's income in the investor's income. In appendices to this chapter, we discuss other types of investments as well as how to deal with an investment whose value has been "other-than-temporarily impaired."

LEARNING OBJECTIVES

After studying this chapter, you should be able to:

- **LO12-1** Describe the key characteristics of a debt investment and demonstrate how to account for a purchase and for interest revenue. (*p. 644*)
- **LO12-2** Demonstrate how to identify and account for debt investments classified for reporting purposes as held-to-maturity. (*p. 648*)
- **LO12-3** Demonstrate how to identify and account for debt investments classified for reporting purposes as trading securities. (*p. 649*)
- **LO12-4** Demonstrate how to identify and account for debt investments classified for reporting purposes as available-for-sale securities. (*p. 653*)
- **LO12-5** Demonstrate how to identify and account for equity investments classified for reporting purposes as fair value through net income. (*p. 667*)
- **LO12-6** Demonstrate how to identify and account for equity investments accounted for under the equity method. (*p. 672*)
- **LO12-7** Explain the adjustments made in the equity method when the fair value of the net assets underlying an investment exceeds their book value at acquisition. (*pp. 661* and *674*)
- **LO12-8** Explain how electing the fair value option and how impairment recognition affect accounting for investments. (*p. 661* and *679*)
- **LO12-9** Discuss the primary differences between U.S. GAAP and IFRS with respect to investments. (*pp. 660–663, 671, 680,* and *690*)

FINANCIAL REPORTING CASE

A Case of Coke

You are the lone accounting major in your five-member group in your Business Policy class. A part of the case your group is working on is the analysis of the financial statements of The Coca-Cola Company.

The marketing major in the group is confused by the following disclosure note included in Coca-Cola's 2015 annual report:

NOTE 3: INVESTMENTS (in part)

Investments in debt securities that the Company has the positive intent and ability to hold to maturity are carried at amortized cost and classified as held-to-maturity. Investments in debt securities that are not classified as held-to-maturity are carried at fair value and classified as either trading or available-for-sale. Realized and unrealized gains and losses on trading securities and realized gains and losses on available-for-sale securities are included in net income. Unrealized gains and losses, net of deferred taxes, on available-for-sale securities are included in our consolidated balance sheets as a component of AOCI . . .

"So they have held-to-maturity securities, trading securities, and available-for-sale securities. What's the difference? And they say that unrealized gains and losses on available-for-sale securities are reported as part of AOCI. What's that? I don't see these gains and losses in the income statement," he complained. "And what about equity method investments? On the balance sheet they have over $12 *billion* of investments accounted for under the equity method! They made almost $500 million on those investments in 2015. Is that cash they can use?"

QUESTIONS

By the time you finish this chapter, you should be able to respond appropriately to the questions posed in this case. Compare your response to the solution provided at the end of the chapter.

1. Why are held-to-maturity securities treated differently from other investment securities? (*p. 648*)
2. Why are unrealized gains and losses on trading securities reported in the income statement? (*p. 650*)
3. Why are unrealized gains and losses on available-for-sale securities not reported in the income statement, but instead are reported in other comprehensive income, and then shown in accumulated other comprehensive income (AOCI) in the balance sheet? (*p. 655*)
4. Explain why Coke accounts for some of its investments by the equity method and what that means. (*p. 672*)

Corporations raise funds to finance their operations by selling equity securities (common and preferred stock) and debt securities (bonds and notes). These securities, also called financial instruments, are purchased as investments by individual investors, mutual funds, and also by other corporations. In later chapters we discuss equity and debt securities from the perspective of the issuing company. Our focus in this chapter is on the corporations that invest in debt and equity securities issued by other corporations as well as in debt securities issued by governmental units (bonds, Treasury bills, and Treasury bonds).

Most companies invest in financial instruments issued by other companies. For some investors, these investments represent ongoing affiliations with the companies whose securities are acquired. Recent examples of those sorts of investments include Microsoft's acquisition of LinkedIn for over $25 billion and Anheuser-Busch InBev's acquisition of SABMiller for over $100 billion. Some investments, though, are not made to obtain a favorable business relationship with another firm. Instead, companies seek only to earn a return from the dividends or interest the securities pay or from increases in the market prices of the securities—the same reasons that might motivate you to buy stocks, bonds, or other investment securities.

With such diversity in investment objectives, it's not surprising that there is diversity in the approaches used to account for investments. As you'll discover when reading this chapter, investments are accounted for in several different ways, depending on whether the investment is in a debt or equity security, the investor's purpose for holding the investment, and the nature of the investment relationship. In Part A, we discuss accounting for debt investments. In Part B, we discuss accounting for equity investments.

PART A

Accounting for Debt Investments

Example of a Debt Investment

LO12–1

Have you ever bought a CD (Certificate of Deposit) at a bank? If so, you've invested in a debt instrument. Let's say you buy a $500, 2-year, 4% CD. What's happened is that you are lending the bank $500 for 2 years, and the bank is promising to pay you 4% interest each year before returning your $500 after two years. The bank's debt (the $500 borrowed from you) is represented by a debt instrument (the CD), which specifies the maturity date (2 years), the principal (or face amount, $500), and the annual rate of interest (4%).

Companies invest in debt too. Like a CD, a bond or other debt security has a specified date when it matures, and on that maturity date, the *principal* (also called the *face amount*) is paid to investors. In the meantime, interest equal to some *stated interest rate* multiplied by the principal is paid to investors on specified interest dates (usually twice a year). Think of the principal and interest payments of the bond as a stream of cash flows that an investor will receive in the future in exchange for purchasing the bond today. The investor values that stream of future cash flows based on the prevailing *market interest rate* for debt of similar risk and maturity at the time the investor purchases the bond.

For an example of how an investor would determine how much to pay for a bond, see Illustration 12–1.

Illustration 12–1

Example of a Debt Investment: Bonds Purchased at a Discount

Because interest is paid semiannually, the present value calculations use:

a. one-half the stated rate (6%),
b. one-half the market rate (7%), and
c. 6 (= 3 × 2) semiannual periods.

On July 1, 2018, Masterwear Industries issued $700,000 of 12% bonds, dated July 1. Interest of $42,000 is payable semiannually on June 30 and December 31. The bonds mature in three years, on June 30, 2021. The market interest rate for bonds of similar risk and maturity is 14%. The entire bond issue was purchased by United Intergroup, Inc.*

Calculation of the Price of the Bonds		**Present Values**
Interest	$ 42,000 × 4.76654**	= $200,195
Principal (face amount)	$700,000 × 0.66634†	= 466,438
Present value (price) of the bonds		$666,633

*The numbers in this illustration are the same as those in Illustration 14–3 in Chapter 14 (except for some differences in dates between the two chapters). This helps us to better appreciate in Chapter 14 how Masterwear's accounting for its bond liability to United compares to United's accounting for its investment in Masterwear bonds. You can find further explanation of why we calculate the bond price this way in Chapter 14.
**Present value of an ordinary annuity of $1: $n = 6$, $i = 7\%$ (Table 4).
†Present value of $1: $n = 6$, $i = 7\%$ (Table 2).
Note: Present value tables are provided at the end of this textbook. If you need to review the concept of the time value of money, refer to the discussions in Chapter 6.

Illustration 12–1 shows that United will pay Masterwear $666,633 on July 1, 2018. In return, United expects to receive from Masterwear $42,000 every six months for the next three years plus the face amount of $700,000 when the bonds mature on June 30, 2021. Of course, if United sells the bonds to another investor, that investor will receive the remaining payments of interest and principal.

Notice that United paid $666,633 to purchase the $700,000 bonds. Why the difference? To determine the issue price of the bonds, it's important to understand how investors compare the bond's stated rate with the market rate. If the interest rate paid by the bond (the stated rate) is higher than the market rate, investors are willing to purchase the bond for more than its maturity value (so it's sold at a *premium*). If the bond's stated rate is lower than the market rate, then investors are willing to purchase the bond only at an amount less than its maturity value (so it's sold at a *discount*). Masterwear was offering its bonds for 12%, but investors could have obtained bonds of similar risk and maturity at a more favorable, higher rate of 14%. To attract investors, Masterwear had to sell its bonds at a discount.

The Masterwear bonds have the key characteristics of all debt investments. Over the three-year life of the bonds, United has to determine how it will account for four events:

1. Purchasing the debt investment.
2. Receiving interest every six months.
3. Holding the bonds during periods in which the bonds' fair value changes (and thus incurring *unrealized holding gains and losses,* since the bonds have not been sold).
4. Either selling the bonds before maturity or receiving the principal payment at their maturity date.

As we discuss below, companies classify debt investments as one of three types: held-to-maturity, trading, or available-for-sale. Accounting for the first two events—the purchase of a bond and the receipt of interest payments—is handled the same way regardless of how the debt investment is classified. We'll look at those events first. Then we'll look at the second two events, which are accounted for differently depending on how the debt investment is classified.

Recording the Purchase of a Debt Investment

All investment securities are initially recorded at cost.

When debt investments are purchased, they are recorded at cost—that is, the total amount paid for the investment, including any brokerage fees. Referring back to Illustration 12–1, we see that United paid $666,633 to purchase Masterwear's $700,000 bonds. United would record the purchase as:

July 1, 2018		
Investment in bonds (face amount)	700,000	
Discount on bond investment (difference)		33,367
Cash (price paid for the bonds)		666,633

Because United purchased the bonds for an amount that's less than their face amount, it credits *Discount on bond investment* for the difference. Discount on bond investment is a contra-asset to the investment account that serves to reduce the carrying value of the investment to its cost at the date of purchase. If United instead had purchased the bonds for an amount (say, $725,000) that is higher than the face amount of the bond ($700,000), it would instead debit *Premium on bond investment* (for $25,000) to record the investment at its cost at the date of purchase.[1]

Recording Interest Revenue

United will record interest revenue using the effective interest method. Here's how it works.

Masterwear's bonds have a *stated rate* of 12%, payable semiannually. This means that every six months, United will receive exactly $42,000 in cash from Masterwear:

[1]This is called the gross method. An alternative would be to record the cost ($666,633 or $725,000) directly in the investment account, called the net method.

$700,000	×	(12% ÷ 2)	=	**$42,000**
Face amount		Stated rate		Interest received

However, recall that United purchased the $700,000 bonds at a discounted amount of $666,633. Why could United pay less than the $700,000 face value for the bonds (and why was Masterwear willing to sell the bonds for less than $700,000)? At the time United purchased the bonds, the *market rate* of interest for bonds of similar risk was 14%. So, United would only be willing to invest in these bonds if it could earn the 14% it could get elsewhere (not the 12% stated rate). To earn this higher rate, United needed to pay only $666,633. Paying the lower amount means United lowered its investment cost and effectively increased its rate of return to 14% (refer back to Illustration 12–1 to see the details of this calculation). While United will receive $42,000 (6%) in interest from Masterwear in the first six months, it will effectively earn interest revenue of $46,664 (7%) on its investment.

$666,633	×	(14% ÷ 2)	=	$46,664
Outstanding balance		Market rate		Interest revenue

Under the *effective interest method*, interest for a period equals the market rate of interest when the debt was purchased multiplied by the outstanding balance of the debt at the beginning of the period.

The amount by which interest revenue exceeds interest received ($46,664 − $42,000 = $4,664 in the first six months) represents a piece of the cost savings from purchasing the investment at a discount. This piece of the cost savings increases United's investment return from the rate the bond pays (12%) to the higher rate (14%) that investors could have earned on other similar bonds at the time they purchased the bond. In fact, this approach is called the *effective interest method* because interest revenue is based on the effective interest rate that the investment earns over its lifetime.

The journal entry to record the interest received for the first six months as investment revenue is:

December 31, 2018		
Cash (stated rate × face amount)	**42,000**	
Discount on bond investment (difference)	4,664	
Interest revenue (market rate × outstanding balance)		46,664

This entry reduces the discount by $4,664 (from $33,367 to $28,703). Because the discount gets smaller, the "amortized cost" of the investment (equal to $700,000 less discount) gets larger by the same amount (from $666,633 to $671,297).

Illustration 12–2 demonstrates interest revenue being recorded at the effective rate over the life of this investment. As you can see, amortization of the discount gradually increases the amortized cost of the investment, until the investment reaches its face amount of $700,000, which is the amount to be received when the debt matures.

Illustration 12–2

Amortization Schedule—Discount

If a bond is purchased at a discount, less cash is received each period than the effective interest earned by the investor, so the unpaid difference increases the outstanding balance of the investment.

Date	Cash Interest	Effective Interest (Interest Revenue)	Amortization of Discount	Discount Balance	Amortized Cost
	(6% × Face amount)	(7% × Outstanding balance)	(Difference)		(Face amount less discount)
7/1/2018				33,367	666,633
12/31/2018	42,000	0.07(666,633) = 46,664	4,664	28,703	671,297
6/30/2019	42,000	0.07(671,297) = 46,991	4,991	23,712	676,288
12/31/2019	42,000	0.07(676,288) = 47,340	5,340	18,372	681,628
6/30/2020	42,000	0.07(681,628) = 47,714	5,714	12,658	687,342
12/31/2020	42,000	0.07(687,342) = 48,114	6,114	6,544	693,456
6/30/2021	42,000	0.07(693,456) = 48,544*	6,544	0	700,000
	252,000	285,367	33,367		

*Rounded

If the bonds were instead purchased at a premium, a similar amortization schedule would *reduce* the premium over time until the bond's amortized cost reached the face amount of $700,000, which is the amount to be received when the debt matures.

Three Classifications of Debt Investments

The amortization schedule shown in Illustration 12–2 is based on the market interest rate (14%) that prevailed at the time United purchased the Masterwear bonds. United will use that amortization schedule for the life of the investment, and *won't change it* in response to changes in prevailing interest rates. However, the prevailing market rate may not always be 14%. The fair value of the bonds will change with changes in the prevailing market interest rate, because market participants will use the prevailing rate to compute the present value of the cash flows provided by the bond. United will incur unrealized holding gains and losses as a result of holding the bond during periods in which its fair value changes.

If the market rate of interest *rises* after a bond is purchased, the market will compute the present value of the cash flows provided by the bond using that higher discount rate, so the fair value of the bond falls. In that case, the person holding the bond suffers an *unrealized holding loss.* The fair value of the bond has decreased, but that loss hasn't been realized, because the investment has not been sold.

The fair value of a fixed-rate investment moves in the opposite direction of market interest rates.

Conversely, if the market rate of interest *falls* after a bond is purchased, the market will calculate the present value of the cash flows provided by the bond using that lower rate, so the fair value of the bond rises. In that case, the investor holding the bond enjoys an *unrealized holding gain.* The fair value of the bond has increased but that gain hasn't yet been realized, because the investment hasn't been sold.

Changes in fair value give rise to unrealized holding gains and losses.

Accounting for changes in fair value depends on the classification of the debt investment. As shown in Illustration 12–3, debt investments are classified in one of three categories: held-to-maturity (HTM) securities, trading securities (TS), or available-for-sale (AFS) securities.

Illustration 12–3
Accounting for Unrealized Holding Gains and Losses on Debt Investments

Reporting Approach	Treatment of Unrealized Holding Gains and Losses	Carried in Balance Sheet at
Held-to-maturity (HTM): used for debt for which the investor has the "positive intent and ability" to hold to maturity.	Not recognized*	Amortized Cost
Trading (TS): used for debt that is held in an active trading account for immediate resale.	Recognized in net income, and therefore in retained earnings as part of shareholders' equity.	Fair Value
Available-for-sale (AFS): used for debt that does not qualify as held-to-maturity or trading.	Recognized in other comprehensive income, and therefore in accumulated other comprehensive income in shareholders' equity*.	Fair Value

*If the investor elects the *fair value option (FVO),* this type of investment also can be accounted for using the same approach that's used for trading securities, with the investment reported at fair value and unrealized holding gains and losses included in net income.

Illustration 12–4 provides a description from a recent annual report of how the Bank of America accounts for its debt investments in each of the three reporting categories.

Illustration 12–4
Disclosure about Investments—Bank of America

Real World Financials

Note 1 (in part): Securities

Debt securities which management has the intent and ability to hold to maturity are classified as held-to-maturity (HTM) and reported at amortized cost. Debt securities that are bought and held principally for the purpose of resale in the near term are classified as trading and are carried at fair value with unrealized gains and losses included in trading account profits (losses). Other debt securities are classified as AFS and carried at fair value with net unrealized gains and losses included in accumulated OCI on an after-tax basis.

FINANCIAL Reporting Case

Q1, p. 643

Why treat unrealized holding gains and losses differently depending on the type of investment? As you know, the primary purpose of accounting is to provide information useful for making decisions. What's most relevant for that purpose is not necessarily the same for each investment a company might make. For example, a company might invest in corporate bonds to provide a steady return until the bonds mature, in which case day-to-day changes in fair value may not be viewed as very relevant, so the held-to-maturity approach is preferable. On the other hand, a company might invest in the same bonds because it plans to sell them at a profit in the near future, in which case the day-to-day changes in fair value could be viewed as very relevant, and the trading security or available-for-sale approach is preferable.

We'll discuss each reporting approach in turn, including how that approach accounts for unrealized holding gains and losses.

Debt Investments to Be Held to Maturity (HTM)

Unrealized Holding Gains and Losses Are Not Recognized for HTM Investments

Held to maturity (HTM) investments require the "positive intent and ability" to hold the investments to maturity.

LO12–2

Unrealized holding gains and losses are less important if sale before maturity isn't an alternative, because those gains and losses will never be realized by sale. For this reason, if an investor has the "positive intent and ability" to hold the securities to maturity, investments in debt securities typically are classified as held-to-maturity (HTM) and reported at their *amortized cost* in the balance sheet.[2] A debt security cannot be classified as held-to-maturity if the investor might sell it before maturity in response to changes in market prices or interest rates, to meet the investor's liquidity needs, or similar factors.

Held to maturity (HTM) investments are reported at amortized cost in the balance sheet.

To consider accounting for unrealized gains and losses, suppose that on December 31, 2018, the market interest rate for securities similar to the Masterwear bonds has fallen to 11%. An investor valuing the Masterwear bonds at that time would do so considering the current market interest rate (11%) because that's the rate of return available for similar bonds. Calculating the present value of the bonds using a lower discount rate results in a higher present value (price).

Let's say that checking market prices in *The Wall Street Journal* indicates that the fair value of the Masterwear bonds on December 31, 2018, is $714,943. As shown in Illustration 12–2, those same bonds have an amortized cost of $671,297. This means there is an unrealized gain of $43,646 for the difference. How will United account for this increase in the fair value of its debt investment? If United views the bonds as HTM investments, that change in fair value will be *ignored* so long as it is viewed as temporary.[3] The investment simply will be shown in the balance sheet at amortized cost of $671,297. United will *disclose* the fair value of its HTM investments in a note to the financial statements, but will not recognize any fair value changes in the income statement or balance sheet.[4]

Sale of HTM Investments

Typically, held-to-maturity investments are—you guessed it—held to maturity. However, suppose that due to unforeseen circumstances the company decided to sell its debt investment for $725,000 on January 5, 2019.[5] United would record the sale as follows (for simplicity we ignore interest earned during the first five days of 2019):[6]

[2]FASB ASC 320–10–25–1: Investments–Debt Securities–Overall–Recognition (previously "Accounting for Certain Investments in Debt and Equity Securities," *Statement of Financial Accounting Standards No. 115* (Norwalk, Conn.: FASB, 1993)).

[3]If an unrealized loss from holding an HTM investment is not viewed as temporary, an "other-than-temporary impairment" (OTT impairment) may have to be recorded. We discuss OTT impairments in more detail in Appendix 12B.

[4]If United had chosen the fair value option for this investment, it would classify the investment as a trading security rather than as an HTM security. We'll illustrate the fair value option when we discuss trading securities.

[5]GAAP [FASB ASC 320–10–25–6: Investments–Debt Securities–Overall–Recognition, previously *Statement of Financial Accounting Standards No. 115*] lists major unforeseen events that could justify sale of an HTM investment. Sale for other reasons could call into question whether the company actually had the intent and ability to hold the investment to maturity. In that case, the company's HTM classification is viewed as "tainted," and the company can be required to reclassify *all* of its HTM investments as AFS investments and avoid using the HTM classification for two years. Similar provisions exist under IFRS for public companies.

[6]For purposes of this example, we ignore any interest accrued for the first five days of 2019. In practice, United would accrue five days of interest revenue and record five days of amortization of the discount, which would produce a revised amortized cost of the bonds that would be used to calculate any gain or loss on sale.

January 5, 2019		
Cash	725,000	
Discount on bond investment (account balance)	28,703	
Investment in Masterwear bonds (account balance)		700,000
Gain on sale of investments (to balance)		53,703

In other words, United would record this sale just like any other asset sale, with a realized gain or loss determined by comparing the cash received with the carrying value (in this case, the amortized cost) of the asset sold.

Additional Consideration

Recall from Chapter 1 that GAAP identifies different ways a firm can determine fair value. If the Masterwear bonds are publicly traded, United can find the fair value by looking up the current market price (this way of obtaining fair value is consistent with "level 1" of the fair value hierarchy). On the other hand, if the bonds are not publicly traded, United can calculate the fair value by using the present value techniques shown in Illustration 12–1 (this way of obtaining fair value is consistent with "level 2" of the fair value hierarchy). With five interest periods remaining, and a current market rate of 11% (5.5% semiannually), the present value would be $714,943.

			Present Values
Interest	$ 42,000 × 4.27028*	=	$179,352
Principal	$700,000 × 0.76513†	=	535,591
Present value of the bonds			$714,943

*Present value of an ordinary annuity of $1: $n = 5$, $i = 5.5\%$. (Table 4)
†Present value of $1: $n = 5$, $i = 5.5\%$. (Table 2)

Using Excel, enter:
=PV(.055,5, −42000, −700000)
Output: 714,946

Using a calculator:
enter: N 5 I 5.5 PMT −42000 FM −700000
Output: = PV 714,946

Financial Statement Presentation

HTM securities appear in the financial statements as follows:

- **Income Statement and Statement of Comprehensive Income:** *Realized* gains and losses are shown in net income in the period in which securities are sold. *Unrealized* holding gains and losses are disclosed in the notes to financial statements. Investments in HTM securities do not affect other comprehensive income.
- **Balance Sheet:** Investments in HTM securities are reported at amortized cost. Fair values of those investments are disclosed in the notes to financial statements.
- **Cash Flow Statement:** Cash flows from buying and selling HTM securities typically are classified as investing activities.

Assuming United sold its investment on January 5, 2019, United's 2018 and 2019 financial statements will include the amounts shown in Illustration 12–5.

Debt Investments Classified as Trading Securities

Some companies—primarily financial institutions—actively and frequently buy and sell securities, expecting to earn profits on short-term price fluctuations. Investments in debt acquired principally for the purpose of selling them in the near term are classified as **trading securities**. The holding period for trading securities generally is measured in hours and days rather than months or years. These investments typically are reported among the investor's current assets. Usually only banks and other financial operations invest in securities in the manner and for the purpose necessary to be categorized as trading securities.

Trading securities are actively managed in a trading account for the purpose of profiting from short-term price changes.

LO12–3

Just like HTM investments, trading securities are recorded at cost when they are purchased, and any discount or premium is amortized to interest revenue over time as periodic

Illustration 12–5
Reporting Held-to-Maturity Investments

(Ignoring income taxes)	2018	2019
Statement of Comprehensive Income		
Revenues	$ ◆	$ ◆
Expenses	◆	◆
Other income (expense):		
Interest revenue	46,664	–0–
Realized gain on sale of investments	–0–	53,703
Net income	46,664	53,703
Other comprehensive income (OCI)	–0–	–0–
Comprehensive income (Net income + OCI)	46,664	53,703
Balance Sheet		
Assets:		
HTM investments	671,297	–0–
Shareholders' equity:		
Retained Earnings	46,664	100,367*
Statement of Cash Flows (direct method)		
Operating Activities:		
Cash from interest received	42,000	–0–
Investing Activities:		
Purchase of HTM securities	(666,633)	–0–
Sale of HTM securities	–0–	725,000

*Net income of $46,664 (2018) + $53,703 (2019) = $100,367 accumulates in retained earnings by the end of 2019.

Only *realized* gains and losses are included in net income.

HTM securities are reported at amortized cost.

Cash flows from buying and selling HTM securities are classified as investing activities.

interest payments are received. However, in subsequent periods, there are two important differences between trading securities and HTM investments.

1. Trading securities are written up or down to their fair value, or "marked to market", in the balance sheet. (HTM securities are kept at amortized cost.)
2. Corresponding unrealized holding gains and losses on trading securities are included in net income in the income statement. (HTM securities do not include unrealized holdings gains and losses in net income.)

FINANCIAL Reporting Case

Q2, p. 643

Be sure to notice that reporting trading securities at their fair value is a departure from amortized cost, which is the way many assets are reported in the balance sheet. Why the difference? For trading securities, fair value information is more relevant than for other assets intended primarily to be used in company operations, like buildings, land and equipment, or for debt investments intended to be held to maturity. Changes in fair values provide an indication of management's success in deciding when to acquire the investment, when to sell it, whether to invest in fixed-rate or variable-rate securities, and whether to invest in long-term or short-term securities. For that reason, it makes sense to report unrealized holding gains and losses on trading securities in net income during a period that fair values change, even though those gains and losses haven't yet been realized through the sale of the securities.

To see how we account for trading securities, let's return to our Masterwear bond example, but assume that those debt investments are held in an active trading portfolio. As of December 31, 2018, United has recorded the purchase of the bonds as well as receipt of the first semiannual interest payment, so the bonds have an amortized cost of $671,297 (refer back to Illustration 12–2).

Adjust Trading Security Investments to Fair Value (2018)

Trading securities are adjusted to their fair value in each reporting period.

Unlike HTM securities, trading securities are carried at fair value in the balance sheet, so their carrying value must be adjusted to fair value by the end of every reporting period. In fact, many companies adjust trading securities to fair value at the end of every day. Rather than increasing or decreasing the investment account itself, we use a valuation allowance, *fair value adjustment,* to increase or decrease the carrying value of the investment. At the same time, we record an unrealized holding gain or loss that is included in net income in the period in which fair value changes (remember, the gain or loss is *unrealized* because the securities haven't been sold).

Assuming the Masterwear bonds have a fair value of $714,943 as of December 31, 2018, the next table shows the calculation of the balance in the fair value adjustment account that is required on that date.

December 31, 2018

Security	**Amortized Cost**	**Fair Value**	**Necessary Fair Value Adjustment Balance**
Masterwear	$671,297	$714,943	$43,646

The bonds need to be reported at their fair value of $714,943. Because the bonds currently are recorded at their amortized cost of $671,297, the fair value adjustment account needs a debit balance of $43,646. United will recognize whatever unrealized holding gain or loss is necessary to move the fair value adjustment from its current balance of $0 (at purchase date) to $43,646 (on December 31, 2018). In this case, the calculation is simple:

	Fair Value Adjustment
Beginning balance on 7/1/2018	$ 0
± Adjustment needed to update fair value	?
Balance needed on 12/31/2018	$43,646

Fair Value Adjustment

Debit	Credit
0	
43,646	
43,646	

The journal entry to record the $43,646 change in United's fair value adjustment and the corresponding unrealized holding gain is:

December 31, 2018

	Debit	Credit
Fair value adjustment (calculated above)*	43,646	
Unrealized holding gain on trading securities—NI†		43,646

*Sometimes companies don't bother with a separate fair value adjustment account and simply adjust the investment account to fair value.

†We title this account "Unrealized. . .—NI" to highlight that, for trading securities, unrealized holding gains and losses are included in the income statement in the period in which they occur.

Each period United owns the Masterwear bonds, it will recognize whatever unrealized holding gain or loss is necessary to move the fair value adjustment to the value it needs to have at the end of the accounting period. Increases in the fair value adjustment produce gains on trading securities that increase net income; decreases produce losses that decrease net income.

Unrealized holding gains and losses for trading securities are included in net income in the period in which fair value changes.

Additional Consideration

Accounting for Portfolios

We have focused on accounting for an individual security, but United would use the same approach to account for a *portfolio* of trading securities. For example, assume that United has the following portfolio of trading securities as of December 31, 2018, as shown below:

Security	**Amortized Cost**	**Fair Value**	**Necessary Fair Value Adjustment Balance**
Miley Inc.	$ 800,000	$ 875,000	$ 75,000
Perry Corp.	950,000	790,000	(160,000)
Total	$1,750,000	$1,665,000	$ (85,000)

(continued)

(concluded)

As of December 31, 2019, the portfolio's status is as follows:

Security	Amortized Cost	Fair Value	Necessary Fair Value Adjustment Balance
Miley Inc.	$ 600,000	$575,000	$ (25,000)
Swift Co.	450,000	325,000	(125,000)
Total	$1,050,000	$900,000	$(150,000)

Fair Value Adjustment

Debit	Credit
	85,000
	65,000
	150,000

On December 31, 2019, the balance of the fair value adjustment needs to change from a credit of $85,000 to a credit of $150,000, requiring an additional credit of $65,000 and recognition of a corresponding loss in net income.

To make that happen, United records the following journal entry:

	Debit	Credit
Unrealized holding loss on trading securities—NI	65,000	
Fair value adjustment		65,000

Sale of Trading Security Investments

Now assume that United sells the bonds for $725,000 on January 5, 2019. To account for the sale, United needs to do two things. First, United needs to update the carrying value of the bonds to fair value and record in net income any unrealized holding gains and losses that occurred during 2019 up to the date of sale. Second, on the date of sale, United needs to record the receipt of cash and remove the amounts associated with the investment from the relevant balance sheet accounts. Let's record each of these entries. (As in our example for HTM investments, for simplicity we ignore interest earned during the first five days of 2019.)

For trading securities, unrealized holding gains and losses from fair value changes are recorded up to the date an investment is sold.

1. Adjust Trading Securities to Fair Value (2019). We first need to update the fair value adjustment and recognize any unrealized holding gains or losses that have occurred during the current reporting period prior to the date of sale. We already have accounted for fair value changes that occurred during 2018. Now we need to record the additional fair value changes and their related unrealized holding gains and losses that have occurred each day in 2019 up to the moment of sale. Companies might record these changes in fair value at the end of each day, but we use a single summary entry that captures those changes in fair value up to the moment of sale.

Remember that on December 31, 2018, the amortized cost of the Masterwear bonds was $671,297, and the fair value was $714,943. We recorded a fair value adjustment of $43,646 for this unrealized holding gain. Now, on January 5, 2019, the fair value has increased further to $725,000, so we need to update the fair value adjustment for the additional $10,057 increase in fair value.

December 31, 2018

Security	Amortized Cost	Fair Value	Necessary Fair Value Adjustment Balance
Masterwear	$671,297	$725,000	$53,703

Fair Value Adjustment

Debit	Credit
43,646	
10,057	
53,703	

	Fair Value Adjustment
Beginning balance on 12/31/2018	$43,646
± Adjustment needed to update fair value	?
Balance needed as of date of sale	$53,703

United needs to record an increase in the fair value adjustment and an additional unrealized holding gain of $10,057 that occurred during the first week of 2019. The journal entry is:

January 5, 2019

	Debit	Credit
Fair value adjustment	10,057	
Unrealized holding gain on trading securities—NI (to balance)		10,057

2. Record the Sale Transaction. After making the previous journal entry, the investment is carried at its fair value as of the date it is being sold, and already has included in net income any gain or loss arising from the difference between amortized cost and fair value as of the date of sale. All that remains is for United to record receipt of cash and remove the investment-related accounts from the balance sheet (again, for simplicity we ignore interest earned during the first five days of 2019).

When a trading security is sold, all of the gain or loss already has been included in net income, so no additional gain or loss is recognized.

January 5, 2019		
Cash	725,000	
Discount on bond investment (account balance)	28,703	
Investment in Masterwear bonds (account balance)		700,000
Fair value adjustment (account balance)		53,703

As with the sale of the HTM investment, we record the receipt of $725,000 cash and remove all the balance sheet accounts associated with the investment. However, unlike the HTM investment, our TS investment has an additional balance sheet account, the fair value adjustment, that needs to be removed when we record the sale. Another difference between the HTM and TS approach is that, because we carry trading securities at fair value as of the the date of sale and already have included in net income the entire gain associated with changes in the fair value of the investment, there is no gain or loss to recognize on the date of sale.[7] However, over the life of the investments, United recognized the same amount of gain under the TS approach ($43,646 + 10,057 = $53,703) as it recognized upon sale under the HTM approach ($53,703). The only difference is timing, with trading securities recognizing unrealized holding gains and losses from fair value changes as they occur but the HTM approach recognizing gains or losses only when they are realized upon sale.

Financial Statement Presentation

Trading securities appear in the financial statements as follows:

- **Income Statement and Statement of Comprehensive Income:** For trading securities, gains and losses are included in the income statement in the periods in which fair value changes, *regardless of whether they are realized or unrealized.* Investments in trading securities do not affect other comprehensive income.
- **Balance Sheet:** Investments in trading securities are reported at fair value, typically as current assets.
- **Cash Flow Statement:** Cash flows from buying and selling trading securities typically are classified as operating activities, because the financial institutions that routinely hold trading securities consider them as part of their normal operations.

Assuming United sold its investment on January 5, 2019, United's 2018 and 2019 financial statements will include the amounts shown in Illustration 12–6.

Debt Investments Classified as Available-for-Sale Securities

LO12–4

The HTM treatment assumes we hold the bonds for their entire life. The trading securities treatment assumes we are planning to sell the bonds in the very near future. Our third treatment, available-for-sale (AFS) securities, falls in the middle. We aren't planning to trade

AFS investments aren't held for trading or designated as held to maturity.

[7]As noted in FASB ASC 320-10-40: Investments–Debt Securities–Overall–Derecognition, for expediency companies may not update the fair value adjustment to the fair value as of the date of sale before recording the sale. In that case, the investment is carried at fair value as of the last balance sheet date, and this second entry would include a gain or loss based on the difference between the cash received and the carrying value of the investment. In our example, the fair value adjustment balance was $43,646 on December 31, 2018, and United would record the following sale entry on January 5, 2019:

Cash	725,000	
Discount on bond investment (account balance)	28,703	
Investment in Masterwear bonds (account balance)		700,000
Fair value adjustment (account balance)		43,646
Gain on trading securities - NI (to balance)		10,057

Illustration 12–6
Reporting Trading Securities

For trading securities, fair value changes affect net income in the period in which they occur.

Trading securities are reported at fair value in the balance sheet.

Cash flows from buying and selling trading securities are classified as operating activities.

(Ignoring income taxes) **Statement of Comprehensive Income**	**2018**	**2019**
Revenues	$ ◆	$ ◆
Expenses	◆	◆
Other income (expense):		
Interest revenue	46,664	–0–
Gains and losses on trading securities	43,646	10,057
Net income	90,310	10,057
Other comprehensive income (OCI)	–0–	–0–
Comprehensive income (Net income + OCI)	$ 90,310	$ 10,057
Balance Sheet		
Assets:		
Trading securities	714,943	–0–
Shareholders' equity:		
Retained Earnings	90,310	100,367*
Statement of Cash Flows (direct method)		
Operating Activities:		
Cash from interest received	42,000	–0–
Purchase of trading securities	(666,633)	–0–
Sale of trading securities	–0–	725,000

*Net income of $90,310 (2018) + $10,057 (2019) = $100,367 accumulates in retained earnings by the end of 2019.

AFS investments are reported at their fair values.

the debt investment actively, but the investment is available to sell if, for example, cash needs arise or the market is particularly favorable. In that case, the company classifies its debt investment as AFS. Like trading securities, we report AFS securities in the balance sheet at fair value. Unlike trading securities, though, unrealized holding gains and losses on AFS securities are *not* included in net income. Instead, they are reported in the statement of comprehensive income as other comprehensive income (OCI).

Additional Consideration

Don't Shoot the Messenger. Or, as written in *The Economist*, "Messenger, Shot: Accounting rules are under attack. Standard-setters should defend them. Politicians and banks should back off."[8] Using fair values that are hard to estimate is controversial. For example, during the financial crisis of 2008/2009 many financial-services companies had to recognize huge unrealized losses associated with their investments. Some blamed their losses on GAAP for requiring estimates of fair value that were driven by depressed current market prices, argued that those losses worsened the financial crisis, and lobbied for a move away from fair-value accounting. Others countered that these companies were using GAAP's requirement for fair value accounting as a "scapegoat" for their bad investment decisions. "Fair value accounting . . . does not create losses but rather reflects a firm's present condition," says Georgene Palacky, director of the CFA's financial reporting group."[9]

Comprehensive Income

Recall from Chapter 4 that comprehensive income is a more all-encompassing view of operations than net income. It includes not only net income but also all other changes in equity that do not arise from transactions with owners.[10] Comprehensive income therefore includes net

[8]Transactions with owners primarily include dividends and the sale or purchase of shares of the company's stock.
[9]"Messenger, Shot," *The Economist*, April 8, 2009.
[10]Sarah Johnson, "The Fair Value Blame Game," CFO.com, March 19, 2008.

income as well as *other comprehensive income (OCI).* You know that net income is closed to retained earnings at the end of each accounting period, and therefore accumulates in retained earnings over time in the shareholders' equity section of the balance sheet. Similarly, OCI is closed to *accumulated other comprehensive income (AOCI)* at the end of each accounting period, and therefore accumulates in AOCI in the shareholders' equity section of the balance sheet. OCI relates to AOCI the same way that net income relates to retained earnings.

Rationale for AFS Treatment of Unrealized Holding Gains and Losses

Why use an approach for accounting for AFS securities that differs from that used for trading securities? Because AFS securities are likely to be held for multiple reporting periods, one could argue that there is sufficient time for unrealized holding gains in some periods to balance out with unrealized holding losses in other periods, so including unrealized holding gains and losses in income each period would confuse investors by making income appear more volatile than it really is over the long run.[11] But how can we show AFS investments at fair value in the balance sheet without recording in net income the unrealized gains and losses associated with changes in fair value? The solution is to show those unrealized gains and losses in OCI as they occur and then only include realized gains and losses in net income in the period in which an investment is actually sold.

FINANCIAL Reporting Case

Q3, p. 643

Adjust AFS Investments to Fair Value (2018)

To see how we adjust AFS investments to their fair value, let's assume the Masterwear bond investment is classified as AFS. As of December 31, 2018, United has recorded the purchase of the bonds on July 1, 2018, as well as receipt of the first semiannual interest payment, so the bonds have an amortized cost of $671,297 (refer back to Illustration 12–2). The fair value of the bonds on December 31, 2018, is $714,943. The next table shows the calculation of the balance in the fair value adjustment account that is required on that date.

December 31, 2018

Security	Amortized Cost	Fair Value	Necessary Fair Value Adjustment Balance
Masterwear	$671,297	$714,943	$43,646

United needs to adjust the balance of the fair value adjustment account from its current balance of $0 (at purchase date) to a debit balance of $43,646 (on December 31, 2018).

	Fair Value Adjustment
Beginning balance on 7/1/2018	$ 0
± Adjustment needed to update fair value	?
Balance needed on 12/31/2018	$43,646

Fair Value Adjustment

Debit	Credit
0	
43,646	
43,646	

The journal entry to record the $43,646 change in United's fair value adjustment and the corresponding unrealized holding gain is:

December 31, 2018		
Fair value adjustment*..	43,646	
Unrealized holding gain on AFS investments—OCI†........................		43,646

*Sometimes companies don't bother with a separate fair value adjustment account and simply adjust the investment account to fair value.
†We title this account "Unrealized . . .—OCI" to highlight that, for available-for-sale securities, unrealized holding gains and losses are included in other comprehensive income (OCI) in the period in which they occur.

For AFS securities, unrealized holding gains and losses from fair value changes are not included in net income, but instead are reported as OCI.

Notice that the amount of unrealized holding gain is the same for these AFS securities as it was for the trading securities in the previous section. What differs is that the

[11] Of course, one could counter-argue that these unrealized holding gains and losses still are relevant, given that each period an investor has discretion over whether or not to continue holding the security or sell that security to realize a gain or loss. For that reason, many accountants would prefer that the FASB do away with the AFS approach and just treat these investments as trading securities.

unrealized holding gain is included in OCI for AFS securities instead of net income as it is for trading securities. At the end of the reporting period, the unrealized holding gain is closed to a shareholders' equity account for both approaches. What differs is that net income gets closed to retained earnings, and OCI gets closed to Accumulated Other Comprehensive Income (AOCI). As with trading securities, the fair value adjustment will be adjusted up or down each period, either for individual securities or for a portfolio of securities, and a corresponding unrealized holding gain or loss reported in OCI. Net income normally is not affected by AFS investments until the period an AFS investment is sold, as we'll discuss next.

Sale of AFS Investments

Let's once again assume that United sells its Masterwear bonds for $725,000 on January 5, 2019 (as with our HTM and TS examples, for simplicity we ignore any interest earned during 2019). For AFS securities, United needs to record three journal entries.[12]

For AFS investments, unrealized holding gains and losses from fair value changes are recorded up to the date an investment is sold.

1. **Adjust AFS Investments to Fair Value (2019).** As with trading securities, we first need to update the fair value adjustment and recognize any unrealized holding gains or losses that have occurred during the current reporting period prior to the date of sale. Remember that on December 31, 2018, the amortized cost of the Masterwear bonds was $671,297, and the fair value was $714,943. We recorded a fair value adjustment of $43,646 for this unrealized holding gain. Now, on January 5, 2019, the fair value has increased further to $725,000, so we need to update the fair value adjustment for the additional $10,057 increase in fair value.

January 5, 2019

Security	Amortized Cost	Fair Value	Necessary Fair Value Adjustment Balance
Masterwear	$671,297	$725,000	$53,703

Fair Value Adjustment

Debit	Credit
43,646	
10,057	
53,703	

	Fair Value Adjustment
Balance as of 12/31/2018	$43,646
± Adjustment needed to update fair value	?
Balance needed as of date of sale	$53,703

United needs to record an increase in the fair value adjustment and an additional unrealized holding gain of $10,057 that occurred during the first week of 2019. The journal entry to record the gain is:

January 5, 2019		
Fair value adjustment	10,057	
Unrealized holding gain on AFS investments—OCI		10,057

At this point, the investment is carried in the balance sheet at its fair value as of the date it is being sold, and all unrealized gains and losses associated with the investment have been included in OCI. Because OCI gets closed to AOCI, the unrealized gains and losses accumulate in AOCI, which acts as a sort of "holding tank" in the shareholders' equity section of the balance sheet. Unrealized holding gains in some years offset unrealized losses in other years as they accumulate in the tank.

When an AFS investment is sold, accumulated unrealized gains and losses are removed from AOCI using a reclassification entry.

2. **Reverse Previous Fair Value Adjustments.** United has been recording changes in fair value over the life of the investment. If United now sells that investment, the effects of those fair value changes must be reversed. United reverses previous unrealized holding gains included in OCI by debiting a reclassification adjustment to OCI for the same amount. Similarly, the account balance of the fair value adjustment is eliminated.

[12]This description of accounting for sales of AFS investments is adapted from the example of journal entries and financial statement presentation shown by FASB ASC 220-10-55 (para. 24-27): Comprehensive Income—Overall—Implementation Guidance and Illustrations—Case B: Available-for-Sale Debt Securities. The three journal entries we describe could be combined into one or two entries in practice.

January 5, 2019		
Reclassification adjustment—OCI	53,703	
Fair value adjustment (account balance)		53,703

Fair Value Adjustment

43,646	53,703
10,057	
0	

After this journal entry is recorded, the fair value adjustment account has a zero balance. Also, after the reclassification adjustment is closed to AOCI, all of the unrealized gains that are associated with the investment have been removed from the AOCI holding tank in shareholders' equity.[13] It's as if no accounting for unrealized gains and losses had ever taken place.[14] That's important, because in the next entry United recognizes in net income a gain or loss on sale . If United didn't use the reclassification entry to back out the unrealized gains and losses from AOCI, it would end up having double counted them in comprehensive income and shareholders equity after it records the sale in the next entry.

AOCI (after closing)

53,703	43,646
	10,057
	0

3. **Record the Sale Transaction.** Now that all of the unrealized holding gains and losses and the fair value adjustment have been cleared away, the final step is to "plug" for the realized gain or loss (a gain in this case).

January 5, 2019		
Cash	725,000	
Discount on bond investment (account balance)	28,703	
Investment in Masterwear bonds (account balance)		700,000
Gain on AFS investments—NI (to balance)		53,703

This entry is identical to the entry United made to record sale of the investment under the HTM approach. As with the HTM investments, no gain or loss is recognized in net income over the life of the investment. Instead, the entire gain or loss is recognized in net income at the time of the sale. So, with this entry and the one preceding it, United has reclassified its $53,703 gain from OCI to net income. That's why the process is called reclassification.

When an AFS investment is sold, realized gains and losses are included in net income.

Additional Consideration

More About Reclassification

Look back through the three entries that are shown for recording a sale of an AFS investment. Think about what has happened. First, United recorded unrealized holding gains in OCI each period as fair value changed over time, and at the end of each period it closed OCI to AOCI in shareholders' equity. Then, once the investment was sold, United backed those unrealized gains out of OCI (and thus out of AOCI) and included them in net income (which is closed to retained earnings in shareholders' equity). From the perspective of shareholders' equity, the unrealized gains were first accumulated in AOCI and then were reclassified from AOCI to retained earnings in the period of sale.

We can rearrange the second and third journal entries to highlight this reclassification process:

Reclassification adjustment—OCI	**53,703**	
Gain on AFS investments—NI (to balance)		**53,703**
Cash	725,000	
Discount on bond investment (account balance)	28,703	
Investment in Masterwear bonds (account balance)		700,000
Fair value adjustment (account balance)		53,703

Once the investment is sold, all the balance sheet accounts are removed and the unrealized holding gains and losses that have been accumulating in AOCI are transferred out of AOCI (via the reclassification entry) and included in net income.

[13]As noted in FASB ASC 320-10-40: Investments—Debt Securities—Overall—Derecognition, for expediency companies might not update the fair value adjustment to fair value before recording the sale. In that case, this second entry would be based on the fair value adjustment as of the last balance sheet date. In our example, the fair value adjustment balance would be $43,646, so that is the amount by which it would be reduced and that is the amount of reclassification adjustment that would be recorded in OCI.

[14]Companies may choose to make this journal entry at the end of the reporting period when they update their fair value adjustment. The order doesn't matter, so long as the journal entry is recorded in the correct reporting period.

It may seem odd that we bother to put all of the unrealized holding gains and losses into OCI and then take them out again, but that approach makes it very clear when gains and losses are moving in and out of AOCI and getting recognized in net income. Here's what happens in the financial statements.

Financial Statement Presentation

AFS securities appear in the financial statements as follows:

- **Income Statement and Statement of Comprehensive Income:** Gains and losses are shown in OCI in the periods in which changes in fair value occur. Those amounts are reclassified out of OCI and recognized in net income in the periods in which securities are sold.
- **Balance Sheet:** Investments in AFS securities are reported at fair value. *Unrealized* holding gains and losses become part of AOCI in shareholders' equity, and are reclassified out of AOCI in the periods in which securities are sold.
- **Cash Flow Statement:** Cash flows from buying and selling AFS securities typically are classified as investing activities.

Assuming United sold its investment on January 5, 2019, United's 2018 and 2019 financial statements will include the amounts shown in Illustration 12–7.

Illustration 12–7
Reporting Available-for-Sale Securities

Only *realized* gains and losses are included in net income.

Other comprehensive income includes *unrealized* holding gains and losses *that occur during the reporting period.*

AFS securities are reported at fair value.

AOCI (in shareholders' equity) includes net unrealized holding gains or losses *accumulated over the current and prior periods.*

Cash flows from buying and selling AFS securities usually are classified as investing activities.

(Ignoring income taxes) **Statement of Comprehensive Income**	**2018**	**2019**
Revenues	$ ♦	$ ♦
Expenses	♦	♦
Other income (expense):		
Interest revenue	46,664	–0–
Realized gain on sale of investments	–0–	53,703
Net income	46,664	53,703
Other comprehensive income (loss) items (OCI):*		
Unrealized holding gains (losses) on investments	43,646	10,057
Reclassification adjustment for net gains and losses included in net income	–0–	(53,703)
Total OCI	43,646	(43,646)
Comprehensive income (Net income + OCI)	$ 90,310	$ 10,057
Balance Sheet		
Assets:		
Available-for-sale securities	$714,943	$ –0–
Shareholders' equity:		
Accumulated other comprehensive income (AOCI)	43,646	–0–
Retained Earnings	46,664	100,367†
Statement of Cash Flows (direct method)		
Operating activities:		
Cash from interest received	42,000	–0–
Investing activities:		
Purchase of available-for-sale securities	(666,633)	–0–
Sale of available-for-sale securities	–0–	725,000

*As we discuss in more detail in Chapter 18, the statement of comprehensive income can be presented as a continuation of the income statement as shown here, or in a separate statement that immediately follows the income statement.
†Net income of $46,664 (2018) + $53,703 (2019) = $100,367 accumulates in retained earnings by the end of 2019.

Individual securities available for sale are classified as either current or noncurrent assets, depending on how long they're likely to be held. An example from the 2015 annual report of Cisco Systems is shown in Illustration 12–8.

Item 1A: Risk Factors (in part)

We maintain an investment portfolio of various holdings, types, and maturities. These securities are generally classified as available-for-sale and, consequently, are recorded on our Consolidated Balance Sheets at fair value with unrealized gains or losses reported as a component of accumulated other comprehensive income.

Note 8: Investments (in part)

The following tables summarize the Company's available-for-sale investments ($ in millions):

July 25, 2015	Amortized Cost	Gross Unrealized Gains	Gross Unrealized Losses	Fair Value
Fixed income securities:				
U.S. Government	$29,904	$41	$ (6)	$29,939
U.S. Government agency	3,662	2	(1)	3,663
Non-U.S. Gov't agency	1,128	1	(1)	1,128
Corporate debt securities	15,802	34	(53)	15,783
U.S. agency mortgage-backed	1,456	8	(3)	1,461
Total fixed income securities	51,952	86	(64)	51,974

Illustration 12–8

Investments in Securities Available-for-Sale—Cisco Systems

Real World Financials

Comparison of HTM, TS, and AFS Approaches

Illustration 12–9 compares accounting for the Masterwear bonds under the three different approaches.

Illustration 12–9 Comparison of HTM, TS, and AFS Approaches

	Held-to-Maturity (HTM)			Trading (TS)			Available-for-Sale (AFS)		
Purchase bonds at a discount	Investments	700,000		Same as HTM			Same as HTM		
	Discount		33,367						
	Cash		666,633						
Record interest revenue	Cash	42,000		Same as HTM			Same as HTM		
	Discount	4,664							
	Interest rev.		46,664						
Adjust to fair value, 2018	No entry			FV adjustment	43,646		FV adjustment	43,646	
				Holding gain—NI		43,646	Holding gain—OCI		43,646
Sell bonds in 2019									
1. Adjust to fair value, 2019	No entry			FV adjustment	10,057		FV adjustment	10,057	
				Holding gain—NI		10,057	Holding gain—OCI		10,057
2. Reclassify unrealized holding gains/losses	No entry			No entry			Reclassification—OCI	53,703	
							FV adjustment		53,703
3. Record sale of bonds	Cash	725,000		Cash	725,000		Cash	725,000	
	Discount	28,703		Discount	28,703		Discount	28,703	
	Investments		700,000	Investments		700,000	Investments		700,000
	Gain—NI		53,703	FV Adjustment		53,703	Gain—NI		53,703
	Note: Total gain of $53,703 is recognized in net income in the period of the sale.			Note: Total gain of $53,703 is recognized in net income over the periods in which the investment is held (43,646 + 10,057).			Note: Reclassification backs out unrealized gains from OCI (and therefore from AOCI), so total gain of $53,703 is recognized in net income in the period of the sale.		

AOCI

	43,646
	10,057
53,703	
	0

This side-by-side comparison highlights several aspects of these accounting approaches:

- To record the purchase of an investment and the receipt of interest revenue, we use identical entries in all three approaches.
- To record changes in fair value, the entries we use for TS and AFS securities have the same effect on the investment (via the fair value adjustment valuation allowance) and the same eventual effect on total shareholders' equity. What differs is whether the unrealized holding gain or loss is recognized in net income and then in retained earnings (TS) or recognized in OCI and then in AOCI (AFS). No fair value adjustment is reported for HTM securities.
- Regardless of approach, the cash flows are the same, and the same total amount of gain or loss is recognized in the income statement (TS: \$43,646 in 2018 + \$10,057 in 2019 = \$53,703 total; AFS and HTM: \$53,703 in 2019). The question is not *how much* total net income is recognized, but *when* the amounts are recognized in net income.

Additional Consideration

Available-for-Sale Investments and Income Taxes. When comparing accounting for TS and AFS securities, we saw that total shareholders' equity ends up being the same amount, regardless of whether unrealized gains and losses are included in net income and closed to retained earnings in shareholders' equity (for TS) or included only in OCI and shown in AOCI in shareholders' equity (for AFS securities). But what about taxes? Tax expense affects net income, so retained earnings includes after-tax amounts. For AOCI to be equivalent to retained earnings, it also should include only after-tax amounts. Therefore, adjustments must be made to OCI and AOCI to account for tax effects. Typically these adjustments also give rise to deferred tax assets and liabilities, as unrealized holding gains and losses rarely affect the current period's taxes payable. Deferred tax assets and liabilities are discussed in Chapter 16.

International Financial Reporting Standards

Accounting for Debt Investments. Until recently, *IAS No. 39* was the standard that specified appropriate accounting for all investments under IFRS.[15] The primary categories in *IAS No. 39* are similar to those in U.S. GAAP, consisting of Fair Value through Profit & Loss (FVPL), similar to TS, HTM, and AFS.

IFRS No. 9, amended on July 24, 2014, will be required after January 1, 2018, and earlier adoption is permitted, so until 2018 either *IAS No. 39* or *IFRS No. 9* might be in effect for a particular company.[16] *IFRS No. 9* eliminates the HTM and AFS classifications, replaced by new classifications that are more restrictive. Specifically, under *IFRS No. 9,* investments in debt securities are classified either as amortized cost (accounted for like HTM investments in U.S. GAAP), fair value through other comprehensive income ("FVOCI," accounted for like AFS investments, except for different impairment recognition criteria) or fair value through profit or loss ("FVPL," accounted for like trading securities). Classification depends on two criteria: (1) whether the investment's contractual cash flows consist solely of payments of principal and interest (SPPI), and (2) whether the business purpose of the investment is to hold it for purposes of collecting contractual cash flows, sell the investment at a profit, or both. If the investment qualifies as SPPI and is held only to collect cash flows, it is classified as amortized cost. If it qualifies as SPPI and is held both to collect cash flows and potentially be sold, it is classified as FVOCI. Otherwise it is classified as FVPL.

One other difference between U.S. GAAP and IFRS is worth noting. U.S. GAAP allows specialized accounting (beyond the scope of this textbook) for particular industries like securities brokers/dealers, investment companies, and insurance companies. IFRS does not.

[15] "Financial Instruments: Recognition and Measurement," *International Accounting Standard No. 39* (IASCF), as amended effective January 1, 2009.

[16] "Financial Instruments," *International Financial Reporting Standard No. 9* (IASCF), November 12, 2009, as amended effective January 1, 2016.

Transfers between Reporting Categories

At each reporting date, the appropriateness of the classification of a debt investment is reassessed. For instance, if the investor no longer has the ability to hold certain securities to maturity and will now hold them for resale, those securities would be reclassified from HTM to AFS. When a security is reclassified between two reporting categories, the security is transferred at its fair value on the date of transfer. Any unrealized holding gain or loss at reclassification should be accounted for *in a manner consistent with the classification into which the security is being transferred.* A summary is provided in Illustration 12–10.

A transfer of a security between reporting categories is accounted for at fair value and in accordance with *the new reporting classification.*

Illustration 12–10

Transfer between Investment Categories

Transfer from:	To:	Unrealized Gain or Loss from Transfer at Fair Value
Either HTM or AFS	Trading	Include in current net income the total unrealized gain or loss, as if it all occurred in the current period.
Trading	Either HTM or AFS	Include in current net income any unrealized gain or loss that occurred in the current period prior to the transfer. (Unrealized gains and losses that occurred in prior periods already were included in net income in those periods.)
Held-to-maturity	Available-for-sale	No current income effect. Report total unrealized gain or loss as a separate component of shareholders' equity (in AOCI).
Available-for-sale	Held-to-maturity	No current income effect. Don't write off any existing unrealized holding gain or loss in AOCI, but amortize it to net income over the remaining life of the security (fair value amount becomes the security's amortized cost basis).

Reclassifications are quite unusual, so when they occur, disclosure notes should describe the circumstances that resulted in the transfers. Other disclosure notes are described in a later section.

International Financial Reporting Standards

Transfers Between Investment Categories. *IAS No. 39* allows transfers of debt investments out of the FVPL category into AFS or HTM in "rare circumstances." Under *IFRS No. 9*, transfers of debt investments between the amortized cost, FVOCI, and FVPL categories occurs if and only if the company changes its business model with respect to the debt investment.

● LO12–8

Fair Value Option

You may recall from Chapter 1 that GAAP allows a **fair value option** (FVO) that permits companies to elect to account for most financial assets and liabilities at fair value. Under the FVO, HTM and AFS investments are shown in the balance sheet at their fair values, and unrealized gains and losses are recognized in net income in the period in which they occur. That accounting approach should sound familiar—it's the same approach we use to account for trading securities. However, unlike trading securities, purchases and sales of investments accounted for under the FVO are likely to be classified as investing activities in the statement of cash flows, because those investments are not held for sale in the near term and therefore are not operational in nature.

Choosing the *fair value option* for HTM and AFS investments means accounting for them like trading securities.

● LO12–7

The company decides whether to elect the FVO on the date the company purchases the investment. The company can elect the FVO for some securities and not for identical others—it's entirely up to the company, but the company has to explain in the notes why it made a partial election. The election is *irrevocable.* So, for example, if a company elects the FVO and later believes that the fair value of an investment is likely to decline, it can't change the election and discontinue use of fair value accounting to avoid recognizing a loss.

Why allow the FVO? As described in Appendix A of this book, companies sometimes enter into *hedging arrangements* that are intended to reduce earnings volatility by offsetting changes in the fair value of assets with changes in the fair value of liabilities. Complex rules apply to many hedging arrangements. The FVO simplifies this process by allowing companies to choose whether to use fair value for most types of financial assets and liabilities. Thus, when a company enters into a hedging arrangement, it just has to make sure to elect the FVO for each asset and liability in the hedging arrangement, and fair value changes of those assets and liabilities will be included in earnings.

International Financial Reporting Standards

LO12–8

Fair Value Option. International accounting standards are more restrictive than U.S. standards for determining when firms are allowed to elect the FVO. Under both *IAS No. 39* and *IFRS No. 9,* companies can elect the FVO only in specific circumstances. For example, a firm could elect the FVO for an asset or liability in order to avoid the "accounting mismatch" that occurs when some parts of a fair value risk-hedging arrangement are accounted for at fair value and others are not. Although U.S. GAAP indicates that the intent of the FVO is to address these sorts of circumstances, it does not require that those circumstances exist.

Impairment of Debt Investments

An "other-than-temporary" impairment loss is recognized in net income even though the security hasn't been sold.

In this chapter we've seen that declines (as well as increases) in the fair value of some investments are reported in earnings. For instance, if the fair value of an investment in trading securities declines, we reduce the reported amount of that investment in the balance sheet and include the loss from the fair value decline in the income statement. Likewise, if the investor has elected the FVO for HTM or AFS investments, those investments are accounted for as trading securities, so fair value changes always are recognized in earnings. Otherwise, fair value changes for HTM and AFS investments typically are not recognized in earnings.

However, there is an exception. If the fair value of an HTM or AFS investment declines below the amortized cost of the investment, and that decline is deemed to be *other-than-temporary (OTT),* the company recognizes an OTT impairment loss in earnings. Accounting for OTT impairments is complicated, both with respect to determining whether an impairment is OTT and in determining the amount of the impairment to include in earnings. After an OTT impairment is recognized, the ordinary treatment of unrealized gains and losses is resumed; that is, further changes in fair value are reported in OCI for AFS investments and not recognized for HTM investments.

CURRENT EXPECTED CREDIT LOSS (CECL) MODEL FOR DEBT INVESTMENTS. Guidance in this area is changing. Starting in 2020, companies will be required to use the CECL ("Current Expected Credit Loss") model to account for impairments of HTM and AFS investments, and companies can choose to use that approach starting in 2019.[17] The CECL model uses the allowance method to account for impairments that you learned to use to account for bad debts in Chapter 7. It requires recognizing impairments of HTM and AFS investments regardless of whether they are judged to be other than temporary. Therefore impairments of debt investments are likely to be recognized sooner under the CECL model than under the current approach.

An in-depth discussion of accounting for impairments of debt investments is provided in Appendix 12B.

[17] "Financial Instruments--Credit Losses (Topic 326)" *Accounting Standards Update 2016-13* (Norwalk, Conn: FASB, 2016).

International Financial Reporting Standards

LO12–9

Impairments. *IFRS No. 9,* amended on July 24, 2014, will be required after January 1, 2018, and earlier adoption is permitted.[18] *IFRS No. 9* calculates impairment of debt investments measured at amortized cost or FVOCI using the *expected credit loss (ECL)* model, which is somewhat similar to the CECL model that will be required soon in U.S. GAAP. Both the U.S. CECL model, and the IFRS ECL model calculate expected credit losses over the remaining life of the investment if there has been a significant increase in credit risk. The U.S. CECL model also does that if there has not been a significant increase in credit risk. In contrast, under the IFRS ECL model, if the credit risk of a debt investment has not increased, the estimate of credit losses only has to include credit losses that result from default events that are possible within the *next 12 months.* For many debt investments, this approach accrues very little credit loss, because the credit risk of the investment hasn't changed and default within the next twelve months is very unlikely. Companies can elect to always recognize lifetime credit losses, but it is unlikely that many will choose to do so. That means that U.S. GAAP will tend to recognize impairment losses earlier, and in higher amounts, than are recognized under IFRS. Further convergence in this area is unlikely in the near future.

Concept Review Exercise

VARIOUS INVESTMENT SECURITIES

Diversified Services, Inc. offers a variety of business services, including financial services through its escrow division. Diversified's fiscal year ends on December 31. Diversified entered into the following investment activities during the last month of 2018 and the first week of 2019:

2018

Dec. 1	**Purchased $30 million of 12% bonds of Vince-Gill Amusement Corporation and $24 million of 10% bonds of Eastern Waste Disposal Corporation, both at face value. The Vince-Gill bonds are to be held until they mature. The Eastern Waste bonds are to be held but might be sold if cash needs require it. Interest on each bond issue is payable semiannually on November 30 and May 31.**
30	**Purchased U.S. Treasury bonds for $5.8 million as trading securities hoping to earn profits on short-term differences in prices.**
31	**Recorded the necessary adjusting entries relating to the investments.**

As of December 31, 2018, the fair value of the Vince-Gill bonds was $32 million, the fair value of the Eastern Waste bonds was $25 million, and the fair value of the Treasury bonds was $5.7 million.

2019

Jan. 7	**Sold the Eastern Waste bonds for $22 million and sold the U.S Treasury bonds for $6 million.**

Required:

1. Prepare the appropriate journal entry for each transaction or event and show the amounts that would be reported in the company's 2018 income statement relative to these investments. Record interest accruing in 2018, but ignore any interest accruing in 2019.
2. Determine the effects of the Eastern Waste investment on net income, other comprehensive income, and comprehensive income for 2018, 2019, and combined over both years. Ignore interest revenue.

[18]"Financial Instruments," *International Financial Reporting Standard No. 9* (IASCF), November 12, 2009, as amended effective January 1, 2016.

1. Journal entries:

2018

Dec. 1 **Purchased $30 million of 12% bonds of Vince-Gill Amusement Corporation and $24 million of 10% bonds of Eastern Waste Disposal Corporation, both at face value. The Vince-Gill bonds are to be held until they mature, but the Eastern Waste bonds are to be held but might be sold if cash needs require it. Interest on each bond issue is payable semiannually on November 30 and May 31.**

	($ in millions)	
Investment in HTM securities (Vince-Gill)	30	
Investment in AFS securities (Eastern Waste)	24	
Cash		54

Dec. 30 **Purchased U.S. Treasury bonds for $5.8 million as trading securities, hoping to earn profits on short-term differences in prices.**

	($ in millions)	
Investment in trading securities (U.S. Treasury bonds)	5.8	
Cash		5.8

Dec. 31 **Recorded the necessary adjusting entries relating to the investments.**

Accrued Interest (one month)	($ in millions)	
Interest receivable—Vince-Gill		
($30 million × 12% × 1/12)	0.3	
Interest receivable—Eastern Waste		
($24 million × 10% × 1/12)	0.2	
Interest revenue		0.5
Fair Value Adjustments		
Unrealized holding loss—NI ($5.7 − 5.8)	0.1	
Fair value adjustment, TS investments		0.1
Fair value adjustment, AFS investments		
($25 million cost − 24 million fair value)	1	
Unrealized holding gain—OCI		1

Note: Securities held-to-maturity are not adjusted to fair value.

Reported in the 2018 Income Statement	($ in millions)
Interest revenue ($0.5 interest)	$0.5
Loss on investments (trading securities)	(0.1)

Note: The $1 million unrealized holding gain for the Eastern Waste bonds is not included in net income because it pertains to available-for-sale securities rather than trading securities, and so is reflected in OCI.

2019

Jan. 7 **Sold the Eastern Waste bonds for $22 million and sold the U.S Treasury bonds for $6 million.**

First consider the AFS investment (Eastern Waste). The fair value of the Eastern Waste bonds at the time of sale is $22 million. Those bonds were carried at a fair value of $25 million as of December 31, 2018, so have suffered an unrealized loss of $3 million during the first part of 2019.

	($ in millions)	
Unrealized holding loss—OCI ($25 − 22)	3	
Fair value adjustment, AFS investments		3

Second, given that the fair value adjustment for the Eastern Waste bonds now has a $2 million credit balance, we need to remove that amount and record the corresponding reclassification entry for OCI:

FV Adjustment, AFS Investments

Debit	Credit	
1		2018 unrealized gain
	3	2019 unrealized loss
	2	Preadjustment balance
2		Reclassification entry
	0	

	($ in millions)	
Fair value adjustment, AFS investments (account balance)	2	
Reclassification adjustment—OCI		2

Third, we need to record the receipt of cash and the loss realized upon sale of the investment:

	($ in millions)	
Cash	22	
Loss—NI (to balance)	2	
Investment in AFS securities (Eastern Waste)		24

Next consider the investment in trading securities (U.S. Treasuries). The fair value of the U.S. Treasury bonds at the time of sale is $6 million. Those bonds were carried at a fair value of $5.7 million as of December 31, 2018, so have enjoyed an unrealized holding gain of $0.3 million during the first part of 2019.

	($ in millions)	
Fair value adjustment, trading securities	0.3	
Unrealized holding gain—NI		0.3

FV Adjustment, U.S. Treasuries

Debit	Credit	
	0.1	2018 unrealized loss
0.3		2019 unrealized gain
0.2		Preadjustment balance
	0.2	Sale entry
0		

On the date of sale, we also need to record the receipt of cash and remove the accounts associated with the trading security from the balance sheet:

	($ in millions)	
Cash	6	
Fair value adjustment, trading securities (account balance)		0.2
Investment in trading securities (U.S. Treasury bonds)		5.8

2. Effects of the Eastern Waste investments on net income, other comprehensive income, and comprehensive income for 2018, 2019, and combined over both years. Ignore interest revenue.

	2018	2019	Cumulatively
Net Income	$0	($2)	($2)
OCI	$1	($3) + 2 = ($1)	$0
Comprehensive Income	$1	($3)	($2)

Financial Statement Presentation and Disclosure

Trading securities, held-to-maturity securities and available-for-sale securities are either current or noncurrent depending on when they are expected to mature or to be sold. However, it's not necessary that a company report individual amounts for the three categories of investments—held-to-maturity, available-for-sale, or trading—on the face of the balance sheet as long as that information is presented in the disclosure notes.[19]

Investors should disclose the following in the disclosure notes for each year presented:

- Aggregate fair value
- Gross realized and unrealized holding gains
- Gross realized and unrealized holding losses
- Change in net unrealized holding gains and losses
- Amortized cost basis by major security type

The notes also include disclosures designed to help financial statement users understand the quality of the inputs companies use when determining fair values and to identify parts of the financial statements that are affected by those fair value estimates. For example, the notes should include the level of the fair value hierarchy (levels 1, 2, or 3) in which all fair value measurements fall. For level 2 or 3 fair values, the notes to the financial statements must include a description of the valuation technique(s) and the inputs used in the fair value measurement process. For level 3 fair values, the notes must indicate the significant inputs used in the fair value measurement, the sensitivity of fair values to significant changes in those inputs, and information about the effect of fair value measurements on earnings, including a reconciliation of beginning and ending balances of the investment that identifies the following:

- Total gains or losses for the period (realized and unrealized), unrealized gains and losses associated with assets and liabilities still held at the reporting date, and where those amounts are included in earnings or shareholders' equity
- Purchases, sales, issuances, and settlements
- Transfers in and out of the level 3 category

All of this disclosure is designed to provide financial statement users with information about those fair values that are most vulnerable to bias or error in the estimation process. For example, as shown in Illustration 12–11, note 2 of HP Inc.'s 2015 annual report includes the following discussion of fair values.

Illustration 12–11

Fair Value Disclosures of Investment Securities—HP Incorporated

Real World Financials

Fair Value (partial)

	As of October 31, 2015			
	Fair Value Measured Using			
($ in millions)	**Level 1**	**Level 2**	**Level 3**	**Total**
Assets:				
Cash equivalents and Investments:				
Time deposits	$ –	$3,584	$ –	$ 3,584
Money market funds	8,895	–	–	8,895
Mutual funds	–	246	–	246
Marketable equity securities	52	10	–	62
Foreign bonds	8	347	–	355
Other debt securities	–	2	40	42
Derivative Instruments:				
Interest rate contracts	–	38	–	38
Foreign exchange contracts	–	1,029	2	1,031
Other derivatives	–	8	–	8
Total assets	$8,955	$5,264	$42	$14,261

[19]FASB ASC 320-10-45-13: Investments–Debt Securities–Overall–Other Presentation Matters (previously *Statement of Financial Accounting Standards No. 115*, "Accounting for Certain Investments in Debt and Equity Securities" (Norwalk, Conn.: FASB, 1993), par. 18).

We can see from these disclosures that HP has relatively few level 3 investments (which are those with the most subjectively estimated fair values). That fact should give financial statement users more faith in the reliability of HP's fair value estimates.

Accounting for Equity Investments

PART B

The critical events over the life of an investment in the equity of another company, such as shares of common stock, include the following:

1. Purchasing the equity security
2. Receiving dividends (for some equity securities)
3. Holding the investment during periods in which the investment's fair value changes (and thus incurring *unrealized holding* gains and losses, since the security has not yet been sold)
4. Selling the investment (and thus incurring *realized* gains and losses, since the security has been sold and the gains or losses actually incurred)

Also, equity investors typically get to vote on key decisions made by the company, such as who will serve on the company's board of directors. Each share of common stock gets a vote, so if an equity investor owns enough shares, the investor has enough votes to influence the operations of the company whose shares it owns. Therefore, accounting for equity investments also considers the extent to which the investor can influence the activities of the investee. As shown in Illustration 12–12, we use three different approaches to account for equity investments.

Illustration 12–12
Reporting Categories for Equity Investments

Characteristics of the Equity Investment	Reporting Method Used by the Investor
The investor ***lacks significant influence*** over the operating and financial policies of the investee (typically owns less than 20% of voting stock):	**Fair Value Through Net Income**—similar to the trading-securities approach used for debt; investment reported at fair value (with unrealized holding gains and losses included in net income), unless fair value is not readily determinable*
The investor ***has significant influence*** over the operating and financial policies of the investee (typically owns between 20% and 50% of the voting stock):	**Equity method**—investment reported at cost adjusted for investor's share of subsequent earnings and dividends of the investee**
The investor ***controls*** the investee (typically owns more than 50% of voting stock):	**Consolidation**—the financial statements of the investor and investee are combined as if they are a single company

*Later in this chapter we discuss in an Additional Consideration box the alternative approach that is used if fair value is not readily determinable.
**If the investor elects the *fair value option*, this type of investment also can be accounted for using the fair-value-through-net-income approach.

We'll first discuss the *fair value through net income* approach that is used when the investor lacks significant influence over the investee. Then we'll cover the *equity method* that's used when the investor does have significant influence. We won't cover *consolidation accounting,* which is used when the investor controls the investee, as that topic is beyond the scope of this book. However, we will discuss consolidations briefly when we discuss the equity method, as the two approaches are related.

When the Investor Lacks Significant Influence: Fair Value through Net Income

LO12–5

If an investor owns less than 20% of the voting shares of an investee, the investor is typically assumed to lack significant influence over the investee. In other words, the investor is in the same position you would be in if you bought a share of the company's stock—the investor hopes to receive dividends and that the value of the shares appreciate over time, but can't really tell the company what to do.

Until very recently, those sorts of equity investments were accounted for as either trading securities or available-for-sale investments, just like we would treat debt investments that weren't intended to be held to maturity. However, starting in 2018, investors are not allowed to use the AFS approach for equity investments. Instead, all equity investments are accounted for like trading securities, using a classification commonly referred to as *fair value through net income.* That means that equity investments for which the investor lacks significant influence are reported the same way we report debt investments that are classified as trading securities (Part A of this chapter). The equity investments are carried at fair value in the balance sheet, with unrealized holding gains and losses recognized in net income in whatever period they occur.[20] Illustration 12–13 provides a simple example of an equity investment that we'll use throughout this section. Let's walk through the key events in the life of United's Arjent investment to see how the fair value through net income approach works for an equity investment.

Illustration 12–13

Example of an Equity Investment Accounted for as Fair Value Through Net Income

The following events during 2018 and 2019 pertain to United Intergroup's investment in the common stock of Arjent, Inc.

July 1, 2018	**Purchase** Arjent, Inc., common stock for $1,500,000
December 31, 2018	**Recognize investment revenue** for a $75,000 cash dividend received from Arjent.
December 31, 2018	**Record a fair value adjustment** to recognize a decline in the value of the Arjent stock investment to $1,450,000.
January 5, 2019	**Sell** the Arjent stock for $1,446,000.

Purchase Investments

All equity investments are recorded initially at cost.

The journal entry to record the purchase of an equity investment is simple, just exchanging one asset (cash) for another (investment):

July 1, 2018		
Investment in Arjent stock	1,500,000	
Cash		1,500,000

Recognize Investment Revenue

Dividends received for equity investments are included in income.

The journal entry to record the receipt of dividends related to the Arjent equity investment also is straightforward.

December 31, 2018		
Cash	75,000	
Dividend revenue		75,000

Adjust Equity Investments to Fair Value (2018)

Equity investments are adjusted to their fair value at each reporting date.

The carrying value of equity investments must be adjusted to fair value at the end of every reporting period. As with trading securities, we use a valuation allowance, *fair value adjustment,* to increase or decrease the carrying value of the investment, and we simultaneously record an unrealized holding gain or loss that is included in net income in the period in which fair value changes. The next table shows the calculation of the balance in the fair value adjustment that is required on December 31, 2018.

December 31, 2018

Security	Cost	Fair Value	Necessary Fair Value Adjustment Balance
Arjent	$1,500,000	$1,450,000	$(50,000)

[20]FASB ASC 321–10–35–1: Investments–Equity Securities–Overall–General (previously *Accounting Standards Update No. 2016-1*, "Recognition and Measurement of Financial Assets and Financial Liabilities" (Norwalk, Conn.: FASB, 2016)).

United needs to move the fair value adjustment from a balance of $0 (at purchase date) to a credit balance of $50,000:

	Fair Value Adjustment
Beginning balance	$ 0
± Adjustment needed to update fair value	?
Balance needed on 12/31/2018	$(50,000)

Fair Value Adjustment	
0	
	50,000
	50,000

The journal entry to record United's unrealized holding loss of $50,000 and the corresponding decrease in United's fair value adjustment account is:

December 31, 2018		
Unrealized holding loss—NI*	50,000	
Fair value adjustment†		50,000

*We title this account "Unrealized . . .—NI" to highlight that, for equity investments accounted for as fair value through net income, unrealized holding gains and losses are included in net income in the period in which they occur.
†Sometimes companies don't bother with a separate fair value adjustment account and simply adjust the investment account to fair value.

What if Arjent's investment instead had a fair value of, say, $1,550,000 as of December 31, 2018? In that case, United would have an unrealized holding *gain* of $50,000, which would require a *debit* to the fair value adjustment account to *increase* the carrying value of the equity to fair value.

Sell the Equity Investment

Now assume United sells the Arjent stock for $1,446,000 on January 5, 2019. According to the FASB, "because all changes in an equity security's fair value are reported in earnings as they occur, the sale of an equity security does not necessarily give rise to a gain or loss. Generally, a debit to cash . . . is recorded for the sales proceeds, and a credit is recorded to remove the security at its fair value (or sales price)."[21] Thus, as with trading securities, United must make two journal entries. United first records in net income any unrealized holding gains and losses that occurred during 2019 prior to the date of sale. Then, on the date of sale, United records the receipt of cash and removes the amounts associated with the investment from the relevant balance sheet accounts.

1. **Adjust Securities to Fair Value (2019).** We first need to update the fair value adjustment and recognize any unrealized holding gains or losses that have occurred during the current reporting period prior to the date of sale.

January 5, 2019

Security	Cost	Fair Value	Necessary Fair Value Adjustment Balance
Arjent	$1,500,000	$1,446,000	$(54,000)

United needs to move the fair value adjustment from a credit balance of $50,000 to a credit balance of $54,000, which requires a credit of $4,000 to this asset valuation account:

	Fair Value Adjustment
Beginning balance on 1/1/2019	$ (50,000)
± Adjustment needed to update fair value	?
Balance needed on 12/31/2018	$(54,000)

Fair Value Adjustment	
0	50,000
	4,000
	54,000

The journal entry to record the investment's decrease in fair value is:

[21]FASB ASC 321-10-40: Investments–Equity Securities–Overall–Derecognition, (previously *Accounting Standards Update No. 2016-1*, "Recognition and Measurement of Financial Assets and Financial Liabilities" (Norwalk, Conn.: FASB, 2016)).

January 5, 2019		
Unrealized holding loss—NI	4,000	
Fair value adjustment		4,000

2. **Record the Sale.** After making the previous journal entry, the investment is carried at its fair value as of the date it is being sold, and all unrealized holding gains and losses associated with the investment have been included in net income. All that remains is for United to record receipt of cash and remove the investment-related accounts from the balance sheet:

January 5, 2019		
Cash	1,446,000	
Fair value adjustment (account balance)	54,000	
Investment in Arjent stock (account balance)		1,500,000

If all of the unrealized holding gains or losses have been included in net income, no additional gain or loss is recognized.

A *realized* gain or loss for the difference between carrying value and the cash received from selling an equity investment is included in net income.

Because United carries the investment at fair value as of the date of sale, and already included in net income the entire loss associated with the investment, there is no realized gain or loss to recognize on the date of sale.[22] Over the life of the investment, United has recognized a total loss of $54,000, but that loss is spread over the life of the investment, recognized as the fair value of the investment changes:

2018 loss recognized in NI:	$(50,000)
2019 loss recognized in NI:	(4,000)
Total over 2018 and 2019:	$(54,000)

Adjust Equity Investments to Fair Value (2019)

If United hadn't sold the Arjent investment during 2019, it would just keep recording whatever fair value adjustment would be necessary to carry the investment at fair value in the balance sheet. For example, if the Arjent investment had a fair value of $1,300,000 at December 31, 2019, United would face the following situation:

December 31, 2019

Security	Cost	Fair Value	Necessary Fair Value Adjustment Balance
Arjent	$1,500,000	$1,300,000	$(200,000)

United would need to credit the fair value adjustment account by another $150,000 to account for the large drop in fair value that occurred during 2019.

Fair Value Adjustment

	50,000
	150,000
	200,000

	Fair Value Adjustment
12/31/2018 balance	$ (50,000)
± Adjustment needed to update fair value	?
12/31/2019 balance	$(200,000)

[22]As noted in FASB ASC 321-10-40: Investments–Equity Securities–Overall–Derecognition, for expediency companies may not update the fair value adjustment to the fair value that exists on the date of sale before recording the sale. In that case, this second entry would include a realized gain or loss based on the difference between the cash received and the fair value of the investment recorded on the last balance sheet date. In our example, the fair value adjustment balance was $50,000 as of December 31, 2018, and United would record the following sale entry on January 5, 2019:

Cash	1,446,000	
Fair value adjustment (account balance)	50,000	
Unrealized holding loss - NI	4,000	
Investment in Arjent		1,500,000

The necessary journal entry is shown below:

December 31, 2019		
Unrealized holding loss—NI	150,000	
Fair value adjustment (calculated above)		150,000

Additional Consideration

What if Fair Value is Not Readily Determinable?. Equity investments are accounted for using the *fair value through net income* approach when the fair value of shares is *readily determinable* by referencing prices on a security exchange or over-the-counter market. But what if fair value isn't readily determinable? In that case, investors can elect to base measurement of fair value on an adjusted cost of the security. Specifically, the investor estimates fair value as cost, minus any impairments that have been recognized previously, and plus or minus adjustments indicated by changes in the prices of similar equity issued by the same investee. Every accounting period, the investor needs to reevaluate whether fair value still is not readily determinable, and also needs to assess whether the investment has been impaired. The investor considers various qualitative factors to assess whether an investment is impaired, such as whether the earnings, cash flows, or business prospects of the investee have deteriorated. If the investor concludes the investment is impaired, it recognizes in net income whatever amount of impairment loss is necessary to reduce the carrying value of the investment to fair value.

International Financial Reporting Standards

LO12–8

Accounting for Equity Investments When the Investor Lacks Significant Influence. As indicated previously, until recently *IAS No. 39* was the standard that specified appropriate accounting for all investments under IFRS.[23] The primary categories in *IAS No. 39* are similar to those used for debt investments in U.S. GAAP, consisting of Fair Value through Profit & Loss (FVPL), similar to TS, HTM, and AFS. *IFRS No. 9,* amended on July 24, 2014, will be required after January 1, 2018, and earlier adoption is permitted, so until 2018 either *IAS No. 39* or *IFRS No. 9* might be in effect for a particular company.[24] Under *IFRS No. 9,* investments in equity securities are classified as either FVPL or FVOCI (Fair Value through Other Comprehensive Income). If the equity is held for trading, it must be classified as FVPL, but otherwise the company can irrevocably elect to classify it as FVOCI. FVOCI is similar to the AFS treatment used for debt investments in U.S. GAAP, but there is an important difference. Unlike AFS, realized gains and losses are not reclassified out of OCI and into net income when the investment is later sold. Rather, the accumulated unrealized gain or loss associated with a sold investment is just transferred from AOCI to retained earnings (both shareholders' equity accounts), without passing through the income statement.

Financial Statement Presentation

We present investments in equity securities in the financial statements the same way we present debt investments classified as trading securities, but they are shown on their own separate line. Equity investments that are held for trading should be classified as current assets in the balance sheet, with cash flows treated as operating activities on the statement of cash flows. On the other hand, equity investments that are held for more long-term purposes should be classified as noncurrent assets in the balance sheet, with cash flows typically treated as investing activities in the statement of cash flows. Notes to the financial

[23]"Financial Instruments: Recognition and Measurement," *International Accounting Standard No. 39* (IASCF), as amended effective January 1, 2009.

[24]"Financial Instruments," *International Financial Reporting Standard No. 9* (IASCF), November 12, 2009, as amended effective January 1, 2016.

statements should disclose the portion of unrealized holding gains and losses for the period that relate to any equity securities still held by the company at the end of the reporting period. Notes also should provide information about how the carrying value was calculated for equity investments for which fair value is not readily determinable.

Additional Consideration

Transition from Prior GAAP. Our discussion of investments in equity securities is based on *ASU 2016-01*, which becomes effective for fiscal years beginning after December 15, 2017.[25] Prior to that ASU, equity investments could be treated as trading securities or AFS investments, similar to debt investments. When companies adopt *ASU 2016-01*, they will make a cumulative-effect adjustment to the balance sheet as of the beginning of the period of adoption, adjusting equity AFS investments to fair value on that date and adjusting retained earnings to appear as if those investments had been accounted for at fair value through net income all along.

When the Investor Has Significant Influence: The Equity Method

Control and Significant Influence

● LO12–6

Usually an investor can *control* the investee if it owns more than 50% of the investees voting shares.

Consolidated financial statements combine the individual elements of the parent and subsidiary statements.

If a company acquires more than 50% of the voting stock of another company, it's said to have **control**, because by voting those shares, the investor actually can control the company acquired. The investor is called the *parent;* the investee is called the *subsidiary.* Both companies continue to operate as separate legal entities, and the subsidiary reports separate financial statements. However, because of the controlling interest, the parent company reports **consolidated financial statements** which treat the parent and the subsidiary as if there were only one company. This entails an item-by-item combination of the parent and subsidiary statements (after first eliminating any amounts that are shared by the separate financial statements).[26] For instance, if the parent has $8 million cash and the subsidiary has $3 million cash, the consolidated balance sheet would report $11 million cash.

Usually an investor can exercise *significant influence* over the investee when it owns at least 20% of the investee's voting shares.

Even if effective control is absent, the investor still may be able to exercise **significant influence** over the operating and financial policies of the investee. This would be the case if the investor owns a large percentage of the outstanding shares relative to other shareholders. By voting those shares as a block, decisions often can be swayed in the direction the investor desires. It is presumed, in the absence of evidence to the contrary, that the investor exercises significant influence over the investee when it owns at least 20% of the investee's voting shares.[27]

The equity method is used when an investor can't control, but can significantly influence, the investee.

When significant influence exists but the investor does not have effective control, the investment should be accounted for by the **equity method**. Under the equity method, the investment is initially recorded at cost. After that, the investment balance is:

Under the *equity method*, the investor recognizes on its own income statement its proportionate share of the investee's income.

- Increased by the investor's percentage share of the investee's net income (or decreased by its share of a loss).
- Decreased by the investor's percentage share of the investee's dividends paid.
- Potentially adjusted for other items (discussed next).

[25] FASB ASC 321–10–35–1: Investments–Equity Securities–Overall–General (previously *Accounting Standards Update No. 2016-1*, "Recognition and Measurement of Financial Assets and Financial Liabilities" (Norwalk, Conn.: FASB, 2016)).

[26] This avoids double counting those amounts in the consolidated statements. For example, amounts owed by one company to the other are represented by accounts payable in one set of financial statements and accounts receivable in the other. These amounts are not included in the statements of the consolidated entity because a company can't "owe itself."

[27] Shareholders are the owners of the corporation. By voting their shares, it is they who determine the makeup of the board of directors—who, in turn, appoint officers—who, in turn, manage the company. Common stock usually is the class of shares that has voting privileges. However, a corporation can create classes of preferred shares that also have voting rights. This is discussed at greater length in Chapter 18.

Additional Consideration

It's possible that a company owns more than 20% of the voting shares but still cannot exercise significant influence over the investee. If, for instance, another company or a small group of shareholders owns 51% or more of the shares, they control the investee regardless of how other investors vote their shares. GAAP provides this and other examples of indications that an investor may be unable to exercise significant influence.

- The investee challenges the investor's ability to exercise significant influence (through litigation or complaints to regulators).
- The investor surrenders significant shareholder rights in a signed agreement.
- The investor is unable to acquire sufficient information about the investee to apply the equity method.
- The investor tries and fails to obtain representation on the board of directors of the investee.[28]

Conversely, it's also possible that a company owns less than 20% of the voting shares but is able to exercise significant influence over the investee. Ability to exercise significant influence with less than 20% ownership might be indicated, for example, by having an officer of the investor corporation on the board of directors of the investee corporation or by having, say, 18% of the voting shares while no other single investor owns more than 50%. In such cases the equity method would be appropriate.

FINANCIAL Reporting Case

Q4, p. 643

The rationale for this approach is the presumption that the fortunes of the investor and investee are so intertwined that, as the investee prospers, the investor prospers proportionately. Stated differently, as the investee earns additional net assets (income), the investor's share of those net assets increases. When the investee pays out assets (dividends), the investor's share of the remaining net assets decreases.

To see how the equity method works, let's turn to Illustration 12–14. In that illustration, we assume that United Intergroup purchased **30%** of Arjent, Inc.'s, common stock for $1,500,000 cash on January 2, 2018. Let's start by thinking about Arjent overall, and then we'll account for United's 30% investment.

Illustration 12–14
Information for Arjent, Inc., at the time United Intergroup purchased 30% for $1,500,000.

	Book Value on Arjent's Financial Statements	**Fair Value at Time of United's Investment**	
Total fair value of Arjent (1/2/2018)			$5,000,000*
Buildings**	$1,000,000	$2,000,000	
Land	500,000	1,000,000	
Other net assets†	600,000	600,000	
Net assets	$2,100,000		3,600,000
Goodwill			$1,400,000
Other information (12/31/2018):			
Arjent's 2018 net income:	$ 500,000		
Arjent's 2018 dividends:	$ 250,000		

*$5,000,000 × 30% purchased = **$1,500,000 purchase price.**
**10-year remaining useful life, no salvage value.
†Other net assets = other assets – total liabilities.

As shown in Illustration 12–14, buying 30% of Arjent for $1,500,000 implies that the full (100%) *fair value* of Arjent's assets and liabilities is $5,000,000 (because $5,000,000 × 30% purchased = $1,500,000 purchase price). However, notice that the *book value* of Arjent's net assets is only $2,100,000. Why do fair value and book value differ? Part of the difference in total fair value and book value represents assets (in this case, buildings and

[28]FASB ASC 323–10–15–10: Investments–Equity Method and Joint Ventures–Overall–Scope and Scope Exceptions (previously "Criteria for Applying the Equity Method of Accounting for Investments in Common Stock," FASB Interpretation No. 35 (Stamford, Conn.: FASB, 1981)).

land) that have fair values greater than their book values. Arjent recorded those assets at historical cost and recognized depreciation of the buildings over time, so the book values of those assets don't reflect their fair values. The remaining difference is previously unrecognized goodwill (e.g., because of loyal customers, well-trained workers, etc.) that GAAP doesn't capture as separate assets but nevertheless represents value for which United was willing to pay. We will see that, under the equity method, all of these amounts are shown in a single investment account, but we still need to track their individual information to account for them correctly.

Purchase of Investment

Recording United's purchase of 30% of Arjent is straightforward. The investment is recorded at cost:

Investment in Arjent stock	1,500,000	
Cash		1,500,000

Recording Investment Revenue

As the investee earns additional net assets, the investor's investment in those net assets increases.

Under the equity method, the investor includes in net income its proportionate share of the investee's net income. The reasoning is that, as the investee earns additional net assets, the value of the investor's share of those net assets also increases, so the investor increases its investment by the amount of income recognized. United's entry would be:

Investment in Arjent stock	150,000	
Investment revenue (30% × $500,000)		150,000

Of course, if Argent had recorded a net loss rather than net income, United would *reduce* its investment in Arjent and recognize a *loss* on investment for its share of the loss. You won't always see these amounts called "investment revenue" or "investment loss." Rather, United might call this line "equity in earnings (losses) of affiliate" or some other title that suggests it is using the equity method.

Receiving Dividends

As the investee distributes net assets as dividends, the investor does not recognize revenue. Rather, the investor's investment in the investee's net assets is reduced.

Because we recognize investment revenue as it is earned by the investee, it would be inappropriate to recognize revenue again when earnings are distributed as dividends. That would be double counting. Instead, we view the dividend distribution as reducing the investee's net assets. The rationale is that the investee is returning assets to its investors in the form of a cash payment, so each investor's equity interest in the remaining net assets declines proportionately.

Cash	75,000	
Investment in Arjent stock (30% × $250,000)		75,000

Further Adjustments

LO12–7

When the investor's expenditure to acquire an equity-method investment exceeds the book value of the underlying net assets acquired, additional adjustments to both the investment account and investment revenue might be needed. The purpose is to approximate the effects of consolidation, without actually consolidating financial statements. More specifically, both the investment account and investment revenue are adjusted for differences between net income reported by the investee and what that amount would have been if consolidation procedures had been followed. This process is often referred to as "amortizing the differential," because it mimics the process of expensing some of the difference between the price paid for the investment and the book value of the investment. Let's look closer at what that means.

Consolidated financial statements report (a) the acquired company's assets at their fair values on the date of acquisition rather than their book values on the investee's balance sheet, and (b) goodwill for the excess of the acquisition price over the fair value of the identifiable net assets acquired. This matters because increasing asset balances to their fair values can result in higher expenses in the future. If it's land or goodwill that's increased, there is no income effect because we don't depreciate or amortize those assets over time.[29] On the other hand, if buildings, equipment, or other depreciable assets are recorded at higher values, depreciation expense will be higher during their remaining useful lives. Likewise, if the recorded amount of inventory is increased, cost of goods sold will be higher when the inventory is sold. When expenses rise, income falls. It is this negative effect on income that the equity method seeks to imitate.

In our example, United needs to make adjustments for the fact that, at the time it purchased its investment in Arjent, the fair values of Arjent's assets and liabilities were higher than the book values of those assets and liabilities in Arjent's balance sheet (refer back to Illustration 12–14). Illustration 12–15 shows United's 30% proportionate share of the amounts shown in Illustration 12–14:

Illustration 12–15

Explanation for Differences Between the Investment and the Book Value of Net Assets Acquired

	Investee Net Assets		Net Assets Purchased		
Purchase price	$5,000,000	× 30% =	$1,500,000		
Fair value (identifiable)	3,600,000	× 30% =	1,080,000		
Difference	$1,400,000	× 30% =	$ 420,000	Goodwill	
Fair value (identifiable)	$3,600,000	× 30% =	$1,080,000		
Book value (identifiable)	2,100,000	× 30% =	630,000		
Difference	$1,500,000	× 30% =	$ 450,000	Buildings	$300,000
				Land	$150,000

Notice in Illustration 12–15 that United paid $1,500,000 for 30% of the identifiable net assets that, sold separately, would have a fair value of $1,080,000. The $420,000 difference between the price paid and the fair value of United's share of Arjent's identifiable net assets is attributable to goodwill. The 30% of identifiable net assets with a fair value of $1,080,000 have a book value on Arjent's balance sheet of only $630,000. The $450,000 difference is attributable to undervalued buildings ($300,000) and land ($150,000). Now let's see what adjustments, if any, United needs to make for these differences.

Adjustments for Additional Depreciation

The investor adjusts its share of the investee's net income to reflect revenues and expenses associated with differences between the fair value and book value of the investee's assets and liabilities that existed at the time the investment was made.

When Arjent determines its net income, it bases depreciation expense on the book value of its buildings on its own balance sheet. United, however, needs to depreciate its share of the *fair value* of those buildings at the time it made its investment. To account for this higher amount of depreciation expense, United reduces investment revenue as if Arjent had included the additional expense in its earnings.

As shown in Illustration 12–14, the book value of Argent's buildings is $1,000,000 and the fair value is $2,000,000, which creates a difference of $1,000,000. United will need to recognize its 30% share of additional depreciation expense for this difference, totaling $300,000 over the remaining life of the buildings. Assuming a 10-year life of the buildings and straight-line depreciation, United must recognize $30,000 of additional depreciation each year for ten years. Had Arjent recorded that additional depreciation in its income statement, United's portion of Arjent's net income would have been lower by $30,000 (ignoring taxes). So, to act as if Arjent had recorded the additional depreciation, United reduces investment revenue and reduces its investment in Arjent stock by $30,000.

[29]Goodwill is not amortized periodically to expense. Only if the asset's value is subsequently judged to be impaired will all or a portion of the recorded amount charged against earnings. FASB ASC 350–20–35: Intangibles–Goodwill and Other–Goodwill–Subsequent Measurement (previously "Goodwill and Other Intangible Assets," *Statement of Financial Accounting Standards No. 141* (Norwalk, Conn.: FASB, 2001)). For review, see Chapter 11.

Investment revenue	30,000	
Investment in Arjent stock [30% × ($2,000,000 – 1,000,000) ÷ 10 years]		30,000

No Adjustments for Land or Goodwill

United makes no adjustments for land or goodwill. Land is not an asset we depreciate. As a result, the difference between the fair value and book value of the land would not cause higher expenses, and we have no need to adjust investment revenue or the investment in Arjent stock for the land.

Recall from Chapter 11 that goodwill, unlike most other intangible assets, is not amortized. In that sense, goodwill resembles land. Thus, acquiring goodwill will not cause higher expenses, so we have no need to adjust investment revenue or the investment in Arjent stock for goodwill.

Adjustments for Other Assets and Liabilities

If the fair value of purchased inventory exceeds its book value, we usually assume the inventory is sold in the next year and reduce investment revenue in the next year by the entire difference.

Also, because in our example there is no difference between the book value and fair value of the remaining net assets, we don't need an adjustment for them either. However, that often will not be the case. For example, Arjent's inventory could have had a fair value that exceeded its book value at the time United purchased its Arjent investment. To recognize expense associated with that higher fair value, United would need to identify the period in which that inventory is sold (usually the next year) and, in that period, reduce its investment revenue and its investment in Arjent stock by its 30% share of the difference between the fair value and book value of the inventory. If, for instance, the $1,000,000 difference between fair value and book value had been attributable to inventory rather than buildings, and that inventory was sold by Arjent in the year following United's investment, United would reduce investment revenue by its 30% share of the difference ($300,000) in the year following the investment. More generally, an equity method investor needs to make these sorts of adjustments whenever there are revenues or expenses associated with an asset or liability that had a difference between book value and fair value at the time the investment was made.

Additional Consideration

Effect on Deferred Income Taxes. Investment revenue is recorded by the equity method when income is earned by the investee, but that revenue is not taxed until it's actually received as cash dividends. This creates a temporary difference between book income and taxable income. You will learn in Chapter 16 that the investor must report a deferred tax liability for the income tax that ultimately will be paid when the income eventually is received as dividends.

Reporting the Investment

The carrying amount of the investment is its initial cost plus the investor's equity in the undistributed earnings of the investee.

The fair value of the investment shares at the end of the reporting period is not reported when using the equity method. The investment account is reported at its original cost, increased by the investor's share of the investee's net income (adjusted for additional expenses like depreciation), and decreased by the portion of those earnings actually received as dividends.

The balance of United's 30% investment in Arjent at December 31, 2018, would be calculated as follows:

Investment in Arjent Stock

Purchase price	1,500,000		
Share of income	150,000		
		75,000	Dividends
		30,000	Depreciation adjustment
	1,545,000		

In the statement of cash flows, we report the purchase and sale of the investment as outflows and inflows of cash in the investing activities section, and the receipt of dividends is reported as an inflow of cash in the operating activities section.[30]

Additional Consideration

Much like consolidation, the equity method views the investor and investee collectively as a special type of single entity (as if the two companies were one company). However, the equity method doesn't require the investor to record separate financial statement items of the investee on an item-by-item basis as in consolidation. Instead, the investor reports its equity interest in the investee as a single investment account. Also, the adjustments that investors make when applying the equity method are designed to mimic what would happen if an investment were consolidated. For those reasons, the equity method sometimes is referred to as a "one-line consolidation," because it essentially collapses the consolidation approach into single lines in the balance sheet and income statement, while having the same effect on total income and shareholders' equity.

When the Investment is Acquired in Mid-Year

Obviously, we've simplified the illustration by assuming the investment was acquired at the beginning of 2018, entailing a full year's income, dividends, and adjustments to account for the income effects of any differences between book value and fair value on the date the investment was acquired. In the more likely event that an investment is acquired sometime after the beginning of the year, applying the equity method is easily modified to include the appropriate fraction of each of those amounts. For example, if United's purchase of 30% of Arjent had occurred on October 1 rather than January 2, we would simply record income, dividends, and adjustments for three months (3/12) of the year. This would result in the following entries to the investment account:

Investment in Arjent Stock

Cost	1,500,000		
Share of income (3/12 × $150,000)	37,500		
		7,500	Depreciation adjustment (3/12 × $30,000)
		18,750	Dividends (3/12 × $75,000)
	1,511,250		

Changes in the investment account the first year are adjusted for the fraction of the year the investor has owned the investment.

AT&T reported its 2015 investments in affiliated companies for which it exercised significant influence using the equity method as shown in Illustration 12–16.

When the Investee Reports a Net Loss

Our illustration assumed the investee earned net income. If the investee reports a *net loss* instead, the investment account would be *decreased* by the investor's share of the investee's net loss (adjusted for additional expenses).

What If Conditions Change?

A CHANGE FROM THE EQUITY METHOD TO ANOTHER METHOD. When the investor's level of influence changes, it may be necessary to change from the equity method

[30]Most companies prepare a statement of cash flows using the indirect method of reporting operating activities. In that case, the operating section begins with net income and adjustments are made to back out the effects of accrual accounting and calculate cash from operations. For companies with equity method investments, net income will include investment revenue and gains or losses associated with sold investments, but cash from operations should include only cash dividends. As an example, because United's 2018 net income includes $120,000 of investment revenue from Arjent ($150,000 portion of income - $30,000 depreciation adjustment), but United received only $75,000 of dividends from Arjent, an indirect method statement of cash flows would include an adjustment, often titled "undistributed earnings of investee," that reduces net income by $45,000 ($75,000 - $120,000) when determining cash from operations.

Illustration 12–16
Equity Method Investments in the Balance Sheet—AT&T

Real World Financials

	Dec 31, 2015	Dec 31, 2014
Total current assets	$ 35,992	$ 33,606
Property, plant, and equipment—Net	124,450	112,898
Goodwill	104,568	69,692
Licenses	93,093	60,824
Customer lists and relationships—Net	18,208	812
Other intangible assets—net	9,409	5,327
Investments in equity affiliates	1,606	250
Other assets	15,346	13,425
Total assets	$402,672	$296,834

Additional Consideration

It's possible that the investor's proportionate share of investee losses could exceed the carrying amount of the investment. If this happens, the investor should discontinue applying the equity method until the investor's share of subsequent investee earnings has equaled losses not recognized during the time the equity method was discontinued. This avoids reducing the investment account below zero.

to another method. For example, when Air-France/KLM's ownership interest in WAM (Amadeus) declined from 22% to 15% during the 2011 fiscal year, it had to stop using the equity method to account for its investment.

When this situation happens, *no adjustment* is made to the remaining carrying amount of the investment. Instead, the equity method is simply discontinued and the new method applied from then on. The balance in the investment account when the equity method is discontinued would serve as the new cost basis for writing the investment up or down to fair value on the next set of financial statements.

A CHANGE FROM ANOTHER METHOD TO THE EQUITY METHOD. Sometimes companies change from another method to the equity method. For example, when the Mitsubishi UFJ Financial Group converted its investment in the convertible preferred stock of Morgan Stanley into common stock, its ownership interest was large enough to qualify for accounting for the investment under the equity method. When a change *to* the equity method is appropriate, the previous method is discontinued and the balance in the investment account at the date of the change (including any unrealized holding gains or losses that occurred prior to the date the investment qualifies for the equity method) is used as the starting balance for applying the equity method. Any cost of acquiring additional shares is added to that balance, and going forward that balance is adjusted for the investor's portion of investee earnings and dividends. A disclosure note also should describe the change.[31]

IF AN EQUITY METHOD INVESTMENT IS SOLD. When an investment reported by the equity method is sold, we recognize a gain or loss if the selling price is more or less than the carrying amount (book value) of the investment. For example, let's continue our illustration and assume United sells its investment in Arjent on January 1, 2019, for $1,446,000. A journal entry would record a loss as follows:

When an equity method investment is sold, a gain or loss is recognized for the difference between its selling price and its carrying amount.

Cash	1,446,000	
Loss on sale of investments (to balance)	99,000	
Investment in Arjent stock (account balance)		1,545,000

[31]Retroactive restatement used to be required when a company changed to the equity method, but as of 2017 that is no longer necessary, per FASB ASC 323–10–35–33: Investments–Equity Method and Joint Ventures–Overall–Increase in Level of Ownership or Degree of Influence (previously "Investments—Equity Method and Joint Ventures (Topic 323): Simplifying the Transition to the Equity Method of Accounting," *Accounting Standards Update No. 2016-07* (Norwalk, Conn.: FASB, 2016)).

COMPARISON OF FAIR VALUE AND THE EQUITY METHOD. Illustration 12–17 compares accounting for the Arjent investment at fair value through net income and under the equity method:

Illustration 12–17 Comparison of Fair Value and Equity Methods

	Fair Value Through Net Income			Equity Method		
Purchase equity investment	Investment in Arjent	1,500,000		Investment in Arjent	1,500,000	
	Cash		1,500,000	Cash		1,500,000
Recognize proportionate share of investee's net income and any related adjustments	No entry			Investment in Arjent	150,000	
				Investment revenue		150,000
				Investment revenue	30,000	
				Investment in Arjent		30,000
Adjust to fair value, 2018	Holding loss—NI	50,000		No entry		
	FV adjustment		50,000			
Receive dividend	Cash	75,000		Cash	75,000	
	Dividend revenue		75,000	Investment in Arjent		75,000
Sell equity investment						
1. Adjust to fair value, 2019	Holding loss—NI	4,000		No entry		
	FV adjustment		4,000			
2. Record sale	Cash	1,446,000		Cash	1,446,000	
	FV adjustment	54,000		Loss—IN (to balance)	99,000	
	Investment in Arjent		1,500,000	Investment in Arjent		1,545,000

This side-by-side comparison highlights several aspects of these accounting approaches.

- To record the purchase of an investment, we use identical entries for both approaches.
- The two approaches differ in whether we record investment revenue when dividends are received and whether we recognize unrealized holding gains and losses associated with changes in the fair value of the investment.
- The differences in how the two approaches account for unrealized holding gains and losses result in different carrying values for the investment at the time the investment is sold, and therefore result in different realized gains or losses when the investment is sold.
- Regardless of approach, the same cash flows occur, and the same total amount of net income is recognized over the life of the investment. In the case of Arjent:
  - **Fair value through net income:** A total of $21,000 of net income is recognized over the life of the investment, equal to $75,000 of dividend revenue minus $54,000 ($50,000 + $4,000) loss on the investment.
  - **Equity method:** A total of $21,000 of net income is recognized over the life of the investment, equal to $150,000 of United's portion of Arjent's net income minus $30,000 depreciation adjustment and minus $99,000 loss realized on sale of investment.
  - Thus, the question is not how much total net income is recognized, but *when* that net income is recognized.

Fair Value Option

LO12–8

If the fair value option is chosen for investments otherwise accounted for by the equity method, the amount that is reported at fair value is clearly indicated.

Companies can choose the fair value option (FVO) for "significant influence" investments that otherwise would be accounted for under the equity method. The company makes an irrevocable decision about whether to elect the FVO, and can make that election for some investments and not for others. As shown in Illustration 12–17, the company carries the investment at fair value in the balance sheet and includes unrealized gains and losses in earnings. These investments are shown on their own line in the balance sheet or are combined with equity method investments with the amount at fair value shown parenthetically. Also, all of the disclosures that are required when reporting fair values as well as some of those that would be required under the equity method still must be provided.[32]

Exactly how a company does the bookkeeping necessary to comply with these broad requirements is up to the company. One alternative is to account for the investment using the entries that would be used if the investor lacked significant influence and accounted for it at fair value through net income. A second alternative is to record all of the accounting entries during the period under the equity method, and then record a fair value adjustment at the end of the period. Regardless of which alternative the company uses, though, the same fair value is reported in the balance sheet at the end of the period, and the same total amount is shown in the income statement (the fair value adjustment amount plus the investment revenue recorded).

International Financial Reporting Standards

LO12–9

Equity Method. Like U.S. GAAP, international accounting standards require the equity method for use with significant influence investees (which they call "associates"), but there are a few important differences. First, *IAS No. 28* governs application of the equity method and requires that the accounting policies of investees be adjusted to correspond to those of the investor when applying the equity method.[33] U.S. GAAP has no such requirement.

Second, IFRS does not provide the fair value option for most investments that qualify for the equity method. U.S. GAAP provides the fair value option for all investments that qualify for the equity method.

Concept Review Exercise

THE EQUITY METHOD

Delta Apparatus bought 40% of Clay Crating Corp.'s outstanding common shares on January 2, 2018, for $540 million. The carrying amount of Clay Crating's net assets (shareholders' equity) at the purchase date totaled $900 million. Book values and fair values were the same for all financial statement items except for inventory and buildings, for which fair values exceeded book values by $25 million and $225 million, respectively. All inventory on hand at the acquisition date was sold during 2018. The buildings have average remaining useful lives of 18 years. During 2018, Clay Crating reported net income of $220 million and paid an $80 million cash dividend.

Required:

1. Prepare the appropriate journal entries during 2018 for the investment.
2. Determine the amounts relating to the investment that Delta Apparatus should report in the 2018 financial statements
   a. as an investment in the balance sheet
   b. as an investment revenue in the income statement
   c. as investing and/or operating activities in the statement of cash flows (direct method)

Solution

1. Prepare the appropriate journal entries during 2018 for the investment.

[32] FASB ASC 825–10–50–28: Financial Instruments–Overall–Disclosure–Fair Value Option (previously "The Fair Value Option for Financial Assets and Financial Liabilities," *Statement of Financial Accounting Standards No. 159* (Norwalk, Conn.: FASB, 2007), para.18.f).

[33] "Investments in Associates," *International Accounting Standard 28* (London, UK: IASCF, 2003), as amended, effective January 1, 2016.

	($ in millions)	
Purchase		
Investment in Clay Crating shares	540	
Cash		540
Net income		
Investment in Clay Crating shares (40% × $220 million)	88	
Investment revenue		88
Dividends		
Cash (40% × $80 million)	32	
Investment in Clay Crating shares		32
Inventory		
Investment revenue (as if 2018 cost of goods sold is higher because beginning inventory was adjusted to fair value)	10	
Investment in Clay Crating shares (40% × $25 million)		10
Buildings		
Investment revenue [($225 million × 40%) ÷ 18 years]	5	
Investment in Clay Crating shares		5

	Investee Net Assets		**Net Assets Purchased**
Fair value (identifiable)	$1,150*	× 40% =	$460
Book value (identifiable)	900	× 40% =	360
Difference	$ 250	× 40% =	$100

*($900 + 25 + 225)

2. Determine the amounts that Delta Apparatus should report in the 2018 financial statements.

a. As an investment in the balance sheet:

Investment in Clay Crating
($ in millions)

	Debit	Credit	
Purchase price	540		
40% of Clay Crating net income	88		
		32	Dividends
		10	Cost of goods sold adjustment for inventory (all sold in 2018)
		5	Depreciation adjustment for buildings ($90,000 ÷ 18)
Balance	581		

b. As investment revenue in the income statement:

$88 million − ($10 + 5) million = $73 million
(share of income) (adjustments)

c. In the statement of cash flows (direct method):

- Investing activities: $540 million cash outflow
- Operating activities: $32 million cash inflow

Decision Makers' Perspective

The various approaches used to account for investments can have very different effects on an investor's income statement and balance sheet. Consequently, it's critical that both managers and external decision makers clearly understand those effects and make decisions accordingly.

To highlight key considerations, suppose that, on January 1, 2018, BigCo spent $5,000,000 to purchase 20% of TechStart, a small start-up company that is developing products that apply an exciting new technology. The purchase price included $500,000 for BigCo's share of the difference between the fair value and book value of TechStart's inventory, all of which was then sold in 2018. TechStart paid a small dividend of $100,000 in 2018, so BigCo received 20% of it, or $20,000. TechStart incurs and expenses large amounts of research and development costs as it develops new technology, so it had a net loss in 2018 of $1,000,000. Yet, the future income-generating potential of the products that TechStart is developing has made TechStart a hot stock, and the fair value of BigCo's 20% investment increased to $5,500,000 by the end of 2018. Illustration 12–18 shows how BigCo's investment would be accounted for under two alternative approaches.

Illustration 12–18

Comparison of Methods Used to Account for Investments

	Fair Value Through Net Income	Equity Method
Share of investee net income (loss)*	$ –0–	$ (700,000)
Dividend income**	20,000	–0–
Increase in investee's fair value†	500,000	–0–
Total 2018 effect on net income (loss)	$ 520,000	$ (700,000)
December 31, 2018 investment book value††	$5,500,000	$4,280,000

*Not recognized if account for the investment at fair value through net income. Under the equity method, investment revenue (loss) is 20% × ($1,000,000 loss) + ($500,000) additional expense for fair value inventory adjustment = ($700,000).
**Not recognized for equity method investments. Instead, dividends reduce book value of the investment.
†Recognized in net income if accounted for at fair value through net income. Not recognized under the equity method.
††Equals fair value if accounted for at fair value through net income. Equals initial cost plus income (or minus loss) and minus dividends for equity method.

The way an investment is accounted for affects net income, investment book value, and the amount of gain or loss recognized when the investment is sold.

The accounting method does not affect cash flows, but it has a big effect on net income in current and future periods. Also, because the accounting method affects the book value of the investment, it affects gain or loss on sale of that investment. In our example, if BigCo sold its TechStart investment at the beginning of 2019 for $5,000,000, it would recognize a $720,000 gain on sale if the investment was accounted for under the equity method, but a $500,000 loss if it was accounted for at fair value through net income. All of these income effects are predictable, but only if a user understands the relevant accounting methods and the fact that those methods all end up recognizing the same amount of total gain or loss over the life of an investment. Nevertheless, sometimes even experienced analysts get confused.[34]

Managers may structure equity investments to qualify for their preferred accounting approach.

A benefit of fair value accounting is that it prevents managers from timing the sale of investments to recognize gains or losses in particular accounting periods.

One strength of the equity method is that it prevents the income manipulation that would be possible if a company recognized income when it received dividends and could significantly influence an investee to pay dividends whenever the company needed an income boost. Remember, under the equity method dividends aren't income, but rather reduce the book value of the investment. Nevertheless, users still need to realize that managers may choose and apply methods in ways that make their company appear most attractive. For example, research suggests that investments sometimes are structured to avoid crossing the 20 to 25 percent threshold that typically requires using the equity method, presumably to avoid the negative effect on earnings that comes from having to recognize the investor's share of investee losses and other income adjustments.[35] Also, a company might smooth income by timing the sale of equity method investments to realize gains in otherwise poor periods and realize losses in otherwise good periods. While consistent with GAAP, mixing these sorts of one-time gains and losses with operating income could encourage users to think that operating income is less volatile than it really is.

[34]For example, in 2000, analysts were accustomed to including Intel's investment gains as ordinary income, because those amounts were not particularly large and could be viewed as part of Intel's business. However, in the 2nd quarter of 2000, Intel recorded a net $2.1 billion gain from selling securities in its available-for-sale portfolio. Analysts were surprised and confused, with some eliminating the gain from their earnings estimates but others including them ("Intel Says Net Jumped 79%; Analysts Upset," *The Wall Street Journal*, July 19, 2000, p. A3).

[35]E. E. Comiskey and C. W. Mulford, "Investment Decisions and the Equity Accounting Standard," *The Accounting Review* 61, no. 3 (July 1986), pp. 519–525.

Regarding the fair value through net income approach, of particular concern is the potential for inaccurate fair value estimates. Even if management is trying to provide the most accurate fair value estimate possible, there is much potential for error, particularly when making estimates at level 3 of the fair value hierarchy. Also, a company conceivably could use the discretion inherent in fair value estimation to manage earnings with respect to trading securities or other investments for which they have elected the fair value option. Given this potential for error and bias, it's not surprising that investors are nervous about the accuracy of fair value estimates. To address these sorts of concerns, the FASB has required extensive note disclosure about the quality of inputs associated with estimates of fair value, but financial statement users need to know to look for those disclosures and still must understand that they cannot assess fully the accuracy of fair value estimates. ●

A concern with fair value accounting is that management has much discretion over fair values, and may not be able to estimate fair values accurately.

FINANCIAL INSTRUMENTS AND INVESTMENT DERIVATIVES A financial instrument is defined as one of the following:

1. Cash
2. Evidence of an *ownership interest* in an entity[36]
3. A contract that (a) imposes on one entity an obligation to *deliver* cash (say accounts payable) or another financial instrument and (b) conveys to the second entity a right to *receive* cash (say accounts receivable) or another financial instrument
4. A contract that (a) imposes on one entity an obligation to *exchange* financial instruments on potentially unfavorable terms (say the issuer of a stock option) and (b) conveys to a second entity a right to *exchange* other financial instruments on potentially favorable terms (say the holder of a stock option)[37]

A complex class of financial instruments exists in financial markets in response to the desire of firms to manage risks. In fact, these financial instruments would not exist in their own right, but have been created solely to hedge against risks created by other financial instruments or by transactions that have yet to occur but are anticipated. Financial futures, interest rate swaps, forward contracts, and options have become commonplace.[38] These financial instruments often are called derivatives because they "derive" their values or contractually required cash flows from some other security or index. For instance, an option to buy an asset in the future at a preset price has a value that is dependent on, or derived from, the value of the underlying asset. Their rapid acceptance as indispensable components of the corporate capital structure has left the accounting profession scrambling to keep pace.

Derivatives are financial instruments that "derive" their values from some other security or index.

The urgency to establish accounting standards for financial instruments has been accelerated by headline stories in the financial press reporting multimillion-dollar losses on exotic derivatives by Enron Corporation, Procter & Gamble, Orange County (California), Piper Jaffrey, and Gibson Greetings, to mention a few. The headlines have tended to focus attention on the misuse of these financial instruments rather than their legitimate use in managing risk.

The FASB has been involved for many years in a project to provide a consistent framework for resolving financial instrument accounting issues, including those related to derivatives and other "off-balance-sheet" instruments. The financial instruments project has three separate but related parts: disclosure, recognition and measurement, and distinguishing between liabilities and equities. Unfortunately, issues to be resolved are extremely complex and will likely require several more years to resolve. To help fill the disclosure gap in the meantime, the FASB has offered a series of temporary, "patchwork" solutions. These are primarily in the form of additional disclosures for financial instruments. More recently, the FASB has tackled the issues of recognition and measurement of derivatives. We discuss these requirements in Appendix A to this book.

The FASB's ongoing financial instruments project is expected to lead to a consistent framework for accounting for all financial instruments.

[36]This category includes not just shares of stock, but also partnership agreements and stock options.

[37]FASB ASC Master Glossary: Financial Instrument (previously "Disclosure of Information about Financial Instruments with Off-Balance-Sheet Risk and Financial Instruments with Concentrations of Credit Risk," *Statement of Financial Accounting Standards No. 105* (Stamford, Conn.: FASB, 1990), par. 6).

[38]Interest rate futures were traded for the first time in 1975 on the Chicago Board of Trade. Interest rate swaps were invented in the early 1980s. They now comprise over 70% of derivatives in use.

Financial Reporting Case Solution

1. **How should you respond? Why are held-to-maturity securities treated differently from other investment securities?** *(p. 648)* You should explain that if an investor has the positive intent and ability to hold the securities to maturity, investments in debt securities are classified as held-to-maturity and reported at amortized cost in the balance sheet. Increases and decreases in fair value are not reported in the financial statements. The reasoning is that the changes are not as relevant to an investor who will hold a security to its maturity regardless of those changes. Changes in the fair value between the time a debt security is acquired and the day it matures to a prearranged maturity value aren't as important if sale before maturity isn't an alternative.
2. **Why are unrealized gains and losses on trading securities reported in the income statement?** *(p. 650)* Trading securities are acquired for the purpose of profiting from short-term market price changes, so gains and losses from holding these securities while prices change are often viewed as relevant performance measures that should be included in net income.
3. **Why are unrealized gains and losses on available-for-sale securities not reported in the income statement, but instead are in other comprehensive income, and then shown in accumulated other comprehensive income (AOCI) in the balance sheet?** *(p. 655)* Available-for-sale securities are not acquired for the purpose of profiting from short-term market price changes, so gains and losses from holding these securities while prices change are viewed as insufficiently relevant performance measures to be included in net income. Instead, those amounts are shown in other comprehensive income (OCI) and accumulated in an owners' equity account (AOCI). It's likely that holding gains in some periods will be offset by holding losses in other periods. When the investment is sold, the net amount of gain or loss is removed from AOCI and recognized in net income.
4. **Explain why Coca-Cola accounts for some of its investments by the equity method and what that means.** *(p. 672)* When an investor does not have "control," but still is able to exercise *significant influence* over the operating and financial policies of the investee, the investment should be accounted for by the equity method. Apparently Coke owns between 20% and 50% of the voting shares of some of the companies it invests in. By the equity method, Coke recognizes investment income in an amount equal to its percentage share of the net income earned by those companies, instead of the amount of that net income it receives as cash dividends. The rationale is that as the investee earns additional net assets, Coke's share of those net assets increases. ●

The Bottom Line

- **LO12-1** Key events in the life of a debt investment are purchase, recording interest revenue, incurring unrealized holding gains and losses due to fair value changes, and recording sale or maturity. *(p. 644)*
- **LO12-2** If an investor has the positive intent and ability to hold the securities to maturity, investments in debt securities are classified as HTM and reported at amortized cost in the balance sheet. These investments are recorded at cost, and holding gains or losses from fair value changes are ignored. *(p. 648)*
- **LO12-3** Investments in debt securities acquired principally for the purpose of selling them in the near term are classified as trading securities. They are reported at their fair values. Holding gains and losses for trading securities are included in earnings. *(p. 649)*
- **LO12-4** Investments in debt securities that don't fit the definitions of the other reporting categories are classified as available-for-sale. They are reported at their fair values. Holding gains and losses from retaining securities during periods of price change are not included in the determination of income for the period; they are reported as a separate component of other comprehensive income in shareholders' equity. *(p. 653)*
- **LO12-5** Investments in equity securities for which the investor lacks the ability to exercise significant influence over the investee are accounted for using a fair value through net income approach. They are reported at their fair values. Holding gains and losses are included in earnings. *(p. 667)*

LO12-6 The equity method requires the investor to recognize investment income equal to its percentage share (based on share ownership) of the net income earned by the investee, rather than the amount received as cash dividends. The investment account is adjusted for the investor's percentage share of net income or loss reported by the investee. When the investor actually receives dividends, the investment account is reduced accordingly. *(p. 672)*

LO12-7 When the fair value of identifiable net assets acquired exceeds the book value of the underlying net assets acquired in the purchase of an equity investment, both the investment account and investment revenue are adjusted for differences between net income reported by the investee and what that amount would have been if consolidation procedures had been followed. *(pp. 661* and *674)*

LO12-8 Impairment recognition requires that, even if a debt investment is accounted for as HTM or AFS, unrealized holding losses are included in net income when the impairment is judged to be other than temporary. The fair value option allows companies to account for most financial assets and liabilities in the same way they account for trading securities, with unrealized holding gains and losses included in net income and the investment carried at fair value in the balance sheet. For equity method investments, this requires clearly identifying the portion of those investments classified in the significant-influence category that is being accounted for at fair value. *(p. 661* and *679)*

LO12-9 U.S. GAAP and IFRS are similar in most respects concerning how they account for investments, but accounting in this area is being overhauled by both the IASB and the FASB, and IFRS companies may report under two different standards (either *IAS No. 39* or *IFRS No. 9*) until 2018. IFRS allows proportionate consolidation as well as the equity method to account for joint ventures, although the option to use proportionate consolidation may be eliminated soon. IFRS is more restrictive in terms of the circumstances in which the fair-value option can be used. Finally, as discussed in Appendix 12B, IFRS recognizes different amounts of OTT impairment for HTM and AFS debt investments, and allows recovery of OTT impairments for debt investments (but not equity investments). *(pp. 660–663, 671, 680,* and *690)*

Other Investments (Special Purpose Funds, Investments In Life Insurance Policies)

APPENDIX 12A

Special Purpose Funds

It's often convenient for companies to set aside money to be used for specific purposes. You learned about one such special purpose fund in Chapter 7 when we discussed petty cash funds. Recall that a petty cash fund is money set aside to conveniently make small expenditures using currency rather than having to follow the time-consuming, formal procedures normally used to process checks. Similar funds sometimes are used to pay interest, payroll, or other short-term needs. Like petty cash, these short-term special purpose funds are reported as current assets.

Some special purpose funds—like petty cash—are current assets.

Special purpose funds also are sometimes established to serve longer-term needs. It's common, for instance, to periodically set aside cash into a fund designated to repay bonds and other long-term debt. Such funds usually accumulate cash over the debt's term to maturity and are composed of the company's periodic contributions plus interest or dividends from investing the money in various return-generating investments. In fact, some debt contracts require the borrower to establish such a fund to repay the debt. In similar fashion, management might voluntarily choose to establish a fund to accumulate money to expand facilities, provide for unexpected losses, buy back shares of stock, or any other special purpose that might benefit from an accumulation of funds. Of course, funds that won't be used within the upcoming operating cycle are noncurrent assets. They typically are reported as part of investments. The same criteria for classifying securities into reporting categories that we discussed previously should be used to classify securities in which funds are invested. Any investment revenue from these funds is reported as such in the income statement.

A special purpose fund can be established for *virtually any purpose.*

Noncurrent special purpose funds are reported within the category *investments and funds.*

Investments in Life Insurance Policies

Companies frequently buy life insurance policies on the lives of their key officers. Under normal circumstances, the company pays the premium for the policy and, as beneficiary,

Certain life insurance policies can be surrendered while the *insured is still alive in* exchange for its *cash surrender value.*

receives the proceeds when the officer dies. Of course, the objective is to compensate the company for the untimely loss of a valuable resource in the event the officer dies. However, some types of life insurance policies can be surrendered while the insured is still alive in exchange for a determinable amount of money, called the cash surrender value. In effect, a portion of each premium payment is not used by the insurance company to pay for life insurance coverage, but instead is invested on behalf of the insured company in a fixed-income investment. Accordingly, the cash surrender value increases each year by the portion of premiums invested plus interest on the previous amount invested. This is simply a characteristic of whole life insurance, unlike term insurance that has lower premiums and provides death benefits only.

Part of each insurance premium represents an increase in the cash surrender value.

From an accounting standpoint, the periodic insurance premium should not be expensed in its entirety. Rather, part of each premium payment, the investment portion, is recorded as an asset. Illustration 12A–1 provides an example.

Illustration 12A–1
Cash Surrender Value

Several years ago, American Capital acquired a $1 million insurance policy on the life of its chief executive officer, naming American Capital as beneficiary. Annual premiums are $18,000, payable at the beginning of each year. In 2018, the cash surrender value of the policy increased according to the contract from $5,000 to $7,000. The CEO died at the end of 2018.

Part of the annual premium represents a build-up in the cash surrender value.

Insurance expense (difference)	16,000	
Cash surrender value of life insurance ($7,000 – 5,000)	2,000	
Cash (2018 premium)		18,000
To record insurance expense and the increase in the investment.		

The cash surrender value is considered to be a noncurrent investment and would be reported in the investments and funds section of the balance sheet. Of course when the insured officer dies, the corporation receives the death benefit of the insurance policy, and the cash surrender value ceases to exist because canceling the policy no longer is an option. The corporation recognizes a gain for the amount of the death benefit less the cash surrender value.

When the death benefit is paid, the cash surrender value becomes null and void.

Cash (death benefit)	1,000,000	
Cash surrender value of life insurance (balance)		7,000
Gain on life insurance settlement (difference)		993,000
To record the proceeds at death.		

APPENDIX 12B Impairment of Debt Investments

An "other-than-temporary" impairment loss is recognized in net income even though the security hasn't been sold.

We saw in Chapter 11 that intangible assets and property, plant, and equipment are subject to impairment losses that reduce earnings if a decline in fair value indicates that the assets' value has been impaired. The same is true for investments. As indicated in Chapter 12, if the fair value of an investment declines to a level below cost, and that decline is not viewed as temporary, companies typically have to recognize an other-than-temporary (OTT) impairment loss in earnings. We don't need to worry about OTT impairments for trading securities, equity investments for which the investor lacks significant influence, or other investments for which a company has chosen the fair value option, because all changes in the fair values of those investments (whether temporary or OTT) always are recognized in earnings. However, that is not the case for held-to-maturity (HTM) and available-for-sale (AFS) debt investments. Declines in fair value typically are ignored for HTM investments and recorded in OCI for AFS investments. Therefore, companies need to evaluate HTM and AFS investments to determine whether an OTT impairment loss has occurred.

We use a three-step process to determine whether an OTT impairment loss must be recognized and how that loss is to be measured and recorded: (1) determine if the investment is impaired, (2) determine whether any impairment is OTT, and (3) determine where to report the OTT impairment.[39] Illustration 12B–1 summarizes those steps.

Is the investment impaired?	Yes, if the fair value is less than the investment's amortized cost.
Is any of the impairment *other-than-temporary (OTT)?*	Yes, if the investor (a) intends to sell the investment, (b) believes it is "more likely than not" that the investor will be required to sell the investment prior to recovering the amortized cost of the investment, less any current-period credit loss, or (c) has incurred credit losses.
Where is the OTT impairment reported?	In net income, if the investor intends to sell the security or is "more likely than not" to be required to sell it before recovery of its amortized cost. Otherwise: • Credit loss portion in net income (Credit loss = amortized cost − PV of expected cash flows) • Noncredit loss portion in OCI (Noncredit loss portion = total impairment − credit loss)

Illustration 12B–1
Other-Than-Temporary Impairment of Debt Investments

A three-step process is used to determine whether an impairment loss on debt investments must be recognized and how that loss is to be measured and recorded.[40] We'll start with the assumption that the investment is AFS, and then indicate what is different if it is HTM.

Debt impairments can be divided into credit losses and noncredit losses.

Credit losses are due to anticipated reductions in cash flows from the debt investment; all others are *noncredit losses*.

1. **Is the investment impaired?** Impairment of a debt investment occurs when fair value has declined to a level below amortized cost. It also may be necessary to split the total amount of impairment into credit losses and noncredit losses. *Credit losses* reflect expected reductions in future cash flows from anticipated defaults on interest or principal payments. We calculate credit losses as the difference between the amortized cost of the debt and the *present value of the cash flows* expected to be collected, using a discount rate equal to the effective interest rate that existed at the date the investment was acquired. *Noncredit losses* capture other reductions in fair value such as those due to changes in general economic conditions.

Debt impairments are OTT if the investor:
a. intends to sell the investment, or
b. believes it is more likely than not that they will sell the investment prior to fair value recovery, or
c. has suffered a credit loss.

2. **Is any impairment other-than-temporary (OTT)?** We view a debt impairment as OTT if one of three conditions holds:
   a. The investor intends to sell the investment,
   b. The investor believes it is "more likely than not" that the investor will be required to sell the investment prior to recovering the amortized cost of the investment less any current-period credit losses, or
   c. The investor determines that a credit loss exists on the investment.

The rationale for 2a and 2b is that an impairment is OTT if the investor is likely to sell the investment before fair value can recover. The rationale for 2c is that an impairment is OTT if the company believes the cash flows provided by the investment won't be enough to allow it to recover the amortized cost of the investment over the life of the investment.

3. **Where is the OTT impairment reported?** If the debt impairment is considered OTT, the investor always writes the investment down to fair value in the balance sheet, but the

[39]FASB ASC 320–10–35: Investments–Debt Securities–Overall–Subsequent Measurement (originally "The Meaning of Other-Than-Temporary Impairment and Its Application to Certain Investments," *FASB Staff Position No. 115-1 and 124-1* (Norwalk, Conn.: FASB, November 5, 2005)).
[40]FASB ASC 320–10–35: Investments–Debt Securities–Overall–Subsequent Measurement (previously "Recognition and Presentation of Other-Than-Temporary Impairments," *FASB Staff Position No. 115-2 and 124-2* (Norwalk, Conn.: FASB, April 9, 2009)).

amount included in net income or other comprehensive income depends on the reason the impairment is considered OTT:

- If the impairment is considered OTT due to reasons 2a or 2b above, the entire impairment loss is included in net income, because it is likely the company will incur a loss equal to the entire difference between fair value and amortized cost.
- If the impairment is considered OTT due to reason 2c above, *only the credit loss* component is included in net income, as that amount of amortized cost is unlikely to be recovered. Any noncredit loss component reduces OCI, similar to how we normally account for unrealized gains and losses on AFS investments.

If a debt impairment is OTT:

- Investment is written down to fair value.
- If OTT because of 2a or 2b, all of the OTT impairment loss is recognized in net income.
- If OTT because of 2c, only the credit loss is recognized in net income; noncredit loss in OCI.

Also, if the debt investment is classified as AFS, recognizing an OTT impairment may involve reclassifying amounts out of OCI that were recorded previously as unrealized gains or losses.

Illustration 12B–2 provides a description of the OTT debt impairment process from Bank of America's recent annual report.

Illustration 12B–2

Disclosure about OTT Impairments of Debt Investments—Bank of America

Real World Financials

Note 1 (in part): Securities

The Corporation regularly evaluates each AFS and HTM debt security where the value has declined below amortized cost to assess whether the decline in fair value is other-than-temporary. In determining whether an impairment is other-than-temporary, the Corporation considers the severity and duration of the decline in fair value, the length of time expected for recovery, the financial condition of the issuer, and other qualitative factors, as well as whether the Corporation either plans to sell the security or it is more likely than not that it will be required to sell the security before recovery of its amortized cost. Beginning in 2009, under new accounting guidance for impairments of debt securities that are deemed to be other-than-temporary, the credit component of an other-than-temporary impairment (OTTI) loss is recognized in earnings and the noncredit component is recognized in accumulated OCI in situations where the Corporation does not intend to sell the security and it is not more-likely-than-not that the Corporation will be required to sell the security prior to recovery. If there is an OTTI on any individual security classified as HTM, the Corporation writes down the security to fair value with a corresponding charge to other income (loss).

For an example of an OTT impairment for an AFS debt investment, see Illustration 12B–3.

In both Cases 1 and 2 of Illustration 12B–3, the amortized cost of the investment is reduced by the amount of OTT impairment that is recognized in earnings ($50,000 for Case 1, $30,000 for Case 2). United achieves this by crediting a contra-asset, discount on bond investment, which United amortizes over the remaining life of the debt the same way it would if it had initially purchased the debt at that discounted amount. In Case 2, the carrying value of the investment also is decreased by the *noncredit loss* component of the impairment ($20,000). United achieves this by crediting a second contra-asset account, fair value adjustment—noncredit loss, with the offsetting loss recognized in OCI, the same way it would be if it were viewed as an unrealized loss under normal accounting for fair value declines of AFS investments.

Note that in both cases the carrying value of the debt becomes $950,000, reduced by the entire amount of the OTT impairment. In Case 1 this occurs via the $50,000 discount, and in Case 2 via the combination of the $30,000 discount and $20,000 fair value adjustment. Also, in both cases all of the OTT impairment is reflected in comprehensive income. The question is how much is reflected in net income as opposed to OCI. To clarify this distinction, GAAP requires that the entire OTT impairment be shown in the income statement, and then the portion attributed to noncredit losses backed out, such that only the credit loss portion reduces net income. That way, financial statement users are aware of the total amount as

Illustration 12B–3
Other-than-temporary Impairment of Debt Investment

United Intergroup, Inc., buys and sells debt securities of other companies as investments, and classifies these investments as AFS. United's fiscal year-end is December 31. The following events occurred during 2018.

Purchase Investment

July 1, 2018	Purchased $1,000,000 of Bendac bonds, maturing on December 31, 2019.

Adjust Investment to Fair Value

December 31, 2018	Valued the Bendac bonds at $950,000. Of the $50,000 impairment, $30,000 is credit loss and $20,000 is noncredit loss.

We'll consider two cases:

- **Case 1:** United either plans to sell the investment or believes it is more likely than not that it will have to sell the investment before fair value recovers (such that the impairment is viewed as OTT under 2a or 2b above).
- **Case 2:** United does *not* intend to sell the investment and does *not* believe it is more likely than not that it will have to sell the Bendac investment before fair value recovers, but estimates that $30,000 of credit losses have occurred (such that the impairment is viewed as OTT under 2c above).

	Case 1		Case 2	
December 31, 2018				
OTT impairment loss—NI	50,000		30,000	
Discount on bond investment		50,000		30,000
OTT impairment loss—OCI			20,000	
Fair value adjustment—Noncredit loss				20,000

Note: If United had included unrealized gains or losses for this investment in OCI in a prior period, it also would have to make a reclassification entry, as demonstrated for an equity OTT impairment in Illustration 12B–3.

well as the amount included in net income. Continuing Illustration 12B–3, income statement presentation of the two cases would be as follows:

Income Statement Presentation, December 31, 2018	Case 1	Case 2
OTT impairment of AFS investments:		
Total OTT impairment loss	$50,000	$50,000
Less: portion recognized in OCI	-0-	20,000
Net impairment loss recognized in net income	$50,000	$30,000

What if a debt investment is classified as HTM rather than AFS? Most of the accounting is the same, but an important difference relates to the recognition of *noncredit* losses in OCI. HTM investments normally don't include unrealized gains and losses in OCI, so these won't routinely be adjusted up or down over time. Therefore, for HTM investments, GAAP requires that companies gradually reverse any amounts included in OCI over the remaining life of the investment, debiting the fair value adjustment and crediting OCI each period.

After an OTT impairment is recorded, the usual treatment of unrealized gains or losses is resumed. Changes in fair value are reported in OCI for AFS investments, and are ignored for HTM investments. Any impairment loss recognized in earnings is not eligible for reversal should fair value recover.

CURRENT EXPECTED CREDIT LOSS (CECL) MODEL FOR DEBT INVESTMENTS As indicated earlier in this chapter and in Chapter 7, guidance is changing with respect to accounting for impairments. These changes will be mandatory starting in 2020, and companies can choose to adopt them starting in 2019.[41]

[41]"Financial Instruments--Credit Losses (Topic 326)" *Accounting Standards Update 2016-13* (Norwalk, Conn: FASB, 2016).

For HTM investments, companies will be required to use the CECL ("Current Expected Credit Loss") model to account for impairments. That means that companies will recognize bad debts for HTM investments the same way they recognize bad debts for any other note receivable. They will use a contra-asset account, the allowance for credit losses, to reduce the carrying value of HTM investments to the net amount expected to be collected, and each period will record whatever credit loss (bad debt expense) or recovery of credit loss is necessary to adjust that allowance to its appropriate balance. Unlike current practice for OTT impairments, reversal of impairments will be allowed if the fair value of the HTM investment recovers. Estimates of the allowance for credit losses will incorporate historical and current data as well as reasonable and supportable forecasts about the future.

For AFS investments, companies won't apply the CECL model. Instead, they'll apply a new AFS Credit Loss model that is very similar to what companies currently use for OTT impairments. It still will be the case that, if companies plan to sell the investment or think it is more likely than not that they will have to sell the investment before fair value recovers, they will recognize in net income an amount of impairment loss equal to the entire difference between amortized cost and fair value. Also, it still will be the case that, in the remaining circumstance in which companies don't think they will have to sell the investment before fair value recovers, companies will recognize credit losses in net income and noncredit losses in OCI. The main difference is that, when companies recognize credit losses in net income using the new AFS Credit Loss model, they will credit an allowance for credit losses (an allowance for bad debts), rather than reducing the amortized cost of the investment directly by crediting a discount on investment account. Similar to HTM investments, the allowance for credit losses will be adjusted upward or downward as necessary to reflect credit losses, with the offsetting expense or recovery of expense shown in net income. However, the allowance for credit losses is not permitted to exceed the difference between amortized cost and fair value of the investment (because the company can always sell the investment at fair value to avoid additional credit losses).

International Financial Reporting Standards

LO12–8

Accounting for Impairments. Our coverage of impairments focuses on *IFRS No. 9*, which is required after 2018 and can be used in practice in periods before then. Under *IFRS No. 9*, companies recognize impairments for debt investments that are accounted for at amortized cost (rather than fair value through net income) or at fair value through other comprehensive income (FVOCI). There is no distinction made for OTT status. The impairment is calculated using the ECL model discussed previously, and is measured either as the 12-month expected credit loss (if the credit risk on the investment has increased significantly) or the lifetime expected credit loss (if the credit risk on the investment has not increased significantly. The entire impairment is recognized in earnings (there is no equivalent to recognizing in OCI any noncredit losses on debt investments), with an offsetting allowance reducing the carrying value of the investment to the appropriate amount.

IFRS allows recoveries of impairments of debt investments to be recognized in earnings. This is a difference from current U.S. GAAP, which does not allow recoveries of any OTT impairment, but not the CECL model that will be required in U.S. GAAP, which allows recoveries.

To illustrate, let's modify our Bendac debt example from Illustration 12B–3 to assume amortized cost of €1,000,000, €30,000 of 12-month expected credit losses and €20,000 of additional credit losses expected for default events occurring after 12 months. Assuming there has not been a significant increase in credit risk, Bendac would recognize an impairment of €30,000:

Impairment loss—NI	30,000	
Allowance for credit losses		30,000

Assuming instead that there has been a significant increase in credit risk, Bendac would recognize an impairment of €50,000:

Impairment loss—NI	50,000	
Allowance for credit losses		50,000

(continued)

(concluded)

If in a subsequent period the fair value of the debt investment improved by €15,000, IFRS would allow *reversal* of that amount of impairment charge.

Allowance for credit losses	15,000	
Reversal of impairment loss—NI		15,000

Companies can elect to always recognize lifetime credit losses, but only have to do so when a significant increase in credit loss has occurred.

Questions For Review of Key Topics

Q 12–1 All investments in *debt* securities are classified for reporting purposes in one of three categories, and can be accounted for differently depending on the classification. What are these three categories?

Q 12–2 When market rates of interest *rise* after a fixed-rate security is purchased, the value of the now-below-market, fixed-interest payments declines, so the market value of the investment falls. On the other hand, if market rates of interest *fall* after a fixed-rate security is purchased, the fixed-interest payments become relatively attractive, and the market value of the investment rises. Assuming these price changes are not viewed as giving rise to an other-than-temporary impairment, how are they reflected in the investment account for a security classified as held-to-maturity?

Q 12–3 Does GAAP distinguish between fair values that are readily determinable from current market prices versus those needing to be calculated based on the company's own assumptions? Explain how a user will know about the reliability of the inputs used to determine fair value.

Q 12–4 When a debt investment is acquired to be held for an unspecified period of time as opposed to being held to maturity, it is reported at the fair value of the investment securities on the reporting date. Why?

Q 12–5 Reporting an investment at its fair value means adjusting its carrying amount for changes in fair value after its acquisition (or since the last reporting date if it was held at that time). Such changes are called unrealized holding gains and losses because they haven't yet been realized through the sale of the security. If the security is classified as available-for-sale, how are unrealized holding gains and losses typically reported?

Q 12–6 What is "comprehensive income"? Its composition varies from company to company but may include which items related to available-for-sale investments that are not included in net income?

Q 12–7 Why are holding gains and losses treated differently for trading securities and securities available-for-sale?

Q 12–8 Western Die-Casting Company holds an investment in unsecured bonds of LGB Heating Equipment, Inc. When the investment was acquired, management's intention was to hold the bonds for resale. Now management has the positive intent and ability to hold the bonds to maturity. How should Western account for the reclassification of the investment?

Q 12–9 Is it necessary for an investor to report individual amounts for the three categories of investments—held-to-maturity, available-for-sale, or trading—in the financial statements? What information should be disclosed about these investments?

IFRS Q 12–10 Under *IFRS No. 9,* what reporting categories are used to account for debt investments? What about for equity investments when the investor lacks the ability to significantly influence the operations of the investee?

IFRS Q 12–11 Under *IFRS No. 9,* which reporting categories are used to account for equity investments when the investor lacks the ability to significantly influence the operations of the investee?

Q 12–12 What is the effect of a company electing the fair value option with respect to a held-to-maturity investment or an available-for-sale investment?

IFRS Q 12–13 Do U.S. GAAP and IFRS differ in the amount of flexibility that companies have in electing the fair value option? Explain.

Q 12–14 Under what circumstances is the equity method used to account for an investment in stock?

Q 12–15 The equity method has been referred to as a *one-line consolidation.* What might prompt this description?

Q 12–16 In the application of the equity method, how should dividends from the investee be accounted for? Why?

Q 12–17 The fair value of depreciable assets of Penner Packaging Company exceeds their book value by $12 million. The assets' average remaining useful life is 10 years. They are being depreciated by the straight-line method. Finest Foods Industries buys 40% of Penner's common shares. When adjusting investment revenue and the investment by the equity method, how will the situation described affect those two accounts?

Q 12–18 Superior Company owns 40% of the outstanding stock of Bernard Company. During 2018, Bernard paid a $100,000 cash dividend on its common shares. What effect did this dividend have on Superior's 2018 financial statements?

Q 12–19 Sometimes an investor's level of influence changes, making it necessary to change from the equity method to another method. How should the investor account for this change in accounting method?

IFRS **Q 12–20** How does IFRS differ from U.S. GAAP with respect to using the equity method?

Q 12–21 What is the effect of a company electing the fair value option with respect to an investment that otherwise would be accounted for using the equity method?

Q 12–22 Define a financial instrument. Provide three examples of current liabilities that represent financial instruments.

Q 12–23 Some financial instruments are called derivatives. Why?

Q 12–24 (Based on Appendix 12A) Northwest Carburetor Company established a fund in 2015 to accumulate money for a new plant scheduled for construction in 2018. How should this special purpose fund be reported in Northwest's balance sheet?

Q 12–25 (Based on Appendix 12A) Whole-life insurance policies typically can be surrendered while the insured is still alive in exchange for a determinable amount of money called the *cash surrender value.* When a company buys a life insurance policy on the life of a key officer to protect the company against the untimely loss of a valuable resource in the event the officer dies, how should the company account for the cash surrender value?

Q 12–26 (Based on Appendix 12B) When market rates of interest *rise* after a fixed-rate security is purchased, the value of the now-below-market, fixed-interest payments declines, so the market value of the investment falls. If that drop in fair value is viewed as giving rise to an other-than-temporary impairment, how would it be reflected in the investment account for a security classified as held-to-maturity?

Q 12–27 (Based on Appendix 12B) Reporting an investment at its fair value requires adjusting its carrying amount for changes in fair value after its acquisition (or since the last reporting date if it was held at that time). Such changes are called unrealized holding gains and losses because they haven't yet been realized through the sale of the security. If a security is classified as available-for-sale, and an unrealized holding loss is viewed as giving rise to an other-than-temporary (OTT) impairment, how is it reported in the financial statements?

Q 12–28 (Based on Appendix 12B) The market value of Helig Forestry and Mining Corporation bonds dropped 6⅛ points when the federal government passed new legislation banning one of the company's primary techniques for extracting ore. Harris Corporation owns Helig bonds and classifies its investment as securities available-for-sale. How should the decline in market value be handled by Harris?

Q 12–29 Explain how the CECL model (introduced in *ASU No. 2016-13* and required in 2020) differs from current GAAP in its calculation of impairment losses.

IFRS **Q 12–30** (Based on Appendix 12B) How does IFRS differ from current U.S. GAAP in accounting for other-than-temporary impairments?

Brief Exercises

connect

BE 12–1
Securities held-to-maturity; bond investment; effective interest
● LO12-1

Lance Brothers Enterprises acquired $720,000 of 3% bonds, dated July 1, on July 1, 2018, as a long-term investment. Management has the positive intent and ability to hold the bonds until maturity. The market interest rate (yield) was 4% for bonds of similar risk and maturity. Lance Brothers paid $600,000 for the investment in bonds and will receive interest semiannually on June 30 and December 31. Prepare the journal entries (a) to record Lance Brothers' investment in the bonds on July 1, 2018, and (b) to record interest on December 31, 2018, at the effective (market) rate.

BE 12–2
Trading securities
● LO12-3

S&L Financial buys and sells securities expecting to earn profits on short-term differences in price. On December 27, 2018, S&L purchased Coca-Cola bonds at par for $875,000 and sold the bonds on January 3, 2019, for $880,000. At December 31, the bonds had a fair value of $873,000. What pretax amounts did S&L include in its 2018 and 2019 net income as a result of this investment (ignoring interest)?

BE 12–3
Trading securities
● LO12-3

For the Coca-Cola bonds described in BE 12-2, prepare journal entries to record (a) any unrealized gains or losses occurring in 2018 and (b) the sale of the bonds in 2019.

BE 12–4
Available-for-sale securities
● LO12-4

S&L Financial buys and sells securities which it classifies as available-for-sale. On December 27, 2018, S&L purchased Coca-Cola bonds at par for $875,000 and sold the bonds on January 3, 2019, for $880,000. At December 31, the bonds had a fair value of $873,000, and S&L has the intent and ability to hold the investment until fair value recovers. What pretax amounts did S&L include in its 2018 and 2019 net income as a result of this investment?

BE 12–5
Available-for-sale securities
● LO12-4

For the Coca-Cola bonds described in BE 12-4, prepare journal entries to record (a) any unrealized gains or losses occurring in 2018 and (b) the sale of the bonds in 2019, including recognition of any unrealized gains in 2019 prior to sale and reclassification of amounts out of OCI.

BE 12–6
Fair value option; available-for-sale securities
● LO12-8

S&L Financial buys and sells securities that it typically classifies as available-for-sale. On December 27, 2018, S&L purchased Coca-Cola bonds at par for $875,000 and sold the bonds on January 3, 2019, for $880,000. At December 31, the bonds had a fair value of $873,000. When it purchased the Coca-Cola bonds, S&L Financial decided to elect the fair value option for this investment. What pretax amounts did S&L include in its 2018 and 2019 net income as a result of this investment (ignoring interest)?

BE 12–7
Available-for-sale securities
● LO12-4

For several years Fister Links Products has held Microsoft bonds, considered by the company to be securities available-for-sale. The bonds were acquired at a cost of $500,000. At the end of 2018, their fair value was $610,000 and their amortized cost was $510,000. At the end of 2019, their fair value was $600,000 and their amortized cost was $520,000. At what amount will the investment be reported in the December 31, 2019, balance sheet? What adjusting entry is required to accomplish this objective (ignore interest)?

BE 12–8
Debt investments under IFRS
● LO12-4, LO12-9
IFRS

Fowler Inc. purchased $75,000 of bonds on January 1, 2018. The bonds pay interest semiannually and mature in 20 years, at which time the $75,000 principal will be paid. The bonds do not pay any amounts other than interest and principal. Fowler's intention is to collect contractual cash flows and eventually sell the bonds within the next couple of years if the price is right. During 2018, the fair value of the bonds increased to $80,000. Fowler reports investments under *IFRS No. 9*. How much unrealized gain or loss will Fowler include in 2018 net income with respect to the bonds?

BE 12–9
Debt investments under IFRS
● LO12-2, LO12-9
IFRS

Assume the same facts as in BE 12–8, but that Fowler intends to hold the bonds until maturity. How much unrealized gain or loss would Fowler include in 2018 net income with respect to the bonds?

BE 12–10
Equity securities
● LO12-5

Adams Industries holds 40,000 shares of FedEx common stock, which is not a large enough ownership interest to allow Adams to exercise significant influence over FedEx. On December 31, 2018, and December 31, 2019, the market value of the stock is $95 and $100 per share, respectively. What is the appropriate reporting category for this investment and at what amount will it be reported in the 2019 balance sheet?

BE 12–11
Equity investments and dividends
● LO12-5

Turner Company owns 10% of the outstanding stock of ICA Company. During the current year, ICA paid a $5 million cash dividend on its common shares. What effect did this dividend have on Turner's 2018 financial statements? Explain the reasoning for this effect.

BE 12–12
Equity method and dividends
● LO12-6

Turner Company owns 40% of the outstanding stock of ICA Company. During the current year, ICA paid a $5 million cash dividend on its common shares. What effect did this dividend have on Turner's 2018 financial statements? Explain the reasoning for this effect.

BE 12–13
Equity method
● LO12-6, LO12-7

The fair value of Wallis, Inc.'s depreciable assets exceeds their book value by $50 million. The assets have an average remaining useful life of 15 years and are being depreciated by the straight-line method. Park Industries buys 30% of Wallis's common shares. When Park adjusts its investment revenue and the investment by the equity method, how will the situation described affect those two accounts?

BE 12–14
Equity method investments
● LO12-6, LO12-9
IFRS

Kim Company bought 30% of the shares of Phelps, Inc., at the start of 2018. Kim paid $10 million for the shares. Thirty percent of the book value of Phelps's net assets is $8 million, and the difference of $2 million is due to land that Phelps owns that has appreciated in value. During 2018, Phelps reported net income of $1 million and paid a cash dividend of $0.5 million. At what amount does Kim carry the Phelps investment on its balance sheet as of December 31, 2018?

BE 12–15
Change in principle; change to the equity method
● LO12-7

At the beginning of 2018, Pioneer Products' ownership interest in the common stock of LLB Co. increased to the point that it became appropriate to begin using the equity method of accounting for the investment. The balance in the investment account was $44 million at the time of the change but would have been $56 million if Pioneer had used the equity method since first investing in LLB. How should Pioneer report the change? Would your answer be the same if Pioneer is changing *from* the equity method rather than *to* the equity method?

BE 12–16
Fair value option; equity method investments
● LO12-8

Turner Company purchased 40% of the outstanding stock of ICA Company for $10,000,000 on January 2, 2018. Turner elects the fair value option to account for the investment. During 2018, ICA earns $750,000 of income and on December 30 pays a dividend of $500,000. On December 31, 2018, the fair value of Turner's investment has increased to $11,500,000. What journal entries would Turner make to account for this investment during 2018, assuming Turner will account for the investment similar to how it would account for a trading security?

BE 12–17
Available-for-sale securities and impairment (Appendix 12B)
● LO12-4, LO12-8

LED Corporation owns $1,000,000 of Branch Pharmaceuticals bonds and classifies its investment as securities available-for-sale. The market price of Branch's bonds fell by $450,000, due to concerns about one of the company's principal drugs. The concerns were justified when the FDA banned the drug. $100,000 of that decline in value already had been included in OCI as a temporary unrealized loss in a prior period. LED views $200,000 of the $450,000 loss as related to *credit* losses, and the other $250,000 as *noncredit* losses. LED thinks it is more likely than not that it will have to sell the investment before fair value recovers. What journal entries should LED record to account for the decline in market value in the current period? How should the decline affect net income and comprehensive income?

BE 12–18
Impairments (AFS Credit Loss Model) (Appendix 12B)
● LO12-4, LO12-8

Answer BE 12-17 under the assumption that LED Corporation used the AFS Credit Loss Model introduced in *ASU 2016-13* and required after 2020.

BE 12–19
Available-for-sale securities and impairment (Appendix 12B)
● LO12-4, LO12-8

LED Corporation owns $1,000,000 of Branch Pharmaceuticals bonds and classifies its investment as securities available-for-sale. The market price of Branch's bonds fell by $450,000, due to concerns about one of the company's principal drugs. The concerns were justified when the FDA banned the drug. $100,000 of that decline in value already had been included in OCI as a temporary unrealized loss in a prior period. LED views $200,000 of the $450,000 loss as related to *credit* losses, and the other $250,000 as *noncredit* losses. LED does not plan to sell the investment and does not think it is more likely than not that it will have to sell the investment before fair value recovers. What journal entries should LED record to account for the decline in market value in the current period? How should the decline affect net income and comprehensive income?

BE 12–20
Recovery of impairments under IFRS (Appendix 12B)
● LO12-3, LO12-8, LO12-9

Wickum Corporation reports under IFRS, and recognized a $500,000 other-than-temporary impairment of an HTM debt investment in Right Corporation. Subsequently, the fair value of Wickum's investment in Right increased by $300,000. How would Wickum account for that increase in fair value?

Exercises

connect

E 12–1
Securities held-to-maturity; bond investment; effective interest, discount
● LO12-1

Tanner-UNF Corporation acquired as a long-term investment $240 million of 6% bonds, dated July 1, on July 1, 2018. Company management has the positive intent and ability to hold the bonds until maturity. The market interest rate (yield) was 8% for bonds of similar risk and maturity. Tanner-UNF paid $200 million for the bonds. The company will receive interest semiannually on June 30 and December 31. As a result of changing market conditions, the fair value of the bonds at December 31, 2018, was $210 million.

Required:

1. Prepare the journal entry to record Tanner-UNF's investment in the bonds on July 1, 2018.
2. Prepare the journal entries by Tanner-UNF to record interest on December 31, 2018, at the effective (market) rate.
3. At what amount will Tanner-UNF report its investment in the December 31, 2018, balance sheet? Why?
4. Suppose Moody's bond rating agency downgraded the risk rating of the bonds motivating Tanner-UNF to sell the investment on January 2, 2019, for $190 million. Prepare the journal entry to record the sale.

E 12–2
Securities held-to-maturity; bond investment; effective interest, premium
● LO12-1

Mills Corporation acquired as a long-term investment $240 million of 6% bonds, dated July 1, on July 1, 2018. Company management has the positive intent and ability to hold the bonds until maturity. The market interest rate (yield) was 4% for bonds of similar risk and maturity. Mills paid $280 million for the bonds. The company will receive interest semiannually on June 30 and December 31. As a result of changing market conditions, the fair value of the bonds at December 31, 2018, was $270 million.

Required:

1. Prepare the journal entry to record Mills' investment in the bonds on July 1, 2018.
2. Prepare the journal entries by Mills to record interest on December 31, 2018, at the effective (market) rate.
3. At what amount will Mills report its investment in the December 31, 2018, balance sheet? Why?
4. Suppose Moody's bond rating agency upgraded the risk rating of the bonds, and Mills decided to sell the investment on January 2, 2019, for $290 million. Prepare the journal entry to record the sale.

E 12–3
Securities held-to-maturity
● LO12-1

FF&T Corporation is a confectionery wholesaler that frequently buys and sells securities to meet various investment objectives. The following selected transactions relate to FF&T's investment activities during the last two months of 2018. At November 1, FF&T held $48 million of 20-year, 10% bonds of Convenience, Inc., purchased May 1, 2018, at face value. Management has the positive intent and ability to hold the bonds until maturity. FF&T's fiscal year ends on December 31.

Nov. 1	Received semiannual interest of $2.4 million from the Convenience, Inc., bonds.
Dec. 1	Purchased 12% bonds of Facsimile Enterprises at their $30 million face value, to be held until they mature in 2024. Semiannual interest is payable May 31 and November 30.
31	Purchased U.S. Treasury bills to be held until they mature in two months for $8.9 million.
31	Recorded any necessary adjusting entry(s) relating to the investments.

The fair values of the investments at December 31 were:

Convenience bonds	$44.7 million
Facsimile Enterprises bonds	30.9 million
U.S. Treasury bills	8.9 million

Required:

Prepare the appropriate journal entry for each transaction or event.

E 12–4
FASB codification research
● LO12-2

CODE

The *FASB Accounting Standards Codification* represents the single source of authoritative U.S. generally accepted accounting principles.

Required:

1. Obtain the relevant authoritative literature on accounting for investments in held-to-maturity securities using the FASB's Codification Research System at the FASB website www.fasb.org.
2. What is the specific citation that describes examples of circumstances under which an investment in debt is available to be sold and therefore should not be classified as held-to-maturity?
3. List the circumstances and conditions.

E 12–5
Trading securities
● LO12-2

[This is a variation of E 12–1 focusing on trading securities.]
Tanner-UNF Corporation acquired as a long-term investment $240 million of 6% bonds, dated July 1, on July 1, 2018. The market interest rate (yield) was 8% for bonds of similar risk and maturity. Tanner-UNF paid $200 million for the bonds. The company will receive interest semiannually on June 30 and December 31. Company management is holding the bonds in its trading portfolio. As a result of changing market conditions, the fair value of the bonds at December 31, 2018, was $210 million.

Required:

1. Prepare the journal entry to record Tanner-UNF's investment in the bonds on July 1, 2018.
2. Prepare the journal entries by Tanner-UNF to record interest on December 31, 2018, at the effective (market) rate.
3. Prepare any additional journal entry necessary for Tanner-UNF to report its investment in the December 31, 2018, balance sheet.
4. Suppose Moody's bond rating agency downgraded the risk rating of the bonds motivating Tanner-UNF to sell the investment on January 2, 2019, for $190 million. Prepare the journal entry to record the sale.

E 12–6
Trading securities
● LO12-1

[This is a variation of E 12–2 focusing on trading securities.]
Mills Corporation acquired as a long-term investment $240 million of 6% bonds, dated July 1, on July 1, 2018. Company management has the positive intent and ability to hold the bonds until maturity. The market interest rate (yield) was 4% for bonds of similar risk and maturity. Mills paid $280 million for the bonds. The company will receive interest semiannually on June 30 and December 31. As a result of changing market conditions, the fair value of the bonds at December 31, 2018, was $270 million.

Required:

1. Prepare the journal entry to record Mills' investment in the bonds on July 1, 2018.
2. Prepare the journal entries by Mills to record interest on December 31, 2018, at the effective (market) rate.

3. At what amount will Mills report its investment in the December 31, 2018, balance sheet? Why?
4. Suppose Moody's bond rating agency upgraded the risk rating of the bonds, and Mills decided to sell the investment on January 2, 2019, for $290 million. Prepare the journal entry to record the sale.

E 12–7
Various transactions relating to trading securities
● LO12-1, LO12-3

Rantzow-Lear Company buys and sells debt securities expecting to earn profits on short-term differences in price. The company's fiscal year ends on December 31. The following selected transactions relating to Rantzow-Lear's trading account occurred during December 2018 and the first week of 2019.

2018	
Dec. 17	Purchased 100 Grocers' Supply Corporation bonds at par for $350,000.
28	Received interest of $2,000 from the Grocers' Supply Corporation bonds.
31	Recorded any necessary adjusting entry relating to the Grocers' Supply Corporation bonds. The market price of the stock was $4,000 per bond.
2019	
Jan. 5	Sold the Grocers' Supply Corporation bonds for $395,000.

Required:
1. Prepare the appropriate journal entry for each transaction.
2. Indicate any amounts that Rantzow-Lear Company would report in its 2018 balance sheet and income statement as a result of this investment.

E 12–8
FASB codification research
● LO12-3, LO12-4, LO12-6, LO12-7

CODE

Access the *FASB's Codification Research System* at the FASB website www.fasb.org.

Required:
Determine the specific citation for accounting for each of the following items:
1. Unrealized holding gains for trading securities should be included in earnings.
2. Under the equity method, the investor accounts for its share of the earnings or losses of the investee in the periods they are reported by the investee in its financial statements.
3. Transfers of securities between categories are accounted for at fair value.
4. Disclosures for available-for-sale securities should include total losses for securities that have net losses included in accumulated other comprehensive income.

E 12–9
Securities available-for-sale; adjusting entries
● LO12-4

Loreal-American Corporation purchased several marketable securities during 2018. At December 31, 2018, the company had the investments in bonds listed below. None was held at the last reporting date, December 31, 2017, and all are considered securities available-for-sale.

	Cost	Fair Value	Unrealized Holding Gain (Loss)
Short term:			
Blair, Inc.	$ 480,000	$ 405,000	$(75,000)
ANC Corporation	450,000	480,000	30,000
Totals	$ 930,000	$ 885,000	$(45,000)
Long term:			
Drake Corporation	$ 480,000	$ 560,000	$ 80,000
Aaron Industries	720,000	660,000	(60,000)
Totals	$1,200,000	$1,220,000	$ 20,000

Required:
1. Prepare appropriate adjusting entries at December 31, 2018.
2. What amounts would be reported in the income statement at December 31, 2018, as a result of these adjusting entries?

E 12–10
Available-for-sale securities
● LO12-1, LO12-4

[This is a variation of E 12–1 focusing on available-for-sale securities.]
Tanner-UNF Corporation acquired as a long-term investment $240 million of 6% bonds, dated July 1, on July 1, 2018. The market interest rate (yield) was 8% for bonds of similar risk and maturity. Tanner-UNF paid $200 million for the bonds. The company will receive interest semiannually on June 30 and December 31. Company management has classified the bonds as available-for-sale investments. As a result of changing market conditions, the fair value of the bonds at December 31, 2018, was $210 million.

Required:
1. Prepare the journal entry to record Tanner-UNF's investment in the bonds on July 1, 2018.
2. Prepare the journal entries by Tanner-UNF to record interest on December 31, 2018, at the effective (market) rate.

3. Prepare any additional journal entry necessary for Tanner-UNF to report its investment in the December 31, 2018, balance sheet.
4. Suppose Moody's bond rating agency downgraded the risk rating of the bonds motivating Tanner-UNF to sell the investment on January 2, 2019, for $190 million. Prepare the journal entries necessary to record the sale, including updating the fair-value adjustment, recording any reclassification adjustment, and recording the sale.

E 12–11
Available-for-sale securities
● LO12-1, LO12-4

[This is a variation of E 12–2 focusing on available-for-sale securities.]
Mills Corporation acquired as a long-term investment $240 million of 6% bonds, dated July 1, on July 1, 2018. Company management has the positive intent and ability to hold the bonds until maturity. The market interest rate (yield) was 4% for bonds of similar risk and maturity. Mills paid $280 million for the bonds. The company will receive interest semiannually on June 30 and December 31. As a result of changing market conditions, the fair value of the bonds at December 31, 2018, was $270 million.

Required:
1. Prepare the journal entry to record Mills' investment in the bonds on July 1, 2018.
2. Prepare the journal entries by Mills to record interest on December 31, 2018, at the effective (market) rate.
3. At what amount will Mills report its investment in the December 31, 2018, balance sheet? Why?
4. Suppose Moody's bond rating agency upgraded the risk rating of the bonds, and Mills decided to sell the investment on January 2, 2019, for $290 million. Prepare the journal entry to record the sale.

E 12–12
Available-for-sale securities
● LO12-1, LO12-4

Colah Company purchased $1 million of Jackson, Inc., 5% bonds at par on July 1, 2018, with interest paid semi-annually. Colah determined that it should account for the bonds as an available-for-sale investment. At December 31, 2018, the Jackson bonds had a fair value of $1.2 million. Colah sold the Jackson bonds on July 1, 2019 for $900,000.

Required:
1. Prepare Colah's journal entries to record:
   a. The purchase of the Jackson bonds on July 1
   b. Interest revenue for the last half of 2018
   c. Any year-end 2018 adjusting entries
   d. Interest revenue for the first half of 2019
   e. Any entries necessary upon sale of the Jackson bonds on July 1, 2019, including updating the fair-value adjustment, recording any reclassification adjustment, and recording the sale
2. Fill out the following table to show the effect of the Jackson bonds on Colah's net income, other comprehensive income, and comprehensive income for 2018, 2019, and cumulatively over 2018 and 2019.

	2018	2019	Total
Net Income			
OCI			
Comprehensive Income			

E 12–13
Classification of securities; adjusting entries
● LO12-4

On February 18, 2018, Union Corporation purchased 10,000 shares of IBM bonds as a long-term investment for $600,000. Union will hold the bonds indefinitely, and may sell them if their price increases sufficiently. On December 31, 2018, and December 31, 2019, the market value of the bonds was $580,000 and $610,000, respectively.

Required:
1. What is the appropriate reporting category for this investment? Why?
2. Prepare the adjusting entry for December 31, 2018.
3. Prepare the adjusting entry for December 31, 2019.

E 12–14
Various investment securities
● LO12-3, LO12-4

At December 31, 2018, Hull-Meyers Corp. had the following investments that were purchased during 2018, its first year of operations:

	Cost	Fair Value
Trading Securities:		
Security A	$ 900,000	$ 910,000
Security B	105,000	100,000
Totals	$1,005,000	$1,010,000

(continued)

(concluded)

Securities Available-for-Sale:		
Security C	$ 700,000	$ 780,000
Security D	900,000	915,000
Totals	$1,600,000	$1,695,000
Securities to Be Held-to-Maturity:		
Security E	$ 490,000	$ 500,000
Security F	615,000	610,000
Totals	$1,105,000	$1,110,000

No investments were sold during 2018. All securities except Security D and Security F are considered short-term investments. None of the fair value changes is considered permanent.

Required:

Determine the following amounts at December 31, 2018.

1. Investments reported as current assets
2. Investments reported as noncurrent assets
3. Unrealized gain (or loss) component of income before taxes
4. Unrealized gain (or loss) component of accumulated other comprehensive income in shareholders' equity

E 12–15
Equity investments; fair value through net income
LO12-4

On March 31, 2018, Chow Brothers, Inc., bought 10% of KT Manufacturing's capital stock for $50 million. KT's net income for the year ended December 31, 2018, was $80 million. The fair value of the shares held by Chow was $35 million at December 31, 2018. KT did not declare or pay a dividend during 2018.

Required:

1. Prepare all appropriate journal entries related to the investment during 2018.
2. Assume that Chow sold the stock on January 20, 2019 for $30 million. Prepare the journal entry Sanborn would use to record the sale.

E 12–16
Equity investments; fair value through net income
LO12-4

On January 2, 2018, Sanborn Tobacco Inc. bought 5% of Jackson Industry's capital stock for $90 million. Jackson Industry's net income for the year ended December 31, 2018, was $120 million. The fair value of the shares held by Sanborn was $98 million at December 31, 2018. During 2018, Jackson declared a dividend of $60 million.

Required:

1. Prepare all appropriate journal entries related to the investment during 2018.
2. Assume that Sanborn sold the stock on January 2, 2019 for $110 million. Prepare the journal entry Sanborn would use to record the sale.

E 12–17
Equity investments; fair value through net income
LO12-4

The accounting records of Jamaican Importers, Inc., at January 1, 2018, included the following:

Assets:	
Investment in IBM common shares	$1,345,000
Less: Fair value adjustment	(145,000)
	$1,200,000
Shareholders' Equity:	
Accumulated unrealized holding gains and losses	$ 145,000

No changes occurred during 2018 in the investment portfolio.

Required:

Prepare appropriate adjusting entry(s) at December 31, 2018, assuming the fair value of the IBM common shares was:

1. $1,175,000
2. $1,275,000
3. $1,375,000

E 12–18
Equity investments; fair value through net income
LO12-4

The investments of Harlon Enterprises included the following cost and fair value amounts ($ in millions):

		Fair Value, Dec. 31	
Equity Investments	**Cost**	**2018**	**2019**
A Corporation shares	$ 20	$14	na
B Corporation bonds	35	35	$ 37
C Corporation shares	15	na	14
D Industries shares	45	46	50
Totals	$115	$95	$101

Harlon accounts for its equity investment portfolio at fair value through net income. Harlon sold its holdings of A Corporation shares on June 1, 2019, for $15 million. On September 12, it purchased the C Corporation shares.

Required:

1. What is the effect of the sale of the A Corporation shares and the purchase of the C Corporation shares on Harlon's 2019 pretax earnings?
2. At what amount should Harlon's securities equity investment portfolio be reported in its 2019 balance sheet?

E 12–19
Investment securities and equity method investments compared
LO12-5, LO12-6

As a long-term investment, Painters' Equipment Company purchased 20% of AMC Supplies Inc.'s 400,000 shares for $480,000 at the beginning of the fiscal year of both companies. On the purchase date, the fair value and book value of AMC's net assets were equal. During the year, AMC earned net income of $250,000 and distributed cash dividends of 25 cents per share. At year-end, the fair value of the shares is $505,000.

Required:

1. Assume no significant influence was acquired. Prepare the appropriate journal entries from the purchase through the end of the year.
2. Assume significant influence was acquired. Prepare the appropriate journal entries from the purchase through the end of the year.

E 12–20
Equity method; purchase; investee income; dividends
LO12-6

As a long-term investment at the beginning of the 2018 fiscal year, Florists International purchased 30% of Nursery Supplies Inc.'s 8 million shares for $56 million. The fair value and book value of the shares were the same at that time. During the year, Nursery Supplies earned net income of $40 million and distributed cash dividends of $1.25 per share. At the end of the year, the fair value of the shares is $52 million.

Required:

Prepare the appropriate journal entries from the purchase through the end of the year.

E 12–21
Error corrections; equity method investment
LO12-6, LO12-7

On December 12, 2018, an equity investment costing $80,000 was sold for $100,000. The investment was carried in the balance sheet at $75,000, and was accounted for under the equity method. An error was made in which the total of the sale proceeds was credited to the investment account.

Required:

1. Prepare the journal entry to correct the error assuming it is discovered before the books are adjusted or closed in 2018. (Ignore income taxes.)
2. Prepare the journal entry to correct the error assuming it is not discovered until early 2019. (Ignore income taxes.)

E 12–22
Equity method; adjustment for depreciation
LO12-6, LO12-7

Fizer Pharmaceutical paid $68 million on January 2, 2018, for 4 million shares of Carne Cosmetics common stock. The investment represents a 25% interest in the net assets of Carne and gave Fizer the ability to exercise significant influence over Carne's operations. Fizer received dividends of $1 per share on December 21, 2018, and Carne reported net income of $40 million for the year ended December 31, 2018. The fair value of Carne's common stock at December 31, 2018, was $18.50 per share.

- The book value of Carne's net assets was $192 million.
- The fair value of Carne's depreciable assets exceeded their book value by $32 million. These assets had an average remaining useful life of eight years.
- The remainder of the excess of the cost of the investment over the book value of net assets purchased was attributable to goodwill.

Required:

Prepare all appropriate journal entries related to the investment during 2018.

E 12–23
Equity method
LO12-6, LO12-7

On January 1, 2018, Cameron Inc. bought 20% of the outstanding common stock of Lake Construction Company for $300 million cash. At the date of acquisition of the stock, Lake's net assets had a fair value of $900 million. Their book value was $800 million. The difference was attributable to the fair value of Lake's buildings and its land exceeding book value, each accounting for one-half of the difference. Lake's net income for the year ended December 31, 2018, was $150 million. During 2018, Lake declared and paid cash dividends of $30 million. The buildings have a remaining life of 10 years.

Required:

1. Prepare all appropriate journal entries related to the investment during 2018, assuming Cameron accounts for this investment by the equity method.
2. Determine the amounts to be reported by Cameron:
   a. As an investment in Cameron's 2018 balance sheet

b. As investment revenue in the income statement
c. Among investing activities in the statement of cash flows

E 12–24
Equity method, partial year
● LO12-6, LO12-7

On July 1, 2018, Gupta Corporation bought 25% of the outstanding common stock of VB Company for $100 million cash. At the date of acquisition of the stock, VB's net assets had a total fair value of $350 million and a book value of $220 million. Of the $130 million difference, $20 million was attributable to the appreciated value of inventory that was sold during the last half of 2018, $80 million was attributable to buildings that had a remaining depreciable life of 10 years, and $30 million related to equipment that had a remaining depreciable life of 5 years. Between July 1, 2018, and December 31, 2018, VB earned net income of $32 million and declared and paid cash dividends of $24 million.

Required:
1. Prepare all appropriate journal entries related to the investment during 2018, assuming Gupta accounts for this investment by the equity method.
2. Determine the amounts to be reported by Gupta:
   a. As an investment in Gupta's December 31, 2018, balance sheet
   b. As investment revenue or loss in Gupta's 2018 income statement
   c. Among investing activities in Gupta's 2018 statement of cash flows

E 12–25
Fair value option; held-to-maturity investments
● LO12-1, LO12-2, LO12-3, LO12-8

[This is a variation of E12–1 focusing on the fair value option.]
Tanner-UNF Corporation acquired as a long-term investment $240 million of 6% bonds, dated July 1, on July 1, 2018. Company management has the positive intent and ability to hold the bonds until maturity, but when the bonds were acquired Tanner-UNF decided to elect the fair value option for accounting for its investment. The market interest rate (yield) was 8% for bonds of similar risk and maturity. Tanner-UNF paid $200 million for the bonds. The company will receive interest semiannually on June 30 and December 31. As a result of changing market conditions, the fair value of the bonds at December 31, 2018, was $210 million.

Required:
1. Would this investment be classified on Tanner-UNF's balance sheet as held-to-maturity securities, trading securities, available-for-sale securities, significant-influence investments, or other? Explain.
2. Prepare the journal entry to record Tanner-UNF's investment in the bonds on July 1, 2018.
3. Prepare the journal entries by Tanner-UNF to record interest on December 31, 2018, at the effective (market) rate.
4. Prepare any journal entry necessary to recognize fair value changes as of December 31, 2018.
5. At what amount will Tanner-UNF report its investment in the December 31, 2018, balance sheet? Why?
6. Suppose Moody's bond rating agency downgraded the risk rating of the bonds motivating Tanner-UNF to sell the investment on January 2, 2019, for $190 million. Prepare the journal entry to record the sale.

E 12–26
Fair value option; available-for-sale investments
● LO12-2, LO12-3, LO12-8

[This is a variation of E12–12 focusing on the fair value option.]
Colah Company purchased $1 million of Jackson, Inc. 5% bonds at par on July 1, 2018, with interest paid semiannually. When the bonds were acquired Colah decided to elect the fair value option for accounting for its investment. At December 31, 2018, the Jackson bonds had a fair value of $1.2 million. Colah sold the Jackson bonds on July 1, 2019 for $900,000.

Required:
3. Prepare Colah's journal entries to record:
   a. The purchase of the Jackson bonds on July 1
   b. Interest revenue for the last half of 2018
   c. Any year-end 2018 adjusting entries
   d. Interest revenue for the first half of 2019
   e. Any entry or entries necessary upon sale of the Jackson bonds on July 1, 2019
4. Fill out the following table to show the effect of the Jackson bonds on Colah's net income, other comprehensive income, and comprehensive income for 2018, 2019, and cumulatively over 2018 and 2019.

	2018	2019	Total
Net Income			
OCI			
Comprehensive Income			

E 12–27
Fair value option; equity method investments
● LO12-6, LO12-8

[This is a variation of E 12–20 focusing on the fair value option.]
As a long-term investment at the beginning of the 2018 fiscal year, Florists International purchased 30% of Nursery Supplies Inc.'s 8 million shares for $56 million. The fair value and book value of the shares were the same at that time. The company realizes that this investment typically would be accounted for under the equity method, but instead chooses the fair value option. During the year, Nursery Supplies earned net income of $40 million and distributed cash dividends of $1.25 per share. At the end of the year, the fair value of the shares is $52 million.

Required:

1. Would this investment be classified on Florists' balance sheet as held-to-maturity securities, trading securities, available-for-sale securities, significant-influence investments, or other? Explain.
2. Prepare all appropriate journal entries related to the investment during 2018.
3. Indicate the effect of this investment on 2018 income before taxes.

E 12–28
Life insurance policy (Appendix 12A)

Edible Chemicals Corporation owns a $4 million whole life insurance policy on the life of its CEO, naming Edible Chemicals as beneficiary. The annual premiums are $70,000 and are payable at the beginning of each year. The cash surrender value of the policy was $21,000 at the beginning of 2018.

Required:

1. Prepare the appropriate 2018 journal entry to record insurance expense and the increase in the investment assuming the cash surrender value of the policy increased according to the contract to $27,000.
2. The CEO died at the end of 2018. Prepare the appropriate journal entry.

E 12–29
Life insurance policy (Appendix 12A)

Below are two unrelated situations relating to life insurance.

Required:

Prepare the appropriate journal entry for each situation.

1. Ford Corporation owns a whole life insurance policy on the life of its president. Ford Corporation is the beneficiary. The insurance premium is $25,000. The cash surrender value increased during the year from $2,500 to $4,600.
2. Petroleum Corporation received a $250,000 life insurance settlement when its CEO died. At that time, the cash surrender value was $16,000.

E 12–30
Held-to-maturity securities; impairments (Appendix 12B)
● LO12-2, LO12-8

Bloom Corporation purchased $1,000,000 of Taylor Company 5% bonds at par with the intent and ability to hold the bonds until they matured in 2025, so Bloom classifies their investment as HTM. Unfortunately, a combination of problems at Taylor Company and in the debt market caused the fair value of the Taylor investment to decline to $600,000 during 2018.

Required:

For each of the following scenarios, prepare appropriate entry(s) at December 31, 2018, and indicate how the scenario will affect the 2018 income statement (ignoring income taxes).

1. Bloom now believes it is more likely than not that it will have to sell the Taylor bonds before the bonds have a chance to recover their fair value. Of the $400,000 decline in fair value, Bloom attributes $250,000 to credit losses, and $150,000 to noncredit losses.
2. Bloom does not plan to sell the Taylor bonds prior to maturity, and does not believe it is more likely than not that it will have to sell the Taylor bonds before the bonds have a chance to recover their fair value. Of the $400,000 decline in fair value, Bloom attributes $250,000 to credit losses, and $150,000 to noncredit losses.

E 12–31
Available-for-sale debt securities; impairments (Appendix 12B)
● LO12-4, LO12-8

[Note: This exercise is a variation of E 12–30, modified to categorize the investment as securities available-for-sale.] Assume all of the same facts and scenarios as E 12–30, except that Bloom Corporation classifies their Taylor investment as AFS.

Required:

1. For each of the scenarios shown in E 12–30, prepare the appropriate entry(s) at December 31, 2018. Indicate how the scenario will affect the 2018 income statement, OCI, and comprehensive income.
2. Repeat requirement 1, but now assume that, at the end of 2017, Bloom had recorded a temporary unrealized loss (not an OTT impairment) of $100,000 on the Taylor investment.

E 12–32
Impairments (AFS Credit Loss Model) (Appendix 12B)
● LO12-4, LO12-8

Answer E 12-31 under the assumption that Bloom Corporation used the AFS Credit Loss Model introduced in *ASU 2016-13* and required after 2020.

Required:

Prepare appropriate entry(s) at December 31, 2018, and for each year indicate how the scenario will affect net income, OCI, and comprehensive income.

E 12–33
Accounting for impairments under IFRS (Appendix 12B)
● LO12-2, LO12-8, LO12-9
IFRS

Rell Corporation reports under IFRS No. 9. Rell has an investment in Tirish, Inc. bonds that Rell accounts for at amortized cost, given that the bonds pay only interest and principal and Rell's business purpose is to hold the bonds to maturity. Rell purchased the bonds for €10,000,000. As of December 31, 2018, Rell calculates €750,000 of credit losses expected for default events occurring during 2019 and €450,000 of credit losses expected for default events occurring after 2019.

Required:

1. Assume the Tirish bonds have not had a significant increase in credit risk. Prepare the journal entry to record any impairment loss as of December 31, 2018.
2. Assume the Tirish bonds have had a significant increase in credit risk. Prepare the journal entry to record any impairment loss as of December 31, 2018.
3. Assume the Tirish bonds have not had a significant increase in credit risk, and that as of December 31, 2019, Rell calculates €650,000 of credit losses expected for default events occurring during 2020 and €350,000 of credit losses expected for default events occurring after 2020. Prepare the journal entry Rell would make with respect to any impairment loss as of December 31, 2019.

Problems

connect

P 12–1
Securities held-to-maturity; bond investment; effective interest
● LO12-1, LO12-2

Fuzzy Monkey Technologies, Inc., purchased as a long-term investment $80 million of 8% bonds, dated January 1, on January 1, 2018. Management has the positive intent and ability to hold the bonds until maturity. For bonds of similar risk and maturity the market yield was 10%. The price paid for the bonds was $66 million. Interest is received semiannually on June 30 and December 31. Due to changing market conditions, the fair value of the bonds at December 31, 2018, was $70 million.

Required:

1. Prepare the journal entry to record Fuzzy Monkey's investment on January 1, 2018.
2. Prepare the journal entry by Fuzzy Monkey to record interest on June 30, 2018 (at the effective rate).
3. Prepare the journal entries by Fuzzy Monkey to record interest on December 31, 2018 (at the effective rate).
4. At what amount will Fuzzy Monkey report its investment in the December 31, 2018, balance sheet? Why?
5. How would Fuzzy Monkey's 2018 statement of cash flows be affected by this investment?

P 12–2
Trading securities; bond investment; effective interest
● LO12-1, LO12-3

[This problem is a variation of P12–1, modified to categorize the investment as trading securities.]

Fuzzy Monkey Technologies, Inc., purchased as a short-term investment $80 million of 8% bonds, dated January 1, on January 1, 2018. Management intends to include the investment in a short-term, active trading portfolio. For bonds of similar risk and maturity the market yield was 10%. The price paid for the bonds was $66 million. Interest is received semiannually on June 30 and December 31. Due to changing market conditions, the fair value of the bonds at December 31, 2018, was $70 million.

Required:

1. Prepare the journal entry to record Fuzzy Monkey's investment on January 1, 2018.
2. Prepare the journal entry by Fuzzy Monkey to record interest on June 30, 2018 (at the effective rate).
3. Prepare the journal entries by Fuzzy Monkey to record interest on December 31, 2018 (at the effective rate).
4. At what amount will Fuzzy Monkey report its investment in the December 31, 2018, balance sheet? Why? Prepare any entry necessary to achieve this reporting objective.
5. How would Fuzzy Monkey's 2018 statement of cash flows be affected by this investment?

P 12–3
Securities available-for-sale; bond investment; effective interest
● LO 12-1, LO12-4

(Note: This problem is a variation of P12–1, modified to categorize the investment as securities available-for-sale.)

Fuzzy Monkey Technologies, Inc., purchased as a long-term investment $80 million of 8% bonds, dated January 1, on January 1, 2018. Management intends to have the investment available for sale when circumstances warrant. For bonds of similar risk and maturity the market yield was 10%. The price paid for the bonds was $66 million. Interest is received semiannually on June 30 and December 31. Due to changing market conditions, the fair value of the bonds at December 31, 2018, was $70 million.

Required:

1. Prepare the journal entry to record Fuzzy Monkey's investment on January 1, 2018.
2. Prepare the journal entry by Fuzzy Monkey to record interest on June 30, 2018 (at the effective rate).
3. Prepare the journal entries by Fuzzy Monkey to record interest on December 31, 2018 (at the effective rate).
4. At what amount will Fuzzy Monkey report its investment in the December 31, 2018, balance sheet? Why? Prepare any entry necessary to achieve this reporting objective.
5. How would Fuzzy Monkey's 2018 statement of cash flows be affected by this investment?

P 12–4
Fair value option; bond investment; effective interest
LO12-1, LO12-2, LO12-3, LO12-4, LO12-8

[This problem is a variation of P 12–3, modified to cause the investment to be accounted for under the fair value option.]

Fuzzy Monkey Technologies, Inc., purchased as a long-term investment $80 million of 8% bonds, dated January 1, on January 1, 2018. Management intends to have the investment available for sale when circumstances warrant. When the company purchased the bonds, management elected to account for them under the fair value option. For bonds of similar risk and maturity the market yield was 10%. The price paid for the bonds was $66 million. Interest is received semiannually on June 30 and December 31. Due to changing market conditions, the fair value of the bonds at December 31, 2018, was $70 million.

Required:

1. Prepare the journal entry to record Fuzzy Monkey's investment on January 1, 2018.
2. Prepare the journal entry by Fuzzy Monkey to record interest on June 30, 2018 (at the effective rate).
3. Prepare the journal entries by Fuzzy Monkey to record interest on December 31, 2018 (at the effective rate).
4. At what amount will Fuzzy Monkey report its investment in the December 31, 2018, balance sheet? Why? Prepare any entry necessary to achieve this reporting objective.
5. How would Fuzzy Monkey's 2018 statement of cash flows be affected by this investment?
6. How would your answers to requirements 1–5 differ if management had the intent and ability to hold the investments until maturity?

P 12–5
Various transactions related to trading securities
LO12-1, LO12-3

The following selected transactions relate to investment activities of Ornamental Insulation Corporation during 2018. The company buys debt securities, intending to profit from short-term differences in price and maintaining them in an active trading portfolio. Ornamental's fiscal year ends on December 31. No investments were held by Ornamental on December 31, 2017.

Mar. 31	Acquired 8% Distribution Transformers Corporation bonds costing $400,000 at face value.	
Sep. 1	Acquired $900,000 of American Instruments' 10% bonds at face value.	
Sep. 30	Received semiannual interest payment on the Distribution Transformers bonds.	
Oct. 2	Sold the Distribution Transformers bonds for $425,000.	
Nov. 1	Purchased $1,400,000 of M&D Corporation 6% bonds at face value.	
Dec. 31	Recorded any necessary adjusting entry(s) relating to the investments. The market prices of the investments are:	
	American Instruments bonds	$ 850,000
	M&D Corporation bonds	$1,460,000
	(Hint: Interest must be accrued.)	

Required:

1. Prepare the appropriate journal entry for each transaction or event during 2018, as well as any adjusting entries necessary at year end.
2. Indicate any amounts that Ornamental Insulation would report in its 2018 income statement, 2018 statement of comprehensive income, and 12/31/2018 balance sheet as a result of these investments.

P 12–6
Various transactions related to securities available-for-sale
LO12-1, LO12-4

(Note: This problem is a variation of P 12–5, modified to categorize the investments as securities available-for-sale.)

The following selected transactions relate to investment activities of Ornamental Insulation Corporation during 2018. The company buys debt securities, *not* intending to profit from short-term differences in price and *not* necessarily to hold debt securities to maturity, but to have them available for sale when circumstances warrant. Ornamental's fiscal year ends on December 31. No investments were held by Ornamental on December 31, 2017.

Mar. 31	Acquired 8% Distribution Transformers Corporation bonds costing $400,000 at face value.	
Sep. 1	Acquired $900,000 of American Instruments' 10% bonds at face value.	
Sep. 30	Received semiannual interest payment on the Distribution Transformers bonds.	
Oct. 2	Sold the Distribution Transformers bonds for $425,000.	
Nov. 1	Purchased $1,400,000 of M&D Corporation 6% bonds costing at face value.	
Dec. 31	Recorded any necessary adjusting entry(s) relating to the investments. The market prices of the investments are:	
	American Instruments bonds	$ 850,000
	M&D Corporation bonds	$1,460,000
	(Hint: Interest must be accrued.)	

Required:

1. Prepare the appropriate journal entry for each transaction or event during 2018, as well as any adjusting entries necessary at year end. For any sales, prepare entries to update the fair-value adjustment, record any reclassification adjustment, and record the sale.
2. Indicate any amounts that Ornamental Insulation would report in its 2018 income statement, 2018 statement of comprehensive income, and 12/31/2018 balance sheet as a result of these investments.

P 12–7
Various transactions related to equity investments: fair value through net income
● LO12-5

(Note: This problem is a variation of P12–5, modified to consider equity investments.)

The following selected transactions relate to investment activities of Ornamental Insulation Corporation during 2018. The company buys equity securities as investments. None of Ornamental's investments are large enough to exert significant influence on the investee. Ornamental's fiscal year ends on December 31. No investments were held by Ornamental on December 31, 2017.

Mar. 31	Acquired Distribution Transformers Corporation common stock for $400,000.
Sep. 1	Acquired $900,000 of American Instruments' common stock.
Sep. 30	Received a $16,000 dividend on the Distribution Transformers common stock.
Oct. 2	Sold the Distribution Transformers common stock for $425,000.
Nov. 1	Purchased $1,400,000 of M&D Corporation common stock.
Dec. 31	Recorded any necessary adjusting entry(s) relating to the investments. The market prices of the investments are:

American Instruments common stock	$ 850,000
M&D Corporation common stock	$1,460,000

Required:

1. Prepare the appropriate journal entry for each transaction or event during 2018, as well as any adjusting entries necessary at year end.
2. Indicate any amounts that Ornamental Insulation would report in its 2018 income statement, 2018 statement of comprehensive income, and 12/31/2018 balance sheet as a result of these investments.

P 12–8
Various transactions relating to trading securities and equity investments
● LO12-1, LO12-3, LO12-5

American Surety and Fidelity buys and sells securities expecting to earn profits on short-term differences in price. For the first 11 months of 2018, gains from selling trading securities totaled $8 million, losses were $11 million, and the company had earned $5 million in investment revenue. The following selected transactions relate to American's trading account and equity securities investment account during December 2018, and the first week of 2019. The company's fiscal year ends on December 31. No trading securities were held by American on December 1, 2018.

2018	
Dec. 12	Purchased FF&G Corporation bonds for $12 million.
13	Purchased 2 million Ferry Intercommunications common shares for $22 million.
15	Sold the FF&G Corporation bonds for $12.1 million.
22	Purchased U.S. Treasury bills for $56 million and Treasury bonds for $65 million.
23	Sold half the Ferry Intercommunications common shares for $10 million.
26	Sold the U.S. Treasury bills for $57 million.
27	Sold the Treasury bonds for $63 million.
28	Received cash dividends of $200,000 from the Ferry Intercommunications common shares.
31	Recorded any necessary adjusting entry(s) and closing entries relating to the investments. The market price of the Ferry Intercommunications stock was $10 per share.
2019	
Jan. 2	Sold the remaining Ferry Intercommunications common shares for $10.2 million.
5	Purchased Warehouse Designs Corporation bonds for $34 million.

Required:

1. Prepare the appropriate journal entry for each transaction or event during 2018.
2. Indicate any amounts that American would report in its 2018 balance sheet and income statement as a result of these investments.
3. Prepare the appropriate journal entry for each transaction or event during 2019.

P 12–9
Securities held-to-maturity; securities available for sale; trading securities and equity investments
● LO12-1, LO12-2, LO12-3, LO12-4, LO12-5

Amalgamated General Corporation is a consulting firm that also offers financial services through its credit division. From time to time the company buys and sells securities. The following selected transactions relate to Amalgamated's investment activities during the last quarter of 2018 and the first month of 2019. The only securities held by Amalgamated at October 1 were $30 million of 10% bonds of Kansas Abstractors, Inc., purchased on May 1 at face value and held in Amalgamated's trading portfolio. The company's fiscal year ends on December 31.

2018	
Oct. 18	Purchased 2 million preferred shares of Millwork Ventures Company for $58 million.
31	Received semiannual interest of $1.5 million from the Kansas Abstractors bonds.
Nov. 1	Purchased 10% bonds of Holistic Entertainment Enterprises at their $18 million face value, to be held until they mature in 2025. Semiannual interest is payable April 30 and October 31.

(continued)

(concluded)

1	Sold the Kansas Abstractors bonds for $28 million because rising interest rates are expected to cause their fair value to continue to fall. No unrealized gains and losses had been recorded on these bonds previously.
Dec. 1	Purchased 12% bonds of Household Plastics Corporation at their $60 million face value, to be held until they mature in 2028. Semiannual interest is payable May 31 and November 30.
20	Purchased U. S. Treasury bonds for $5.6 million as trading securities, hoping to earn profits on short-term differences in prices.
21	Purchased 4 million common shares of NXS Corporation for $44 million, planning to earn profits from dividends or gains if prevailing market conditions encourage sale.
23	Sold the Treasury bonds for $5.7 million.
29	Received cash dividends of $3 million from the Millwork Ventures Company preferred shares.
31	Recorded any necessary adjusting entry(s) and closing entries relating to the investments. The market price of the Millwork Ventures Company preferred stock was $27.50 per share and $11.50 per share for the NXS Corporation common. The fair values of the bond investments were $58.7 million for Household Plastics Corporation and $16.7 million for Holistic Entertainment Enterprises.
2019	
Jan. 7	Sold the NXS Corporation common shares for $43 million.

Required:
Prepare the appropriate journal entry for each transaction or event.

P 12–10
Investment securities and equity method investments compared
● LO12-6, LO12-7

On January 4, 2018, Runyan Bakery paid $324 million for 10 million shares of Lavery Labeling Company common stock. The investment represents a 30% interest in the net assets of Lavery and gave Runyan the ability to exercise significant influence over Lavery's operations. Runyan received dividends of $2.00 per share on December 15, 2018, and Lavery reported net income of $160 million for the year ended December 31, 2018. The market value of Lavery's common stock at December 31, 2018, was $31 per share. On the purchase date, the book value of Lavery's net assets was $800 million and:

a. The fair value of Lavery's depreciable assets, with an average remaining useful life of six years, exceeded their book value by $80 million.
b. The remainder of the excess of the cost of the investment over the book value of net assets purchased was attributable to goodwill.

Required:
1. Prepare all appropriate journal entries related to the investment during 2018, assuming Runyan accounts for this investment by the equity method.
2. Prepare the journal entries required by Runyan, assuming that the 10 million shares represent a 10% interest in the net assets of Lavery rather than a 30% interest.

P 12–11
Fair value option; equity method investments
● LO12-5, LO12-8

[This problem is a variation of P 12–10 focusing on the fair value option.]

On January 4, 2018, Runyan Bakery paid $324 million for 10 million shares of Lavery Labeling Company common stock. The investment represents a 30% interest in the net assets of Lavery and gave Runyan the ability to exercise significant influence over Lavery's operations. Runyan chose the fair value option to account for this investment. Runyan received dividends of $2.00 per share on December 15, 2018, and Lavery reported net income of $160 million for the year ended December 31, 2018. The market value of Lavery's common stock at December 31, 2018, was $31 per share. On the purchase date, the book value of Lavery's net assets was $800 million and:

a. The fair value of Lavery's depreciable assets, with an average remaining useful life of six years, exceeded their book value by $80 million.
b. The remainder of the excess of the cost of the investment over the book value of net assets purchased was attributable to goodwill.

Required:
Assuming Runyan accounts for this investment under the fair value option, prepare all appropriate journal entries in a manner similar to accounting for securities for which there is not significant influence.

P 12–12
Fair value option; equity method investments
● LO12-5, LO12-6, LO12-7, LO12-8

[This problem is an expanded version of P 12–11 that considers alternative ways in which a firm might apply the fair value option to account for significant-influence investments that would normally be accounted for under the equity method.]

Companies can choose the fair value option for investments that otherwise would be accounted for under the equity method. If the fair value option is chosen, the investment is shown at fair value in the balance sheet, and unrealized holding gains and losses are recognized in the income statement. However, exactly how a company complies with those broad requirements is up to the company. This problem requires you to consider alternative ways in which a company might apply the fair value option for investments that otherwise would be accounted for under the equity method.

On January 4, 2018, Runyan Bakery paid $324 million for 10 million shares of Lavery Labeling Company common stock. The investment represents a 30% interest in the net assets of Lavery and gave Runyan the ability to exercise significant influence over Lavery's operations. Runyan chose the fair value option to account for this investment. Runyan received dividends of $2.00 per share on December 15, 2018, and Lavery reported net income of $160 million for the year ended December 31, 2018. The market value of Lavery's common stock at December 31, 2018, was $31 per share. On the purchase date, the book value of Lavery's net assets was $800 million and:

a. The fair value of Lavery's depreciable assets, with an average remaining useful life of six years, exceeded their book value by $80 million.
b. The remainder of the excess of the cost of the investment over the book value of net assets purchased was attributable to goodwill.

Required:

1. Prepare all appropriate journal entries related to the investment during 2018, assuming Runyan accounts for this investment under the fair value option, and accounts for the Lavery investment in a manner similar to what it would use for securities for which there is not significant influence. Indicate the effect of these journal entries on 2018 net income, and indicate the amount at which the investment is carried in the December 31, 2018, balance sheet.
2. Prepare all appropriate journal entries related to the investment during 2018, assuming Runyan accounts for this investment under the fair value option, but uses equity method accounting to account for Lavery's income and dividends, and then records a fair value adjustment at the end of the year that allows it to comply with GAAP. Indicate the effect of these journal entries on 2018 net income, and indicate the amount at which the investment is carried in the December 31, 2018, balance sheet. (Note: You should end up with the same total 2018 income effect and same carrying value on the balance sheet for requirements 1 and 2.)

P 12–13
Equity method
● LO12-6, LO12-7

Northwest Paperboard Company, a paper and allied products manufacturer, was seeking to gain a foothold in Canada. Toward that end, the company bought 40% of the outstanding common shares of Vancouver Timber and Milling, Inc., on January 2, 2018, for $400 million.

At the date of purchase, the book value of Vancouver's net assets was $775 million. The book values and fair values for all balance sheet items were the same except for inventory and plant facilities. The fair value exceeded book value by $5 million for the inventory and by $20 million for the plant facilities.

The estimated useful life of the plant facilities is 16 years. All inventory acquired was sold during 2018.

Vancouver reported net income of $140 million for the year ended December 31, 2018. Vancouver paid a cash dividend of $30 million.

Required:

1. Prepare all appropriate journal entries related to the investment during 2018.
2. What amount should Northwest report as its income from its investment in Vancouver for the year ended December 31, 2018?
3. What amount should Northwest report in its balance sheet as its investment in Vancouver?
4. What should Northwest report in its statement of cash flows regarding its investment in Vancouver?

P 12–14
Equity method
● LO12-6, LO12-7

On January 2, 2018, Miller Properties paid $19 million for 1 million shares of Marlon Company's 6 million outstanding common shares. Miller's CEO became a member of Marlon's board of directors during the first quarter of 2018.

The carrying amount of Marlon's net assets was $66 million. Miller estimated the fair value of those net assets to be the same except for a patent valued at $24 million above cost. The remaining amortization period for the patent is 10 years.

Marlon reported earnings of $12 million and paid dividends of $6 million during 2018. On December 31, 2018, Marlon's common stock was trading on the NYSE at $18.50 per share.

Required:

1. When considering whether to account for its investment in Marlon under the equity method, what criteria should Miller's management apply?
2. Assume Miller accounts for its investment in Marlon using the equity method. Ignoring income taxes, determine the amounts related to the investment to be reported in its 2018:
   a. Income statement
   b. Balance sheet
   c. Statement of cash flows

P 12–15
Classifying investments
● LO12-2 through LO12-6

Indicate (by letter) the way each of the investments listed below most likely should be accounted for based on the information provided.

Item	Reporting Category
____ 1. 35% of the nonvoting preferred stock of American Aircraft Company	T. Trading securities
____ 2. Treasury bills to be held to maturity	M. Securities held-to-maturity
____ 3. Two-year note receivable from affiliate	A. Securities available-for-sale
____ 4. Accounts receivable	
____ 5. Treasury bond maturing in one week	F. Fair value through net income
____ 6. Common stock held in an investment account for immediate resale	E. Equity method
____ 7. Bonds acquired to profit from short-term differences in price	C. Consolidation
____ 8. 35% of the voting common stock of Computer Storage Devices Company	N. None of these
____ 9. 90% of the voting common stock of Affiliated Peripherals, Inc	
____ 10. Corporate bonds of Primary Smelting Company to be sold if interest rates fall ½%	
____ 11. 25% of the voting common stock of Smith Foundries Corporation (51% family-owned by Smith family; fair value readily determinable)	
____ 12. 17% of the voting common stock of Shipping Barrels Corporation (Investor's CEO on the board of directors of Shipping Barrels Corporation)	

P 12–16
Fair value option; held-to-maturity investments
LO12-1, LO12-2, LO12-8

On January 1, 2018, Ithaca Corp. purchases Cortland Inc. bonds that have a face value of $150,000. The Cortland bonds have a stated interest rate of 6%. Interest is paid semiannually on June 30 and December 31, and the bonds mature in 10 years. For bonds of similar risk and maturity, the market yield on particular dates is as follows:

January 1, 2018	7.0%
June 30, 2018	8.0%
December 31, 2018	9.0%

Required:

1. Calculate the price Ithaca would have paid for the Cortland bonds on January 1, 2018 (ignoring brokerage fees), and prepare a journal entry to record the purchase.
2. Prepare all appropriate journal entries related to the bond investment during 2018, assuming Ithaca accounts for the bonds as a held-to-maturity investment. Ithaca calculates interest revenue at the effective interest rate as of the date it purchased the bonds.
3. Prepare all appropriate journal entries related to the bond investment during 2018, assuming that Ithaca chose the fair value option when the bonds were purchased, and that Ithaca determines fair value of the bonds semi-annually. Ithaca calculates interest revenue at the effective interest rate as of the date it purchased the bonds.

P 12–17
Accounting for debt and equity investments
LO12-1, LO12-4, LO12-5, LO12-9
IFRS

Feherty, Inc., accounts for its investments under *IFRS No. 9* and purchased the following investments during December 2018:

1. Fifty of Donald Company's $1,000 bonds. The bonds pay semiannual interest, return principal in eight years, and include no other cash flows or other features. Feherty plans to hold 10 of the bonds to collect contractual cash flows over the life of the investment and to hold 40, both to collect contractual cash flows but also to sell them if their price appreciates sufficiently. Subsequent to Feherty's purchase of the bonds, but prior to December 31, the fair value of the bonds increased to $1,040 per bond, and Feherty sold 10 of the 40 bonds. Feherty also sold 5 of the 10 bonds it had planned to hold to collect contractual cash flows over the life of the investment. The fair value of the bonds remained at $1,040 as of December 31, 2018.
2. $25,000 of Watson Company common stock. Feherty does not have the ability to significantly influence the operations of Watson. Feherty elected to account for this equity investment at fair value through OCI (FVOCI). Subsequent to Feherty's purchase of the stock, the fair value of the stock investment increased to $30,000 as of December 31, 2018.

Required:

1. Indicate how Feherty would account for its investments when it acquired the Donald bonds and Watson stock.
2. Calculate the effect of realized and unrealized gains and losses associated with the Donald bonds and the Watson stock on Feherty's net income, other comprehensive income, and comprehensive income for the year ended December 31, 2018. Ignore interest revenue and taxes.

P 12–18
Accounting for other-than-temporary impairments (Appendix 12B)
LO12-2, LO12-3, LO12-4, LO12-8

Stewart Enterprises has the following investments, all purchased prior to 2018:

1. Bee Company 5% bonds, purchased at face value, with an amortized cost of $4,000,000, and classified as held to maturity. At December 31, 2018, the Bee investment had a fair value of $3,500,000, and Stewart calculated that $240,000 of the fair value decline is a credit loss and $260,000 is a noncredit loss. At December 31, 2019, the Bee investment had a fair value of $3,700,000, and Stewart calculated that $140,000 of the difference between fair value and amortized cost was a credit loss and $160,000 was a noncredit loss.

2. Oliver Corporation 4% bonds, purchased at face value, with an amortized cost of $2,500,000, classified as a trading security. Because of unrealized losses prior to 2018, the Oliver bonds have a fair value adjustment account with a credit balance of $200,000, such that the carrying value of the Oliver investment is $2,300,000 prior to making any adjusting entries in 2018. At December 31, 2018, the Oliver investment had a fair value of $2,200,000, and Stewart calculated that $120,000 of the difference between amortized cost and fair value is a credit loss and $180,000 is a noncredit loss. At December 31, 2019, the Oliver investment had a fair value of $2,700,000.
3. Jones Inc. 6% bonds, purchased at face value, with an amortized cost of $3,500,000, and classified as an available-for-sale investment. Because of unrealized losses prior to 2018, the Jones bonds have a fair value adjustment account with a credit balance of $400,000, such that the carrying value of the Jones investment is $3,100,000 prior to making any adjusting entries in 2018. At December 31, 2018, the Jones investment had a fair value of $2,700,000, and Stewart calculated that $225,000 of the difference between amortized cost and fair value is a credit loss and $575,000 is a noncredit loss. At December 31, 2019, the Jones investment had a fair value of $2,900,000, and Stewart calculated that $125,000 of the difference between amortized cost and fair value is a credit loss and $475,000 is a noncredit loss.

Stewart does not intend to sell any of these investments and does not believe it is more likely than not that it will have to sell any of the bond investments before fair value recovers.

Required:

Prepare the appropriate adjusting journal entries to account for fair value changes during 2018 and 2019, assuming that each investment is viewed as qualifying as an other-than-temporary (OTT) impairment as of December 31, 2018, and then is accounted for normally during 2019 (with no additional OTT impairment in 2019).

Broaden Your Perspective

Apply your critical-thinking ability to the knowledge you've gained. These cases will provide you an opportunity to develop your research, analysis, judgment, and communication skills. You also will work with other students, integrate what you've learned, apply it in real world situations, and consider its global and ethical ramifications. This practice will broaden your knowledge and further develop your decision-making abilities.

Real World Case 12–1
Intel's investments
● LO12-4

The following disclosure note appeared in the December 26, 2015, annual report of the Intel Corporation.

Note 5: Cash and Investments (partial)

Available-for-sale investments as of December 26, 2015, and December 27, 2014, were as follows:

	December 26, 2015				December 27, 2014			
($ in millions)	Adjusted Cost	Gross Unrealized Gains	Gross Unrealized Losses	Fair Value	Adjusted Cost	Gross Unrealized Gains	Gross Unrealized Losses	Fair Value
Asset-backed securities	$ 5	$ —	$ (1)	$ 4	$ 8	$ —	$(2)	$ 6
Corporate debt	4,164	3	(10)	4,157	2,040	13	(5)	2,048
Financial institution instruments	11,140	1	(2)	11,139	3,146	2	(1)	3,147
Government debt	748	—	(1)	747	741	—	(1)	740
Marketable equity securities	3,254	2,706	—	5,960	3,318	3,779	—	7,097
Total available-for-sale investments	$19,311	$2,710	$(14)	$22,007	$9,253	$3,794	$(9)	$13,038

Intel also indicates the following: "During 2015, we sold available-for-sale investments for proceeds of $2.2 billion . . . The gross realized gains on sales of available-for-sale investments were $133 million in 2015. Intel's Note 24 (Other Comprehensive Income) indicates unrealized holding losses of $999 million during 2015, and a reclassification adjustment of $93 for gains that had previously been included in OCI and recorded in the fair value adjustment but which were now being included in net income after being realized upon sale. Note: Intel's 2015 financial statements were issued prior to the effective date of *ASU 2016-01*, so Intel includes equity investments among its available-for-sale investments. That difference from current GAAP will not affect your answer to the case questions.

Required:

1. Draw a T-account that shows the change between the December 27, 2014, and December 26, 2015, balances for the fair value adjustment associated with Intel's AFS investments for 2015. By how much did the fair value adjustment change during 2015?
2. Prepare a journal entry that records any unrealized holding gains and losses that occurred during 2015. Ignore income taxes.
3. Prepare a journal entry that records any reclassification adjustment for available-for-sale investments sold during 2015. Ignore income taxes.
4. Using your journal entries from requirements 2 and 3, adjust your T-account from requirement 1. Have you accounted for the entire change in the fair value adjustment that occurred during 2015? Speculate as to the cause of any difference.

Real World Case 12–2
Reporting securities available-for-sale; obtain and critically evaluate an annual report
● LO12-4

All publicly traded domestic companies use EDGAR, the Electronic Data Gathering, Analysis, and Retrieval system, to make the majority of their filings with the SEC. You can access EDGAR at www.sec.gov.

Required:

1. Locate a recent annual report of a public company that includes a footnote that describes an investment in securities available-for-sale. You can use EDGAR at www.sec.gov.
2. Under what caption are the investments reported in the comparative balance sheets? Are they reported as current or noncurrent assets?
3. Are realized gains or losses reported in the comparative income statements?
4. Are unrealized gains or losses reported in the comparative statements and shareholders' equity?
5. Are accumulated unrealized gains or losses identifiable in the comparative balance sheets? If so, under what caption? Why are unrealized gains or losses reported here rather in the income statement?
6. Are cash flow effects of these investments reflected in the company's comparative statements of cash flows? If so, what information is provided by this disclosure?

International Case 12–3
Comparison of equity method between IFRS and U.S. GAAP
● LO12-5, LO12-6, LO12-7, LO12-9

IFRS

The following are excerpts from the 2015 financial statements of Renault, a large French automobile manufacturer.

14 – INVESTMENT IN NISSAN

A – Nissan consolidation method

Renault's percentage interest in Nissan is 43.7% and Renault holds 43.4% of voting rights in Nissan. Renault and Nissan have chosen to develop a unique type of alliance between two distinct companies with common interests, uniting forces to achieve optimum performance. The Alliance is organized so as to preserve individual brand identities and respect each company's corporate culture.

Consequently:

- Renault is not assured of holding the majority of voting rights in Nissan's Shareholders' Meeting.
- The terms of the Renault-Nissan agreement do not entitle Renault to appoint the majority of Nissan directors, nor to hold the majority of voting rights at meetings of Nissan's Board of Directors; Renault cannot unilaterally appoint the President of Nissan; on December 31, 2015, Renault occupied two of the nine seats on Nissan's Board of Directors (unchanged since December 31, 2014).
- Renault-Nissan B.V., owned 50% by Renault and 50% by Nissan, is the Alliance's joint decision-making body for strategic issues concerning either group individually. Its decisions are applicable to both Renault and Nissan. This decision-making power was conferred on Renault-Nissan B.V. to generate synergies and bring both automakers worldwide economies of scale. This entity does not enable Renault to direct Nissan's financial and operating strategies, which are governed by Nissan's Board of Directors and cannot therefore be considered to represent contractual control by Renault over Nissan. The matters examined by Renault-Nissan B.V. since it was formed have remained strictly within this contractual framework, and are not an indication that Renault exercises control over Nissan.
- Renault can neither use nor influence the use of Nissan's assets in the same way as its own assets.
- Renault provides no guarantees in respect of Nissan's debt.

In view of this situation, Renault is considered to exercise significant influence over Nissan, and therefore uses the equity method to include its investment in Nissan in the consolidation.

Renault's Note D lists various restatements that Renault makes when accounting for its Nissan investment under the equity method. Some of those changes harmonize Nissan's accounting (under Japanese accounting standards). Others reflect adjustments to fair value of assets and liabilities applied by Renault at the time of acquisitions in 1999 and 2002.

Required:

1. Go to Deloitte's IAS Plus website and examine the summary of the IASB's *IAS No. 28* (http://www.iasplus.com/standard/ias28.htm), which governs application of the equity method. Focus on two areas: Identification of Associates and Applying the Equity Method of Accounting.

2. Evaluate Renault's decision to use the equity method to account for its investment in Nissan. Does Renault have insignificant influence, significant influence, or control?
3. Evaluate the fact that, when accounting for its investment in Nissan under the equity method, Renault makes adjustments that take into account the fair value of assets and liabilities at the time Renault invested in Nissan. Give an example of the sorts of adjustments that might be made. Are such adjustments consistent with IFRS? With U.S. GAAP? Explain.
4. Evaluate the fact that, when accounting for its investment in Nissan under the equity method, Renault makes adjustments for harmonization of accounting standards. Are such adjustments consistent with IFRS? With U.S. GAAP? Explain.

International Case 12–4
Comparison of equity method and proportionate consolidation under IFRS
● LO12-6, LO12-9

IFRS

Obtain the 2015 annual report of FCA Group (www.fcagroup.com), which manufactures Fiat-brand automobiles as well as other products.

Required:

Find FCA's discussion of "Interests in other companies" in the "Significant Accounting Policies" note that follows the financial statements. Is FCA accounting for its equity investments in a way that is consistent with U.S. GAAP? Explain.

Research Case 12–5
Researching the way investments are reported; retrieving information from the Internet
● LO12-2, LO12-3, LO12-4, LO12-5, LO12-6

All publicly traded domestic companies use EDGAR, the Electronic Data Gathering, Analysis, and Retrieval system, to make the majority of their filings with the SEC. You can access EDGAR at www.sec.gov.

Required:

1. Search for a public company with which you are familiar. Access its most recent 10-K filing. Search or scroll to find financial statements and related notes.
2. Answer the following questions. (If the chosen company does not report investments in the securities of other companies, choose another company.)
   a. What is the amount and classification of any investment securities reported in the balance sheet? Are unrealized gains or losses reported in the shareholders' equity section?
   b. Are any investments reported by the equity method?
   c. What amounts from these investments are reported in the comparative income statements? Has that income increased or decreased over the years reported?
   d. Are any acquisitions or disposals of investments reported in the statement of cash flows?

Real World Case 12–6
Merck's investments
● LO12-4, LO12-5, LO12-6

Corporations frequently invest in securities issued by other corporations. Some investments are acquired to secure a favorable business relationship with another company. On the other hand, others are intended only to earn an investment return from the dividends or interest the securities pay or from increases in the market prices of the securities—the same motivations that might cause you to invest in stocks, bonds, or other securities. This diversity in investment objectives means no single accounting method is adequate to report every investment.

Merck & Co., Inc., invests in securities of other companies. Access Merck's 2015 10-K (which includes financial statements) using EDGAR at www.sec.gov. Note: Merck's 2015 financial statements were issued prior to the effective date of *ASU 2016-01*, so do not be surprised by the fact that Merck includes equity investments among its available-for-sale investments.

Required:

1. What is the amount and classification of any investment securities reported on the balance sheet? In which current and noncurrent asset categories are investments reported by Merck? What criteria are used to determine the classifications?
2. How are unrealized gains or losses reported? Realized gains and losses?
3. Are any investments reported by the equity method?
4. What amounts from equity method investments are reported in the comparative income statements?
5. Are cash flow effects of these investments reflected in the company's comparative statements of cash flows? If so, what information is provided by this disclosure?

Real World Case 12–7
Comprehensive income—Microsoft
● LO12-4

Microsoft's 2015 10-K includes the following information in Note 20—Accumulated Other Comprehensive Income relevant to its available-for-sale investments:

($ in millions)	Year Ended June 30, 2015	2014	2013
Investments			
Accumulated other comprehensive income balance, beginning of period	$3,531	$1,794	$1,431
Unrealized gains, net of tax effects of $59, $1,067 and $244	110	2,053	453
Reclassification adjustments for gains included in other income (expense), net	(728)	(447)	(139)
Tax expense included in provision for income taxes	256	131	49
Amounts reclassified from accumulated other comprehensive income	(472)	(316)	(90)
Net current period other comprehensive income (loss)	(362)	1,737	363
Accumulated other comprehensive income balance, end of period	$3,169	$3,531	$1,794

Required:

1. Prepare a journal entry to record unrealized gains for 2015. (*Hint*: $110 is net tax effects, so you will need to add back tax effects to show the amount of unrealized gain gross taxes.)
2. Prepare a journal entry to record Microsoft's reclassification adjustment for 2015.

Trueblood Accounting Case 12–8
Impairments (Appendix 12B)
LO12-4

The following Trueblood case is recommended for use with this chapter. The case provides an excellent opportunity for class discussion, group projects, and writing assignments. The case, along with Professor's Discussion Material, can be obtained from the Deloitte Foundation at its website: www.deloitte.com/us/truebloodcases.

Case: 14-9: O.T.T. Incorporated

This case gives students an opportunity to discuss accounting for other-than-temporary impairments.

Research Case 12–9
Changes in accounting for other-than-temporary impairments (Appendix 12B)
LO12-2, LO12-4, LO12-8

In Appendix 12B, you learned that accounting for other-than-temporary impairments has changed recently. You also learned that these changes were controversial. In fact, two of the five members of the FASB voted against the changes and provided an explanation for their position when the standard that defined the changes was issued. That information isn't included in the FASB's Accounting Standards Codification, but you can find it in the original standard, "Recognition and Presentation of Other-Than-Temporary Impairments," FASB Staff Position (FSP) No. 115-2 and 124-2 (Norwalk, Conn.: FASB, April 9, 2009), which is available under the "Reference Library" and "Superseded Standards" link at www.fasb.org.

Required:

Access the FSP, turn to page 17, and read why FASB members Linsmeier and Siegel dissented. What were their major concerns with the new approach for accounting for OTT impairments? Do you find those concerns compelling?

Continuing Cases

Target Case
LO12-4, LO12-6

Target Corporation prepares its financial statements according to U.S. GAAP. Target's financial statements and disclosure notes for the year ended January 30, 2016, are available Connect. This material also is available under the Investor Relations link at the company's website (www.target.com). Target does not have investments in stock or bonds. However, CVS Health Corp., which purchased Target's pharmacy and clinical business during 2015, does have some investments. Access CVS's 2015 10K (issued on February 9, 2016) at investors.cvshealth.com to answer the following questions,

Required:

1. CVS indicates in Note 1 that it has some short-term investments that consist of certificates of deposit (CDs).
   a. How has CVS classified those CDs for accounting purposes?
   b. Per CVS's balance sheet, what was the balance in CVS's short-term investments as of December 31, 2015 and December 31, 2014?
   c. Per CVS's statement of cash flows, what cash transactions affected short-term investments during 2015?
   d. Prepare a T-account that summarizes transactions affecting CVS's short-term investments during 2015. Speculate as to the explanation for any "plug" figure necessary to make the T-account balance.

2. Per Note 1, CVS has equity-method investments in SureScripts, LLC and in Heartland Healthcare Services. CVS indicates that those investments are immaterial for the year ended December 31, 2015. Assuming that the Heartland investment is material,
   a. How would Heartland's earnings affect CVS's income statement?
   b. How would Heartland's earnings affect CVS's balance sheet?

Air France–KLM Case

IFRS

Air France-KLM (AF), a Franco-Dutch company, prepares its financial statements according to International Financial Reporting Standards. AF's financial statements and disclosure notes for the year ended December 31, 2015, are available in Connect. This material is also available under the Finance link at the company's website (www.airfranceklm.com).

Required:

1. Read Notes 24 and 36.4. Focusing on investments accounted for at fair value through profit and loss (FVTPL):
   a. As of December 31, 2015, what is the total balance of those investments in the balance sheet?
   b. How much of that balance is classified as current and how much as noncurrent?
   c. How much of the fair value of those investments is accounted for using level 1, level 2, and level 3 inputs of the fair value hierarchy? Given that information, assess the reliability (representational faithfulness) of this fair value estimate.
2. Complete Requirement 1 again, but for investments accounted for as available for sale.
3. Read Notes 4.3 and 22.
   a. When AF can exercise significant influence over an investee, what accounting approach does it use to account for the investment? How does AF determine if it can exercise significant influence?
   b. If AF is involved in a joint venture, what accounting approach does it use to account for the investment?
   c. What is the carrying value of AF's equity-method investments in its December 31, 2015 balance sheet?
   d. How did AF's equity-method investments affect AF's 2015 net income from continuing operations?

CPA Exam Questions and Simulations

ROGER *CPA Review*

Sample CPA Exam questions from Roger CPA Review are available in Connect as support for the topics in this chapter. These Multiple Choice Questions and Task-Based Simulations include expert-written explanations and solutions, and provide a starting point for students to become familiar with the content and functionality of the actual CPA Exam.

APPENDIX

A Derivatives

"... derivatives are financial weapons of mass destruction ..."

— Warren Buffett, Berkshire Hathaway CEO

"... the growing use of complex financial instruments known as derivatives does not pose a threat to the country's financial system ..."

— Alan Greenspan, Federal Reserve Chairman

"Total world derivatives are $1000 trillion or 19 times the total world GDP of $54 trillion."

— Chuck Burr, *Culture Change*

In today's global economy and evolving financial markets, businesses are increasingly exposed to a variety of risks, which, unmanaged, can have major impacts on earnings or even threaten a company's very existence. Risk management, then, has become critical. Derivative financial instruments have become the key tools of risk management.[1]

Derivatives are financial instruments that "derive" their values from some other security or index.

Derivatives are financial instruments that "derive" their values or contractually required cash flows from some other security or index. For instance, a contract allowing a company to buy a particular asset (say steel, gold, or flour) at a designated future date at a predetermined price is a financial instrument that derives its value from expected and actual changes in the price of the underlying asset. Financial futures, forward contracts, options, and interest rate swaps are the most frequently used derivatives. Derivatives are valued as tools to manage or hedge companies' increasing exposures to risk, including interest rate risk, price risk, and foreign exchange risk. The variety, complexity, and magnitude of derivatives have grown rapidly in recent years. Accounting standard-setters have scrambled to keep pace.

Derivatives serve as a form of "insurance" against risk.

A persistent stream of headline stories has alerted us to multimillion-dollar losses by many companies and the financial collapse of Bear Stearns and AIG.[2] Focusing on these headlines, it would be tempting to conclude that derivatives are risky business indeed. Certainly they can be quite risky if misused, but the fact is, these financial instruments exist to lessen, not increase, risk. Properly used, they serve as a form of "insurance" against risk. In fact, if a company is exposed to a substantial risk and does not hedge that risk, it is taking a gamble. On the other hand, if a derivative is used improperly, it can be a huge gamble itself.

The notional amount of the derivatives market vastly exceeds the total value of the assets they are intended to mimic or mirror. This implies that firms are using derivatives for purposes other than risk management. Many observers are fearful that the size of the derivatives market poses significant risk to the economy. Some caution that the vast derivatives market could even cause the entire global financial system to crash. Why? If interest rates rise, then many speculative interest rate swaps would incur losses. But it's the size of the interest rate swap market, and thus the size of the resultant losses, that prompts the anxiety. At the start of 2014, the over-the-counter derivatives market was $702 trillion. Yes, that's 702 with twelve zeroes ($702,000,000,000,000). And, that's over 30 times the U.S. Gross Domestic Product. Eighty-two percent of those derivatives ($584 trillion) are interest rate swaps.[3] Our focus here, though, is not on the risk posed by the speculative use of derivatives, but instead on the use of derivatives to reduce company risk.

[1] Almost all financial institutions and over half of all nonfinancial companies use derivatives.

[2] Bear Sterns has since been sold at a bargain basement price to JP Morgan, and AIG has since recovered from its difficulties.

[3] Bank for International Settlements, *BIS Quarterly Review*, June 2014.

Derivatives Used to Hedge Risk

Hedging means taking a risk position that is opposite to an actual position that is exposed to risk.

Hedging means taking an action that is expected to produce exposure to a particular type of risk that is precisely the *opposite* of an actual risk to which the company already is exposed. For instance, the volatility of interest rates creates exposure to interest-rate risk for companies that issue debt—which, of course, includes most companies. So, a company that frequently arranges short-term loans from its bank under a floating (variable) interest rate agreement is exposed to the risk that interest rates might increase and adversely affect borrowing costs. Similarly, a company that regularly reissues commercial paper as it matures faces the possibility that new rates will be higher and cut into forecasted income. When borrowings are large, the potential cost can be substantial. So, the firm might choose to hedge its position by entering into a transaction that would produce a *gain* of roughly the same amount as the potential loss if interest rates do, in fact, increase.

Hedging is used to deal with three areas of risk exposure: fair value risk, cash flow risk, and foreign currency risk. Let's look at some of the more common derivatives.

A *futures contract* allows a firm to sell (or buy) a financial instrument at a designated future date, at today's price.

FINANCIAL FUTURES A futures contract is an agreement between a seller and a buyer that requires the seller to deliver a particular commodity (say corn, gold, or pork bellies) at a designated future date, at a *predetermined* price. These contracts are actively traded on regulated futures exchanges. When the "commodity" is a *financial instrument,* such as a Treasury bond, Treasury bill, commercial paper, or a certificate of deposit, the agreement is referred to as a *financial futures contract.*[4]

To appreciate the way these hedges work, you need to remember that when interest rates rise, the market price of interest-bearing securities goes down. For instance, if you have an investment in a 10% bond and market interest rates go up to, say, 12%, your 10% bond is less valuable relative to other bonds paying the higher rate. Conversely, when interest rates decline, the market price of interest-bearing securities goes up. This risk that the investment's value might change is referred to as *fair value risk.* The company that issued the securities is faced with fair value risk also. If interest rates decline, the fair value of that company's debt would rise, a risk the borrower may want to hedge against. Later in this section, we'll look at an illustration of how the borrower would account for and report such a hedge.

The seller in a financial futures contract realizes a gain (loss) when interest rates rise (decline).

Now let's look at the effect on a contract to sell or buy securities (or any asset for that matter) at preset prices. One who is contracted to *sell* securities at a *preset* price after their market price has fallen benefits from the rise in interest rates. Consequently, the value of the contract that gives one the right to sell securities at a preset price goes up as the market price declines. The seller in a futures contract derives a gain (loss) when interest rates rise (decline).[5] Conversely, the one obligated to buy securities at a preset price experiences a loss. This risk of having to pay more cash or receive less cash is referred to as *cash flow risk.*

Another example of cash flow risk would be borrowing money by issuing a variable (floating) rate note. If market interest rates rise, the borrower would have to pay more interest. Similarly, the lender (investor) in the variable (floating) rate note transaction would face cash flow risk that interest rates would decline, resulting in lower cash interest receipts.

Let's look closer at how a futures contract can mitigate cash flow risk. Consider a company in April that will replace its $10 million of 8.5% bank notes with a bond issue when the notes mature in June. The company is exposed to the risk that interest rates in June will have risen, increasing borrowing costs. To counteract that possibility, the firm might enter a contract in April to deliver (sell) bonds in June at their *current* price. Since there are no corporate bond futures contracts, the company buys Treasury bond futures, which will accomplish essentially the same purpose. In essence, the firm agrees to sell Treasury bonds in June at a price established now (April). Let's say it's April 6 and the price of Treasury bond futures on the International Monetary Market of the Chicago Mercantile Exchange is quoted as 95.24.[6] Since the trading unit of Treasury bond futures is a 15-year, $100,000, 8% Treasury bond,

[4]Note that a financial futures contract meets the definition of a financial instrument because it entails the exchange of financial instruments (cash for Treasury bonds, for instance). But, a futures contract for the sale or purchase of a nonfinancial commodity like corn or gold does not meet the definition because one of the items to be exchanged is not a financial instrument.

[5]The seller of a futures contract is obligated to sell the bonds at a future date. The buyer of a futures contract is obligated to buy the bonds at a future date. The company in our example, then, is the seller of the futures contract.

[6]Price quotes are expressed as a percentage of par.

the company might sell 105 Treasury bond futures to hedge the June issuance of debt. This would effectively provide a hedge of 105 × $100,000 × 95.24% = $10,000,200.[7]

Here's what happens then. If interest rates rise, borrowing costs will go up for our example company because it will have to sell debt securities at a higher interest cost (or lower price). But that loss will be offset (approximately) by the gain produced by being in the opposite position on Treasury bond futures. Take note, though, this works both ways. If interest rates go down causing debt security prices to rise, the potential benefit of being able to issue debt at that lower interest rate (higher price) will be offset by a loss on the futures position.

A very important point about futures contracts is that the seller does not need to have actual possession of the commodity (the Treasury bonds, in this case), nor is the purchaser of the contract required to take possession of the commodity. In fact, virtually all financial futures contracts are "netted out" before the actual transaction is to take place. This is simply a matter of reversing the original position. A seller closes out his transaction with a purchase. Likewise, a purchaser would close out her transaction with a sale. After all, the objective is not to actually buy or sell Treasury bonds (or whatever the commodity might be), but to incur the financial impact of movements in interest rates as reflected in changes in Treasury bond prices. Specifically, it will buy at the lower price (to reverse the original seller position) at the same time it's selling its new bond issue at that same lower price. The financial futures market is an "artificial" exchange in that its reason for existing is to provide a mechanism to transfer risk from those exposed to it to those willing to accept the risk, not to actually buy and sell the underlying financial instruments.

If the impending debt issue being hedged is a short-term issue, the company may attain a more effective hedge by selling Treasury *bill* futures since Treasury bills are 90-day securities, or maybe certificate of deposit (CD) futures that also are traded in futures markets. The object is to get the closest association between the financial effects of interest rate movements on the actual transaction and the effects on the financial instrument used as a hedge.

The effectiveness of a hedge is influenced by the closeness of the match between the item being hedged and the financial instrument chosen as a hedge.

FINANCIAL FORWARD CONTRACTS A forward contract is similar to a futures contract but differs in three ways:

1. A forward contract calls for delivery on a specific date, whereas a futures contract permits the seller to decide later which specific day within the specified month will be the delivery date (if it gets as far as actual delivery before it is closed out).
2. Unlike a futures contract, a forward contract usually is not traded on a market exchange.
3. Unlike a futures contract, a forward contract does not call for a daily cash settlement for price changes in the underlying contract. Gains and losses on forward contracts are paid only when they are closed out.

OPTIONS Options frequently are purchased to hedge exposure to the effects of changing interest rates. Options serve the same purpose as futures in that respect but are fundamentally different. An option on a financial instrument—say a Treasury bill—gives its holder the right either to buy or to sell the Treasury bill at a specified price and within a given time period. Importantly, though, the option holder has no obligation to exercise the option. On the other hand, the holder of a futures contract must buy or sell within a specified period unless the contract is closed out before delivery comes due.

FOREIGN CURRENCY FUTURES Foreign loans frequently are denominated in the currency of the lender (Japanese yen, Swiss franc, Euro, and so on). When loans must be repaid in foreign currencies, a new element of risk is introduced. This is because if exchange rates change, the dollar equivalent of the foreign currency that must be repaid differs from the dollar equivalent of the foreign currency borrowed.

To hedge against "foreign exchange risk" exposure, some firms buy or sell foreign currency futures contracts. These are similar to financial futures except specific foreign

Foreign exchange risk often is hedged in the same manner as interest rate risk.

[7] This is a simplification of the more sophisticated way financial managers determine the optimal number of futures.

currencies are specified in the futures contracts rather than specific debt instruments. They work the same way to protect against foreign exchange risk as financial futures protect against fair value or cash flow risk.

Interest rate swaps exchange fixed interest payments for floating rate payments, or vice versa, without exchanging the underlying notional amounts.

INTEREST RATE SWAPS Over 82% of derivatives are interest rate contracts, of which 75% are interest rate swaps. These contracts exchange fixed interest payments for floating rate payments, or vice versa, without exchanging the underlying principal amounts. For example, suppose you owe $100,000 on a 10% fixed rate home loan. You envy your neighbor who also is paying 10% on her $100,000 mortgage, but hers is a floating rate loan, so if market rates fall, so will her loan rate. To the contrary, she is envious of your fixed rate, fearful that rates will rise, increasing her payments. A solution would be for the two of you to effectively swap interest payments using an interest rate swap agreement. The way a swap works, you both would continue to actually make your own interest payments, but you would exchange the net cash difference between payments at specified intervals. So, in this case, if market rates (and thus floating payments) increase, you would pay your neighbor; if rates fall, she pays you. The net effect is to exchange the consequences of rate changes. In other words, you have effectively converted your fixed-rate debt to floating-rate debt; your neighbor has done the opposite.

Of course, this technique is not dependent on happening into such a fortuitous pairing of two borrowers with opposite philosophies on interest rate risk. Instead, banks or other intermediaries offer, for a fee, one-sided swap agreements to companies desiring to be either fixed-rate payers or variable-rate payers. Intermediaries usually strive to maintain a balanced portfolio of matched, offsetting swap agreements.

Theoretically, the two parties to such a transaction exchange principal amounts, say the $100,000 amount above, in addition to the interest on those amounts. It makes no practical sense, though, for the companies to send each other $100,000. So, instead, the principal amount is not actually exchanged, but serves merely as the computational base for interest calculations and is called the *notional amount.* Similarly, the fixed-rate payer doesn't usually send the entire fixed interest amount (say 10% × $100,000 = $10,000) and receive the entire variable interest amount (say 9% × $100,000 = $9,000). Generally, only the net amount ($1,000 in this case) is exchanged. This is illustrated in Illustration A–1.

Illustration A–1
Interest Rate Swap—Shortcut Method

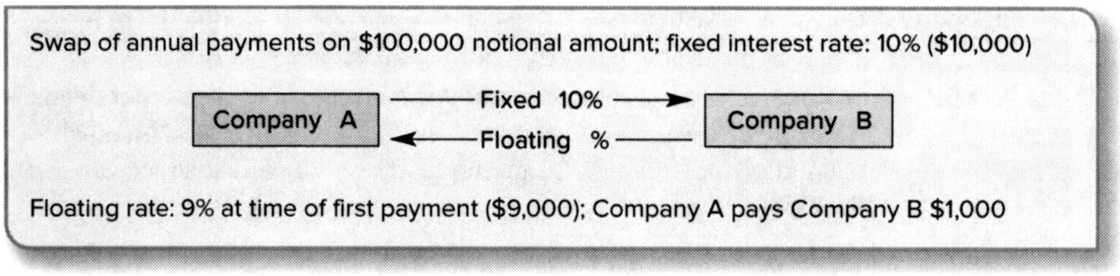

From an accounting standpoint, the central issue is not the operational differences among various hedge instruments, but their similarities in functioning as hedges against risk.

Accounting for Derivatives

A key to accounting for derivatives is knowing the purpose for which a company holds them and whether the company is effective in serving that purpose. Derivatives, for instance, may be held for risk management (hedging activities). The desired effect, and often the real effect, is a reduction in risk. On the other hand, derivatives sometimes are held for speculative position taking, hoping for large profits. The effect of this activity usually is to *increase* risk. Perhaps more important, derivatives acquired as hedges and intended to reduce risk may, in fact, unintentionally increase risk instead.

Derivatives not serving as hedges are extremely speculative due to the high leverage inherent in such investments.

It's important to understand that, serving as investments rather than as hedges, derivatives are extremely speculative. This is due to the high leverage inherent in derivatives. Here's why. The investment outlay usually is negligible, but the potential gain or loss on the investment usually is quite high. A small change in interest rates or another underlying event can trigger a large change in the fair value of the derivative. Because the initial investment was minimal, the change in value relative to the investment itself represents a huge percentage gain or loss. Their extraordinarily risky nature prompted Warren Buffett, one of the country's most celebrated financiers, to refer to derivatives as "financial weapons of mass destruction." Accounting for derivatives is designed to treat differently (a) derivatives designated as hedges and those not designated as hedges as well as (b) the effective portion and the ineffective portion of gains and losses from intended hedges.

The basic approach to accounting for derivatives is fairly straightforward, although implementation can be quite cumbersome. All derivatives, no exceptions, are carried on the balance sheet as either assets or liabilities at fair (or market) value.[8] The reasoning is that (a) derivatives create either rights or obligations that meet the definition of assets or liabilities, and (b) fair value is the most meaningful measurement.

Each derivative contract has a "fair value," which is an amount that one side owes the other at a particular moment.

Accounting for the gain or loss on a derivative depends on how it is used. Specifically, if the derivative is not designated as a hedging instrument or doesn't qualify as one, any gain or loss from fair value changes is recognized immediately in earnings. On the other hand, if a derivative is used to hedge against exposure to risk, any gain or loss from fair value changes is either (a) recognized immediately in earnings along with an offsetting loss or gain on the item being hedged or (b) deferred in comprehensive income until it can be recognized in earnings at the same time as earnings are affected by a hedged transaction. Which way depends on whether the derivative is designated as a (a) fair value hedge, (b) cash flow hedge, or (c) foreign currency hedge. Let's look now at each of the three hedge designations.

FAIR VALUE HEDGES A company can be adversely affected when a change in either prices or interest rates causes a change in the fair value of one of its assets, its liabilities, or a commitment to buy or sell assets or liabilities. If a derivative is used to hedge against the exposure to changes in the fair value of an asset, liability, or a firm commitment, it can be designated as a fair value hedge. In that case, when the derivative is adjusted to reflect changes in fair value, the other side of the entry recognizes a gain or loss to be included *currently* in earnings. At the same time, though, the loss or gain from changes in the fair value (due to the risk being hedged)[9] of the item being hedged also is included currently in earnings. This means that, to the extent the hedge is effective in serving its purpose, the gain or loss on the derivative will be offset by the loss or gain on the item being hedged. In fact, this is precisely the concept behind the procedure.

A gain or loss from a *fair value hedge* is recognized immediately in earnings, along with the loss or gain from the item being hedged.

The reasoning is that as interest rates or other underlying events change, a hedge instrument will produce a gain approximately equal to a loss on the item being hedged (or vice versa). These income effects are interrelated and offsetting, so it would be improper to report the income effects in different periods. More critically, the intent and effect of having the hedge instrument is to *lessen* risk. And yet, recognizing gains in one period and counterbalancing losses in another period would tend to cause fluctuations in income that convey an *increase* in risk. However, to the extent that a hedge is ineffective and produces gains or losses different from the losses or gains being hedged, the ineffective portion is recognized in earnings immediately.

The income effects of the hedge instrument and the income effects of the item being hedged should affect earnings at the same time.

Some of the more common fair value hedges use as follows:

- An interest rate swap to synthetically convert fixed-rate debt (for which interest rate changes could change the fair value of the debt) into floating-rate debt
- A futures contract to hedge changes in the fair value (due to price changes) of aluminum, sugar, or some other type of inventory
- A futures contract to hedge the fair value (due to price changes) of a firm commitment to sell natural gas or some other asset

ILLUSTRATION Because interest rate swaps comprise the majority of derivatives in use, we will use swaps to illustrate accounting for derivatives. Let's look at the example in Illustration A–2.

[8]FASB ASC 815–10: Derivatives and Hedging–Overall (previously "Accounting for Derivative Instruments and Hedging Activities," *Statement of Financial Accounting Standards No. 133* (Norwalk, Conn.: FASB, 1998)).

[9]The fair value of a hedged item might also change for reasons other than from effects of the risk being hedged. For instance, the hedged risk may be that a change in interest rates will cause the fair value of a bond to change. The bond price might also change, though, if the market perceives that the bond's default risk has changed.

Illustration A–2

Interest Rate Swap—Shortcut Method

Wintel Semiconductors issued $1 million of 18-month, 10% bank notes on January 1, 2018. Wintel is exposed to the risk that general interest rates will decline, causing the fair value of its debt to rise. (If the fair value of Wintel's debt increases, its effective borrowing cost is higher relative to the market.) To hedge against this fair value risk, the firm entered into an 18-month interest rate swap agreement on January 1 and designated the swap as a hedge against changes in the fair value of the note. The swap calls for the company to receive payment based on a 10% fixed interest rate on a notional amount of $1 million and to make payment based on a floating interest rate tied to changes in general rates.* As the Illustration will show, this effectively converts Wintel's fixed-rate debt to floating-rate debt. Cash settlement of the net interest amount is made semiannually at June 30 and December 31 of each year, with the net interest being the difference between the $50,000 fixed interest [$1 million × (10% × ½)] and the floating interest rate, times $1 million at those dates.

Floating (market) settlement rates were 9% at June 30, 2018, 8% at December 31, 2018, and 9% at June 30, 2019. Net interest receipts can be calculated as shown below. Fair values of both the derivative and the note resulting from those market rate changes are assumed to be quotes obtained from securities dealers.

	1/1/18	6/30/18	12/31/18	6/30/19
Fixed rate	10%	10%	10%	10%
Floating rate	10%	9%	8%	9%
Fixed payments [$1 million × (10% × ½)]		$ 50,000	$ 50,000	$ 50,000
Floating payments ($1 million × ½ floating rate)		45,000	40,000	45,000
Net interest receipts		$ 5,000	$ 10,000	$ 5,000
Fair value of interest rate swap	0	$ 9,363	$ 9,615	0
Fair value of note payable	$1,000,000	$1,009,363	$1,009,615	$1,000,000

*A common measure for benchmarking variable interest rates is LIBOR, the London Interbank Offered Rate, a base rate at which large international banks lend funds to each other.

When the floating rate declined from 10% to 9%, the fair values of both the derivative (swap) and the note increased. This created an offsetting gain on the derivative and a holding loss on the note. Both are recognized in earnings at the same time (at June 30, 2018).

The interest rate swap is designated as a fair value hedge on this note at issuance.

The swap settlement is the difference between the fixed interest (5%) and variable interest (4.5%).

The fair value of derivatives is recognized in the balance sheet.

The hedged liability (or asset) is adjusted to fair value as well.

	Debit	Credit
January 1, 2018		
Cash	1,000,000	
Notes payable		1,000,000
To record the issuance of the note.		
June 30, 2018		
Interest expense (10% × ½ × $1 million)	50,000	
Cash		50,000
To record interest.		
Cash [$50,000 – (9% × ½ × $1 million)]	5,000	
Interest expense		5,000
To record the net cash settlement.		
Interest rate swap* ($9,363 – 0)	9,363	
Holding gain—interest rate swap		9,363
To record change in fair value of the derivative.		
Holding loss—hedged note	9,363	
Note payable ($1,009,363 – 1,000,000)		9,363
To record change in fair value of the note due to interest rate changes.		

*This would be a liability rather than an investment (asset) if the fair value had declined.

The net interest settlement on June 30, 2018, is $5,000 because the fixed rate is 5% (half of the 10% annual rate) and the floating rate is 4.5% (half of the 9% annual rate).

December 31, 2018

Interest expense	50,000	
Cash (10% × ½ × $1,000,000)		50,000
To record interest.		
Cash [$50,000 − (8% × ½ × $1 million)]	10,000	
Interest expense		10,000
To record the net cash settlement.		
Interest rate swap ($9,615 − 9,363)	252	
Holding gain—interest rate swap		252
To record the change in fair value of the derivative.		
Holding loss—hedged note	252	
Note payable ($1,009,615 − 1,009,363)		252
To record the change in fair value of the note due to interest rate changes.		

As with any debt, interest expense is the effective rate times the outstanding balance.

The settlement is the difference between the fixed interest (5%) and variable interest (4%).

The derivative is increased by the change in fair value. The note is increased by the change in fair value.

The fair value of the swap increased by $252 (from $9,363 to $9,615). Similarly, we adjust the note's book value by the amount necessary to increase it to fair value. This produces a holding loss on the note that exactly offsets the gain on the swap. This result is the hedging effect that motivated Wintel to enter the fair value hedging arrangement in the first place.

At June 30, 2019, Wintel repeats the process of adjusting to fair value both the derivative investment and the note being hedged.

June 30, 2019

Interest expense	50,000	
Cash (10% × ½ × $1,000,000)		50,000
To record interest.		
Cash [$50,000 − (9% × ½ × $1 million)]	5,000	
Interest expense		5,000
To record the net cash settlement.		
Holding loss—interest rate swap	9,615	
Interest rate swap ($0 − 9,615)		9,615
To record the change in fair value of the derivative.		
Note payable ($1,000,000 − 1,009,615)	9,615	
Holding gain—hedged note		9,615
To record the change in fair value of the note due to interest rate changes.		
Note payable	1,000,000	
Cash		1,000,000
To repay the loan.		

The net interest received is the difference between the fixed interest (5%) and floating interest (4.5%).

The swap's fair value now is zero.

The net interest received is the difference between the fixed rate (5%) and floating rate (4.5%) times $1 million. The fair value of the swap decreased by $9,615 (from $9,615 to zero).[10] That decline represents a holding *loss* that we recognize in earnings. Similarly, we record an offsetting holding gain on the note for the change in its fair value.

Now let's see how the book values changed for the swap account and the note:

	Swap (Debit)	Swap (Credit)	Note (Debit)	Note (Credit)
Jan. 1, 2018				1,000,000
June 30, 2018	9,363			9,363
Dec. 31, 2018	252			252
June 30, 2019		9,615	9,615	
			1,000,000	
	0			0

[10]Because there are no future cash receipts from the swap arrangement at this point, the fair value of the swap is zero.

The income statement is affected as follows:

	Income Statement + (−)	
June 30, 2018	(50,000)	Interest expense—fixed payment
	5,000	Interest expense—net cash settlement
	9,363	Holding gain—interest rate swap
	(9,363)	Holding loss—hedged note
	(45,000)	Net effect—same as floating interest payment
Dec. 31, 2018	(50,000)	Interest expense—fixed payment
	10,000	Interest expense—net cash settlement
	252	Holding gain—interest rate swap
	(252)	Holding loss—hedged note
	(40,000)	Net effect—same as floating interest payment
June 30, 2019	(50,000)	Interest expense—fixed payment
	5,000	Interest expense—net cash settlement
	9,615	Holding gain—interest rate swap
	(9,615)	Holding loss—hedged note
	(45,000)	Net effect—same as floating interest payment

As this demonstrates, the swap effectively converts fixed-interest debt to floating-interest debt.

Additional Consideration

Fair Value of the Swap

The fair value of a derivative typically is based on a quote obtained from a derivatives dealer. That fair value will approximate the present value of the expected net interest settlement receipts for the remaining term of the swap. In fact, we can actually calculate the fair value of the swap that we accepted as given in our illustration.

Since the June 30, 2018, floating rate of 9% caused the cash settlement on that date to be $5,000, it's reasonable to look at 9% as the best estimate of future floating rates and therefore assume the remaining two cash settlements also will be $5,000 each. We can then calculate at June 30, 2018, the present value of those expected net interest settlement receipts for the remaining term of the swap.

Fixed interest	10% × ½ × $1 million	$ 50,000
Expected floating interest	9% × ½ × $1 million	45,000
Expected cash receipts for both Dec. 31, 2018 and June 30, 2019		$ 5,000
		× 1.87267*
Present value		$ 9,363

*Present value of an ordinary annuity of $1: $n = 2$, $i = 4.5\%$ (½ of 9%) (from Table 4)

Fair Value of the Notes

The fair value of the note payable will be the present value of principal and remaining interest payments discounted at the market rate. The market rate will vary with the designated floating rate but might differ due to changes in default (credit) risk and the term structure of interest rates. Assuming it's 9% at June 30, 2018, we can calculate the fair value (present value) of the notes.

Interest	$50,000* × 1.87267† =	$ 93,633
Principal	$1,000,000 × 0.91573‡ =	915,730
		$1,009,363

*½ of 10% × $1,000,000
†Present value of an ordinary annuity of $1: $n = 2$, $i = 4.5\%$ (from Table 4)
‡Present value of $1: $n = 2$, $i = 4.5\%$ (from Table 2)

(continued)

(concluded)

Note: Often the cash settlement rate is "reset" as of each cash settlement date. Thus, the floating rate actually used at the end of each period to determine the payment is the floating market rate as of the beginning of the same period. In our illustration, for instance, there would have been no cash settlement at June 30, 2018, since we would use the beginning floating rate of 10% to determine payment. Similarly, we would have used the 9% floating rate at June 30, 2018, to determine the cash settlement six months later at December 31. In effect, each cash settlement would be delayed six months. Had this arrangement been in effect in the current illustration, there would have been one fewer cash settlement payment (two rather than three), but would not have affected the fair value calculations above because, either way, our expectation would be cash receipts of $5,000 for both Dec. 31, 2018, and June 30, 2019.

CASH FLOW HEDGES The risk in some transactions or events is the risk of a change in cash flows, rather than a change in fair values. We noted earlier, for instance, that *fixed-rate* debt subjects a company to the risk that interest rate changes could change the fair value of the debt. On the other hand, if the obligation is *floating-rate* debt, the fair value of the debt will not change when interest rates do, but cash flows will. If a derivative is used to hedge against the exposure to changes in cash inflows or cash outflows of an asset or liability or a forecasted transaction (like a future purchase or sale), it can be designated as a cash flow hedge. In that case, when the derivative is adjusted to reflect changes in fair value, the other side of the entry is a gain or loss to be deferred as a component of other comprehensive income and included in earnings later, at the same time as earnings are affected by the hedged transaction. Once again, the effect is matching the earnings effect of the derivative with the earnings effect of the item being hedged, precisely the concept behind hedge accounting.

A gain or loss from a *cash flow hedge* is deferred as other comprehensive income until it can be recognized in earnings along with the earnings effect of the item being hedged.

To understand the deferral of the gain or loss, we need to revisit the concept of comprehensive income. Comprehensive income, as you may recall from Chapters 4, 12, 17, and 18, is a more expansive view of the change in shareholders' equity than traditional net income. In fact, it encompasses all changes in equity other than from transactions with owners.[11] So, in addition to net income itself, comprehensive income includes up to four other changes in equity that don't (yet) belong in net income, namely, net holding gains (losses) on investments in debt securities (Chapter 12), gains (losses) from and amendments to postretirement benefit plans (Chapter 17), gains (losses) from foreign currency translation, and deferred gains (losses) from derivatives designated as cash flow hedges.[12]

Some of the more commonly used cash flow hedges are:

- An interest rate swap to synthetically convert floating rate debt (for which interest rate changes could change the cash interest payments) into fixed rate debt.
- A futures contract to hedge a forecasted sale (for which price changes could change the cash receipts) of natural gas, crude oil, or some other asset.

FOREIGN CURRENCY HEDGES Today's economy is increasingly a global one. The majority of large "U.S." companies are, in truth, multinational companies that may receive only a fraction of their revenues from U.S. operations. Many operations of those companies are located abroad. Foreign operations often are denominated in the currency of the foreign country (the Euro, Japanese yen, Russian rubles, and so on). Even companies without foreign operations sometimes hold investments, issue debt, or conduct other transactions denominated in foreign currencies. As exchange rates change, the dollar equivalent of the

The possibility that foreign currency exchange rates might change exposes many companies to foreign currency risk.

[11]Transactions with owners primarily include dividends and the sale or purchase of shares of the company's stock.
[12]FASB ASC 220–10–55–2: Comprehensive Income–Overall–Implementation Guidance and Illustrations (previously "Reporting Comprehensive Income," *Statement of Financial Accounting Standards No. 130* (Norwalk, Conn.: FASB, 1997)).

foreign currency changes. The possibility of currency rate changes exposes these companies to the risk that some transactions require settlement in a currency other than the entities' functional currency or that foreign operations will require translation adjustments to reported amounts.

A foreign currency hedge can be a hedge of foreign currency exposure of the following:

- A firm commitment—treated as a fair value hedge
- An available-for-sale security—treated as a fair value hedge
- A forecasted transaction—treated as a cash flow hedge
- A company's net investment in a foreign operation—the gain or loss is reported in *other comprehensive income* as part of unrealized gains and losses from foreign currency translation[13]

To qualify as a hedge, the hedging relationship must be highly effective in achieving offsetting changes in fair values or cash flows.

HEDGE EFFECTIVENESS When a company elects to apply hedge accounting, it must establish at the inception of the hedge the method it will use to assess the effectiveness of the hedging derivative, as well as the measurement approach it will use to determine the ineffective portion of the hedge.[14] The key criterion for qualifying as a hedge is that the hedging relationship must be "highly effective" in achieving offsetting changes in fair values or cash flows based on the hedging company's specified risk management objective and strategy.

An assessment of this effectiveness must be made at least every three months and whenever financial statements are issued. There are no precise guidelines for assessing effectiveness, but it generally means a high correlation between changes in the fair value or cash flows of the derivative and of the item being hedged, not necessarily a specific reduction in risk. Hedge accounting must be terminated for hedging relationships that no longer are highly effective.

HEDGE INEFFECTIVENESS In Illustration A–2, the loss on the hedged note exactly offset the gain on the swap. This is because the swap in this instance was highly effective in hedging the risk due to interest rate changes. However, the loss and gain would not have exactly offset each other if the hedging arrangement had been ineffective. For instance, suppose the swap's term had been different from that of the note (say a three-year swap term compared with the 18-month term of the note) or if the notional amount of the swap differed from that of the note (say $500,000 rather than $1 million). In that case, changes in the fair value of the swap and changes in the fair value of the note would not be the same. The result would be a greater (or lesser) amount recognized in earnings for the swap than for the note. Because there would not be an exact offset, earnings would be affected, an effect resulting from hedge ineffectiveness. That is a desired effect of hedge accounting; to the extent that a hedge is effective, the earnings effect of a derivative cancels out the earnings effect of the item being hedged. However, even if a hedge is highly effective, all ineffectiveness is recognized currently in earnings.

Imperfect hedges result in part of the derivative gain or loss being included in current earnings.

FAIR VALUE CHANGES UNRELATED TO THE RISK BEING HEDGED In Illustration A–2, the fair value of the hedged note and the fair value of the swap changed by the same amounts each year because we assumed the fair values changed only due to interest rate changes. It's also possible, though, that the note's fair value would change by an amount different from that of the swap for reasons unrelated to interest rates. Remember from our earlier discussion that the market's perception of a company's creditworthiness,

---

[13]This is the same treatment previously prescribed for these translation adjustments by FASB ASC 830: Foreign Currency Matters (previously *Statement of Financial Accounting Standards No. 52*).

[14]Remember, if a derivative is not designated as a hedge, any gains or losses from changes in its fair value are recognized immediately in earnings.

and thus its ability to pay interest and principal when due, also can affect the value of debt, whether interest rates change or not. In hedge accounting, we ignore those changes. We recognize only the fair value changes in the hedged item that we can attribute to the risk being hedged (interest rate risk in this case). For example, if a changing perception of default risk had caused the note's fair value to increase by an additional, say $5,000, our journal entries in Illustration A–2 would have been unaffected. Notice, then, that although we always mark a *derivative* to fair value, the reported amount of the *item being hedged* may not be its fair value. We mark a hedged item to fair value only to the extent that its fair value changed due to the risk being hedged.

Fair value changes unrelated to the risk being hedged are ignored.

Disclosure of Derivatives and Risk

To be adequately informed about the effectiveness of a company's risk management, investors and creditors need information about strategies for holding derivatives and specific hedging activities. Toward that end, extensive disclosure requirements provide information that includes the following:

- Objectives and strategies for holding and issuing derivatives
- A description of the items for which risks are being hedged
- For forecasted transactions: a description, time before the transaction is expected to occur, the gains and losses accumulated in other comprehensive income, and the events that will trigger their recognition in earnings
- Beginning balance of, changes in, and ending balance of the derivative component of other comprehensive income
- The net amount of gain or loss reported in earnings (representing aggregate hedge ineffectiveness)
- Qualitative and quantitative information about failed hedges: canceled commitments or previously hedged forecasted transactions no longer expected to occur

The intent is to provide information about the company's success in reducing risks and, consequently, about risks not managed successfully. Remember, too, that when derivatives are employed ineffectively, risks can escalate. Ample disclosures about derivatives are essential to maintain awareness of potential opportunities and problems with risk management.

In addition, GAAP requires companies to provide enhanced disclosures indicating (a) how and why the company uses derivative instruments, (b) how the company accounts for derivative instruments and related hedged items, and (c) how derivative instruments and related hedged items affect the company's balance sheet, income statement, and cash flows.[15] The required disclosures include two tables, one that highlights the location and fair values of derivative instruments in the balance sheet, and another that indicates the location and amounts of gains and losses on derivative instruments in the income statement. The two tables distinguish between derivative instruments that are designated as hedging instruments and those that are not. The tables also categorize derivative instruments by each major type—interest rate contracts, foreign exchange contracts, equity contracts, commodity contracts, credit contracts, and other types of contracts.

Even for some traditional liabilities, the amounts reported on the face of the financial statements provide inadequate disclosure about the degree to which a company is exposed to risk of loss. To provide adequate disclosure about a company's exposure to risk, additional information must be provided about (a) concentrations of credit risk and (b) the fair value of all financial instruments.[16]

[15]FASB ASC 815: Derivatives and Hedging (previously "Disclosures about Derivative Instruments and Hedging Activities—an amendment of FASB Statement No. 133," *Statement of Financial Accounting Standards No. 161* (Stamford, Conn.: FASB, 2008)).

[16]FASB ASC 825–10–50–1: Financial Instruments–Overall–Disclosure (previously "Disclosures About Fair Values of Financial Instruments," *Statement of Financial Accounting Standards No. 107* (Norwalk, Conn.: FASB, 1991), as amended by *Statement of Financial Accounting Standards No. 133*, "Accounting for Derivative Instruments and Hedging Activities" (Norwalk, Conn.: FASB, 1998)).

Extended Method for Interest Rate Swap Accounting

A shortcut method for accounting for an interest rate swap is permitted when a hedge meets certain criteria. In general, the criteria are designed to see if the hedge supports the assumption of "no ineffectiveness." Illustration A–2 of a fair value hedge met those criteria, in particular, (a) the swap's notional amount matches the note's principal amount, (b) the swap's expiration date matches the note's maturity date, (c) the fair value of the swap is zero at inception, and (d) the floating payment is at the market rate.[17] Because Wintel can conclude that the swap will be highly effective in offsetting changes in the fair value of the debt, it can use the changes in the fair value of the swap to measure the offsetting changes in the fair value of the debt. That's the essence of the shortcut method used in Illustration A–2. The extended method required when the criteria are *not* met for the short-cut method is described in this section (Illustration A–3 begins by describing the same scenario as in Illustration A–2). It produces the same effect on earnings and in the balance sheet as does the procedure shown in Illustration A–2.

Illustration A–3

Interest Rate Swap—Extended Method

Wintel Semiconductors issued $1 million of 18-month, 10% bank notes on January 1, 2018. Wintel is exposed to the risk that general interest rates will decline, causing the fair value of its debt to rise. (If the fair value of Wintel's debt increases, its effective borrowing cost is higher relative to the market.) To hedge against this fair value risk, the firm entered into an 18-month interest rate swap agreement on January 1 and designated the swap as a hedge against changes in the fair value of the note. The swap calls for the company to receive payment based on a 10% fixed interest rate on a notional amount of $1 million and to make payment based on a floating interest rate tied to changes in general rates. Cash settlement of the net interest amount is made semiannually at June 30 and December 31 of each year, with the net interest being the difference between the $50,000 fixed interest [$1 million × (10% × ½)] and the floating interest rate, times $1 million at those dates.

Floating (market) settlement rates were 9% at June 30, 2018, 8% at December 31, 2018, and 8% at June 30, 2019. Net interest receipts can be calculated as shown below. Fair values of both the derivative and the note resulting from those market rate changes are assumed to be quotes obtained from securities dealers.

	1/1/18	6/30/18	12/31/18	6/30/19
Fixed rate	10%	10%	10%	10%
Floating rate	10%	9%	8%	9%
Fixed payments				
[$1 million × (10% × ½)]		$ 50,000	$ 50,000	$ 50,000
Floating payments				
($1 million × ½ floating rate)		45,000	40,000	45,000
Net interest receipts		$ 5,000	$ 10,000	$ 5,000
Fair value of interest rate swap	0	$ 9,363	$ 9,615	0
Fair value of note payable	$1,000,000	$1,009,363	$1,009,615	$1,000,000

When the floating rate declined in Illustration A–3 from 10% to 9%, the fair values of both the derivative (swap) and the note increased. This created an offsetting gain on the derivative and holding loss on the note. Both are recognized in earnings the same period (June 30, 2018).

The interest rate swap is designated as a fair value hedge on this note at issuance.

January 1, 2018		
Cash	1,000,000	
Notes payable		1,000,000
To record the issuance of the note.		

[17]There is no precise minimum interval, though it generally is three to six months or less. Other criteria are specified by FASB ASC 815–20–25–104: Derivatives and Hedging–Hedging-General–Recognition–Shortcut Method, *SFAS No. 133* (para. 68), in addition to the key conditions listed here.

June 30, 2018		
Interest expense (10% × ½ × $1 million)	50,000	
Cash		50,000
To record interest.		
Cash [$50,000 – (9% × ½ × $1 million)]	5,000	
Interest rate swap ($9,363 – 0)	9,363	
Interest revenue (10% × ½ × $0)		0
Holding gain—interest rate swap (to balance)		14,363
To record the net cash settlement, accrued interest on the swap, and change in the fair value of the derivative.		
Holding loss—hedged note	9,363	
Notes payable ($1,009,363 – 1,000,000)		9,363
To record change in fair value of the note due to interest rate changes.		

The swap settlement is the difference between the fixed interest (5%) and variable interest (4.5%).

The fair value of derivatives is recognized in the balance sheet.

The hedged liability (or asset) is adjusted to fair value as well.

The net interest settlement on June 30, 2018, is $5,000 because the fixed rate is 5% (half of the 10% annual rate) and the floating rate is 4.5% (half of the 9% annual rate). A holding gain ($14,363) is produced by holding the derivative security during a time when an interest rate decline caused an increase in the value of that asset. A portion ($5,000) of the gain was received in cash, and another portion ($9,363) is reflected as an increase in the value of the asset.

We also have a holding loss of the same amount. This is because we also held a liability during the same time period, and the interest rate change caused its fair value to increase as well.

December 31, 2018		
Interest expense (9% × ½ × $1,009,363)	45,421	
Notes payable (difference)*	4,579	
Cash (10% × ½ × $1,000,000)		50,000
To record interest.		
Cash [$50,000 – (8% × ½ × $1 million)]	10,000	
Interest rate swap ($9,615 – 9,363)	252	
Interest revenue (9% × ½ × $9,363)		421
Holding gain—interest rate swap (to balance)		9,831
To record the net cash settlement, accrued interest on the swap, and change in the fair value of the derivative.		
Holding loss—hedged note	4,831	
Notes payable ($1,009,615 – 1,009,363 + 4,579)		4,831
To record the change in fair value of the note due to interest rate changes.		

*We could use a premium on the note to adjust its book value.

As with any debt, interest expense is the effective rate times the outstanding balance.

The cash settlement is the difference between the fixed interest (5%) and variable interest (4%).

Interest ($421) accrues on the asset.

The note is increased by the change in fair value.

We determine interest on the note the same way we do for any liability, as you learned earlier—at the effective rate (9% × ½) times the outstanding balance ($1,009,363). This results in reducing the note's book value for the cash interest paid in excess of the interest expense.

The fair value of the swap increased due to the interest rate decline by $252 (from $9,363 to $9,615). The holding gain we recognize in earnings consists of that increase (a) plus the $10,000 cash settlement also created by the interest rate decline and (b) minus the $421 increase that results not from the interest rate decline, but from interest accruing on the asset.[18] Similarly, we adjust the note's book value by the amount necessary to increase it to fair value, allowing for the $4,579 reduction in the note in the earlier entry to record interest.

At June 30, 2019, Wintel repeats the process of adjusting to fair value both the derivative investment and the note being hedged.

[18]The investment in the interest rate swap represents the present value of expected future net interest receipts. As with other such assets, interest accrues at the effective rate times the outstanding balance. You also can think of the accrued interest mathematically as the increase in present value of the future cash flows as we get one period nearer to the dates when the cash will be received.

Interest expense is the effective rate times the outstanding balance.

The net interest received is the difference between the fixed interest (5%) and floating interest (4.5%).

The swap's fair value now is zero.

June 30, 2019		
Interest expense (8% × ½ × $1,009,615)	40,385	
Notes payable (difference)	9,615	
Cash (10% × ½ × $1,000,000)		50,000
To record interest.		
Cash [$50,000 − (9% × ½ × $1 million)]	5,000	
Holding loss—interest rate swap (to balance)	5,000	
Interest rate swap ($0 − $9,615)		9,615
Interest revenue (8% × ½ × $9,615)		385
To record the net cash settlement, accrued interest on the swap, and change in the fair value of the derivative.		
Notes payable ($1,000,000 − 1,009,615 + 9,615)	0	
Holding gain—hedged note		0
To record the change in fair value of the note due to interest rate changes.		
Note payable	1,000,000	
Cash		1,000,000
To repay the loan.		

The net interest received is the difference between the fixed rate (5%) and floating rate (4.5%), times $1 million. The fair value of the swap decreased by $9,615 (from $9,615 to zero).[19] The holding loss we recognize in earnings consists of that decline (a) minus the $5,000 portion of the decline resulting from it being realized in cash settlement and (b) plus the $385 increase that results not from the interest rate change, but from interest accruing on the asset.

Now let's see how the book values changed for the swap account and the note.

	Swap (Dr.)	Swap (Cr.)	Note (Dr.)	Note (Cr.)
Jan. 1, 2018				1,000,000
June 30, 2018	9,363			9,363
Dec. 31, 2018	252		4,579	4,831
June 30, 2019		9,615	9,615	
			1,000,000	
	0			0

The income statement is affected as follows:

Income Statement + (—)

June 30, 2018	(50,000)	Interest expense
	0	Interest revenue (no time has passed)
	14,363	Holding gain interest rate swap
	(9,363)	Holding loss—hedged note
	(45,000)	Net effect—same as floating interest payment
Dec. 31, 2018	(45,421)	Interest expense
	421	Interest revenue
	9,831	Holding gain—interest rate swap
	(4,831)	Holding loss—hedged note
	(40,000)	Net effect—same as floating interest payment
June 30, 2019	(40,385)	Interest expense
	385	Interest revenue
	(5,000)	Holding gain—interest rate swap
	0	Holding loss—hedged note
	(45,000)	Net effect—same as floating interest payment

As this demonstrates, the swap effectively converts Wintel's fixed-interest debt to floating interest debt.

[19]Because there are no future cash receipts or payments from the swap arrangement at this point, the fair value of the swap is zero.

Additional Consideration

Private Company GAAP – Derivatives and Hedging. The Private Company Council (PCC) sought feedback from private company stakeholders and found that most users of private company financial statements find it difficult to obtain fixed-rate borrowing and often enter into an interest rate swap to economically convert their variable-rate borrowing into a fixed-rate borrowing, which under GAAP caused significant variability in the income statements. As a result, the PCC concluded that the cost and complexity of hedge accounting outweigh the benefits for private companies.

In response to the PCC's conclusion, the FASB issued an Accounting Standards Update in 2014 that allows an accounting alternative to make it easier for certain interest rate swaps to qualify for hedge accounting for private companies that is quite different from what is required for public companies.[20] This alternative allows a nonpublic company (that's not a financial institution) to apply hedge accounting to its interest rate swaps as long as the terms of the swap and the related debt are aligned. If the conditions are met, the company can assume the cash flow hedge is fully effective. Those applying the simplified hedge accounting approach will be able to recognize the swap at its settlement value, instead of at its fair value.

This alternative should significantly reduce the cost and complexity of accounting for derivatives and hedging transactions of private companies.

Where We're Headed

One phase of the FASB's *Financial Instruments* project aspires to improve, simplify, and converge the financial reporting requirements for hedging activities. In May 2010, the FASB proposed revisions of standards for hedge accounting in its proposed Accounting Standards Update, *Accounting for Financial Instruments and Revisions to the Accounting for Derivative Instruments and Hedging Activities—Financial Instruments (Topic 825) and Derivatives and Hedging (Topic 815).*

In July 2014, the International Accounting Standards Board (IASB) issued a revision of IFRS 9 *Financial Instruments*. This guidance differs significantly from the FASB's proposal.

At the time this textbook was written, the FASB was actively developing a proposed new standard intended to make hedge accounting easier for companies to apply and for users of the financial statements to understand. The FASB had reached several tentative decisions that included:

- Helping companies take advantage of the favorable accounting treatment that reduces income-statement volatility.
- Changing language that currently can result in restating financial statements.
- Allowing companies to defer the recognition of ineffectiveness for cash flow hedges until the hedged item affects earnings.
- Allowing companies to hedge contractually specified components of nonfinancial items.
- Expanding the types of interest rates that could be designated as the hedged risk in cash flow and fair value hedges.
- Relaxing certain hedge effectiveness assessment requirements.
- Eliminating the burden to complete ongoing analysis associated with the long-haul method (when the short-cut method is not allowed) for fair value hedges of financial items.

[20] *Accounting Standards Update No. 2014-03,* "Derivatives and Hedging (Topic 815): Accounting for Certain Receive-Variable, Pay-Fixed Interest Rate Swaps—Simplified Hedge Accounting Approach (a consensus of the Private Comapny Council)," (Norwalk, Conn.: FASB, January 2014).

The Bottom Line

- **LOA–1** All derivatives are reported in the balance sheet at fair value.
- **LOA–2** *Hedging* means taking a risk position that is opposite to an actual position that is exposed to risk. For a derivative used to hedge against exposure to risk, treatment of any gain or loss from fair value changes depends on whether the derivative is designated as (a) a fair value hedge, (b) a cash flow hedge, or (c) a foreign currency hedge.
- **LOA–3** We recognize a gain or loss from a *fair value hedge* immediately in earnings along with the loss or gain from the item being hedged. This is so the income effects of the hedge instrument and the income effects of the item being hedged will affect earnings at the same time.
- **LOA–4** We defer a gain or loss from a *cash flow hedge* as part of other comprehensive income until it can be recognized in earnings along with the earnings effect of the item being hedged.
- **LOA–5** Imperfect hedges result in part of the derivative gain or loss being included in current earnings. We ignore market value changes unrelated to the risk being hedged.
- **LOA–6** Extensive disclosure requirements about derivatives are designed to provide investors and creditors information about the adequacy of a company's risk management and the company's success in reducing risks, including risks not managed successfully.

Questions For Review of Key Topics

Q A–1 Some financial instruments are called derivatives. Why?

Q A–2 Should gains and losses on a fair value hedge be recorded as they occur, or should they be recorded to coincide with losses and gains on the item being hedged?

Q A–3 Hines Moving Company held a fixed-rate debt of $2 million. The company wanted to hedge its fair value exposure with an interest rate swap. However, the only notional available at the time, on the type of swap it desired, was $2.5 million. What will be the effect of any gain or loss on the $500,000 notional difference?

Q A–4 What is a futures contract?

Q A–5 What is the effect on interest of an interest rate swap?

Q A–6 How are derivatives reported on the balance sheet? Why?

Q A–7 When is a gain or a loss from a cash flow hedge reported in earnings?

Exercises

connect

E A–1
Derivatives; hedge classification

Indicate (by abbreviation) the type of hedge each activity described below would represent.

Hedge Type

FV	Fair value hedge
CF	Cash flow hedge
FC	Foreign currency hedge
N	Would not qualify as a hedge

Activity

____ 1. An options contract to hedge possible future price changes of inventory

____ 2. A futures contract to hedge exposure to interest rate changes prior to replacing bank notes when they mature

____ 3. An interest rate swap to synthetically convert floating rate debt into fixed rate debt

____ 4. An interest rate swap to synthetically convert fixed rate debt into floating rate debt

____ 5. A futures contract to hedge possible future price changes of timber covered by a firm commitment to sell

____ 6. A futures contract to hedge possible future price changes of a forecasted sale of tin

____ 7. ExxonMobil's net investment in a Kuwait oil field

____ 8. An interest rate swap to synthetically convert floating rate interest on a stock investment into fixed rate interest

____ 9. An interest rate swap to synthetically convert fixed rate interest on a held-to-maturity debt investment into floating rate interest

(continued)

(concluded)

____10. An interest rate swap to synthetically convert floating rate interest on a held-to-maturity debt investment into fixed rate interest

____11. An interest rate swap to synthetically convert fixed rate interest on a stock investment into floating rate interest

E A–2
Derivatives; interest rate swap; fixed rate debt

On January 1, 2018, LLB Industries borrowed $200,000 from Trust Bank by issuing a two-year, 10% note, with interest payable quarterly. LLB entered into a two-year interest rate swap agreement on January 1, 2018, and designated the swap as a fair value hedge. Its intent was to hedge the risk that general interest rates will decline, causing the fair value of its debt to increase. The agreement called for the company to receive payment based on a 10% fixed interest rate on a notional amount of $200,000 and to pay interest based on a floating interest rate. The contract called for cash settlement of the net interest amount quarterly.

Floating (LIBOR) settlement rates were 10% at January 1, 8% at March 31, and 6% June 30, 2018. The fair values of the swap are quotes obtained from a derivatives dealer. Those quotes and the fair values of the note are as indicated below.

	January 1	March 31	June 30
Fair value of interest rate swap	0	$ 6,472	$ 11,394
Fair value of note payable	$200,000	$206,472	$211,394

Required:

1. Calculate the net cash settlement at March 31 and June 30, 2018.
2. Prepare the journal entries through June 30, 2018, to record the issuance of the note, interest, and necessary adjustments for changes in fair value.

E A–3
Derivatives; interest rate swap; fixed rate investment

(This is a variation of E A–2, modified to consider an investment in debt securities.)

On January 1, 2018, S&S Corporation invested in LLB Industries' negotiable two-year, 10% notes, with interest receivable quarterly. The company classified the investment as available-for-sale. S&S entered into a two-year interest rate swap agreement on January 1, 2018, and designated the swap as a fair value hedge. Its intent was to hedge the risk that general interest rates will decline, causing the fair value of its investment to increase. The agreement called for the company to make payment based on a 10% fixed interest rate on a notional amount of $200,000 and to receive interest based on a floating interest rate. The contract called for cash settlement of the net interest amount quarterly.

Floating (LIBOR) settlement rates were 10% at January 1, 8% at March 31, and 6% June 30, 2018. The fair values of the swap are quotes obtained from a derivatives dealer. Those quotes and the fair values of the investment in notes are as follows:

	January 1	March 31	June 30
Fair value of interest rate swap	0	$ 6,472	$ 11,394
Fair value of the investment in notes	$200,000	$206,472	$211,394

Required:

1. Calculate the net cash settlement at March 31 and June 30, 2018.
2. Prepare the journal entries through June 30, 2018, to record the investment in notes, interest, and necessary adjustments for changes in fair value.

E A–4
Derivatives; interest rate swap; fixed rate debt; fair value change unrelated to hedged risk

(This is a variation of E A–2, modified to consider fair value change unrelated to hedged risk.)

LLB Industries borrowed $200,000 from Trust Bank by issuing a two-year, 10% note, with interest payable quarterly. LLB entered into a two-year interest rate swap agreement on January 1, 2018, and designated the swap as a fair value hedge. Its intent was to hedge the risk that general interest rates will decline, causing the fair value of its debt to increase. The agreement called for the company to receive payment based on a 10% fixed interest rate on a notional amount of $200,000 and to pay interest based on a floating interest rate.

Floating (LIBOR) settlement rates were 10% at January 1, 8% at March 31, and 6% at June 30, 2018. The fair values of the swap are quotes obtained from a derivatives dealer. Those quotes and the fair values of the note are as indicated below. The additional rise in the fair value of the note (higher than that of the swap) on June 30 was due to investors' perceptions that the creditworthiness of LLB was improving.

	January 1	March 31	June 30
Fair value of interest rate swap	0	$ 6,472	$ 11,394
Fair value of note payable	$200,000	$206,472	$220,000

Required:

1. Calculate the net cash settlement at June 30, 2018.
2. Prepare the journal entries on June 30, 2018, to record the interest and necessary adjustments for changes in fair value.

E A–5
Derivatives; interest rate swap; fixed rate debt; extended method

(This is a variation of Exercise A–2, modified to consider the extended method.)

On January 1, 2018, LLB Industries borrowed $200,000 from Trust Bank by issuing a two-year, 10% note, with interest payable quarterly. LLB entered into a two-year interest rate swap agreement on January 1, 2018, and designated the swap as a fair value hedge. Its intent was to hedge the risk that general interest rates will decline, causing the fair value of its debt to increase. The agreement called for the company to receive payment based on a 10% fixed interest rate on a notional amount of $200,000 and to pay interest based on a floating interest rate. The contract called for cash settlement of the net interest amount quarterly.

Floating (LIBOR) settlement rates were 10% at January 1, 8% at March 31, and 6% at June 30, 2018. The fair values of the swap are quotes obtained from a derivatives dealer. Those quotes and the fair values of the note are as follows:

	January 1	March 31	June 30
Fair value of interest rate swap	0	$ 6,472	$ 11,394
Fair value of note payable	$200,000	$206,472	$211,394

Required:

Prepare the journal entries through June 30, 2018, to record the issuance of the note, interest, and necessary adjustments for changes in fair value. Use the extended method demonstrated in Illustration A–3.

E A–6
Derivatives; interest rate swap; fixed-rate debt; fair value change unrelated to hedged

(Note: This is a variation of Exercise A–5, modified to consider fair value change unrelated to hedged risk.)

On January 1, 2018, LLB Industries borrowed $200,000 from Trust Bank by issuing a two-year, 10% note, with interest payable quarterly. LLB entered into a two-year interest rate swap agreement on January 1, 2018, and designated the swap as a fair value hedge. Its intent was to hedge the risk that general interest rates will decline, causing the fair value of its debt to increase. The agreement called for the company to receive payment based on a 10% fixed interest rate on a notional amount of $200,000 and to pay interest based on a floating interest rate. The contract called for cash settlement of the net interest amount quarterly.

Floating (LIBOR) settlement rates were 10% at January 1, 8% at March 31, and 6% June 30, 2018. The fair values of the swap are quotes obtained from a derivatives dealer. Those quotes and the fair values of the note are as indicated below. The additional rise in the fair value of the note (higher than that of the swap) on June 30 was due to investors' perceptions that the creditworthiness of LLB was improving.

	January 1	March 31	June 30
Fair value of interest rate swap	0	$ 6,472	$ 11,394
Fair value of note payable	$200,000	206,472	220,000

Required:

1. Calculate the net cash settlement at June 30, 2018.
2. Prepare the journal entries on June 30, 2018, to record the interest and necessary adjustments for changes in fair value. Use the extended method demonstrated in Illustration A–3.

Problems

connect

P A–1
Derivatives; interest rate swap

On January 1, 2018, Labtech Circuits borrowed $100,000 from First Bank by issuing a three-year, 8% note, payable on December 31, 2020. Labtech wanted to hedge the risk that general interest rates will decline, causing the fair value of its debt to increase. Therefore, Labtech entered into a three-year interest rate swap agreement on January 1, 2018, and designated the swap as a fair value hedge. The agreement called for the company to receive payment based on an 8% fixed interest rate on a notional amount of $100,000 and to pay interest based on a floating interest rate tied to LIBOR. The contract called for cash settlement of the net interest amount on December 31 of each year.

Floating (LIBOR) settlement rates were 8% at inception and 9%, 7%, and 7% at the end of 2018, 2019, and 2020, respectively. The fair values of the swap are quotes obtained from a derivatives dealer. These quotes and the fair values of the note are as follows:

	January 1	December 31		
	2018	2018	2019	2020
Fair value of interest rate swap	0	$ (1,759)	$ 935	0
Fair value of note payable	$100,000	$98,241	$100,935	$100,000

Required:

1. Calculate the net cash settlement at the end of 2018, 2019, and 2020.
2. Prepare the journal entries during 2018 to record the issuance of the note, interest, and necessary adjustments for changes in fair value.
3. Prepare the journal entries during 2019 to record interest, net cash interest settlement for the interest rate swap, and necessary adjustments for changes in fair value.
4. Prepare the journal entries during 2020 to record interest, net cash interest settlement for the interest rate swap, necessary adjustments for changes in fair value, and repayment of the debt.
5. Calculate the book values of both the swap account and the note in each of the three years.
6. Calculate the net effect on earnings of the hedging arrangement in each of the three years. (Ignore income taxes.)
7. Suppose the fair value of the note at December 31, 2018, had been $97,000 rather than $98,241, with the additional decline in fair value due to investors' perceptions that the creditworthiness of Labtech was worsening. How would that affect your entries to record changes in the fair values?

P A–2
Derivatives; interest rate swap; comprehensive

CMOS Chips is hedging a 20-year, $10 million, 7% bond payable with a 20-year interest rate swap and has designated the swap as a fair value hedge. The agreement called for CMOS to receive payment based on a 7% fixed interest rate on a notional amount of $10 million and to pay interest based on a floating interest rate tied to LIBOR. The contract calls for cash settlement of the net interest amount on December 31 of each year.

At December 31, 2018, the fair value of the derivative and of the hedged bonds has increased by $100,000 because interest rates declined during the reporting period.

Required:

1. Does CMOS have an unrealized gain or loss on the derivative for the period? On the bonds? Will earnings increase or decrease due to the hedging arrangement? Why?
2. Suppose interest rates increased, rather than decreased, causing the fair value of both the derivative and of the hedged bonds to decrease by $100,000. Would CMOS have an unrealized gain or loss on the derivative for the period? On the bonds? Would earnings increase or decrease due to the hedging arrangement? Why?
3. Suppose the fair value of the bonds at December 31, 2018, had increased by $110,000 rather than $100,000, with the additional increase in fair value due to investors' perceptions that the creditworthiness of CMOS was improving. Would CMOS have an unrealized gain or loss on the derivative for the period? On the bonds? Would earnings increase or decrease due to the hedging arrangement? Why?
4. Suppose the notional amount of the swap had been $12 million, rather than the $10 million principal amount of the bonds. As a result, at December 31, 2018, the swap's fair value had increased by $120,000 rather than $100,000. Would CMOS have an unrealized gain or loss on the derivative for the period? On the bonds? Would earnings increase or decrease due to the hedging arrangement? Why?
5. Suppose BIOS Corporation is an investor, having purchased all $10 million of the bonds issued by CMOS as described in the original situation above. BIOS is hedging its investment, classified as available-for-sale, with a 20-year interest rate swap and has designated the swap as a fair value hedge. The agreement called for BIOS to make *payment* based on a 7% fixed interest rate on a notional amount of $10 million and to *receive* interest based on a floating interest rate tied to LIBOR. Would BIOS have an unrealized gain or loss on the derivative for the period due to interest rates having declined? On the bonds? Would earnings increase or decrease due to the hedging arrangement? Why?

P A–3
Derivatives; interest rate swap; fixed rate debt; extended method

(Note: This is a variation of P A–1, modified to consider the extended method demonstrated in Illustration A–3.)

On January 1, 2018, Labtech Circuits borrowed $100,000 from First Bank by issuing a three-year, 8% note, payable on December 31, 2020. Labtech wanted to hedge the risk that general interest rates will decline, causing the fair value of its debt to increase. Therefore, Labtech entered into a three-year interest rate swap agreement on January 1, 2018, and designated the swap as a fair value hedge. The agreement called for the company to receive payment based on an 8% fixed interest rate on a notional amount of $100,000 and to pay interest based on a floating interest rate tied to LIBOR. The contract called for cash settlement of the net interest amount on December 31 of each year.

Floating (LIBOR) settlement rates were 8% at inception and 9%, 7%, and 7% at the end of 2018, 2019, and 2020, respectively. The fair values of the swap are quotes obtained from a derivatives dealer. Those quotes and the fair values of the note are as follows:

	January 1	December 31		
	2018	2018	2019	2020
Fair value of interest rate swap	0	$ (1,759)	$ 935	0
Fair value of note payable	$100,000	$ 98,241	100,935	$100,000

Required:

Use the extended method demonstrated in Illustration A–3.

1. Calculate the net cash settlement at the end of 2018, 2019, and 2020.
2. Prepare the journal entries during 2018 to record the issuance of the note, interest, and necessary adjustments for changes in fair value.
3. Prepare the journal entries during 2019 to record interest, net cash interest settlement for the interest rate swap, and necessary adjustments for changes in fair value.
4. Prepare the journal entries during 2020 to record interest, net cash interest settlement for the interest rate swap, necessary adjustments for changes in fair value, and repayment of the debt.
5. Calculate the book values of both the swap account and the note in each of the three years.
6. Calculate the net effect on earnings of the hedging arrangement in each of the three years. (Ignore income taxes.)
7. Suppose the fair value of the note at December 31, 2018, had been $97,000 rather than $98,241, with the additional decline in fair value due to investors' perceptions that the creditworthiness of Labtech was worsening. How would that affect your entries to record changes in the fair values?

Broaden Your Perspective

Apply your critical-thinking ability to the knowledge you've gained. These cases will provide you an opportunity to develop your research, analysis, judgment, and communication skills. You also will work with other students, integrate what you've learned, apply it in real-world situations, and consider its global and ethical ramifications. This practice will broaden your knowledge and further develop your decision-making abilities.

Real World Case A–1
Derivative losses; recognition in earnings

The following is an excerpt from a disclosure note of Johnson & Johnson:

6. Fair Value Measurements (in part)
As of January 3, 2016, the balance of deferred net losses on derivatives included in accumulated other comprehensive income was $36 million after-tax. The Company expects that substantially all of the amounts related to forward foreign exchange contracts will be reclassified into earnings over the next 12 months as a result of transactions that are expected to occur over that period.

Required:

1. Johnson & Johnson indicates that it expects that substantially all of the balance of deferred net losses on derivatives will be reclassified into earnings over the next 12 months as a result of transactions that are expected to occur over that period. What is meant by "reclassified into earnings"?
2. What type(s) of hedging transaction might be accounted for in this way?

Communication Case A–2
Derivatives; hedge accounting

A conceptual question in accounting for derivatives is this: Should gains and losses on a hedge instrument be recorded as they occur, or should they be recorded to coincide (match) with income effects of the item being hedged?

ABI Wholesalers plans to issue long-term notes in May that will replace its $20 million of 9.5% bonds when they mature in July. ABI is exposed to the risk that interest rates in July will have risen, increasing borrowing costs (reducing the selling price of its notes). To hedge that possibility, ABI entered a (Treasury bond) futures contract in May to deliver (sell) bonds in July at their *current* price.

As a result, if interest rates rise, borrowing costs will go up for ABI because it will sell notes at a higher interest cost (or lower price). But that loss will be offset (approximately) by the gain produced by being in the opposite position on Treasury bond futures.

Two opposing viewpoints are:

View 1: Gains and losses on instruments designed to hedge anticipated transactions should be recorded as they occur.

View 2: Gains and losses on instruments designed to hedge anticipated transactions should be recorded to coincide (match) with income effects of the item being hedged.

In considering this question, focus on conceptual issues regarding the practicable and theoretically appropriate treatment, unconstrained by GAAP. Your instructor will divide the class into two to six groups, depending on the size of the class. The mission of your group is to reach consensus on the appropriate accounting for the gains and losses on instruments designed to hedge anticipated transactions.

Required:

1. Each group member should deliberate the situation independently and draft a tentative argument prior to the class session for which the case is assigned.
2. In class, each group will meet for 10 to 15 minutes in different areas of the classroom. During that meeting, group members will take turns sharing their suggestions for the purpose of arriving at a single group treatment.
3. After the allotted time, a spokesperson for each group (selected during the group meetings) will share the group's solution with the class. The goal of the class is to incorporate the views of each group into a consensus approach to the situation.

Real World Case A–3
Researching the way interest rate futures prices are quoted on the Chicago Mercantile Exchange; retrieving information from the Internet

The Chicago Mercantile Exchange, or Merc, at 30 S. Wacker Drive in Chicago, is the world's largest financial exchange, an international marketplace enabling institutions and businesses to trade futures and options contracts including currencies, interest rates, stock indexes, and agricultural commodities.

Required:

1. Access the Merc on the Internet. The web address is www.cmegroup.com.
2. Access the daily settlements within the site. In the Search box, enter "U.S. Treasury Bond." Choose U.S. Treasury Bond.
3. What are the settlement prices for September futures contracts?

Research Case A–4
Issue related to the derivatives standard; research an article

In an effort to keep up with the rapidly changing global financial markets, the FASB issued standards on accounting for and disclosure of derivative financial instruments. A *Journal of Accountancy* article that discusses this standard is "The Decision on Derivatives," by Arlette C. Wilson, Gary Waters, and Barry J. Bryan, November 1998.

Required:

On the Internet, go to the AICPA site at www.aicpa.org and find the article mentioned.

1. What are the primary problems or issues the FASB attempts to address regarding accounting for derivative financial instruments?
2. In considering the issues, the FASB made four fundamental decisions that became the cornerstones of the statement issued in 1998. What are those fundamental decisions? Which do you think is most critical to fair financial reporting?

chapter 9

Foreign Currency Transactions and Hedging Foreign Exchange Risk

Today, international business transactions are a regular occurrence. In its 2015 annual report, Lockheed Martin Corporation reported export sales of $9.5 billion, representing 21 percent of total sales. Some businesses are very significantly involved in transactions occurring throughout the world as evidenced by this excerpt from Cirrus Logic, Inc.'s fiscal year 2015 annual report: "Export sales, principally to Asia, including sales to U.S.-based customers that manufacture at plants overseas, were approximately $869.9 million in fiscal year 2015, $673.7 million in fiscal year 2014, and $764.9 million in fiscal year 2013. Export sales to customers located in Asia were 92 percent of net sales in fiscal years 2015 and 2014 and 91 percent in fiscal year 2013. All other export sales represented 3 percent of net sales in each of fiscal years 2015, 2014, and 2013."

Collections from export sales or payments for imported items might be made not in U.S. dollars but in pesos, pounds, yen, and the like depending on the negotiated terms of the transaction. As foreign currency exchange rates fluctuate, so does the U.S. dollar value of these export sales and import purchases. Companies often find it necessary to engage in some form of hedging activity to reduce losses arising from fluctuating exchange rates. At the end of fiscal year 2015, in conjunction with its foreign currency hedging activities, Apple, Inc., reported having outstanding foreign exchange contracts with a notional value of $119.2 billion.

This chapter covers accounting issues related to foreign currency transactions and foreign currency hedging activities. To provide background for subsequent discussions of the accounting issues, the chapter begins by describing foreign exchange markets. The chapter then discusses accounting for import and export transactions, followed by coverage of various hedging techniques. Because they are most popular, the discussion concentrates on foreign currency forward contracts and options. Understanding how to account for these items is important for any company engaged in international transactions.

Learning Objectives

After studying this chapter, you should be able to:

LO 9-1 Understand concepts related to foreign currency, exchange rates, and foreign exchange risk.

LO 9-2 Account for foreign currency transactions using the two-transaction perspective, accrual approach.

LO 9-3 Account for foreign currency borrowings.

LO 9-4 Understand the different types of foreign exchange risk that can be hedged and how foreign currency forward contracts and foreign currency options can be used to hedge those risks.

LO 9-5 Understand the accounting guidelines for derivative financial instruments.

LO 9-6 Understand the basic concepts of hedge accounting.

LO 9-7 Account for forward contracts and options used as hedges of foreign currency denominated assets and liabilities.

LO 9-8 Account for forward contracts and options used as hedges of foreign currency firm commitments.

LO 9-9 Account for forward contracts and options used as hedges of forecasted foreign currency transactions.

LO 9-1

Understand concepts related to foreign currency, exchange rates, and foreign exchange risk.

Foreign Exchange Markets

Each country (or group of countries) uses its own currency as the unit of value for the purchase and sale of goods and services. The currency used in the United States is the U.S. dollar, the currency used in Mexico is the Mexican peso, the currency used by a subset of European Union countries is the euro, and so on. If a U.S. citizen travels to Mexico and wishes to purchase local goods, Mexican merchants require payment to be made in Mexican pesos. To make a purchase in Mexico, a U.S. citizen would need to acquire pesos using U.S. dollars. The foreign currency *exchange rate* is the price at which the foreign currency can be acquired (or sold). A variety of factors determine the exchange rate between two currencies; unfortunately for those engaged in international business, the exchange rate can fluctuate over time.[1]

Exchange Rate Mechanisms

Exchange rates have not always fluctuated. During the period 1945–1973, countries fixed the value of their currency in terms of the U.S. dollar, and the value of the U.S. dollar was fixed in terms of gold. In March 1973, most countries allowed their currencies to float in value. Today, several different currency arrangements exist. Some of the more important ones and the countries affected follow:

1. *Independent float:* The value of the currency is allowed to fluctuate freely according to market forces with little or no intervention from the central bank (example countries include Australia, Brazil, Canada, Japan, Sweden, Switzerland, the United Kingdom, and the United States).
2. *Pegged to another currency:* The value of the currency is fixed (pegged) in terms of a particular foreign currency and the central bank intervenes as necessary to maintain the fixed value. For example, Bahrain, Panama, and Saudi Arabia peg their currency to the U.S. dollar. China has pegged its currency, the yuan (or Renminbi), to the U.S. dollar since 1994, while allowing a revaluation in 2005 and again in 2015. By managing the value of its currency (downward) rather than allowing it to float freely, the Chinese government has made it easier for Chinese companies to export their products overseas.
3. *European Monetary System (euro):* In 1998, the countries comprising the European Monetary System adopted a common currency called the *euro* and established a European Central Bank.[2] Until 2002, local currencies such as the German mark and French franc continued to exist but were fixed in value in terms of the euro. On January 1, 2002, local currencies disappeared, and the euro became the currency in 12 European countries. Today, 19 countries are part of the euro zone. The value of the euro floats against other currencies such as the Swiss franc, British pound, and U.S. dollar.

Foreign Exchange Rates

Exchange rates between the U.S. dollar and many foreign currencies are published on a daily basis in *The Wall Street Journal* and major U.S. newspapers. Exchange rates also are available online at websites such as www.oanda.com and www.x-rates.com. To illustrate exchange rates and the foreign currency market, next we examine exchange rates for selected currencies reported for December 1-2, 2015, as shown in Exhibit 9.1.

The exchange rates shown in Exhibit 9.1 are for trades between banks; that is, these are interbank or wholesale prices. Prices charged by banks to retail customers, such as companies engaged in international business, are higher. These are selling rates at which banks will sell currency to one another. The prices that banks are willing to pay to buy foreign currency are

[1] Several theories attempt to explain exchange rate fluctuations but with little success, at least in the short term. An understanding of the causes of exchange rate changes is not necessary to comprehend the concepts underlying the accounting for changes in exchange rates.

[2] Most longtime members of the European Union (EU) are "euro zone" countries. The major exception is the United Kingdom, which elected not to participate. Switzerland is another important European country not part of the euro zone because it is not a member of the EU.

EXHIBIT 9.1
Exchange Rates for Selected Currencies (December 1-2, 2015)

	December 1, 2015		December 2, 2015	
Country/Currency	**Direct***	**Indirect†**	**Direct***	**Indirect†**
Euro zone euro.	1.0607	0.9428	1.0685	0.9359
UK pound	1.5078	0.6632	1.5027	0.6655
Canada dollar	0.7491	1.3349	0.7480	1.3369
Brazil real.	0.2584	3.8700	0.2595	3.8536
China yuan	0.1560	6.4103	0.1560	6.4103

Source: http://www.oanda.com/currency/historical-rates.
*www.oanda.com/currency/historical-rates.
†Indirect quotes have been calculated by the author.

somewhat less than the selling rates. The difference between the buying and selling rates is the spread through which the banks earn a profit on foreign exchange trades. For example, the December 1, 2015, selling rate for the euro was $1.0607, while the the buying rate was $1.0596. On that date, banks were willing to buy euros for $1.0596 and sell them for $1.0607, earning a profit of $0.0011 per euro.

Two columns of information are shown for each day's exchange rates. The first column reports *direct quotes,* which indicate the number of U.S. dollars needed to purchase one unit of foreign currency. The direct quote for the Brazilian real on December 1 was $0.2584; in other words, 1.0 Brazilian real (BRL) could be purchased for $0.2584. The second column reports *indirect quotes,* which indicate the number of foreign currency units that could be purchased with one U.S. dollar. These rates are simply the inverse of direct quotes (indirect quote = 1 ÷ direct quote). If one BRL can be purchased with $0.2584, then 3.87 BRL can be purchased with $1.00. To avoid confusion, *direct quotes are used exclusively in this chapter.*

The third and fourth columns in Exhibit 9.1 show exchange rates for December 2, 2015. Two of the currencies shown increased in U.S. dollar price (appreciated) from December 1 to December 2, namely the euro and Brazilian real. For example, the euro increased in price by $0.0078 from one day to the next. As a result, the purchase of 100,000 euros on December 2, 2015, would have cost $780 more than on the previous day. In contrast, the U.S. dollar price for two currencies decreased (depreciated) from one day to the next, namely the British pound and Canadian dollar. The Chinese yuan did not change in U.S. dollar value because this currency was effectively pegged to the U.S. dollar.

Foreign Currency Forward Contracts

Foreign currency trades can be executed on a spot or forward basis. The *spot rate* is the price at which a foreign currency can be purchased or sold today. In contrast, the *forward rate* is the price available today at which foreign currency can be purchased or sold sometime in the future. Because many international business transactions take some time to be completed, the ability to lock in a price today at which foreign currency can be purchased or sold at some future date has definite advantages.

A *foreign currency forward contract* can be negotiated by a firm with its bank to exchange foreign currency for U.S. dollars, or vice versa, on a specified future date at a predetermined exchange rate. A forward contract can be written for whatever currency and for whatever future date is required. Entering into a forward contract has no up-front cost; the firm and its bank simply agree today to exchange foreign currency for U.S. dollars at the forward rate on a future date. Similar to how banks make a profit in the spot market, there is a spread between the buying and selling rates in the forward market. For example, on February 1 a bank might agree to buy 500,000 British pounds in three months from one customer at a forward rate of $1.50 and simultaneously agree to sell 500,000 British pounds (GBP) in three months to another customer at a rate of $1.51. In this way, the bank generates a profit of $5,000 (500,000 GBP x $0.01) from entering into these two forward contracts.

The forward rate can exceed the spot rate on a given date, in which case the foreign currency is said to be selling at a *premium* in the forward market, or the forward rate can be less than the spot rate, in which case the currency is selling at a *discount.* Currencies sell at a premium or a discount because of differences in interest rates between two countries. When the interest rate in the foreign country exceeds the domestic interest rate, the foreign currency sells at a discount in the forward market. Conversely, if the foreign interest rate is less than the domestic rate, the foreign currency sells at a premium.[3]

The forward exchange rate for a specific future settlement date will change over time due to changes in the spot exchange rate and/or changes in the differential interest rates between two countries. For example, assume on April 15 the U.S. dollar (USD) per Mexican peso (MXN) spot rate is $0.11 and the forward rate for a forward contract to be settled on June 15 is $0.105. The peso is selling at a discount of $0.005 in the two-month forward market due to a higher interest rate in Mexico than in the United States. If the USD/MXN spot rate decreases to $0.08 on May 15, the forward rate for a June 15 settlement-date forward contract also will decrease, to an amount less than $0.08. The peso will continue to sell at a discount in the one-month forward market because of the higher interest rate in Mexico.

Until December 2014, *The Wall Street Journal* published forward rates offered by New York banks for several major currencies on a daily basis. Since then, it has been difficult for third parties to obtain data on foreign currency forward rates. The spot rate for Swiss francs (CHF) on December 8, 2014, was reported to be $1.0245. On the same day, the one-month forward rate was reported as $1.0250, so the CHF was selling at a premium in the forward market. By entering into a forward contract on December 8, 2014, it would have been possible for a firm to guarantee that CHF could be purchased on January 8, 2015, at a price of $1.0250, regardless of what the spot rate turned out to be on January 8. Entering into the forward contract to purchase CHF would have been beneficial if the spot rate on January 8 was more than $1.0250. On the other hand, such a forward contract would have been detrimental if the spot rate was less than $1.0250. In either case, the firm must execute the forward contract and purchase CHF on January 8 at $1.0250.

As it turned out, the spot rate for CHF on January 8, 2015, was $0.9819, so entering into a one-month forward contract on December 8, 2014, to purchase CHF at $1.0250 on January 8, 2015, would have resulted in a loss because CHF could have been purchased at a lower price using the spot rate on that date.

Foreign Currency Options

To provide companies more flexibility than exists with a forward contract, a market for *foreign currency options* has developed. A foreign currency option gives the holder of the option *the right but not the obligation* to trade foreign currency in the future. A *put* option is for the sale of foreign currency by the holder of the option; a *call* option is for the purchase of foreign currency by the holder of the option. The *strike price* is the exchange rate at which the option will be executed if the option holder decides to exercise the option. The strike price is similar to a forward rate. There are generally several strike prices to choose from at any particular time. Foreign currency options can be purchased on the Philadelphia Stock Exchange or the Chicago Mercantile Exchange, but most foreign currency options are purchased directly from a bank in the so-called over-the-counter (OTC) market. Options purchased in the OTC market usually have a strike price that is equal to the spot rate on that date. These options are said to be "at-the-money."

Unlike a forward contract, for which banks earn their profit through the spread between buying and selling rates, options must actually be purchased by paying an *option premium,* which is a function of two components: intrinsic value and time value. An option's *intrinsic value* is equal to the gain that could be realized by exercising the option immediately. For example, if the spot rate for the euro is $1.00, a *call* option (to purchase euros) with a strike price of $0.97 has an intrinsic value of $0.03 per euro. Euros can be purchased for $0.97 and sold for $1.00, generating a gain of $0.03 per euro. On the other hand, when the spot rate for the euro is $1.00, a *put* option (to sell euros) with a strike price of $0.97 has an intrinsic

[3] This relationship is based on the theory of interest rate parity that indicates the difference in national interest rates should be equal to, but opposite in sign to, the forward rate discount or premium. This topic is covered in detail in international finance textbooks.

value of zero. An option with a positive intrinsic value is said to be "in-the-money." The *time value* of an option relates to the fact that the spot rate can change over time and cause the option's intrinsic value to increase. Even though a call option with a strike price of $1.00 has zero intrinsic value when the spot rate is $1.00, it will have a positive time value because there is a chance that the spot rate could increase over the next 90 days and bring the option into the money. As time passes, the time value of an option decreases because there is less time remaining for the option to increase in intrinsic value. The fair value of a foreign currency option on a specific date is the sum of its intrinsic and time values on that date.

The fair value of a foreign currency option can be determined by applying an adaptation of the Black-Scholes option pricing formula. This formula is discussed in detail in international finance books. In very general terms, the value of an option is a function of the difference between the current spot rate and strike price, the difference between domestic and foreign interest rates, the length of time to expiration, and the potential volatility of changes in the spot rate. For purposes of this book, the premium originally paid for a foreign currency option and its subsequent fair value up to the date of expiration derived from applying the pricing formula will be given.

On December 17, 2015, when the USD spot rate for euros was $1.09, the Chicago Mercantile Exchange indicated that a January 2016 call option in euros with a strike price of $1.09 could have been purchased by paying a premium of $0.0068 per euro. Thus, the right to purchase a standard contract of 125,000 euros in December 2016 at a price of $1.09 per euro could have been acquired by paying $850 ($0.0068 × 125,000 euros). Because the spot rate and the strike price were both $1.09, the euro call option had zero intrinsic value and a time value of $850. If the spot rate for euros on January 17, 2016, is more than $1.09, the option will be exercised and euros purchased at the strike price of $1.09. If, on the other hand, the January 17, 2016, spot rate is less than $1.09, the option will not be exercised; instead, euros will be purchased at the lower spot rate. The call option establishes the maximum amount that would have to be paid for euros but does not lock in a disadvantageous price should the spot rate fall below the option strike price. The actual spot rate for euros on January 17, 2016, turned out to be $1.091, so the option would have been exercised and euros purchased for $1.09.

Foreign Currency Transactions

LO 9-2

Account for foreign currency transactions using the two-transaction perspective, accrual approach.

Export sales and import purchases are international transactions; they are components of what is called *trade*. When two parties from different countries enter into a transaction, they must decide which of the two countries' currencies to use to settle the transaction. For example, if a U.S. computer manufacturer sells to a customer in Japan, the parties must decide whether the transaction will be denominated (payment will be made) in U.S. dollars or in Japanese yen.

Assume that a U.S. exporter (Amerco) sells goods to a German importer that will pay in euros (€). In this situation, Amerco has entered into a foreign currency transaction. It must restate the euro amount that it actually will receive into U.S. dollars to account for this transaction. This happens because Amerco keeps its books and prepares financial statements in U.S. dollars. Although the German importer has entered into an international transaction, it does not have a foreign currency transaction (payment will be made in its currency) and no restatement is necessary.

Assume that, as is customary in its industry, Amerco does not require immediate payment and allows its German customer 30 days to pay for its purchases. By doing this, Amerco runs the risk that the euro might depreciate against the U.S. dollar between the sale date and the date of payment. If so, the sale would generate fewer U.S. dollars than it would have had the euro not decreased in value, and the sale is less profitable because it was made on a credit basis. In this situation Amerco is said to have an *exposure to foreign exchange risk.* Specifically, Amerco has a transaction exposure that can be summarized as follows:

- *Export sale:* A transaction exposure exists when the exporter *allows the buyer to pay in a foreign currency* and *allows the buyer to pay sometime after the sale has been made.* The exporter is exposed to the risk that the foreign currency might depreciate (decrease in value) between the date of sale and the date payment is received, thereby decreasing the U.S. dollars ultimately collected.
  - Note that there is no exposure to foreign exchange risk if the exporter requires the foreign customer to make payment on the date of sale. In that case, the exporter would receive foreign currency and immediately convert it into U.S. dollars at the spot rate on the date of sale.
- *Import purchase:* A transaction exposure exists when the importer *is required to pay in foreign currency* and *is allowed to pay sometime after the purchase has been made.* The importer is exposed to the risk that the foreign currency might appreciate (increase in price) between the date of purchase and the date of payment, thereby increasing the U.S. dollars that have to be paid for the imported goods.
  - Note that there is no exposure to foreign exchange risk if the importer makes payment in foreign currency on the date of purchase. In that case, the importer converts U.S. dollars into foreign currency at the spot rate on the date of purchase and immediately makes payment.

Accounting Issue

The major issue in accounting for foreign currency transactions is how to deal with the change in U.S. dollar value of the sales revenue and account receivable resulting from the export when the foreign currency changes in value. (The corollary issue is how to deal with the change in the U.S. dollar value of the account payable and goods being acquired in an import purchase.) For example, assume that Amerco, a U.S. company, sells goods to a German customer at the price of 1 million euros when the spot exchange rate is $1.32 per euro. If payment were received at the sale date, Amerco could have converted 1 million euros into $1,320,000; this amount clearly would be the amount at which the sales revenue would be recognized. Instead, Amerco allows the German customer 30 days to pay for its purchase. At the end of 30 days, the euro has depreciated to $1.30 and Amerco is able to convert the 1 million euros received on that date into only $1,300,000. How should Amerco account for this $20,000 decrease in value?

FASB *ASC* 830-20 Foreign Currency Matters–Foreign Currency Transactions requires companies to use what can be referred to as a *two-transaction perspective* in accounting for foreign currency transactions. This perspective treats the export sale and the subsequent collection of cash as two separate transactions. Because management has made two decisions—(1) to make the export sale and (2) to extend credit in foreign currency to the customer—the company should report the income effect from each of these decisions separately. The U.S. dollar value of the sale is recorded at the date the sale occurs. At that point, the sale has been completed; there are no subsequent adjustments to the Sales account. Any difference between the number of U.S. dollars that could have been received at the date of sale and the number of U.S. dollars actually received at the date of collection due to fluctuations in the exchange rate is a result of the decision to extend foreign currency credit to the customer. This difference is treated as a foreign exchange gain or loss that is reported separately from Sales in the income statement.

Similarly, an import purchase denominated in a foreign currency and the subsequent payment of cash must be accounted for separately. The U.S. dollar value of the goods purchased is recorded at the date of purchase, with no subsequent adjustments to the cost of the goods. Any difference between the number of U.S. dollars that could have been paid on the date of purchase and the actual number of U.S. dollars that is paid on the payment date due to a change in the exchange rate is treated as a foreign exchange gain or loss.

Using the two-transaction perspective to account for its export sale to the German customer, Amerco would make the following journal entries:

Date of Sale:	Accounts Receivable (€)	1,320,000	
	Sales		1,320,000
	To record the sale and euro receivable at the spot rate of $1.32.		
Date of Collection:	Foreign Exchange Loss	20,000	
	Accounts Receivable (€)		20,000
	To adjust the value of the euro receivable to the new spot rate of $1.30 and record a foreign exchange loss resulting from the depreciation in the euro.		
	Cash	1,300,000	
	Accounts Receivable (€)		1,300,000
	To record the receipt of 1 million euros and conversion into U.S. dollars at the spot rate of $1.30.		

Sales are reported in income at the amount that would have been received if the customer had not been given 30 days to pay the 1 million euros—that is, $1,320,000. A separate Foreign Exchange Loss of $20,000 is reported in net income to indicate that because of the decision to extend foreign currency credit to the German customer and because the euro decreased in value, Amerco actually received fewer U.S. dollars.[4]

Note that Amerco keeps its Account Receivable (€) account separate from its U.S. dollar receivables. Companies engaged in international trade need to keep separate receivable and payable accounts in each of the currencies in which they have transactions. Each foreign currency receivable and payable should have a separate account number in the company's chart of accounts.

We can summarize the relationship between fluctuations in exchange rates and foreign exchange gains and losses as follows:

		Foreign Currency (FC)	
Transaction	**Type of Exposure**	**Appreciates**	**Depreciates**
Export sale	Asset (receivable)	Gain	Loss
Import purchase	Liability (payable)	Loss	Gain

A foreign currency receivable arising from an export sale creates an *asset exposure* to foreign exchange risk. If the foreign currency appreciates, the foreign currency asset increases in U.S. dollar value and a foreign exchange gain arises; depreciation of the foreign currency causes a foreign exchange loss. A foreign currency payable arising from an import purchase creates a *liability exposure* to foreign exchange risk. If the foreign currency appreciates, the foreign currency liability increases in U.S. dollar value and a foreign exchange loss results; depreciation of the currency results in a foreign exchange gain.

Balance Sheet Date before Date of Payment

The question arises as to what adjustments should be made if a balance sheet date falls between the date of sale (or purchase) and the date of collection (or payment). For example, assume that Amerco shipped goods to its German customer on December 1, 2017, with payment to be received on March 1, 2018. Assume that at December 1, the spot rate for the euro was $1.32, but by December 31, the euro has appreciated to $1.33. Is any adjustment needed at December 31, 2017, when the books are closed to account for the fact that the foreign currency receivable has changed in U.S. dollar value since December 1?

Authoritative accounting literature requires foreign currency balances such as a foreign currency receivable or a foreign currency payable to be revalued at the balance sheet date to account for the change in exchange rates. Under the two-transaction perspective, this means that a foreign exchange gain or loss arises at the balance sheet date. The next question then is

[4] Note that the foreign exchange loss results because the customer is allowed to pay in euros and is given 30 days to pay. If the transaction were denominated in U.S. dollars, no loss would result, nor would there be a loss if the euros had been received at the date the sale was made.

what should be done with these foreign exchange gains and losses that have not yet been realized in cash. Should they be included in net income?

U.S. GAAP requires unrealized foreign exchange gains and losses to be reported in net income in the period in which the exchange rate changes. This is consistent with accrual accounting as it results in reporting the effect of a rate change that will have an impact on cash flow in the period when the event causing the impact takes place. Thus, any change in the exchange rate from the date of sale to the balance sheet date results in a foreign exchange gain or loss to be reported in net income in that period. Any change in the exchange rate from the balance sheet date to the date of collection results in a second foreign exchange gain or loss that is reported in net income in the second accounting period. Amerco makes the following journal entries under this approach:

12/1/17	Accounts Receivable (€)......................	1,320,000	
	Sales		1,320,000
	To record the sale and euro receivable at the spot rate of $1.32.		
12/31/17	Accounts Receivable (€)......................	10,000	
	Foreign Exchange Gain		10,000
	To adjust the value of the euro receivable to the new spot rate of $1.33 and record a foreign exchange gain in 2017 net income resulting from the appreciation in the euro since December 1.		
3/1/18	Foreign Exchange Loss	30,000	
	Accounts Receivable (€)		30,000
	To adjust the value of the euro receivable to the new spot rate of $1.30 and record a foreign exchange loss in 2018 net income resulting from the depreciation in the euro since December 31.		
	Cash..	1,300,000	
	Accounts Receivable (€)		1,300,000
	To record the receipt of 1 million euros and conversion at the spot rate of $1.30.		

The net impact on income in 2017 is a sale of $1,320,000 and a foreign exchange gain of $10,000; in 2018, Amerco records a foreign exchange loss of $30,000. This results in a net increase of $1,300,000 in Retained Earnings that is balanced by an equal increase in Cash over the two-year period. Over the two-year period Amerco recognizes a net foreign exchange loss of $20,000.

One criticism of the accrual approach is that it leads to a violation of conservatism when an unrealized foreign exchange gain arises at the balance sheet date. In fact, this is one of only a few situations in U.S. GAAP in which it is acceptable to recognize an unrealized gain in net income. (This treatment is similar to how changes in the fair value of equity investments are recognized.)

Restatement at the balance sheet date is required for all foreign currency assets and liabilities carried on a company's books. In addition to foreign currency payables and receivables arising from import and export transactions, companies might have dividends receivable from foreign subsidiaries, loans payable to foreign lenders, or lease payments receivable from foreign customers that are denominated in a foreign currency and therefore must be restated at the balance sheet date. Each of these foreign currency denominated assets and liabilities is exposed to foreign exchange risk; therefore, fluctuation in exchange rates result in foreign exchange gains and losses on all foreign currency denominated assets and liabilities.

Many U.S. companies report foreign exchange gains and losses on the income statement in a line item often titled Other income (expense). Companies include other incidental gains and losses such as gains and losses on sales of assets in this line item as well. Companies are required to disclose the magnitude of foreign exchange gains and losses if material. For example, in the Notes to Financial Statements in its 2014 annual report, Merck indicated that the income statement item Other (Income) Expense, Net, included exchange losses of $180 million in 2014, $290 million in 2013, and $185 million in 2012.

International Accounting Standard 21—The Effects of Changes in Foreign Exchange Rates

Similar to U.S. GAAP, *IAS 21,* "The Effects of Changes in Foreign Exchange Rates," also requires the use of a two-transaction perspective in accounting for foreign currency transactions with unrealized foreign exchange gains and losses accrued in net income in the period of exchange rate change. There are no substantive differences between IFRS and U.S. GAAP in the accounting for foreign currency transactions.

Foreign Currency Borrowing

LO 9-3

Account for foreign currency borrowings.

In addition to the receivables and payables that arise from import and export activities, companies often must account for foreign currency borrowings, another type of foreign currency transaction. Companies borrow foreign currency from foreign lenders either to finance foreign operations or perhaps to take advantage of more favorable interest rates. The facts that both the principal and interest are denominated in foreign currency and both create an exposure to foreign exchange risk complicate accounting for a foreign currency borrowing.

To demonstrate the accounting for foreign currency debt, assume that on July 1, 2017, Multicorp International borrowed 1 billion Japanese yen (¥) on a one-year note at a per annum interest rate of 5 percent. Interest is payable and the note comes due on July 1, 2018. The following exchange rates apply:

Date	U.S. Dollars per Japanese Yen Spot Rate
July 1, 2017	$0.00921
December 31, 2017	0.00932
July 1, 2018	0.00937

On July 1, 2017, Multicorp borrows ¥1 billion and converts it into $9,210,000 in the spot market. On December 31, 2017, Multicorp must revalue the Japanese yen note payable with an offsetting foreign exchange gain or loss reported in income and must accrue interest expense and interest payable. Interest is calculated by multiplying the loan principal in yen by the relevant interest rate. The amount of interest payable in yen is then translated to U.S. dollars at the spot rate to record the accrual journal entry. On July 1, 2018, any difference between the amount of interest accrued at year-end and the actual U.S. dollar amount that must be spent to pay the accrued interest is recognized as a foreign exchange gain or loss. These journal entries account for this foreign currency borrowing:

7/1/17	Cash	9,210,000	
	Note Payable (¥)		9,210,000
	To record the ¥ note payable at the spot rate of $0.00921 and the conversion of ¥1 billion into U.S. dollars.		
12/31/17	Interest Expense	233,000	
	Accrued Interest Payable (¥)		233,000
	To accrue interest for the period July 1–December 31, 2017: ¥1 billion × 5% × ½ year = ¥25 million × $0.00932 = $233,000.		

(continued)

(continued)

	Foreign Exchange Loss	110,000	
	Note Payable (¥)		110,000
	To revalue the ¥ note payable at the spot rate of $0.00932 and record a foreign exchange loss of $110,000 [¥1 billion × ($0.00932 – $0.00921)].		
7/1/18	Interest Expense	234,250	
	Accrued Interest Payable (¥)............		234,250
	To accrue interest for the period January 1–July 1, 2018: ¥1 billion × 5% × ½ year = ¥25 million × $0.00937 = $234,250.		
	Foreign Exchange Loss	1,250	
	Accrued Interest Payable (¥)		1,250
	To revalue the ¥ interest payable that was accrued on December 31, 2017, at the spot rate of $0.00937 and record a foreign exchange loss of $1,250 [¥25 million × ($0.00937 – $0.00932)].		
	Accrued Interest Payable (¥)	468,500	
	Cash....................................		468,500
	To record the cash interest payment of $468,500 [¥50 million x the spot rate of $0.00937] and remove the ¥ accrued interest payable from the books.		
	Foreign Exchange Loss	50,000	
	Note Payable (¥)		50,000
	To revalue the ¥ note payable at the spot rate of $0.00937 and record a foreign exchange loss of $50,000 [¥1 billion × ($0.00937 – $0.00932)].		
	Note Payable (¥)..........................	9,370,000	
	Cash....................................		9,370,000
	To record repayment of the ¥1 billion note through purchase of ¥1 billion at the spot rate of $0.00937 and remove the ¥ note payable from the books..		

The total U.S. dollar borrowing cost on the 1 billion Japanese yen note payable is equal to the difference between the U.S. dollar cash outflows and cash inflow: $9,370,000 + $468,500 – $9,210,000 = $628,500. This borrowing cost is reflected in Multicorp's financial statements as a combination of interest expense ($467,250) and foreign exchange loss ($161,250). Taking the exchange rate effect on the cost of borrowing into consideration results in an "effective" interest rate of 6.8% ($628,500/$9,210,000), even though the stated interest rate is only 5%.

Foreign Currency Loan

At times companies lend foreign currency to related parties, creating the opposite situation from a foreign currency borrowing. The accounting involves keeping track of a note receivable and related interest receivable, both of which are denominated in foreign currency. Fluctuations in the U.S. dollar value of the principal and interest generally give rise to foreign exchange gains and losses that would be included in net income. An exception arises when the foreign currency loan is made on a long-term basis to a foreign branch, subsidiary, or equity method affiliate. Foreign exchange gains and losses on "intra-entity foreign currency transactions that are of a long-term investment nature (that is, settlement is not planned or anticipated in the foreseeable future)" are deferred in accumulated other comprehensive income until the loan is repaid.[5] Only the foreign exchange gains and losses related to the interest receivable are recorded currently in net income.

LO 9-4

Understand the different types of foreign exchange risk that can be hedged and how foreign currency forward contracts and foreign currency options can be used to hedge those risks.

Hedges of Foreign Exchange Risk

In the example provided in the earlier section on foreign currency transactions, Amerco has an asset exposure in euros when it sells goods to the German customer and allows the customer three months to pay for its purchase. If the euro depreciates over the next three months, Amerco will incur a net foreign exchange loss. For many companies, the uncertainty of not knowing exactly how many U.S. dollars an export sale will generate is of great concern. To avoid this uncertainty, companies often use derivative financial instruments to hedge against the effect of unfavorable changes in the value of foreign currencies. A derivative financial instrument, or simply derivative, derives its value from some "underlying." In the case of foreign currency derivatives, the underlying is the currency exchange rate. The two most common derivatives used to hedge foreign exchange risk are *foreign currency forward contracts* and *foreign currency options.* In our example, Amerco will receive euros in three months when it collects the receivable and it will need to sell those euros at that time. Through a forward contract, Amerco can lock in the price at which it will sell the euros it receives in three months. An option establishes a price at which Amerco will be able, but is not required, to sell the euros it receives in three months. If Amerco enters into a forward contract or purchases a put option on the date the sale is made, the derivative is being used as a *hedge of a recognized foreign currency denominated asset* (the euro account receivable).

Companies engaged in foreign currency activities often enter into hedging arrangements as soon as they receive a noncancelable sales order or place a noncancelable purchase order. A noncancelable order that specifies the foreign currency price and date of delivery is known as a *foreign currency firm commitment.* Assume that on June 1, Amerco accepts an order to sell parts to a customer in South Korea at a price of 5 million Korean won. The parts will be delivered and payment will be received on August 15. On June 1, before the sale has been made, Amerco enters into a forward contract to sell 5 million Korean won on August 15. In this case, Amerco is using a foreign currency derivative as a *hedge of an unrecognized foreign currency firm commitment.*

Some companies have foreign currency transactions that occur on a regular basis and can be reliably forecasted. For example, Amerco regularly purchases materials from a supplier in Hong Kong for which it pays in Hong Kong dollars. Even if Amerco has no contract to make future purchases, it has an exposure to foreign currency risk if it plans to continue making purchases from the Hong Kong supplier. Assume that on October 1, Amerco forecasts that it will make a purchase from the Hong Kong supplier in one month. To hedge against a possible increase in the price of the Hong Kong dollar, Amerco acquires a call option on October 1 to purchase Hong Kong dollars in one month. The foreign currency option represents a *hedge of a forecasted foreign currency denominated transaction.*

LO 9-5

Understand the accounting guidelines for derivative financial instruments.

Derivatives Accounting

FASB *ASC* Topic 815, "Derivatives and Hedging," governs the accounting for derivatives, including those used to hedge foreign exchange risk. This authoritative literature provides guidance for hedges of the following sources of foreign exchange risk:

1. Recognized foreign currency denominated assets and liabilities.
2. Unrecognized foreign currency firm commitments.
3. Forecasted foreign currency denominated transactions.
4. Net investments in foreign operations.

Different accounting applies to each type of foreign currency hedge. This chapter demonstrates the accounting for the first three types of hedges. The next chapter covers hedges of net investments in foreign operations.

[5] FASB ASC (para. 830-20-35-3b).

Fundamental Requirement of Derivatives Accounting

The fundamental requirement of FASB *ASC* 815 is that companies carry all derivatives on the balance sheet at their fair value. Derivatives are reported on the balance sheet as assets when they have a positive fair value and as liabilities when they have a negative fair value. The first issue in accounting for derivatives is the determination of fair value.

The fair value of derivatives can change over time, causing adjustments to be made to the carrying values of the assets and liabilities. The second issue in accounting for derivatives is the treatment of the gains and losses that arise from these fair value changes.

Determination of Fair Value of Derivatives

The *fair value of a foreign currency forward contract* is determined by reference to changes in the forward rate over the life of the contract, discounted to the present value. Three pieces of information are needed to determine the fair value of a forward contract at any point in time:

1. The forward rate when the forward contract was entered into.
2. The current forward rate for a contract that matures on the same date as the forward contract entered into.
3. A discount rate—typically, the company's incremental borrowing rate.

Assume that Exim Company enters into a forward contract with its bank on December 1 to sell 1 million Mexican pesos on March 1 at a forward rate of $0.085 per peso, or a total of $85,000. Exim incurs no cost to enter into the forward contract, which has no value on December 1. On December 31, when Exim closes its books to prepare financial statements, the forward rate to sell Mexican pesos on March 1 has changed to $0.082. On that date, a forward contract for the delivery of 1 million pesos could be negotiated, resulting in a cash inflow of only $82,000 on March 1. This represents a favorable change in the value of Exim's forward contract of $3,000 ($85,000 – $82,000). The undiscounted fair value of the forward contract on December 31 is $3,000. Assuming that the company's incremental borrowing rate is 12 percent per annum, the undiscounted fair value of the forward contract must be discounted at the rate of 1 percent per month for two months (from the current date of December 31 to the settlement date of March 1). The fair value of the forward contract at December 31 is $2,940.90 ($3,000 × 0.9803).[6]

The manner in which the *fair value of a foreign currency option* is determined depends on whether the option is traded on an exchange or has been acquired in the over-the-counter market. The fair value of an exchange-traded foreign currency option is its current market price quoted on the exchange. For over-the-counter options, fair value can be determined by obtaining a price quote from an option dealer (such as a bank). If dealer price quotes are unavailable, the company can estimate the value of an option using the modified Black-Scholes option pricing model (briefly mentioned earlier). Regardless of who does the calculation, principles similar to those of the Black-Scholes pricing model can be used to determine the fair value of the option.

Accounting for Changes in the Fair Value of Derivatives

Changes in the fair value of derivatives must be included in *comprehensive income,* which consists of two components: *net income* and *other comprehensive income.* Other comprehensive income consists of income items that current authoritative accounting literature require to be deferred in stockholders' equity such as unrealized gains and losses on available-for-sale debt securities. Other comprehensive income is accumulated and reported as a separate line in the stockholders' equity section of the balance sheet. This book uses the account title *Accumulated Other Comprehensive Income* to describe this stockholders' equity line item.

In accordance with U.S. GAAP, gains and losses arising from changes in the fair value of derivatives are recognized initially either (1) in net income or (2) in other comprehensive income (reflected on the balance sheet in accumulated other comprehensive income).

[6] The present value factor for two months at 1 percent per month is calculated as $1/1.01^2$, or 0.9803.

Recognition treatment depends partly on whether the company uses derivatives for hedging purposes or for speculation.

Although using derivatives for speculation is not commonly done by nonfinancial institutions, financial entities might acquire derivative financial instruments as investments for speculative purposes. For example, assume that the three-month forward rate for British pounds is \$2.00, and a speculator believes the British pound spot rate in three months will be \$1.97. In that case, the speculator would enter into a three-month forward contract to sell British pounds. At the future date, the speculator purchases pounds at the spot rate of \$1.97 and sells them at the contracted forward rate of \$2.00, reaping a gain of \$0.03 per British pound. Of course, such an investment might as easily generate a loss if the spot rate does not move as expected. For speculative derivatives, the change in the fair value of the derivative must be recognized immediately as a gain or loss in net income.[7]

The accounting for changes in the fair value of derivatives used for hedging depends on the nature of the foreign exchange risk being hedged and on whether the derivative qualifies for *hedge accounting.*

Hedge Accounting

LO 9-6

Understand the basic concepts of hedge accounting.

Companies enter into hedging relationships to minimize the adverse effect that changes in exchange rates have on cash flows and net income. As such, companies would like to account for hedges in a way that recognizes the gain or loss from the hedge in net income in the same period as the loss or gain on the risk being hedged. This approach is known as *hedge accounting.* U.S. GAAP allows hedge accounting for foreign currency derivatives only if three conditions are satisfied:

1. The derivative is used to hedge either a cash flow exposure or a fair value exposure to foreign exchange risk.
2. The derivative is highly effective in offsetting changes in the cash flows or fair value related to the hedged item.
3. The derivative is properly documented as a hedge.

Each of these conditions is discussed in turn.

Nature of the Hedged Risk

Derivatives for which companies wish to use hedge accounting must be designated as either a *cash flow hedge* or a *fair value hedge.* For hedges of recognized foreign currency assets and liabilities and hedges of foreign currency firm commitments, companies must choose between the two types of designation. Hedges of forecasted foreign currency transactions can qualify only as cash flow hedges. Accounting procedures differ for the two types of hedges. In general, gains and losses on cash flow hedges are included in other comprehensive income (and therefore deferred on the balance sheet in accumulated other comprehensive income), and gains and losses on fair value hedges are recognized immediately in net income.

A *fair value exposure* exists if changes in exchange rates can affect the fair value of an asset or liability reported on the balance sheet. To qualify for hedge accounting, the fair value risk must have the potential to affect net income if it is not hedged. For example, a fair value risk is associated with a foreign currency account receivable. If the foreign currency depreciates, the receivable must be written down with an offsetting loss recognized in net income. The authoritative literature has determined that a fair value exposure also exists for foreign currency firm commitments.

A *cash flow exposure* exists if changes in exchange rates can affect the amount of cash flow to be realized from a foreign currency transaction with changes in cash flow reflected in net income. A foreign currency account receivable, for example, has both a fair value exposure and a cash flow exposure. A cash flow exposure exists for (1) recognized foreign currency

[7] In the next section we will see that the change in fair value of a derivative designated as the fair value hedge of a foreign currency denominated asset or liability also is recognized immediately in net income.

assets and liabilities, (2) foreign currency firm commitments, and (3) forecasted foreign currency transactions.

Hedge Effectiveness

For hedge accounting to be used initially, the hedge must be expected to be highly effective in generating gains and losses that offset losses and gains on the item being hedged. The hedge actually must be effective in generating offsetting gains and losses for hedge accounting to continue to be applied over the life of the hedge.

At inception, a foreign currency derivative can be considered an effective hedge if the critical terms of the hedging instrument match those of the hedged item. Critical terms include the currency type, currency amount, and settlement date. For example, a forward contract to purchase 100,000 Canadian dollars in 30 days would be an effective hedge of a 100,000 Canadian dollar liability that is payable in 30 days.

Hedge Documentation

For hedge accounting to be applied, U.S. GAAP requires formal documentation of the hedging relationship at the inception of the hedge (i.e., on the date a foreign currency forward contract is entered into or a foreign currency option is acquired). The hedging company must prepare a document that identifies the hedged item (for example, a 100,000 Canadian dollar liability), the hedging instrument (a forward contract to purchase 100,000 Canadian dollars), the nature of the risk being hedged (a cash flow exposure), how the hedging instrument's effectiveness will be assessed (through reference to changes in the forward rate), and the risk management objective and strategy for undertaking the hedge (to minimize risk associated with a possible Canadian dollar appreciation).

Hedging Combinations

The specific accounting procedures followed and journal entries needed to account for a foreign currency hedging relationship are determined by a combination of the following factors:

1. The type of foreign currency item being hedged:
   a. Foreign currency denominated asset or liability.
   b. Foreign currency firm commitment.
   c. Forecasted foreign currency transaction.
2. The type of hedging instrument used:
   a. Forward contract.
   b. Option.
3. The nature of the hedged risk:
   a. Cash flow exposure.
   b. Fair value exposure.
4. The nature of the foreign currency item being hedged:
   a. Asset (existing or future).
   b. Liability (existing or future).

In the next three sections in this chapter we discuss the accounting for hedges of (1) foreign currency denominated assets/liabilities, (2) foreign currency firm commitments, and (3) forecasted foreign currency transactions. We demonstrate through examples the use of both forward contracts and options to hedge these items, and we selectively demonstrate the accounting for both cash flow and fair value hedges. We focus on hedges entered into by an exporter that has a current or future foreign currency asset that is exposed to foreign exchange risk. The comprehensive example at the end of this chapter demonstrates the accounting for hedges entered into by an importer that has an existing or future foreign currency liability. Exhibit 9.2 provides an overall summary of the procedures followed in accounting for hedges of foreign exchange risk for those combinations presented in this chapter. By examining this exhibit, the similarities and differences in the procedures followed and accounting entries prepared to account for each hedge combination can be discerned.

EXHIBIT 9.2 Summary of Accounting for Hedges of Foreign Exchange Risk

	Hedge of a Foreign Currency Denominated Asset or Liability				Hedge of a Foreign Currency Firm Commitment		Hedge of a Forecasted Foreign Currency Transaction	
	Cash Flow Hedge		Fair Value Hedge		Fair Value Hedge		Cash Flow Hedge	
Date	Forward Contract	Option	Forward Contract	Option	Forward Contract	Option	Forward Contract	Option
A. Initiation Date	1. Recognize the transaction (sale or purchase) and foreign currency denominated asset or liability	1. Recognize the transaction (sale or purchase) and foreign currency denominated asset or liability	1. Recognize the transaction (sale or purchase) and foreign currency denominated asset or liability	1. Recognize the transaction (sale or purchase) and foreign currency denominated asset or liability	1. No entry related to the firm commitment (zero value)	1. No entry related to the firm commitment	1. No entry related to the forecasted transaction	1. No entry related to the forecasted transaction
	2. No entry related to forward contract (zero fair value)	2. Recognize option as an asset (purchase price is fair value)	2. No entry related to forward contract (zero fair value)	2. Recognize option as an asset (purchase price is fair value)	2. No entry related to forward contract (zero fair value)	2. Recognize option as an asset (purchase price is fair value)	2. No entry related to forward contract (zero fair value)	2. Recognize option as an asset (purchase price is fair value)
B. Balance Sheet Date	1. Adjust hedged asset or liability to fair value, with counterpart (change in fair value) reported as foreign exchange gain or loss in net income	1. Adjust hedged asset or liability to fair value, with counterpart (change in fair value) reported as foreign exchange gain or loss in net income	1. Adjust hedged asset or liability to fair value, with counterpart (change in fair value) reported as foreign exchange gain or loss in net income	1. Adjust hedged asset or liability to fair value, with counterpart (change in fair value) reported as foreign exchange gain or loss in net income	1. Adjust forward contract to fair value (either an asset or a liability), with counterpart (change in fair value) reported as gain or loss in net income	1. Adjust option to fair value (either an asset or zero value), with counterpart (change in fair value) reported as gain or loss in net income	1. N/A	1. N/A
	2. Adjust forward contract to fair value (either an asset or a liability), with counterpart (change in fair value) reported in AOCI	2. Adjust option to fair value (either an asset or zero value), with counterpart (change in fair value) reported in AOCI	2. Adjust forward contract to fair value (either an asset or a liability), with counterpart (change in fair value) reported as gain or loss in net income	2. Adjust option to fair value (either an asset or zero value), with counterpart (change in fair value) reported as gain or loss in net income	2. Adjust firm commitment to fair value (based on change in forward rate), with counterpart (change in fair value) reported as gain or loss in net income	2. Adjust firm commitment to fair value (based on change in spot rate), with counterpart (change in fair value) reported as gain or loss in net income	2. Adjust forward contract to fair value (either an asset or a liability), with counterpart (change in fair value) reported in AOCI	2. Adjust option to fair value (either an asset or zero value), with counterpart (change in fair value) reported in AOCI

(continued)

EXHIBIT 9.2 (Continued)

Date	Hedge of a Foreign Currency Denominated Asset or Liability				Hedge of a Foreign Currency Firm Commitment		Hedge of a Forecasted Foreign Currency Transaction	
	Cash Flow Hedge		Fair Value Hedge		Fair Value Hedge		Cash Flow Hedge	
	Forward Contract	Option	Forward Contract	Option	Forward Contract	Option	Forward Contract	Option
	3. Transfer an amount from AOCI to net income to offset the foreign exchange gain or loss on the hedged asset or liability recognized in B.1	3. Transfer an amount from AOCI to net income to offset the foreign exchange gain or loss on the hedged asset or liability recognized in B.1	3. N/A	3. N/A	3. N/A	3. N/A	3. N/A	3. N/A
	4. Transfer from AOCI to net income (as discount expense or premium revenue) the current period's amortization of discount or premium	4. Transfer from AOCI to net income (as expense) the change in time value on the option	4. N/A	4. N/A	4. N/A	4. N/A	4. Transfer from AOCI to net income (as discount expense or premium revenue) the current period's amortization of discount or premium	4. Transfer from AOCI to net income (as option expense) the change in time value on the option
C. Settlement Date	1.–4. Repeat steps B.1.–B.4	1.–4. Repeat steps B.1.–B.4	1.–2. Repeat steps B.1. and B.2	1.–2. Repeat steps B.1. and B.2	1.–2. Repeat steps B.1. and B.2	1.–2. Repeat steps B.1. and B.2	1.–2. Repeat steps B.2. and B.4	1.–2. Repeat steps B.2. and B.4
	5. Recognize settlement of the foreign currency denominated asset or liability	5. Recognize settlement of the foreign currency denominated asset or liability	3. Recognize settlement of the foreign currency denominated asset or liability	3. Recognize settlement of the foreign currency denominated asset or liability	3. Recognize the transaction (sale or purchase)	3. Recognize the transaction (sale or purchase)	3. Recognize the transaction (sale or purchase)	3. Recognize the transaction (sale or purchase)
	6. Recognize settlement of the forward contract*	6. Recognize exercise (or expiration) of the option*	4. Recognize settlement of the forward contract&	4. Recognize exercise (or expiration) of the option&	4. Recognize settlement of the forward contract#	4. Recognize exercise (or expiration) of the option#	4. Recognize settlement of the forward contract#	4. Recognize exercise (or expiration) of the option#
					5. Close the balance in the firm commitment account as an adjustment to net income	5. Close the balance in the firm commitment account as an adjustment to net income	5. Close the balance in AOCI related to the forward contract as an adjustment to net income	5. Close the balance in AOCI related to the option as an adjustment to net income

*Step 6 precedes step 5 in the case of a foreign currency denominated liability.
&Step 4 precedes step 3 in the case of a foreign currency denominated liability.
#Step 4 precedes step 3 in the case of a foreign currency purchase transaction.

LO 9-7

Account for forward contracts and options used as hedges of foreign currency denominated assets and liabilities.

Hedges of Foreign Currency Denominated Assets and Liabilities

Hedges of foreign currency denominated assets and liabilities, such as accounts receivable and accounts payable, can qualify as either *cash flow hedges* or *fair value hedges*. To qualify as a cash flow hedge, the hedging instrument must completely offset the variability in the cash flows associated with the foreign currency receivable or payable. If the hedging instrument does not qualify as a cash flow hedge or if the company elects not to designate the hedging instrument as a cash flow hedge, the hedge is designated as a fair value hedge. The following summarizes the basic accounting for the two types of hedges of foreign currency denominated assets and liabilities.

Cash Flow Hedge

At each balance sheet date, the following procedures are required:

1. The hedged asset (foreign currency account receivable) or liability (foreign currency account payable) is adjusted to fair value based on changes in the spot exchange rate, and a foreign exchange gain or loss is recognized in net income (Cash Flow Hedge Step B.1. in Exhibit 9.2).
2. To comply with the fundamental requirement of derivatives accounting, the derivative hedging instrument (forward contract or option) is adjusted to fair value (resulting in an asset or liability reported on the balance sheet) with the counterpart recognized as a change in Accumulated Other Comprehensive Income (AOCI) (Cash Flow Hedge Step B.2. in Exhibit 9.2).
3. An amount equal to the foreign exchange gain or loss on the hedged asset or liability is then transferred from AOCI to net income; the net effect is to offset any gain or loss on the hedged asset or liability (Cash Flow Hedge Step B.3. in Exhibit 9.2).
4. An additional amount is removed from AOCI and recognized in net income to reflect (a) the current period's amortization of the original discount or premium on the forward contract (if a forward contract is the hedging instrument) or (b) the change in the *time value* of the option (if an option is the hedging instrument) (Cash Flow Hedge Step B.4. in Exhibit 9.2).

Fair Value Hedge

At each balance sheet date, the following procedures are required:

1. Adjust the hedged asset or liability to fair value based on changes in the spot exchange rate and recognize a foreign exchange gain or loss in net income (Fair Value Hedge Step B.1. in Exhibit 9.2).
2. Adjust the derivative hedging instrument to fair value (resulting in an asset or liability reported on the balance sheet) and recognize the counterpart as a gain or loss in net income (Fair Value Hedge Step B.2. in Exhibit 9.2).

Forward Contract Used to Hedge a Foreign Currency Denominated Asset

We now return to the Amerco example in which the company has a foreign currency account receivable to demonstrate the accounting for a hedge of a recognized foreign currency denominated asset.[8] In the preceding example, Amerco has an asset exposure in euros when it sells goods to the German customer and allows the customer three months to pay for its purchase. To hedge its exposure to a possible decline in the U.S. dollar value of the euro, Amerco enters into a forward contract.

[8] The comprehensive illustration at the end of this chapter demonstrates the accounting for the hedge of a foreign currency denominated liability.

Assume that on December 1, 2017, the three-month forward rate for euros is $1.305 and Amerco signs a contract with New Manhattan Bank to deliver 1 million euros in three months in exchange for $1,305,000. No cash changes hands on December 1, 2017. Because the spot rate on December 1 is $1.32, the euro (€) is selling at a discount in the three-month forward market (the forward rate is less than the spot rate). Because the euro is selling at a discount of $0.015 ($1.305 - $1.320) per euro, Amerco receives $15,000 less than it would had payment been received at the date the goods are delivered ($1,305,000 versus $1,320,000). This $15,000 reduction in cash flow can be considered as an expense; it is the cost of extending foreign currency credit to the foreign customer.[9] Conceptually, this expense is similar to the transaction loss that arises on the export sale. It exists only because the transaction is denominated in a foreign currency. The major difference is that Amerco knows the exact amount of the discount expense at the date of sale, whereas when it is left unhedged, Amerco does not know the size of the transaction loss until three months pass. (In fact, it is possible that the unhedged receivable could result in a transaction gain rather than a transaction loss.)

Because the future spot rate turns out to be only $1.30, selling euros at a forward rate of $1.305 is obviously better than leaving the euro receivable unhedged: Amerco will receive $5,000 more as a result of the hedge. This can be viewed as a gain resulting from the use of the forward contract. Unlike the discount expense, the exact size of this gain is not known until three months pass. (In fact, it is possible that use of the forward contract could result in an additional loss. This would occur if the spot rate on March 1, 2018, is more than the forward rate of $1.305.)

Amerco must account for its foreign currency transaction and the related forward contract simultaneously but separately. The process can be better understood by referring to the steps involving the three parties—Amerco, the German customer, and New Manhattan Bank—shown in Exhibit 9.3.

Because the settlement date, currency type, and currency amount of the forward contract match the corresponding terms of the account receivable, the hedge is expected to be highly effective. If Amerco properly designates the forward contract as a hedge of its euro account receivable position, it may apply hedge accounting. Because it completely offsets the variability in the cash flows related to the account receivable, Amerco may designate the forward

EXHIBIT 9.3
Hedge of a Foreign Currency Account Receivable with a Forward Contract

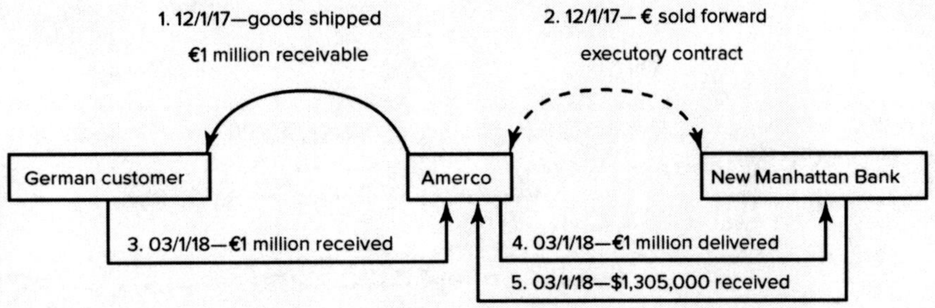

Steps on December 1, 2017

1. Amerco ships goods to the German customer, thereby creating an Account Receivable of €1 million.
2. Amerco then sells €1 million three months forward to New Manhattan Bank, creating an executory contract to pay €1 million and receive $1,305,000.

Steps on March 1, 2018

3. The German customer remits €1 million to Amerco—the € Account Receivable has been received and Amerco has €1 million reflected in an account Foreign Currency (€).
4. Amerco delivers €1 million to New Manhattan Bank.
5. New Manhattan Bank pays Amerco $1,305,000.

[9] This should not be confused with the cost associated with normal credit risk—that is, the risk that the customer will not pay for its purchase. That is a separate issue unrelated to the currency in which the transaction is denominated.

contract as a cash flow hedge. Alternatively, because changes in the spot rate affect not only the cash flows but also the fair value of the foreign currency receivable, Amerco may elect to account for this forward contract as a fair value hedge.

In either case, Amerco determines the fair value of the forward contract by referring to the change in the forward rate for a contract maturing on March 1, 2018. The relevant exchange rates, U.S. dollar value of the euro receivable, and fair value of the forward contract are determined as follows:

		Account Receivable (€)		Forward Rate to 3/1/18	Forward Contract	
Date	Spot Rate	U.S. Dollar Value	Change in U.S. Dollar Value		Fair Value	Change in Fair Value
12/1/17	$1.32	$1,320,000	—	$1.305	$ –0–	—
12/31/17	1.33	1,330,000	+$10,000	1.316	(10,783)*	–$10,783
3/1/18	1.30	1,300,000	– 30,000	1.30	5,000†	+ 15,783

*$1,305,000 – $1,316,000 = $(11,000) × 0.9803 = $(10,783), where 0.9803 is the present value factor for two months at an annual interest rate of 12 percent (1 percent per month) calculated as $1/1.01^2$.

†$1,305,000 – $1,300,000 = $5,000. This is the difference between the dollars that will be received when the forward contract is executed (based on the original forward rate) and the dollars that would have been received if no forward contract had been entered into (based on the spot rate on the date the euros are received).

Amerco pays nothing to enter into the forward contract at December 1, 2017, and the forward contract has a fair value of zero on that date. The original discount on the forward contract is $15,000, determined by the difference in the euro spot rate and three-month forward rate on December 1, 2017 [($1.305 – $1.32) × €1 million]. At December 31, 2017, the forward rate for a contract to deliver euros on March 1, 2018, is $1.316. Amerco could enter into a forward contract on December 31, 2017, to sell 1 million euros for $1,316,000 on March 1, 2018. Because Amerco is committed to sell 1 million euros for $1,305,000, the nominal value of the forward contract is $(11,000). The fair value of the forward contract is the present value of this amount. Assuming that Amerco has an incremental borrowing rate of 12 percent per year (1 percent per month) and discounting for two months (from December 31, 2017, to March 1, 2018), the fair value of the forward contract at December 31, 2017, is $(10,783). Because the fair value is negative, the forward contract is a liability on December 31, 2017. On March 1, 2018, the forward rate to sell euros on that date is, by definition, the spot rate of $1.30. At that rate, Amerco could sell 1 million euros for $1,300,000. Because Amerco has a contract to sell euros for $1,305,000, the fair value of the forward contract on March 1, 2018, is $5,000. At this point, the forward contract is an asset because it has a positive fair value. From December 31, 2017, to March 1, 2018, the fair value of the forward contract has increased by $15,783.

Forward Contract Designated as Cash Flow Hedge

Assume that Amerco designates the forward contract as a *cash flow hedge* of a foreign currency denominated asset. In this case, it allocates the original forward discount or premium to net income over the life of the forward contract using an effective interest method. The company prepares the following journal entries to account for the foreign currency transaction and the related forward contract:

2017 Journal Entries—Forward Contract Designated as a Cash Flow Hedge

12/1/17	Accounts Receivable (€)	1,320,000	
	Sales		1,320,000
	To record the sale and €1 million account receivable at the spot rate of $1.32 (Cash Flow Hedge Step A.1. in Exhibit 9.2).		
	Amerco makes no formal entry for the forward contract because it is an executory contract (no cash changes hands) and has a fair value of zero (Cash Flow Hedge Step A.2. in Exhibit 9.2).		

Amerco prepares a memorandum designating the forward contract as a hedge of the risk of changes in the cash flow to be received on the foreign currency account receivable resulting from changes in the U.S. dollar–euro exchange rate. Following steps B.1.-B.4. in accounting for a cash flow hedge presented in Exhibit 9.2, the company prepares the following journal entries on December 31:

12/31/17	Accounts Receivable (€).	10,000	
	Foreign Exchange Gain		10,000
	To adjust the value of the € receivable to the new spot rate of $1.33 and record a foreign exchange gain resulting from the appreciation of the € since December 1 (Cash Flow Hedge Step B.1. in Exhibit 9.2).		
	Accumulated Other Comprehensive Income (AOCI).	10,783	
	Forward Contract.		10,783
	To record the forward contract as a liability at its fair value of $10,783 with a corresponding debit to AOCI (Cash Flow Hedge Step B.2. in Exhibit 9.2).		
	Loss on Forward Contract	10,000	
	Accumulated Other Comprehensive Income (AOCI)		10,000
	To record a loss on forward contract to offset the foreign exchange gain on account receivable with a corresponding credit to AOCI (Cash Flow Hedge Step B.3. in Exhibit 9.2).		
	Discount Expense	5,019	
	Accumulated Other Comprehensive Income (AOCI)		5,019
	To allocate the forward contract discount to net income over the life of the contract using the effective interest method with a corresponding credit to AOCI (Cash Flow Hedge Step B.4. in Exhibit 9.2).		

The first entry at December 31, 2017, serves to revalue the foreign currency account receivable and recognize a foreign exchange gain of $10,000 in net income. Because the forward contract has a negative fair value of $(10,783), GAAP requires it to be reported on the balance sheet as a liability. Thus, the second entry makes a credit of $10,783 to Forward Contract. Under cash flow hedge accounting, the change in the fair value of the forward contract, which has gone from $0 to $(10,783) is not recognized immediately in income, but is instead deferred in stockholders' equity. Thus, the debit of $10,783 in the second entry is made to AOCI. The third entry achieves the objective of hedge accounting by transferring $10,000 from AOCI to a loss on forward contract. As a result of this entry, the loss on forward contract of $10,000 and the foreign exchange gain on the account receivable of $10,000 exactly offset one another, and the net impact on income is zero. As a result of the second and third entries, the forward contract is reported on the balance sheet as a liability at fair value of $(10,783); a loss on forward contract is recognized in the amount of $10,000 to offset the foreign exchange gain; and AOCI has a negative (debit) balance of $783. The second and third entries could be combined into one entry as follows:

Loss on Forward Contract.	10,000	
Accumulated Other Comprehensive Income (AOCI)	783	
Forward Contract		10,783

The negative balance in AOCI of $783 can be viewed as that portion of the loss on the forward contract (decrease in fair value of the forward contract) that is not recognized in net income but instead is deferred in stockholders' equity. Under cash flow hedge accounting, a loss on the hedging instrument (forward contract) is recognized only to the extent that it offsets a gain on the item being hedged (account receivable).

The last entry uses the effective interest method to allocate a portion of the $15,000 forward contract discount as an expense to net income. The company calculates the implicit interest rate associated with the forward contract by considering the fact that the forward contract will generate cash flow of $1,305,000 from a foreign currency asset with an initial value of $1,320,000. Because the discount of $15,000 accrues over a three-month period, the effective interest rate is calculated as $1-\sqrt[3]{[\$1,305,000/\$1,320,000]}$ = .0038023 The amount of discount to be allocated to net income for the month of December 2017 is $1,320,000 × .0038023 = $5,019. A debit of $5,019 is made to Discount Expense in the last journal entry on December 31, 2017. By making the credit in this journal entry to AOCI, the theoretically correct amounts are reported in net income and on the balance sheet, and the balance sheet remains in balance.

The impact on net income for the year 2017 follows:

Sales.		$1,320,000
Foreign exchange gain.	$10,000	
Loss on forward contract	(10,000)	
Net gain (loss).		–0–
Discount expense		(5,019)
Impact on net income.		$1,314,981

Assets		Liabilities and Stockholders' Equity	
Accounts receivable (€)	$1,330,000	Forward contract	$ 10,783
		Retained earnings	1,314,981
		AOCI.	4,236
			$1,330,000

2018 Journal Entries—Forward Contract Designated as Cash Flow Hedge

From December 31, 2017, to March 1, 2018, the euro account receivable decreases in value by $30,000 and the forward contract increases in value by $15,873. In addition, on March 1, 2018, the remaining discount on forward contract must be amortized to expense. The company prepares the following journal entries on March 1 to reflect these changes:

3/1/18	Foreign Exchange Loss	30,000	
	Accounts Receivable (€)		30,000
	To adjust the value of the € receivable to the new spot rate of $1.30 and record a foreign exchange loss resulting from the depreciation of the € since December 31 (Cash Flow Hedge Step C.1. in Exhibit 9.2).		
	Forward Contract	15,783	
	Accumulated Other Comprehensive Income (AOCI)		15,783
	To adjust the carrying value of the forward contract to its current fair value of $5,000 with a corresponding credit to AOCI (Cash Flow Hedge Step C.2. in Exhibit 9.2).		
	Accumulated Other Comprehensive Income (AOCI)	30,000	
	Gain on Forward Contract.		30,000
	To record a gain on forward contract to offset the foreign exchange loss on account receivable with a corresponding debit to AOCI (Cash Flow Hedge Step C.3. in Exhibit 9.2).		
	Discount Expense.	9,981	
	Accumulated Other Comprehensive Income (AOCI)		9,981
	To allocate the remaining forward contract discount to net income ($15,000 – 5,019 = $9,981) with a corresponding credit to AOCI (Cash Flow Hedge Step C.4. in Exhibit 9.2).		

As a result of these entries, the balance in AOCI is zero: $4,236 + $15,783 − $30,000 + $9,981 = $0.

The next two journal entries recognize the receipt of euros from the customer, close out the euro account receivable, and record the settlement of the forward contract.

3/1/18	Foreign Currency (€)	1,300,000	
	Accounts Receivable (€)		1,300,000
	To record receipt of €1 million from the German customer as an asset (Foreign Currency) at the spot rate of $1.30 (Cash Flow Hedge Step C.5. in Exhibit 9.2).		
	Cash	1,305,000	
	Foreign Currency (€)		1,300,000
	Forward Contract		5,000
	To record settlement of the forward contract (i.e., record receipt of $1,305,000 in exchange for delivery of €1 million) and remove the forward contract from the accounts (Cash Flow Hedge Step C.6. in Exhibit 9.2).		

The impact on net income for the year 2018 follows:

Foreign exchange loss	$(30,000)	
Gain on forward contract	30,000	
Net gain (loss)		–0–
Discount expense		$(9,981)
Impact on net income		$(9,981)

The net effect on the balance sheet over the two years is a $1,305,000 increase in Cash with a corresponding increase in Retained Earnings of $1,305,000 ($1,314,981 – $9,981). The cumulative amount recognized as Discount Expense of $15,000 reflects the cost of extending credit to the German customer.

The net benefit from entering into the forward contract is $5,000. This "gain" is not directly reflected in net income. However, it can be calculated as the difference between the net gain on the forward contract ($10,000 loss in 2017 plus $30,000 gain in 2018 = $20,000 net gain) and the cumulative amount of discount expense ($15,000) recognized over the two periods: $20,000 – $15,000 = $5,000.

Effective Interest versus Straight-Line Methods

Use of the effective interest method results in allocating the forward contract discount $5,019 at the end of the first month and $9,981 at the end of the next two months. Straight-line allocation of the $15,000 discount on a monthly basis results in a reasonable approximation of these amounts:

12/31/17	$15,000 × ⅓ = $5,000
3/1/18	$15,000 × ⅔ = $10,000

Determining the effective interest rate is complex and provides no conceptual insights. For the remainder of this chapter, we use straight-line allocation of forward contract discounts and premiums. The important thing to keep in mind in this example is that with a cash flow hedge, an expense equal to the original forward contract discount is recognized in net income over the life of the contract.

What if the forward rate on December 1, 2017, had been $1.326 (i.e., the euro was selling at a premium in the forward market)? In that case, Amerco would receive $6,000 more through the forward sale of euros ($1,326,000) than had it received the euros at the date of sale ($1,320,000). Amerco would allocate the forward contract premium as an increase in net income at the rate of $2,000 per month: $2,000 at December 31, 2017, and $4,000 at March 1, 2018.

Forward Contract Designated as Fair Value Hedge

Assume that Amerco decides to designate the forward contract not as a cash flow hedge but as a fair value hedge. In that case, it takes the gain or loss on the forward contract directly to net income and does not separately amortize the original discount on the forward contract.

2017 Journal Entries—Forward Contract Designated as a Fair Value Hedge

12/1/17	Accounts Receivable (€).	1,320,000	
	Sales		1,320,000
	To record the sale and €1 million account receivable at the spot rate of $1.32 (Fair Value Hedge Step A.1. in Exhibit 9.2).		

The forward contract requires no formal entry (Fair Value Hedge Step A.2. in Exhibit 9.2). A memorandum designates the forward contract as a hedge of the risk of changes in the fair value of the foreign currency account receivable resulting from changes in the U.S. dollar–euro exchange rate.

Following the two steps in accounting for a fair value hedge presented in Exhibit 9.2, the company prepares the following entries on December 31:

12/31/17	Accounts Receivable (€).	10,000	
	Foreign Exchange Gain		10,000
	To adjust the value of the € receivable to the new spot rate of $1.33 and record a foreign exchange gain resulting from the appreciation of the € since December 1 (Fair Value Hedge Step B.1. in Exhibit 9.2).		
	Loss on Forward Contract	10,783	
	Forward Contract.		10,783
	To record the forward contract as a liability at its fair value of $10,783 and record a forward contract loss for the change in the fair value of the forward contract since December 1 (Fair Value Hedge Step B.2. in Exhibit 9.2).		

The first entry at December 31, 2017, serves to revalue the foreign currency account receivable and recognize a foreign exchange gain of $10,000. The second entry recognizes the forward contract as a liability of $10,783 on the balance sheet. Because the forward contract has been designated as a fair value hedge, the debit in the second entry recognizes the entire change in fair value of the forward contract as a loss in net income; there is no deferral of loss in stockholders' equity. A net loss of $783 is reported in net income as a result of these two entries.

The impact on net income for the year 2017 is as follows:

Sales.		$1,320,000
Foreign exchange gain.	$10,000	
Loss on forward contract	(10,783)	
Net gain (loss).		(783)
Impact on net income		$1,319,217

The effect on the December 31, 2017, balance sheet follows:

Assets		**Liabilities and Stockholders' Equity**	
Accounts receivable (€).	$1,330,000	Forward contract	$ 10,783
		Retained earnings	1,319,217
			$1,330,000

Discussion Question

DO WE HAVE A GAIN OR WHAT?

Ahnuld Corporation, a health juice producer, recently expanded its sales through exports to foreign markets. Earlier this year, the company negotiated the sale of several thousand cases of turnip juice to a retailer in the country of Tcheckia. The customer is unwilling to assume the risk of having to pay in U.S. dollars. Desperate to enter the Tcheckian market, the vice president for international sales agrees to denominate the sale in tchecks, the national currency of Tcheckia. The current exchange rate for 1 tcheck is $2.00. In addition, the customer indicates that it cannot pay until it sells all of the juice. Payment of 100,000 tchecks is scheduled for six months from the date of sale.

Fearful that the tcheck might depreciate in value over the next six months, the head of the risk management department at Ahnuld Corporation enters into a forward contract to sell tchecks in six months at a forward rate of $1.80. The forward contract is designated as a fair value hedge of the tcheck receivable. Six months later, when Ahnuld receives payment from the Tcheckian customer, the exchange rate for the tcheck is $1.70. The corporate treasurer calls the head of the risk management department into her office.

Treasurer: I see that your decision to hedge our foreign currency position on that sale to Tcheckia was a bad one.

Department head: What do you mean? We have a gain on that forward contract. We're $10,000 better off from having entered into that hedge.

Treasurer: That's not what the books say. The accountants have recorded a net loss of $20,000 on that particular deal. I'm afraid I'm not going to be able to pay you a bonus this year. Another bad deal like this one and I'm going to have to demote you back to the interest rate swap department.

Department head: Those bean counters have messed up again. I told those guys in international sales that selling to customers in Tcheckia was risky, but at least by hedging our exposure, we managed to receive a reasonable amount of cash on that deal. In fact, we ended up with a gain of $10,000 on the hedge. Tell the accountants to check their debits and credits again. I'm sure they just put a debit in the wrong place or some accounting thing like that.

Have the accountants made a mistake? Does the company have a loss, a gain, or both from this forward contract?

2018 Journal Entries—Forward Contract Designated as a Fair Value Hedge

The company prepares the following entries on March 1:

3/1/18	Foreign Exchange Loss	30,000	
	Accounts Receivable (€)		30,000
	To adjust the value of the € receivable to the new spot rate of $1.30 and record a foreign exchange loss resulting from the depreciation of the € since December 31 (Fair Value Hedge Step C.1. in Exhibit 9.2).		
	Forward Contract	15,783	
	Gain on Forward Contract		15,783
	To adjust the carrying value of the forward contract to its current fair value of $5,000 and record a forward contract gain for the change in the fair value since December 31 (Fair Value Hedge Step C.2. in Exhibit 9.2).		

(continued)

(continued)

3/1/18	Foreign Currency (€)	1,300,000	
	Accounts Receivable (€)		1,300,000
	To record receipt of €1 million from the German customer as an asset at the spot rate of $1.30 (Fair Value Hedge Step C.3. in Exhibit 9.2).		
	Cash	1,305,000	
	Foreign Currency (€)		1,300,000
	Forward Contract		5,000
	To record settlement of the forward contract (i.e., record receipt of $1,305,000 in exchange for delivery of €1 million) and remove the forward contract from the accounts (Fair Value Hedge Step C.4. in Exhibit 9.2).		

The impact on net income for the year 2018 follows:

Foreign exchange loss	$ (30,000)
Gain on forward contract	15,783
Impact on net income	$(14,217)

The net effect on the balance sheet for the two periods is an increase of $1,305,000 in Cash with a corresponding increase in Retained Earnings of $1,305,000 ($1,319,217 – $14,217).

Under fair value hedge accounting, the company does not amortize the original forward contract discount systematically over the life of the contract. Instead, it recognizes the discount in income as the difference between the foreign exchange Gain (Loss) on the account receivable and the Gain (Loss) on the forward contract—that is, $(783) in 2017 and $(14,217) in 2018. The net impact on net income over the two years is $(15,000), which reflects the cost of extending credit to the German customer. The net gain on the forward contract of $5,000 ($10,783 loss in 2017 and $15,783 gain in 2018) reflects the net benefit (i.e., increase in cash inflow) from Amerco's decision to hedge the euro receivable.

Companies often cannot or do not bother to designate as hedges the forward contracts they use to hedge foreign currency denominated assets and liabilities. In those cases, the company accounts for the forward contract as if it were a speculative investment. The company reports an undesignated forward contract on the balance sheet at fair value as an asset or liability and immediately recognizes changes in the fair value of the forward contract in net income. This accounting treatment is exactly the same as if the forward contract had been designated as a fair value hedge. The only difference between a forward contract designated as a fair value hedge of a foreign currency denominated asset or liability and an undesignated (speculative) forward contract is the manner in which the company discloses it in the notes to the financial statements. E.I. du Pont de Nemours and Company provided the following disclosure related to this in its 2014 Form 10-K (page F-43):

Derivatives Not Designated in Hedging Relationships

Foreign Currency Contracts

The company routinely uses forward exchange contracts to reduce its net exposure, by currency, related to foreign currency-denominated monetary assets and liabilities of its operations so that exchange gains and losses resulting from exchange rate changes are minimized. The netting of such exposures precludes the use of hedge accounting; however, the required revaluation of the forward contracts and the associated foreign currency-denominated monetary assets and liabilities intends to achieve a minimal earnings impact, after taxes.

Cash Flow Hedge versus Fair Value Hedge

A forward contract used to hedge a foreign currency denominated asset or liability can be designated as either a cash flow hedge or a fair value hedge when it completely offsets the variability in cash flows associated with the hedged item. The total impact on income is the same regardless of whether the forward contract is designated as a fair value hedge or as a cash flow hedge. In our example, Amerco recognized an expense (or loss) of $15,000 in both cases, and the company knew what the total expense was going to be as soon as the contract was signed.

A benefit to designating a forward contract as a cash flow hedge is that the company knows the forward contract's effect on net income *each year* as soon as the contract is signed. The net impact on income is the periodic amortization of the forward contract discount or premium. In our example, Amerco knew on December 1, 2017, that it would recognize a discount expense of $5,000 in 2017 and $10,000 in 2018. The impact on each year's income is not as systematic when the forward contract is designated as a fair value hedge—loss of $783 in 2017 and $14,217 in 2018. Moreover, the company does not know what the net impact on 2017 income will be until December 31, 2017, when the euro account receivable and the forward contract are revalued. Because of the potential for greater volatility in periodic net income that results from a fair value hedge, companies may prefer to designate forward contracts used to hedge a foreign currency denominated asset or liability as cash flow hedges.

Foreign Currency Option Used to Hedge a Foreign Currency Denominated Asset

As an alternative to a forward contract, Amerco could hedge its exposure to foreign exchange risk arising from the euro account receivable by purchasing a foreign currency put option. A put option would give Amerco the right but not the obligation to sell 1 million euros on March 1, 2018, at a predetermined strike price. Assume that on December 1, 2017, Amerco purchases an over-the-counter option from its bank with a strike price of $1.32 when the spot rate is $1.32 and pays a premium of $0.009 per euro.[10] Thus, the purchase price for the option is $9,000 (€1 million × $0.009).

Because the strike price and spot rate are the same, no intrinsic value is associated with this option. The premium is based solely on time value; that is, it is possible that the euro will depreciate and the spot rate on March 1, 2018, will be less than $1.32, in which case the option will be "in the money." If the spot rate for euros on March 1, 2018, is less than the strike price of $1.32, Amerco will exercise its option and sell its 1 million euros at the strike price of $1.32. If the spot rate for euros in three months is more than the strike price of $1.32, Amerco will not exercise its option but will sell euros at the higher spot rate. By purchasing this option, Amerco is guaranteed a minimum cash flow from the export sale of $1,311,000 ($1,320,000 from exercising the option less the $9,000 cost of the option). There is no limit to the maximum number of U.S. dollars that Amerco could receive.

As is true for other derivative financial instruments, authoritative accounting literature requires foreign currency options to be reported on the balance sheet at fair value. The fair value of a foreign currency option at the balance sheet date is determined by reference to the premium quoted by banks on that date for an option with a similar expiration date. Banks (and other sellers of options) determine the current premium by incorporating relevant variables at the balance sheet date into the modified Black-Scholes option pricing model. Changes in value for the euro account receivable and the foreign currency option are summarized as follows:

	Account Receivable (€)				Foreign Currency Option	
Date	**Spot Rate**	**U.S. Dollar Value**	**Change in U.S. Dollar Value**	**Option Premium for 3/1/18**	**Fair Value**	**Change in Fair Value**
12/1/17	$1.32	$1,320,000	$ –0–	$0.009	$9,000	$ –0–
12/31/17	1.33	1,330,000	+ 10,000	0.006	6,000	– 3,000
3/1/18	1.30	1,300,000	– 30,000	0.020	20,000	+ 14,000

The fair value of the foreign currency put option at December 1 is its cost of $9,000. The spot rate for the euro increases during December, which causes a decrease in the fair value of the put

[10] The seller of the option determined the price of the option (the premium) by using a variation of the Black-Scholes option pricing formula.

option; the right to sell euros at $1.32 is of even less value when the spot rate is $1.33 (on December 31) than when the spot rate was $1.32 (on December 1). The bank determines the fair value of the option at December 31 to be $6,000. By March 1, the euro spot rate has decreased to $1.30. By exercising its option on March 1 at the strike price of $1.32, Amerco will receive $1,320,000 from its export sale, rather than only $1,300,000 if it were required to sell euros in the spot market on March 1. Thus, the option has a fair value of $20,000 on March 1.

We can decompose the fair value of the foreign currency option into its intrinsic value and time value components as follows:

Date	Fair Value	Intrinsic Value	Time Value	Change in Time Value
12/1/17	$ 9,000	$ –0–	$9,000	$ –0–
12/31/17	6,000	–0–	6,000	–3,000
3/1/18	20,000	20,000	–0–	–6,000

Because the option strike price is less than or equal to the spot rate at both December 1 and December 31, the option has no intrinsic value at those dates. The entire fair value is attributable to time value only. On March 1, the date of expiration, no time value remains, and the entire amount of fair value is attributable to intrinsic value.

Option Designated as Cash Flow Hedge

Assume that Amerco designates the foreign currency option as a *cash flow hedge* of a foreign currency denominated asset. In this case, Amerco recognizes the change in the option's time value immediately in net income. The company prepares the following journal entries to account for the foreign currency transaction and the related foreign currency option:

2017 Journal Entries—Option Designated as a Cash Flow Hedge

12/1/17	Accounts Receivable (€)	1,320,000	
	Sales		1,320,000
	To record the sale and €1 million account receivable at the spot rate of $1.32 (Cash Flow Hedge Step A.1. in Exhibit 9.2).		
	Foreign Currency Option	9,000	
	Cash		9,000
	To record the purchase of the foreign currency option as an asset at its fair value of $9,000 (Cash Flow Hedge Step A.2. in Exhibit 9.2).		

From December 1 to December 31, the euro account receivable increases in value by $10,000 and the option decreases in value by $3,000. The company prepares the following journal entries on December 31 to reflect these changes:

12/31/17	Accounts Receivable (€)	10,000	
	Foreign Exchange Gain		10,000
	To adjust the value of the € receivable to the new spot rate of $1.33 and record a foreign exchange gain resulting from the appreciation of the € since December 1 (Cash Flow Hedge Step B.1. in Exhibit 9.2).		
	Accumulated Other Comprehensive Income (AOCI)	3,000	
	Foreign Currency Option		3,000
	To adjust the fair value of the option from $9,000 to $6,000 with a corresponding debit to AOCI (Cash Flow Hedge Step B.2. in Exhibit 9.2).		
	Loss on Foreign Currency Option	10,000	
	Accumulated Other Comprehensive Income (AOCI)		10,000

(*continued*)

(continued)

	To record a loss on foreign currency option to offset the foreign exchange gain on the account receivable with a corresponding credit to AOCI (Cash Flow Hedge Step B.3. in Exhibit 9.2).		
	Option Expense.	3,000	
	Accumulated Other Comprehensive Income (AOCI) . . .		3,000
	To recognize the change in the time value of the option as a decrease in net income with a corresponding credit to AOCI (Cash Flow Hedge Step B.4. in Exhibit 9.2).		

The first three journal entries prepared on December 31 result in the euro account receivable and the foreign currency option being reported on the balance sheet at fair value with a net gain (loss) of zero reflected in net income, which is consistent with the concept of hedge accounting. The final entry serves to amortize a portion of the option cost to expense in net income. On March 1, the remaining $6,000 of option cost will be expensed.

The impact on net income for the year 2017 follows:

Sales.		$1,320,000
Foreign exchange gain.	$ 10,000	
Loss on foreign currency option	(10,000)	
Net gain (loss).		–0–
Option expense		(3,000)
Impact on net income		$1,317,000

The effect on the December 31, 2017, balance sheet is as follows:

Assets		**Liabilities and Stockholders' Equity**	
Cash.	$ (9,000)	Retained earnings	$1,317,000
Accounts receivable (€)	1,330,000	AOCI.	10,000
Foreign currency option.	6,000		$1,327,000
	$1,327,000		

At March 1, 2018, the option has increased in fair value by $14,000—time value decreases by $6,000 and intrinsic value increases by $20,000. The accounting entries made in 2018 are presented next:

2018 Journal Entries—Option Designated as a Cash Flow Hedge

3/1/18	Foreign Exchange Loss.	30,000	
	Accounts Receivable (€).		30,000
	To adjust the value of the € receivable to the new spot rate of $1.30 and record a foreign exchange loss resulting from the depreciation of the € since December 31 (Cash Flow Hedge Step C.1. in Exhibit 9.2).		
	Foreign Currency Option.	14,000	
	Accumulated Other Comprehensive Income (AOCI) . . .		14,000
	To adjust the fair value of the option from $6,000 to $20,000 with a corresponding credit to AOCI (Cash Flow Hedge Step C.2. in Exhibit 9.2).		
	Accumulated Other Comprehensive Income (AOCI)	30,000	
	Gain on Foreign Currency Option.		30,000
	To record a gain on foreign currency option to offset the foreign exchange gain on account receivable with a corresponding debit to AOCI (Cash Flow Hedge Step C.3. in Exhibit 9.2).		
	Option Expense.	6,000	
	Accumulated Other Comprehensive Income (AOCI) . . .		6,000
	To recognize the change in the time value of the option as a decrease in net income with a corresponding credit to AOCI (Cash Flow Hedge Step C.4. in Exhibit 9.2).		

The first three entries on March 1 result in the euro account receivable and the foreign currency option being reported at their fair values, with a net gain (loss) of zero. The fourth entry amortizes the remaining cost of the option to expense. As a result of these entries, the balance in AOCI is zero: $10,000 + $14,000 – $30,000 + $6,000 = $0.

The next two journal entries recognize the receipt of euros from the customer, close out the euro account receivable, and record the exercise of the foreign currency option.

3/1/18	Foreign Currency (€)	1,300,000	
	Accounts Receivable (€)		1,300,000
	To record receipt of €1 million from the German customer as an asset at the spot rate of $1.30 (Cash Flow Hedge Step C.5. in Exhibit 9.2).		
	Cash	1,320,000	
	Foreign Currency (€)		1,300,000
	Foreign Currency Option		20,000
	To record exercise of the option (i.e., record receipt of $1,320,000 in exchange for delivery of €1 million) and remove the foreign currency option from the accounts (Cash Flow Hedge Step C.6. in Exhibit 9.2).		

The impact on net income for the year 2018 follows:

Foreign exchange loss	$(30,000)	
Gain on foreign currency option	30,000	
Net gain (loss)		–0–
Option expense		(6,000)
Impact on net income		$(6,000)

Over the two accounting periods, Amerco reports sales of $1,320,000 and a cumulative option expense of $9,000. The net effect on the balance sheet is an increase in the cash account of $1,311,000 ($1,320,000 – $9,000) with a corresponding increase in the retained earnings account of $1,311,000 ($1,317,000 – $6,000).

The net benefit from having acquired the option is $11,000. This is the difference between the amount Amerco received from executing the option ($1,320,000) and the amount Amerco would have received if it had not acquired the option ($1,300,000), net of the option's cost ($9,000): $1,320,000 – $1,300,000 – $9,000 = $11,000. Amerco indirectly reflects this "gain" in net income as the net gain on foreign currency option ($10,000 loss in 2017 plus $30,000 gain in 2018) less the cumulative option expense ($9,000) recognized over the two accounting periods: $20,000 – $9,000 = $11,000.

Option Designated as Fair Value Hedge

Assume that Amerco decides not to designate the foreign currency option as a cash flow hedge but to treat it as a fair value hedge. In that case, it takes the gain or loss on the option directly to net income. The change in the time value of the option is not recognized, so there is no option expense recorded.

2017 Journal Entries—Option Designated as a Fair Value Hedge

12/1/17	Accounts Receivable (€)	1,320,000	
	Sales		1,320,000
	To record the sale and €1 million account receivable at the spot rate of $1.32 (Fair Value Hedge Step A.1. in Exhibit 9.2).		

(continued)

(continued)

	Foreign Currency Option.	9,000	
	Cash		9,000
	To record the purchase of the foreign currency option as an asset at its fair value of $9,000 (Fair Value Hedge Step A.2. in Exhibit 9.2).		
12/31/17	Accounts Receivable (€)	10,000	
	Foreign Exchange Gain.		10,000
	To adjust the value of the € receivable to the new spot rate of $1.33 and record a foreign exchange gain resulting from the appreciation of the € since December 1 (Fair Value Hedge Step B.1. in Exhibit 9.2).		
	Loss on Foreign Currency Option	3,000	
	Foreign Currency Option.		3,000
	To adjust the fair value of the option from $9,000 to $6,000 and record a loss on foreign currency option for the change in the fair value of the option since December 1 (Fair Value Hedge Step B.2. in Exhibit 9.2).		

The impact on net income for the year 2017 follows:

Sales.		$1,320,000
Foreign exchange gain.	$10,000	
Loss on foreign currency option	(3,000)	
Net gain (loss).		7,000
Impact on net income		$1,327,000

2018 Journal Entries—Option Designated as a Fair Value Hedge

3/1/18	Foreign Exchange Loss	30,000	
	Accounts Receivable (€)		30,000
	To adjust the value of the € receivable to the new spot rate of $1.30 and record a foreign exchange loss resulting from the depreciation of the € since December 31 (Fair Value Hedge Step C.1. in Exhibit 9.2).		
	Foreign Currency Option	14,000	
	Gain on Foreign Currency Option		14,000
	To adjust the fair value of the option from $6,000 to $20,000 and record a gain on foreign currency option for the change in fair value since December 31 (Fair Value Hedge Step C.2. in Exhibit 9.2).		
	Foreign Currency (€).	1,300,000	
	Accounts Receivable (€)		1,300,000
	To record receipt of €1 million from the German customer as an asset at the spot rate of $1.30 (Fair Value Hedge Step C.3. in Exhibit 9.2).		
	Cash.	1,320,000	
	Foreign Currency (€).		1,300,000
	Foreign Currency Option		20,000
	To record exercise of the option (i.e., record receipt of $1,320,000 in exchange for delivery of €1 million) and remove the foreign currency option from the accounts (Fair Value Hedge Step C.4. in Exhibit 9.2).		

The impact on net income for the year 2018 follows:

Foreign exchange loss	$(30,000)
Gain on foreign currency option	14,000
Impact on net income	$(16,000)

Over the two accounting periods, Amerco reports sales of $1,320,000 and a cumulative net loss of $9,000 ($7,000 net gain in 2017 and $16,000 net loss in 2018). The net effect on the balance sheet is an increase in cash of $1,311,000 ($1,320,000 – $9,000) with a corresponding increase in retained earnings of $1,311,000 ($1,327,000 – $16,000). The net benefit from having acquired the option is $11,000. Amerco reflects this in net income through the net gain on foreign currency option ($3,000 loss in 2017 and $14,000 gain in 2018) recognized over the two accounting periods.

The accounting for an option used as a fair value hedge of a foreign currency denominated asset or liability is the same as if the option had been considered a speculative derivative. The only advantage to designating the option as a fair value hedge relates to the disclosures made in the notes to the financial statements.

Spot Rate Exceeds Strike Price

If the spot rate at March 1, 2018, had been more than the strike price of $1.32, Amerco would allow its option to expire unexercised. Instead it would sell its foreign currency (€) at the spot rate. The fair value of the foreign currency option on March 1, 2018, would be zero. The journal entries for 2017 to reflect this scenario would be the same as the preceding ones. The option would be reported as an asset on the December 31, 2017, balance sheet at $6,000 and the € receivable would have a carrying value of $1,330,000. The entries on March 1, 2018, assuming a spot rate on that date of $1.325 (rather than $1.30), would be as follows:

3/1/18	Foreign Exchange Loss	5,000	
	Accounts Receivable (€)		5,000
	To adjust the value of the € receivable to the new spot rate of $1.325 and record a foreign exchange loss resulting from the depreciation of the € since December 31 (Fair Value Hedge Step C.1. in Exhibit 9.2).		
	Loss on Foreign Currency Option.	6,000	
	Foreign Currency Option		6,000
	To adjust the fair value of the option from $6,000 to $0 and record a loss on foreign currency option for the change in fair value since December 31 (Fair Value Hedge Step C.2. in Exhibit 9.2).		
	Foreign Currency (€).	1,325,000	
	Accounts Receivable (€)		1,325,000
	To record receipt of €1 million from the German customer as an asset at the spot rate of $1.325 (Fair Value Hedge Step C.3. in Exhibit 9.2).		
	Cash	1,325,000	
	Foreign Currency (€).		1,325,000
	To record the sale of €1 million at the spot rate of $1.325 (Fair Value Hedge Step C.4. in Exhibit 9.2).		

The overall impact on net income for the year 2018 is as follows:

Foreign exchange loss	$ (5,000)
Loss on foreign currency option	(6,000)
Impact on net income	$(11,000)

LO 9-8

Account for forward contracts and options used as hedges of foreign currency firm commitments.

Hedges of Unrecognized Foreign Currency Firm Commitments

In the examples thus far, Amerco does not enter into a hedge of its export sale until it actually makes the sale. Assume now that on December 1, 2017, Amerco receives and accepts an order from a German customer to deliver goods on March 1, 2018, at a price of 1 million euros. Assume further that under the terms of the sales agreement, Amerco will ship the goods to the German customer on March 1, 2018, and will receive immediate payment on delivery. In other words, Amerco will not extend credit to the German customer. Although Amerco will not make the sale until March 1, 2018, it has a firm commitment to make the sale and receive 1 million euros in three months. This creates a euro asset exposure to foreign exchange risk as of December 1, 2017. On that date, Amerco wants to hedge against an adverse change in the value of the euro over the next three months. This is known as a *hedge of a foreign currency firm commitment.* U.S. GAAP allows hedges of firm commitments to be designated either as cash flow or fair value hedges. However, because the results of fair value hedge accounting are intuitively more appealing, we do not cover cash flow hedge accounting for firm commitments.

A firm commitment is an executory contract; the company has not delivered goods nor has the customer paid for them. Normally, executory contracts are not recognized in financial statements. However, when a firm commitment is hedged using a derivative financial instrument, hedge accounting requires explicit recognition on the balance sheet at fair value of both the derivative financial instrument (forward contract or option) and the firm commitment. The change in fair value of the firm commitment results in a gain or loss that offsets the loss or gain on the hedging instrument (forward contract or option), thus achieving the goal of hedge accounting. This raises the conceptual question of how to measure the fair value of the firm commitment. When a forward contract is used as the hedging instrument, the fair value of the firm commitment is determined through reference to changes in the forward exchange rate. Changes in the spot exchange rate are used to determine the fair value of the firm commitment when a foreign currency option is the hedging instrument.

Forward Contract Used as Fair Value Hedge of a Firm Commitment

To hedge its firm commitment exposure to a decline in the U.S. dollar value of the euro, Amerco decides to enter into a forward contract on December 1, 2017. Assume that on that date, the three-month forward rate for euros is $1.305 and Amerco signs a contract with New Manhattan Bank to deliver 1 million euros in three months in exchange for $1,305,000. No cash changes hands on December 1, 2017. Amerco measures the fair value of the firm commitment through changes in the forward rate. Because the fair value of the forward contract is also measured using changes in the forward rate, the gains and losses on the firm commitment and forward contract exactly offset. The fair value of the forward contract and firm commitment are determined as follows:

		Forward Contract		Firm Commitment	
Date	Forward Rate to 3/1/18	Fair Value	Change in Fair Value	Fair Value	Change in Fair Value
12/1/17	$ 1.305	$ –0–	$ –0–	$ –0–	$ –0–
12/31/17	1.316	(10,783)*	– 10,783	10,783*	+ 10,783
3/1/18	1.30 (spot)	5,000†	+ 15,783	(5,000)†	– 15,783

*($1,305,000 – $1,316,000) = $(11,000) × 0.9803 = $(10,783), where 0.9803 is the present value factor for two months at an annual interest rate of 12 percent (1 percent per month) calculated as $1/1.01^2$.
†($1,305,000 – $1,300,000) = $5,000.

Amerco pays nothing to enter into the forward contract at December 1, 2017. Both the forward contract and the firm commitment have a fair value of zero on that date. As a result, there are no journal entries needed on December 1, 2017. At December 31,

2017, the forward rate for a contract to deliver euros on March 1, 2018, is $1.316. A forward contract could be entered into on December 31, 2017, to sell 1 million euros for $1,316,000 on March 1, 2018. Because Amerco is committed to sell 1 million euros for $1,305,000, the value of the forward contract is $(11,000); present value is $(10,783), a liability. The fair value of the firm commitment is also measured through reference to changes in the forward rate. As a result, the fair value of the firm commitment is equal in amount but of opposite sign to the fair value of the forward contract. At December 31, 2017, the firm commitment is an asset of $10,783. To apply the two steps in accounting for a fair value hedge of a firm commitment at the balance sheet date, on December 31, 2017, Amerco will:

1. Adjust the forward contract to fair value, which results in the recognition of a liability of $10,783, and recognize the counterpart as a loss in net income (Fair Value Hedge Step B.1. in Exhibit 9.2).
2. Adjust the firm commitment to fair value, which results in the recognition of an asset of $10,783, and recognize the counterpart as a gain on firm commitment in net income (Fair Value Hedge Step B.2. in Exhibit 9.2).

The journal entries in 2017 to account for the forward contract fair value hedge of a foreign currency firm commitment are as follows:

2017 Journal Entries—Forward Contract Fair Value Hedge of Firm Commitment

12/1/17	There is no entry to record either the sales agreement or the forward contract because both are executory contracts. A memorandum designates the forward contract as a hedge of the risk of changes in the fair value of the firm commitment resulting from changes in the U.S. dollar–euro forward exchange rate (Fair Value Hedge Steps A.1. and A.2. in Exhibit 9.2).		
12/31/17	Loss on Forward Contract	10,783	
	Forward Contract.		10,783
	To record the forward contract as a liability at its fair value of $(10,783) and record a forward contract loss for the change in the fair value of the forward contract since December 1 (Fair Value Hedge Step B.1. in Exhibit 9.2).		
	Firm Commitment.	10,783	
	Gain on Firm Commitment.		10,783
	To record the firm commitment as an asset at its fair value of $10,783 and record a firm commitment gain for the change in the fair value of the firm commitment since December 1 (Fair Value Hedge Step B.2. in Exhibit 9.2).		

Consistent with the objective of hedge accounting, the gain on the firm commitment offsets the loss on the forward contract, and the impact on 2017 net income is zero. Amerco reports the forward contract as a liability and reports the firm commitment as an asset on the December 31, 2017, balance sheet. This achieves the objective of making sure that derivatives are reported on the balance sheet and ensures that there is no impact on net income.

On March 1, 2018, the forward rate to sell euros on that date, by definition, is the spot rate, $1.30. At that rate, Amerco could sell 1 million euros for $1,300,000. Because Amerco has a contract to sell euros for $1,305,000, the fair value of the forward contract on March 1, 2018, is $5,000 (an asset). The firm commitment has a value of $(5,000), a liability.

On March 1, 2018, Amerco first recognizes changes in the fair value of the forward contract and firm commitment since December 31. The company then records the sale and the settlement of the forward contract. Finally, the $5,000 balance in the firm commitment account is closed as an adjustment to net income. The required journal entries are as follows:

2018 Journal Entries—Forward Contract Fair Value Hedge of Firm Commitment

3/1/18	Forward Contract	15,783	
	Gain on Forward Contract		15,783
	To adjust the fair value of the forward contract from $(10,783) to $5,000 and record a forward contract gain for the change in fair value since December 31 (Fair Value Hedge Step C.1. in Exhibit 9.2).		
	Loss on Firm Commitment	15,783	
	Firm Commitment		15,783
	To adjust the fair value of the firm commitment from $10,783 to $(5,000) and record a firm commitment loss for the change in fair value since December 31 (Fair Value Hedge Step C.2. in Exhibit 9.2).		
	Foreign Currency (€)	1,300,000	
	Sales		1,300,000
	To record the sale and the receipt of €1 million as an asset at the spot rate of $1.30 (Fair Value Hedge Step C.3. in Exhibit 9.2).		
	Cash	1,305,000	
	Foreign Currency (€)		1,300,000
	Forward Contract		5,000
	To record settlement of the forward contract (receipt of $1,305,000 in exchange for delivery of €1 million) and remove the forward contract from the accounts (Fair Value Hedge Step C.4. in Exhibit 9.2).		
	Firm Commitment	5,000	
	Adjustment to Net Income—Firm Commitment		5,000
	To close the firm commitment as an adjustment to net income (Fair Value Hedge Step C.5. in Exhibit 9.2).		

Once again, the gain on forward contract and the loss on firm commitment offset. As a result of the last entry, the export sale increases 2018 net income by $1,305,000 ($1,300,000 in sales plus a $5,000 adjustment to net income). This exactly equals the amount of cash received. In practice, companies use a variety of account titles for the adjustment to net income that results from closing the firm commitment account.

The net gain on forward contract of $5,000 ($10,783 loss in 2017 plus $15,783 gain in 2018) measures the net benefit to the company from hedging its firm commitment. Without the forward contract, Amerco would have sold the 1 million euros received on March 1, 2018, at the spot rate of $1.30 generating cash flow of $1,300,000. Through the forward contract, Amerco is able to sell the euros for $1,305,000, a net gain of $5,000.

Option Used as Fair Value Hedge of Firm Commitment

Now assume that to hedge its exposure to a decline in the U.S. dollar value of the euro, Amerco purchases a put option to sell 1 million euros on March 1, 2018, at a strike price of $1.32. The premium for such an option on December 1, 2017, is $0.009 per euro. With this option, Amerco is guaranteed a minimum cash flow from the export sale of $1,311,000 ($1,320,000 from option exercise less $9,000 cost of the option).

Amerco measures the fair value of the firm commitment by referring to changes in the U.S. dollar–euro spot rate. In this case, Amerco must discount the fair value of the firm commitment to its present value. The fair value and changes in fair value for the firm commitment and foreign currency option are summarized here:

	Option Premium	Foreign Currency Option			Firm Commitment	
Date	for 3/1/18	Fair Value	Change in Fair Value	Spot Rate	Fair Value	Change in Fair Value
12/1/17	$0.009	$ 9,000	$ –0–	$1.32	$ –0–	$ –0–
12/31/17	0.006	6,000	– 3,000	1.33	9,803*	+ 9,803
3/1/18	0.020	20,000	+14,000	1.30	(20,000)†	–29,803

*$1,330,000 – $1,320,000 = $10,000 × 0.9803 = $9,803, where 0.9803 is the present value factor for two months at an annual interest rate of 12 percent (1 percent per month) calculated as $1/1.01^2$.
†$1,300,000 – $1,320,000 = $(20,000).

At December 1, 2017, given the spot rate of $1.32, the firm commitment to receive 1 million euros in three months would generate a cash flow of $1,320,000. At December 31, 2017, the cash flow that the firm commitment could generate increases by $10,000 to $1,330,000. The fair value of the firm commitment at December 31, 2017, is the present value of $10,000 discounted at 1 percent per month for two months. Amerco determines the fair value of the firm commitment on March 1, 2018, by referring to the change in the spot rate from December 1, 2017, to March 1, 2018. Because the spot rate declines by $0.02 over that period, the firm commitment to receive 1 million euros has a fair value of $(20,000) on March 1, 2018. The journal entries to account for the foreign currency option and related foreign currency firm commitment are discussed next:

2017 Journal Entries—Option Fair Value Hedge of Firm Commitment

12/1/17	Foreign Currency Option	9,000	
	Cash.		9,000
	To record the purchase of the foreign currency option as an asset (Fair Value Hedge Step A.2. in Exhibit 9.2).		

There is no entry to record the sales agreement because it is an executory contract (Fair Value Hedge Step A.1. in Exhibit 9.2). Amerco prepares a memorandum to designate the option as a hedge of the risk of changes in the fair value of the firm commitment resulting from changes in the spot exchange rate.

12/31/17	Loss on Foreign Currency Option	3,000	
	Foreign Currency Option.		3,000
	To adjust the fair value of the option from $9,000 to $6,000 and record the change in the value of the option as a loss (Fair Value Hedge Step B.1. in Exhibit 9.2).		
	Firm Commitment	9,803	
	Gain on Firm Commitment		9,803
	To record the firm commitment as an asset at its fair value of $9,803 and record a firm commitment gain for the change in the fair value of the firm commitment since December 1 (Fair Value Hedge Step B.2. in Exhibit 9.2).		

Because the fair value of the firm commitment is based on changes in the spot rate whereas the fair value of the option is based on a variety of factors, the gain on the firm commitment and loss on the option do not exactly offset.

The impact on net income for the year 2017 is as follows:

Gain on firm commitment	$ 9,803
Loss on foreign currency option	(3,000)
Impact on net income	$ 6,803

The effect on the December 31, 2017, balance sheet follows:

Assets		Liabilities and Stockholders' Equity	
Cash	$ (9,000)	Retained earnings	$6,803
Foreign currency option	6,000		
Firm commitment	9,803		
	$ 6,803		

On March 1, 2018, following fair value hedge accounting procedures, Amerco first recognizes changes in the fair value of the option and of the firm commitment since December 31. The company then records the sale and the exercise of the option. Finally, the $20,000 balance in the firm commitment account is closed as an adjustment to net income. The required journal entries are as follows:

2018 Journal Entries—Option Fair Value Hedge of Firm Commitment

3/1/18	Foreign Currency Option	14,000	
	Gain on Foreign Currency Option		14,000
	To adjust the fair value of the foreign currency option from $6,000 to $20,000 and record a gain on foreign currency option for the change in fair value since December 31 (Fair Value Hedge Step C.1. in Exhibit 9.2)		
	Loss on Firm Commitment	29,803	
	Firm Commitment		29,803
	To adjust the fair value of the firm commitment from $9,803 to $(20,000) and record a firm commitment loss for the change in fair value since December 31 (Fair Value Hedge Step C.2. in Exhibit 9.2)		
	Foreign Currency (€)	1,300,000	
	Sales		1,300,000
	To record the sale and the receipt of €1 million as an asset at the spot rate of $1.30 (Fair Value Hedge Step C.3. in Exhibit 9.2).		
	Cash	1,320,000	
	Foreign Currency (€)		1,300,000
	Foreign Currency Option		20,000
	To record exercise of the foreign currency option (receipt of $1,320,000 in exchange for delivery of €1 million) and remove the foreign currency option from the accounts (Fair Value Hedge Step C.4. in Exhibit 9.2).		
	Firm Commitment	20,000	
	Adjustment to Net Income—Firm Commitment		20,000
	To close the firm commitment as an adjustment to net income (Fair Value Hedge Step C.5. in Exhibit 9.2).		

The following is the impact on net income for the year 2018:

Sales	$1,300,000
Loss on firm commitment	(29,803)
Gain on foreign currency option	14,000
Adjustment to net income–firm commitment	20,000
Impact on net income	$1,304,197

The net increase in net income over the two accounting periods is $1,311,000 ($6,803 in 2017 plus $1,304,197 in 2018), which exactly equals the net cash flow realized on the export sale ($1,320,000 from exercising the option less $9,000 to purchase the option). The net gain on the option of $11,000 (loss of $3,000 in 2017 plus gain of $14,000 in 2018) reflects the net benefit from having entered into the hedge. Without the option, Amerco would have sold the 1 million euros received on March 1, 2018, at the spot rate of $1.30 for $1,300,000.

LO 9-9

Account for forward contracts and options used as hedges of forecasted foreign currency transactions.

Hedge of Forecasted Foreign Currency Denominated Transaction

Cash flow hedge accounting also is used for foreign currency derivatives used to hedge the cash flow risk associated with a forecasted foreign currency transaction. For hedge accounting to apply, the forecasted transaction must be probable (likely to occur), the hedge must be highly effective in offsetting fluctuations in the cash flow associated with the foreign currency risk, and the hedging relationship must be properly documented.

Accounting for a hedge of a forecasted transaction differs from accounting for a hedge of a foreign currency firm commitment in two ways:

1. Unlike the accounting for a firm commitment, there is no recognition of the forecasted transaction or gains and losses on the forecasted transaction. (Because there is no recognition of an asset or liability, there is no fair value exposure to foreign exchange risk. Thus, fair value hedge accounting is not appropriate for hedges of forecasted transactions.)
2. The company reports the hedging instrument (forward contract or option) at fair value, but because no gain or loss occurs on the forecasted transaction to offset against, the company does not report changes in the fair value of the hedging instrument as gains and losses in net income. Instead, it reports them in other comprehensive income. On the projected date of the forecasted transaction, the company transfers the cumulative change in the fair value of the hedging instrument from accumulated other comprehensive income (balance sheet) to net income (income statement).

Forward Contract Cash Flow Hedge of a Forecasted Transaction

To demonstrate the accounting for a hedge of a forecasted foreign currency transaction, assume that Amerco has a long-term relationship with its German customer and can reliably forecast that the customer will require delivery of goods costing 1 million euros in March 2018. Confident that it will receive 1 million euros on March 1, 2018, Amerco enters into a forward contract on December 1, 2017, to sell 1 million euros on March 1, 2018, at a rate of $1.30. The facts are essentially the same as those for the hedge of a firm commitment except that Amerco does not receive a sales order from the German customer until late February 2018. Relevant exchange rates and the fair value of the forward contract are as follows:

		Forward Contract	
Date	**Forward Rate to 3/1/18**	**Fair Value**	**Change in Fair Value**
12/1/17	$1.305	$ –0–	$ –0–
12/31/17	1.316	(10,783)*	– 10,783
3/1/18	1.30 (spot)	5,000	+ 15,783

*($1,305,000 – $1,316,000) = $(11,000) × 0.9803 = $(10,783), where 0.9803 is the present value factor for two months at an annual interest rate of 12 percent (1 percent per month) calculated as $1/1.01^2$. The original discount on the forward contract is determined by the difference in the € spot rate and the three-month forward rate on December 1, 2017: ($1.305 – $1.32) × €1 million = $15,000.

2017 Journal Entries—Forward Contract Hedge of a Forecasted Transaction

12/1/17 There is no entry to record either the forecasted sale or the forward contract. A memorandum designates the forward contract as a hedge of the risk of changes in the cash flows related to the forecasted sale resulting from changes in the spot rate (Cash Flow Hedge Steps A.1. and A.2. in Exhibit 9.2).

On December 31, the forward contract is recognized as a liability at its fair value, with the counterpart reflected in AOCI, and discount expense is recognized due to the passage of time, with the counterpart also reflected in AOCI. The necessary journal entries are:

12/31/17	Accumulated Other Comprehensive Income (AOCI)	10,783	
	Forward Contract		10,783
	To record the forward contract as a liability at its fair value of $10,783 with a corresponding debit to AOCI (Cash Flow Hedge Step B.2. in Exhibit 9.2).		
	Discount Expense.	5,000	
	Accumulated Other Comprehensive Income (AOCI) . .		5,000
	To record straight-line allocation of the forward contract discount: $15,000 x ⅓ = $5,000 (Cash Flow Hedge Step B.4. in Exhibit 9.2).		

Discount expense reduces 2017 net income by $5,000. The impact on the December 31, 2017, balance sheet is as follows:

Assets	Liabilities and Stockholders' Equity	
No effect	Forward contract	$10,783
	Retained earnings	(5,000)
	AOCI.	(5,783)
		$ -0-

On March 1, 2018, the carrying value of the forward contract is adjusted to fair value and the discount is amortized to expense. Then, the sale and the settlement of the forward contract are recorded. Finally, the balance in AOCI related to the hedge of the forecasted transaction is closed as an adjustment to net income. The following entries are required:

2018 Journal Entries—Forward Contract Hedge of a Forecasted Transaction

3/1/18	Forward Contract.	15,783	
	Accumulated Other Comprehensive Income (AOCI). . .		15,783
	To adjust the carrying value of the forward contract to its current fair value of $5,000 with a corresponding credit to AOCI (Cash Flow Hedge Step C.1. in Exhibit 9.2).		
3/1/18	Discount Expense	10,000	
	Accumulated Other Comprehensive Income (AOCI). . .		10,000
	To record straight-line allocation of the forward contract discount: $15,000 x ⅔ = $10,000 (Cash Flow Hedge Step C.2. in Exhibit 9.2).		
	Foreign Currency (€).	1,300,000	
	Sales		1,300,000
	To record the sale and the receipt of €1 million as an asset at the spot rate of $1.30 (Cash Flow Hedge Step C.3. in Exhibit 9.2).		
	Cash	1,305,000	
	Foreign Currency (€).		1,300,000
	Forward Contract.		5,000
	To record settlement of the forward contract (receipt of $1,305,000 in exchange for delivery of €1 million) and remove the forward contract from the accounts (Cash Flow Hedge Step C.4. in Exhibit 9.2).		
	Accumulated Other Comprehensive Income (AOCI).	20,000	
	Adjustment to Net Income–Forecasted Transaction. . . .		20,000
	To close AOCI as an adjustment to net income (Cash Flow Hedge Step C.5. in Exhibit 9.2).		

As a result of these entries, the forward contract liability reported at December 31, 2017, has been reduced to zero, as has the balance in AOCI related to this forward contract.

The impact on net income for the year 2018 follows:

Sales	$1,300,000
Discount expense	(10,000)
Adjustment to net income–forecasted transaction	20,000
Impact on net income	$1,310,000

Over the two accounting periods, the net impact on net income is $1,305,000, which equals the amount of net cash inflow realized from the sale.

Option Designated as a Cash Flow Hedge of a Forecasted Transaction

Now assume that Amerco hedges its forecasted foreign currency transaction by purchasing a 1 million euro put option on December 1, 2017. The option, which expires on March 1, 2018, has a strike price of $1.32 and a premium of $0.009 per euro. The fair value of the option at relevant dates is as follows (same as in previous examples):

Date	Option Premium for 3/1/18	Foreign Currency Option				
		Fair Value	Change in Fair Value	Intrinsic Value	Time Value	Change in Time Value
12/1/17	$0.009	$ 9,000	$ –0–	$ –0–	$9,000	$ –0–
12/31/17	0.006	6,000	– 3,000	–0–	6,000	– 3,000
3/1/18	0.020	20,000	+14,000	20,000	–0–	– 6,000

2017 Journal Entries—Option Hedge of a Forecasted Transaction

12/1/17	Foreign Currency Option	9,000	
	Cash		9,000
	To record the purchase of the foreign currency option as an asset (Cash Flow Hedge Step A.2. in Exhibit 9.2). There is no entry to record the forecasted sale. A memorandum designates the foreign currency option as a hedge of the risk of changes in the cash flows related to the forecasted sale (Cash Flow Hedge Step A.1. in Exhibit 9.2).		

At December 31, the carrying value of the option is decreased for the change in fair value since December 1, and the change in the time value of the option is recognized as option expense. The required journal entries are as follows:

12/31/17	Accumulated Other Comprehensive Income (AOCI)	3,000	
	Foreign Currency Option		3,000
	To adjust the carrying value of the option to its fair value with a corresponding debit to AOCI (Cash Flow Hedge Step B.2. in Exhibit 9.2).		
	Option Expense	3,000	
	Accumulated Other Comprehensive Income (AOCI)		3,000
	To recognize the change in the time value of the option as a decrease in net income with a corresponding credit to AOCI (Cash Flow Hedge Step B.4. in Exhibit 9.2).		

The impact on net income for the year 2017 follows:

Option expense	$(3,000)
Impact on net income	$(3,000)

A foreign currency option of $6,000 is reported as an asset on the December 31, 2017, balance sheet. Cash is decreased by $9,000, and Retained Earnings is decreased by $3,000.

On March 1, 2018, first the carrying value of the option is adjusted to fair value and the change in the time value of the option is recognized as option expense. Then, the sale and the exercise of the foreign currency option are recorded. Finally, the balance in AOCI related to the hedge of the forecasted transaction is closed as an adjustment to net income. The following entries are required:

2018 Journal Entries—Option Hedge of a Forecasted Transaction

3/1/18	Foreign Currency Option	14,000	
	Accumulated Other Comprehensive Income (AOCI)		14,000
	To adjust the carrying value of the option to its fair value with a corresponding credit to AOCI (Cash Flow Hedge Step C.1. in Exhibit 9.2).		
	Option Expense	6,000	
	Accumulated Other Comprehensive Income (AOCI)		6,000
	To recognize the change in the time value of the option as a decrease in net income with a corresponding credit to AOCI (Cash Flow Hedge Step C.2. in Exhibit 9.2).		
	Foreign Currency (€)	1,300,000	
	Sales		1,300,000
	To record the sale and the receipt of €1 million as an asset at the spot rate of $1.30 (Cash Flow Hedge Step C.3. in Exhibit 9.2).		
	Cash	1,320,000	
	Foreign Currency (€)		1,300,000
	Foreign Currency Option		20,000
	To record the exercise of the foreign currency option (receipt of $1,320,000 in exchange for delivery of €1 million) and remove the foreign currency option from the accounts (Cash Flow Hedge Step C.4. in Exhibit 9.2).		
	Accumulated Other Comprehensive Income (AOCI)	20,000	
	Adjustment to Net Income–Forecasted Transaction		20,000
	To close AOCI as an adjustment to net income (Cash Flow Hedge Step C.5. in Exhibit 9.2).		

The following is the impact on net income for the year 2018:

Sales	$1,300,000
Option expense	(6,000)
Adjustment to net income–forecasted transaction	20,000
Impact on net income	$1,314,000

Over the two periods, a total of $1,311,000 is recognized as net income, which is equal to the net cash inflow realized from the export sale ($1,320,000 from the sale less $9,000 for the option).

Use of Hedging Instruments

There are probably as many different corporate strategies regarding hedging foreign exchange risk as there are companies exposed to that risk. Some companies require hedges of all foreign currency transactions. Others require the use of a forward contract hedge when the forward rate results in a larger cash inflow or smaller cash outflow than with the spot rate. Still other companies have proportional hedging policies that require hedging on some predetermined percentage (e.g., 50 percent, 60 percent, or 70 percent) of transaction exposure. For example, on page 79 of its 2014 annual report, Johnson Controls, Inc., states: "The Company hedges 70% to 90% of the nominal amount of each of its known foreign exchange transactional exposures."

Companies are required to provide information on the use of derivative financial instruments to hedge foreign exchange risk in the notes to financial statements. Exhibit 9.4 presents disclosures made by Abbott Laboratories in its 2014 annual report. Abbott Labs uses forward contracts to hedge foreign exchange risk associated with anticipated foreign currency transactions, foreign currency denominated payables and receivables, and foreign currency borrowings. Much of its hedging activity relates to intra-entity transactions involving foreign subsidiaries. The table in Exhibit 9.4 discloses that (1) Abbott's forward contracts primarily are to sell foreign currencies to receive U.S. dollars, (2) 49 percent of Abbott's $15,562 million in forward contracts at December 31, 2014, was in euros, and (3) the net fair value of all the company's forward contracts was positive and reported on the balance sheet as an asset (receivable).

Abbott Labs uses forward contracts exclusively to manage its foreign exchange risk. Thermo Fischer Scientific uses foreign currency forward contracts as well as options to hedge exposures resulting from changes in currency exchange rates. In contrast, The Coca-Cola Company employs a combination of forward contracts, currency options, and collars[11] in its foreign exchange risk-hedging strategy.

EXHIBIT 9.4 Disclosures Related to Hedging Foreign Exchange Risk in Abbott Laboratories' 2014 Annual Report

Foreign Currency Sensitive Financial Instruments

Certain Abbott foreign subsidiaries enter into foreign currency forward exchange contracts to manage exposures to changes in foreign exchange rates for anticipated intercompany purchases by those subsidiaries whose functional currencies are not the U.S. dollar. These contracts are designated as cash flow hedges of the variability of the cash flows due to changes in foreign exchange rates and are marked-to-market with the resulting gains or losses reflected in Accumulated other comprehensive income (loss). Gains or losses will be included in Cost of products sold at the time the products are sold, generally within the next twelve to eighteen months. At December 31, 2014 and 2013, Abbott held $1.5 billion and $135 million, respectively, of such contracts. Contracts held at December 31, 2014 will mature in 2015 or 2016 depending on the contract. Contacts held at December 31, 2013 matured in 2014.

Abbott enters into foreign currency forward exchange contracts to manage its exposure to foreign currency denominated intercompany loans and trade payables and third-party trade payables and receivables. The contracts are marked-to-market, and resulting gains or losses are reflected in income and are generally offset by losses or gains on the foreign currency exposure being managed. At December 31, 2014 and 2013, Abbott held $14.1 billion and $13.8 billion, respectively, of such contracts, which generally mature in the next twelve months.

The following table reflects the total foreign currency forward contracts outstanding at December 31, 2014.

(dollars in millions)	**Contract Amount**	**Weighted Average Exchange Rate**	**Fair and Carrying Value Receivable/ (Payable)**
Receive primarily U.S. Dollars in exchange for the following currencies:			
Euro	$ 7,574	1.2458	$ 19
British pound	1,295	1.5790	9
Japanese yen	2,258	115.0311	56
Canadian dollar	371	1.1197	13
All other currencies	4,064	N/A	31
Total	$15,562		$128

[11] A foreign currency collar is created by simultaneously purchasing a call option and selling a put option in a foreign currency to fix a range of prices at which the foreign currency can be purchased at a predetermined future date.

The Euro

The introduction of the euro as a common currency throughout much of Europe in 2002 reduced the need for hedging in that region of the world. For example, a German company purchasing goods from a Spanish supplier no longer has an exposure to foreign exchange risk because both countries use a common currency. This is also true for German subsidiaries of U.S. parent companies. However, any euro-denominated transactions between the U.S. parent and its German (or other euro zone) subsidiary continue to be exposed to foreign exchange risk.

One advantage of the euro for U.S. companies is that a euro account receivable from sales to a customer in, say, the Netherlands acts as a natural hedge of a euro account payable on purchases from, say, a supplier in Italy. Assuming that similar amounts and time periods are involved, any foreign exchange loss (gain) arising from the euro payable is offset by a foreign exchange gain (loss) on the euro receivable. A company does not need to hedge the euro account payable with a hedging instrument such as a foreign currency option.

International Financial Reporting Standard 9— Financial Instruments

IFRS 9, "Financial Instruments," provides guidance on the accounting for hedging instruments including those used to hedge foreign exchange risk. Rules and procedures in *IFRS 9* related to foreign currency hedge accounting generally are consistent with U.S. GAAP. Similar to current U.S. standards, *IFRS 9* allows hedge accounting for foreign currency–denominated assets and liabilities, firm commitments, and forecasted transactions when documentation requirements and effectiveness tests are met and requires hedges to be designated as cash flow or fair value hedges. While the hedge accounting models in U.S. GAAP and IFRS are based on similar principles, a number of differences exist in the application guidance provided by the two sets of standards.

One difference between the two sets of standards relates to the type of financial instrument that can be designated as a foreign currency cash flow hedge. Under U.S. GAAP, only derivative financial instruments can be used as a cash flow hedge, whereas *IFRS 9* also allows nonderivative financial instruments, such as foreign currency loans, to be designated as hedging instruments in a foreign currency cash flow hedge.

The standards also differ with regard to the recognition of changes in fair value of forward contracts used as fair value hedges. *IFRS 9* allows companies to choose between recognizing these changes either in net income (as is required under U.S. GAAP) or in other comprehensive income.

Another difference relates to the accounting for the time value of options. Under *IFRS 9,* the initial time value of an option must be amortized to net income on a systematic and rational (e.g., straight-line) basis. To achieve this, changes in time value are reflected initially in AOCI rather than in net income, with an amount equal to the current period's amortization reclassified from AOCI to net income. The total amount recognized as option expense in net income will be the same under both IFRS and U.S. GAAP, but the timing of income statement recognition is likely to differ.

Summary

1. Several exchange rate systems are used around the world. Most national currencies fluctuate in value against other currencies over time. However, some countries have pegged their national currency to the U.S. dollar.
2. Exposure to foreign exchange risk exists when a payment to be made or to be received is denominated (stated) in terms of a foreign currency. Appreciation in a foreign currency results in a foreign exchange gain when the foreign currency is to be received and a foreign exchange loss when the foreign currency is to be paid. Conversely, a decrease in the value of a foreign currency results in a foreign exchange loss when the foreign currency is to be received and a foreign exchange gain when the foreign currency is to be paid.
3. Companies must revalue foreign currency assets and liabilities to their current U.S. dollar value using current exchange rates when financial statements are prepared. The change in U.S. dollar

value of foreign currency balances is recognized as a foreign exchange gain or loss in net income in the period in which the exchange rate change occurs. This is known as the two-transaction perspective, accrual approach.

4. Borrowing foreign currency creates two exposures to foreign exchange risk. Foreign exchange gains and losses both on the foreign currency note payable and on the accrued foreign currency interest payable are recognized in net income over the life of the debt.
5. IFRS rules related to the accounting for foreign currency transactions generally are consistent with U.S. GAAP. *IAS 21* requires a two-transaction, accrual approach in accounting for foreign currency transactions.
6. Exposure to foreign exchange risk can be eliminated through hedging. Hedging involves establishing a price today at which a foreign currency to be received in the future can be sold in the future or at which a foreign currency to be paid in the future can be purchased in the future.
7. The two most popular derivative financial instruments for hedging foreign exchange risk are foreign currency forward contracts and foreign currency options. A *forward contract* is a binding agreement to exchange currencies at a predetermined rate. An *option* gives the buyer the right, but not the obligation, to exchange currencies at a predetermined rate.
8. Hedge accounting is appropriate when three criteria are met: (1) the derivative is used to hedge either a fair value exposure or cash flow exposure to foreign exchange risk, (2) the derivative is highly effective in offsetting changes in the fair value or cash flows related to the hedged item, and (3) the derivative is properly documented as a hedge. Hedge accounting requires reporting gains and losses on the hedging instrument in net income in the same period as gains and losses on the item being hedged.
9. Companies must report all derivatives, including forward contracts and options, on the balance sheet at their fair value. Changes in fair value are included in accumulated other comprehensive income if the derivative is designated as a cash flow hedge and in net income if it is designated as a fair value hedge.
10. Authoritative accounting literature provides guidance for hedges of (a) recognized foreign currency denominated assets and liabilities, (b) unrecognized foreign currency firm commitments, and (c) forecasted foreign currency denominated transactions. Cash flow hedge accounting can be used for all three types of hedges; fair value hedge accounting can be used only for (a) and (b).
11. If a company hedges a foreign currency firm commitment and designates the hedging instrument as a fair value hedge, it should recognize gains and losses on the hedging instrument as well as on the underlying firm commitment in net income. The firm commitment account created to offset the gain or loss on firm commitment is treated as an adjustment to the underlying transaction when it takes place.
12. If a company hedges a forecasted transaction, it must designate the hedging instrument as a cash flow hedge and report changes in the fair value of the hedging instrument in accumulated other comprehensive income. The cumulative change in fair value reported in other comprehensive income is included in net income in the period in which the forecasted transaction was originally anticipated to take place.
13. Similar to U.S. GAAP, *IFRS 9* allows hedge accounting for hedges of foreign currency assets and liabilities, firm commitments, and forecasted transactions, provided that the hedge is properly documented and is effective. Foreign currency hedging instruments are designated either as a cash flow or a fair value hedge; in either case the hedging instrument must be reported at fair value. Unlike U.S. GAAP, when a fair value hedge is designated, *IFRS 9* allows fair value changes to be reported in accumulated other comprehensive income. Similarly, the change in time value of an option is reported in AOCI.

Comprehensive Illustration

Problem

(*Estimated Time: 60 to 75 minutes*) Zelm Company is a U.S. company that produces electronic switches for the telecommunications industry. Zelm regularly imports component parts from a supplier located in Guadalajara, Mexico, and makes payments in Mexican pesos. The following spot exchange rates, forward exchange rates, and call option premium for Mexican pesos exist during the period August to October.

	U.S. Dollar per Mexican Peso		
Date	**Spot Rate**	**Forward Rate to October 31**	**Call Option Premium for October 31 (strike price $0.080)**
August 1	$0.080	$0.085	$0.0052
September 30	0.086	0.088	0.0095
October 31	0.091	0.091	0.0110

Part A

On August 1, Zelm imports parts from its Mexican supplier at a price of 1 million Mexican pesos. It receives the parts on August 1 but does not pay for them until October 31. In addition, on August 1, Zelm enters into a forward contract to purchase 1 million pesos on October 31. It appropriately designates the forward contract as a *cash flow hedge* of the Mexican peso liability exposure. Zelm's incremental borrowing rate is 12 percent per annum (1 percent per month), and the company uses a straight-line method on a monthly basis for allocating forward discounts and premiums.

Part B

The facts are the same as in Part A with the exception that Zelm designates the forward contract as a *fair value hedge* of the Mexican peso liability exposure.

Part C

On August 1, Zelm imports parts from its Mexican supplier at a price of 1 million Mexican pesos. It receives the parts on August 1 but does not pay for them until October 31. In addition, on August 1 Zelm purchases a three-month call option on 1 million Mexican pesos with a strike price of $0.080. The option is appropriately designated as a *cash flow hedge* of the Mexican peso liability exposure.

Part D

On August 1, Zelm orders parts from its Mexican supplier at a price of 1 million Mexican pesos. It receives the parts and pays for them on October 31. On August 1, Zelm enters into a forward contract to purchase 1 million Mexican pesos on October 31. It designates the forward contract as a *fair value hedge* of the Mexican peso firm commitment. Zelm determines the fair value of the firm commitment by referring to changes in the forward exchange rate.

Part E

On August 1, Zelm orders parts from its Mexican supplier at a price of 1 million Mexican pesos. It receives the parts and pays for them on October 31. On August 1, Zelm purchases a three-month call option on 1 million Mexican pesos with a strike price of $0.080. The option is appropriately designated as a *fair value hedge* of the Mexican peso firm commitment. The fair value of the firm commitment is by reference to changes in the spot exchange rate.

Part F

Zelm anticipates that it will import component parts from its Mexican supplier in the near future. On August 1, Zelm purchases a three-month call option on 1 million Mexican pesos with a strike price of $0.080. It appropriately designates the option as a *cash flow hedge* of a forecasted Mexican peso transaction. Zelm receives and pays for parts costing 1 million Mexican pesos on October 31.

Required

Prepare journal entries for each of these independent situations in accordance with U.S. GAAP and determine the impact each situation has on the September 30 and October 31 trial balances.

Solution

Part A. Forward Contract Cash Flow Hedge of a Recognized Foreign Currency Liability

8/1	Parts Inventory	80,000	
	Accounts Payable (Mexican pesos)		80,000
	To record the purchase of parts and a peso account payable at the spot rate of $0.080.		

The forward contract requires no formal entry. Zelm prepares a memorandum to designate the forward contract as a hedge of the risk of changes in the cash flow to be paid on the foreign currency payable resulting from changes in the U.S. dollar–Mexican peso exchange rate.

9/30	Foreign Exchange Loss	6,000	
	Accounts Payable (Mexican pesos)		6,000
	To adjust the value of the Mexican peso payable to the new spot rate of $0.086 and record a foreign exchange loss resulting from the appreciation of the peso since August 1.		
	Forward Contract	2,970	
	Accumulated Other Comprehensive Income (AOCI)		2,970
	To record the forward contract as an asset at its fair value of $2,970 with a corresponding credit to AOCI.		

Zelm determines the fair value of the forward contract by referring to the change in the forward rate for a contract that settles on October 31: ($0.088 – $0.085) × 1 million pesos = $3,000. The present value of $3,000 discounted for one month (from October 31 to September 30) at an interest rate of 12 percent per year (1 percent per month) is calculated as follows: $3,000 × 0.9901 = $2,970.

Accumulated Other Comprehensive Income (AOCI)	6,000	
Gain on Forward Contract		6,000
To record a gain on forward contract to offset the foreign exchange loss on account payable with a corresponding debit to AOCI.		
Premium Expense	3,333	
Accumulated Other Comprehensive Income (AOCI)		3,333
To allocate the forward contract premium to income over the life of the contract using a straight-line method on a monthly basis ($5,000 × ⅔ = $3,333).		

The original premium on the forward contract is determined by the difference in the peso spot rate and three-month forward rate on August 1: ($0.085 – $0.080) × 1 million pesos = $5,000.

Trial Balance—September 30	Debit	Credit
Parts inventory	$80,000	$ –0–
Accounts Payable (Mexican pesos)		86,000
Forward Contract (asset)	2,970	
AOCI		303
Foreign exchange loss	6,000	
Gain on forward contract		6,000
Premium expense	3,333	–0–
	$92,303	$92,303

10/31	Foreign Exchange Loss	5,000	
	Accounts Payable (Mexican pesos)		5,000
	To adjust the value of the Mexican peso payable to the new spot rate of $0.091 and record a foreign exchange loss resulting from the appreciation of the peso since September 30.		
	Forward Contract	3,030	
	Accumulated Other Comprehensive Income (AOCI)		3,030
	To adjust the carrying value of the forward contract to its current fair value of $6,000 with a corresponding credit to AOCI.		

The current fair value of the forward contract is determined by referring to the difference in the spot rate on October 31 and the original forward rate: ($0.091 – $0.085) × 1 million pesos = $6,000. The forward contract adjustment on October 31 is calculated as the difference in the current fair value and the carrying value at September 30: $6,000 – $2,970 = $3,030.

		Debit	Credit
	Accumulated Other Comprehensive Income (AOCI).....	5,000	
	Gain on Forward Contract		5,000
	To record a gain on forward contract to offset the foreign exchange loss on account payable with a corresponding debit to AOCI.		
	Premium Expense	1,667	
	Accumulated Other Comprehensive Income (AOCI) ..		1,667
	To allocate the forward contract premium to income over the life of the contract using a straight-line method on a monthly basis ($5,000 x ⅓ = $1,667).		
	Foreign Currency (Mexican pesos)....................	91,000	
	Cash..		85,000
	Forward Contract..................................		6,000
	To record settlement of the forward contract: Record payment of $85,000 in exchange for 1 million pesos, record the receipt of 1 million pesos as an asset at the spot rate of $0.091, and remove the forward contract from the accounts.		
	Accounts Payable (pesos)	91,000	
	Foreign Currency (pesos)........................		91,000
	To record remittance of 1 million pesos to the Mexican supplier.		

Trial Balance—October 31	**Debit**	**Credit**
Cash		$85,000
Parts inventory....................................	$80,000	–0–
Retained earnings, 9/30	3,333	–0–
Foreign exchange loss...............................	5,000	–0–
Gain on forward contract............................	–0–	5,000
Premium expense....................................	1,667	–0–
	$90,000	$90,000

Part B. Forward Contract Fair Value Hedge of a Recognized Foreign Currency Liability

		Debit	Credit
8/1	Parts Inventory	80,000	
	Accounts Payable (Mexican pesos)		80,000
	To record the purchase of parts and a Mexican peso account payable at the spot rate of $0.080.		

The forward contract requires no formal entry. A memorandum designates the forward contract as a hedge of the risk of changes in the cash flow to be paid on the foreign currency payable resulting from changes in the U.S. dollar–peso exchange rate.

		Debit	Credit
9/30	Foreign Exchange Loss	6,000	
	Accounts Payable (Mexican pesos)		6,000
	To adjust the value of the peso payable to the new spot rate of $0.086 and record a foreign exchange loss resulting from the appreciation of the peso since August 1.		
	Forward Contract.................................	2,970	
	Gain on Forward Contract		2,970
	To record the forward contract as an asset at its fair value of $2,970 and record a forward contract gain for the change in the fair value of the forward contract since August 1.		

Trial Balance—September 30	Debit	Credit
Parts inventory	$80,000	$ –0–
Accounts payable (Mexican pesos)		86,000
Forward contract (asset)	2,970	–0–
Foreign exchange loss	6,000	–0–
Gain on forward contract	–0–	2,970
	$88,970	$88,970

10/31	Foreign Exchange Loss	5,000	
	Accounts Payable (Mexican pesos)		5,000
	To adjust the value of the peso payable to the new spot rate of $0.091 and record a foreign exchange loss resulting from the appreciation of the peso since September 30.		
	Forward Contract	3,030	
	Gain on Forward Contract		3,030
	To adjust the carrying value of the forward contract to its current fair value of $6,000 and record a forward contract gain for the change in fair value since September 30.		
	Foreign Currency (Mexican pesos)	91,000	
	Cash		85,000
	Forward Contract		6,000
	To record settlement of the forward contract: Record payment of $85,000 in exchange for 1 million pesos, record the receipt of 1 million pesos as an asset at the spot rate of $0.091, and remove the forward contract from the accounts.		
	Accounts Payable (pesos)	91,000	
	Foreign Currency (pesos)		91,000
	To record remittance of 1 million pesos to the Mexican supplier.		

Trial Balance—October 31	Debit	Credit
Cash	$ –0–	$85,000
Parts inventory	80,000	–0–
Retained earnings, 9/30	3,030	–0–
Foreign exchange loss	5,000	–0–
Gain on forward contract	–0–	3,030
	$88,030	$88,030

Part C. Option Cash Flow Hedge of a Recognized Foreign Currency Liability

The following schedule summarizes the changes in the components of the fair value of the peso call option with a strike price of $0.080:

Date	Spot Rate	Option Premium	Fair Value	Change in Fair Value	Intrinsic Value	Time Value	Change in Time Value
8/1	$0.080	$0.0052	$ 5,200	$ –0–	$ –0–	$5,200*	$ –0–
9/30	0.086	0.0095	9,500	+4,300	6,000†	3,500†	– 1,700
10/31	0.091	0.0110	11,000	+1,500	11,000	–0–‡	– 3,500

*Because the strike price and spot rate are the same, the option has no intrinsic value. Fair value is attributable solely to the time value of the option.

†With a spot rate of $0.086 and a strike price of $0.08, the option has an intrinsic value of $6,000. The remaining $3,500 of fair value is attributable to time value.

‡The time value of the option at maturity is zero.

		Debit	Credit
8/1	Parts Inventory	80,000	
	Accounts Payable (Mexican pesos)		80,000
	To record the purchase of parts and a peso account payable at the spot rate of $0.080.		
	Foreign Currency Option	5,200	
	Cash		5,200
	To record the purchase of a foreign currency option as an asset.		
9/30	Foreign Exchange Loss	6,000	
	Accounts Payable (pesos)		6,000
	To adjust the value of the peso payable to the new spot rate of $0.086 and record a foreign exchange loss resulting from the appreciation of the peso since August 1.		
	Foreign Currency Option	4,300	
	Accumulated Other Comprehensive Income (AOCI)		4,300
	To adjust the fair value of the option from $5,200 to $9,500 with a corresponding credit to AOCI.		
	Accumulated Other Comprehensive Income (AOCI)	6,000	
	Gain on Foreign Currency Option		6,000
	To record a gain on forward currency option to offset the foreign exchange loss on account payable with a corresponding debit to AOCI.		
	Option Expense	1,700	
	Accumulated Other Comprehensive Income (AOCI)		1,700
	To recognize the change in the time value of the foreign currency option as an expense with a corresponding credit to AOCI.		

Trial Balance—September 30	**Debit**	**Credit**
Cash		$ 5,200
Parts inventory	$80,000	–0–
Foreign currency option (asset)	9,500	–0–
Accounts payable (Mexican pesos)	–0–	86,000
Foreign exchange loss	6,000	–0–
Gain on foreign currency option	–0–	6,000
Option expense	1,700	–0–
	$97,200	$97,200

		Debit	Credit
10/31	Foreign Exchange Loss	5,000	
	Accounts Payable (Mexican pesos)		5,000
	To adjust the value of the peso payable to the new spot rate of $0.091 and record a foreign exchange loss resulting from the appreciation of the peso since September 30.		
	Foreign Currency Option	1,500	
	Accumulated Other Comprehensive Income (AOCI)		1,500
	To adjust the carrying value of the foreign currency option to its current fair value of $11,000 with a corresponding credit to AOCI.		
	Accumulated Other Comprehensive Income (AOCI)	5,000	
	Gain on Foreign Currency Option		5,000
	To record a gain on foreign currency option to offset the foreign exchange loss on account payable with a corresponding debit to AOCI.		
	Option Expense	3,500	
	Accumulated Other Comprehensive Income (AOCI)		3,500
	To recognize the change in the time value of the foreign currency option as an expense with a corresponding credit to AOCI.		

Foreign Currency (Mexican pesos)	91,000	
Cash		80,000
Foreign Currency Option		11,000
To record exercise of the foreign currency option: Record payment of $80,000 in exchange for 1 million pesos, record the receipt of 1 million pesos as an asset at the spot rate of $0.091, and remove the option from the accounts.		
Accounts Payable (pesos)	91,000	
Foreign Currency (pesos)		91,000
To record remittance of 1 million pesos to the Mexican supplier.		

Trial Balance—October 31	**Debit**	**Credit**
Cash ($5,200 credit balance + $80,000 credit)	$ –0–	$85,200
Parts inventory	80,000	–0–
Retained earnings, 9/30	1,700	–0–
Foreign exchange loss	5,000	–0–
Gain on foreign currency option	–0–	5,000
Option expense	3,500	–0–
	$90,200	$90,200

Part D. Forward Contract Fair Value Hedge of a Foreign Currency Firm Commitment

8/1	The forward contract or the purchase order requires no formal entry. A memorandum would be prepared designating the forward contract as a fair value hedge of the foreign currency firm commitment.		
9/30	Forward Contract	2,970	
	Gain on Forward Contract		2,970
	To record the forward contract as an asset at its fair value of $2,970 and record a forward contract gain for the change in the fair value of the forward contract since August 1.		
	Loss on Firm Commitment	2,970	
	Firm Commitment		2,970
	To record the firm commitment as a liability at its fair value of $2,970 based on changes in the forward rate and record a firm commitment loss for the change in fair value since August 1.		

Trial Balance—September 30	**Debit**	**Credit**
Forward contract (asset)	$2,970	$ –0–
Firm commitment (liability)	–0–	2,970
Gain on forward contract	–0–	2,970
Loss on firm commitment	2,970	–0–
	$5,940	$5,940

10/31	Forward Contract	3,030	
	Gain on Forward Contract		3,030
	To adjust the carrying value of the forward contract to its current fair value of $6,000 and record a forward contract gain for the change in fair value since September 30.		
	Loss on Firm Commitment	3,030	
	Firm Commitment		3,030
	To adjust the value of the firm commitment to $6,000 based on changes in the forward rate and record a firm commitment loss for the change in fair value since September 30.		

Foreign Currency (Mexican pesos)	91,000	
Cash		85,000
Forward Contract		6,000
To record settlement of the forward contract: Record payment of $85,000 in exchange for 1 million pesos, record the receipt of 1 million pesos as an asset at the spot rate of $0.091, and remove the forward contract from the accounts.		
Parts Inventory	91,000	
Foreign Currency (Mexican pesos)		91,000
To record the purchase of parts through the payment of 1 million pesos to the Mexican supplier.		
Firm Commitment	6,000	
Adjustment to Net Income–Firm Commitment		6,000
To close the firm commitment account as an adjustment to net income.		

(*Note:* The final entry to close the Firm Commitment account to Adjustment to Net Income must be made *only* in the period in which Parts Inventory affects net income through Cost of Goods Sold. The Firm Commitment account remains on the books as a liability until that point in time.)

Trial Balance—October 31	Debit	Credit
Cash	$ –0–	$85,000
Parts inventory (cost of goods sold)	91,000	–0–
Gain on forward contract	–0–	3,030
Loss on firm commitment	3,030	–0–
Adjustment to net income–firm commitment	–0–	6,000
	$94,030	$94,030

Part E. Option Fair Value Hedge of a Foreign Currency Firm Commitment

8/1	Foreign Currency Option	5,200	
	Cash		5,200
	To record the purchase of a foreign currency option as an asset.		
9/30	Foreign Currency Option	4,300	
	Gain on Foreign Currency Option		4,300
	To adjust the fair value of the option from $5,200 to $9,500 and record an option gain for the change in fair value since August 1.		
	Loss on Firm Commitment	5,940	
	Firm Commitment		5,940
	To record the firm commitment as a liability at its fair value of $5,940 based on changes in the spot rate and record a firm commitment loss for the change in fair value since August 1.		

The fair value of the firm commitment is determined by referring to changes in the spot rate from August 1 to September 30: ($0.080 – $0.086) × 1 million pesos = $(6,000). This amount must be discounted for one month at 12 percent per annum (1 percent per month): $(6,000) × 0.9901 = $(5,940).

Trial Balance—September 30	Debit	Credit
Cash	$ –0–	$ 5,200
Foreign currency option (asset)	9,500	–0–
Firm commitment (liability)	–0–	5,940
Gain on foreign currency option	–0–	4,300
Loss on firm commitment	5,940	–0–
	$15,440	$15,440

10/31	Foreign Currency Option	1,500	
	Gain on Foreign Currency Option		1,500
	To adjust fair value of the option from $9,500 to $11,000 and record an option gain for the change in fair value since September 30.		
	Loss on Firm Commitment	5,060	
	Firm Commitment		5,060
	To adjust the fair value of the firm commitment from $5,940 to $11,000 and record a firm commitment loss for the change in fair value since September 30.		

The fair value of the firm commitment is determined by referring to changes in the spot rate from August 1 to October 31: ($0.080 – $0.091) × 1 million pesos = $(11,000).

	Foreign Currency (Mexican pesos)	91,000	
	Cash		80,000
	Foreign Currency Option		11,000
	To record exercise of the foreign currency option: Record payment of $80,000 in exchange for 1 million pesos, record the receipt of 1 million pesos as an asset at the spot rate of $0.091, and remove the option from the accounts.		
	Parts Inventory	91,000	
	Foreign Currency (pesos)		91,000
	To record the purchase of parts through the payment of 1 million pesos to the Mexican supplier.		
	Firm Commitment	11,000	
	Adjustment to Net Income–Firm Commitment		11,000
	To close Firm Commitment account to Adjustment to Net Income.		

(*Note:* The final entry to close the Firm Commitment to Adjustment to Net Income is made *only* in the period in which Parts Inventory affects net income through Cost of Goods Sold. The Firm Commitment account remains on the books as a liability until that point in time.)

Trial Balance—October 31	Debit	Credit
Cash ($5,200 credit balance + $80,000 credit)	$ –0–	$85,200
Parts inventory (cost of goods sold)	91,000	–0–
Retained earnings, 9/30	1,640	–0–
Gain on foreign currency option	–0–	1,500
Loss on firm commitment	5,060	–0–
Adjustment to net income–firm commitment	–0–	11,000
	$97,700	$97,700

Part F. Option Cash Flow Hedge of a Forecasted Foreign Currency Transaction

8/1	Foreign Currency Option	5,200	
	Cash		5,200
	To record the purchase of a foreign currency option as an asset.		
9/30	Foreign Currency Option	4,300	
	Accumulated Other Comprehensive Income (AOCI)		4,300
	To adjust the fair value of the option from $5,200 to $9,500 with a corresponding adjustment to AOCI.		
	Option Expense	1,700	
	Accumulated Other Comprehensive Income (AOCI)		1,700
	To recognize the change in the time value of the foreign currency option as an expense with a corresponding credit to AOCI.		

Trial Balance—September 30	Debit	Credit
Cash	$ -0-	$ 5,200
Foreign currency option (asset)	9,500	-0-
Accumulated other comprehensive income	-0-	6,000
Option expense	1,700	-0-
	$11,200	$11,200

		Debit	Credit
10/31	Foreign Currency Option	1,500	
	Accumulated Other Comprehensive Income (AOCI)		1,500
	To adjust the fair value of the option from $9,500 to $11,000 with a corresponding adjustment to AOCI.		
	Option Expense	3,500	
	Accumulated Other Comprehensive Income (AOCI)		3,500
	To recognize the change in the time value of the foreign currency option as an expense with a corresponding credit to AOCI.		
	Foreign Currency (Mexican pesos)	91,000	
	Cash		80,000
	Foreign Currency Option		11,000
	To record exercise of the foreign currency option: Record payment of $80,000 in exchange for 1 million pesos, record the receipt of 1 million pesos as an asset at the spot rate of $0.091, and remove the option from the accounts.		
	Parts Inventory	91,000	
	Foreign Currency (Mexican pesos)		91,000
	To record the purchase of parts through the payment of 1 million pesos to the Mexican supplier.		
	Accumulated Other Comprehensive Income (AOCI)	11,000	
	Adjustment to Net Income–Forecasted Transaction		11,000
	To close AOCI as an adjustment to net income.		

(*Note:* The final entry to close AOCI to Adjustment to Net Income is made at the date that the forecasted transaction was expected to occur, regardless of when the parts inventory affects net income.)

Trial Balance—October 31	Debit	Credit
Cash ($5,200 credit balance + $80,000 credit)	$ -0-	$85,200
Parts inventory (cost of goods sold)	91,000	-0-
Retained earnings, 9/30	1,700	-0-
Foreign currency option expense	3,500	-0-
Adjustment to net income–forecasted transaction	-0-	11,000
	$96,200	$96,200

Questions

1. What concept underlies the two-transaction perspective in accounting for foreign currency transactions?
2. A company makes an export sale denominated in a foreign currency and allows the customer one month to pay. Under the two-transaction perspective, accrual approach, how does the company account for fluctuations in the exchange rate for the foreign currency?
3. What factors create a foreign exchange gain on a foreign currency transaction? What factors create a foreign exchange loss?
4. In what way is the accounting for a foreign currency borrowing more complicated than the accounting for a foreign currency account payable?
5. What does the term *hedging* mean? Why do companies elect to follow this strategy?
6. How does a foreign currency option differ from a foreign currency forward contract?
7. How does the timing of hedges of (*a*) foreign currency denominated assets and liabilities, (*b*) foreign currency firm commitments, and (*c*) forecasted foreign currency transactions differ?

8. Why would a company prefer a foreign currency option over a forward contract in hedging a foreign currency firm commitment? Why would a company prefer a forward contract over an option in hedging a foreign currency asset or liability?
9. How do companies report foreign currency derivatives, such as forward contracts and options, on the balance sheet?
10. How does a company determine the fair value of a foreign currency forward contract? How does it determine the fair value of an option?
11. What is hedge accounting?
12. Under what conditions can companies use hedge accounting to account for a foreign currency option used to hedge a forecasted foreign currency transaction?
13. What are the differences in accounting for a forward contract used as *(a)* a cash flow hedge and *(b)* a fair value hedge of a foreign currency denominated asset or liability?
14. What are the differences in accounting for a forward contract used as a fair value hedge of *(a)* a foreign currency denominated asset or liability and *(b)* a foreign currency firm commitment?
15. What are the differences in accounting for a forward contract used as a cash flow hedge of *(a)* a foreign currency denominated asset or liability and *(b)* a forecasted foreign currency transaction?
16. How are changes in the fair value of an option accounted for in a cash flow hedge? In a fair value hedge?

Problems

LO 9-1

1. Which of the following combinations correctly describes the relationship between foreign currency transactions, exchange rate changes, and foreign exchange gains and losses?

Type of Transaction	Foreign Currency	Foreign Exchange Gain or Loss
a. Export sale	Appreciates	Loss
b. Import purchase	Appreciates	Gain
c. Import purchase	Depreciates	Gain
d. Export sale	Depreciates	Gain

LO 9-2

2. In accounting for foreign currency transactions, which of the following approaches is used in the United States?
   a. One-transaction perspective; accrue foreign exchange gains and losses.
   b. One-transaction perspective; defer foreign exchange gains and losses.
   c. Two-transaction perspective; defer foreign exchange gains and losses.
   d. Two-transaction perspective; accrue foreign exchange gains and losses.

LO 9-2

3. On October 1, 2017, Tile Co., a U.S. company, purchased products from Azulejo, a Portuguese company, with payment due on December 1, 2017. If Tile's 2017 operating income included no foreign exchange gain or loss, the transaction could have
   a. Been denominated in U.S. dollars.
   b. Resulted in an unusual gain.
   c. Generated a foreign exchange gain to be reported as a deferred charge on the balance sheet.
   d. Generated a foreign exchange loss to be reported as a separate component of stockholders' equity.

LO 9-2

4. Brief, Inc., had a receivable from a foreign customer that is payable in the customer's local currency. On December 31, 2017, Brief correctly included this receivable for 200,000 local currency units (LCU) in its balance sheet at $110,000. When Brief collected the receivable on February 15, 2018, the U.S. dollar equivalent was $120,000. In Brief's 2018 consolidated income statement, how much should it report as a foreign exchange gain?
   a. $-0-
   b. $10,000
   c. $15,000
   d. $25,000

LO 9-2, 9-3

5. On July 1, 2017, Mifflin Company borrowed 200,000 euros from a foreign lender evidenced by an interest-bearing note due on July 1, 2018. The note is denominated in euros. The U.S. dollar equivalent of the note principal is as follows:

Date	Amount
July 1, 2017 (date borrowed)	$225,000
December 31, 2017 (Mifflin's year-end)	220,000
July 1, 2018 (date repaid)	210,000

In its 2018 income statement, what amount should Mifflin include as a foreign exchange gain or loss on the note?

a. $15,000 gain
b. $15,000 loss
c. $10,000 gain
d. $10,000 loss

LO 9-1, 9-2

6. Grace Co. had a Chinese yuan payable resulting from imports from China and a Mexican peso receivable resulting from exports to Mexico. Grace recorded foreign exchange losses related to both its yuan payable and peso receivable. Did the foreign currencies increase or decrease in dollar value from the date of the transaction to the settlement date?

Yuan	Peso
a. Increase	Increase
b. Increase	Decrease
c. Decrease	Increase
d. Decrease	Decrease

LO 9-2, 9-3

7. Matthias Corp. had the following foreign currency transactions during 2017:
   - Purchased merchandise from a foreign supplier on January 20 for the U.S. dollar equivalent of $60,000 and paid the invoice on April 20 at the U.S. dollar equivalent of $50,000.
   - On September 1, borrowed the U.S. dollar equivalent of $300,000 evidenced by a note that is payable in the lender's local currency in one year. On December 31, the U.S. dollar equivalent of the principal amount was $320,000.

In Matthias's 2017 income statement, what amount should be included as a net foreign exchange gain or loss?

a. $10,000 gain
b. $10,000 loss
c. $20,000 gain
d. $30,000 loss

LO 9-7

8. A U.S. exporter has a Thai baht account receivable resulting from an export sale on June 1 to a customer in Thailand. The exporter signed a forward contract on June 1 to sell Thai baht and designated it as a cash flow hedge of a recognized Thai baht receivable. The spot rate was $0.022 on that date, and the forward rate was $0.021. Which of the following did the U.S. exporter report in net income?

a. Discount expense
b. Discount revenue
c. Premium expense
d. Premium revenue

LO 9-8

9. St. Philip Company ordered parts costing €100,000 from a foreign supplier on January 15 when the spot rate was $0.20 per €. A one-month forward contract was signed on that date to purchase €100,000 at a forward rate of $0.23. The forward contract is properly designated as a fair value hedge of the €100,000 firm commitment. On February 15, when the company receives the parts, the spot rate is $0.22. At what amount should St. Philip Company carry the parts inventory on its books?

a. $20,000
b. $21,000
c. $22,000
d. $23,000

LO 9-5

10. On December 1, 2017, Ringling Company (a U.S.-based company) entered into a three-month forward contract to purchase 1,000,000 pesos on March 1, 2018. The following U.S. dollar per peso exchange rates apply:

Date	Spot Rate	Forward Rate (to March 1, 2018)
December 1, 2017	$0.044	$0.047
December 31, 2017	0.046	0.049
March 1, 2018	0.050	N/A

Ringling's incremental borrowing rate is 12 percent. The present value factor for two months at an annual interest rate of 12 percent (1 percent per month) is 0.9803.

Which of the following correctly describes the manner in which Ringling Company will report the forward contract on its December 31, 2017, balance sheet?

a. As an asset in the amount of $1,960.60.

b. As an asset in the amount of $2,940.90.

c. As a liability in the amount of $980.30.

d. As a liability in the amount of $2,940.90.

Use the following information for Problems 11 and 12.

MNC Corp. (a U.S.-based company) sold parts to a South Korean customer on December 1, 2017, with payment of 10 million South Korean won to be received on March 31, 2018. The following exchange rates apply:

Date	Spot Rate	Forward Rate (to March 31, 2018)
December 1, 2017	$0.0035	$0.0034
December 31, 2017	0.0033	0.0032
March 31, 2018	0.0038	N/A

MNC's incremental borrowing rate is 12 percent. The present value factor for three months at an annual interest rate of 12 percent (1 percent per month) is 0.9706.

LO 9-2

11. Assuming that MNC did not enter into a forward contract, how much foreign exchange gain or loss should it report on its 2017 income statement with regard to this transaction?

a. $5,000 gain

b. $3,000 gain

c. $2,000 loss

d. $1,000 loss

LO 9-7

12. Assuming that MNC entered into a forward contract to sell 10 million South Korean won on December 1, 2017, as a fair value hedge of a foreign currency receivable, what is the net impact on its net income in 2017 resulting from a fluctuation in the value of the won?

a. No impact on net income.

b. $58.80 decrease in net income.

c. $2,000 decrease in net income.

d. $1,941.20 increase in net income.

LO 9-9

13. On March 1, Pimlico Corporation (a U.S.-based company) expects to order merchandise from a supplier in Sweden in three months. On March 1, when the spot rate is $0.10 per Swedish krona, Pimlico enters into a forward contract to purchase 500,000 Swedish kroner at a three-month forward rate of $0.12. At the end of three months, when the spot rate is $0.115 per Swedish krona, Pimlico orders and receives the merchandise, paying 500,000 kroner. What amount does Pimlico report in net income as a result of this cash flow hedge of a forecasted transaction?

a. $10,000 premium expense plus a $7,500 positive adjustment to net income when the merchandise is purchased.

b. $10,000 Discount expense plus a $5,000 positive adjustment to net income when the merchandise is purchased.

c. $2,500 premium expense plus a $5,000 negative adjustment to net income when the merchandise is purchased.

d. $2,500 premium expense plus a $2,500 positive adjustment to net income when the merchandise is purchased.

LO 9-9

14. Torres Corporation (a U.S.-based company) expects to order goods from a foreign supplier at a price of 100,000 pounds, with delivery and payment to be made on September 20. On July 20, Torres purchased a two-month call option on 100,000 pounds and designated this option as a cash flow hedge of a forecasted foreign currency transaction. The option has a strike price of $1.25 per pound and costs $600. The spot rate for pounds is $1.25 on June 20 and $1.30 on September 20. What amount will Torres Corporation report as an option expense in net income for the quarter ended September 30?

a. $300

b. $600

c. $2,000

d. $5,000

Use the following information for Problems 15 through 17.

On September 1, 2017, Jensen Company received an order to sell a machine to a customer in Canada at a price of 100,000 Canadian dollars. Jensen shipped the machine and received payment on March 1, 2018. On September 1, 2017, Jensen purchased a put option giving it the right to sell 100,000 Canadian dollars on March 1, 2018, at a price of $80,000. Jensen properly designated the option as a fair value hedge of the Canadian dollar firm commitment. The option cost $2,000 and had a fair value of $2,300 on December 31, 2017. The fair value of the firm commitment was measured by referring to changes in the spot rate. The following spot exchange rates apply:

Date	U.S. Dollar per Canadian Dollar
September 1, 2017	$0.80
December 31, 2017	0.79
March 1, 2018	0.77

Jensen Company's incremental borrowing rate is 12 percent. The present value factor for two months at an annual interest rate of 12 percent (1 percent per month) is 0.9803.

LO 9-8

15. What was the net impact on Jensen Company's 2017 income as a result of this fair value hedge of a firm commitment?

a. $–0–.

b. $680.30 decrease in income.

c. $300 increase in income.

d. $980.30 increase in income.

LO 9-8

16. What was the net impact on Jensen Company's 2018 income as a result of this fair value hedge of a firm commitment?

a. $–0–.

b. $1,319.70 decrease in income.

c. $77,980.30 increase in income.

d. $78,680.30 increase in income.

LO 9-8

17. What was the net increase or decrease in cash flow from having purchased the foreign currency option to hedge this exposure to foreign exchange risk?

a. $–0–.

b. $1,000 increase in cash flow.

c. $1,500 decrease in cash flow.

d. $3,000 increase in cash flow.

Use the following information for Problems 18 through 20.

On June 1, 2017, Micro Corp. received an order for parts from a Mexican customer at a price of 1,000,000 Mexican pesos with a delivery date of July 31, 2017. On June 1, when the U.S. dollar–Mexican peso spot rate is $0.115, Micro Corp. entered into a two-month forward contract to sell 1,000,000 pesos at a forward rate of $0.12 per peso. Micro designates the forward contract as a fair value hedge of the firm commitment to receive pesos, and the fair value of the firm commitment is measured by referring to changes in the peso forward rate. Micro delivers the parts and receives payment on July 31, 2017, when the peso spot rate is $0.118. On June 30, 2017, the Mexican peso spot rate is $0.123, and the forward contract has a fair value of $2,400.

LO 9-8

18. What is the net impact on Micro's net income for the quarter ended June 30, 2017, as a result of this forward contract hedge of a firm commitment?
    a. $–0–.
    b. $2,400 increase in net income.
    c. $4,000 decrease in net income.
    d. $8,000 increase in net income.

LO 9-8

19. What is the net impact on Micro's net income for the quarter ended September 30, 2017, as a result of this forward contract hedge of a firm commitment?
    a. $–0–.
    b. $115,000 increase in net income.
    c. $118,000 increase in net income.
    d. $120,000 increase in net income.

LO 9-8

20. What is Micro's net increase or decrease in cash flow from having entered into this forward contract hedge?
    a. $–0–.
    b. $1,000 increase in cash flow.
    c. $1,500 decrease in cash flow.
    d. $2,000 increase in cash flow.

Use the following information for Problems 21 and 22.
On November 1, 2017, Dos Santos Company forecasts the purchase of raw materials from a Brazilian supplier on February 1, 2018, at a price of 200,000 Brazilian reals. On November 1, 2017, Dos Santos pays $1,500 for a three-month call option on 200,000 reals with a strike price of $0.40 per real. Dos Santos properly designates the option as a cash flow hedge of a forecasted foreign currency transaction. On December 31, 2017, the option has a fair value of $1,100. The following spot exchange rates apply:

Date	U.S. Dollar per Brazilian Real
November 1, 2017	$0.40
December 31, 2017	0.38
February 1, 2018	0.41

LO 9-9

21. What is the net impact on Dos Santos Company's 2017 net income as a result of this hedge of a forecasted foreign currency transaction?
    a. $–0–.
    b. $400 decrease in net income.
    c. $1,000 decrease in net income.
    d. $1,400 decrease in net income.

LO 9-9

22. What is the net impact on Dos Santos Company's 2018 net income as a result of this hedge of a forecasted foreign currency transaction? Assume that the raw materials are consumed and become a part of the cost of goods sold in 2018.
    a. $80,000 decrease in net income.
    b. $80,600 decrease in net income.
    c. $81,100 decrease in net income.
    d. $83,100 decrease in net income.

LO 9-2

23. Turbo Corporation (a U.S.-based company) acquired merchandise on account from a foreign supplier on November 1, 2017, for 100,000 markkas. It paid the foreign currency account payable on January 17, 2018. The following exchange rates for 1 markka are known:

November 1, 2017	$0.754
December 31, 2017	0.742
January 15, 2018	0.747

a. How does the fluctuation in exchange rates affect Turbo's 2017 income statement?

b. How does the fluctuation in exchange rates affect Turbo's 2018 income statement?

LO 9-2

24. On December 20, 2017, Butanta Company (a U.S. company headquartered in Miami, Florida) sold parts to a foreign customer at a price of 50,000 ostras. Payment is received on January 10, 2018. Currency exchange rates for 1 ostra are as follows:

December 20, 2017	$1.05
December 31, 2017	1.02
January 10, 2018	0.98

a. How does the fluctuation in exchange rates affect Butanta's 2017 income statement?

b. How does the fluctuation in exchange rates affect Butanta's 2018 income statement?

LO 9-2

25. Peerless Corporation (a U.S. company) made a sale to a foreign customer on September 15, for 100,000 crowns. It received payment on October 15. The following exchange rates for 1 crown apply:

September 15	$0.60
September 30	0.66
October 15	0.62

Prepare all journal entries for Peerless in connection with this sale, assuming that the company closes its books on September 30 to prepare interim financial statements.

LO 9-2

26. On December 15, 2017, Lisbeth Inc. (a U.S. company) purchases merchandise inventory from a foreign supplier for 50,000 schillings. Lisbeth agrees to pay in 45 days after it sells the merchandise. Lisbeth makes sales rather quickly and pays the entire obligation on January 25, 2018. Currency exchange rates for 1 schilling are as follows:

December 15, 2017	$0.28
December 31, 2017	0.30
January 25, 2018	0.33
January 31, 2018	0.34

Prepare all journal entries for Lisbeth Company in connection with this purchase and payment.

LO 9-2

27. Voltac Corporation (a U.S. company located in Charlotte, North Carolina) has the following import/export transactions denominated in Mexican pesos in 2017:

March 1	Bought inventory costing 100,000 pesos on credit.
May 1	Sold 60 percent of the inventory for 80,000 pesos on credit.
August 1	Collected 70,000 pesos from customers.
September 1	Paid 60,000 pesos to suppliers.

Currency exchange rates for 1 peso for 2017 are as follows:

March 1	$0.10
May 1	0.12
August 1	0.13
September 1	0.14
December 31	0.15

For each of the following accounts, how much will Voltac report on its 2017 financial statements?

a. Inventory.

b. Cost of Goods Sold.

c. Sales.

d. Accounts Receivable.

e. Accounts Payable.

f. Cash.

LO 9-3

28. On April 1, 2017, Mendoza Company borrowed 500,000 euros for one year at an interest rate of 5 percent per annum. Mendoza must make its first interest payment on the loan on October 1, 2017, and will make a second interest payment on March 31, 2018, when the loan is repaid. Mendoza prepares U.S.-dollar financial statements and has a December 31 year-end. Prepare all journal entries related to this foreign currency borrowing assuming the following exchange rates for 1 euro:

April 1, 2017	$1.10
October 1, 2017	1.20
December 31, 2017	1.24
March 31, 2018	1.28

LO 9-2

29. Benjamin, Inc., operates an export/import business. The company has considerable dealings with companies in the country of Camerrand. The denomination of all transactions with these companies is alaries (AL), the Camerrand currency. During 2017, Benjamin acquires 20,000 widgets at a price of 8 alaries per widget. It will pay for them when it sells them. Currency exchange rates for 1 AL are as follows:

September 1, 2017	$0.46
December 1, 2017	0.44
December 31, 2017	0.48
March 1, 2018	0.45

a. Assume that Benjamin acquired the widgets on December 1, 2017, and made payment on March 1, 2018. What is the effect of the exchange rate fluctuations on reported income in 2017 and in 2018?

b. Assume that Benjamin acquired the widgets on September 1, 2017, and made payment on December 1, 2017. What is the effect of the exchange rate fluctuations on reported income in 2017?

c. Assume that Benjamin acquired the widgets on September 1, 2017, and made payment on March 1, 2018. What is the effect of the exchange rate fluctuations on reported income in 2017 and in 2018?

LO 9-3

30. On September 30, 2017, Ericson Company negotiated a two-year, 1,000,000 dudek loan from a foreign bank at an interest rate of 2 percent per year. It makes interest payments annually on September 30 and will repay the principal on September 30, 2019. Ericson prepares U.S.-dollar financial statements and has a December 31 year-end.

a. Prepare all journal entries related to this foreign currency borrowing assuming the following exchange rates for 1 dudek:

September 30, 2017	$0.100
December 31, 2017	0.105
September 30, 2018	0.120
December 31, 2018	0.125
September 30, 2019	0.150

b. Taking the exchange rate effect on the cost of borrowing into consideration, determine the effective interest rate in dollars on the loan in each of the three years 2017, 2018, and 2019.

LO 9-7

31. Brandlin Company of Anaheim, California, sells parts to a foreign customer on December 1, 2017, with payment of 16,000 korunas to be received on March 1, 2018. Brandlin enters into a forward

contract on December 1, 2017, to sell 16,000 korunas on March 1, 2018. Relevant exchange rates for the koruna on various dates are as follows:

Date	Spot Rate	Forward Rate (to March 1, 2018)
December 1, 2017	$2.70	$2.775
December 31, 2017	2.80	2.900
March 1, 2018	2.95	N/A

Brandlin's incremental borrowing rate is 12 percent. The present value factor for two months at an annual interest rate of 12 percent (1 percent per month) is 0.9803. Brandlin must close its books and prepare financial statements at December 31.

a. Assuming that Brandlin designates the forward contract as a cash flow hedge of a foreign currency receivable and recognizes any premium or discount using the straight-line method, prepare journal entries for these transactions in U.S. dollars. What is the impact on 2017 net income? What is the impact on 2018 net income? What is the impact on net income over the two accounting periods?

b. Assuming that Brandlin designates the forward contract as a fair value hedge of a foreign currency receivable, prepare journal entries for these transactions in U.S. dollars. What is the impact on 2017 net income? What is the impact on 2018 net income? What is the impact on net income over the two accounting periods?

LO 9-7

32. Use the same facts as in Problem 31 except that Brandlin Company purchases materials from a foreign supplier on December 1, 2017, with payment of 16,000 korunas to be made on March 1, 2018. The materials are consumed immediately and recognized as cost of goods sold at the date of purchase. On December 1, 2017, Brandlin enters into a forward contract to purchase 16,000 korunas on March 1, 2018.

a. Assuming that Brandlin designates the forward contract as a cash flow hedge of a foreign currency payable and recognizes any premium or discount using the straight-line method, prepare journal entries for these transactions in U.S. dollars. What is the impact on 2017 net income? What is the impact on 2018 net income? What is the impact on net income over the two accounting periods?

b. Assuming that Brandlin designates the forward contract as a fair value hedge of a foreign currency payable, prepare journal entries for these transactions in U.S. dollars. What is the impact on net income in 2017 and in 2018? What is the impact on net income over the two accounting periods?

LO 9-7

33. On June 1, Alexander Corporation sold goods to a foreign customer at a price of 1,000,000 pesos and will receive payment in three months on September 1. On June 1, Alexander acquired an option to sell 1,000,000 pesos in three months at a strike price of $0.062. Relevant exchange rates and option premiums for the peso are as follows:

Date	Spot Rate	Put Option Premium for September 1 (strike price $0.062)
June 1	$0.062	$0.0025
June 30	0.066	0.0018
September 1	0.061	N/A

Alexander must close its books and prepare its second-quarter financial statements on June 30.

a. Assuming that Alexander designates the foreign currency option as a cash flow hedge of a foreign currency receivable, prepare journal entries for these transactions in U.S. dollars. What is the impact on net income over the two accounting periods?

b. Assuming that Alexander designates the foreign currency option as a fair value hedge of a foreign currency receivable, prepare journal entries for these transactions in U.S. dollars. What is the impact on net income over the two accounting periods?

LO 9-7

34. On June 1, Cairns Corporation purchased goods from a foreign supplier at a price of 1,000,000 francs and will make payment in three months on September 1. On June 1, Cairns acquired an

option to purchase 1,000,000 francs in three months at a strike price of $0.852. Relevant exchange rates and option premiums for the franc are as follows:

Date	Spot Rate	Call Option Premium for September 1 (strike price $0.852)
June 1	$0.852	$0.002
June 30	0.858	0.007
September 1	0.872	N/A

Cairns must close its books and prepare its second-quarter financial statements on June 30.

a. Assuming that Cairns designates the foreign currency option as a cash flow hedge of a foreign currency payable, prepare journal entries for these transactions in U.S. dollars. What is the impact on net income over the two accounting periods?

b. Assuming that Cairns designates the foreign currency option as a fair value hedge of a foreign currency payable, prepare journal entries for these transactions in U.S. dollars. What is the impact on net income over the two accounting periods?

LO 9-7

35. On November 1, 2017, Bernard Company (a U.S.-based company) sold merchandise to a foreign customer for 100,000 FCUs with payment to be received on April 30, 2018. At the date of sale, Bernard entered into a six-month forward contract to sell 100,000 FCUs. The company properly designates the forward contract as a cash flow hedge of a foreign currency receivable. The following exchange rates apply:

Date	Spot Rate	Forward Rate (to April 30, 2018)
November 1, 2017	$0.21	$0.20
December 31, 2017	0.19	0.17
April 30, 2018	0.18	N/A

Bernard's incremental borrowing rate is 12 percent. The present value factor for four months at an annual interest rate of 12 percent (1 percent per month) is 0.9610.

a. Prepare all journal entries, including December 31 adjusting entries, to record the sale and forward contract.

b. What is the impact on net income in 2017?

c. What is the impact on net income in 2018?

LO 9-7

36. Eximco Corporation (based in Champaign, Illinois) has a number of transactions with companies in the country of Mongagua, where the currency is the mong. On November 30, 2017, Eximco sold equipment at a price of 500,000 mongs to a Mongaguan customer that will make payment on January 31, 2018. In addition, on November 30, 2017, Eximco purchased raw materials from a Mongaguan supplier at a price of 300,000 mongs; it will make payment on January 31, 2018. To hedge its net exposure in mongs, Eximco entered into a two-month forward contract on November 30, 2017, to deliver 200,000 mongs to the foreign currency broker in exchange for $104,000. Eximco properly designates its forward contract as a fair value hedge of a foreign currency receivable. The following rates for the mong apply:

Date	Spot Rate	Forward Rate (to January 31, 2018)
November 30, 2017	$0.53	$0.52
December 31, 2017	0.50	0.48
January 31, 2018	0.49	N/A

Eximco's incremental borrowing rate is 12 percent. The present value factor for one month at an annual interest rate of 12 percent (1 percent per month) is 0.9901.

a. Prepare all journal entries, including December 31 adjusting entries, to record these transactions and the forward contract.

b. What is the impact on net income in 2017?

c. What is the impact on net income in 2018?

LO 9-7, 9-8

37. On October 1, 2017, Sharp Company (based in Denver, Colorado) entered into a forward contract to sell 100,000 rubles in four months (on January 31, 2018) and receive $39,000 in U.S. dollars. Exchange rates for the ruble follow:

Date	Spot Rate	Forward Rate (to January 31, 2018)
October 1, 2017	$0.35	$0.39
December 31, 2017	0.38	0.41
January 31, 2018	0.40	N/A

Sharp's incremental borrowing rate is 12 percent. The present value factor for one month at an annual interest rate of 12 percent (1 percent per month) is 0.9901. Sharp must close its books and prepare financial statements on December 31.

a. Prepare journal entries, assuming that Sharp entered into the forward contract as a fair value hedge of a 100,000 ruble receivable arising from a sale made on October 1, 2017. Include entries for both the sale and the forward contract.

b. Prepare journal entries, assuming that Sharp entered into the forward contract as a fair value hedge of a firm commitment related to a 100,000 ruble sale that will be made on January 31, 2018. Include entries for both the firm commitment and the forward contract. The fair value of the firm commitment is measured by referring to changes in the forward rate.

LO 9-8

38. On August 1, Ling-Harvey Corporation (a U.S.-based importer) placed an order to purchase merchandise from a foreign supplier at a price of 400,000 ringgits. Ling-Harvey will receive and make payment for the merchandise in three months on October 31. On August 1, Ling-Harvey entered into a forward contract to purchase 400,000 ringgits in three months at a forward rate of $0.60. It properly designates the forward contract as a fair value hedge of a foreign currency firm commitment. The fair value of the firm commitment is measured by referring to changes in the forward rate. Relevant exchange rates for the ringgit are as follows:

Date	Spot Rate	Forward Rate (to October 31)
August 1	$0.60	$0.60
September 30	0.63	0.66
October 31	0.68	N/A

Ling-Harvey's incremental borrowing rate is 12 percent. The present value factor for one month at an annual interest rate of 12 percent (1 percent per month) is 0.9901. Ling-Harvey must close its books and prepare its third-quarter financial statements on September 30.

a. Prepare journal entries for the forward contract and firm commitment through October 31.

b. Assuming the inventory is sold in the fourth quarter, what is the impact on net income over the two accounting periods?

c. What net cash outflow results from the purchase of merchandise from the foreign supplier?

LO 9-8

39. On June 1, Vandervelde Corporation (a U.S.-based manufacturing firm) received an order to sell goods to a foreign customer at a price of 100,000 leks. Vandervelde will ship the goods and receive payment in three months on September 1. On June 1, Vandervelde purchased an option to sell 100,000 leks in three months at a strike price of $1.00. It properly designated the option as a fair value hedge of a foreign currency firm commitment. The fair value of the firm commitment is measured by referring to changes in the spot rate. Relevant exchange rates and option premiums for the lek are as follows:

Date	Spot Rate	Put Option Premium for September 1 (strike price $1.00)
June 1	$1.00	$0.020
June 30	0.94	0.028
September 1	0.88	N/A

Vandervelde's incremental borrowing rate is 12 percent. The present value factor for two months at an annual interest rate of 12 percent (1 percent per month) is 0.9803. Vandervelde Corporation must close its books and prepare its second-quarter financial statements on June 30.

a. Prepare journal entries for the foreign currency option and firm commitment.

b. What is the impact on net income over the two accounting periods?

c. What is the net cash inflow resulting from the sale of goods to the foreign customer?

LO 9-8

40. Spitz Company ordered merchandise from a foreign supplier on November 20 at a price of 100,000 forints when the spot rate was $0.50 per forint. Delivery and payment were scheduled for December 20. On November 20, Spitz acquired a call option on 100,000 forints at a strike price of $0.50, paying a premium of $0.01 per forint. It designates the option as a fair value hedge of a foreign currency firm commitment. The fair value of the firm commitment is measured by referring to changes in the spot rate. The merchandise arrives and Spitz makes payment according to schedule. Spitz sells the merchandise by December 31, when it closes its books.

a. Assuming a spot rate of $0.53 per forint on December 20, prepare all journal entries to account for the foreign currency option, foreign currency firm commitment, and purchase of inventory.

b. Assuming a spot rate of $0.48 per forint on December 20, prepare all journal entries to account for the foreign currency option, foreign currency firm commitment, and purchase of inventory.

LO 9-9

41. Based on past experience, Leickner Company expects to purchase raw materials from a foreign supplier at a cost of 1,000,000 marks on March 15, 2018. To hedge this forecasted transaction, the company acquires a three-month call option to purchase 1,000,000 marks on December 15, 2017. Leickner selects a strike price of $0.58 per mark, paying a premium of $0.005 per unit, when the spot rate is $0.58. The spot rate increases to $0.584 at December 31, 2017, causing the fair value of the option to increase to $8,000. By March 15, 2018, when the raw materials are purchased, the spot rate has climbed to $0.59, resulting in a fair value for the option of $10,000.

a. Prepare all journal entries for the option hedge of a forecasted transaction and for the purchase of raw materials, assuming that December 31 is Leickner's year-end and that the raw materials are included in the cost of goods sold in 2018.

b. What is the overall impact on net income over the two accounting periods?

c. What is the net cash outflow to acquire the raw materials?

LO 9-7, 9-7, 9-8

42. Vino Veritas Company, a U.S.-based importer of wines and spirits, placed an order with a French supplier for 1,000 cases of wine at a price of 200 euros per case. The total purchase price is 200,000 euros. Relevant exchange rates for the euro are as follows:

Date	Spot Rate	Forward Rate to October 31	Call Option Premium for October 31 (strike price $1.00)
September 15	$1.00	$1.06	$0.035
September 30	1.05	1.09	0.070
October 31	1.10	1.10	0.100

Vino Veritas Company has an incremental borrowing rate of 12 percent (1 percent per month) and closes the books and prepares financial statements at September 30.

a. Assume that the wine arrived on September 15, and the company made payment on October 31. There was no attempt to hedge the exposure to foreign exchange risk. Prepare journal entries to account for this import purchase.

b. Assume that the wine arrived on September 15, and the company made payment on October 31. On September 15, Vino Veritas entered into a 45-day forward contract to purchase 200,000 euros. It properly designated the forward contract as a fair value hedge of a foreign currency payable. Prepare journal entries to account for the import purchase and foreign currency forward contract.

c. Vino Veritas ordered the wine on September 15. The wine arrived and the company paid for it on October 31. On September 15, Vino Veritas entered into a 45-day forward contract to purchase 200,000 euros. The company properly designated the forward contract as a fair value hedge of a foreign currency firm commitment. The fair value of the firm commitment is measured by referring to changes in the forward rate. Prepare journal entries to account for the foreign currency forward contract, firm commitment, and import purchase.

d. The wine arrived on September 15, and the company made payment on October 31. On September 15, Vino Veritas purchased a 45-day call option for 200,000 euros. It properly designated the option as a cash flow hedge of a foreign currency payable. Prepare journal entries to account for the import purchase and foreign currency option.

e. The company ordered the wine on September 15. It arrived on October 31, and the company made payment on that date. On September 15, Vino Veritas purchased a 45-day call option for 200,000 euros. It properly designated the option as a fair value hedge of a foreign currency firm commitment. The fair value of the firm commitment is measured by referring to changes in the spot rate. Prepare journal entries to account for the foreign currency option, firm commitment, and import purchase.

Develop Your Skills

RESEARCH CASE—INTERNATIONAL FLAVORS AND FRAGRANCES

CPA skills

Many companies make annual reports available on their corporate web page, often under an Investors tab. Annual reports also can be accessed through the SEC's EDGAR system at www.sec.gov (under Filings, click Company Filings Search, type in Company Name, and under Filing Type, search for 10-K).

Access the most recent annual report for International Flavors and Fragrances (IFF) to complete the following requirements.

Required

1. Identify the location(s) in the annual report where IFF provides disclosures related to its management of foreign exchange risk.
2. Determine the types of hedging instruments the company uses and the types of hedges in which it engages.
3. Determine the manner in which the company discloses the fact that its foreign exchange hedges are effective in offsetting gains and losses on the underlying items being hedged.

ACCOUNTING STANDARDS CASE—FORECASTED TRANSACTIONS

CPA skills

Fergusson Corporation, a U.S. company, manufactures components for the automobile industry. In the past, Fergusson purchased actuators used in its products from a supplier in the United States. The company plans to shift its purchases to a supplier in Portugal. Fergusson's CFO expects to place an order with the Portuguese supplier in the amount of 200,000 euros in three months. In contemplation of this future import, the CFO purchased a euro call option to hedge the cash flow risk that the euro might appreciate against the U.S. dollar over the next three months. The CFO is aware that a foreign currency option used to hedge the cash flow risk associated with a forecasted foreign currency transaction may be designated as a hedge for accounting purposes only if the forecasted transaction is probable. However, he is unsure how he should demonstrate that the anticipated import purchase from Portugal is likely to occur. He wonders whether management's intention to make the purchase is sufficient.

Required

Search current U.S. authoritative accounting literature to determine whether management's intent is sufficient to assess that a forecasted foreign currency transaction is likely to occur. If not, what additional evidence must be considered? Identify the FASB ASC guidance for answering these questions.

EXCEL CASE—DETERMINE FOREIGN EXCHANGE GAINS AND LOSSES

CPA skills

Import/Export Company, a U.S. company, made a number of import purchases and export sales denominated in foreign currency in 2015. Information related to these transactions is summarized in the following table. The company made each purchase or sale on the date in the Transaction Date column and made payment in foreign currency or received payment on the date in the Settlement Date column.

Foreign Currency	Type of Transaction	Amount in Foreign Currency	Transaction Date	Settlement Date
Brazilian real (BRL)	Import purchase	(130,000)	1/10/2015	5/10/2015
Chilean peso (CLP)	Import purchase	(30,000,000)	1/10/2015	5/10/2015
Swiss franc (CHF)	Export sale	50,000	1/10/2015	4/10/2015
Swiss franc (CHF)	Import purchase	(50,000)	4/10/2015	7/10/2015
Euro	Export sale	45,000	1/10/2015	4/10/2015
Euro	Export sale	45,000	4/10/2015	7/10/2015
Chinese yuan (CNY)	Import purchase	(300,000)	1/10/2015	7/10/2015

Required

1. Create an electronic spreadsheet with the information from the preceding table. Label columns as follows:
   Foreign Currency
   Type of Transaction
   Amount in Foreign Currency
   Transaction Date
   Exchange Rate at Transaction Date
   $ Value at Transaction Date
   Settlement Date
   Exchange Rate at Settlement Date
   $ Value at Settlement Date
   Foreign Exchange Gain (Loss)
2. Use historical exchange rate information available on the Internet at www.x-rates.com, Historic Lookup, to find the 2015 exchange rates between the U.S. dollar and each foreign currency on the relevant transaction and settlement dates.
3. Complete the electronic spreadsheet to determine the foreign exchange gain (loss) on each transaction. Determine the total net foreign exchange gain (loss) reported in Import/Export Company's 2015 income statement.
4. Explain why a foreign exchange gain arises for some transactions and a foreign exchange loss occurs for other transactions.

ANALYSIS CASE—CASH FLOW HEDGE

CPA *skills*

On February 1, 2017, Linber Company forecasted the purchase of component parts on May 1, 2017, at a price of 100,000 euros. On that date, Linber entered into a forward contract to purchase 100,000 euros on May 1, 2017. It designated the forward contract as a cash flow hedge of the forecasted transaction. The spot rate for euros on February 1, 2017, was $1 per euro. On May 1, 2017, the forward contract was settled, and the component parts were received and paid for. The parts were consumed in the second quarter of 2017.

Linber's financial statements reported the following amounts related to this cash flow hedge (credit balances in parentheses):

Income Statement	First Quarter 2017	Second Quarter 2017
Premium expense	$4,000	$ 2,000
Cost of goods sold	–0–	103,000
Adjustment to net income	–0–	3,000

Balance Sheet	3/31/17	5/1/17
Forward contract (liability)	$(1,980)*	$ –0–
AOCI (credit)	(2,020)	–0–
Change in cash	–0–	(106,000)

*$2,000 × 0.9901 = $1,980, where 0.9901 is the present value factor for one month at an annual interest rate of 12 percent calculated as 1/1.01.

Required

1. On February 1, 2017, what was the U.S. dollar per euro forward rate to May 1, 2017?
2. On March 31, 2017, what was the U.S. dollar per euro forward rate to May 1, 2017?
3. Was Linber better off or worse off as a result of having entered into this cash flow hedge of a forecasted transaction? By what amount?
4. What does the total premium expense of $6,000 reflect?

INTERNET CASE—HISTORICAL EXCHANGE RATES

CPA skills

The Pier Ten Company, a U.S. company, made credit sales to four customers in Asia on September 15, 2015, and received payment on October 15, 2015. Information related to these sales is as follows:

Customer	Location	Invoice Price
Rama Properties Ltd.	New Delhi	3,319,000 Indian rupees (INR)
Luzon Island Group	Manila	2,337,000 Philippine pesos (PHP)
Mishima Industries Inc.	Tokyo	6,017,000 Japanese yen (JPY)
Melayu Trading Company	Kuala Lumpur	214,800 Malaysian ringgit (MYR)

The Pier Ten Company's fiscal year ends September 30.

Required

1. Use historical exchange rate information available on the Internet at www.x-rates.com, Historical Lookup, to find exchange rates between the U.S. dollar and each foreign currency for September 15, September 30, and October 15, 2015.
2. Determine the foreign exchange gains and losses that Pier Ten would have recognized in net income in the fiscal years ended September 30, 2015, and September 30, 2016, and the overall foreign exchange gain or loss for each transaction. Determine for which transaction, if any, it would have been important for Pier Ten to hedge its foreign exchange risk.
3. Pier Ten could have acquired a one-month put option on September 15, 2015, to hedge the foreign exchange risk associated with each of the four export sales. In each case, the put option would have cost $100 with the strike price equal to the September 15, 2015, spot rate. Determine for which hedges, if any, Pier Ten would have recognized a net gain on the foreign currency option.

COMMUNICATION CASE—FORWARD CONTRACTS AND OPTIONS

CPA skills

Palmetto Bug Extermination Corporation (PBEC), a U.S. company, regularly purchases chemicals from a supplier in Switzerland with the invoice price denominated in Swiss francs. PBEC has experienced several foreign exchange losses in the past year due to increases in the U.S. dollar price of the Swiss currency. As a result, Dewey Nukem, PBEC's CEO, has asked you to investigate the possibility of using derivative financial instruments, specifically foreign currency forward contracts and foreign currency options, to hedge the company's exposure to foreign exchange risk.

Required

Draft a memo to CEO Nukem comparing the advantages and disadvantages of using forward contracts and options to hedge foreign exchange risk. Recommend the type of hedging instrument you believe the company should employ and justify this recommendation.

chapter

12

Financial Reporting and the Securities and Exchange Commission

Learning Objectives

After studying this chapter, you should be able to:

- LO 12-1 Understand the origin and expansive role of the Securities and Exchange Commission.
- LO 12-2 Describe the purpose(s) of various federal securities laws.
- LO 12-3 Understand the Congressional rationale for enacting the Sarbanes–Oxley Act and the responsibilities of the Public Company Accounting Oversight Board.
- LO 12-4 Describe the SEC's role in establishing generally accepted accounting principles (GAAP).
- LO 12-5 Define and describe an issuer's filings with the Securities and Exchange Commission.
- LO 12-6 Describe an issuer's registration process, various forms used by the issuers, and the exemption(s) from registration.

The Securities and Exchange Commission was born on June 6, 1934—a time of despair in the markets. Americans were still suffering from the 1929 market crash after a roaring 1920s when they bought about $50 billion in new securities—half of which turned out to be worthless. Their confidence also was eroded by the 1932 indictment (later acquittal) of Samuel Insull for alleged wrongs in the collapse of his utility "empire," and by the 1933–34 Senate hearings on improper market activity.[1]

The financing of U.S. industry depends on raising vast amounts of capital. During every business day in the United States, many billions of dollars of stocks, bonds, and other securities are sold to thousands of individuals, corporations, trust funds, pension plans, mutual funds, and other investors. Such investors cannot be expected to venture their money without forethought. They have to be able to assess the risks involved: the possibility of either a profit or loss being returned to them as well as the expected amount.

Consequently, disclosure of sufficient, accurate information is absolutely necessary to stimulate the inflow of large quantities of capital. Enough data must be available to encourage investors to consider buying and selling securities in hopes of generating profits. With inadequate or unreliable information on which to base these decisions, investing becomes little more than gambling.

The Work of the Securities and Exchange Commission

In the United States, the responsibility for ensuring that complete and reliable information is available to investors lies with the Securities and Exchange Commission (SEC), an independent agency of the federal government created by the Securities Exchange Act of 1934. Although the SEC's authority applies mainly to publicly held companies, the commission's guidelines and requirements have had a major influence in the United States on the development of all generally accepted accounting principles (GAAP).

[1] The relative size of ownership is most often the key factor in assessing one company's degree of influence over another. However, as discussed later in this chapter, other factors (e.g., contractual relationships between firms) can also provide influence or control over firms regardless of the percentage of shares owned.

LO 12-1

Understand the origin and expansive role of the Securities and Exchange Commission.

As described on the SEC's website:

> The mission of the U.S. Securities and Exchange Commission is to protect investors, maintain fair, orderly, and efficient markets, and facilitate capital formation.
>
> As more and more first-time investors turn to the markets to help secure their futures, pay for homes, and send children to college, our investor protection mission is more compelling than ever.
>
> As our nation's securities exchanges mature into global for-profit competitors, there is even greater need for sound market regulation.
>
> And the common interest of all Americans in a growing economy that produces jobs, improves our standard of living, and protects the value of our savings means that all of the SEC's actions must be taken with an eye toward promoting the capital formation that is necessary to sustain economic growth.
>
> The world of investing is fascinating and complex, and it can be very fruitful. But unlike the banking world, where deposits are guaranteed by the federal government, stocks, bonds and other securities can lose value. There are no guarantees. That's why investing is not a spectator sport. By far the best way for investors to protect the money they put into the securities markets is to do research and ask questions.
>
> The laws and rules that govern the securities industry in the United States derive from a simple and straightforward concept: all investors, whether large institutions or private individuals, should have access to certain basic facts about an investment prior to buying it, and so long as they hold it. To achieve this, the SEC requires public companies to disclose meaningful financial and other information to the public. This provides a common pool of knowledge for all investors to use to judge for themselves whether to buy, sell, or hold a particular security. Only through the steady flow of timely, comprehensive, and accurate information can people make sound investment decisions.[2]

The SEC is headed by five commissioners appointed by the president of the United States (with the consent of the Senate) to serve five-year staggered terms. To ensure the bipartisan nature of this group, no more than three of these individuals can belong to the same political party. The chairman is from the same political party as the president. The commissioners provide leadership for an agency that has grown over the years into an organization with approximately 4,600 employees in 11 regional locations. Despite its importance, the SEC is a relatively small component of the federal government. However, the SEC generates significant fees primarily from issuers, relative to 8–K, 10–K, 10–Q, and registration statement fees. This results in a fully self-funded SEC.

The SEC is composed of five divisions and 23 offices including the following:

- The *Division of Corporation Finance* has responsibility to ensure that publicly held companies meet disclosure requirements. This division reviews registration statements, annual and quarterly filings, proxy materials, annual reports, and tender offers.
- The *Division of Trading and Markets* oversees the securities markets in this country and is responsible for registering and regulating brokerage firms. This division also oversees the Securities Investor Protection Corporation (SIPC), a nonprofit corporation that provides insurance for cash and securities held by customers in member brokerage firms. This insurance protects ("insures") against the failure of the member brokerage firms.
- The *Division of Enforcement* helps to ensure compliance with federal securities laws. This division investigates possible violations of securities laws and recommends appropriate remedies. The most common issues facing this division are insider trading, misrepresentation or omission of important information about securities, manipulation of the market price of a security, and issuance of securities without proper registration. According to the SEC's annual report, 807 investigations of possible violations were initiated in 2015.
- The *Division of Investment Management* oversees the $66.8 trillion investment management industry and administers the securities laws affecting investment companies including mutual funds and investment advisers. This division also interprets laws and regulations for the public and the SEC staff.

[2] The U.S. Securities and Exchange Commission, SEC website, March 2016. Available at www.sec.gov/about/whatwedo.shtml.

- The *Division of Economic and Risk Analysis* assists the SEC in efforts to protect investors, maintain efficient markets, and facilitate capital creation. This Division interacts with every SEC Division and office and provides access to sophisticated economic and risk analysis to help advise and inform policy makers and rule makers.
- The *Office of Information Technology* supports the SEC and its staff in all aspects of information technology. This office operates the Electronic Data Gathering Analysis and Retrieval (EDGAR) system, which electronically receives, processes, and disseminates more than half a million financial statements every year. This office also maintains a very active website that contains a tremendous amount of data about the SEC and the securities industry and free access to EDGAR.[3]
- The *Office of Compliance Inspections and Examinations* determines whether brokers, dealers, and investment companies and advisers comply with federal securities laws. One of the most important goals of this office is the quick and often informal correction of compliance problems.
- The *Office of the Chief Accountant* is the principal adviser to the commission on accounting and auditing matters that arise in connection with the securities laws. The office also works closely with private sector bodies such as the FASB and the AICPA that set various accounting and auditing standards.

This chapter provides an overview of the workings of the Securities and Exchange Commission as well as the agency's relationship to the accounting profession. Because complete examination of the organization is beyond the scope of this textbook, we discuss only a portion of the SEC's extensive functions here. This coverage introduces the role the agency currently plays in the world of U.S. business.

LO 12-2

Describe the purpose(s) of various federal securities laws.

Purpose of the Federal Securities Laws

Before examining the SEC and its various functions in more detail, a historical perspective should be established. The development of laws regulating companies involved in interstate commerce was discussed as early as 1885. In fact, the Industrial Commission created by Congress suggested in 1902 that all publicly held companies should be required to disclose material information including annual financial reports. However, the crisis following the stock market crash of 1929 and the widespread fraud that was subsequently discovered were necessary to prompt Congress to act in hope of reestablishing the trust and stability needed for the capital markets.

> Before the Great Crash of 1929, there was little support for federal regulation of the securities markets. This was particularly true during the post–World War I surge of securities activity. Proposals that the federal government require financial disclosure and prevent the fraudulent sale of stock were never seriously pursued. Tempted by promises of "rags to riches" transformations and easy credit, most investors gave little thought to the systemic risk that arose from widespread abuse of margin financing and unreliable information about the securities in which they were investing. During the 1920s, approximately 20 million large and small shareholders took advantage of post-war prosperity and set out to make their fortunes in the stock market. It is estimated that of the $50 billion in new securities offered during this period, half became worthless. When the stock market crashed in October 1929, the fortunes of countless investors were lost. . . . When the stock market crashed in October 1929, public confidence in the markets plummeted. There was a consensus that for the economy to recover, the public's faith in the capital markets needed to be restored.[4]

As a result, Congress enacted two primary pieces of securities legislation designed to restore investor trust in the capital markets by providing more structure and government oversight:

- The Securities Act of 1933, often referred to as the *truth in securities law,* regulates the initial offering of securities by a company or underwriter.
- The Securities Exchange Act of 1934, which actually created the SEC, regulates the subsequent trading of securities through brokers and exchanges.

[3] www.sec.gov/edgar/searchedgar/webusers.htm.

[4] U.S. Securities and Exchange Commission, SEC website, March 2016. Available at www.sec.gov/about/whatwedo.shtml.

These laws put an end to the legality of many abuses that had been common practices such as the manipulation of stock market prices and the misuse of corporate information by officials and directors (often referred to as *inside parties*[5]) for their own personal gain. Just as important, these two legislative actions were designed to help rebuild public confidence in the capital market system. Because of the large losses suffered during the 1929 market crash and the subsequent depression, many investors had begun to avoid buying stocks, bonds, or other securities.

This reduction in the pool of available capital dramatically compounded the economic problems of the day.

The creation of federal securities laws did not end with the 1933 Act and the 1934 Act. During the decades since the first commissioners were appointed, the SEC has administered rules and regulations created by a number of different congressional actions. Despite the passage of subsequent legislation, this organization's major objectives have remained relatively constant. Over the years, the SEC has attempted to achieve several interconnected goals including

- Ensuring that full and fair information is disclosed to all investors before the securities of a company are allowed to be bought and sold.
- Prohibiting the dissemination of materially misstated information.
- Preventing the misuse of information especially by inside parties.
- Regulating the operation of securities markets such as the New York Stock Exchange and the various over-the-counter exchanges.

In many regards, the SEC's work has been a success. The value of the securities that have been registered as well as the volume of these securities bought and sold each business day is staggering by any standard. Over the decades, the number of individuals and institutions (from both inside and outside the United States) willing to take the risk of making financial investments has grown to incredible numbers. In 2015 alone, more than 4.2 trillion shares were exchanged on just the New York Stock Exchange.[6] However, a cloud has rested over the entire U.S. capital market system. Since the early 2000s when a number of highly publicized corporate scandals shook public confidence in the financial information available for decision-making purposes. Where once most investors appeared to believe in the overall integrity of the stock markets, that faith clearly diminished although the problem did not reach the magnitude seen in the 1930s. This lack of confidence was a drag on the general willingness to invest and, thus, on the economy as a whole.

An unlimited number of reasons can be put forth for these scandals. Some of them are

- Greed by corporate executives.
- Failure in the corporate governance process as practiced by many boards of directors.
- Failure of public accounting firms to apply appropriate quality control measures to ensure independent judgments.
- Shortcomings in promulgated standards used to self-regulate the accounting profession.
- Unreasonable market expectations brought on by years of skyrocketing stock values fueled in part by technology stocks.
- A workload that overburdened the Securities and Exchange Commission, which the relatively small agency could not handle in an adequate fashion.

As a result, on July 30, 2002, President George W. Bush signed the Sarbanes–Oxley Act of 2002. This wide-ranging legislation was designed to end many of the problems that have

[5] *Inside parties* usually are identified as the officers of a company as well as its directors and any owners of more than 10 percent of any class of equity security. An individual's level of ownership is measured by a person's own holdings of equity securities as well as ownership by related parties such as a spouse, minor children, relatives living in the same house as the person in question, or a trust in which the person is the beneficiary.

[6] NYSE website, March 2016. Available at www.nyxdata.com/.

plagued corporate reporting and the securities markets in recent years in the hope of restoring public confidence. This law has had an enormous impact on public accounting as well as the reporting required in connection with the issuance of securities.

In light of additional financial market scandals, Congress passed and President Obama signed the Wall Street Reform and Consumer Protection Act of 2010.[7] This new legislation marks a significant expansion of the federal government's role in regulating corporate governance and provides expanded authority to the SEC to require extensive disclosures concerning corporate compensation.

Full and Fair Disclosure

No responsibility of the SEC is more vital than that of ensuring that a company has disclosed sufficient, reliable information before its stocks, bonds, or other securities are publicly traded. The noted reporting problems that became the scandals at companies such as Enron, WorldCom, Adelphia, and Tyco still draw increased attention to this role.

Unless specifically exempted, all publicly held companies (frequently referred to as *issuers* or *registrants*) must periodically file detailed reports with the SEC. The SEC requires and regulates these filings as a result of a number of laws passed by Congress over the years:

1. *Securities Act of 1933*: Requires the registration of new securities offered for public sale so that potential investors can have adequate information. The act is also intended to prevent deceit and misrepresentation in connection with the sale of securities.[8]
2. *Securities Exchange Act of 1934*: Created the SEC and empowered it to require reporting by publicly owned companies and registration of securities, security exchanges, and certain brokers and dealers. This act prohibits fraudulent and unfair behavior such as sales practice abuses and insider trading.
3. *Public Utility Holding Company Act of 1935*: Requires registration of interstate holding companies of public utilities covered by this law. This act was passed because of abuses in the 1920s in which huge, complex utility empires were created to minimize the need for equity financing.
4. *Trust Indenture Act of 1939*: Requires registration of trust indenture documents and supporting data in connection with the public sale of bonds, debentures, notes, and other debt securities.
5. *Investment Company Act of 1940*: Requires registration of investment companies, including mutual funds, that engage in investing and trading in securities. This act is designed in part to minimize conflicts of interest that arise with fund management.
6. *Investment Advisers Act of 1940* and *Securities Investor Protection Act of 1970*: Require investment advisers to register and to follow certain standards created to protect investors.
7. *Foreign Corrupt Practices Act of 1977*: Affects registration indirectly through amendment to the Securities Exchange Act of 1934. This act requires the maintenance of accounting records and adequate internal accounting controls.
8. *Insider Trading Sanctions Act of 1984* and *Insider Trading and Securities Fraud Enforcement Act of 1988*: Also affect registration indirectly. Increase the penalties against persons who profit from illegal use of inside information and who are associated with market manipulation and securities fraud.
9. *Sarbanes–Oxley Act of 2002*: Designed as an answer to the numerous corporate accounting scandals that came to light in 2001 and 2002. As discussed in a later section of this chapter, this act mandated a number of reforms to bolster corporate responsibility, strengthen disclosure, and combat fraud. It also created the Public Company Accounting Oversight Board (PCAOB) to oversee the accounting profession.

[7] Public Law No. 111–203, 124 stat. 1376 (2010). This statute is commonly referred to as the "Dodd–Frank Act."

[8] Interestingly, one of the provisions originally suggested for this act would have created a federal corps of auditors. The defeat of this proposal (after some debate) has allowed for the rise of the independent auditing profession as it is currently structured in the United States. For more information, see Mark Moran and Gary John Previts, "The SEC and the Profession, 1934–1984: The Realities of Self-Regulation," *Journal of Accountancy*, July 1984.

SEC Requirements

As is obvious from the previous list of statutes, the SEC administers extensive filing requirements. Thus, accountants who specialize in working with the federal securities laws must develop a broad knowledge of a great many reporting rules and regulations. The SEC specifies most of these disclosure requirements in two basic documents, *Regulation S–K* and *Regulation S–X,* which are supplemented by periodic releases and staff bulletins.

Regulation S–K established requirements for all nonfinancial information contained in filings with the SEC. Descriptions of the registrant's business and its securities are just two items covered by these regulations. A partial list of other nonfinancial data to be disclosed includes specified data about the company's directors, officers, and other management; management's discussion and analysis of the current financial condition and the results of operations; and descriptions of both legal proceedings and the company's properties.

Regulation S–X prescribed the form and content of the financial statements (and the accompanying notes and related schedules) included in the various reports filed with the SEC. Thus, before being accepted, all financial information must meet a number of clearly specified requirements established by Regulation S-X.

The SEC's Impact on Financial Reporting to Stockholders

The SEC's disclosure and accounting requirements are not limited to the filings made directly with that body. *Rule 14c–3* of the 1934 Act states that the annual reports of publicly held companies should include financial statements that have been audited. This information (referred to as *proxy information* because it accompanies the management's request to cast votes for absentee stockholders at the annual shareholders meeting) must present balance sheets as of the end of the two most recent fiscal years along with income statements and cash flow statements for the three most recent fiscal years. *Rule 14c–3* also states that additional information, as specified in *Regulation S–K,* should be included in this annual report. The result has been a significant demand for CPAs to provide services as independent auditors.

Over the years, the SEC has moved toward an *integrated disclosure system.* Under this approach, much of the same reported information that the SEC requires must also go to the shareholders. Thus, the overall reporting process is simplified because only a single set of information must be generated in most cases. The integrated disclosure system is also intended as a way to improve the quality of the disclosures received directly by the shareholders.

Information required in proxy statements, which the shareholders receive directly, includes the following:

1. Five-year summary of operations including sales, total assets, income from continuing operations, and cash dividends per share.
2. Description of the business activities including principal products and sources and availability of raw materials.
3. Three-year summary of industry segments, export sales, and foreign and domestic operations.
4. List of company directors and executive officers.
5. Market price of the company's common stock for each quarterly period within the two most recent fiscal years.
6. Any restrictions on the company's ability to continue paying dividends.
7. Management's discussion and analysis of financial condition, changes in financial condition, and results of operations. This discussion should include liquidity, trends and significant events, causes of material changes in the financial statements, and the impact of inflation on the company.

In addition, even prior to passage of the Sarbanes–Oxley Act, the SEC required certain disclosures in proxy statements describing the services provided by the registrant's independent external auditor. This information helped to ensure that true independence was not endangered. Apparently, mere disclosure was not adequate in all cases.

Such disclosure must include the following:

1. All nonaudit services provided by the independent audit firm.
2. A statement as to whether the board of directors (or its audit committee) approved all nonaudit services after considering the possibility that such services might impair the external auditor's independence.
3. The percentage of nonaudit fees to the total annual audit fee. This disclosure helps indicate the importance of the audit work to the firm versus the reward from any other services provided to the registrant.
4. Individual nonaudit fees that are more than 3 percent of the annual audit fee.

LO 12-3

Understand the Congressional rationale for enacting the Sarbanes-Oxley Act and the responsibilities of the Public Company Accounting Oversight Board.

Corporate Accounting Scandals and the Sarbanes–Oxley Act

When William H. Donaldson entered his cavernous corner office on the sixth floor of the Securities and Exchange Commission in 2003, he headed an agency at one of its lowest points since its creation 80 years ago.[9]

Enron's former chairman and chief executive, Kenneth Lay, received $152.7 million in payments and stock in the year leading up to the company's collapse amid revelations that it hid debt and inflated profit for years. Lay's take in 2001 was more than 11,000 times the maximum amount of severance paid to laid-off workers.

Former WorldCom CEO Bernard Ebbers borrowed $408 million from the telecommunications company that had improperly accounted for $9 billion and was forced into bankruptcy. Ebbers had pledged company shares as collateral, but with those shares, once valued at $286 million, worthless, he was said to be considering forgoing his $1.5 million annual pension to help settle the debt.

Adelphia Communications's founder and former CEO, John J. Rigas, allegedly conspired with four other executives to loot the company, leading prosecutors to seek the forfeiture of more than $2.5 billion.[10]

Hardly a day passed during 2002 without a new revelation of corporate wrongdoing. The list of companies whose executives virtually robbed the corporate treasury or whose accounting practices ranged from dubious to outrageous is unfortunately long. Throughout this excruciating disclosure process, many in the investing public began to raise two related questions:

Why didn't the independent auditor stop these practices?

How can the SEC allow such activities to occur?

As indicated previously, a number of theories can suggest the cause of the ethical meltdown during this period, ranging from human greed to inappropriate auditing practices. In truth, as the history of this time continues to unfold, a variety of culprits share the blame for such reprehensible behavior on both the corporate and the individual levels.

Regardless of the reasons, drastic actions had to be taken to reduce or eliminate future abuses (actual and perceived) to begin restoring public confidence in publicly traded entities and their disclosed accounting information. A capitalistic economy needs readily accepted investments, and that is possible only if investors believe they can make wise decisions to buy and sell securities based on the information available. Thus, Congress passed the Sarbanes–Oxley Act in July 2002[11] by a virtually unanimous vote. The scope

[9] Stephen Labaton, "Can a Bloodied S.E.C. Dust Itself Off and Get Moving?" *The New York Times,* December 16, 2002, p. C-2.

[10] Brad Foss, "Unearthing of Corporate Scandals Exposed Market's Vulnerabilities," Associated Press Newswires, December 12, 2002.

[11] Public Law 107–204; 107th Congress, July 30, 2002.

and potential consequences of this legislation are extremely broad; the actual impact will probably not be determined for decades. "The Sarbanes–Oxley Act of 2002 is a major reform package mandating the most far-reaching changes Congress has imposed on the business world since FDR's New Deal."[12]

The act is so wide ranging that this text describes only a general overview of some of the more frequently discussed statutory provisions here.

Creation of the Public Company Accounting Oversight Board

The public accounting profession has long taken pride in its own self-regulation. Through its major professional body, the American Institute of Certified Public Accountants (AICPA), the profession has established and enforced its own code of conduct and, through its Auditing Standards Board (ASB), created its own auditing standards for decades. The maintenance of public trust was often heard as a litany for the creation of such professional guidelines. Unfortunately, self-regulation obviously was not always successful in the public auditing arena. One of the inherent flaws in the system was that the professional body, the AICPA, was considerably smaller than many of the international audit firms that it sought to control. Discipline and conformity are simply difficult to maintain when the students are many times bigger, richer, and more powerful than the principal.

The Sarbanes–Oxley Act created the Public Company Accounting Oversight Board (PCAOB) to oversee auditors of public companies. The creation of the Oversight Board—a governmental board under the control of the SEC—effectively minimizes self-regulation in the accounting profession. The board

- Has five members appointed by the SEC to staggered five-year terms.[13]
- Allows only two members to be accountants, past or present.[14]
- Enforces auditing, quality control, and independence standards and rules.
- Is under the oversight and enforcement authority of the SEC.
- Is funded from fees levied on all publicly traded companies.

These few provisions show that this Oversight Board rather than the accounting profession is now ultimately in charge of regulating public accounting firms whose clients are publicly traded companies. Although the board itself is not a government agency, the SEC has control of it and, thus, is a much more active participant in the work of the independent auditor. For example, the SEC is to pick the five members of the board (after consultation with the chair of the Board of Governors of the Federal Reserve System and the secretary of the U.S. Department of the Treasury). The Act requires the board members to be prominent individuals of integrity and good reputation who must cease all other professional and business activities to help ensure independence and adequate time commitment.

One of the most interesting issues is how the Oversight Board interacts with the Auditing Standards Board to promulgate audit and attestation standards. While the AICPA authorizes the ASB to issue such pronouncements, the mandate of the Sarbanes-Oxley Act requires the Oversight Board to play a significant role in this process. Although directed to cooperate with the accounting profession, the PCAOB has the authority to amend, modify, repeal, or reject any auditing standard.[15] ASB standards, unless later modified or superseded by the PCAOB, are adopted for audits of securities issuers. The Oversight Board has since taken an active role in developing its own pronouncements and many new ASB pronouncements apply only to nonissuers.

[12] Richard I. Miller and Paul H. Pashkoff, "Regulations under the Sarbanes–Oxley Act," *Journal of Accountancy*, October 2002, p. 33.

[13] Sarbanes–Oxley Act of 2002, Sec. 101(e)(1).

[14] Ibid., Sec. 101(e)(2).

[15] Ibid., Sec. 103(a)(1).

Registration of Public Accounting Firms

Registration of public accounting firms is required only of firms that prepare, issue, or participate in preparing an audit report for an issuer—basically an entity that issues securities on a publicly traded exchange. Consequently, virtually all public accounting firms of significant size must register, but most small firms do not need to register. Even foreign firms that play a substantial role in the audit of an organization that has securities registered in the United States must register with the PCAOB and follow the rules of the Sarbanes–Oxley Act. This act has a significant impact on the activities of foreign companies that sell their securities on U.S. markets, an impact not necessarily appreciated outside the United States. "Under the law, CEOs are required to vouch for financial statements, boards must have audit committees drawn from independent directors, and companies can no longer make loans to corporate directors. All of that conflicts with some other countries' rules and customs."[16]

The application process for PCAOB registration provides the Oversight Board a significant amount of information about the audit firms. The firms must identify each of their audit clients that qualifies as an issuer and the Oversight Board then assesses an annual fee on the issuer based on the size of its market capitalization. These fees serve, in part, as the financial support for the work of the Oversight Board.[17]

Other information required of the accounting firms in this application process includes the following:

- A list of all accountants participating in the audit report of any client qualifying as an issuer.
- Annual fees received from each issuer with the amounts separated as to audit and nonaudit services.
- Information about any criminal, civil, or administrative actions pending against the firm or any person associated with the firm.
- Information regarding disagreements between the issuer and the auditing firm during the previous year.

Inspections of Registered Firms

After registration, each audit firm is subject to periodic inspections by the PCAOB. Any firm that audits more than 100 issuers per year will be inspected annually. All other registered firms will be inspected every three years. The Oversight Board has the power to take disciplinary action as a result of the findings of these inspections. In addition, deficiencies can be made public if the firm does not address them in an appropriate fashion within 12 months.

The PCAOB's power is not limited just to reacting to the findings of annual inspections. "The new board has a full range of sanctions at its disposal, including suspension or revocation of registration, censure, and significant fines. It has authority to investigate any act or practice that may violate the act, the new board's rules, the provisions of the federal securities laws relating to audit reports, or applicable professional standards."[18] Clearly, Congress provided the new Oversight Board extensive powers to enable it to clean up any problems discovered in public accounting.

Auditor Independence

One of the most discussed issues surrounding accounting scandals is the failure of audit firms to act independently in dealing with audit clients. Not surprisingly, a significant portion of the Sarbanes-Oxley Act ensures that public accounting firms are, indeed, independent. Certain services that could previously have been provided to an audit client are now forbidden.[19] These

[16] Louis Lavelle and Mike McNamee, "Will Overseas Boards Play by American Rules?" *BusinessWeek*, December 16, 2002, p. 36.

[17] Sarbanes–Oxley Act of 2002, Sec. 102(b)(2).

[18] Miller and Pashkoff, "Regulations under the Sarbanes–Oxley Act," pp. 35 and 36.

[19] Sarbanes–Oxley Act of 2002, Sec. 201.

include financial information system design and implementation as well as internal audit outsourcing. The client's audit committee must preapprove any allowed services and disclose them in reports to the SEC.

Audit committees have long been considered an important element in maintaining an appropriate distance between the external auditors and the management of the client. The committee has been composed of members of the company's board of directors and served as a liaison with the auditors. However, in actual practice, the work and the composition of the audit committee tended to vary greatly from company to company, until the Sarbanes–Oxley Act formalized the liaison role by making the audit committee responsible for the appointment and compensation of the external auditor. To help ensure impartiality, the committee must be made up of individuals who are independent from management. The Act directs the auditor to report to the audit committee rather than to company management. To further ensure independence from management, the lead partner of the audit firm must be rotated off the job after five years.[20]

These provisions, as well as the many other elements of the Sarbanes–Oxley Act, have changed public accounting as it was known in the past. Drastic action was needed and was taken.[21] This Act has strengthened the independent audit to help eliminate the dubious practices that haunted public accounting. Some of these steps may not have been necessary, but the need to reestablish public confidence in the capital market system forced the legislators to avoid any "quick-fix" solutions.

LO 12-4

Describe the SEC's role in establishing generally accepted accounting principles (GAAP).

The SEC's Authority and SEC Filings

The SEC's Authority over Generally Accepted Accounting Principles

The primary focus of the Sarbanes–Oxley Act was on the regulation of independent auditors and auditing standards. Therefore, it had little impact on accounting standards and the registration of securities. Those regulations continue to evolve over time. Because financial reporting standards can be changed merely by amending *Regulation S–X*, the SEC holds the ultimate legal authority for establishing accounting principles for most publicly held companies in this country. In the past, the SEC has usually restricted the application of this power to disclosure issues while looking to the private sector (with the SEC's oversight) to formulate accounting principles. For this reason, the FASB rather than the SEC is generally viewed as the main standards-setting body for financial accounting in the United States. "Under federal law, the SEC has the mandate to determine accounting principles for publicly traded companies. But it has generally ceded that authority to private-sector accounting bodies such as the Financial Accounting Standards Board."[22]

On the accounting side of self-regulation, from its inception, the FASB has been a freestanding organization entirely separate from the AICPA. As we discuss later, the SEC has always had the ability to significantly impact accounting standards. Furthermore, the problems that led to the largest corporate scandals were less about accounting issues and more about audit failures. Some observers, however, contend that the rules-based orientation of U.S. generally accepted accounting principles encourages income manipulation, which also could encourage more investigative activity by the SEC in this area.

However, the SEC does retain the ability to exercise its power with regard to the continuing evolution of accounting principles. The chief accountant of the SEC (described earlier in this chapter) is responsible for providing the commissioners and the commission staff with

[20] Ibid., Sec. 203.

[21] The Sarbanes–Oxley Act, particularly Section 404 requirements, adds a significant cost to reporting operations for public companies. However, the SEC attempted to provide "Section 404 relief" from the "multimillion-dollar expenses," while still ensuring proper disclosure. "Getting It Right," *Journal of Accountancy*, March 2007, p. 29.

[22] Kevin G. Salwen and Robin Goldwyn Blumenthal, "Tackling Accounting, SEC Pushes Changes with Broad Impact," *The Wall Street Journal*, September 27, 1990, p. A1.

advice on all current accounting and auditing matters and helps to draft rules for the form and content of financial statement disclosure and other reporting requirements. Because he or she is the principal adviser to the SEC on all accounting and auditing matters,[23] the most powerful accounting position in the United States is that of chief accountant of the SEC. The work of the chief accountant can lead the SEC to pass amendments as needed to alter various aspects of *Regulation S–X.*

The SEC had issued *Financial Reporting Releases (FRRs)* to supplement *Regulation S–X* and *Regulation S–K.* They explain desired changes in the reporting requirements. By the end of 1998, 50 FRRs had been issued.[24] By 2004 this number was 72. In addition, the staff of the SEC publishes a series of *Staff Accounting Bulletins (SABs)* as a means of informing the financial community of its positions.

> Staff Accounting Bulletins reflect the SEC staff's views regarding accounting-related disclosure practices. They represent interpretations and policies followed by the Division of Corporation Finance and the Office of the Chief Accountant in administering the disclosure requirements of the federal securities laws.

For example, *SAB 101* was released in 1999 to provide guidance in connection with the recognition of revenue. The bulletin first stated that any transaction that fell within the scope of specific authoritative literature (e.g., a FASB statement) should be reported based on that pronouncement. *SAB 101* then established guidelines for revenue recognition situations when authoritative standards were not available. In such cases, a reporting entity should recognize revenue when realized (or realizable) and earned. However, *SAB 101* then went further to establish four criteria for revenue recognition: evidence that an arrangement exists, delivery has occurred or services have been rendered, the price is fixed or can be determined, and collectibility is reasonably assured. To help apply these criteria in actual practice, *SAB 101* included nine examples to show how to judge revenue recognition in such cases as the receipt of money in layaway programs and annual membership fees received by discount retailers.

Additional Disclosure Requirements

Historically, the SEC has restricted the use of its authority (as in *SAB 101*) to the gray areas of accounting for which official guidance is not available. New reporting problems arise each year while no authoritative body has ever completely addressed many other accounting issues, even after years of discussion. As another response to such problems, the SEC often requires the disclosure of additional data if current rules are viewed as insufficient.

> It was in the 1970s that the SEC seemed to single out disclosure as the area in which it would take the standard-setting lead, leaving measurement issues to the FASB. This was when the SEC was expanding the coverage of Management's Discussion & Analysis (MD&A), an extensive narrative disclosure that is required to be appended to the financial statements.[25]

For example, in the early part of 1997, while the FASB worked on a project concerning the accounting for derivatives, the SEC approved rules so that more information would be available immediately. Note disclosure in financial statements had to include more information about accounting policies used. In addition, information about the risk of loss from market rate or price changes inherent in derivatives and other financial instruments was required. By means of these disclosures, the SEC enabled investors to have data about the potential consequences of the company's financial position.

[23] www.sec.gov/about/whatwedo.shtml , March 2016.

[24] From 1937 until 1982, the SEC issued more than 300 *Accounting Series Releases* (ASRs) to (1) amend *Regulation S-X,* (2) express interpretations regarding accounting and auditing issues, and (3) report disciplinary actions against public accountants. The SEC codified the ASRs that dealt with financial reporting matters of continuing interest and issued it as *Financial Reporting Release No. 1.*

[25] Stephen A. Zeff, "A Perspective on the U.S. Public/Private-Sector Approach to the Regulation of Financial Reporting," *Accounting Horizons,* March 1995, pp. 58–59.

Moratorium on Specific Accounting Practices

The commission also can exert its power by declaring a moratorium on the use of specified accounting practices. When authoritative guidance is not present, the SEC can simply prohibit a particular method from being applied. As an example, in the 1980s, companies utilized a variety of procedures to account for internal computer software costs because no official pronouncement had yet been issued. Consequently, the SEC

> imposed a moratorium that will prohibit companies that plan to go public from capitalizing the internal costs of developing computer software for sale or lease or marketed to customers in other ways. . . . The decision doesn't prevent companies currently capitalizing internal software expenses from continuing, but the companies must disclose the effect of not expensing such costs as incurred. The moratorium continues until the Financial Accounting Standards Board issues a standard on the issue.[26]

Two years later when the FASB eventually arrived at a resolution of this question and issued *SFAS 86,* "Accounting for the Costs of Computer Software to Be Sold, Leased, or Otherwise Marketed," the SEC dropped the moratorium. Hence, the FASB set the accounting rule, but the SEC ensured appropriate reporting until that time.

Challenging Individual Statements

As described, officially requiring additional disclosure and prohibiting the application of certain accounting practices are two methods the SEC uses to control the financial reporting process. Forcing a specific registrant to change its filed statements is another, less formal approach that can create the same control. For example,

> Advanced Micro Devices, Inc., agreed to settle an investigation by the Securities and Exchange Commission of the semiconductor company's public disclosures. The SEC found AMD "made inaccurate and misleading statements" concerning development of its 486 microprocessor. In 1992 and 1993, AMD "led the public to believe that it was independently designing the microcode for its 486 microprocessor without access" to the code of its rival chipmaker, Intel Corp., the SEC said, "when, in fact, AMD had provided its engineers . . . with Intel's copyrighted 386 microcode to accelerate the company's development efforts." Without admitting or denying the commission's findings, AMD, based in Sunnyvale, California, consented to an order barring it from committing future violations of SEC rules. No fines were imposed.[27]

Following the SEC's action, any company involved in a similar event would certainly be well advised to provide the suggested disclosure. Failing to do so could result in the SEC's refusal to approve an issuer's future registrations.

The Dodd–Frank Act strengthens the SEC's role in challenging, or at least questioning, financial statements. The act added a new provision to the Securities Exchange Act, pursuant to which the SEC may require listed companies to adopt and publish policies by which they will disgorge or "claw back" executive compensation when restated financial statements are necessitated by executive misconduct. Failure to adopt such policies results in mandatory delisting.[28]

Overruling the FASB

The SEC's actions are not necessarily limited, however, to the gray areas of accounting. Although the commission generally has allowed the FASB (and previous authoritative groups) to establish accounting principles, the SEC retains the authority to override or negate any pronouncements produced in the private sector. This power was dramatically demonstrated in 1977 when the FASB issued *SFAS 19,* "Financial Accounting and Reporting by Oil and Gas Producing Companies." After an extended debate over the merits of alternative methods, the FASB issued this statement requiring oil- and gas-producing companies to apply the successful-efforts method when accounting for unsuccessful exploration and drilling costs.

[26] "SEC Imposes 'Software Costs' Moratorium," *Journal of Accountancy,* September 1983, p. 3.

[27] "SEC Inquiry on Disclosure to Public Is Being Settled," *The Wall Street Journal,* October 1, 1996, p. B4.

[28] Dodd–Frank §954.

In response, the SEC almost immediately invoked a moratorium on the use of this practice until an alternative approach could be evaluated. Thus, companies filing with the SEC were not allowed to follow the method established by the FASB (after years of formal study and deliberation by that body). Although the commission's reaction toward the accounting profession was a unique instance, the handling of this one issue clearly demonstrates the veto power that the SEC maintains over the work of the FASB.[29]

LO 12-5

Define and describe an issuer's filings with the Securities and Exchange Commission.

Filings with the SEC

Because of legislation and regulations, registrants may be required to make numerous different filings with the SEC. The SEC actually receives hundreds of thousands of filings per year. However, for the overview presented here, the reporting process is divided into two very broad categories:

1. Registration statements.
2. Periodic filings.

Registration statements ensure the disclosure of sufficient, relevant financial data before either a company or its underwriters can *initially offer* a security to the public. The Securities Act of 1933 mandates dissemination of such information. Registration is necessary except in certain situations described at a later point in this chapter. The SEC charges a registration fee based on the value of the securities offered.[30] This fee is a very small fraction of the value of the securities being issued. In 2013, it was $136.40 for each $1 million of security offering. The SEC collects fees vastly in excess of its operating costs and, in fact, has a net position at the end of most fiscal years.

For years, the existence of this surplus has caused debate. Some view it as a source of general revenue for the federal government, and others have argued that it indicated that corporations were being overcharged for the registration process. However, another possibility emerged as a result of the corporate accounting scandals in 2001 and 2002: The surplus probably meant that the resources being invested in the SEC's work were not adequate. In other words, the agency could simply not meet its responsibilities with the money allotted. Not surprisingly, the Sarbanes–Oxley Act authorized a 77 percent increase in the agency's budget as well as a substantial increase in the size of its staff. However, this authorization did not necessarily mean that the SEC would actually receive more money in the budgeting process.

> Instead of supporting the 77 percent budget hike promised by Congress, the White House wants the SEC to make do with a more modest $568 million next year. The Commission's 2002 budget was $438 million. While this might seem like a lot, Harvey Goldschmid [SEC Commissioner] said that it is not enough to pay for the effective policing of 17,000 companies, 34,000 investment portfolios, and 7,500 financial advisers, especially in a climate where so much emphasis is placed on the quality of oversight.[31]

After initial registration, a number of federal laws, the most important of which is the Securities Exchange Act of 1934, require registrants to provide periodic filings. This legislation has resulted in the *continual reporting of specified data* by all companies that have securities publicly traded on either a national securities exchange or an over-the-counter market.

For registration statements as well as periodic filings, the SEC has established forms that give the format and content to be followed in providing required information. "These

[29] For a detailed account of the activities surrounding the SEC's rejection of *SFAS 19,* see Donald Gorton, "The SEC Decision Not to Support SFAS 19: A Case Study of the Effect of Lobbying on Standard Setting," *Accounting Horizons,* March 1991.

[30] Self-Regulatory Organizations also impose similar fees. For instance, the National Association of Security Dealers imposes a .01 percent initial filing fee (with a $75,000.00 cap) based on the proposed maximum aggregate offering price. This permits the NASD to fulfill its functions in regard to its role with the SEC. SEC Release No. 34-50984, File No. SR-NASD-2004-177.

[31] Howard Stock, "Don't Short-Change SEC, Goldschmid Tells Bush," *Investors Relations Business,* December 16, 2002.

forms contain no blanks to be filled in as do tax forms. Instead, they are narrative in character, giving general instructions about the items of information to be furnished. Detailed information must be assembled by the companies using the form designed for the type of security being offered as well as the type of company making the offer."[32]

Registration Statements (1933 Act)

As indicated, a registration statement must be filed with and made effective by the Securities and Exchange Commission before a company can offer a security publicly. A security is very broadly defined to include items such as a note, stock, treasury stock, bond, debenture, investment contract, evidence of indebtedness, or transferable share.

The SEC's role is not to evaluate the quality of the investment. Rather, the SEC seeks to ensure that the content and disclosure of the filing comply with all applicable regulations. The responsibility for the information always rests with corporate officials. The SEC is charged with ensuring full and fair disclosure of relevant financial information. The registrant has the responsibility to provide such data, but the decision to invest must remain with the public.

A number of different forms are available for this purpose, depending on the specific circumstances. Some of the most commonly encountered registration statement forms follow:[33]

- S–1 Used when no other form is prescribed. Usually used by new registrants or by companies that have been filing reports with the SEC for less than 36 months.
- S–3 Used by companies that are large and already have a significant following in the stock market (at least $75 million of the voting stock is held by nonaffiliates). Disclosure is reduced for these organizations because the public is assumed to already have access to a considerable amount of information. Form F–3 is used if registration is by a foreign issuer.
- S–4 Used for securities issued in connection with business combination transactions.
- S–8 Used as a registration statement for employee stock plans.
- S–11 Used for the registration of securities by certain real estate companies.

The use of several of these forms, especially Form S–3, offers a distinct advantage to established companies that are issuing securities. Rather than duplicate voluminous information already disclosed in other filings with the SEC—frequently the annual report to shareholders—the registrant can simply indicate the location of the data in these other documents, a process referred to as *incorporation by reference.*

LO 12-6

Describe an issuer's registration process, various forms used by the issuers, and the exemption(s) from registration.

Registration Procedures

The actual registration process is composed of a series of events leading up to the SEC's permission to "go effective." Because the registrant is seeking to obtain significant financial resources through the issuance of new securities in public markets, each of these procedures is vitally important.

After selecting the appropriate form, the company accumulates information according to the requirements of ***Regulation S–K*** and ***Regulation S–X.*** If it anticipates problems or questions, the company may request a prefiling conference with the SEC staff to seek guidance prior to beginning the registration. For example, if uncertainty concerning the handling or disclosure of an unusual transaction exists, a prefiling conference can save all parties considerable time and effort.

> The Commission has a long-established policy of holding its staff available for conferences with prospective registrants or their representatives in advance of filing a registration statement. These conferences may be held for the purpose of discussing generally the problems confronting a registrant in effecting registration or to resolve specific problems of an unusual nature which are sometimes presented by involved or complicated financial transactions.[34]

[32] K. Fred Skousen, *An Introduction to the SEC* (Cincinnati: South-Western Publishing, 1991), p. 47.

[33] www.sec.gov/info/edgar/forms/edgform.pdf.

[34] Stanley Weinstein, Daniel Schechtman, and Michael A. Walker, *SEC Compliance*, vol. 4 (Englewood Cliffs, NJ: Prentice Hall, 1999), para. 30,641.

When the SEC receives it, the Division of Corporation Finance reviews the registration statement.[35] An analyst determines whether all nonfinancial information complies with the SEC's disclosure requirements in *Regulation S–K.* At the same time, an accountant verifies that the financial statement data included in the filing meet the standards of *Regulation S–X* and have been prepared according to generally accepted accounting principles. *Because the SEC does not conduct a formal audit, the report of the company's independent CPA is essential to this particular evaluation.* In addition, an SEC lawyer reviews the registration statement to verify its legal aspects.

The Division of Corporation Finance regularly requests clarifications, changes, or additional information, especially for those filings involving an initial registration. A *letter of comments* (also known as a *deficiency letter*) is issued to the company to communicate these findings. In most cases, the registrant attempts to provide the necessary data or changes to expedite the process. However, in controversial areas, the issuer may begin discussions directly with the SEC staff in hope of resolving the problem without making the requested adjustments or disclosure or, at least, with limited inconvenience.

When the Division of Corporation Finance is eventually satisfied that the company has fulfilled all SEC regulations, the registration statement is made effective and the securities can be sold. *Effectiveness does not, however, indicate an endorsement of the securities by the SEC.* With most offerings, the company actually sells the stock using one or more underwriters (stock brokerage firms) that market the shares to their clients to earn commissions.

For convenience and to save time and money, large companies are allowed to use a process known as *shelf registration.* They file once with the SEC and are then allowed to offer those securities at any time over the subsequent two years without having to go back to the SEC. For example, "Enterprise Products Partners L. P. announced today that it has filed an $800 million universal shelf registration statement with the Securities and Exchange Commission for the proposed sale of debt and equity securities over the next two years."[36]

The registration statement is physically composed of two parts. Part I, referred to as a *prospectus,* contains extensive information that includes these items:

1. Financial statements for the issuing company audited by an independent CPA along with appropriate supplementary data.
2. An explanation of the intended use of the proceeds to be generated by the sale of the new securities.
3. A description of the risks associated with the securities.
4. A description of the business and the properties owned by the issuer.

The registrant must furnish every potential buyer of the securities with a copy of this prospectus, thus ensuring the adequate availability of information for their investment analysis.

Part II of the registration statement is primarily for the informational needs of the SEC staff. Additional data should be disclosed about the company and the securities being issued such as marketing arrangements, expenses of issuance, sales to special parties, and the like. The registrant is not required to provide this information to prospective buyers, although the entire registration statement is available to the public through the SEC.

Securities Exempt from Registration According to the 1933 Act, not all securities issued by companies and their underwriters require registration prior to their sale. For example, securities sold to the residents of the state in which the issuing company is chartered and principally doing business are exempted. However, these offerings may still be regulated by the securities laws of the individual states (commonly known as *blue sky laws*), which vary significantly.[37]

[35] All registration statements filed by issuers offering securities to the public for the first time are reviewed. Subsequent registration statements and periodic filings are reviewed only on a selective basis.

[36] "Enterprise Files $800 Million Universal Shelf Registration with SEC," *Business Wire,* December 27, 1999.

[37] "These early laws became known as 'blue sky' laws after a judicial decision characterized some transactions as 'speculative schemes which have no more basis than so many feet of blue sky.'" (Skousen, *An Introduction to the SEC,* p. 3.)

Other exempt offerings include but are not limited to the following:

- Securities issued by governments, banks, and savings and loan associations.
- Securities issued that are restricted to a company's own existing stockholders for which no commission is paid to solicit the exchange.
- Securities, such as bonds, issued by nonprofit organizations such as religious, educational, or charitable groups.
- Revised Regulation A: Regulation A is an exemption from the requirement to register public offerings. In March 2015, the SEC implemented Section 401 of the Jumpstart Our Business Startups (JOBS) Act by amending Regulation A to create two offering tiers. Tier 1 provides exemption for up to $20 million of securities in a 12-month period. Tier 2 provides exemption for up to $50 million of securities in a 12-month period. Both Tier 1 and Tier 2 securities may be offered publicly utilizing general solicitation and advertising and offered to unaccredited investors.
- Regulation D—Rule 504: Offerings of no more than $1 million made to any number of investors within a 12-month period. No specific disclosure of information is required. General solicitations are allowed. The issuer must give notice of the offering to the SEC within 15 days of the first sale.
- Regulation D—Rule 505: Offerings of no more than $5 million made to 35 or fewer non-accredited and an unlimited number of accredited purchasers in a 12-month period. No general solicitation is allowed for securities issued in this manner. Unaccredited investors must still be furnished an audited balance sheet and other specified information. Parties making purchases have to hold the securities for at least two years or lose the filing exemption.
- Regulation D—Rule 506: The private placement of any dollar amount of issuance to unlimited non-accredited investors and no more than 35 sophisticated investors (having knowledge and experience in financial matters) who already have sufficient information available to them about the issuing company. General solicitation is not permitted, although solicitation is permitted if the entire issuance is to accredited investors. These private placement rules have become quite important in recent years. Private placements in the United States rose from $16 billion in 1980 to more than $200 billion in 1996. By 2004, private equity placements nearly approached this figure, approximating $177 billion. For example, "SYS Technologies, a leading provider of real time information technology solutions to industrial and U.S. government customers, announced today that it has completed a private placement with institutional investors raising gross proceeds of $3.35 million on June 3, 2005."[38]

Periodic Filings with the SEC

Once a company has issued securities that are publicly traded on a securities exchange or an over-the-counter market, it must continually file information with the SEC so that adequate disclosure is available. As with registration statements, several different forms are utilized for this purpose. However, for most companies with actively traded securities, three of these are common: Form 10–K (an annual report), Form 10–Q (a quarterly report), and Form 8–K (disclosure of significant events). Smaller businesses use Form 10–KSB for annual reports and Form 10–QSB for quarterly reports.

In addition, as mentioned previously, proxy statements must be filed with the SEC. Management or another interested party issues these statements to a company's owners in hope of securing voting rights to be used at stockholders' meetings.

Form 10–K A 10–K form is an annual report filed with the SEC to provide information and disclosures required by *Regulation S–K* and *Regulation S–X*. Fortunately, because of the integrated disclosure system, the annual report distributed by companies to their stockholders now includes most of the basic financial disclosures required by the SEC in Form

[38] "SYS Technologies Completes Private Placement Transaction," www.freshnews.com/news/fresh-money/article_24429.html.

10–K. Thus, many companies simply attach the stockholders' annual report to the Form 10–K each year and use the incorporation by reference procedure to meet most of the SEC's filing requirements. This process is sometimes known as a *wraparound filing*.

Form 10–K, as with the various other SEC filings, is constantly undergoing assessment to determine whether it is meeting investor needs.[39] Thus, the SEC's reporting requirements are evolutionary and change over time.

> The Securities and Exchange Commission issued guidelines aimed at making public companies provide a more detailed look at the trends and business changes that management expects in the future. . . . In the main part of yesterday's interpretation, the commissioners said that in the 10–K reports, companies must discuss "trends, demands, commitments or events" that it knows are "reasonably likely" to occur and have a material effect on financial condition or results.[40]

As this quote indicates, the SEC is especially interested in the quality of the information provided by the MD&A section of a registrant's filings. Basically, management should describe the company's past, present, and future. This information can furnish investors with a feel for the prospects of the company; it is a candid narrative to provide statement readers with a sense of management's priorities, accomplishments, and concerns. The SEC staff carefully reviews the MD&A feature. "If the management of a company knows something that could have a material impact on earnings in the future, officials have an obligation to share that information with shareholders."[41]

Form 10–Q A 10–Q form contains condensed interim financial statements for the registrant and must be filed with the SEC shortly after the end of each quarter. However, no Form 10–Q is required following the fourth quarter of the year since a Form 10–K is forthcoming shortly thereafter. A Form 10–Q does not have to be audited by an independent CPA.

Information to be contained in each Form 10–Q includes the following:

- Income statements must be included for the most recent quarter and for the year to date as well as for the comparative periods in the previous year.
- A statement of cash flows is also necessary, but only for the year to date as well as for the corresponding period in the preceding year.
- Two balance sheets are reported: one as of the end of the most recent quarter and the second showing the company's financial position at the end of the previous fiscal year.
- Each Form 10–Q should also include any needed disclosures pertaining to the current period including the MD&A of the financial condition of the company and results of operations.

Form 8–K An 8–K form is used to disclose a unique or significant happening.[42] Consequently, the 8–K is not filed at regular time intervals but within 15 calendar days of the event (or within five business days in certain specified instances). The SEC receives thousands of 8–K reports each year. According to the SEC's guidelines, Form 8–K may be filed to report any action that company officials believe is important to security holders. However, the following events are designated for required disclosure in this manner:

- Resignation of a director.
- Changes in control of the registrant.
- Acquisition or disposition of assets.
- Changes in the registrant's certified public accountants (independent auditors).
- Bankruptcy or receivership.

[39] The current Form 10–K instructions can be viewed at www.sec.gov/about/forms/form10-K.pdf. This version of the Form 10–K has been approved for use through March 31, 2018.

[40] Paul Duke Jr., "SEC Issues Guidelines for 10–K Filings Seeking More Details on Trends, Changes," *The Wall Street Journal*, May 19, 1989, p. A2.

[41] Kevin G. Salwen, "SEC Charges Caterpillar Failed to Warn Holders of Earnings Risk Posed by Unit," *The Wall Street Journal*, April 2, 1992, p. A3.

[42] The current Form 8–K instructions can be viewed at www.sec.gov/about/forms/form8-K.pdf. The SEC estimates that an issuer can complete an 8–K filing in approximately five hours.

Proxy Statements As previously mentioned, most of the significant actions undertaken by a company first must be approved at stockholders' meetings. For example, the members of the board of directors are elected in this meeting to oversee the company's operations. Although such votes are essential to the operations of a business, few major companies could possibly assemble enough shareholders at any one time and place for a voting quorum. The geographic distances are simply too great. Hence, before each of the periodic meetings, the management (or any other interested party) usually requests signed proxies from shareholders granting the legal authority to cast votes for the owners in connection with the various actions to be taken at such stockholders' meetings.[43]

Because of the power conveyed by a proxy, any such solicitation sent to shareholders (by any party) must include specific information as the SEC required in its *Regulation 14A.* This proxy statement has to be filed with the SEC at least 10 days before being distributed. In addition to the disclosed items previously described, other data must be reported to the owners:

- The proxy statement needs to indicate on whose behalf the solicitation is being made.
- The proxy statement must disclose fully all matters that are to be voted on at the meeting.
- In most cases, the proxy statement has to be accompanied (or preceded) by an annual report to the shareholders.

As with all areas of disclosure, the SEC's regulation of proxy statements has greatly enhanced the information available to investors. Historically, shareholders have not always been able to get adequate information.

> Thus was the president of one company able to respond cavalierly to a shareholder's request for information, "I can assure you that the company is in a good financial position. I trust that you will sign and mail your proxy at an early date." Quaint. But that was nothing. One unlisted company printed its proxy on the back of the dividend check—so when you endorsed the check you voted for management.[44]
>
> From a 1902 annual report to shareholders: "The settled plan has been to withhold all information from stockholders and others that is not called for by the stockholders in a body. So far no request for information has been made in the manner prescribed by the directors."[45]

Electronic Data Gathering, Analysis, and Retrieval System (EDGAR)

During recent years, the SEC has been almost overwhelmed by the sheer mountains of documents that it receives, reviews, and makes available to the public. Filings with the SEC contain millions of pieces of paper each year. Not surprisingly, some problems in the capital markets during the last few years have been blamed, in part, on this overload. "[The SEC's] corporation finance division cannot keep up with the deluge of company filings."[46]

In 1984, the SEC began to develop an electronic data gathering, analysis, and retrieval system nicknamed EDGAR. As originally envisioned, all filings would arrive at the SEC on disks or through some other electronic transmission. Each filing could be reviewed, analyzed, and stored by SEC personnel on a computer so they would no longer constantly have to sift through stacks of paper. Perhaps more important, investors would have the ability to access these data through the Internet. Thus, investors throughout the world could have information available for their decisions literally minutes after the documents are made effective by the SEC.

Because of the ambitious nature of the EDGAR project, approximately a decade was required to get the system effectively operational. For years, EDGAR was the object of much scorn; "one member of the House Energy and Commerce Committee suggested renaming the project Mr. Ed, 'since the SEC has a much better chance of finding a talking horse than it does

[43] Any person who owns at least 5 percent of the company's stock or has been an owner for six months or longer has the right to look at a list of shareholders to make a proxy solicitation.

[44] Laura Jereski, "You've Come a Long Way, Shareholder," *Forbes,* July 13, 1987, p. 282.

[45] Skousen, *An Introduction to the SEC,* p. 75.

[46] Stephen Labaton, "Can a Bloodied S.E.C. Dust Itself Off and Get Moving?" *The New York Times,* December 16, 2002.

Discussion Question

IS THE DISCLOSURE WORTH THE COST?

Filing with the SEC requires a very significant amount of time and effort on the registrant's part. Companies frequently resist attempts by the SEC to increase the levels of disclosure. Usually, they argue that additional information will not necessarily be useful to a great majority of investors. Regardless of the issue being debated, critics claim that the cost of the extra data far outweighs any benefits that might be derived from this disclosure.

Such contentions are not necessarily made just to avoid disclosing information. This cost analysis has continued for most of the past four decades. One survey from the late 1970s estimated the cost of SEC disclosures to be more than $400 million in 1975 alone.

> The table reports an estimated $213,500,000 for the fully variable costs of 10–K, 10–Q, and 8–K disclosures in 1975. To this should be added the separate estimate (not shown) of $191,900,000 for disclosure related to new issues in 1975, for a total estimate of about $400,000,000 for SEC disclosure costs in 1975. These estimates are biased downward because they do not include various fixed costs.*

Such costs are either passed along to the consumer in the form of higher prices or serve to retard the growth of the reporting company.

Additional SEC requirements continue to concern issuers, many of which conclude that "the costs of mandatory SEC disclosures outweigh the benefits" and accept delisting from the various exchanges, rather than incurring the costs of such disclosure.† SEC revenues, which constitute real out-of-pocket costs to issuers, exceeded $3 billion in 2012. This represents a 15-fold increase in the past 40 years.

The author of one survey (that has been widely discussed and debated over the years) held that federal securities laws are not actually helpful to investors.

> I found that there was little evidence of fraud related to financial statements in the period prior to the enactment of the Securities Acts. Nor was there a widespread lack of disclosure. . . . Hence, I conclude that there was little justification for the accounting disclosure required by the Acts. . . . These findings indicate that the data required by the SEC do not seem to be useful to investors.‡

The SEC was created, in part, to ensure that the public has fair and full disclosure about companies whose securities are publicly traded. However, the commission must be mindful of the cost of such disclosures. How can the SEC determine whether the cost of a proposed disclosure is more or less than the benefits to be derived by the public? After all, despite SEC investigations, Bernard Madoff avoided detection for decades.

*J. Richard Zecher, "An Economic Perspective of SEC Corporate Disclosure," *The SEC and Accounting: The First 50 Years,* ed. Robert H. Mundheim and Noyes E. Leech (Amsterdam: North-Holland, 1985), pp. 75–76.
† Brian J. Bushee and Christian Leuz, "Economic Consequences of SEC Disclosure Regulation," The Wharton School, University of Pennsylvania, February 2004, p. 3.
‡George J. Benston, "The Value of the SEC's Accounting Disclosure Requirements," *The Accounting Review,* July 1969, p. 351.

of achieving an efficient computer filing system.'"[47] However, the beginning of the explosive use of the Internet in the mid-1990s corresponded with the widespread availability of information on EDGAR. Not surprisingly, EDGAR's popularity has expanded.

[47] Sandra Block, "SEC Gets Closer to Electronic Filing," *The Wall Street Journal,* August 30, 1991, p. C1.

If you're suspicious about a certain stock, then go to the Securities and Exchange Commission's EDGAR database—chockablock with annual reports, prospectuses and all the other paperwork demanded of public companies.[48]

Since Congress went to all the trouble in the 1930s of creating the SEC and requiring these corporate disclosures, it seems like somebody should give them an occasional good read. The EDGAR database at the SEC's Web site gives any individual free access to the filings of thousands of public companies. . . . It's sometimes amazing what kind of information typing someone's name, address or phone number into an EDGAR search engine can generate.[49]

Today virtually all publicly held companies are required to file their SEC reports electronically. Paper filings, when permitted, are also converted to electronic files and available to the general public.[50] The resultant EDGAR filings are typically available via the SEC's website within 24 hours of filing. These public filings, combined with the ease of access via the Internet, have resulted in the virtually immediate dissemination of vital investment-related data to accounting professionals, financial advisers, government regulators, and the investing public. EDGAR users can locate filings based on entity names, standard industrial classification (SIC) codes, central index keys (CIK), addresses, date–time frames, and a variety of other variables. This extensive database has helped move financial reporting to a significantly higher level of transparency.

Summary

1. In the United States, the Securities and Exchange Commission (SEC) has been entrusted with the responsibility for ensuring that complete and reliable information is available to investors who buy and sell securities in public capital markets. Since being created in 1934, this agency has administered numerous reporting rules and regulations created by congressional actions starting with the Securities Act of 1933 and the Securities Exchange Act of 1934.
2. The corporate accounting scandals that rocked the U.S. financial community during 2001 and 2002 led Congress to pass the Sarbanes–Oxley Act. This legislation addressed a number of problems. One main provision was the creation of the Public Company Accounting Oversight Board to monitor and regulate the auditors of public companies. Audit firms of public companies must register with this board and are subject to periodic inspections as well as various types of possible disciplinary actions. This act also contains rules to help ensure the independence of the external auditor.
3. Before a company's securities (either equity or debt) can be publicly traded, appropriate filings must be made with the SEC to ensure that sufficient data are made available to potential investors. Disclosure requirements for this process are outlined in two documents: *Regulation S–K* (for nonfinancial information) and *Regulation S–X* (describing the form and content of all included financial statements).
4. The ability to require the reporting of special information gives the SEC enormous legal power over accounting standards in the United States. Traditionally, this authority has been wielded only on rare occasions and only to increase disclosure requirements and to provide guidance where none was otherwise available. However, in a significant demonstration of its authority, the SEC overruled the FASB's decision in 1977 as to the appropriate method to account for unsuccessful exploration and drilling costs incurred by oil- and gas-producing companies.
5. Filings with the SEC are divided generally into two broad categories: registration statements and periodic filings. Registration statements are designed to provide information about a company prior to its issuance of a security to the public. Depending on the circumstances, several different registration forms are available for this purpose. After the registrant produces the statement and the SEC initially reviews it, a letter of comments describing desired explanations or changes is furnished. These concerns must be resolved before the security can be sold.
6. Not all securities issued in the United States require registration with the SEC. As an example, formal registration is not necessary for securities sold by either government units or banks. Certain

[48] The address for EDGAR is located at the SEC website www.sec.gov. A quick EDGAR tutorial is available at www.sec.gov/edgar/quickedgar.htm to familiarize users with the retrieval system. Joseph R. Garber, "Click Before You Leap," *Forbes,* February 24, 1997, p. 162.

[49] John Emshwiller, "Financial Filings Hold Key to Investigative Pieces, Big and Small," *The Wall Street Journal,* May 31, 2005.

[50] www.sec.gov/edgar/quickedgar.htm.

issues for relatively small amounts are also exempt although some amount of disclosure is normally required. Securities sold solely within the state in which the business operates are not subject to federal securities laws but must comply with state laws frequently referred to as *blue sky laws.*

7. Companies whose stocks or bonds are publicly traded on a securities exchange must also submit periodic filings to the SEC to ensure that adequate disclosure is constantly maintained. Among the most common of these filings are Form 10–K (an annual report) and Form 10–Q (condensed interim financial information). Form 8–K also is required to report any significant events that occur. In addition, proxy statements (documents that are used to solicit votes at stockholders' meetings) also come under the filing requirements monitored by the SEC.
8. The SEC created the EDGAR database to allow companies to make electronic filings with the commission. More importantly, EDGAR allows any person with access to the Internet to review these documents in a timely fashion. Thus, access to financial and other information about filing entities has become much more widely available.

Questions

(Students should visit the SEC website, www.sec.gov, for supplemental resources.)

1. Why were federal securities laws originally enacted by Congress?
2. What are some of the possible reasons for the numerous corporate accounting scandals discovered during 2001 and 2002?
3. List several provisions of the Sarbanes–Oxley Act that are designed to restore public confidence in the U.S. capital market system.
4. What is the SEC's relationship to the Public Company Accounting Oversight Board?
5. Who must register with the Public Company Accounting Oversight Board?
6. What is the impact of being registered with the PCAOB?
7. How has the Sarbanes–Oxley Act attempted to ensure that external auditors will be completely independent in the future?
8. What is the purpose of the inspection process created by the Sarbanes–Oxley Act?
9. What is covered by *Regulation S–K?*
10. What is covered by *Regulation S–X?*
11. What are some of the major divisions and offices within the SEC?
12. What does the Securities Act of 1933 cover?
13. What does the Securities Exchange Act of 1934 cover?
14. What are the goals of the SEC?
15. What information is required in a proxy statement?
16. Why is the content of a proxy statement considered to be so important?
17. How does the SEC affect the development of generally accepted accounting principles in the United States?
18. What is the purpose of *Financial Reporting Releases* and *Staff Accounting Bulletins?*
19. What was the SEC's response to the FASB's handling of accounting for oil- and gas-producing companies, and why was this action considered so significant?
20. What is the purpose of a registration statement?
21. Under what law is a registration statement filed?
22. What are the two parts of a registration statement? What does each part contain?
23. How does the SEC generate revenues?
24. Two forms commonly used in the registration process are Form S–1 and Form S–3. Which registrants should use each form?
25. What is incorporation by reference?
26. What is a prefiling conference, and why might it be helpful to a registrant?
27. What is a letter of comments? By what other name is it often called?
28. What is a prospectus? What does a prospectus contain?
29. Under what circumstances is a company exempt from filing a registration statement with the SEC prior to the issuance of securities?
30. What is a private placement of securities?

31. What are blue sky laws?
32. What is a wraparound filing?
33. When is a Form 8–K issued by a company? What specific information does a Form 8–K convey?
34. What is the purpose of the Management's Discussion and Analysis?
35. What is the difference between a Form 10–K and a Form 10–Q?
36. What was the purpose of creating the EDGAR system?

Problems

LO 12-1

1. Which of the following statements is true?
   a. The Securities Exchange Act of 1934 regulates intrastate stock offerings made by a company.
   b. The Securities Act of 1933 regulates the subsequent public trading of securities through brokers and markets.
   c. The Securities Exchange Act of 1934 is commonly referred to as blue sky legislation.
   d. The Securities Act of 1933 regulates the initial offering of securities by a company.

LO 12-2

2. What is the purpose of *Regulation S–K?*
   a. Defines generally accepted accounting principles in the United States.
   b. Establishes required disclosure of nonfinancial information with the SEC.
   c. Establishes required financial disclosures with the SEC.
   d. Indicates which companies must file with the SEC on an annual basis.

LO 12-2

3. What is the difference between *Regulation S–K* and *Regulation S–X?*
   a. *Regulation S–K* establishes reporting requirements for companies in their initial issuance of securities whereas *Regulation S–X* is directed toward the subsequent issuance of securities.
   b. *Regulation S–K* establishes reporting requirements for companies smaller than a certain size whereas *Regulation S–X* is directed toward companies larger than that size.
   c. *Regulation S–K* establishes regulations for nonfinancial information filed with the SEC whereas *Regulation S–X* prescribes the form and content of financial statements included in SEC filings.
   d. *Regulation S–K* establishes reporting requirements for publicly held companies whereas *Regulation S–X* is directed toward private companies.

LO 12-2

4. The Securities Exchange Act of 1934
   a. Regulates the public trading of previously issued securities through brokers and exchanges.
   b. Prohibits blue sky laws.
   c. Regulates the initial offering of securities by a company.
   d. Requires the registration of investment advisers.

LO 12-3

5. Which of the following is a requirement of the Sarbanes–Oxley Act of 2002?
   a. Registration of all auditing firms with the Public Company Accounting Oversight Board.
   b. Annual inspection of all auditing firms registered with the Public Company Accounting Oversight Board.
   c. A monetary fee assessed on organizations issuing securities.
   d. Overall assessment of the work of the SEC each year.

LO 12-3

6. Which of the following is *not* correct with regard to the Public Company Accounting Oversight Board?
   a. The board can expel a registered auditing firm without SEC approval.
   b. All registered auditing firms must be inspected at least every three years.
   c. The board members must be appointed by Congress.
   d. The board has the authority to set auditing standards rather than utilize the work of the Auditing Standards Board.

LO 12-3

7. Which of the following is *not* a way by which the Sarbanes–Oxley Act attempts to ensure auditor independence from an audit client?
   a. The auditing firm must be appointed by the client's audit committee.
   b. Audit fees must be approved by the Public Company Accounting Oversight Board.
   c. The audit committee must be composed of members of the client's board of directors who are independent of the management.
   d. The external auditor cannot also perform financial information system design and implementation work.

LO 12-5
8. What is a registration statement?
   a. A statement that must be filed with the SEC before a company can begin an initial offering of securities to the public.
   b. A required filing with the SEC before a large amount of stock can be obtained by an inside party.
   c. An annual filing made with the SEC.
   d. A filing made by a company with the SEC to indicate that a significant change has occurred.

LO 12-5
9. Which of the following is a registration statement used by large companies that already have a significant following in the stock market?
   a. Form 8–K
   b. Form 10–K
   c. Form S–1
   d. Form S–3

LO 12-4
10. What was the significance of the controversy in 1977 over the appropriate accounting principles to be used by oil- and gas-producing companies?
   a. Several major lawsuits resulted.
   b. Companies refused to follow the SEC's dictates.
   c. Partners of a major accounting firm were indicted on criminal charges.
   d. The SEC overruled the FASB on its handling of this matter.

LO 12-6
11. Which of the following must be provided to every potential buyer of a new security?
   a. A letter of comments.
   b. A deficiency letter.
   c. A prospectus.
   d. A Form S–16.

LO 12-5
12. What does the term *incorporation by reference* mean?
   a. The legal incorporation of a company in more than one state.
   b. Filing information with the SEC by indicating that the information is already available in another document.
   c. A reference guide indicating informational requirements specified in *Regulation S–X.*
   d. Incorporating a company in a state outside of its base of operations.

LO 12-6
13. What is a letter of comments?
   a. A letter the SEC sends to a company indicating needed changes or clarifications in a registration statement.
   b. A questionnaire supplied to the SEC by a company suggesting changes in *Regulation S–X.*
   c. A letter included in a Form 10–K to indicate the management's assessment of the company's financial position.
   d. A letter composed by a company asking for information or clarification prior to the filing of a registration statement.

LO 12-6
14. What is a prospectus?
   a. A document attached to a Form 8–K.
   b. A potential stockholder as defined by *Regulation S–K.*
   c. A document a company files with the SEC prior to filing a registration statement.
   d. The first part of a registration statement that a company must furnish to all potential buyers of a new security.

LO 12-6
15. Which of the following is *not* exempt from registration with the SEC under the Securities Act of 1933?
   a. Securities issued by a nonprofit religious organization.
   b. Securities issued by a government unit.
   c. A public offering of $40 million to unaccredited investors under Regulation A.
   d. An offering to 40 sophisticated investors.

LO 12-6
16. Which of the following is usually *not* filed with the SEC on a regular periodic basis?
   a. A Form 10–Q
   b. A prospectus
   c. A proxy statement
   d. A Form 10–K

LO 12-6 17. What is a shelf registration?

a. A registration statement that the SEC formally rejects.
b. A registration statement that the SEC rejects due to the lapse of a specified period of time.
c. A registration process for large companies that allows them to offer securities over a period of time without seeking additional approval by the SEC.
d. A registration form that is withdrawn by the registrant without any action having been taken.

LO 12-6 18. What is EDGAR?

a. A system the SEC uses to reject registration statements that do not contain adequate information.
b. The enforcement arm of the SEC.
c. A system designed by the SEC to allow electronic filings.
d. A branch of the government that oversees the work of the SEC.

LO 12-1, 12-3, 12-5, 12-6 19. Identify each of the following as they pertain to the SEC.

a. Blue sky laws.
b. S–8 Statement.
c. Letter of comments.
d. Public Company Accounting Oversight Board.
e. Prospectus.

LO 12-2 20. Discuss the objectives of the Securities Act of 1933 and the Securities Exchange Act of 1934. How are these objectives accomplished?

LO 12-6 21. What are the general steps involved in filing a registration statement with the SEC?

LO 12-4 22. Discuss the methods by which the SEC can influence the development of generally accepted accounting principles in the United States.

LO 12-6 23. Which forms do most companies file with the SEC on a periodic basis? Explain the purpose of each form and its primary contents.

LO 12-5 24. Which forms do most companies file with the SEC in connection with the offering of securities to the public?

LO 12-6 25. What is the importance of a Form 8–K? What is the importance of a proxy statement?

LO 12-3 26. Describe the provisions of the Sarbanes–Oxley Act as they relate to the creation and responsibilities of the Public Company Accounting Oversight Board.

LO 12-1, 12-2, 12-4, 12-5, 12-6 27. Explain each of the following items:

a. Staff Accounting Bulletins.
b. Wraparound filing.
c. Incorporation by reference.
d. Division of Corporation Finance.
e. Integrated disclosure system.
f. Management's discussion and analysis.
g. Chief accountant of the SEC.

LO 12-6 28. Which organizations are normally exempted from the SEC's registration requirements?

Develop Your Skills

RESEARCH CASE 1

CPA skills

Domer Corporation is preparing to issue a relatively small amount of securities and does not want to go to the trouble and expense of filing a registration statement with the SEC. Company officials hope to be exempt under provisions of Regulation A. These officials want to be certain that they meet these provisions precisely so that no later legal problems arise.

Required

Go to the website www.sec.gov and select "Corporate Finance under Divisions." Then select the link for "Statutes, Rules, and Forms," followed by the "Rules, Regulations, and Schedules" link. Based on the information provided for Regulation A (click on "General Rules and Regulations, Securities Act of 1933"), prepare a report for Domer Corporation officials as to the requirements for exemption and advise as to the maximum amount of capital that may be raised through such issuance. Assuming that Domer Corporation is a development stage company, revise the report. Note specifically Regulation §230.251.

RESEARCH CASE 2

CPA skills

Tasch Corporation, a multilevel marketing and sales organization, plans to sell approximately $10,000,000 worth of "service agreements" to many of its customers. These service agreements guarantee a set return to the customer in exchange for an up-front purchase price, with Tasch Corporation managing the various business interests of its customers. Jerry Tasch, the corporation's president, needs advice concerning the necessity of SEC filings prior to the sale of these service agreements.

Required

Assume that the only (initial) question to be addressed is whether the service agreements constitute securities under the Securities Act of 1933. Perform research utilizing an Internet search engine to determine whether the service agreements are in fact securities. Note that courts interpret statutes and regulations, so it is often useful to look at judicial determinations to reach a conclusion. To that end, consider locating and reviewing the following case: *SEC v. Calvo,* 378 F.3d 1211 (11th Cir. 2004). Students can locate this case using many web links including FINDLAW and LexisNexis. This web link will direct the student directly to the specific opinion (https://law.resource.org/pub/us/case/reporter/F3/378/378.F3d.1211.02-13445.html).

ANALYSIS CASE 1

CPA skills

Go to the website www.sec.gov and, under the Filings heading, click on "Filings" and then click on "Company Filing Search." Enter the name of a well-known company such as Facebook. A list of available documents should be shown for that company.

Required

Using these available documents, answer the following questions:

1. Has the company filed an 8–K during the most recent time period? If so, open that document and determine the reason that the form was filed with the SEC.
2. Has the company filed a 10–K during the recent time period? If so, open that document and determine the total reported net income for the latest period of time.
3. Has the company filed a 10–Q during the most recent time period? If so, open that document and determine what issues were addressed and disclosed.

COMMUNICATION CASE 1

The senior partner of Wojtysiak & Co., CPAs, has been approached by a small, publicly traded corporation wishing to change auditors. The Wojtysiak firm does not audit any other public companies. Because of the Sarbanes-Oxley Act of 2002, Mike Wojtysiak, the senior partner, needs to know the regulatory issues facing his firm if it accepts the new engagement.

Required

Draft a report that outlines the Sarbanes–Oxley considerations for a firm such as the Wojtysiak firm. Locate the actual act (Public Law 107-204) or perform a thorough summary and review it prior to preparing the report. The full act may be found at: www.gpo.gov/fdsys/pkg/PLAW-107publ204/pdf/PLAW-107publ204.pdf.

chapter 1

The Equity Method of Accounting for Investments

The first several chapters of this text present the accounting and reporting for investment activities of businesses. The focus is on investments when one firm possesses either significant influence or control over another through ownership of voting shares. When one firm owns enough voting shares to be able to affect the decisions of another, accounting for the investment can become challenging and complex. The source of such complexities typically stems from the fact that transactions among the firms affiliated through ownership cannot be considered independent, arm's-length transactions. As in many matters relating to financial reporting, we look to transactions with *outside parties* to provide a basis for accounting valuation. When firms are affiliated through a common set of owners, measurements that recognize the relationships among the firms help to provide objectivity in financial reporting.

The Reporting of Investments in Corporate Equity Securities

In its recent annual report, The Coca-Cola Company describes its 28 percent investment in Coca-Cola FEMSA, a Mexican bottling company with operations throughout much of Latin America. The Coca-Cola Company uses the equity method to account for several of its bottling company investments, including Coca-Cola FEMSA. The Coca-Cola Company states,

> We use the equity method to account for investments in companies, if our investment provides us with the ability to exercise significant influence over operating and financial policies of the investee. Our consolidated net income includes our Company's proportionate share of the net income or loss of these companies.
>
> Our judgment regarding the level of influence over each equity method investment includes considering key factors such as our ownership interest, representation on the board of directors, participation in policy-making decisions and material intercompany transactions.

Such information is hardly unusual in the business world; corporate investors frequently acquire ownership shares of both domestic and foreign businesses. These investments can range from the purchase of a few shares to the acquisition of 100 percent control. Although purchases of corporate equity securities (such as the ones made by Coca-Cola) are not uncommon, they pose a considerable number of financial reporting issues because a close relationship has been established without the investor gaining actual control. These issues are currently addressed by the *equity method.* This chapter deals with accounting for stock investments that fall under the application of this method.

Learning Objectives

After studying this chapter, you should be able to:

- **LO 1-1** Describe in general the various methods of accounting for an investment in equity shares of another company.
- **LO 1-2** Identify the sole criterion for applying the equity method of accounting and know the guidelines to assess whether the criterion is met.
- **LO 1-3** Describe the financial reporting for equity method investments and prepare basic equity method journal entries for an investor.
- **LO 1-4** Allocate the cost of an equity method investment and compute amortization expense to match revenues recognized from the investment to the excess of investor cost over investee book value.
- **LO 1-5** Understand the financial reporting consequences for:
  - a. A change to the equity method.
  - b. Investee's other comprehensive income.
  - c. Investee losses.
  - d. Sales of equity method investments.
- **LO 1-6** Describe the rationale and computations to defer the investor's share of gross profits on intra-entity inventory sales until the goods are either consumed by the owner or sold to outside parties.
- **LO 1-7** Explain the rationale and reporting implications of fair-value accounting for investments otherwise accounted for by the equity method.

LO 1-1

Describe in general the various methods of accounting for an investment in equity shares of another company.

Generally accepted accounting principles (GAAP) recognize four different approaches to the financial reporting of investments in corporate equity securities:

1. Fair-value method.
2. Cost method for equity securities without readily determinable fair values.
3. Consolidation of financial statements.
4. Equity method.

The financial statement reporting for a particular investment depends primarily on the degree of influence that the investor (stockholder) has over the investee, a factor most often indicated by the relative size of ownership.[1] Because voting power typically accompanies ownership of equity shares, influence increases with the relative size of ownership. The resulting influence can be very little, a significant amount, or, in some cases, complete control.

Fair-Value Method

In many instances, an investor possesses only a small percentage of an investee company's outstanding stock, perhaps only a few shares. Because of the limited level of ownership, the investor cannot expect to significantly affect the investee's operations or decision making. These shares are bought in anticipation of cash dividends or in appreciation of stock market values. Such investments are recorded at cost and periodically adjusted to fair value according to the Financial Accounting Standards Board (FASB) *Accounting Standards Codification* (ASC) Topic 321, "Investments—Equity Securities."

Fair value is defined by the ASC (Master Glossary) as the "price that would be received to sell an asset or paid to transfer a liability in an orderly transaction between market participants at the measurement date." For most investments in equity securities, quoted stock market prices represent fair values.

Because a full coverage of limited ownership investments in equity securities is presented in intermediate accounting textbooks, only the following basic principles are noted here:

- Initial investments in equity securities are recorded at cost and subsequently adjusted to fair value if fair value is readily determinable (typically by reference to market value); otherwise, the investment remains at cost.
- Changes in the fair values of equity securities during a reporting period are recognized as income.[2]
- Dividends declared on the equity securities are recognized as income.

The above procedures are followed for equity security investments (with readily determinable fair values) when the owner possesses neither significant influence nor control.

Cost Method (Investments in Equity Securities without Readily Determinable Fair Values)

When the fair value of an investment in equity securities is not readily determinable, and the investment provides neither significant influence nor control, the investment may be measured at cost. Such investments sometimes can be found in ownership shares of firms that are not publicly traded or experience only infrequent trades.

[1] The relative size of ownership is most often the key factor in assessing one company's degree of influence over another. However, as discussed later in this chapter, other factors (e.g., contractual relationships between firms) can also provide influence or control over firms regardless of the percentage of shares owned.

[2] FASB Accounting Standards Update (ASU) No. 2016-01, Financial Instruments—Overall, requires equity investments (except those accounted for under the equity method of accounting or those that result in consolidation of the investee) to be measured at fair value with changes in fair value recognized in net income, unless fair values are not readily determinable. Thus, the previous available-for-sale category with fair value changes recorded in other comprehensive income will no longer be available. The ASU is effective for fiscal years beginning after December 15, 2017, with early adoption permitted.

Investments in equity securities that employ the cost method often continue to be reported at their original cost over time.[3] Income from cost method equity investments usually consists of the investor's share of dividends declared by the investee. However, despite its emphasis on cost measurements, GAAP allows for two fair value assessments that may affect cost method amounts reported on the balance sheet and the income statement.

- First, cost method equity investments periodically must be assessed for impairment to determine if the fair value of the investment is less than its carrying amount. The ASC allows a qualitative assessment to determine if impairment is likely.[4] Because the fair value of a cost method equity investment is not readily available (by definition), if impairment is deemed likely, an entity must estimate a fair value for the investment to measure the amount (if any) of the impairment loss.
- Second, ASC (321-10-35-2) allows for recognition of "observable price changes in orderly transactions for the identical or a similar investment of the same issuer." Any unrealized holding gains (or losses) from these observable price changes are included in earnings with a corresponding adjustment to the investment account. So even if equity shares are only infrequently traded (and thus fair value is not readily determinable), such trades can provide a basis for financial statement recognition under the cost method for equity investments.

Consolidation of Financial Statements

Many corporate investors acquire enough shares to gain actual control over an investee's operations. In financial accounting, such control may be achieved when a stockholder accumulates more than 50 percent of an organization's outstanding voting stock. At that point, rather than simply influencing the investee's decisions, the investor often can direct the entire decision-making process. A review of the financial statements of America's largest organizations indicates that legal control of one or more subsidiary companies is an almost universal practice. PepsiCo, Inc., as just one example, holds a majority interest in the voting stock of literally hundreds of corporations.

Investor control over an investee presents a special accounting challenge. Normally, when a majority of voting stock is held, the investor-investee relationship is so closely connected that the two corporations are viewed as a single entity for reporting purposes.[5] Hence, an entirely different set of accounting procedures is applicable. Control generally requires the consolidation of the accounting information produced by the individual companies. Thus, a single set of financial statements is created for external reporting purposes with all assets, liabilities, revenues, and expenses brought together. The various procedures applied within this consolidation process are examined in subsequent chapters of this textbook.

The FASB ASC Section 810-10-05 on variable interest entities expands the use of consolidated financial statements to include entities that are financially controlled through special contractual arrangements rather than through voting stock interests. Prior to the accounting requirements for variable interest entities, many firms (e.g., Enron) avoided consolidation of entities that they owned little or no voting stock in but otherwise controlled through special contracts. These entities were frequently referred to as "special purpose entities (SPEs)" and provided vehicles for some firms to keep large amounts of assets and liabilities off their consolidated financial statements. Accounting for these entities is discussed in Chapters 2 and 6.

[3] Dividends received in excess of earnings subsequent to the date of investment are considered returns of the investment and are recorded as reductions of cost of the investment.

[4] Impairment indicators include assessments of earnings performance, economic environment, going-concern ability, etc. If the qualitative assessment does not indicate impairment, no further testing is required. If an equity security without a readily determinable fair value is impaired, the investor recognizes the difference between the investment's fair value and carrying amount as an impairment loss in net income (ASC 321-10-35-3).

[5] As discussed in Chapter 2, ownership of a majority voting interest in an investee does not always lead to consolidated financial statements.

Discussion Question

DID THE COST METHOD INVITE EARNINGS MANIPULATION?

Prior to GAAP for equity method investments, firms used the cost method to account for their unconsolidated investments in common stock regardless of the presence of significant influence. Under the cost method, when the investee declares a dividend, the investor records "dividend income." The investment account typically remains at its original cost—hence the term *cost method.*

Many firms' compensation plans reward managers based on reported annual income. How might the use of the cost method of accounting for significant influence investments have resulted in unintended wealth transfers from owners to managers? Do the equity or fair-value methods provide similar incentives?

Equity Method

Another investment relationship is appropriately accounted for using the equity method. In many investments, although control is not achieved, the degree of ownership indicates the ability of the investor to exercise *significant influence* over the investee. Recall Coca-Cola's 28 percent investment in Coca-Cola FEMSA's voting stock. Through its ownership, Coca-Cola can undoubtedly influence Coca-Cola FEMSA's decisions and operations.

To provide objective reporting for investments with significant influence, FASB ASC Topic 323, "Investments—Equity Method and Joint Ventures," describes the use of the equity method. The equity method employs the accrual basis for recognizing the investor's share of investee income. Accordingly, the investor recognizes income as it is earned by the investee. As noted in FASB ASC (para. 323-10-05-5), because of its significant influence over the investee, the investor

> has a degree of responsibility for the return on its investment and it is appropriate to include in the results of operations of the investor its share of earnings or losses of the investee.

Furthermore, under the equity method, the investor records its share of investee dividends declared as a decrease in the investment account, not as income.

In today's business world, many corporations hold significant ownership interests in other companies without having actual control. The Coca-Cola Company, for example, owns between 20 and 50 percent of several bottling companies, both domestic and international. Many other investments represent joint ventures in which two or more companies form a new enterprise to carry out a specified operating purpose. For example, Ford Motor Company and Sollers formed FordSollers, a passenger and commercial vehicle manufacturing, import, and distribution company in Russia. Each partner owns 50 percent of the joint venture. For each of these investments, the investors do not possess absolute control because they hold less than a majority of the voting stock. Thus, the preparation of consolidated financial statements is inappropriate. However, the large percentage of ownership indicates that each investor possesses some ability to affect the investee's decision-making process.

Finally, as discussed at the end of this chapter, firms may elect a fair-value option in their financial reporting for certain financial assets and financial liabilities. Among the qualifying financial assets for fair-value reporting are significant influence investments otherwise accounted for by the equity method.

International Accounting Standard 28—Investments in Associates

The International Accounting Standards Board (IASB), similar to the FASB, recognizes the need to take into account the significant influence that can occur when one firm holds a certain amount of voting shares of another. The IASB defines significant influence as the power to participate in the financial and operating policy decisions of the investee, but it is not control or joint control over those policies. The following describes the basics of the equity method in International Accounting Standard (IAS) 28:[6]

> If an investor holds, directly or indirectly (e.g., through subsidiaries), 20 per cent or more of the voting power of the investee, it is presumed that the investor has significant influence, unless it can be clearly demonstrated that this is not the case. Conversely, if the investor holds, directly or indirectly (e.g., through subsidiaries), less than 20 per cent of the voting power of the investee, it is presumed that the investor does not have significant influence, unless such influence can be clearly demonstrated. A substantial or majority ownership by another investor does not necessarily preclude an investor from having significant influence.
>
> Under the equity method, the investment in an associate is initially recognised at cost and the carrying amount is increased or decreased to recognise the investor's share of the profit or loss of the investee after the date of acquisition. The investor's share of the profit or loss of the investee is recognised in the investor's profit or loss. Distributions received from an investee reduce the carrying amount of the investment.

As seen from the above excerpt from *IAS 28,* the equity method concepts and applications described are virtually identical to those prescribed by the FASB ASC.

Application of the Equity Method

An understanding of the equity method is best gained by initially examining the FASB's treatment of two questions:

1. What factors indicate when the equity method should be used for an investment in another entity's ownership securities?
2. How should the investor report this investment and the income generated by it to reflect the relationship between the two entities?

Criteria for Utilizing the Equity Method

LO 1-2

Identify the sole criterion for applying the equity method of accounting and guidance in assessing whether the criterion is met.

The rationale underlying the equity method is that an investor begins to gain the ability to influence the decision-making process of an investee as the level of ownership rises. According to FASB ASC Topic 323 on equity method investments, achieving this "ability to exercise significant influence over operating and financial policies of an investee even though the investor holds 50 percent or less of the common stock" is the sole criterion for requiring application of the equity method [FASB ASC (para. 323-10-15-3)].

Clearly, a term such as *the ability to exercise significant influence* is nebulous and subject to a variety of judgments and interpretations in practice. At what point does the acquisition of one additional share of stock give an owner the ability to exercise significant influence? This decision becomes even more difficult in that only the *ability* to exercise significant influence need be present. There is no requirement that any actual influence must ever be applied.

FASB ASC Topic 323 provides guidance to the accountant by listing several conditions that indicate the presence of this degree of influence:

- Investor representation on the board of directors of the investee.
- Investor participation in the policy-making process of the investee.
- Material intra-entity transactions.

[6] International Accounting Standards Board, IAS 28, "Investments in Associates," Technical Summary (www.iasb.org).

- Interchange of managerial personnel.
- Technological dependency.
- Extent of ownership by the investor in relation to the size and concentration of other ownership interests in the investee.

No single one of these guides should be used exclusively in assessing the applicability of the equity method. Instead, all are evaluated together to determine the presence or absence of the sole criterion: the ability to exercise significant influence over the investee.

These guidelines alone do not eliminate the leeway available to each investor when deciding whether the use of the equity method is appropriate. To provide a degree of consistency in applying this standard, the FASB provides a general ownership test: *If an investor holds between 20 and 50 percent of the voting stock of the investee, significant influence is normally assumed and the equity method is applied.*

> An investment (direct or indirect) of 20 percent or more of the voting stock of an investee shall lead to a presumption that in the absence of predominant evidence to the contrary an investor has the ability to exercise significant influence over an investee. Conversely, an investment of less than 20 percent of the voting stock of an investee shall lead to a presumption that an investor does not have the ability to exercise significant influence unless such ability can be demonstrated.[7]

Limitations of Equity Method Applicability

At first, the 20 to 50 percent rule may appear to be an arbitrarily chosen boundary range established merely to provide a consistent method of reporting for investments. However, the essential criterion is still the ability to significantly influence (but not control) the investee, rather than 20 to 50 percent ownership. If the absence of this ability is proven (or control exists), the equity method should not be applied regardless of the percentage of shares held.

For example, the equity method is not appropriate for investments that demonstrate any of the following characteristics regardless of the investor's degree of ownership:[8]

- An agreement exists between investor and investee by which the investor surrenders significant rights as a shareholder.
- A concentration of ownership operates the investee without regard for the views of the investor.
- The investor attempts but fails to obtain representation on the investee's board of directors.

In each of these situations, because the investor is unable to exercise significant influence over its investee, the equity method is not applied.

Alternatively, if an entity can exercise *control* over its investee, regardless of its ownership level, consolidation (rather than the equity method) is appropriate. FASB ASC (para. 810-10-05-8) limits the use of the equity method by expanding the definition of a controlling financial interest and addresses situations in which financial control exists absent majority ownership interest. In these situations, control is achieved through contractual and other arrangements called *variable interests.*

To illustrate, one firm may create a separate legal entity in which it holds less than 50 percent of the voting interests but nonetheless controls that entity through governance document provisions and/or contracts that specify decision-making power and the distribution of profits and losses. Entities controlled in this fashion are typically designated as *variable interest entities,* and their sponsoring firm may be required to include them in consolidated financial reports despite the fact that ownership is less than 50 percent. For example, the Walt Disney Company reclassified several former equity method investees as variable interest entities and now consolidates these investments.[9]

[7] FASB ASC (para. 323-10-15-8).

[8] FASB ASC (para. 323-10-15-10). This paragraph deals specifically with limits to using the equity method for investments in which the owner holds 20 to 50 percent of the outstanding shares.

[9] Chapters 2 and 6 provide further discussions of variable interest entities.

Extensions of Equity Method Applicability

For some investments that either fall short of or exceed 20 to 50 percent ownership, the equity method is nonetheless appropriately used for financial reporting. As an example, The Coca-Cola Company acquired a 16.7 percent investment in Monster Beverage Corporation in 2015. Coca-Cola notes in its annual 2015 financial statements that "Based on our equity ownership percentage, the significance that our expanded distribution and coordination agreements have on Monster's operations, and our representation on Monster's Board of Directors, the Company is accounting for its interest in Monster as an equity method investment."

Conditions can also exist where the equity method is appropriate despite a majority ownership interest. In some instances, rights granted to noncontrolling shareholders restrict the powers of the majority shareholder. Such rights may include approval over compensation, hiring, termination, and other critical operating and capital spending decisions of an entity. If the noncontrolling rights are so restrictive as to call into question whether control rests with the majority owner, the equity method is employed for financial reporting rather than consolidation. For example, prior to its acquisition of BellSouth, AT&T, Inc., stated in its financial reports "we account for our 60 percent economic investment in Cingular under the equity method of accounting because we share control equally with our 40 percent partner BellSouth."

To summarize, the following table indicates the method of accounting that is typically applicable to various stock investments:

Criterion	Normal Ownership Level	Applicable Accounting Method
Inability to significantly influence	Less than 20%	Fair value or cost method
Ability to significantly influence	20%–50%	Equity method or fair value
Control through voting interests	More than 50%	Consolidated financial statements
Control through variable interests (governance documents, contracts)	Primary beneficiary status (no ownership required)	Consolidated financial statements

LO 1-3

Describe the financial reporting for equity method investments and prepare basic equity method journal entries for an investor.

Accounting for an Investment—The Equity Method

Now that the criteria leading to the application of the equity method have been identified, a review of its reporting procedures is appropriate. Knowledge of this accounting process is especially important to users of the investor's financial statements because the equity method affects both the timing of income recognition as well as the carrying amount of the investment account.

In applying the equity method, the accounting objective is to report the investment and investment income to reflect the close relationship between the investor and investee. After recording the cost of the acquisition, two equity method entries periodically record the investment's impact:

1. The investor's investment account *increases as the investee recognizes and reports income.* Also, the investor recognizes investment income using the accrual method—that is, in the same period as reported by the investee in its financial statements. If an investee reports income of $100,000, a 30 percent owner should immediately increase its own income by $30,000. This earnings accrual reflects the essence of the equity method by emphasizing the connection between the two companies; as the owners' equity of the investee increases through the earnings process, the investment account also increases. Although the investor initially records the acquisition at cost, upward adjustments in the asset balance are recorded as soon as the investee makes a profit. The investor reduces the investment account if the investee reports a loss.

2. The investor decreases its investment account for its share of investee cash dividends. When the investee declares a cash dividend, its owners' equity decreases. The investor mirrors this change by recording a reduction in the carrying amount of the investment rather than recognizing the dividend as revenue. Furthermore, because the investor recognizes income when the investee recognizes it, double counting would occur if the investor also recorded its share of subsequent investee dividends as revenue. Importantly, a cash dividend declaration is not an appropriate point for income recognition. As stated in FASB ASC (para. 323-10-35-4),

> Under the equity method, an investor shall recognize its share of the earnings or losses of an investee in the periods for which they are reported by the investee in its financial statements rather than in the period in which an investee declares a dividend.

Because the investor can influence their timing, investee dividends cannot objectively measure income generated from the investment.

Application of Equity Method	
Investee Event	**Investor Accounting**
Income is recognized.	Proportionate share of income is recognized.
Dividends are declared.	Investor's share of investee dividends reduce the investment account.

Application of the equity method thus causes the investment account on the investor's balance sheet to vary directly with changes in the investee's equity.

In contrast, the fair-value method reports investments at fair value if it is readily determinable. Also, income is recognized both from changes in fair value and upon receipt of dividends. Consequently, financial reports can vary depending on whether the equity method or fair-value method is appropriate.

To illustrate, assume that Big Company owns a 20 percent interest in Little Company purchased on January 1, 2017, for $210,000. Little then reports net income of $200,000, $300,000, and $400,000, respectively, in the next three years while declaring dividends of $50,000, $100,000, and $200,000. The fair values of Big's investment in Little, as determined by market prices, were $245,000, $282,000, and $325,000 at the end of 2017, 2018, and 2019, respectively.

Exhibit 1.1 compares the accounting for Big's investment in Little across the two methods. The fair-value method carries the investment at its market values, presumed to be readily available in this example. Income is recognized both through changes in Little's fair value and as Little declares dividends.

In contrast, under the equity method, Big recognizes income as it is recorded by Little. As shown in Exhibit 1.1, Big recognizes $180,000 in income over the three years, and the

EXHIBIT 1.1 Comparison of Fair-Value Method (ASC 321) and Equity Method (ASC 323)

			Accounting by Big Company When Influence Is Not Significant (fair-value method)			Accounting by Big Company When Influence Is Significant (equity method)	
Year	**Income of Little Company**	**Dividends Declared by Little Company**	**Dividend Income**	**Fair-Value Change to Income**	**Carrying Amount of Investment**	**Equity in Investee Income***	**Carrying Amount of Investment†**
2017	$200,000	$ 50,000	$10,000	$ 35,000	$ 245,000	$ 40,000	$240,000
2018	300,000	100,000	20,000	37,000	282,000	60,000	280,000
2019	400,000	200,000	40,000	43,000	325,000	80,000	320,000
Total income recognized			$70,000	$115,000		$180,000	

*Equity in investee income is 20 percent of the current year income reported by Little Company.

†The carrying amount of an investment under the equity method is the original cost plus income recognized less dividends. For 2017, as an example, the $240,000 reported balance is the $210,000 cost plus $40,000 equity income less $10,000 in dividends.

carrying amount of the investment is adjusted upward to $320,000. Dividends from Little are not an appropriate measure of income because of the assumed significant influence over the investee. Big's ability to influence Little's decisions applies to the timing of dividend distributions. Therefore, dividends from Little do not objectively measure Big's income from its investment in Little. As Little records income, however, under the equity method Big recognizes its share (20 percent) of the income and increases the investment account. Thus the equity method reflects the accrual model: The investor recognizes income as it is recognized by the investee, not when the investee declares a cash dividend.

Exhibit 1.1 shows that the carrying amount of the investment fluctuates each year under the equity method. This recording parallels the changes occurring in the net asset figures reported by the investee. If the owners' equity of the investee rises through income, an increase is made in the investment account; decreases such as losses and dividends cause reductions to be recorded. Thus, the equity method conveys information that describes the relationship created by the investor's ability to significantly influence the investee.

Equity Method Accounting Procedures

Once guidelines for the application of the equity method have been established, the mechanical process necessary for recording basic transactions is straightforward. The investor accrues its percentage of the earnings reported by the investee each period. Investee dividend declarations reduce the investment balance to reflect the decrease in the investee's book value.[10]

Referring again to the information presented in Exhibit 1.1, Little Company reported a net income of $200,000 during 2017 and declared and paid cash dividends of $50,000. These figures indicate that Little's net assets have increased by $150,000 during the year. Therefore, in its financial records, Big Company records the following journal entries to apply the equity method:

Investment in Little Company	40,000	
Equity in Investee Income		40,000
To accrue earnings of a 20 percent owned investee ($200,000 × 20%).		
Dividend Receivable	10,000	
Investment in Little Company		10,000
To record a dividend declaration by Little Company ($50,000 × 20%).		
Cash	10,000	
Dividend Receivable		10,000
To record collection of the cash dividend.		

In the first entry, Big accrues income based on the investee's reported earnings. The second entry reflects the dividend declaration and the related reduction in Little's net assets followed then by the cash collection. The $30,000 net increment recorded here in Big's investment account ($40,000 − $10,000) represents 20 percent of the $150,000 increase in Little's book value that occurred during the year.

Excess of Investment Cost over Book Value Acquired

LO 1-4

Allocate the cost of an equity method investment and compute amortization expense to match revenues recognized from the investment to the excess of investor cost over investee book value.

After the basic concepts and procedures of the equity method are mastered, more complex accounting issues can be introduced. Surely one of the most common problems encountered in applying the equity method occurs when the investment cost exceeds the proportionate book value of the investee company.[11]

[10] In this text, the terms *book value* and *carrying amount* are used synonymously. Each refers to either an account balance, an amount appearing in a financial statement, or the amount of net assets (stockholders' equity) of a business entity.

[11] Although encountered less frequently, investments can be purchased at a cost that is less than the underlying book value of the investee. Accounting for this possibility is explored in later chapters.

Discussion Question

DOES THE EQUITY METHOD REALLY APPLY HERE?

Abraham, Inc., a New Jersey corporation, operates 57 bakeries throughout the northeastern section of the United States. In the past, its founder, James Abraham, owned all the company's outstanding common stock. However, during the early part of this year, the corporation suffered a severe cash flow problem brought on by rapid expansion. To avoid bankruptcy, Abraham sought additional investment capital from a friend, Dennis Bostitch, who owns Highland Laboratories. Subsequently, Highland paid $700,000 cash to Abraham, Inc., to acquire enough newly issued shares of common stock for a one-third ownership interest.

At the end of this year, the accountants for Highland Laboratories are discussing the proper method of reporting this investment. One argues for maintaining the asset at its original cost: "This purchase is no more than a loan to bail out the bakeries. Mr. Abraham will continue to run the organization with little or no attention paid to us. After all, what does anyone in our company know about baking bread? I would be surprised if Abraham does not reacquire these shares as soon as the bakery business is profitable again."

One of the other accountants disagrees, stating that the equity method is appropriate. "I realize that our company is not capable of running a bakery. However, the official rules state that we must have only the *ability* to exert significant influence. With one-third of the common stock in our possession, we certainly have that ability. Whether we use it or not, this ability means that we are required to apply the equity method."

How should Highland Laboratories account for its investment in Abraham, Inc.?

Unless the investor acquires its ownership at the time of the investee's conception, paying an amount equal to book value is rare. A number of possible reasons exist for a difference between the book value of a company and its fair value as reflected by the price of its stock. A company's fair value at any time is based on a multitude of factors such as company profitability, the introduction of a new product, expected dividend payments, projected operating results, and general economic conditions. Furthermore, stock prices are based, at least partially, on the perceived worth of a company's net assets, amounts that often vary dramatically from underlying book values. Many asset and liability accounts shown on a balance sheet tend to measure historical costs rather than current value. In addition, these reported figures are affected by the specific accounting methods adopted by a company. Inventory costing methods such as LIFO and FIFO, for example, obviously lead to different book values as does each of the acceptable depreciation methods.

If an investment is acquired at a price in excess of the investee's book value, logical reasons should explain the additional cost incurred by the investor. The source of the excess of cost over book value is important. Income recognition requires matching the income generated from the investment with its cost. Excess costs allocated to fixed assets will likely be expensed over longer periods than costs allocated to inventory. In applying the equity method, the cause of such an excess payment can be divided into two general categories:

1. Specifically identifiable investee assets and liabilities can have fair values that differ from their present book values. The excess payment can be identified directly with individual accounts such as inventory, equipment, franchise rights, and so on.
2. The investor may pay an extra amount because it expects future benefits to accrue from the investment. Such benefits could be anticipated as the result of factors such as the estimated profitability of the investee or the expected relationship between the two companies. When

the additional payment cannot be attributed to any specifically identifiable investee asset or liability, the investor recognizes an intangible asset called *goodwill.* For example, eBay Inc. once disclosed in its annual report that goodwill related to its equity method investments was approximately $27.4 million.

As an illustration, assume that Grande Company is negotiating the acquisition of 30 percent of the outstanding shares of Chico Company. Chico's balance sheet reports assets of $500,000 and liabilities of $300,000 for a net book value of $200,000. After investigation, Grande determines that Chico's equipment is undervalued in the company's financial records by $60,000. One of its patents is also undervalued, but only by $40,000. By adding these valuation adjustments to Chico's book value, Grande arrives at an estimated $300,000 worth for the company's net assets. Based on this computation, Grande offers $90,000 for a 30 percent share of the investee's outstanding stock.

Book value of Chico Company [assets minus liabilities (or stockholders' equity)]	$200,000
Undervaluation of equipment	60,000
Undervaluation of patent	40,000
Value of net assets	$300,000
Percentage acquired	30%
Purchase price	$ 90,000

Although Grande's purchase price is in excess of the proportionate share of Chico's book value, this additional amount can be attributed to two specific accounts: Equipment and Patents. No part of the extra payment is traceable to any other projected future benefit. Thus, the cost of Grande's investment is allocated as follows:

Payment by investor		$90,000
Percentage of book value acquired ($200,000 × 30%)		60,000
Payment in excess of book value		30,000
Excess payment identified with specific assets:		
Equipment ($60,000 undervaluation × 30%)	$18,000	
Patent ($40,000 undervaluation × 30%)	12,000	30,000
Excess payment not identified with specific assets—goodwill		$ -0-

Of the $30,000 excess payment made by the investor, $18,000 is assigned to the equipment whereas $12,000 is traced to a patent and its undervaluation. No amount of the purchase price is allocated to goodwill.

To take this example one step further, assume that Chico's owners reject Grande's proposed $90,000 price. They believe that the value of the company as a going concern is higher than the fair value of its net assets. Because the management of Grande believes that valuable synergies will be created through this purchase, the bid price is raised to $125,000 and accepted. This new acquisition price is allocated as follows:

Payment by investor		$125,000
Percentage of book value acquired ($200,000 × 30%)		60,000
Payment in excess of book value		65,000
Excess payment identified with specific assets:		
Equipment ($60,000 undervaluation × 30%)	$18,000	
Patent ($40,000 undervaluation × 30%)	12,000	30,000
Excess payment not identified with specific assets—goodwill		$ 35,000

As this example indicates, *any extra payment that cannot be attributed to a specific asset or liability is assigned to the intangible asset goodwill.* Although the actual purchase price can be computed by a number of different techniques or simply result from negotiations, goodwill is always the excess amount not allocated to identifiable asset or liability accounts.

Under the equity method, the investor enters total cost in a single investment account regardless of the allocation of any excess purchase price. If all parties accept Grande's bid of $125,000, the acquisition is initially recorded at that amount despite the internal assignments made to equipment, patents and goodwill. The entire $125,000 was paid to acquire this investment, and it is recorded as such.

The Amortization Process

In the above transaction, the extra payment over Grande's book value was made for specific identifiable assets (equipment and patents), and goodwill. Even though the actual dollar amounts are recorded within the investment account, a definite historical cost can be attributed to these assets. With a cost to the investor as well as a specified life, the payment relating to each asset (except land, goodwill, and other indefinite life intangibles) should be amortized over an appropriate time period.[12] However, certain intangibles such as goodwill, are considered to have indefinite lives and thus are not subject to amortization.[13]

Goodwill associated with equity method investments, for the most part, is measured in the same manner as goodwill arising from a business combination (see Chapters 2 through 7). One difference is that goodwill arising from a business combination is subject to annual impairment reviews, whereas goodwill implicit in equity method investments is not. Equity method investments are tested in their entirety for permanent declines in value.[14]

To show the amortization process for definite-lived assets, we continue with our Grande and Chico example. Assume, that the equipment has a 10-year remaining life, the patent a 5-year life, and the goodwill an indefinite life. If the straight-line method is used with no salvage value, *the investor's cost* should be amortized initially as follows:[15]

Account	Cost Assigned	Remaining Useful Life	Annual Amortization
Equipment	$18,000	10 years	$1,800
Patent	12,000	5 years	2,400
Goodwill	35,000	Indefinite	–0–
Annual expense (for five years until patent cost is completely amortized)			$4,200

In recording this annual expense, Grande reduces the investment balance in the same way it would amortize the cost of any other asset that had a limited life. Therefore, at the end of the first year of holding the investment, the investor records the following journal entry under the equity method:

Equity in Investee Income	4,200	
Investment in Chico Company		4,200
To record amortization of excess payment allocated to equipment and patent.		

[12] A 2015 FASB *Proposed Accounting Standards Update,* "Simplifying the Equity Method of Accounting," recommended the elimination of the identification and amortization of excess cost over acquired investee book value. However, at a December 2015 meeting, the FASB did not affirm the proposed elimination of current accounting treatment for the excess cost over acquired investee book value and directed its staff to research additional alternatives for improving the equity method.

[13] Other intangibles (such as certain licenses, trademarks, etc.) also can be considered to have indefinite lives and thus are not amortized unless and until their lives are determined to be limited. Further discussion of intangibles with indefinite lives appears in Chapter 3.

[14] Because equity method goodwill is not separable from the related investment, goodwill should not be separately tested for impairment. See also FASB ASC para. 350-20-35-59.

[15] Unless otherwise stated, all amortization computations are based on the straight-line method with no salvage value.

Because this amortization relates to investee assets, the investor does not establish a specific expense account. Instead, as in the previous entry, the expense is recognized by decreasing the the investor's equity income accruing from the investee company.

To illustrate this entire process, assume that Tall Company purchases 20 percent of Short Company for $200,000. Tall can exercise significant influence over the investee; thus, the equity method is appropriately applied. The acquisition is made on January 1, 2017, when Short holds net assets with a book value of $700,000. Tall believes that the investee's building (10-year remaining life) is undervalued within the financial records by $80,000 and equipment with a 5-year remaining life is undervalued by $120,000. Any goodwill established by this purchase is considered to have an indefinite life. During 2017, Short reports a net income of $150,000 and at year-end declares a cash dividend of $60,000.

Tall's three basic journal entries for 2017 pose little problem:

January 1, 2017		
Investment in Short Company	200,000	
Cash		200,000
To record acquisition of 20 percent of the outstanding shares of Short Company.		

December 31, 2017		
Investment in Short Company	30,000	
Equity in Investee Income		30,000
To accrue 20 percent of the 2017 reported earnings of investee ($150,000 × 20%).		
Dividend Receivable	12,000	
Investment in Short Company		12,000
To record a dividend declaration by Short Company ($60,000 × 20%).		

An allocation of Tall's $200,000 purchase price must be made to determine whether an additional adjusting entry is necessary to recognize annual amortization associated with the extra payment:

Payment by investor		$200,000
Percentage of 1/1/17 book value ($700,000 × 20%)		140,000
Payment in excess of book value		60,000
Excess payment identified with specific assets:		
Building ($80,000 × 20%)	$16,000	
Equipment ($120,000 × 20%)	24,000	40,000
Excess payment not identified with specific assets—goodwill		$ 20,000

As can be seen, $16,000 of the purchase price is assigned to a building and $24,000 to equipment, with the remaining $20,000 attributed to goodwill. For each asset with a definite useful life, periodic amortization is required.

Asset	Attributed Cost	Remaining Useful Life	Annual Amortization
Building	$16,000	10 years	$1,600
Equipment	24,000	5 years	4,800
Goodwill	20,000	Indefinite	–0–
Total for 2017			$6,400

At the end of 2017, Tall must also record the following adjustment in connection with these cost allocations:

Equity in Investee Income	6,400	
Investment in Short Company		6,400
To record 2017 amortization of excess payment allocated to building ($1,600) and equipment ($4,800).		

Although these entries are shown separately here for better explanation, Tall would probably net the income accrual for the year ($30,000) and the amortization ($6,400) to create a single entry increasing the investment and recognizing equity income of $23,600. Thus, the first-year return on Tall Company's beginning investment balance (defined as equity earnings/beginning investment balance) is equal to 11.80 percent ($23,600/$200,000).

Equity Method—Additional Issues

The previous sections on equity income accruals and excess cost amortizations provide the basics for applying the equity method. However, several other non-routine issues can arise during the life of an equity method investment. More specifically, special procedures are required in accounting for each of the following:

1. Reporting a change to the equity method.
2. Reporting investee income from sources other than continuing operations.
3. Reporting investee losses.
4. Reporting the sale of an equity investment.

LO 1-5a

Understand the financial reporting consequences for a change to the equity method.

Reporting a Change to the Equity Method

In many instances, an investor's ability to significantly influence an investee is not achieved through a single stock acquisition. The investor could possess only a minor ownership for some years before purchasing enough additional shares to require conversion to the equity method. Before the investor achieves significant influence, any investment should be reported by either the fair-value method, or if the investment fair value is not readily determinable, the cost method. After the investment reaches the point at which the equity method becomes applicable, a technical question arises about the appropriate means of changing from one method to the other.[16]

FASB ASC (para. 323-10-35-33) addresses the issue of how to account for an investment in the common stock of an investee that, through additional stock acquisition or other means (e.g., increased degree of influence, reduction of investee's outstanding stock, etc.) becomes qualified for use of the equity method.

> If an investment qualifies for use of the equity method . . . , the investor shall add the cost of acquiring the additional interest in the investee (if any) to the current basis of the investor's previously held interest and adopt the equity method of accounting as of the date the investment becomes qualified for equity method accounting.

Thus, the FASB requires a prospective approach by requiring that the cost of any new share acquired simply be added to the current investment carrying amount. By mandating prospective treatment, the FASB avoids the complexity of restating prior period amounts.[17]

To illustrate, assume that on January 1, 2017, Alpha Company exchanges $84,000 for a 10 percent ownership in Bailey Company. At the time of the transaction, officials of Alpha do not believe that their company gained the ability to exert significant influence over Bailey. Alpha properly accounts for the investment using the fair-value method and recognizes in net

[16] A switch to the equity method also can be required if the investee purchases a portion of its own shares as treasury stock. This transaction can increase the investor's percentage of outstanding stock.

[17] Prior to 2017, the FASB required a retrospective adjustment to an investor's previous ownership shares upon achieving significant influence over an investee.

income its 10 percent ownership share of changes in Bailey's fair value. The fair and book values of Bailey's common stock appear below:

Date	Fair Value	Book Value
January 1, 2017	$840,000	$670,000
December 31, 2017	890,000	715,000

At the end of 2017, Alpha recognizes the increase in its 10 percent share of Bailey's fair value and increases its investment account to $89,000. Because the fair-value method is used to account for the investment, Bailey's $670,000 book value balance at January 1, 2017 does not affect Alpha's accounting.

Then on January 1, 2018, Alpha purchases an additional 30 percent of Bailey's outstanding voting stock for $267,000 and achieves the ability to significantly influence the investee's decision making. Alpha will now apply the equity method to account for its investment in Bailey. To bring about the prospective change to the equity method, Alpha prepares the following journal entry on January 1, 2018:

Investment in Bailey Company	267,000	
Cash		267,000
To record an additional 30 percent investment in Bailey Company		

On January 1, 2018, Bailey's carrying amounts for its assets and liabilities equaled their fair values except for a patent, which was undervalued by $175,000 and had a 10-year remaining useful life.

To determine the proper amount of excess fair value amortization required in applying the equity method, Alpha prepares an investment allocation schedule. The fair value of Alpha's total (40 percent) investment serves as the valuation basis for the allocation schedule as of January 1, 2018, the date Alpha achieves the ability to exercise significant influence over Bailey. Below is the January 1, 2018 investment allocation schedule:

Investment Fair Value Allocation Schedule
Investment in Bailey Company
January 1, 2018

Current fair value of initial 10 percent ownership of Bailey	$ 89,000
Payment for additional 30 percent investment in Bailey	267,000
Total fair value of 40 percent investment in Bailey	$356,000
Alpha's share of Bailey's book value (40% x $715,000)	286,000
Investment fair value in excess of Bailey's book value	$ 70,000
Excess fair value attributable to Bailey's patent (40% x $175,000)	$ 70,000
	-0-

We next assume that Bailey reports net income of $130,000 and declares and pays a $50,000 dividend at the end of 2018. Accordingly, Alpha applies the equity method and records the following three journal entries at the end of 2018:

Investment in Bailey Company	45,000	
Equity in Investee Income		45,000
To accrue 40 percent of the year 2018 income reported by Bailey Company ($130,000 × 40%) – $7,000 excess patent amortization (10-year remaining life).		
Dividend Receivable	20,000	
Investment in Bailey Company		20,000
To record the 2018 dividend declaration by Bailey Company ($50,000 × 40%).		
Cash	20,000	
Dividend Receivable		20,000
To record collection of the cash dividend.		

LO 1-5b

Understand the financial reporting consequences for investee's other comprehensive income.

Reporting Investee's Other Comprehensive Income and Irregular Items

In many cases, reported net income and dividends sufficiently capture changes in an investee's owners' equity. By recording its share of investee income and dividends, an investor company typically ensures its investment account reflects its share of the underlying investee equity. However, when an investee company's activities require recognition of other comprehensive income (OCI), its owners' equity (and net assets) will reflect changes not captured in its reported net income.[18]

Equity method accounting requires that the investor record its share of investee OCI which then is included in its balance sheet as Accumulated Other Comprehensive Income (AOCI). As noted by The Coca-Cola Company in its 2014 annual 10-K report,

> AOCI attributable to shareowners of The Coca-Cola Company is separately presented on our consolidated balance sheets as a component of The Coca-Cola Company's shareowners' equity, which also includes our proportionate share of equity method investees' AOCI.

Included in AOCI are items such as accumulated derivative net gains and losses, foreign currency translation adjustments, and certain pension adjustments.

To examine this issue, assume that Charles Company applies the equity method in accounting for its 30 percent investment in the voting stock of Norris Company. No excess amortization resulted from this investment. In 2017, Norris reports net income of $500,000. Norris also reports $80,000 in OCI from pension and other postretirement adjustments. Charles Company accrues earnings of $150,000 based on 30 percent of the $500,000 net figure. However, for proper financial reporting, Charles must recognize an increase in its Investment in Norris account for its 30 percent share of its investee's OCI. This treatment is intended, once again, to mirror the close relationship between the two companies.

The journal entry by Charles Company to record its equity interest in the income and OCI of Norris follows:

Investment in Norris Company	174,000	
Equity in Investee Income		150,000
Other Comprehensive Income of Investee		24,000
To accrue the investee's operating income and other comprehensive income from equity investment.		

OCI thus represents a source of change in investee company net assets that is recognized under the equity method. In the above example, Charles Company includes $24,000 of other comprehensive income in its balance sheet AOCI total.

Other equity method recognition issues arise for irregular items traditionally included within net income. For example, an investee may report income (loss) from discontinued operations as components of its current net income. In such cases, the equity method requires the investor to record and report its share of these items in recognizing equity earnings of the investee.

LO 1-5c

Understand the financial reporting consequences for investee losses.

Reporting Investee Losses

Although most of the previous illustrations are based on the recording of profits, accounting for losses incurred by the investee is handled in a similar manner. The investor recognizes the appropriate percentage of each loss and reduces the carrying amount of the investment account. Even though these procedures are consistent with the concept of the equity method, they fail to take into account all possible loss situations.

Impairments of Equity Method Investments

Investments can suffer permanent losses in fair value that are not evident through equity method accounting. Such declines can be caused by the loss of major customers, changes

[18] OCI is defined as revenues, expenses, gains, and losses that under generally accepted accounting principles are included in comprehensive income but excluded from net income. OCI is accumulated and reported in stockholders" equity.

in economic conditions, loss of a significant patent or other legal right, damage to the company's reputation, and the like. Permanent reductions in fair value resulting from such adverse events might not be reported immediately by the investor through the normal equity entries discussed previously. The FASB ASC (para. 323-10-35-32) provides the following guidance:

> A loss in value of an investment which is other than a temporary decline shall be recognized. Evidence of a loss in value might include, but would not necessarily be limited to, absence of an ability to recover the carrying amount of the investment or inability of the investee to sustain an earnings capacity that would justify the carrying amount of the investment.

Thus, when a permanent decline in an equity method investment's value occurs, the investor must recognize an impairment loss and reduce the asset to fair value.

However, this loss must be permanent before such recognition becomes necessary. Under the equity method, a temporary drop in the fair value of an investment is simply ignored.

Navistar International Corporation, for example, noted the following in its 2015 annual report:

> We assess the potential impairment of our equity method investments and determine fair value based on valuation methodologies, as appropriate, including the present value of estimated future cash flows, estimates of sales proceeds, and market multiples. If an investment is determined to be impaired and the decline in value is other than temporary, we record an appropriate write-down.

Investment Reduced to Zero

Through the recognition of reported losses as well as any permanent drops in fair value, the investment account can eventually be reduced to a zero balance. This condition is most likely to occur if the investee has suffered extreme losses or if the original purchase was made at a low, bargain price. Regardless of the reason, the carrying amount of the investment account is sometimes eliminated in total.

When an investment account is reduced to zero, the investor should discontinue using the equity method rather than establish a negative balance. The investment retains a zero balance until subsequent investee profits eliminate all unrecognized losses. Once the original cost of the investment has been eliminated, no additional losses can accrue to the investor (since the entire cost has been written off).

For example, Sirius XM Holdings Corporation explains in its 2015 financial statements that

> . . . As of December 31, 2015, we had $840 (thousand) in losses related to our investment in Sirius XM Canada that we had not recorded in our consolidated financial statements since our investment balance is zero. Future equity income will be offset by these losses prior to recording equity income in our results.

Reporting the Sale of an Equity Investment

LO 1-5d

Understand the financial reporting consequences for sales of equity method investments.

At any time, the investor can choose to sell part or all of its holdings in the investee company. If a sale occurs, the equity method continues to be applied until the transaction date, thus establishing an appropriate carrying amount for the investment. The investor then reduces this balance by the percentage of shares sold.

As an example, assume that Top Company owns 40 percent of the 100,000 outstanding shares of Bottom Company, an investment accounted for by the equity method. Any excess investment cost over Top's share of Bottom's book value is considered goodwill. Although these 40,000 shares were acquired some years ago for $200,000, application of the equity method has increased the asset balance to $320,000 as of January 1, 2018. On July 1, 2018, Top elects to sell 10,000 of these shares (one-fourth of its investment) for $110,000 in cash, thereby reducing ownership in Bottom from 40 percent to 30 percent. Bottom Company reports net income of $70,000 during the first six months of 2018 and declares and pays cash dividends of $30,000.

Top, as the investor, initially makes the following journal entries on July 1, 2018, to accrue the proper income and establish the correct investment balance:

Investment in Bottom Company	28,000	
Equity in Investee Income		28,000
To accrue equity income for first six months of 2018 ($70,000 × 40%).		
Dividend Receivable	12,000	
Investment in Bottom Company		12,000
To record a cash dividend declaration by Bottom Company ($30,000 × 40%).		
Cash	12,000	
Dividend Receivable		12,000
To record collection of the cash dividend.		

These two entries increase the carrying amount of Top's investment by $16,000, creating a balance of $336,000 as of July 1, 2018. The sale of one-fourth of these shares can then be recorded as follows:

Cash	110,000	
Investment in Bottom Company		84,000
Gain on Sale of Investment		26,000
To record sale of one-fourth of investment in Bottom Company (1/4 × $336,000 = $84,000).		

After the sale is completed, Top continues to apply the equity method to this investment based on 30 percent ownership rather than 40 percent. However, if the sale had been of sufficient magnitude to cause Top to lose its ability to exercise significant influence over Bottom, the equity method would cease to be applicable. For example, if Top Company's holdings were reduced from 40 percent to 15 percent, the equity method might no longer be appropriate after the sale. The remaining shares held by the investor are reported according to the fair-value method with the remaining book value becoming the new *cost* figure for the investment rather than the amount originally paid.

If an investor is required to change from the equity method to the fair-value method, no retrospective adjustment is made. Although, as previously demonstrated, a change to the equity method mandates a restatement of prior periods, the treatment is not the same when the investor's change is to the fair-value method.

LO 1-6

Describe the rationale and computations to defer gross profits on intra-entity inventory sales until the goods are either consumed by the owner or sold to outside parties.

Deferral of Intra-Entity Gross Profits in Inventory[19]

Many equity acquisitions establish ties between companies to facilitate the direct purchase and sale of inventory items. For example, The Coca-Cola Company recently disclosed net sales in excess of $8.9 billion to its equity method investees. The significant influence relationship between an investor and investee in many ways creates its own entity that works to achieve business objectives. Thus, we use the term *intra-entity* to describe sales between an investor and its equity method investee.

Intra-entity sales require special accounting to ensure proper timing for profit recognition. A fundamental accounting concept is that an entity cannot recognize profits through activities with itself. For example, when an investor company sells inventory to its 40 percent-owned investee at a profit, 40 percent of this intra-entity sale effectively is with itself. Consequently, when inventory sales occur between investor and investee, because of their ownership

[19] Intra-entity transfers can involve the sale of items other than inventory. The intra-entity transfer of depreciable fixed assets and land is discussed in a later chapter.

EXHIBIT 1.2
Downstream and Upstream Sales

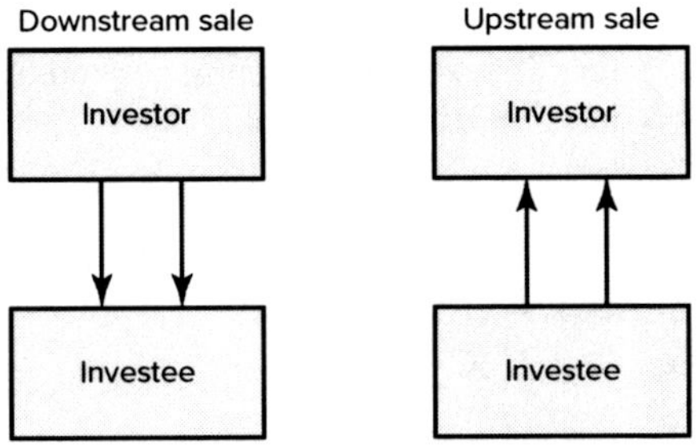

affiliation, the investor delays gross profit recognition until the inventory is sold to an independent party or is consumed.[20]

Importantly, in the presence of significant influence, the amount of profit deferred is limited to the investor's ownership share of the investee. In applying the equity method, the investor therefore defers only its share of the profit from intra-entity sales until the buyer's ultimate disposition of the goods. When the inventory is eventually consumed within operations or resold to an unrelated party, the investor recognizes the remaining gross profit. Accounting for both the profit deferral and subsequent recognition takes place through adjustments to the "Equity in Investee Income" and "Investment" accounts.

Intra-entity inventory sales are identified as either *downstream* or *upstream. Downstream sales* refer to the investor's sale of an item to the investee. Conversely, an *upstream sale* describes one that the investee makes to the investor (see Exhibit 1.2). *Although the direction of intra-entity sales does not affect reported equity method balances for investments when significant influence exists, it has definite consequences when financial control requires the consolidation of financial statements, as discussed in Chapter 5.* Therefore, these two types of intra-entity sales are examined separately even at this introductory stage.

Downstream Sales of Inventory

Assume that Major Company owns a 40 percent share of Minor Company and accounts for this investment through the equity method. In 2018, Major sells inventory to Minor at a price of $50,000. This figure includes a gross profit of 30 percent, or $15,000. By the end of 2018, Minor has sold $40,000 of these goods to outside parties while retaining $10,000 in inventory for sale during the subsequent year.

The investor has made downstream sales to the investee. In applying the equity method, recognition of the related profit must be delayed until the buyer disposes of these goods. Although total intra-entity inventory sales amounted to $50,000 in 2018, $40,000 of this merchandise has already been resold to outsiders, thereby justifying the normal reporting of profits. For the $10,000 still in the investee's inventory, the investor delays gross profit recognition. In computing equity income, the investor's portion of the intra-entity profit must be deferred until Minor disposes of the goods.

The gross profit on the original intra-entity sale was 30 percent of the sale price; therefore, Major's profit associated with these remaining items is $3,000 ($10,000 × 30%). *However, because only 40 percent of the investee's stock is held, just $1,200 ($3,000 × 40%) of this profit is deferred.* Major's ownership percentage reflects the intra-entity portion of the profit. The total $3,000 gross profit within the ending inventory balance is not the amount deferred. Rather, 40 percent of that gross profit is viewed as the currently deferred figure.

Remaining Ending Inventory	Gross Profit Percentage	Gross Profit in Ending Inventory	Investor Ownership Percentage	Deferred Intra-Entity Gross Profit
$10,000	30%	$3,000	40%	$1,200

[20] When inventory is consumed, for example in a manufacturing process, sales of the resulting production are assumed to generate revenues from outside, unrelated parties.

After calculating the appropriate deferral, the investor decreases current equity income by $1,200 to reflect the deferred portion of the intra-entity profit. This procedure temporarily removes this portion of the profit from the investor's books in 2018 until the investee disposes of the inventory in 2019. Major accomplishes the actual deferral through the following year-end journal entry:

Intra-Entity Gross Profit Deferral		
Equity in Investee Income	1,200	
Investment in Minor Company.		1,200
To defer gross profit on sale of inventory to Minor Company.		

In the subsequent year, when this inventory is eventually consumed by Minor or sold to unrelated parties, the deferral is no longer needed. Because a sale to an outside party has now occurred, Major should recognize the $1,200. By merely reversing the preceding deferral entry, the accountant succeeds in moving the investor's profit into the appropriate time period. Recognition shifts from the year of inventory transfer to the year in which the sale to customers outside of the affiliated entity takes place.

Subsequent Recognition of Intra-Entity Gross Profit		
Investment in Minor Company	1,200	
Equity in Investee Income.		1,200
To recognize income on intra-entity sale that now can be recognized after sales to outsiders.		

Upstream Sales of Inventory

Unlike consolidated financial statements (see Chapter 5), the equity method reports upstream sales of inventory in the same manner as downstream sales. Hence, the investor's share of gross profits remaining in ending inventory is deferred until the items are used or sold to unrelated parties. To illustrate, assume that Major Company once again owns 40 percent of Minor Company. During the current year, Minor sells merchandise costing $40,000 to Major for $60,000. At the end of the fiscal period, Major still retains $15,000 of these goods. Minor reports net income of $120,000 for the year.

To reflect the basic accrual of the investee's earnings, Major records the following journal entry at the end of this year:

Income Accrual		
Investment in Minor Company	48,000	
Equity in Investee Income.		48,000
To accrue income from 40 percent owned investee ($120,000 × 40%).		

The amount of the deferred intra-entity gross profit remaining at year-end is computed using the 33⅓ gross profit percentage of the sales price ($20,000/$60,000):

Remaining Ending Inventory	Gross Profit Percentage	Gross Profit in Ending Inventory	Investor Ownership Percentage	Deferred Intra-Entity Gross Profit
$15,000	33⅓%	$5,000	40%	$2,000

Based on this calculation, a second entry is required of the investor at year-end. Once again, a deferral of the gross profit created by the intra-entity sale is necessary for proper timing of income recognition. *Under the equity method for investments with significant influence, the direction of the sale between the investor and investee (upstream or downstream) has no effect on the final amounts reported in the financial statements.*

Intra-Entity Gross Profit Deferral		
Equity in Investee Income	2,000	
Investment in Minor Company		2,000
To defer recognition of intra-entity gross profit until inventory is used or sold to unrelated parties.		

After the adjustment, Major, the investor, reports earnings from this equity investment of \$46,000 (\$48,000 – \$2,000). The income accrual is reduced because the investor defers its portion of the intra-entity gross profit. When the investor eventually consumes or sells the \$15,000 in merchandise, the preceding journal entry is reversed. In this way, the effects of the inventory transfer are reported in the proper accounting period when sales to an outside party allow the recognition of the previously deferred intra-entity gross profit.

In an upstream sale, the investor's own inventory account contains the deferred gross profit. The previous entry, though, defers recognition of this profit by decreasing Major's investment account rather than the inventory balance. An alternative treatment would be the direct reduction of the investor's inventory balance as a means of accounting for this deferred amount. Although this alternative is acceptable, decreasing the investment account remains the traditional approach for deferring gross profits, even for upstream sales.

Whether upstream or downstream, the investor's sales and purchases are still reported as if the transactions were conducted with outside parties. Only the investor's share of the gross profit is deferred, and that amount is adjusted solely through the equity income account. Furthermore, because the companies are not consolidated, the investee's reported balances are not altered at all to reflect the nature of these sales/purchases. Obviously, readers of the financial statements need to be made aware of the inclusion of these amounts in the income statement. Thus, reporting companies must disclose certain information about related-party transactions. These disclosures include the nature of the relationship, a description of the transactions, the dollar amounts of the transactions, and amounts due to or from any related parties at year-end.

Financial Reporting Effects and Equity Method Criticisms

Equity Method Reporting Effects

It is important to realize that business decisions, including equity investments, typically involve the assessment of a wide range of consequences. For example, managers frequently are very interested in how financial statements report the effects of their decisions. This attention to financial reporting effects of business decisions arises because measurements of financial performance often affect the following:

- The firm's ability to raise capital.
- Managerial compensation.
- The ability to meet debt covenants and future interest rates.
- Managers' reputations.

Managers are also keenly aware that measures of earnings per share can strongly affect investors' perceptions of the underlying value of their firms' publicly traded stock. Consequently, prior to making investment decisions, firms will study and assess the prospective effects of applying the equity method on the income reported in financial statements. Additionally, such analyses of prospective reported income effects can influence firms regarding the degree of influence they wish to have, or even on the decision of whether to invest. For example, managers could have a required projected rate of return on an initial investment. In such cases, an analysis of projected income will be made to assist in setting an offer price.

For example, Investmor Co. is examining a potential 25 percent equity investment in Marco, Inc., that will provide a significant level of influence. Marco projects an annual income of $300,000 for the near future. Marco's book value is $450,000, and it has an unrecorded newly developed technology appraised at $200,000 with an estimated useful life of 10 years. In considering offer prices for the 25 percent investment in Marco, Investmor projects equity earnings as follows:

Projected income (25% × $300,000)	$75,000
Excess unpatented technology amortization [(25% × 200,000) ÷ 10 years]	(5,000)
Annual expected equity in Marco earnings	$70,000

Investmor's required first-year rate of return (before tax) on these types of investments is 20 percent. Therefore, to meet the first-year rate of return requirement involves a maximum price of $350,000 ($70,000 ÷ 20% = $350,000). If the shares are publicly traded (leaving the firm a "price taker"), such income projections can assist the company in making a recommendation to wait for share prices to move to make the investment attractive.

Criticisms of the Equity Method

Over the past several decades, thousands of business firms have accounted for their investments using the equity method. Recently, however, the equity method has come under criticism for the following:

- Emphasizing the 20–50 percent of voting stock in determining significant influence versus control.
- Allowing off-balance-sheet financing.
- Potentially biasing performance ratios.

The guidelines for the equity method suggest that a 20–50 percent ownership of voting shares indicates significant influence that falls short of control. But can one firm exert "control" over another firm absent an interest of more than 50 percent? Clearly, if one firm controls another, consolidation is the appropriate financial reporting technique. However, over the years, firms have learned ways to control other firms despite owning less than 50 percent of voting shares. For example, contracts across companies can limit one firm's ability to act without permission of the other. Such contractual control can be seen in debt arrangements, long-term sales and purchase agreements, and agreements concerning board membership. As a result, control is exerted through a variety of contractual arrangements. For financial reporting purposes, however, if ownership is 50 percent or less, a firm can argue that control technically does not exist.

In contrast to consolidated financial reports, when applying the equity method, the investee's assets and liabilities are not combined with the investor's amounts. Instead, the investor's balance sheet reports a single amount for the investment, and the income statement reports a single amount for its equity in the earnings of the investee. If consolidated, the assets, liabilities, revenues, and expenses of the investee are combined and reported in the body of the investor's financial statements.

Thus, for those companies wishing to actively manage their reported balance sheet numbers, the equity method provides an effective means. By keeping its ownership of voting shares below 50 percent, a company can technically meet the rules for applying the equity method for its investments and at the same time report investee assets and liabilities "off balance sheet." As a result, relative to consolidation, a firm employing the equity method will report smaller values for assets and liabilities. Consequently, higher rates of return for its assets and sales, as well as lower debt-to-equity ratios, could result.

On the surface, it appears that firms can avoid balance sheet disclosure of debts by maintaining investments at less than 50 percent ownership. However, the equity method requires summarized information as to assets, liabilities, and results of operations of the investees to be presented in the notes or in separate statements. Therefore, supplementary information could be available under the equity method that would not be separately identified in consolidation. Nonetheless, some companies have contractual provisions (e.g., debt covenants, managerial compensation agreements) based on ratios in the main body of the financial statements. Meeting the provisions of such contracts could provide managers strong incentives to maintain technical eligibility to use the equity method rather than full consolidation.

LO 1-7

Explain the rationale and reporting implications of fair-value accounting for investments otherwise accounted for by the equity method.

Fair-Value Reporting for Equity Method Investments

Financial reporting standards allow a fair-value option under which an entity may irrevocably elect fair value as the initial and subsequent measurement attribute for certain financial assets and financial liabilities. Under the fair-value option, changes in the fair value of the elected financial items are included in earnings. Among the many financial assets available for the fair-value option were investments otherwise accounted for under the equity method.

For example, Citigroup has reported at fair value certain of its investments that previously were reported using the equity method. In its 2015 annual report, Citigroup noted that "certain investments in non-marketable equity securities and certain investments that would otherwise have been accounted for using the equity method are carried at fair value, since the Company has elected to apply fair-value accounting. Changes in fair value of such investments are recorded in earnings." Many other firms, however, have been reluctant to elect the fair-value option for their equity method investments.

Firms using fair-value accounting simply report the investment's fair value as an asset and changes in fair value as earnings. As such, firms neither compute excess cost amortizations nor adjust earnings for intra-entity profits. Dividends from an investee are included in earnings under the fair-value option. Because dividends typically reduce an investment's fair value, an increase in earnings from investee dividends would be offset by a decrease in earnings from the decline in an investment's fair value.

To illustrate, on January 1, 2017, Westwind Co. pays $722,000 in exchange for 40,000 common shares of Armco, Inc., which has 100,000 common shares outstanding, the majority of which continue to trade on the New York Stock Exchange. During the next two years, Armco reports the following information:

Year	Net Income	Cash Dividends	Common Shares Total Fair Value at December 31
2017	$158,000	$25,000	$1,900,000
2018	125,000	25,000	1,870,000

Westwind elects to use fair-value accounting and accordingly makes the following journal entries for its investment in Armco over the next two years.

Investment in Armco, Inc..	722,000	
Cash		722,000
To record Westwind's initial 40 percent investment in Armco, Inc.		
Cash	10,000	
Dividend Income*		10,000
To recognize 2017 dividends received (40%) as investment income.		
Investment in Armco, Inc..	38,000	
Investment Income		38,000
To recognize Westwind's 40 percent of the 2017 change in Armco's fair value [($1,900,000 × 40%) – $722,000].		
Cash	10,000	
Dividend Income*		10,000
To recognize 2018 dividends received (40%) as investment income.		
Investment Loss	12,000	
Investment in Armco, Inc.		12,000
To recognize Westwind's 40 percent of the 2018 change in Armco's fair value [40% × ($1,870,000 – $1,900,000)].		

*This example assumes dividend declaration and payment occur at the same time.

In its December 31, 2018, balance sheet, Westwind thus reports its Investment in Armco account at $748,000, equal to 40 percent of Armco's total fair value (or $722,000 initial cost adjusted for 2017–2018 fair value changes of $38,000 less $12,000).

In addition to the increasing emphasis on fair values in financial reporting, the fair-value option also was motivated by a perceived need for consistency across various balance sheet items. In particular, the fair-value option is designed to limit volatility in earnings that occurs when some financial items are measured using cost-based attributes and others at fair value.

As FASB ASC (para. 825-10-10-1) observes, the objective of the fair-value option is

> to improve financial reporting by providing entities with the opportunity to mitigate volatility in reported earnings caused by measuring related assets and liabilities differently without having to apply complex hedge accounting provisions.

Thus, the fair-value option is designed to match asset valuation with fair-value reporting requirements for many liabilities.

Summary

1. The equity method of accounting for an investment reflects the close relationship that could exist between an investor and an investee. More specifically, this approach is available when the owner achieves the ability to apply significant influence to the investee's operating and financial decisions. Significant influence is presumed to exist at the 20 to 50 percent ownership level. However, the accountant must evaluate each situation, regardless of the percentage of ownership, to determine whether this ability is actually present.
2. To mirror the relationship between the companies, the equity method requires the investor to accrue income when the investee reports it in its financial statements. In recording this profit or loss, the investor separately reports items such as other comprehensive income and discontinued operations, to highlight their special nature. Dividend declarations decrease the owners' equity of the investee company; therefore, the investor reduces the investment account for its share of investee dividends.
3. When acquiring capital stock, an investor often pays an amount that exceeds the investee company's underlying book value. For accounting purposes, such excess payments must be either identified with specific assets and liabilities (such as land or buildings) or allocated to an intangible asset referred to as *goodwill.* The investor then amortizes each assigned cost (except for any amount attributed to land, goodwill, or other indefinite life assets) over the expected useful lives of the assets and liabilities. This amortization affects the amount of equity income recognized by the investor.
4. If the investor sells the entire investment or any portion of it, the equity method is applied until the date of disposal. A gain or loss is computed based on the adjusted book value at that time. Remaining shares are accounted for by means of either the equity method or the fair-value method, depending on the investor's subsequent ability to significantly influence the investee.
5. Inventory (or other assets) can be transferred between investor and investee. Because of the relationship between the two companies, the equity income accrual should be reduced to defer the portion of any gross profit included on these intra-entity sales until the items are either sold to outsiders or consumed. Thus, the amount of intra-entity gross profit in ending inventory decreases the amount of equity income recognized by the investor in the current period although this effect is subsequently reversed.
6. Firms may elect to report significant influence investments at fair value with changes in fair value as earnings. Under the fair-value option, firms simply report the investment's fair value as an asset and changes in fair value as earnings.

Comprehensive Illustration

(Estimated Time: 30 to 50 Minutes) Every chapter in this textbook concludes with an illustration designed to assist students in tying together the essential elements of the material presented. After a careful reading of each chapter, attempt to work through the comprehensive problem. Then review the solution that follows the problem, noting the handling of each significant accounting issue.

Problem

Part A

On January 1, 2016, Red Hawk Company pays $70,000 for a 10 percent interest in Wolf Company's common stock. Because market quotes for Wolf's stock are readily available on a continuing basis, the investment account has been appropriately maintained at fair value.

On January 1, 2017, Red Hawk acquires an additional 20 percent of Wolf Company for $176,000. This second purchase provides Red Hawk the ability to exert significant influence over Wolf, and Red Hawk will now apply the equity method. At the time of this transaction, Wolf had a January 1, 2017 book value of $650,000 although Wolf's equipment with a 4-year remaining life was undervalued by $80,000 relative to its fair value.

During these two years, Wolf reported the following operational results (cash dividends are declared and paid in July each year):

Year	Net Income	Cash Dividends	Fair Value at January 1
2016	$210,000	$110,000	$700,000
2017	270,000	110,000	880,000

Required

a. What income did Red Hawk originally report for 2016 in connection with this investment?

b. On comparative financial statements for 2016 and 2017, what figures should Red Hawk report in connection with this investment?

Part B (Continuation of Part A)

In 2018, Wolf Company reports $400,000 in income and $60,000 in other comprehensive income from foreign currency translation adjustments. The company declares and pays a $120,000 cash dividend. During this fiscal year, Red Hawk sells inventory costing $80,000 to Wolf for $100,000. Wolf continues to hold 50 percent of this merchandise at the end of 2018. Red Hawk maintains 30 percent ownership of Wolf throughout the period.

Required

Prepare all necessary journal entries for Red Hawk for the year 2018.

Solution

Part A

a. Red Hawk Company accounts for its investment in Wolf Company at fair value during 2016. Because Red Hawk held only 10 percent of the outstanding shares, significant influence apparently was absent. Because stock quotes were readily available, the investment was periodically updated to fair value. Therefore, the investor recorded both dividends and changes in fair value in its 2016 financial statements as follows:

Dividend income (10% × $110,000)	$11,000
Increase in fair value [10% × ($880,000 – 700,000)]	18,000
Total income recognized from investment in Wolf in 2016	$29,000

b. Changes to the equity method are accounted for prospectively. Therefore, in comparative statements, Red Hawk's 2016 income from its investment in Wolf is $29,000 as reflected in the fair value method shown in part a. above.

Red Hawk's 2017 financial statements will reflect the equity method as a result of the January 1, 2017 share purchase that resulted in significant influence. To determine the 2017 equity method income Red Hawk first evaluates its combined investments in Wolf to determine whether either goodwill or incremental asset values need to be reflected within the equity method procedures.

Fair Value Allocation of 30 Percent Ownership of Wolf Company on January 1, 2017	
Fair value of initial 10 percent purchase	$ 88,000
Payment for 20 percent investment at January 1, 2017	176,000
Fair value of 30 percent ownership	264,000
Book value acquired ($650,000 × 30%)	195,000
Fair value in excess of book value	69,000
Excess fair value identified with specific assets:	
Equipment ($80,000 × 30%)	24,000
Excess fair value not identified with specific assets—goodwill	$ 45,000

In allocating Wolf's January 1, 2017 fair value, $24,000 of the payment is attributable to the under-valued equipment with $45,000 assigned to goodwill. Because the equipment now has only a four-year remaining life, annual amortization of $6,000 is appropriate ($24,000/4).

Financial Reporting—2017		
Equity in Investee Income (income statement)		
Income reported by Wolf		$270,000
Red Hawk's ownership		30%
Red Hawk's share of Wolf's reported income	$ 81,000	
Less: Amortization expense:		
Equipment ($24,000/4 years)	(6,000)	
Equity in investee income—2017	$ 75,000	
Investment in Wolf (balance sheet)		
Fair value—1/1/17 (above)	$264,000	
Equity in investee income (above)	75,000	
Less: Investee dividends ($110,000 × 30%)	(33,000)	
Investment in Wolf—12/31/17	$306,000	

Part B

In July 2018 Wolf declares and pays a $36,000 cash dividend to Red Hawk (30% × $120,000). According to the equity method, this dividend reduces the carrying amount of the investment account:

Dividend Receivable	36,000	
Investment in Wolf Company		36,000
To record the 2018 cash dividend declaration by Wolf Company.		
Cash	36,000	
Dividend Receivable		36,000
To record collection of the cash dividend.		

Red Hawk records no other journal entries in connection with this investment until the end of 2018. At that time, the annual accrual of income as well as the adjustment to record amortization is made (see Part A for computation of expense). The investee's net income is reported separately from its other comprehensive income.

Investment in Wolf Company	138,000	
Equity in Investee Income		120,000
Investee Other Comprehensive Income		18,000
To recognize reported income of investee based on a 30 percent ownership level of $400,000 net income and $60,000 other comprehensive income.		
Equity in Investee Income	6,000	
Investment in Wolf Company		6,000
To record annual amortization on excess payment made in relation to equipment ($24,000/4 years).		

Red Hawk needs to make only one other equity entry during 2018. Intra-entity sales have occurred and Wolf continues to hold a portion of the inventory. Therefore, the investor's share of gross profit must be deferred. The gross profit rate from the sale was 20 percent ($20,000/$100,000). Because the investee still possesses $50,000 of this merchandise, the related gross profit is $10,000 ($50,000 × 20%). However, Red Hawk owns only 30 percent of Wolf's outstanding stock; thus, the intra-entity gross profit in inventory at year-end is $3,000 ($10,000 × 30%). That amount must be deferred until Wolf either consumes the inventory or sells it to unrelated parties.

Equity in Investee Company	3,000	
Investment in Wolf Company		3,000
To defer the investor's share of intra-entity gross profit in ending inventory.		

Questions

1. A company acquires a rather large investment in another corporation. What criteria determine whether the investor should apply the equity method of accounting to this investment?
2. What accounting treatments are appropriate for investments in equity securities without readily determinable fair values?
3. What indicates an investor's ability to significantly influence the decision-making process of an investee?
4. Why does the equity method record dividends from an investee as a reduction in the investment account, not as dividend income?
5. Jones Company owns a 25 percent interest in shares of Sandridge Company common stock. Under what circumstances might Jones decide that the equity method would not be appropriate to account for this investment?
6. Smith, Inc., has maintained an ownership interest in Watts Corporation for a number of years. This investment has been accounted for using the equity method. What transactions or events create changes in the Investment in Watts Corporation account as recorded by Smith?
7. Although the equity method is a generally accepted accounting principle (GAAP), recognition of equity income has been criticized. What theoretical problems can opponents of the equity method identify? What managerial incentives exist that could influence a firm's percentage ownership interest in another firm?
8. Because of the acquisition of additional investee shares, an investor will now change from the fair-value method to the equity method. Which procedures are applied to accomplish this accounting change?
9. Riggins Company accounts for its investment in Bostic Company using the equity method. During the past fiscal year, Bostic reported other comprehensive income from translation adjustments related to its foreign investments. How would this other comprehensive income affect the investor's financial records?
10. During the current year, Davis Company's common stock suffers a permanent drop in market value. In the past, Davis has made a significant portion of its sales to one customer. This buyer recently announced its decision to make no further purchases from Davis Company, an action that led to the loss of market value. Hawkins, Inc., owns 35 percent of the outstanding shares of Davis, an investment that is recorded according to the equity method. How would the loss in value affect this investor's financial reporting?
11. Wilson Company acquired 40 percent of Andrews Company at a bargain price because of losses expected to result from Andrews's failure in marketing several new products. Wilson paid only $100,000, although Andrews's corresponding book value was much higher. In the first year after acquisition, Andrews lost $300,000. In applying the equity method, how should Wilson account for this loss?
12. In a stock acquisition accounted for by the equity method, a portion of the purchase price often is attributed to goodwill or to specific assets or liabilities. How are these amounts determined at acquisition? How are these amounts accounted for in subsequent periods?
13. Princeton Company holds a 40 percent interest in shares of Yale Company common stock. On June 19 of the current year, Princeton sells part of this investment. What accounting should Princeton make on June 19? What accounting will Princeton make for the remainder of the current year?
14. What is the difference between downstream and upstream sales? How does this difference affect application of the equity method?
15. How is the investor's share of gross profit on intra-entity sales calculated? Under the equity method, how does the deferral of gross profit affect the recognition of equity income?
16. How are intra-entity transfers reported in an investee's separate financial statements if the investor is using the equity method?
17. What is the fair-value option for reporting equity method investments? How do the equity method and fair-value accounting differ in recognizing income from an investee?

Problems

LO 1-3

1. When an investor uses the equity method to account for investments in common stock, the investor's share of cash dividends from the investee should be recorded as
   a. A deduction from the investor's share of the investee's profits.
   b. Dividend income.
   c. A deduction from the stockholders' equity account, Dividends to Stockholders.
   d. A deduction from the investment account.
   (AICPA adapted)

LO 1-2

2. Which of the following does not indicate an investor company's ability to significantly influence an investee?
   a. Material intra-entity transactions.
   b. The investor owns 30 percent of the investee but another owner holds the remaining 70 percent.
   c. Interchange of personnel.
   d. Technological dependency.

LO 1-5a

3. Hawkins Company has owned 10 percent of Larker, Inc., for the past several years. This ownership did not allow Hawkins to have significant influence over Larker. Recently, Hawkins acquired an additional 30 percent of Larker and now will use the equity method. How will the investor report change?
   a. A cumulative effect of an accounting change is shown in the current income statement.
   b. A retrospective adjustment is made to restate all prior years presented using the equity method.
   c. No change is recorded; the equity method is used from the date of the new acquisition.
   d. Hawkins will report the change as a component of accumulated other comprehensive income.

LO 1-7

4. Under fair-value accounting for an equity investment, which of the following affects the income the investor recognizes from its ownership of the investee?
   a. The investee's reported income adjusted for excess cost over book value amortizations.
   b. Changes in the fair value of the investor's ownership shares of the investee.
   c. Intra-entity profits from upstream sales.
   d. Other comprehensive income reported by the investee.

LO 1-5c

5. When an equity method investment account is reduced to a zero balance
   a. The investor should establish a negative investment account balance for any future losses reported by the investee.
   b. The investor should discontinue using the equity method until the investee begins paying dividends.
   c. Future losses are reported as unusual items in the investor's income statement.
   d. The investment retains a zero balance until subsequent investee profits eliminate all unrecognized losses.

LO 1-3

6. On January 1, Puckett Company paid $1.6 million for 50,000 shares of Harrison's voting common stock, which represents a 40 percent investment. No allocation to goodwill or other specific account was made. Significant influence over Harrison is achieved by this acquisition and so Puckett applies the equity method. Harrison declared a $2 per share dividend during the year and reported net income of $560,000. What is the balance in the Investment in Harrison account found in Puckett's financial records as of December 31?
   a. $1,724,000
   b. $1,784,000
   c. $1,844,000
   d. $1,884,000

LO 1-3, 1-4

7. In January 2017, Domingo, Inc., acquired 20 percent of the outstanding common stock of Martes, Inc., for $700,000. This investment gave Domingo the ability to exercise significant influence over Martes, whose balance sheet on that date showed total assets of $3,900,000 with liabilities of $900,000. Any excess of cost over book value of the investment was attributed to a patent having a remaining useful life of 10 years.
   In 2017, Martes reported net income of $170,000. In 2018, Martes reported net income of $210,000. Dividends of $70,000 were declared in each of these two years. What is the equity method balance of Domingo's Investment in Martes, Inc., at December 31, 2018?
   a. $728,000
   b. $748,000
   c. $756,000
   d. $776,000

LO 1-3, 1-4

8. Franklin purchases 40 percent of Johnson Company on January 1 for $500,000. Although Franklin did not use it, this acquisition gave Franklin the ability to apply significant influence to Johnson's operating and financing policies. Johnson reports assets on that date of $1,400,000 with liabilities of $500,000. One building with a seven-year remaining life is undervalued on Johnson's books by $140,000. Also, Johnson's book value for its trademark (10-year remaining life) is undervalued by $210,000. During the year, Johnson reports net income of $90,000 while declaring dividends of $30,000. What is the Investment in Johnson Company balance (equity method) in Franklin's financial records as of December 31?
   a. $504,000
   b. $507,600
   c. $513,900
   d. $516,000

LO 1-3, 1-4

9. Evan Company reports net income of $140,000 each year and declares an annual cash dividend of $50,000. The company holds net assets of $1,200,000 on January 1, 2017. On that date, Shalina purchases 40 percent of Evan's outstanding common stock for $600,000, which gives it the ability to significantly influence Evan. At the purchase date, the excess of Shalina's cost over its proportionate share of Evan's book value was assigned to goodwill. On December 31, 2019, what is the Investment in Evan Company balance (equity method) in Shalina's financial records?
   a. $600,000
   b. $660,000
   c. $690,000
   d. $708,000

LO 1-6

10. Perez, Inc., applies the equity method for its 25 percent investment in Senior, Inc. During 2018, Perez sold goods with a 40 percent gross profit to Senior, which sold all of these goods in 2018. How should Perez report the effect of the intra-entity sale on its 2018 income statement?
   a. Sales and cost of goods sold should be reduced by the amount of intra-entity sales.
   b. Sales and cost of goods sold should be reduced by 25 percent of the amount of intra-entity sales.
   c. Investment income should be reduced by 25 percent of the gross profit on the amount of intra-entity sales.
   d. No adjustment is necessary.

LO 1-6

11. Panner, Inc., owns 30 percent of Watkins and applies the equity method. During the current year, Panner buys inventory costing $54,000 and then sells it to Watkins for $90,000. At the end of the year, Watkins still holds only $20,000 of merchandise. What amount of gross profit must Panner defer in reporting this investment using the equity method?
   a. $2,400
   b. $4,800
   c. $8,000
   d. $10,800

LO 1-3, 1-4, 1-6

12. Alex, Inc., buys 40 percent of Steinbart Company on January 1, 2017, for $530,000. The equity method of accounting is to be used. Steinbart's net assets on that date were $1.2 million. Any excess of cost over book value is attributable to a trade name with a 20-year remaining life. Steinbart immediately begins supplying inventory to Alex as follows:

Year	Cost to Steinbart	Transfer Price	Amount Held by Alex at Year-End (at transfer price)
2017	$70,000	$100,000	$25,000
2018	96,000	150,000	45,000

Inventory held at the end of one year by Alex is sold at the beginning of the next.

Steinbart reports net income of $80,000 in 2017 and $110,000 in 2018 and declares $30,000 in dividends each year. What is the equity income in Steinbart to be reported by Alex in 2018?
   a. $34,050
   b. $38,020
   c. $46,230
   d. $51,450

LO 1-3, 1-4

13. On January 3, 2018, Matteson Corporation acquired 40 percent of the outstanding common stock of O'Toole Company for $1,160,000. This acquisition gave Matteson the ability to exercise significant influence over the investee. The book value of the acquired shares was $820,000. Any excess cost over the underlying book value was assigned to a copyright that was undervalued on its balance sheet. This copyright has a remaining useful life of 10 years. For the year ended December 31, 2018, O'Toole reported net income of $260,000 and declared cash dividends of $50,000. At December 31, 2018, what should Matteson report as its investment in O'Toole under the equity method?

LO 1-3

14. On January 1, 2018, Fisher Corporation paid $2,290,000 for 35 percent of the outstanding voting stock of Steel, Inc., and appropriately applies the equity method for its investment. Any excess of cost over Steel's book value was attributed to goodwill. During 2018, Steel reports $720,000 in net income and a $100,000 other comprehensive income loss. Steel also declares and pays $20,000 in dividends.

    a. What amount should Fisher report as its Investment in Steel on its December 31, 2018, balance sheet?

    b. What amount should Fisher report as Equity in Earnings of Steel on its 2018 income statement?

LO 1-3, 1-4

15. On January 1, 2017, Ridge Road Company acquired 20 percent of the voting shares of Sauk Trail, Inc., for $2,700,000 in cash. Both companies provide commercial Internet support services but serve markets in different industries. Ridge Road made the investment to gain access to Sauk Trail's board of directors and thus facilitate future cooperative agreements between the two firms. Ridge Road quickly obtained several seats on Sauk Trail's board which gave it the ability to significantly influence Sauk Trail's operating and investing activities.

    The January 1, 2017, carrying amounts and corresponding fair values for Sauk Trail's assets and liabilities follow:

	Carrying Amount	Fair Value
Cash and receivables	$ 110,000	$ 110,000
Computing equipment	5,000,000	5,700,000
Patented technology	100,000	4,000,000
Trademark	150,000	2,000,000
Liabilities	(185,000)	(185,000)

    Also as of January 1, 2017, Sauk Trail's computing equipment had a seven-year remaining estimated useful life. The patented technology was estimated to have a three-year remaining useful life. The trademark's useful life was considered indefinite. Ridge Road attributed to goodwill any unidentified excess cost.

    During the next two years, Sauk Trail reported the following net income and dividends:

	Net Income	Dividends Declared
2017	$1,800,000	$150,000
2018	1,985,000	160,000

    a. How much of Ridge Road's $2,700,000 payment for Sauk Trail is attributable to goodwill?

    b. What amount should Ridge Road report for its equity in Sauk Trail's earnings on its income statements for 2017 and 2018?

    c. What amount should Ridge Road report for its investment in Sauk Trail on its balance sheets at the end of 2017 and 2018?

LO 1-3, 1-4, 1-7

16. On January 1, 2017, Alison, Inc., paid $60,000 for a 40 percent interest in Holister Corporation's common stock. This investee had assets with a book value of $200,000 and liabilities of $75,000. A patent held by Holister having a $5,000 book value was actually worth $20,000. This patent had a six-year remaining life. Any further excess cost associated with this acquisition was attributed to goodwill. During 2017, Holister earned income of $30,000 and declared and paid dividends of $10,000. In 2018, it had income of $50,000 and dividends of $15,000. During 2018, the fair value of Allison's investment in Holister had risen from $68,000 to $75,000.

    a. Assuming Alison uses the equity method, what balance should appear in the Investment in Holister account as of December 31, 2018?

    b. Assuming Alison uses fair-value accounting, what income from the investment in Holister should be reported for 2018?

LO 1-3, 1-6

17. On January 1, 2018, Alamar Corporation acquired a 40 percent interest in Burks, Inc., for $210,000. On that date, Burks's balance sheet disclosed net assets with both a fair and book value of $360,000. During 2018, Burks reported net income of $80,000 and declared and paid cash dividends of $25,000. Alamar sold inventory costing $30,000 to Burks during 2018 for $40,000. Burks used all of this merchandise in its operations during 2018. Prepare all of Alamar's 2018 journal entries to apply the equity method to this investment.

LO 1-1, 1-2, 1-3, 1-4, 1-5a

18. Milani, Inc., acquired 10 percent of Seida Corporation on January 1, 2017, for $190,000 and appropriately accounted for the investment using the fair-value method. On January 1, 2018, Milani purchased an additional 30 percent of Seida for $600,000 which resulted in significant influence over Seida. On that date, the fair value of Seida's common stock was $2,000,000 in total. Seida's January 1, 2018, book value equaled $1,850,000, although land was undervalued by $120,000. Any additional excess fair value over Seida's book value was attributable to a trademark with an 8-year remaining life. During 2018, Seida reported income of $300,000 and declared and paid dividends of $110,000. Prepare the 2018 journal entries for Milani related to its investment in Seida.

LO 1-6

19. Tiberend, Inc., sold $150,000 in inventory to Schilling Company during 2017 for $225,000. Schilling resold $105,000 of this merchandise in 2017 with the remainder to be disposed of during 2018. Assuming that Tiberend owns 25 percent of Schilling and applies the equity method, what journal entry is recorded at the end of 2017 to defer the intra-entity gross profit?

LO 1-3, 1-4, 1-6

20. BuyCo, Inc. holds 25 percent of the outstanding shares of Marqueen Company and appropriately applies the equity method of accounting. Excess cost amortization (related to a patent) associated with this investment amounts to $10,000 per year. For 2017, Marqueen reported earnings of $100,000 and declares cash dividends of $30,000. During that year, Marqueen acquired inventory for $50,000, which it then sold to BuyCo for $80,000. At the end of 2017, BuyCo continued to hold merchandise with a transfer price of $32,000.

    a. What Equity in Investee Income should BuyCo report for 2017?

    b. How will the intra-entity transfer affect BuyCo's reporting in 2018?

    c. If BuyCo had sold the inventory to Marqueen, how would the answers to (*a*) and (*b*) have changed?

LO 1-1, 1-2, 1-3, 1-4, 1-5a

21. On January 1, 2016, Halstead, Inc., purchased 75,000 shares of Sedgwick Company common stock for $1,480,000, giving Halstead 25 percent ownership and the ability to apply significant influence over Sedgwick. Any excess of cost over book value acquired was attributed solely to goodwill.

    Sedgwick reports net income and dividends as follows. These amounts are assumed to have occurred evenly throughout these years. Dividends are declared and paid in the same period.

	Net Income	Annual Cash Dividends (paid quarterly)
2016	$340,000	$120,000
2017	480,000	140,000
2018	600,000	160,000

    On July 1, 2018, Halstead sells 12,000 shares of this investment for $25 per share, thus reducing its interest from 25 to 21 percent, but maintaining its significant influence.

    Determine the amounts that would appear on Halstead's 2018 income statement relating to its ownership and partial sale of its investment in Sedgwick's common stock.

LO 1-1, 1-2, 1-3, 1-4, 1-5d

22. Echo, Inc., purchased 10 percent of ProForm Corporation on January 1, 2017, for $345,000 and accounted for the investment using the fair-value method. Echo acquires an additional 15 percent of ProForm on January 1, 2018, for $580,000. The equity method of accounting is now appropriate for this investment. No intra-entity sales have occurred.

    a. How does Echo initially determine the income to be reported in 2017 in connection with its ownership of ProForm?

    b. What factors should have influenced Echo in its decision to apply the equity method in 2018?

    c. What factors could have prevented Echo from adopting the equity method after this second purchase?

    d. What is the objective of the equity method of accounting?

    e. What criticisms have been leveled at the equity method?

f. In comparative statements for 2017 and 2018, how would Echo determine the income to be reported in 2017 in connection with its ownership of ProForm? Why is this accounting appropriate?

g. How is the allocation of Echo's acquisition made?

h. If ProForm declares a cash dividend, what impact does it have on Echo's financial records under the equity method? Why is this accounting appropriate?

i. On financial statements for 2018, what amounts are included in Echo's Investment in ProForm account? What amounts are included in Echo's Equity in Income of ProForm account?

LO 1-3, 1-6

23. Parrot Corporation holds a 42 percent ownership of Sunrise, Inc., and applies the equity method to account for its investment. Parrot assigned the entire original excess purchase price over book value to goodwill. During 2017, the two companies made intra-entity inventory transfers. A portion of this merchandise was not resold until 2018. During 2018, additional transfers were made.

a. What is the difference between upstream transfers and downstream transfers?

b. How does the direction of an intra-entity transfer (upstream versus downstream) affect the application of the equity method?

c. How is the intra-entity gross profit deferral computed in applying the equity method?

d. How should Parrot compute the amount of equity income to be recognized in 2017? What entry is made to record this income?

e. How should Parrot compute the amount of equity income to be recognized in 2018?

f. If none of the transferred inventory had remained at the end of 2017, how would these transfers have affected the application of the equity method?

g. How do these intra-entity transfers affect Sunrise's financial reporting?

LO 1-1, 1-5d

24. Several years ago, Einstein, Inc., bought 40 percent of the outstanding voting stock of Brooks Company. The equity method is appropriately applied. On August 1 of the current year, Einstein sold a portion of these shares.

a. How does Einstein compute the book value of this investment on August 1 to determine its gain or loss on the sale?

b. How should Einstein account for this investment after August 1?

c. If Einstein retains only a 2 percent interest in Brooks so that it holds virtually no influence over Brooks, what figures appear in the investor's income statement for the current year?

d. If Einstein retains only a 2 percent interest in Brooks so that virtually no influence is held, does the investor have to retroactively adjust any previously reported figures?

LO 1-3, 1-4, 1-6

25. Matthew, Inc. owns 30 percent of the outstanding stock of Lindman Company and has the ability to significantly influence the investee's operations and decision making. On January 1, 2018, the balance in the Investment in Lindman account is $335,000. Amortization associated with this acquisition is $9,000 per year. In 2018, Lindman earns an income of $90,000 and declares cash dividends of $30,000. Previously, in 2017, Lindman had sold inventory costing $24,000 to Matthew for $40,000. Matthew consumed all but 25 percent of this merchandise during 2017 and used the rest during 2018. Lindman sold additional inventory costing $28,000 to Matthew for $50,000 in 2018. Matthew did not consume 40 percent of these 2018 purchases from Lindman until 2019.

a. What amount of equity method income would Matthew recognize in 2018 from its ownership interest in Lindman?

b. What is the equity method balance in the Investment in Lindman account at the end of 2018?

LO 1-1, 1-3, 1-4

26. On December 31, 2016, Akron, Inc. purchased 5 Percent of Zip Company's common shares on the open market in exchange for $16,000. On December 31, 2017, Akron, Inc., acquires an additional 25 percent of Zip Company's outstanding common stock for $95,000.

During the next two years, the following information is available for Zip Company:

	Income	Dividends Declared	Common Stock Fair Value (12/31)
2016			$320,000
2017	$ 75,000	$ 7,000	380,000
2018	88,000	15,000	480,000

At December 31, 2017, Zip reports a net book value of $290,000. Akron attributed any excess of its 30 percent share of Zip's fair over book value to its share of Zip's franchise agreements. The franchise agreements had a remaining life of 10 years at December 31, 2017.

a. Assume Akron applies the equity method to its Investment in Zip account:
1. What amount of equity income should Akron report for 2018?
2. On Akron's December 31, 2018, balance sheet, what amount is reported for the Investment in Zip account?

b. Assume Akron uses fair-value accounting for its Investment in Zip account:
1. What amount of income from its investment in Zip should Akron report for 2018?
2. On Akron's December 31, 2018, balance sheet, what amount is reported for the Investment in Zip account?

LO 1-3, 1-4, 1-5d, 1-6

27. Belden, Inc. acquires 30 percent of the outstanding voting shares of Sheffield, Inc. on January 1, 2017, for $312,000, which gives Belden the ability to significantly influence Sheffield. Sheffield has a net book value of $800,000 at January 1, 2017. Sheffield's asset and liability accounts showed carrying amounts considered equal to fair values except for a copyright whose value accounted for Belden's excess cost over book value in its 30 percent purchase. The copyright had a remaining life of 16 years at January 1, 2017. No goodwill resulted from Belden's share purchase.

Sheffield reported net income of $180,000 in 2017 and $230,000 of net income during 2018. Dividends of $70,000 and $80,000 are declared and paid in 2017 and 2018, respectively. Belden uses the equity method.

a. On its 2018 comparative income statements, how much income would Belden report for 2017 and 2018 in connection with the company's investment in Sheffield?

b. If Belden sells its entire investment in Sheffield on January 1, 2019, for $400,000 cash, what is the impact on Belden's income?

c. Assume that Belden sells inventory to Sheffield during 2017 and 2018 as follows:

Year	Cost to Belden	Price to Sheffield	Year-End Balance (at transfer price)
2017	$30,000	$50,000	$20,000 (sold in following year)
2018	33,000	60,000	40,000 (sold in following year)

What amount of equity income should Belden recognize for the year 2018?

LO 1-3, 1-4, 1-5b, 1-6

28. Harper, Inc. acquires 40 percent of the outstanding voting stock of Kinman Company on January 1, 2017, for $210,000 in cash. The book value of Kinman's net assets on that date was $400,000, although one of the company's buildings, with a $60,000 carrying amount, was actually worth $100,000. This building had a 10-year remaining life. Kinman owned a royalty agreement with a 20-year remaining life that was undervalued by $85,000.

Kinman sold inventory with an original cost of $60,000 to Harper during 2017 at a price of $90,000. Harper still held $15,000 (transfer price) of this amount in inventory as of December 31, 2017. These goods are to be sold to outside parties during 2018.

Kinman reported a $40,000 net loss and a $20,000 other comprehensive loss for 2017. The company still manages to declare and pay a $10,000 cash dividend during the year.

During 2018, Kinman reported a $40,000 net income and declared and paid a cash dividend of $12,000. It made additional inventory sales of $80,000 to Harper during the period. The original cost of the merchandise was $50,000. All but 30 percent of this inventory had been resold to outside parties by the end of the 2018 fiscal year.

Prepare all journal entries for Harper for 2017 and 2018 in connection with this investment. Assume that the equity method is applied.

LO 1-3, 1-4, 1-5b, 1-6

29. On January 1, 2018, Pine Company owns 40 percent (40,000 shares) of Seacrest, Inc., which it purchased several years ago for $182,000. Since the date of acquisition, the equity method has been properly applied, and the carrying amount of the investment account as of January 1, 2018, is $293,600. Excess patent cost amortization of $12,000 is still being recognized each year. During 2018, Seacrest reports net income of $342,000 and a $120,000 other comprehensive loss, both incurred uniformly throughout the year. No dividends were declared during the year. Pine sold 8,000 shares of Seacrest on August 1, 2018, for $93,000 in cash. However, Pine retains the ability to significantly influence the investee.

During the last quarter of 2017, Pine sold $50,000 in inventory (which it had originally purchased for only $30,000) to Seacrest. At the end of that fiscal year, Seacrest's inventory retained $10,000 (at sales price) of this merchandise, which was subsequently sold in the first quarter of 2018.

On Pine's financial statements for the year ended December 31, 2018, what income effects would be reported from its ownership in Seacrest?

LO 1-3, 1-4, 1-6

30. On July 1, 2016, Killearn Company acquired 88,000 of the outstanding shares of Shaun Company for $13 per share. This acquisition gave Killearn a 25 percent ownership of Shaun and allowed Killearn to significantly influence the investee's decisions.

As of July 1, 2016, the investee had assets with a book value of $3 million and liabilities of $74,400. At the time, Shaun held equipment appraised at $364,000 above book value; it was considered to have a seven-year remaining life with no salvage value. Shaun also held a copyright with a five-year remaining life on its books that was undervalued by $972,000. Any remaining excess cost was attributable to goodwill. Depreciation and amortization are computed using the straight-line method. Killearn applies the equity method for its investment in Shaun.

Shaun's policy is to declare and pay a $1 per share cash dividend every April 1 and October 1. Shaun's income, earned evenly throughout each year, was $598,000 in 2016, $639,600 in 2017, and $692,400 in 2018.

In addition, Killearn sold inventory costing $91,200 to Shaun for $152,000 during 2017. Shaun resold $92,000 of this inventory during 2017 and the remaining $60,000 during 2018.

a. Determine the equity income to be recognized by Killearn during each of these years.

b. Compute Killearn's investment in Shaun Company's balance as of December 31, 2018.

LO 1-1, 1-2, 1-3, 1-4, 1-5d

31. On January 1, 2017, Fisher Corporation purchased 40 percent (80,000 shares) of the common stock of Bowden, Inc., for $982,000 in cash and began to use the equity method for the investment. The price paid represented a $60,000 payment in excess of the book value of Fisher's share of Bowden's underlying net assets. Fisher was willing to make this extra payment because of a recently developed patent held by Bowden with a 15-year remaining life. All other assets were considered appropriately valued on Bowden's books.

Bowden declares and pays a $100,000 cash dividend to its stockholders each year on September 15. Bowden reported net income of $400,000 in 2017 and $380,000 in 2018. Each income figure was earned evenly throughout its respective years.

On July 1, 2018, Fisher sold 10 percent (20,000 shares) of Bowden's outstanding shares for $330,000 in cash. Although it sold this interest, Fisher maintained the ability to significantly influence Bowden's decision-making process.

Prepare the journal entries for Fisher for the years of 2017 and 2018.

LO 1-3, 1-4, 1-6

32. On January 1, 2017, Stream Company acquired 30 percent of the outstanding voting shares of Q-Video, Inc., for $770,000. Q-Video manufactures specialty cables for computer monitors. On that date, Q-Video reported assets and liabilities with book values of $1.9 million and $700,000, respectively. A customer list compiled by Q-Video had an appraised value of $300,000, although it was not recorded on its books. The expected remaining life of the customer list was five years with straight-line amortization deemed appropriate. Any remaining excess cost was not identifiable with any particular asset and thus was considered goodwill.

Q-Video generated net income of $250,000 in 2017 and a net loss of $100,000 in 2018. In each of these two years, Q-Video declared and paid a cash dividend of $15,000 to its stockholders.

During 2017, Q-Video sold inventory that had an original cost of $100,000 to Stream for $160,000. Of this balance, $80,000 was resold to outsiders during 2017, and the remainder was sold during 2018. In 2018, Q-Video sold inventory to Stream for $175,000. This inventory had cost only $140,000. Stream resold $100,000 of the inventory during 2018 and the rest during 2019.

For 2017 and then for 2018, compute the amount that Stream should report as income from its investment in Q-Video in its external financial statements under the equity method.

Develop Your Skills

EXCEL CASE 1

CPA *skills*

On January 1, 2018, Acme Co. is considering purchasing a 40 percent ownership interest in PHC Co., a privately held enterprise, for $700,000. PHC predicts its profit will be $185,000 in 2018, projects a 10 percent annual increase in profits in each of the next four years, and expects to pay a steady annual dividend of $30,000 for the foreseeable future. Because PHC has on its books a patent that is undervalued by $375,000, Acme realizes that it will have an additional amortization expense of $15,000 per year over the next 10 years—the patent's estimated remaining useful life. All of PHC's other assets and liabilities have book values that approximate market values. Acme uses the equity method for its investment in PHC.

Required

1. Using an Excel spreadsheet, set the following values in cells:
   - Acme's cost of investment in PHC.
   - Percentage acquired.
   - First-year PHC reported income.
   - Projected growth rate in income.
   - PHC annual dividends.
   - Annual excess patent amortization.
2. Referring to the values in (1), prepare the following schedules using columns for the years 2018 through 2022.
   - Acme's equity in PHC earnings with rows showing these:
     - Acme's share of PHC reported income.
     - Amortization expense.
     - Acme's equity in PHC earnings.
   - Acme's Investment in PHC balance with rows showing the following:
     - Beginning balance.
     - Equity earnings.
     - Dividends.
     - Ending balance.
   - Return on beginning investment balance = Equity earnings/Beginning investment balance in each year.
3. Given the preceding values, compute the average of the projected returns on beginning investment balances for the first five years of Acme's investment in PHC. What is the maximum Acme can pay for PHC if it wishes to earn at least a 10 percent average return on beginning investment balance? (*Hint:* Under Excel's Data tab, select What-If Analysis, and the Goal Seek capability to produce a 10 percent average return on beginning investment balance by changing the cell that contains Acme's cost of investment in PHC. Excel's Solver should produce an exact answer while Goal Seek should produce a close approximation. You may need to first add in the Solver capability under Excel's Tools menu.)

EXCEL CASE 2

On January 1, Intergen, Inc., invests $200,000 for a 40 percent interest in Ryan, a new joint venture with two other partners, each investing $150,000 for 30 percent interest. Intergen plans to sell all of its production to Ryan, which will resell the inventory to retail outlets. The equity partners agree that Ryan will buy inventory only from Intergen. Also, Intergen plans to use the equity method for financial reporting.

During the year, Intergen expects to incur costs of $850,000 to produce goods with a final retail market value of $1,200,000. Ryan projects that, during this year, it will resell three-fourths of these goods for $900,000. It should sell the remainder in the following year.

The equity partners plan a meeting to set the price Intergen will charge Ryan for its production. One partner suggests a transfer price of $1,025,000 but is unsure whether it will result in an equitable return across the equity holders. Importantly, Intergen agrees that its total rate of return (including its own operations and its investment in Ryan) should be equal to that of the other investors' return on their investments in Ryan. All agree that Intergen's value including its investment in Ryan is $1,000,000.

Required

1. Create an Excel spreadsheet analysis showing the following:
   - Projected income statements for Intergen and Ryan. Formulate the statements to do the following:
     - Link Ryan's cost of goods sold to Intergen's sales (use a starting value of $1,025,000 for Intergen's sales).
     - Link Intergen's equity in Ryan's earnings to Ryan's net income (adjusted for Intergen's gross profit rate × Ryan's ending inventory × 40 percent ownership percentage).
     - Be able to change Intergen's sales and see the effects throughout the income statements of Ryan and Intergen. Note that the cost of goods sold for Intergen is fixed.

- The rate of return for the two 30 percent equity partners on their investment in Ryan.
- The total rate of return for Intergen based on its $1,000,000 value.

2. What transfer price will provide an equal rate of return for each of the investors in the first year of operation? (*Hint:* Under Excel's Data tab, select What-If Analysis and then the Goal Seek capability to produce a zero difference in rates of return across the equity partners by changing the cell that contains Intergen's sales. Excel's Solver add-in will work as well.)

ANALYSIS CASE

CPA skills

Access The Coca-Cola Company's SEC 10-K filing at www.coca-cola.com and address the following:

1. What companies does Coca-Cola describe as significant equity method investments? How do these investments help Coca-Cola?
2. What criteria does Coca-Cola use in choosing to apply the equity method for these investments?
3. How does Coca-Cola describe its application of the equity method?
4. What amount of equity income did Coca-Cola report?
5. Coca-Cola discloses the fair values of its publicly traded bottlers accounted for as equity method investments. List the book values and fair values for these equity method investments that have publically traded data. Discuss the relevance of each of these two values.

RESEARCH AND ANALYSIS CASE—IMPAIRMENT

CPA skills

Wolf Pack Transport Co. has a 25 percent equity investment in Maggie Valley Depot (MVD), Inc., which owns and operates a warehousing facility used for the collection and redistribution of various consumer goods. Wolf Pack paid $1,685,000 for its 25 percent interest in MVD several years ago, including a $300,000 allocation for goodwill as the only excess cost over book value acquired. Wolf Pack Transport has since appropriately applied the equity method to account for the investment. In its most recent balance sheet, because of recognized profits in excess of dividends since the acquisition, Wolf Pack reported a $2,350,000 amount for its Investment in Maggie Valley Depot, Inc., account.

However, competition in the transit warehousing industry has increased in the past 12 months. In the same area as the MVD facility, a competitor company opened two additional warehouses that are much more conveniently located near a major interstate highway. MVD's revenues declined 30 percent as customers shifted their business to the competitor's facilities and the prices for warehouse services declined. The market value of Wolf Pack's stock ownership in MVD fell to $1,700,000 from a high last year of $2,500,000. MVD's management is currently debating ways to respond to these events but has yet to formulate a firm plan.

Required

1. What guidance does the FASB ASC provide for equity method investment losses in value?
2. Should Wolf Pack recognize the decline in the value of its holdings in MVD in its current year financial statements?
3. Should Wolf Pack test for impairment of the value it had initially assigned to goodwill?

RESEARCH CASE—NONCONTROLLING SHAREHOLDER RIGHTS

CPA skills

Consolidated financial reporting is appropriate when one entity has a controlling financial interest in another entity. The usual condition for a controlling financial interest is ownership of a majority voting interest. But in some circumstances, control does not rest with the majority owner—especially when noncontrolling owners are contractually provided with approval or veto rights that can restrict the actions of the majority owner. In these cases, the majority owner employs the equity method rather than consolidation.

Required

Address the following by searching the FASB ASC Topic 810 on consolidation.

1. What are protective noncontrolling rights?
2. What are substantive participating noncontrolling rights?

3. What noncontrolling rights overcome the presumption that all majority-owned investees should be consolidated?
4. Zee Company buys 60 percent of the voting stock of Bee Company with the remaining 40 percent noncontrolling interest held by Bee's former owners, who negotiated the following noncontrolling rights:
   - Any new debt above $1,000,000 must be approved by the 40 percent noncontrolling shareholders.
   - Any dividends or other cash distributions to owners in excess of customary historical amounts must be approved by the 40 percent noncontrolling shareholders.

   According to the FASB ASC, what are the issues in determining whether Zee should consolidate Bee or report its investment in Bee under the equity method?

chapter 2

Consolidation of Financial Information

Financial statements published and distributed to owners, creditors, and other interested parties appear to report the operations and financial position of a single company. In reality, these statements frequently represent a number of separate organizations tied together through common control (a *business combination*). When financial statements represent more than one corporation, we refer to them as *consolidated financial statements.*

Consolidated financial statements are typical in today's business world. Most major organizations, and many smaller ones, hold control over an array of organizations. For example, from 2000 through 2016, Cisco Systems, Inc., reported more than 100 business acquisitions that now are consolidated in its financial reports. PepsiCo, Inc., as another example, annually consolidates data from a multitude of companies into a single set of financial statements. By gaining control over these companies (often known as *subsidiaries*)—which include Frito-Lay, Gatorade, Quaker Oats, Sabra, and Tropicana Products—PepsiCo (the *parent*) forms a single business combination and single reporting entity.

The consolidation of financial information as exemplified by Cisco Systems and PepsiCo is one of the most complex procedures in all of accounting. Comprehending this process completely requires understanding the theoretical logic that underlies the creation of a business combination. Furthermore, a variety of procedural steps must be mastered to ensure that proper accounting is achieved for this single reporting entity. The following coverage introduces both of these aspects of the consolidation process.

The FASB *Accounting Standards Codification* (ASC) contains the current accounting standards for business combinations under the following topics:

- "Business Combinations" (Topic 805).
- "Consolidation" (Topic 810).

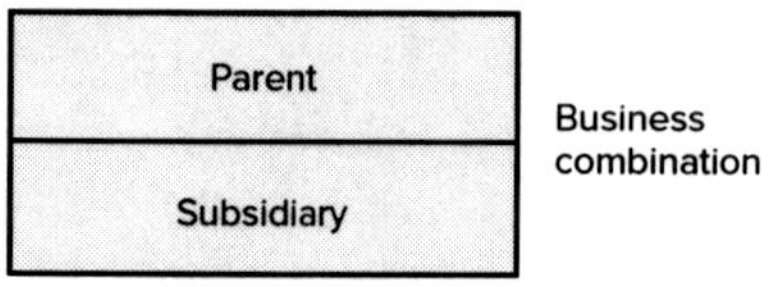

The ASC "Business Combinations" topic provides guidance on the accounting and reporting for business combinations using the *acquisition method.* The acquisition method embraces a *fair-value* measurement attribute. Adoption of this attribute reflects the FASB's increasing emphasis on fair value for measuring and assessing business activity. In the past, financial reporting standards embraced the cost principle to measure and report the

Learning Objectives

After studying this chapter, you should be able to:

LO 2-1 Discuss the motives for business combinations.

LO 2-2 Recognize when consolidation of financial information into a single set of statements is necessary.

LO 2-3 Define the term *business combination* and differentiate across various forms of business combinations.

LO 2-4 Describe the valuation principles of the acquisition method.

LO 2-5 Determine the fair value of the consideration transferred for an acquisition and allocate that fair value to specific assets acquired (including goodwill) and liabilities assumed or to a gain on bargain purchase.

LO 2-6 Prepare an acquiring firm's journal entry to record
a. a business combination when dissolution takes place.
b. the various related costs involved in a business combination.
c. a business combination when the acquired firm retains its separate existence.

LO 2-7 Prepare a worksheet to consolidate the financial statements of two companies that form a business combination in the absence of dissolution.

LO 2-8 Describe the accounting treatment for the various intangible assets often acquired in a business combination.

LO 2-9 Appendix 2A: Identify the general characteristics of the legacy purchase and pooling of interest methods of accounting for past business combinations. Understand the effects that persist today in financial statements from the use of these legacy methods.

LO 2-10 Appendix 2B: Explain the rationale and procedures underlying a subsidiary's election to adopt pushdown accounting.

financial effects of business combinations. This fundamental change from a cost-based to a fair-value model has transformed the way we account for and report business combinations in our society.

The ASC "Consolidation" topic provides guidance on circumstances that require a firm to prepare consolidated financial reports and various other related reporting issues. Basically, consolidated financial reports must be prepared whenever one firm has a controlling financial interest in another. Although ownership of a majority voting interest is the usual condition for a controlling financial interest, the power to control may also exist with a lesser percentage of ownership through governance contracts, leases, or agreement with other stockholders.[1]

In this chapter, we first present expansion through corporate takeovers and present an overview of the consolidation process. Then we present the specifics of the acquisition method of accounting for business combinations where the acquirer obtains complete ownership of another firm. Later, beginning in Chapter 4, we introduce coverage of acquisitions with less than complete ownership.

Financial reporting for business combinations has experienced many changes over the past decade. Prior to the acquisition method requirement, accounting standards allowed either the purchase method or the earlier pooling of interests method of accounting for business combinations. Neither of these methods is now permitted for reporting the formation of new business combinations. However, because of the prospective application of the acquisition method beginning in 2009, legacy effects of these methods remain in many of today's financial statements. Therefore, an appendix to this chapter provides a review of the purchase method and pooling of interests method.

LO 2-1

Discuss the motives for business combinations.

Expansion through Corporate Takeovers

Reasons for Firms to Combine

A frequent economic phenomenon is the combining of two or more businesses into a single entity under common management and control. During recent decades, the United States and the rest of the world have experienced an enormous number of corporate mergers and takeovers, transactions in which one company gains control over another. According to Thomson Reuters, the number of mergers and acquisitions globally in 2015 exceeded 42,300, with a total value of more than $4.7 trillion. Of these deals more than $2.3 trillion involved a U.S. firm. As indicated by Exhibit 2.1, the magnitude of recent combinations continues to be large.

As with any other economic activity, business combinations can be part of an overall managerial strategy to maximize shareholder value. Shareholders—the owners of the firm—hire managers to direct resources so that the firm's value grows over time. In this way, owners receive a return on their investment. Successful firms receive substantial benefits through enhanced share value. Importantly, the managers of successful firms also receive substantial benefits in salaries, especially if their compensation contracts are partly based on stock market performance of the firm's shares.

If the goal of business activity is to maximize the firm's value, in what ways do business combinations help achieve that goal? Clearly, the business community is moving rapidly toward business combinations as a strategy for growth and competitiveness. Size and scale are obviously becoming critical as firms compete in today's markets. Importantly, valuable synergies often accompany business combinations. If large firms can be more efficient in delivering goods and services, they gain a competitive advantage and become more profitable for the owners. Increases in scale can produce larger profits from enhanced sales volume despite smaller (more competitive) profit margins. When two firms integrate successive stages of production and distribution of products, coordinating raw material purchases,

[1] We discuss entities controlled through contractual means (known as variable interest entities) in Chapter 6.

EXHIBIT 2.1
Recent Notable Business Combinations

Acquirer	Target	Deal Value
AT&T	DirecTV	$47.4B
Berkshire Hathaway, Inc.	Precision Castparts	$32.0B
Visa, Inc.	Visa Europe Ltd	$23.3B
Facebook, Inc.	WhatsApp	$17.2B
MeadWestvaco	RockTenn	$16.0B
Intel Corporation	Altera Corporation	$15.0B
CVS Health Corporation	Omnicare, Inc.	$12.9B
Marriott	Starwood Hotels Intl	$12.2B
Merck	Cubist	$ 9.5B
Weyerhaeuser	Plum Creek Timber	$ 8.4B
Celgene Corporation	Receptos, Inc.	$ 7.2B
Cox Automotive	Dealertrack Technologies	$ 4.0B
FedEx	TNT Express	$ 4.8B
Expedia	HomeAway	$ 3.9B
Microsemi Corporation	PMC-Sierra, Inc.	$ 2.5B
Constellation Brands	Ballast Point Brewing & Spirits	$ 1.0B

manufacturing, and delivery, substantial savings can result. As an example, Oracle's acquisition of Sun Microsystems creates synergies by enabling Oracle to integrate its software product lines with Sun's hardware specifications. The acquisition further allows Oracle to offer complete systems made of chips, computers, storage devices, and software with an aim toward increased efficiency and quality.[2] Other cost savings resulting from elimination of duplicate efforts, such as data processing and marketing, can make a single entity more profitable than the separate parent and subsidiary had been in the past. Such synergies often accompany business combinations.

Although no two business combinations are exactly alike, many share one or more of the following characteristics that potentially enhance profitability:

- Vertical integration of one firm's output and another firm's distribution or further processing.
- Cost savings through elimination of duplicate facilities and staff.
- Quick entry for new and existing products into domestic and foreign markets.
- Economies of scale allowing greater efficiency and negotiating power.
- The ability to access financing at more attractive rates. As firm size increases, negotiating power with financial institutions can increase also.
- Diversification of business risk.

Business combinations also occur because many firms seek the continuous expansion of their organizations, often into diversified areas. Acquiring control over a vast network of different businesses has been a strategy utilized by a number of companies (sometimes known as *conglomerates*) for decades. Entry into new industries is immediately available to the parent without having to construct facilities, develop products, train management, or create market recognition. Many corporations have successfully employed this strategy to produce huge, highly profitable organizations. Unfortunately, others discovered that the task of managing a widely diverse group of businesses can be a costly learning experience. Even combinations that are designed to take advantage of operating synergies and cost savings will fail if the integration is not managed carefully.

Overall, the primary motivations for many business combinations can be traced to an increasingly competitive environment. Three recent business combinations provide interesting examples of distinct motivations to combine: Facebook and WhatsApp, AT&T and DirecTV, and Rock-Tenn and MeadwestVaco. Each is discussed briefly in turn.

[2] Ben Worthen, Cari Tuna, and Justin Scheck, "Companies More Prone to Go 'Vertical,'" *The Wall Street Journal*, November 30, 2009.

Facebook and WhatsApp

On October 26, 2014, Facebook completed its acquisition of WhatsApp, the popular internet messaging service with over 600 million users. As stated in its 2014 annual 10-K report, Facebook paid a total of $17.2B in what was one of the largest technology company acquisitions of the year.[3] According to the acquisition agreement, WhatsApp will retain all of its staff and will operate as an independent subsidiary of Facebook, similar to Facebook's 2012 acquisition of Instagram. The steep purchase price was based almost entirely on long-term potential, as in the first six months of 2014, WhatsApp reported just $15M in revenue.[4] Facebook CEO Mark Zuckerberg indicated that his immediate focus was on growing WhatsApp, and that he would not attempt to monetize the service until the number of users reached 1 billion.[5]

Many analysts weighed in on why Facebook would spend over 10% of its net worth for a company with minimal revenue. Aileen Lee, from venture capital firm Kliener Perkins Caufield & Byers, noted that it was important for Facebook to beat out its competition in acquiring a fast growing messaging service like WhatsApp. "These big companies feel like they can't afford to lose mind share and time share to competitors, and they are willing to pay a lot of money for large user bases."[6] Other analysts cited the benefit of an expanded portfolio in protecting against inevitable shifts in online consumer behavior.[7]

Of the total $17.2B purchase consideration, Facebook recognized $15.3B in goodwill. According to Facebook's 2014 10-K, the goodwill value is "primarily attributable to expected synergies from future growth, from potential monetization opportunities, from strategic advantages provided in the mobile ecosystem, and from expansion of our mobile messaging offerings." As is common in high-tech acquisitions, much of the purchase price for WhatsApp was attributed to other intangibles. Facebook reported an additional $2.8B in intangible assets (beyond goodwill) including acquired users, trade name, and acquired technology.

AT&T and DirecTV

On July 24, 2015, AT&T acquired DirecTV for $47.4 billion. According to AT&T's September 30, 2015 10-Q report, $32.7 billion was paid in stock and $14.7 billion in cash. The acquisition made AT&T the nation's leading TV provider, surpassing Comcast for first place.[8] In order to contend with changing consumer demands, many large media companies were turning to mergers as a way to expand offerings. CEO Randall Stephenson commented in a press release that AT&T will now "be able to meet consumers' future entertainment preferences . . .traditional TV service, . . .their favorite content on a mobile device, or video streamed over the Internet to any screen".[9] The acquisition will also provide AT&T access to millions of DirecTV customers in the Latin American market.

The DirecTV acquisition was subject to a series of conditions imposed by the FCC. These conditions included providing discounted broadband service to low-income households, and offering all-fiber access to at least 12.5 million small consumers.[10] Due to antitrust concerns, the FCC and other regulatory agencies had taken an increasingly active role in monitoring mergers in the media industry. Notably, in April of 2015, Comcast withdrew its $45B bid for Time Warner due in large part to resistance from the FCC and Department of Justice.[11]

Intangible assets represented the majority of the value paid for DirecTV. According to its third quarter 2015 10-Q, AT&T reported $35.3 billion in goodwill and $34.7 billion coming

[3] Although some news releases cited prices as high as $22 billion, the larger prices evidently included post-acquisition compensation for continuing employees.

[4] *TechCrunch,* Josh Constine, "WhatsApp's First Half of 2014 Revenue Was $15M, Net Loss of $232.5M Was Mostly Issuing Stock," October 28, 2014.

[5] Bloomberg Business, Sarah Frier, "Facebook $22 Billion WhatsApp Deal Buys $10 Million in Sales," October 28, 2014.

[6] *New York Times Dealbook,* David Gelles, "For Facebook, it's Users First and Profits Later," February 20, 2014.

[7] ibid.

[8] *New York Times,* Credit Jonathan Alcorn/Reuters, "F.C.C. Approves AT&T-DirecTV Deal," July 24, 2015.

[9] AT&T press release, "AT&T Completes Acquisition of DIRECTV," Dallas, TX, July 24, 2015.

[10] AT&T 10-Q report for the quarter ending September 30, 2015.

[11] *Los Angeles Times,* Meg James, "AT&T gets FCC approval, immediately completes $49-billion takeover of DirecTV", July 24, 2015.

from other intangible assets such as customer relationships and satellite access rights. As also reflected in the 10-Q, AT&T expects significant synergies as a result of the acquisition, especially in the area of video content cost savings and expanded video service capabilities.

MeadwestVaco and Rock-Tenn

On March 6, 2015, packaging companies MeadwestVaco (MWV) and Rock-Tenn finalized their business combination agreement to become wholly owned subsidiaries of WestRock, a newly formed parent company. WestRock manufactures a variety of consumer and commercial packaging materials, paperboard, and merchandising displays. The company is also one of the largest recyclers of paper.[12]

As part of the business combination, equity of WestRock was divided almost equally, with MWV shareholders owning 50.1% of the new company and Rock-Tenn shareholders getting 49.9%. According to its 2015 annual 10-K report, for financial reporting purposes, Rock-Tenn was treated as the acquiring party. The consideration transferred in the combination was $8.3 billion and was allocated to assets of $16 billion and liabilities of $7.7 billion.[13]

Rock-Tenn had made acquisitions of $7 billion in the 10 years prior to the business combination with MWV and wanted to continue expanding. MWV was attractive to Rock-Tenn because of its diverse and complimentary products as well as its global reach, with plants in Brazil and India. According to Barclay's analyst Scott Gaffner, Rock-Tenn was not in a position to acquire MWV due to its size, and that a "merger of equals" was the best option.[14] From MWV's standpoint, the business combination served as a means to penetrate new end markets and add to its set of global customers.[15]

The prospect of cost synergies was also a large factor for both companies in deciding to combine. In its presentation to investors, Rock-Tenn noted that $550 million in cost savings were achieved related to its 2011 acquisition of Smurfit-Stone. WestRock expects to generate annual cost synergies of $300M resulting from the business combination, to be realized by the third year of operations. Procurement and supply chain integration, production plant optimization, and corporate and overhead reduction are all expected to contribute to the savings.[16]

LO 2-2

Recognize when consolidation of financial information into a single set of statements is necessary.

Business Combinations, Control, and Consolidated Financial Reporting

The consolidation of financial information into a single set of statements becomes necessary when the business combination of two or more companies creates a single economic entity. As stated in FASB ASC (810-10-10-1): "There is a presumption that consolidated financial statements are more meaningful than separate financial statements and that they are usually necessary for a fair presentation when one of the entities in the consolidated group directly or indirectly has a controlling financial interest in the other entities."

Thus, in producing financial statements for external distribution, the reporting entity transcends the boundaries of incorporation to encompass (i.e., consolidate) all companies for which control is present. Even though the various companies may retain their legal identities as separate corporations, the resulting information is more meaningful to outside parties when consolidated into a single set of financial statements.

To explain the process of preparing consolidated financial statements for a business combination, we address three questions:

1. How is a business combination formed?
2. What constitutes a controlling financial interest?
3. How is the consolidation process carried out?

[12] www.rocktenn.com/products

[13] Westrock Company 2015 annual 10-K report.

[14] *businessfinancenews.com,* Jason Graul, Rock-Tenn Company, MeadWestvaco Corp. (MWV) Merger: Barclays Views Cost & Operational Synergies, July 15, 2015.

[15] MWV and RockTenn, Investor Presentation, "Creating a Global Packaging Leader," January 26, 2015.

[16] *Ibid,* footnote 11.

LO 2-3

Define the term *business combination* and differentiate across various forms of business combinations.

Business Combinations—Creating a Single Economic Entity

A business combination refers to a transaction or other event in which an acquirer obtains control over one or more businesses.

Business combinations are formed by a wide variety of transactions or events with various formats. For example, each of the following is identified as a business combination although it differs widely in legal form. In every case, two or more enterprises are being united into a single economic entity so that consolidated financial statements are required.

1. One company obtains the assets, and often the liabilities, of another company in exchange for cash, other assets, liabilities, stock, or a combination of these. The second organization normally dissolves itself as a legal corporation. Thus, only the acquiring company remains in existence, having absorbed the acquired net assets directly into its own operations. Any business combination in which only one of the original companies continues to exist is referred to in legal terms as a *statutory merger*.

2. One company obtains all of the capital stock of another in exchange for cash, other assets, liabilities, stock, or a combination of these. After gaining control, the acquiring company can decide to transfer all assets and liabilities to its own financial records with the second company being dissolved as a separate corporation.[17] The business combination is, once again, a statutory merger because only one of the companies maintains legal existence. This statutory merger, however, is achieved by obtaining equity securities rather than by buying the target company's assets. Because stock is obtained, the acquiring company must gain 100 percent control of all shares before legally dissolving the subsidiary.

3. Two or more companies transfer either their assets or their capital stock to a newly formed corporation. Both original companies are dissolved, leaving only the new organization in existence. A business combination effected in this manner is a *statutory consolidation*. The use here of the term *consolidation* should not be confused with the accounting meaning of that same word. In accounting, *consolidation* refers to the mechanical process of bringing together the financial records of two or more organizations to form a single set of statements. A statutory consolidation denotes a specific type of business combination that has united two or more existing companies under the ownership of a newly created company.

4. One company achieves legal control over another by acquiring a majority of voting stock. *Although control is present, no dissolution takes place; each company remains in existence as an incorporated operation.* NBC Universal, as an example, continues to retain its legal status as a corporation after being acquired by Comcast Corporation. Separate incorporation is frequently preferred to take full advantage of any intangible benefits accruing to the acquired company as a going concern. Better utilization of such factors as licenses, trade names, employee loyalty, and the company's reputation can be possible when the subsidiary maintains its own legal identity. Moreover, maintaining an independent information system for a subsidiary often enhances its market value for an eventual sale or initial public offering as a stand-alone entity.

Because the asset and liability account balances are not physically combined as in statutory mergers and consolidations, each company continues to maintain an independent accounting system. To reflect the combination, the acquiring company enters the takeover transaction into its own records by establishing a single investment asset account. However, the newly acquired subsidiary omits any recording of this event; its stock is simply transferred to the parent from the subsidiary's shareholders. Thus, the subsidiary's financial records are not directly affected by a takeover.

5. A final vehicle for control of another business entity does not involve a majority voting stock interest or direct ownership of assets. Control of a variable interest entity (VIE) by design often does not rest with its equity holders. Instead, control is exercised through contractual arrangements with a sponsoring firm that, although it technically may not own the VIE, becomes its "primary beneficiary" with rights to its residual profits. These contracts can take the form of leases, participation rights, guarantees, or other interests. Past use of VIEs

[17] Although the acquired company has been legally dissolved, it frequently continues to operate as a separate division within the surviving company's organization.

EXHIBIT 2.2
Business Combinations

Type of Combination	Action of Acquiring Company	Action of Acquired Company
Statutory merger through asset acquisition.	Acquires assets and often liabilities.	Dissolves and goes out of business.
Statutory merger through capital stock acquisition.	Acquires all stock and then transfers assets and liabilities to its own books.	Dissolves as a separate corporation, often remaining as a division of the acquiring company.
Statutory consolidation through capital stock or asset acquisition.	Newly created entity receives assets or capital stock of original companies.	Original companies may dissolve while remaining as separate divisions of newly created company.
Acquisition of more than 50 percent of the voting stock.	Acquires stock that is recorded as an investment; controls decision making of acquired company.	Remains in existence as legal corporation, although now a subsidiary of the acquiring company.
Control through ownership of variable interests (see Chapter 6). Risks and rewards often flow to a sponsoring firm that may or may not hold equity shares.	Establishes contractual control over a variable interest entity to engage in a specific activity.	Remains in existence as a separate legal entity—often a trust or partnership.

was criticized because these structures provided sponsoring firms with off-balance sheet financing and sometimes questionable profits on sales to their VIEs. Prior to 2004, many sponsoring entities of VIEs did not technically meet the definition of a controlling financial interest (i.e., majority voting stock ownership) and thus did not consolidate their VIEs. Current GAAP, however, expands the notion of control and thus requires consolidation of VIEs by their primary beneficiary.

As you can see, business combinations are created in many distinct forms. The specific format is a critical factor in the subsequent consolidation of financial information. Exhibit 2.2 provides an overview of the various combinations.

Control—An Elusive Quality

The definition of control is central to determining when two or more entities become one economic entity and therefore one reporting entity. Control of one firm by another is most often achieved through the acquisition of voting shares. The ASC (810-10-15-8) describes control as follows:

> The usual condition for a controlling financial interest is ownership of a majority voting interest, and, therefore, as a general rule ownership by one reporting entity, directly or indirectly, of more than 50 percent of the outstanding voting shares of another entity is a condition pointing toward consolidation.

By exercising majority voting power, one firm can literally dictate the financing and operating activities of another firm. Accordingly, U.S. GAAP traditionally has pointed to a majority voting share ownership as a controlling financial interest that requires consolidation.

Notably, the power to control may also exist with less than 50 percent of the outstanding shares of another entity. The ASC (810-10-15-8) goes on to observe that:

> The power to control may also exist with a lesser percentage of ownership, for example, by contract, lease, agreement with other stockholders, or by court decree.

Therefore, despite possessing less than 50 percent of the subsidiary's voting stock, one ownership group can enter into contractual arrangement with other ownership groups that provide control.

Alternatively, majority ownership does not always indicate an exclusive ability for one entity to exercise control over another. According to the FASB ASC Glossary, control can also be defined as,

> The direct or indirect ability to determine the direction of management and policies through ownership, contract, or otherwise.

This description recognizes the complex profit-sharing agreements that sometimes accompany economic resource sharing. To reduce their risk, several parties may participate in directing the activities of another entity. For example, a parent with majority ownership may grant certain decision rights to noncontrolling shareholders in exchange for economic support. Such noncontrolling participation rights may be powerful enough to prevent the majority owners from controlling the entity.

As the complexity of ownership arrangements increases, defining when one firm controls another remains a continuing challenge for financial reporting standard setters. Nonetheless, the primary way U.S. firms exercise control remains through the acquisition of a majority of another firm's voting shares. Consequently, in this text, we largely focus on control relationships established through voting interests. In Chapter 6, however, we expand our coverage to include the consolidation of firms where control is exercised through variable interests.

Consolidation of Financial Information

When one company gains control over another, a business combination is established. Financial data gathered from the individual companies are then brought together to form a single set of consolidated statements. Although this process can be complicated, the objectives of a consolidation are straightforward—to report the financial position, results of operations, and cash flows for the combined entity. As a part of this process, reciprocal accounts and intra-entity transactions must be adjusted or eliminated to ensure that all reported balances truly represent the single entity.

Applicable consolidation procedures vary significantly depending on the legal format employed in creating a business combination. *For a statutory merger or a statutory consolidation, when the acquired company (or companies) is (are) legally dissolved, only one accounting consolidation ever occurs.* On the date of the combination, the surviving company simply records the various account balances from each of the dissolving companies. Because the accounts are brought together permanently in this manner, no further consolidation procedures are necessary. After the balances have been transferred to the survivor, the financial records of the acquired companies are closed out as part of the dissolution.

Conversely, in a combination when all companies retain incorporation, a different set of consolidation procedures is appropriate. Because the companies preserve their legal identities, each continues to maintain its own independent accounting records. *Thus, no permanent consolidation of the account balances is ever made. Rather, the consolidation process must be carried out anew each time the reporting entity prepares financial statements for external reporting purposes.*

When separate record-keeping is maintained, the accountant faces a unique problem: The financial information must be brought together periodically without disturbing the accounting systems of the individual companies. Because these consolidations are produced outside the financial records, worksheets traditionally are used to expedite the process. Worksheets are a part of neither company's accounting records nor the resulting financial statements. Instead, they are an efficient structure for organizing and adjusting the information used to prepare externally reported consolidated statements.

Consequently, the legal characteristics of a business combination have a significant impact on the approach taken to the consolidation process:

What is to be consolidated?

- If dissolution takes place, appropriate account balances are physically consolidated in the surviving company's financial records.
- If separate incorporation is maintained, only the financial statement information (not the actual records) is consolidated.

When does the consolidation take place?

- If dissolution takes place, a permanent consolidation occurs at the date of the combination.
- If separate incorporation is maintained, the consolidation process is carried out at regular intervals whenever financial statements are to be prepared.

How are the accounting records affected?

- If dissolution takes place, the surviving company's accounts are adjusted to include appropriate balances of the dissolved company. The dissolved company's records are closed out.
- If separate incorporation is maintained, each company continues to retain its own records. Using worksheets facilitates the periodic consolidation process without disturbing the individual accounting systems.

LO 2-4

Describe the valuation principles of the acquisition method.

Financial Reporting for Business Combinations

The Acquisition Method

Regardless of whether the acquired firm maintains its separate incorporation or dissolution takes place, current standards require the acquisition method to account for business combinations. Applying the acquisition method involves recognizing and measuring

- The consideration transferred for the acquired business and any noncontrolling interest.
- The separately identified assets acquired and liabilities assumed.
- Goodwill, or a gain from a bargain purchase.

Fair value is the measurement attribute used to recognize these and other aspects of a business combination. Therefore, prior to examining specific applications of the acquisition method, we present a brief discussion of the fair-value concept as applied to business combinations.

Consideration Transferred for the Acquired Business

The fair value of the consideration transferred to acquire a business from its former owners is the starting point in valuing and recording a business combination. In describing the acquisition method, the FASB ASC states:

> The consideration transferred in a business combination shall be measured at fair value, which shall be calculated as the sum of the acquisition-date fair values of the assets transferred by the acquirer, the liabilities incurred by the acquirer to former owners of the acquiree, and the equity interests issued by the acquirer. (ASC 805-30-30-7)

The acquisition method thus embraces the fair value of the consideration transferred in measuring the acquirer's interest in the acquired business.[18] Fair value is defined as the price that would be received to sell an asset or paid to transfer a liability in an orderly transaction between market participants at the measurement date. Thus, market values are often the best source of evidence of the fair value of consideration transferred in a business combination. Items of consideration transferred can include cash, securities (either stocks or debt), and other property or obligations.

Contingent Consideration: An Additional Element of Consideration Transferred

Contingent consideration, when present in a business combination, is an additional element of consideration transferred. Contingent consideration can be useful in negotiations when two parties disagree with each other's estimates of future cash flows for the target firm or when

[18] An occasional exception occurs in a bargain purchase in which the fair value of the net assets acquired serves as the valuation basis for the acquired firm. Other exceptions include situations in which control is achieved without a transfer of consideration, or determination of the fair value of the consideration transferred is less reliable than other measures of the business fair value.

valuation uncertainty is high.[19] Acquisition agreements often contain provisions to pay former owners (typically cash or additional shares of the acquirer's stock) upon achievement of specified future performance measures. For example, Walt Disney Company disclosed in its 2015 annual report its 2014 acquisition of 100 percent of the outstanding shares of common stock of Maker Studios, Inc. Disney's agreement with the former owners of Maker Studios provided for:

> up to $450 million of additional cash upon final determination of Maker's achievement of certain performance targets for calendar years 2014 and 2015. The [Walt Disney] Company recognized a $198 million liability for the fair value of the contingent consideration (determined by a probability weighting of potential payouts), of which approximately $100 million was paid in fiscal 2015 for calendar year 2014. Subsequent changes in the estimated fair value, if any, will be recognized in earnings.

Disney thus included the fair value of the contingent consideration as a component of the fair value of the consideration transferred for Maker Studios. The acquisition method treats contingent consideration obligations as a negotiated component of the fair value of the consideration transferred. As seen in the above Disney quote, determining the fair value of contingent future payments typically involves probability and risk assessments based on circumstances existing on the acquisition date.

Regardless of the elements that constitute the consideration transferred, the parent's financial statements must now incorporate its newly acquired ownership interest in a controlled entity. In Chapters 2 and 3, we focus exclusively on combinations that result in complete ownership by the acquirer (i.e., no noncontrolling interest in the acquired firm). As described in Chapter 4, in a less-than-100-percent acquisition, the noncontrolling interest also is measured initially at its fair value. Then, the combined fair values of the parent's consideration transferred and the noncontrolling interest comprise the valuation basis for the acquired firm in consolidated financial reports.

Assets Acquired and Liabilities Assumed

A fundamental principle of the acquisition method is that an acquirer must identify the assets acquired and the liabilities assumed in the business combination. Further, once these have been identified, the acquirer measures the assets acquired and the liabilities assumed at their acquisition-date fair values, with only a few exceptions.[20] As demonstrated in subsequent examples, the principle of recognizing and measuring assets acquired and liabilities assumed at fair value applies across all business combinations.

Fair value, as defined by GAAP, is the price that would be received from selling an asset or paid for transferring a liability in an orderly transaction between market participants at the measurement date. However, determining the acquisition-date fair values of the individual assets acquired and liabilities assumed can prove challenging.[21] The ASC (820-10-35-28) points to three sets of valuation techniques typically employed: the market approach, the income approach, and the cost approach.

Market Approach

The market approach estimates fair values using other market transactions involving similar assets or liabilities. In a business combination, assets acquired such as marketable securities and some tangible assets may have established markets that can provide comparable market values for estimating fair values. Similarly, the fair values of many liabilities assumed can be determined by reference to market trades for similar debt instruments.

Income Approach

The income approach relies on multi-period estimates of future cash flows projected to be generated by an asset. These projected cash flows are then discounted at a required rate of

[19] Cain, Denis, and Denis, "Earnouts: A Study of Financial Contracting in Acquisition Agreements," *Journal of Accounting and Economics* 51 (2011), 151–170.

[20] Exceptions to the fair-value measurement principle include deferred taxes, certain employee benefits, indemnification assets, reacquired rights, share-based awards, and assets held for sale.

[21] Identifying and measuring the acquired firm's financial statement items can take some time. ASC (805-10-25-14) allows an acquirer to adjust the provisional amounts recognized for a business combination up to a year after the acquisition date.

return that reflects the time value of money and the risk associated with realizing the future estimated cash flows. The multi-period income approach is often useful for obtaining fair-value estimates of intangible assets and acquired in-process research and development.

Cost Approach

The cost approach estimates fair values by reference to the current cost of replacing an asset with another of comparable economic utility. Used assets can present a particular valuation challenge if active markets only exist for newer versions of the asset. Thus, the cost to replace a particular asset reflects both its estimated replacement cost and the effects of obsolescence. In this sense obsolescence is meant to capture economic declines in value including both technological obsolescence and physical deterioration. The cost approach is widely used to estimate fair values for many tangible assets acquired in business combinations such as property, plant, and equipment.

Goodwill, and Gains on Bargain Purchases

In a business combination, the parent must account for both the consideration transferred and the individual amounts of the identified assets acquired and liabilities assumed at their acquisition-date fair values. However, in many cases the respective collective amounts of these two values will differ. Current GAAP accounting for the difference requires one of two outcomes—in one the acquirer recognizes an asset (goodwill), in the other a gain.

When the consideration transferred exceeds the acquisition-date net amount of the identified assets acquired and the liabilities assumed, the acquirer recognizes the asset goodwill for the excess.[22] Goodwill is defined as an asset representing the future economic benefits arising in a business combination that are not individually identified and separately recognized. Goodwill often embodies the expected synergies that the acquirer expects to achieve through control of the acquired firm's assets. Goodwill may also capture non-recognized intangibles of the acquired firm such as employee expertise.

Conversely, if the collective fair value of the net identified assets acquired and liabilities assumed exceeds the consideration transferred, the acquirer recognizes a "gain on bargain purchase." In such cases, the fair value of the net assets acquired replaces the consideration transferred as the valuation basis for the acquired firm. Bargain purchases can result from business divestitures forced by regulatory agencies or other types of distress sales. Before recognizing a gain on bargain purchase, however, the acquirer must reassess whether it has correctly identified and measured all of the acquired assets and liabilities. Illustrations and further discussions of goodwill and of bargain purchase gains follow in the next section.

LO 2-5

Determine the total fair value of the consideration transferred for an acquisition, and allocate that fair value to specific subsidiary assets acquired (including goodwill) and liabilities assumed or to a gain on bargain purchase.

Procedures for Consolidating Financial Information

To demonstrate an application of the acquisition method, assume BigNet Company specializes in communications equipment and business software that provide web-based applications for retail companies. BigNet seeks to expand its operations and plans to acquire Smallport on December 31. Smallport Company owns computers, telecommunications equipment, and software that customize website billing and ordering systems for their customers. BigNet hopes to expand Smallport's customer contracts, utilize its recently developed software, and create other synergies by combining with Smallport.

Exhibit 2.3 lists the December 31 account balances for both BigNet and Smallport. In addition, the estimated fair values of Smallport's assets and liabilities are shown. Although Smallport's computers and equipment have a $400,000 book value, their current fair value is $600,000. Smallport's software has only a $100,000 value on its books; the internal development costs were primarily expensed. The software's observable fair value, however, is $1,200,000. Similarly, although not reflected in its financial records, Smallport has several

[22] Assuming a 100% acquisition. For combinations with less than complete ownership, goodwill is computed as the excess of the consideration transferred plus the acquisition-date fair value of the noncontrolling interest over the collective fair values of the net identified assets acquired and liabilities assumed.

EXHIBIT 2.3 Basic Consolidation Information

	BigNet Company Book Values December 31	Smallport Company Book Values December 31	Smallport Company Fair Values December 31
Current assets	$ 1,100,000	$ 300,000	$ 300,000
Computers and equipment (net)	1,300,000	400,000	600,000
Capitalized software (net)	500,000	100,000	1,200,000
Customer contracts	–0–	–0–	700,000
Notes payable	(300,000)	(200,000)	(250,000)
Net assets	**$ 2,600,000**	**$ 600,000**	**$2,550,000**
Common stock—$10 par value	$ (1,600,000)		
Common stock—$5 par value		$ (100,000)	
Additional paid-in capital	(40,000)	(20,000)	
Retained earnings, 1/1	(870,000)	(370,000)	
Dividends declared	110,000	10,000	
Revenues	(1,000,000)	(500,000)	
Expenses	800,000	380,000	
Owners' equity 12/31	**$(2,600,000)**	**$(600,000)**	
Retained earnings, 12/31	(960,000)*	(480,000)*	

*Retained earnings balance after closing out revenues, expenses, and dividends.
Note: Parentheses indicate a credit balance.

large ongoing customer contracts. BigNet estimates the fair value of the customer contracts at $700,000. Smallport also has a $200,000 note payable incurred to help finance the software development. Because interest rates are currently low, this liability (incurred at a higher rate of interest) has a present value of $250,000.

Smallport's net assets (total assets less total liabilities) have a book value of $600,000 but a fair value of $2,550,000. Fair values for only the assets and liabilities are appraised here; the capital stock, retained earnings, dividend, revenue, and expense accounts represent historical measurements rather than any type of future values. Although these equity and income accounts can give some indication of the organization's overall worth, they are not property and thus not transferred in the combination.

Legal as well as accounting distinctions divide business combinations into several separate categories. To facilitate the introduction of consolidation accounting, we present the various procedures utilized in this process according to the following sequence:

1. Acquisition method when dissolution takes place.
2. Acquisition method when separate incorporation is maintained.

Acquisition Method When Dissolution Takes Place

When the acquired firm's legal status is dissolved in a business combination, the continuing firm takes direct ownership of the former firm's assets and assumes its liabilities. Thus, the continuing firm will prepare a journal entry to record

- The fair value of the consideration transferred by the acquiring firm to the former owners of the acquiree, and
- The identified assets acquired and liabilities assumed at their individual fair values.

However, the entry to record the combination further depends on the relation between the consideration transferred and the net amount of the fair values assigned to the identified assets acquired and liabilities assumed. Therefore, we initially provide three illustrations that demonstrate the procedures to record a business combination, each with different amounts of consideration transferred relative to the acquired asset and liability fair values. Each example assumes a merger takes place and, therefore, the acquired firm is dissolved. In each situation, the consideration transferred is compared to the fair value of the net identifiable assets acquired and liabilities assumed to determine if goodwill or a bargain purchase gain should be recorded.

Consideration Transferred Equals Net Fair Values of Identified Assets Acquired and Liabilities Assumed

Assume that after negotiations with the owners of Smallport, BigNet agrees to pay cash of $550,000 and to issue 20,000 previously unissued shares of its $10 par value common stock (currently selling for $100 per share) for all of Smallport's assets and liabilities. Following the acquisition, Smallport then dissolves itself as a legal entity. The consideration transferred from BigNet to Smallport is computed as follows and in this case, exactly equals the collective fair values of Smallport's assets less liabilities:

Cash payment	$ 550,000
Common stock issued by BigNet ($100 x 20,000 shares)	2,000,000
Total consideration transferred	$2,550,000
Fair value of Smallport's net identifiable assets	$2,550,000

The $2,550,000 fair value of the consideration transferred by BigNet represents the fair value of the acquired Smallport business and serves as the basis for recording the combination in total.

BigNet also must record all of Smallport's identified assets and liabilities at their ***individual*** fair values. These two valuations present no difficulties because BigNet's consideration transferred exactly equals the $2,550,000 collective net fair values of the individual assets and liabilities acquired as shown in Exhibit 2.3.

Because Smallport Company will be dissolved, BigNet (the surviving company) enters a journal entry in its financial records to record the combination. BigNet has directly acquired the assets and assumed the liabilities of Smallport. Under the acquisition method, BigNet records Smallport's assets and liabilities at fair value ignoring original book values. Revenue, expense, dividend, and equity accounts cannot be transferred to a parent and are not included in recording the business combination.

LO 2-6a

Prepare the journal entry to consolidate the accounts of a subsidiary if dissolution takes place.

Acquisition Method: Consideration Transferred Equals Net Identified Asset Fair Values—Subsidiary Dissolved

BigNet Company's Financial Records—December 31		
Current Assets	300,000	
Computers and Equipment	600,000	
Capitalized Software	1,200,000	
Customer Contracts	700,000	
Notes Payable		250,000
Cash (paid by BigNet)		550,000
Common Stock (20,000 shares issued by BigNet at $10 par value)		200,000
Additional Paid-In Capital		1,800,000
To record acquisition of Smallport Company. Assets acquired and liabilities assumed are recorded at fair value.		

BigNet's financial records now show $1,900,000 in the Computers and Equipment account ($1,300,000 former balance + $600,000 acquired), $1,700,000 in Capitalized Software ($500,000 + $1,200,000), and so forth. Note that the customer contracts, despite being unrecorded on Smallport's books, are nonetheless identified and recognized on BigNet's financial records as part of the assets acquired in the combination. These items have been added into BigNet's balances (see Exhibit 2.3) at their fair values. Conversely, BigNet's revenue balance continues to report the company's own $1,000,000 with expenses remaining at $800,000 and dividends of $110,000. Under the acquisition method, only the subsidiary's revenues, expenses, dividends, and equity transactions that occur subsequent to the takeover affect the business combination.

Consideration Transferred Exceeds Net Amount of Fair Values of Identified Assets Acquired and Liabilities Assumed

In this next illustration, BigNet transfers to the owners of Smallport consideration of \$1,000,000 in cash plus 20,000 shares of common stock with a fair value of \$100 per share in exchange for ownership of the company. The consideration transferred from BigNet to Smallport is now computed as follows and results in an excess amount exchanged over the fair value of the net assets acquired:

Cash payment	\$1,000,000
Common stock issued by BigNet (\$100 x 20,000 shares)	2,000,000
Total consideration transferred	\$3,000,000
Fair value of Smallport's net identifiable assets	\$2,550,000
Goodwill	\$ 450,000

As presented in the above calculation, when the consideration transferred in an acquisition exceeds total net fair value of the identified assets and liabilities, the excess (\$450,000 in this case) is allocated to an unidentifiable asset known as goodwill.[23] Unlike other assets, we consider goodwill as unidentifiable because we presume it emerges from several other assets acting together to produce an expectation of enhanced profitability. Goodwill essentially captures all sources of profitability beyond what can be expected from simply summing the fair values of the acquired firm's assets and liabilities.

The resulting consideration paid is \$450,000 more than the \$2,550,000 fair value of Smallport's net identifiable assets and is assigned to the unidentifiable asset Goodwill.

Several factors may have affected BigNet's \$3,000,000 acquisition offer. First, BigNet may expect its assets to act in concert with those of Smallport, thus creating synergies that will produce profits beyond the total expected for the separate companies. In our earlier examples, Facebook, WestRock, and AT&T all clearly anticipated substantial synergies from their acquisitions. Other factors such as Smallpot's history of profitability, its reputation, the quality of its personnel, and the current economic condition of the industry in which it operates may also affect the acquisition offer. In general, if a target company is projected to generate unusually high profits relative to its asset base, acquirers frequently are willing to pay a premium price.

Acquisition Method: Consideration Transferred Exceeds Net Identified Asset Fair Values—Subsidiary Dissolved

Returning to BigNet's \$3,000,000 consideration, \$450,000 is in excess of the fair value of Smallport's net assets. Thus, goodwill of that amount is entered into BigNet's accounting system along with the fair value of each individual asset and liability. BigNet makes the following journal entry at the date of acquisition:

BigNet Company's Financial Records—December 31		
Current Assets	300,000	
Computers and Equipment	600,000	
Capitalized Software	1,200,000	
Customer Contracts	700,000	
Goodwill	450,000	
Notes Payable		250,000
Cash (paid by BigNet)		1,000,000
Common Stock (20,000 shares issued by BigNet at \$10 par value)		200,000
Additional Paid-In Capital		1,800,000
To record acquisition of Smallport Company. Assets acquired and liabilities assumed are recorded at individual fair values with excess fair value attributed to goodwill.		

[23] In business combinations, such excess payments are not unusual and can be quite large. When Oracle acquired PeopleSoft, it initially assigned \$4.5 billion of its \$11 billion purchase price to the fair value of the acquired identified net assets. It assigned the remaining \$6.5 billion to goodwill.

Once again, BigNet's financial records now show $1,900,000 in the Computers and Equipment account ($1,300,000 former balance + $600,000 acquired), $1,700,000 in Capitalized Software ($500,000 + $1,200,000), and so forth. As the only change, BigNet records goodwill of $450,000 for the excess consideration paid over the net identified asset fair values.[24]

Bargain Purchase—Consideration Transferred Is Less Than Net Amount of Fair Values of Identified Assets Acquired and Liabilities Assumed

Occasionally, the fair value of the consideration transferred by the acquirer is less than the fair value received in an acquisition. Such bargain purchases typically are considered anomalous. Businesses generally do not sell assets or businesses at prices below their fair values. Nonetheless, bargain purchases do occur—most often in forced or distressed sales.

For example, Westamerica Bank's acquisition of County Bank (California) from the FDIC resulted in a $48.8 million "bargain purchase" gain. The FDIC sold the failed County Bank to Westamerica for $0 and additional guarantees. As a result, Westamerica recorded the combination at the estimated fair value of the net assets acquired and recognized a gain of $48.8 million. This gain treatment is consistent with the view that the acquiring firm is immediately better off by the amount that the fair value acquired in the business combination exceeds the consideration transferred.

To demonstrate accounting for a bargain purchase, our third illustration begins with BigNet transferring consideration of $2,000,000 to the owners of Smallport in exchange for their business. BigNet conveys no cash and issues 20,000 shares of $10 par common stock that has a $100 per share fair value. The consideration transferred from BigNet to Smallport is now computed as follows and results in a gain on bargain purchase:

Cash payment	$ -0-
Common stock issued by BigNet ($100 × 20,000 shares)	2,000,000
Total consideration transferred	$ 2,000,000
Fair value of Smallport's identifiable net assets	$ 2,550,000
Gain on bargain purchase	$ 550,000

In accounting for this acquisition, at least two competing fair values are present. First, the $2,000,000 consideration transferred for Smallport represents a negotiated transaction value for the business. Second, the net amount of fair values individually assigned to the identified assets acquired and liabilities assumed produces $2,550,000. Additionally, based on expected synergies with Smallport, BigNet's management may believe that the fair value of the business exceeds the net asset fair value. Nonetheless, because the consideration transferred is less than the net asset fair value, a bargain purchase has occurred.

The acquisition method records the identified assets acquired and liabilities assumed at their individual fair values. In a bargain purchase situation, this net asset fair value effectively replaces the consideration transferred as the acquired firm's valuation basis for financial reporting. The consideration transferred serves as the acquired firm's valuation basis only if the consideration equals or exceeds the net amount of fair values for the assets acquired and liabilities assumed (as in the first two examples). In this case, however, the $2,000,000 consideration paid is less than the $2,550,000 net asset fair value, indicating a bargain purchase. Thus, the $2,550,000 net asset fair value serves as the valuation basis for the combination. A $550,000 *gain on bargain purchase* results because the $2,550,000 recorded value is accompanied by a payment of only $2,000,000. The acquirer recognizes this gain on its income statement in the period the acquisition takes place.

[24] As discussed in Chapter 3, the assets and liabilities (including goodwill) acquired in a business combination are assigned to reporting units of the combined entity. A reporting unit is simply a line of business (often a segment) in which an acquired asset or liability will be employed. The objective of assigning acquired assets and liabilities to reporting units is to facilitate periodic goodwill impairment testing.

Acquisition Method: Consideration Transferred Is Less Than Net Identified Asset Fair Values—Subsidiary Dissolved

BigNet Company's Financial Records—December 31		
Current Assets	300,000	
Computers and Equipment	600,000	
Capitalized Software	1,200,000	
Customer Contracts	700,000	
Notes Payable		250,000
Common Stock (20,000 shares issued by BigNet at $10 par value)		200,000
Additional Paid-In Capital		1,800,000
Gain on Bargain Purchase		550,000
To record acquisition of Smallport Company. Assets acquired and liabilities assumed are each recorded at fair value. Excess net asset fair value is attributed to a gain on bargain purchase.		

LO 2-6a

Prepare the journal entry to consolidate the accounts of a subsidiary if dissolution takes place.

A consequence of implementing a fair-value concept to acquisition accounting is the recognition of an unrealized gain on the bargain purchase. A criticism of the gain recognition is that the acquirer recognizes profit from a buying activity that occurs prior to traditional accrual measures of earned income (i.e., selling activity). Nonetheless, an exception to the general rule of recording business acquisitions at fair value of the consideration transferred occurs in the rare circumstance of a bargain purchase. Thus, in a bargain purchase, the fair values of the assets received and all liabilities assumed in a business combination are considered more relevant for asset valuation than the consideration transferred.

Summary: Acquisition Method When Dissolution Takes Place

When the acquired firm is dissolved in a business combination, the acquiring firm prepares a journal entry to record the combination on its books. The fair value of the consideration transferred by the acquiring firm provides the starting point for recording the acquisition. With few exceptions, the separately identified assets acquired and liabilities assumed are recorded at their individual fair values. Goodwill is recognized if the fair value of the consideration transferred exceeds the net identified asset fair value. If the net identified asset fair value of the business acquired exceeds the consideration transferred, a gain on a bargain purchase is recognized and reported in current income of the combined entity. Exhibit 2.4 summarizes possible allocations using the acquisition method.

LO 2-6b

Prepare the journal entry to record the various related costs involved in a business combination.

Related Costs of Business Combinations

Three additional categories of costs typically accompany business combinations, regardless of whether dissolution takes place. First, firms often engage attorneys, accountants, investment bankers, and other professionals for combination-related services. The acquisition

EXHIBIT 2.4
Consolidation Values—The Acquisition Method

Consolidation Values	Acquisition Accounting
Consideration transferred equals the fair values of net identified assets acquired.	Identified assets acquired and liabilities assumed are recorded at their fair values.
Consideration transferred is greater than the fair values of net identified assets acquired.	Identified assets acquired and liabilities assumed are recorded at their fair values. The excess consideration transferred over the net identified asset fair value is recorded as goodwill.
Bargain purchase—consideration transferred is less than the fair values of net identified assets acquired. The total of the individual fair values of the net identified assets acquired effectively becomes the acquired business fair value.	Identified assets acquired and liabilities assumed are recorded at their fair values. The excess amount of net identified asset fair value over the consideration transferred is recorded as a gain on bargain purchase.

EXHIBIT 2.5
Acquisition Method—Accounting for Costs Frequently Associated with Business Combinations

Types of Combination Costs	Acquisition Accounting
Direct combination costs (e.g., accounting, legal, investment banking, appraisal fees, etc.)	Expense as incurred
Indirect combination costs (e.g., internal costs such as allocated secretarial or managerial time)	Expense as incurred
Amounts incurred to register and issue securities	Reduce the value assigned to the fair value of the securities issued (typically a debit to additional paid-in capital)

method does not consider such expenditures as part of the fair value received by the acquirer. Therefore, professional service fees are expensed in the period incurred. The second category concerns an acquiring firm's internal costs. Examples include secretarial and management time allocated to the acquisition activity. Such indirect costs are reported as current year expenses, too. Finally, amounts incurred to register and issue securities in connection with a business combination simply reduce the otherwise determinable fair value of those securities. Exhibit 2.5 summarizes the three categories of related payments that accompany a business combination and their respective accounting treatments.

To illustrate the accounting treatment of these costs that frequently accompany business combinations, assume the following in connection with BigNet's acquisition of Smallport.

- BigNet pays an additional $100,000 in accounting and attorney fees.
- Internal secretarial and administrative costs of $75,000 are indirectly attributable to BigNet's combination with Smallport.
- Costs to register and issue BigNet's securities issued in the combination total $20,000.

Following the acquisition method, regardless of whether dissolution occurs or separate incorporation is maintained, BigNet would record these transactions as follows:

BigNet Company's Financial Records		
Professional Services Expense	100,000	
Cash		100,000
To record as expenses of the current period any direct combination costs.		
Salaries and Administrative Expenses	75,000	
Accounts Payable (or Cash)		75,000
To record as expenses of the current period any indirect combination costs.		
Additional Paid-In Capital	20,000	
Cash		20,000
To record costs to register and issue stock in connection with the Smallport acquisition.		

The Acquisition Method When Separate Incorporation Is Maintained

When each company retains separate incorporation in a business combination, many aspects of the consolidation process are identical to those demonstrated in the previous section. Fair value, for example, remains the basis for initially consolidating the subsidiary's assets and liabilities. Also, the acquiring firm records a journal entry on its books reflecting the investment and the consideration transferred in the combination.

However, several significant differences are evident in combinations in which each company remains a legally incorporated separate entity. Most noticeably, the consolidation of the financial information is only simulated; the acquiring company does not physically record the acquired assets and liabilities. *Because dissolution does not occur, each company maintains independent record-keeping.* To facilitate the preparation of consolidated financial statements, a worksheet and consolidation entries are employed using data gathered from these separate companies.

A worksheet provides the structure for generating financial reports for the single economic entity. An integral part of this process employs consolidation worksheet entries that either adjust or eliminate various account balances of the parent and subsidiary. These adjustments and eliminations are entered on the worksheet to produce consolidated statements as if the financial records had been physically combined. *Because no actual union occurs, neither company ever records consolidation worksheet entries in its journals.* Instead, these adjustments and eliminations appear solely on the worksheet to derive consolidated balances for financial reporting purposes.

Example: (includes stock issue, related combination costs, and contingent consideration)

To illustrate the worksheet mechanics, we again use the Exhibit 2.3 example of BigNet and Smallport. We also include combination costs and contingent consideration. Assume that BigNet acquires Smallport Company on December 31 by issuing 26,000 shares of $10 par value common stock valued at $100 per share (or $2,600,000 in total). BigNet pays fees of $40,000 to a third party for its assistance in arranging the transaction.

Then, to settle a difference of opinion regarding Smallport's fair value, BigNet promises to pay an additional $83,200 to the former owners if Smallport's earnings exceed $300,000 during the next annual period. BigNet estimates a 25 percent probability that the $83,200 contingent payment will be required. A discount rate of 4 percent (to represent the time value of money) yields an expected present value of $20,000 for the contingent liability ($83,200 × 25% × 0.961538). The fair-value approach of the acquisition method views such contingent payments as part of the consideration transferred. According to this view, contingencies have value to those who receive the consideration and represent measurable obligations of the acquirer.[25] Therefore, the fair value of the consideration transferred in this example consists of the following two elements:

Fair value of securities issued by BigNet.	$2,600,000
Fair value of contingent performance liability	20,000
Total fair value of consideration transferred.	$2,620,000

To facilitate a possible future spinoff, BigNet maintains Smallport as a separate corporation with its independent accounting information system intact. Therefore, whenever financial statements for the combined entity are prepared, BigNet utilizes a worksheet in simulating the consolidation of these two companies.

LO 2-6c

Prepare the journal entry to record a business combination when the acquired firm retains its separate existence.

Although the assets and liabilities are not transferred, BigNet must still record the consideration provided to Smallport's owners. When the subsidiary remains separate, the parent establishes an investment account that initially reflects the acquired firm's acquisition-date fair value. Because Smallport maintains its separate identity, BigNet prepares the following journal entries on its books to record the business combination.

LO 2-7

Prepare a worksheet to consolidate the accounts of two companies that form a business combination in the absence of dissolution.

Acquisition Method—Subsidiary Is Not Dissolved

BigNet Company's Financial Records—December 31		
Investment in Smallport Company (consideration transferred).	2,620,000	
Contingent Performance Liability.		20,000
Common Stock (26,000 shares issued by BigNet at $10 par value)		260,000
Additional Paid-In Capital (value of shares in excess of par value)		2,340,000
To record acquisition of Smallport Company, which maintains its separate legal identity.		
Professional Services Expense	40,000	
Cash (paid for third-party fees).		40,000
To record combination costs.		

As Exhibit 2.6 demonstrates, a worksheet can be prepared on the date of acquisition to arrive at consolidated totals for this combination. The entire process consists of six steps.

[25] The ASC (805-30-35-1) notes several reasons for contingent consideration including meeting an earnings target, reaching a specified share price, or reaching a milestone on a research and development project.

EXHIBIT 2.6 Acquisition Method—Date of Acquisition

Accounts	BigNet	Smallport	Consolidation Entries: Debits	Consolidation Entries: Credits	Consolidated Totals
Income Statement					
Revenues	(1,000,000)				(1,000,000)
Expenses	840,000*				840,000
Net income	(160,000)				(160,000)
Statement of Retained Earnings					
Retained earnings, 1/1	(870,000)				(870,000)
Net income (above)	(160,000)*				(160,000)
Dividends declared	110,000				110,000
Retained earnings, 12/31	(920,000)				(920,000)
Balance Sheet					
Current assets	1,060,000*	300,000			1,360,000
Investment in Smallport Company	2,620,000*	–0–		(S) 600,000	–0–
				(A) 2,020,000	
Computers and equipment	1,300,000	400,000	(A) 200,000		1,900,000
Capitalized software	500,000	100,000	(A) 1,100,000		1,700,000
Customer contracts	–0–	–0–	(A) 700,000		700,000
Goodwill	–0–	–0–	(A) 70,000		70,000
Total assets	5,480,000	800,000			5,730,000
Notes payable	(300,000)	(200,000)		(A) 50,000	(550,000)
Contingent performance liability	(20,000)*				(20,000)
Common stock	(1,860,000)*	(100,000)	(S) 100,000		(1,860,000)
Additional paid-in capital	(2,380,000)*	(20,000)	(S) 20,000		(2,380,000)
Retained earnings, 12/31 (above)	(920,000)	(480,000)	(S) 480,000		(920,000)
Total liabilities and equities	(5,480,000)	(800,000)	2,670,000	2,670,000	(5,730,000)

Note: Parentheses indicate a credit balance.
*Balances have been adjusted for consideration transferred and payment of direct acquisition costs. Also note follow-through effects to net income and retained earnings from the expensing of the direct acquisition costs.
(S) Elimination of Smallport's stockholders' equity accounts as of December 31 and book value portion of the investment account.
(A) Allocation of BigNet's consideration fair value in excess of book value.
Note: Parentheses indicate a credit balance.
*Balances have been adjusted for consideration transferred and payment of direct acquisition costs. Also note follow-through effects to net income and retained earnings from the expensing of the direct acquisition costs.
(S) Elimination of Smallport's stockholders' equity accounts as of December 31 and book value portion of the investment account.
(A) Allocation of BigNet's consideration fair value in excess of book value.

Step 1

Prior to constructing a worksheet, the parent prepares a formal allocation of the acquisition-date fair value similar to the equity method procedures presented in Chapter 1.[26] Thus, the following schedule is appropriate for BigNet's acquisition of Smallport:

Acquisition-Date Fair-Value Allocation Schedule

Fair value of consideration transferred by BigNet		$2,620,000
Book value of Smallport (see Exhibit 2.3).		600,000
Excess of fair value over book value.		$2,020,000
Allocations made to specific accounts based on acquisition-date fair and book value differences (see Exhibit 2.3):		
Computers and equipment ($600,000 – $400,000).	$ 200,000	
Capitalized software ($1,200,000 – $100,000).	1,100,000	
Customer contracts ($700,000 – 0)	700,000	
Notes payable ($250,000 – $200,000).	(50,000)	1,950,000
Excess fair value not identified with specific items—Goodwill		$ 70,000

[26] This allocation procedure is helpful but not critical if dissolution occurs. The asset and liability accounts are simply added directly into the parent's books at their acquisition-date fair value with any excess assigned to goodwill as shown in the previous sections of this chapter.

Note that this schedule initially subtracts Smallport's acquisition-date book value. The resulting $2,020,000 difference represents the total amount needed on the Exhibit 2.6 worksheet to adjust Smallport's individual assets and liabilities from book value to fair value (and to recognize goodwill). Next, the schedule shows how this $2,020,000 total is allocated to adjust each individual item to fair value. The fair-value allocation schedule thus effectively serves as a convenient supporting schedule for the Exhibit 2.6 worksheet and is routinely prepared for every consolidation.

No part of the $2,020,000 excess fair value is attributed to the current assets because their book values equal their fair values. The Notes Payable account shows a negative allocation because the debt's present value exceeds its book value. An increase in debt decreases the fair value of the company's net assets.

Step 2

The consolidation process begins with preparing the first two columns of the worksheet (see Exhibit 2.6) containing the separate companies' acquisition-date book value financial figures (see Exhibit 2.3). BigNet's accounts have been adjusted for the journal entries recorded earlier for the investment and the combination costs. As another preliminary step, Smallport's revenue, expense, and dividend accounts have been closed into its Retained Earnings account. The subsidiary's operations prior to the December 31 takeover have no direct bearing on the operating results of the business combination. These activities occurred before Smallport was acquired; thus, the new owner should not include any precombination subsidiary revenues or expenses in the consolidated statements.

Step 3

Consolidation Entry S eliminates Smallport's stockholders' equity accounts (S is a reference to beginning subsidiary stockholders' equity) as follows:

Consolidation Entry S

Common Stock (Smallport Company)	100,000	
Additional Paid-In Capital (Smallport Company)	20,000	
Retained Earnings (Smallport Company).	480,000	
Investment in Smallport Company.		600,000

Consolidation Entry S is a worksheet entry and accordingly does not affect the financial records of either company. The subsidiary balances (Common Stock, Additional Paid-In Capital, and Retained Earnings) represent ownership interests that are now held by the parent—thus they are not represented as equity in the parent's consolidated balance sheet. Moreover, by removing these account balances on the worksheet, only Smallport's assets and liabilities remain to be combined with the parent company figures.

Consolidation Entry S also removes the $600,000 component of the parent's Investment in Smallport Company account balance that equates to the book value of the subsidiary's net assets. For external reporting purposes, BigNet should include each of Smallport's assets and liabilities rather than a single investment balance. In effect, this portion of the parent's Investment in Smallport Company account balance is eliminated and replaced by the specific subsidiary assets and liabilities that are already listed in the second column of the worksheet.

Step 4

Consolidation Entry A removes the $2,020,000 excess payment in the Investment in Smallport Company and assigns it to the specific accounts indicated by the fair-value allocation schedule as follows:

Consolidation Entry A

Computers and Equipment	200,000	
Capitalized Software	1,100,000	
Customer Contracts	700,000	
Goodwill	70,000	
Note Payable		50,000
Investment in Smallport Company		2,020,000

Consequently, Computers and Equipment is increased by $200,000 to agree with Smallport's fair value: $1,100,000 is attributed to Capitalized Software, $700,000 to Customer Contracts, and $50,000 to Notes Payable. The unidentified excess of $70,000 is allocated to Goodwill. This entry for the consolidation worksheet is labeled Entry A to indicate that it represents the allocations made in connection with Smallport's acquisition-date fair value.

Consolidation Entry A also completes the Investment in Smallport Company account balance elimination on the worksheet. The investment remains on BigNet's books, but it does not appear on the consolidated balance sheet. Instead the investment account is replaced on the worksheet with Smallport's actual assets and liabilities as shown in Step 5.

Step 5

All accounts are extended into the Consolidated Totals column. For accounts such as Current Assets, this process simply adds Smallport and BigNet book values. However, when applicable, this extension also includes any allocations to establish the acquisition-date fair values of Smallport's assets and liabilities. Computers and Equipment, for example, is increased by $200,000. By increasing the subsidiary's book value to fair value, the reported balances are the same as in the previous examples when dissolution occurred. The use of a worksheet does not alter the consolidated figures but only the method of deriving those numbers.

Step 6

We subtract consolidated expenses from revenues to arrive at a $160,000 net income. Note that because this is an acquisition-date worksheet, we consolidate no amounts for Smallport's revenues and expenses. Having just been acquired, Smallport has not yet earned any income for BigNet owners. Consolidated revenues, expenses, and net income are identical to BigNet's balances. Subsequent to acquisition, of course, Smallport's revenue and expense accounts will be consolidated with BigNet's (coverage of this topic begins in Chapter 3).

Worksheet Mechanics

In general, totals (such as net income and ending retained earnings) are not directly consolidated across on the worksheet. Rather, the components (such as revenues and expenses) are extended across and then combined vertically to derive the appropriate figure. Net income is then carried down on the worksheet to the statement of retained earnings and used (along with beginning retained earnings and dividends) to compute the December 31 retained earnings balance. In the same manner, ending retained earnings of $920,000 is entered into the balance sheet to arrive at total liabilities and equities of $5,730,000, a number that reconciles with the total of consolidated assets.

Although it remains on BigNet's books, the Investment in Smallport account is eliminated entirely in consolidation. On the worksheet, the investment account is effectively replaced with the acquisition-date fair values of Smallport's assets and liabilities along with goodwill created by the combination.

The balances in the final column of Exhibit 2.6 are used to prepare consolidated financial statements for the business combination of BigNet Company and Smallport Company. The worksheet entries serve as a catalyst to bring together the two independent sets of financial information. The actual accounting records of both BigNet and Smallport remain unaltered by this consolidation process.

Bargain Purchase of a Separately Incorporated Subsidiary

Finally, although not addressed directly by the above example, bargain purchase gains can also occur in acquisitions of separately incorporated subsidiaries. If the consideration transferred is less than the fair value of a newly acquired subsidiary's identifiable net assets, then the parent records a bargain purchase gain on its books as part of the investment journal entry. The bargain purchase gain then appears on the the consolidated income statement for the reporting period that contains the acquisition date.

LO 2-8

Describe the accounting treatment for the various intangible assets often acquired in a business combination.

Acquisition-Date Fair-Value Allocations—Additional Issues

Intangibles

An important element of acquisition accounting is the acquirer's recognition and measurement of the assets acquired and liabilities assumed in the combination. In particular, the advent of the information age brings new measurement challenges for a host of intangible assets that provide value in generating future cash flows. Intangible assets often comprise the largest proportion of an acquired firm. For example, when AT&T acquired AT&T Broadband, it allocated approximately $19 billion of the $52 billion purchase price to franchise costs. These franchise costs form an intangible asset representing the value attributed to agreements with local authorities that allow access to homes.

Intangible assets include both current and noncurrent assets (not including financial instruments) that lack physical substance. In determining whether to recognize an intangible asset in a business combination, two specific criteria are essential.

1. Does the intangible asset arise from contractual or other legal rights?
2. Is the intangible asset capable of being sold or otherwise separated from the acquired enterprise?

Intangibles arising from contractual or legal rights are commonplace in business combinations. Often identified among the assets acquired are trademarks, patents, copyrights, franchise agreements, and a number of other intangibles that derive their value from governmental protection (or other contractual agreements) that allow a firm exclusive use of the asset. Most intangible assets recognized in business combinations meet the contractual-legal criterion.

Also seen in business combinations are intangible assets meeting the separability criterion. An acquired intangible asset is recognized if it is capable of being separated or divided from the acquiree and sold, transferred, licensed, rented, or exchanged individually or together with a related contract, identifiable asset, or liability. The acquirer is not required to have the intention to sell, license, or otherwise exchange the intangible in order to meet the separability criterion. For example, an acquiree may have developed internally a valuable customer list or other noncontractual customer relationships. Although the value of these items may not have arisen from a specific legal right, they nonetheless convey benefits to the acquirer that may be separable through sale, license, or exchange.

Exhibit 2.7 provides an extensive listing of intangible assets with indications of whether they typically meet the legal/contractual or separability criteria.

The FASB (Exposure Draft, *Business Combinations and Intangible Assets,* para. 271) recognized the inherent difficulties in estimating the separate fair values of many intangibles and stated that:

> difficulties may arise in assigning the acquisition cost to individual intangible assets acquired in a basket purchase such as a business combination. Measuring some of those assets is less difficult than measuring other assets, particularly if they are exchangeable and traded regularly in the marketplace. . . . Nonetheless, even those assets that cannot be measured on that basis may have more cash flow streams directly or indirectly associated with them than can be used as the basis for measuring them. While the resulting measures may lack the precision of other measures, they provide information that is more representationally faithful than would be the case if those assets were simply subsumed into goodwill on the grounds of measurement difficulties.

EXHIBIT 2.7 Illustrative Examples of Intangible Assets That Meet the Criteria for Recognition Separately from Goodwill (FASB ASC paragraphs 805-20-55-11 through 45)

The following are examples of intangible assets that meet the criteria for recognition as an asset apart from goodwill. The following illustrative list is not intended to be all-inclusive; thus, an acquired intangible asset could meet the recognition criteria of this statement but not be included on that list. Assets designated by the symbol (c) are those that would generally be recognized separately from goodwill because they meet the contractual-legal criterion. Assets designated by the symbol (s) do not arise from contractual or other legal rights but should nonetheless be recognized separately from goodwill because they meet the separability criterion. The determination of whether a specific acquired intangible asset meets the criteria in this statement for recognition apart from goodwill should be based on the facts and circumstances of each individual business combination.*

Marketing-Related Intangible Assets

1. Trademarks, trade names.[c]
2. Service marks, collective marks, certification marks.[c]
3. Trade dress (unique color, shape, or package design).[c]
4. Newspaper mastheads.[c]
5. Internet domain names.[c]
6. Noncompetition agreements.[c]

Customer-Related Intangible Assets

1. Customer lists.[s]
2. Order or production backlog.[c]
3. Customer contracts and related customer relationships.[c]
4. Noncontractual customer relationships.[s]

Artistic-Related Intangible Assets

1. Plays, operas, and ballets.[c]
2. Books, magazines, newspapers, and other literary works.[c]
3. Musical works such as compositions, song lyrics, and advertising jingles.[c]
4. Pictures and photographs.[c]
5. Video and audiovisual material, including motion pictures, music videos, and television programs.[c]

Contract-Based Intangible Assets

1. Licensing, royalty, standstill agreements.[c]
2. Advertising, construction, management, service, or supply contracts.[c]
3. Lease agreements.[c]
4. Construction permits.[c]
5. Franchise agreements.[c]
6. Operating and broadcast rights.[c]
7. Use rights such as landing, drilling, water, air, mineral, timber cutting, and route authorities.[c]
8. Servicing contracts such as mortgage servicing contracts.[c]
9. Employment contracts.[c]

Technology-Based Intangible Assets

1. Patented technology.[c]
2. Computer software and mask works.[c]
3. Unpatented technology.[s]
4. Databases, including title plants.[s]
5. Trade secrets, including secret formulas, processes, and recipes.[c]

*The intangible assets designated by the symbol (c) also could meet the separability criterion. However, separability is not a necessary condition for an asset to meet the contractual-legal criterion.

Undoubtedly, as our knowledge economy continues its rapid growth, asset allocations to items such as those identified in Exhibit 2.7 are expected to be frequent.

Preexisting Goodwill on Subsidiary's Books

In our examples of business combinations so far, the assets acquired and liabilities assumed have all been specifically identifiable (e.g., current assets, capitalized software, computers and equipment, customer contracts, and notes payable). However, in many cases, an acquired firm has an unidentifiable asset (i.e., goodwill recorded on its books in connection with a previous business combination of its own). A question arises as to the parent's treatment of this preexisting goodwill on the newly acquired subsidiary's books.

By its very nature, such preexisting goodwill is not considered identifiable by the parent. Therefore, in calculating the new goodwill acquired in the combination, the new owner simply excludes the carrying amount of any preexisting goodwill from the subsidiary's acquisition-date book value. The new owner effectively reallocates any preexisting subsidiary goodwill via a credit in consolidation worksheet Entry A. This worksheet credit to the subsidiary's goodwill balance is then offset by worksheet enties to identifiable assets and liabilities, followed by a debit to the new goodwill from the combination. The logic is that the total business fair value is first allocated to the identified assets and liabilities. Only if an excess amount remains after recognizing the fair values of the net identified assets is any goodwill recognized. Thus, in all business combinations, only goodwill reflected in the current acquisition is brought forward in the consolidated entity's financial reports.

Acquired In-Process Research and Development

The negotiations for a business combination begin with the identification of the tangible and intangible assets acquired and liabilities assumed by the acquirer. The fair values of the acquired individual assets and liabilities then provide the basis for financial statement valuations. Many firms—especially those in pharmaceutical and high-tech industries—have allocated significant portions of acquired businesses to in-process research and development (IPR&D).

Current accounting standards require that acquired IPR&D be measured at acquisition-date fair value and recognized in consolidated financial statements as an asset. However, this was not always the case. Past standards required immediate expense treatment for acquired IPR&D. Nonetheless, arguments about the future economic benefits of IPR&D ultimately persuaded the FASB to require asset recognition. For example, in commenting on the nature of IPR&D as an asset, Pfizer in an October 28, 2005, comment letter to the FASB observed that:

> board members know that companies frame business strategies around IPR&D, negotiate for it, pay for it, fair value it, and nurture it and they view those seemingly rational actions as inconsistent with the notion that IPR&D has no probable future economic benefit.

Asset recognition for acquired IPR&D is now standard even though benefits must be estimated and may be uncertain. To illustrate, when ARCA Biopharma acquired a significant in-process research and development asset through a merger with Nuvelo, Inc., it disclosed the following in its financial statements:

> A valuation firm was engaged to assist ARCA in determining the estimated fair values of these (IPR&D) assets as of the acquisition date. Discounted cash flow models are typically used in these valuations, and the models require the use of significant estimates and assumptions including but not limited to:

- Projecting regulatory approvals.
- Estimating future cash flows from product sales resulting from completed products and in-process projects.
- Developing appropriate discount rates and probability rates by project.

The IPR&D asset is initially considered an indefinite-lived intangible asset and is not subject to amortization. IPR&D is then tested for impairment annually or more frequently if events or changes in circumstances indicate that the asset might be impaired.

Recognizing acquired IPR&D as an asset is clearly consistent with the FASB's fair-value approach to acquisition accounting. Similar to costs that result in goodwill and other internally generated intangibles (e.g., customer lists, trade names, etc.), IPR&D costs are expensed as incurred in ongoing business activities. However, a business combination is considered a significant recognition event for which all fair values transferred in the transaction should be fully accounted for, including any values assigned to IPR&D. Moreover, because the acquirer paid for the IPR&D, an expectation of future economic benefit is assumed and, therefore, the amount is recognized as an asset.

To illustrate further, assume that ClearTone Company pays $2,300,000 in cash for all assets and liabilities of Newave, Inc., in a merger transaction. ClearTone manufactures components for cell phones. The primary motivation for the acquisition is a particularly attractive research and development project under way at Newave that will extend a cell phone's battery life by up to 50 percent. ClearTone hopes to combine the new technology with its manufacturing process and projects a resulting substantial revenue increase. ClearTone is optimistic that Newave will finish the project in the next two years. At the acquisition date, ClearTone prepares the following schedule that recognizes the items of value it expects to receive from the Newave acquisition:

Consideration transferred		$2,300,000
Receivables	$ 55,000	
Patents	220,000	
In-process research and development	1,900,000	
Accounts payable	(175,000)	
Fair value of identified net assets acquired		2,000,000
Goodwill		$ 300,000

ClearTone records the transaction as follows:

Receivables	55,000	
Patents	220,000	
Research and Development Asset	1,900,000	
Goodwill	300,000	
Accounts Payable		175,000
Cash		2,300,000

Research and development expenditures incurred subsequent to the date of acquisition will continue to be expensed. Acquired IPR&D assets initially should be considered indefinite-lived until the project is completed or abandoned. As with other indefinite-lived intangible assets, an acquired IPR&D asset is tested for impairment and is not amortized until its useful life is determined to be no longer indefinite.

Convergence between U.S. and International Accounting Standards

The FASB ASC Topics "Business Combinations" (805) and "Consolidation" (810) represent outcomes of a joint project between the FASB and the International Accounting Standards Board (IASB). The primary objective of the project was stated as follows:

> to develop a single high-quality standard for business combinations that can be used for both domestic and cross-border financial reporting. The goal is to develop a standard that includes a common set of principles and related guidance that produces decision-useful information and minimizes exceptions to those principles. The standard should improve the completeness, relevance, and comparability of financial information about business combinations . . . (FASB Project Updates: *Business Combinations: Applying the Acquisition Method—Joint Project of the IASB and FASB:* October 25, 2007)

The IASB subsequently issued International Financial Reporting Standard 3 (*IFRS 3*) Revised (effective July 2009), which along with FASB ASC Topics 805, "Business Combinations," and 810, "Consolidation," effectively converged the accounting for business combinations internationally. The two standards are identical in most important aspects of accounting for business combinations although differences can result in noncontrolling interest valuation and some other limited applications.[27] The joint project on business combinations represents one of the first successful implementations of the agreement between the two standard-setting groups to coordinate efforts on future work with the goal of developing high-quality comparable standards for both domestic and cross-border financial accounting.

Summary

1. Consolidation of financial information is required for external reporting purposes when one organization gains control of another, thus forming a single economic entity. In many combinations, all but one of the companies is dissolved as a separate legal corporation. Therefore, the consolidation process is carried out fully at the date of acquisition to bring together all accounts into a single set of financial records. In other combinations, the companies retain their identities as separate enterprises and continue to maintain their own separate accounting systems. For these cases, consolidation is a periodic process necessary whenever the parent produces external financial statements. This periodic procedure is frequently accomplished through the use of a worksheet and consolidation entries.
2. Current financial reporting standards require the acquisition method in accounting for business combinations. Under the acquisition method, the fair value of the consideration transferred provides the starting point for valuing the acquired firm. The fair value of the consideration transferred by the acquirer includes the fair value of any contingent consideration. The acquired company assets and liabilities are consolidated at their individual acquisition-date fair values. Direct combination costs are expensed as incurred because they are not part of the acquired business fair value. Also, the fair value of all acquired in-process research and development is recognized as an asset in business combinations and is subject to subsequent impairment reviews.

[27] Chapter 4 of this text provides further discussion of noncontrolling interest accounting differences across U.S. GAAP and IFRS. Other differences are presented in chapters where the applicable topics are covered.

3. If the consideration transferred for an acquired firm exceeds the total fair value of the acquired firm's net assets, the residual amount is recognized in the consolidated financial statements as goodwill, an intangible asset. When a bargain purchase occurs, individual assets and liabilities acquired continue to be recorded at their fair values and a gain on bargain purchase is recognized.
4. Particular attention should be given to the recognition of intangible assets in business combinations. An intangible asset must be recognized in an acquiring firm's financial statements if the asset arises from a legal or contractual right (e.g., trademarks, copyrights, artistic materials, royalty agreements). If the intangible asset does not represent a legal or contractual right, the intangible will still be recognized if it is capable of being separated from the firm (e.g., customer lists, noncontractual customer relationships, unpatented technology).

Comprehensive Illustration

Problem

(*Estimated Time: 45 to 65 Minutes*) Following are the account balances of Miller Company and Richmond Company as of December 31. The fair values of Richmond Company's assets and liabilities are also listed.

	Miller Company Book Values 12/31	Richmond Company Book Values 12/31	Richmond Company Fair Values 12/31
Cash	$ 600,000	$ 200,000	$ 200,000
Receivables	900,000	300,000	290,000
Inventory	1,100,000	600,000	820,000
Buildings and equipment (net)	9,000,000	800,000	900,000
Unpatented technology	–0–	–0–	500,000
In-process research and development	–0–	–0–	100,000
Accounts payable	(400,000)	(200,000)	(200,000)
Notes payable	(3,400,000)	(1,100,000)	(1,100,000)
Totals	$ 7,800,000	$ 600,000	$1,510,000
Common stock—$20 par value	$ (2,000,000)		
Common stock—$5 par value		$ (220,000)	
Additional paid-in capital	(900,000)	(100,000)	
Retained earnings, 1/1	(2,300,000)	(130,000)	
Revenues	(6,000,000)	(900,000)	
Expenses	3,400,000	750,000	
Totals	$ (7,800,000)	$ (600,000)	

Note: Parentheses indicate a credit balance.

Additional Information (not reflected in the preceding figures)

- On December 31, Miller issues 50,000 shares of its $20 par value common stock for all of the outstanding shares of Richmond Company.
- As part of the acquisition agreement, Miller agrees to pay the former owners of Richmond $250,000 if certain profit projections are realized over the next three years. Miller calculates the acquisition-date fair value of this contingency at $100,000.
- In creating this combination, Miller pays $10,000 in stock issue costs and $20,000 in accounting and legal fees.

Required

a. Miller's stock has a fair value of $32 per share. Using the acquisition method:
1. Prepare the necessary journal entries if Miller dissolves Richmond so it is no longer a separate legal entity.
2. Assume instead that Richmond will retain separate legal incorporation and maintain its own accounting systems. Prepare a worksheet to consolidate the accounts of the two companies.

b. If Miller's stock has a fair value of $26 per share, describe how the consolidated balances would differ from the results in requirement (*a*).

Solution

a. 1. In a business combination, the accountant first determines the total fair value of the consideration transferred. Because Miller's stock is valued at $32 per share, the 50,000 issued shares are worth $1,600,000 in total. Included in the consideration transferred is the $100,000 acquisition-date fair value of the contingent performance obligation.

This $1,700,000 total fair value is compared to the $1,510,000 fair value of Richmond's assets and liabilities (including the fair value of IPR&D). Miller recognizes the $190,000 excess fair value ($1,700,000 – $1,510,000) as goodwill. Because dissolution occurs, Miller records on its books the individual fair values of Richmond's identifiable assets and liabilities with the excess recorded as goodwill.

The $10,000 stock issue cost reduces Additional Paid-In Capital. The $20,000 direct combination costs (accounting and legal fees) are expensed when incurred.

Miller Company's Financial Records—December 31

Cash	200,000	
Receivables	290,000	
Inventory	820,000	
Buildings and Equipment	900,000	
Unpatented Technology	500,000	
Research and Development Asset	100,000	
Goodwill	190,000	
Accounts Payable		200,000
Notes Payable		1,100,000
Contingent Performance Obligation		100,000
Common Stock (Miller) (par value)		1,000,000
Additional Paid-In Capital (fair value in excess of par value)		600,000
To record acquisition of Richmond Company		
Professional Services Expense	20,000	
Cash (paid for combination costs)		20,000
To record legal and accounting fees related to the combination.		
Additional Paid-In Capital	10,000	
Cash (stock issuance costs)		10,000
To record payment of stock issuance costs		

2. Under this scenario, the acquisition fair value is equal to that computed in part (*a*1).

50,000 shares of stock at $32.00 each	$1,600,000
Contingent performance obligation	100,000
Acquisition-date fair value of consideration transferred	$1,700,000

Because the subsidiary is maintaining separate incorporation, Miller establishes an investment account to reflect the $1,700,000 acquisition consideration:

Miller's Financial Records—December 31

Investment in Richmond Company	1,700,000	
Contingent Performance Obligation		100,000
Common Stock (Miller) (par value)		1,000,000
Additional Paid-In Capital (fair value in excess of par value)		600,000
To record investment in Richmond Company		
Professional Services Expense	20,000	
Cash (paid for combination costs)		20,000
To record legal and accounting fees related to the combination.		
Additional Paid-In Capital	10,000	
Cash (stock issuance costs)		10,000
To record payment of stock issuance costs		

Because Richmond maintains separate incorporation and its own accounting system, Miller prepares a worksheet for consolidation. To prepare the worksheet, Miller first allocates Richmond's fair value to assets acquired and liabilities assumed based on their individual fair values:

Fair value of consideration transferred by Miller......	$1,700,000
Book value of Richmond..........................	600,000
Excess fair value over book value..................	$1,100,000

Allocations are made to specific accounts based on differences in fair values and book values:

Receivables ($290,000 – $300,000)........................	$(10,000)	
Inventory ($820,000 – $600,000)...........................	220,000	
Buildings and equipment ($900,000 – $800,000)............	100,000	
Unpatented technology ($500,000 – 0)	500,000	
In-process research and development	100,000	910,000
Goodwill		$190,000

The following steps produce the consolidated financial statements total in Exhibit 2.8:

Exhibit 2.8 Comprehensive Illustration—Solution—Acquisition Method

MILLER COMPANY AND RICHMOND COMPANY
Consolidation Worksheet
For Period Ending December 31

Accounts	Miller Company	Richmond Company	Consolidation Entries Debit	Consolidation Entries Credit	Consolidated Totals
Income Statement					
Revenues	(6,000,000)				(6,000,000)
Expenses	3,420,000*				3,420,000*
Net income	(2,580,000)				(2,580,000)
Statement of Retained Earnings					
Retained earnings, 1/1	(2,300,000)				(2,300,000)
Net income (above)	(2,580,000)				(2,580,000)
Retained earnings, 12/31	(4,880,000)				(4,880,000)
Balance Sheet					
Cash	570,000*	200,000			770,000
Receivables	900,000	300,000		(A) 10,000	1,190,000
Inventory	1,100,000	600,000	(A) 220,000		1,920,000
Investment in Richmond Company	1,700,000*	–0–		(A) 1,100,000	–0–
				(S) 600,000	
Buildings and equipment (net)	9,000,000	800,000	(A) 100,000		9,900,000
Goodwill	–0–	–0–	(A) 190,000		190,000
Unpatented technology	–0–	–0–	(A) 500,000		500,000
Research and development asset	–0–	–0–	(A) 100,000		100,000
Total assets	13,270,000	1,900,000			14,570,000
Accounts payable	(400,000)	(200,000)			(600,000)
Notes payable	(3,400,000)	(1,100,000)			(4,500,000)
Contingent performance obligation	(100,000)*	–0–			(100,000)
Common stock	(3,000,000)*	(220,000)	(S) 220,000		(3,000,000)
Additional paid-in capital	(1,490,000)*	(100,000)	(S) 100,000		(1,490,000)
Retained earnings, 12/31 (above)	(4,880,000)*	(280,000)†	(S) 280,000		(4,880,000)
Total liabilities and equities	(13,270,000)	(1,900,000)	1,710,000	1,710,000	(14,570,000)

Note: Parentheses indicate a credit balance.
*Balances have been adjusted for issuance of stock, payment of combination expenses, and recognition of contingent performance obligation.
†Beginning retained earnings plus revenues minus expenses.

- Miller's balances have been updated on this worksheet to include the effects of both the newly issued shares of stock, the recognition of the contingent performance liability, and the combination expenses.
- Richmond's revenue and expense accounts have been closed to Retained Earnings. The acquisition method consolidates only postacquisition revenues and expenses.
- Worksheet Entry S eliminates the $600,000 book value component of the Investment in Richmond Company account along with the subsidiary's stockholders' equity accounts.

  Entry A adjusts all of Richmond's assets and liabilities to fair value based on the allocations determined earlier.

b. If the fair value of Miller's stock is $26.00 per share, then the fair value of the consideration transferred in the Richmond acquisition is recomputed as follows:

Fair value of shares issued ($26 × 50,000 shares)	$1,300,000
Fair value of contingent consideration	100,000
Total consideration transferred at fair value	$1,400,000

Because the consideration transferred is $110,000 less than the $1,510,000 fair value of the net assets received in the acquisition, a bargain purchase has occurred. In this situation, Miller continues to recognize each of the separately identified assets acquired and liabilities assumed at their fair values. Resulting differences in the consolidated balances relative to the requirement (*a*) solution are as follows:

- The $110,000 excess fair value recognized over the consideration transferred is recognized as a "gain on bargain purchase."
- Consolidated net income increases by the $110,000 gain to $2,690,000.
- No goodwill is recognized.
- Miller's additional paid-in capital decreases by $300,000 to $1,190,000.
- Consolidated retained earnings increase by the $110,000 gain to $4,990,000.

Also, because of the bargain purchase, the "Investment in Richmond Company" account balance on Miller's separate financial statements shows the $1,510,000 fair value of the net identified assets received. This valuation measure is an exception to the general rule of using the consideration transferred to provide the valuation basis for the acquired firm.

Appendix A

LO 2-9

Identify the general characteristics of the legacy purchase and pooling of interest methods of accounting for past business combinations. Understand the effects that persist today in financial statements from the use of these legacy methods.

Legacy Methods of Accounting For Business Combinations

The acquisition method provides the accounting for business combinations occurring in 2009 and thereafter. However, for decades, business combinations were accounted for using either the **purchase** or **pooling of interests** method. From 2002 through 2008, the purchase method was used exclusively for business combinations. Prior to 2002, financial reporting standards allowed two alternatives: the purchase method and the pooling of interests method. Because the FASB required prospective application of the acquisition method for 2009 and beyond, the purchase and pooling of interests methods continue to provide the basis for financial reporting for pre-2009 business combinations and thus will remain relevant for many years. Literally tens of thousands of past business combinations will continue to be reported in future statements under one of these legacy methods.

The following sections describe the purchase and pooling of interests methods along with comparisons to the acquisition method.

The Purchase Method: An Application of the Cost Principle

A basic principle of the purchase method was to record a business combination at the cost to the new owners. For example, several years ago MGM Grand, Inc., acquired Mirage Resorts, Inc., for approximately $6.4 billion. This purchase price continued to serve as the valuation basis for Mirage Resorts' assets and liabilities in the preparation of MGM Grand's consolidated financial statements.

Several elements of the purchase method reflect a strict application of the cost principle. The following items represent examples of how the cost-based purchase method differs from the fair-value–based acquisition method.

- Acquisition date allocations (including bargain purchases).
- Direct combination costs.
- Contingent consideration.
- In-process research and development.

We next briefly discuss the accounting treatment for these items across the current and previous financial reporting regimes.

Purchase-Date Cost Allocations (Including Bargain Purchases)

In pre-2009 business combinations, the application of the cost principle often was complicated because literally hundreds of separate assets and liabilities were acquired. Accordingly, for asset valuation and future income determination, firms needed a basis to allocate the total cost among the various assets and liabilities received in the bargained exchange. Similar to the acquisition method, the purchase method based its cost allocations on the combination-date fair values of the acquired assets and liabilities. Also closely related to the acquisition method procedures, any excess of cost over the sum of the net identified asset fair values was attributed to goodwill.

But the purchase method stands in marked contrast to the acquisition method in bargain purchase situations. Under the purchase method, a bargain purchase occurred when the sum of the individual fair values of the acquired net assets exceeded the purchase cost. To record a bargain purchase at cost, however, the purchase method required that certain long-term assets be recorded at amounts below their assessed fair values.

For example, assume Adams Co. paid $520,000 for Brook Co. in 2008. Brook has the following assets with appraised fair values:

Accounts receivable	$ 15,000
Land	200,000
Building	400,000
Accounts payable	(5,000)
Total net fair value	$610,000

However, to record the combination at its $520,000 cost, Adams cannot use all of the above fair values. The purchase method solution was to require that Adams reduce the valuation assigned to the acquired long-term assets (land and building) proportionately by $90,000 ($610,000 – $520,000). The total fair value of the long-term assets, in this case $600,000, provided the basis for allocating the reduction. Thus, Adams would reduce the acquired land by (2/6 × $90,000) = $30,000 and the building by (4/6 × $90,000) = $60,000. Adams's journal entry to record the combination using the purchase method would then be as follows:

Accounts Receivable	15,000	
Land ($200,000 – $30,000)	170,000	
Building ($400,000 – $60,000)	340,000	
Accounts Payable		5,000
Cash		520,000

Note that current assets and liabilities did not share in the proportionate reduction to cost. Long-term assets were subject to the reduction because their fair-value estimates were considered less reliable than current items and liabilities. Finally, in rare situations firms recognized an extraordinary gain on a purchase, but only in the very unusual case that the long-term assets were reduced to a zero valuation.

In contrast, the acquisition method embraces the fair-value concept and discards the consideration transferred as a valuation basis for the business acquired in a bargain purchase. Instead, the acquirer measures and recognizes the fair values of each of the assets acquired and liabilities assumed at the date of combination, regardless of the consideration transferred in the transaction. As a result, (1) no assets are recorded at amounts below their assessed fair values, as is the case with bargain purchases accounted for by the purchase method, and (2) a gain on bargain purchase is recognized at the acquisition date.

Direct Combination Costs

Almost all business combinations employ professional services to assist in various phases of the transaction. Examples include target identification, due diligence regarding the value of an acquisition, financing, tax planning, and preparation of formal legal documents. Prior to 2009, under the purchase method, the investment cost basis included direct combination costs. In contrast, the acquisition method considers these costs as payments for services received, not part of the fair value exchanged for the business. Thus, under the acquisition method, direct combination costs are expensed as incurred.

Contingent Consideration

Often business combination negotiations result in agreements to provide additional payments to former owners if they meet specified future performance measures. The purchase method accounted for such contingent consideration obligations as postcombination adjustments to the purchase cost (or stockholders' equity if the contingency involved the parent's equity share value) upon resolution of the contingency. The acquisition method treats contingent consideration obligations as a negotiated component of the fair value of the consideration transferred, consistent with the fair-value measurement attribute.

In-Process Research and Development (IPR&D)

Prior to 2009, financial reporting standards required the immediate expensing of acquired IPR&D if the project had not yet reached technological feasibility and the assets had no future alternative uses. Expensing acquired IPR&D was consistent with the accounting treatment for a firm's ongoing research and development costs.

The acquisition method, however, requires tangible and intangible assets acquired in a business combination to be used in a particular research and development activity, including those that may have no alternative future use, to be recognized and measured at fair value at the acquisition date. These capitalized research and development costs are reported as intangible assets with indefinite lives subject to periodic impairment reviews. Moreover, because the acquirer identified and paid for the IPR&D, the acquisition method assumes an expectation of future economic benefit and therefore recognizes an asset.

The Pooling of Interests Method: Continuity of Previous Ownership

Historically, former owners of separate firms would agree to combine for their mutual benefit and continue as owners of a combined firm. It was asserted that the assets and liabilities of the former firms were never really bought or sold; former owners merely exchanged ownership shares to become joint owners of the combined firm. Combinations characterized by exchange of voting shares and continuation of previous ownership became known as pooling of interests. Rather than an exchange transaction with one ownership group replacing another, a pooling of interests was characterized by a continuity of ownership interests before and after the business combination. Prior to its elimination, this method was applied to a significant number of business combinations.[26] To reflect the continuity of ownership, two important steps characterized the pooling of interests method:

1. The book values of the assets and liabilities of both companies became the book values reported by the combined entity.
2. The revenue and expense accounts were combined retrospectively as well as prospectively. The idea of continuity of ownership gave support for the recognition of income accruing to the owners both before and after the combination.

Therefore, in a pooling, reported income was typically higher than under the contemporaneous purchase accounting. Under pooling, not only did the firms retrospectively combine incomes, but also the smaller asset bases resulted in smaller depreciation and amortization expenses. Because net income reported in financial statements often is used in a variety of contracts, including managerial compensation, managers considered the pooling method an attractive alternative to purchase accounting.

Prior to 2002, accounting and reporting standards allowed both the purchase and pooling of interest methods for business combinations. However, standard setters established strict criteria for use of the pooling method. The criteria were designed to prevent managers from engaging in purchase transactions and then reporting them as poolings of interests. Business combinations that failed to meet the pooling criteria had to be accounted for by the purchase method.

These criteria had two overriding objectives. First, to ensure the complete fusion of the two organizations, one company had to obtain substantially all (90 percent or more) of the voting stock of the other. The second general objective of these criteria was to prevent purchase combinations from being disguised as poolings. Past experience had shown that combination transactions were frequently manipulated so that they would qualify for pooling of interests treatment (usually to increase reported earnings). However, subsequent events, often involving cash being paid or received by the parties, revealed the true nature of the combination: One company was purchasing the other in a bargained exchange. A number of qualifying criteria for pooling of interests treatment were designed to stop this practice.

[26] Past prominent business combinations accounted for by the pooling of interests method include Exxon-Mobil, Pfizer-Warner Lambert, Yahoo!-Broadcast.com, and Pepsi-Quaker Oats, among thousands of others.

EXHIBIT 2.9
Precombination Information for Baker Company

January 1	Book Values	Fair Values
Current assets	$ 30,000	$ 30,000
Internet domain name	160,000	300,000
Licensing agreements	–0–	500,000
In-process research and development	–0–	200,000
Notes payable	(25,000)	(25,000)
Total net assets	$165,000	$1,005,000

Note: Parentheses indicate a credit balance.

Comparisons across the Pooling of Interests, Purchase, and Acquisition Methods

To illustrate some of the differences across the purchase, pooling of interests, and acquisition methods, assume that on January 1, Archer Inc. acquired Baker Company in exchange for 10,000 shares of its $1.00 par common stock having a fair value of $1,200,000 in a transaction structured as a merger. In connection with the acquisition, Archer paid $25,000 in legal and accounting fees. Also, Archer agreed to pay the former owners additional cash consideration contingent upon the completion of Baker's existing contracts at specified profit margins. The current fair value of the contingent obligation was estimated to be $150,000. Exhibit 2.9 provides Baker's combination-date book values and fair values.

Purchase Method Applied

Archer's valuation basis for its purchase of Baker is computed and allocated as follows:

Fair value of shares issued		$1,200,000
Direct combination costs (legal and accounting fees)		25,000
Cost of the Baker purchase		$1,225,000
Cost allocation:		
Current assets	$ 30,000	
Internet domain name	300,000	
Licensing agreements	500,000	
Research and development expense	200,000	
Notes payable	(25,000)	
Total net fair value of items acquired		1,005,000
Goodwill		$ 220,000

Note the following characteristics of the purchase method from the above schedule.

- The valuation basis is cost and includes direct combination costs but excludes the contingent consideration.
- The cost is allocated to the assets acquired and liabilities assumed based on their individual fair values (unless a bargain purchase occurs and then the long-term items may be recorded as amounts less than their fair values).
- Goodwill is the excess of cost over the fair values of the net assets purchased.
- Acquired in-process research and development is expensed immediately at the purchase date.

Pooling of Interests Method Applied

Because a purchase sale was deemed not to occur, the pooling method relied on previously recorded values reflecting a continuation of previous ownership. Thus, the following asset would be recorded by Archer in a business combination accounted for as a pooling of interests.

	Values Assigned
Current assets	$ 30,000
Internet domain name	160,000
Licensing agreements	–0–
In-process research and development	–0–
Notes payable	(25,000)
Total value assigned within the combination	$165,000

Note the following characteristics of the pooling of interests method from the above schedule.

- Because a pooling of interests was predicated on a continuity of ownership, the accounting incorporated a continuation of previous book values and ignored fair values exchanged in a business combination.
- Previously unrecognized (typically internally developed) intangibles continue to be reported at a zero value postcombination.
- Because the pooling of interests method values an acquired firm at its previously recorded book value, no new amount for goodwill was ever recorded in a pooling.

Acquisition Method Applied

According to the acquisition method, Archer's valuation basis for its acquisition of Baker is computed as follows:

Fair value of shares issued		$1,200,000
Fair value of contingent performance obligation		150,000
Total consideration transferred for the Baker acquisition		$1,350,000
Cost allocation:		
Current assets	$ 30,000	
Internet domain name	300,000	
Licensing agreements	500,000	
Research and development asset	200,000	
Notes payable	(25,000)	
Total net fair value of items acquired		1,005,000
Goodwill		$ 345,000

Note the following characteristics of the acquisition method from the above schedule.

- The valuation basis is fair value of consideration transferred and includes the contingent consideration but excludes direct combination costs.
- The assets acquired and liabilities assumed are recorded at their individual fair values.
- Goodwill is the excess of the consideration transferred over the fair values of the net assets acquired.
- Acquired in-process research and development is recognized as an asset.
- Professional service fees to help accomplish the acquisition are expensed.

The following table compares the amounts from Baker that Archer would include in its combination-date consolidated financial statements under the pooling of interests method, the purchase method, and the acquisition method.

Values Incorporated in Archer's Consolidated Balance Sheet Resulting from the Baker Transaction

	Pooling of Interests Method	Purchase Method	Acquisition Method
Current assets	$ 30,000	$ 30,000	$ 30,000
Internet domain name	160,000	300,000	300,000
Licensing agreements	–0–	500,000	500,000
In-process research and development asset*	–0–	–0–	200,000
Goodwill	–0–	220,000	345,000
Notes payable	(25,000)	(25,000)	(25,000)
Contingent performance obligation	–0–	–0–	(150,000)
Total net assets recognized by Archer	$165,000	$1,025,000	$1,200,000

*Acquired in-process research and development was expensed under the purchase method and not recognized at all under the pooling of interests method.

Several comparisons should be noted across these methods of accounting for business combinations:

- In consolidating Baker's assets and liabilities, the purchase and acquisition methods record fair values. In contrast, the pooling method uses previous book values and ignores fair values. Consequently, although a fair value of $1,350,000 is exchanged, only a net value of $165,000 (assets less liabilities) is reported in the pooling.
- The pooling method, as reflected in the preceding example, typically shows smaller asset values and consequently lowers future depreciation and amortization expenses. Thus, higher future net income was usually reported under the pooling method compared to similar situations that employed the purchase method.
- Under pooling, financial ratios such as Net Income/Total Assets were dramatically inflated. Not only was this ratio's denominator understated through failure to recognize internally developed assets acquired (and fair values in general), but the numerator was overstated through smaller depreciation and amortization expenses.
- Although not shown, the pooling method retrospectively combined the acquired firm's revenues, expenses, dividends, and retained earnings. The purchase and acquisition methods incorporate only postcombination values for these operational items. Also all costs of the combination (direct and indirect acquisition costs and stock issue costs) were expensed in the period of combination under the pooling of interests method.
- Finally, with adoption of the acquisition method, the FASB has moved clearly in the direction of increased management accountability for the fair values of all assets acquired and liabilities assumed in a business combination.

Appendix B

Pushdown Accounting

In the analysis of business combinations to this point, discussion has focused on (1) the recording of the combination by the parent company and (2) required consolidation procedures. An additional reporting issue, however, arises concerning the separate postacquisition financial statements of subsidiary companies than maintain separate incorporation.

This issue has become especially significant in recent years because of business acquisitions by private-equity firms. An organization, for example, might acquire a company, work to improve its business model, and subsequently offer the shares back to the public in hopes of making a large profit. What valuation basis should be used in reporting the subsidiary's financial statements that accompany the initial public offering? In other situations, a subsidiary company may need to provide its own separate financial statements in connection with a new public debt issue. Should the subsidiary's financial statements utilize the new basis of accounting that the parent company established in the acquisition or continue its financial statement carrying amounts established prior to the acquisition?

To illustrate, assume that Strand Company owns one asset: a production machine with a carrying amount of $200,000 but a fair value of $900,000. Parker Corporation pays exactly $900,000 in cash to acquire Strand. Consolidation offers no real problem here: The machine will be reported by the business combination at $900,000.

However, if Strand continues to issue separate financial statements (for example, to its creditors or potential stockholders), should the machine be reported at $200,000 or $900,000? If adjusted, should the $700,000 increase be reported as a gain by the subsidiary or as an addition to contributed capital? Should depreciation be based on $200,000 or $900,000? If the subsidiary is to be viewed as a new entity with a new basis for its assets and liabilities, should Retained Earnings be returned to zero? If the parent acquires only 51 percent of Strand, does that change the answers to the previous questions?

Proponents of pushdown accounting argue that a change in ownership creates a new basis for subsidiary assets and liabilities. An unadjusted balance ($200,000 in the preceding illustration) is a cost figure applicable to previous stockholders. That amount is no longer relevant information. Rather, according to this argument, the fair value at the date control of the company changes is now relevant, a figure best reflected by the consideration transferred to acquire the subsidiary. Balance sheet accounts should be reported at the asset's acquisition-date fair value. ($900,000 in the illustration) rather than the cost incurred by the previous owners of the company. Moreover, the subsidiary can now recognize any previously unrecognized intangible assets as valued by its new owner concurrently with the acquisition.

External Reporting Option for Pushdown Accounting

To address the valuation issues for a subsidiary's separately issued financial statements, the FASB issued Accounting Standards Update (ASU) No. 2014-17, *Business Combinations: Pushdown Accounting* in November 2014. The ASU does not require pushdown accounting, but instead provides an option to apply pushdown accounting following a business combination in which the acquirer obtains control of an acquired entity and the acquired entity maintains separate incorporation. A newly acquired entity (e.g., subsidiary firm) may elect the option to apply pushdown accounting in the reporting period immediately following the acquisition.[27] Alternatively, a newly acquired company may simply choose to continue using its previous accounting valuations in separately issued financial statements.

When an acquired entity elects to apply pushdown accounting, it reflects in its financial statements the valuations for the individual assets and liabilities used by the parent in allocating the consideration transferred in the acquisition. Thus, the parent's acquisition-date valuations for its newly acquired subsidiary are "pushed down" to the subsidiary's financial statements.

As discussed below, the FASB (ASC 805-50-30) provides particular guidance for three accounting issues: goodwill, bargain purchase gains, and acquisition-related liabilities. We then discuss other accounting issues including acquisition-date retained earnings and other owners' equity effects.

Goodwill

When an entity elects pushdown accounting, any goodwill recognized in the combination is reported in the acquired entity's separate financial statements.

Bargain Purchase Gains

An exception to pushdown accounting's general rule of using the parent's valuations for the subsidiary's separate financial statement occurs for bargain purchases. Recall that when the fair values assigned to the subsidiary's collective net assets exceeds the parent's consideration transferred, the parent recognizes a bargain purchase gain on its income statement. In this case, however, pushdown accounting requires that the acquired entity not recognize the gain in its income statement, but instead as an adjustment to its additional paid-in capital. The reflection of the bargain purchase gain in additional paid-in capital prevents income recognition by both the acquirer and the acquiree for the same event.

Acquisition-Related Liabilities

When acquisition-related liabilities arise, pushdown accounting recognizes only the debt that the acquired firm must recognize under other generally accepted accounting principles. Thus if an acquired firm is either jointly or severally liable for repayment of the debt, such debt is pushed down to its separate financial statements, possibly including debt incurred by the acquirer.

Acquisition-Date Subsidiary Retained Earnings

After recognizing the new basis for its assets and liabilities, the acquired firm must then report the effects of the acquisition in its owners' equity section. Because pushdown accounting treats the acquired firm as a new reporting entity, the acquired firm reports zero acquisition-date retained earnings. The elimination of acquisition-date subsidiary retained earnings is consistent with consolidated financial reporting.

Additional Paid-In Capital from Pushdown Accounting

The overall effect of the combined pushdown accounting adjustments to the previous carrying amounts of the subsidiary's assets and liabilities then is reported as an adjustment to the subsidiary's additional paid-in capital attributable to the common shareholders. For example, a subsidiary may report "Additional paid-in capital from pushdown accounting" in its separate balance sheet. The total effect in the additional paid-in capital from pushdown accounting results from both the elimination of acquisition-date retained earnings and the revaluation of the acquired firm's assets and liabilities to the parent's basis.

[27] The acquired entity can also elect to apply pushdown accounting in periods subsequent to the acquisition, but must report the election as a retrospective change in accounting principle (ASC Topic 250, Accounting Changes and Error Corrections). Once made, the decision to apply pushdown accounting to a specific change-in-control event is irrevocable.

EXHIBIT 2.10
Pushdown Accounting—Date of Acquisition

Smallport Company Balance Sheet at January 1	
Current assets	$ 300,000
Computers and equipment	600,000
Capitalized software	1,200,000
Customer contracts	700,000
Goodwill	70,000
Total assets	$ 2,870,000
Liabilities	$ (250,000)
Common stock	(100,000)
Additional paid-in capital excess over par	(20,000)
Additional paid-in capital from pushdown accounting	(2,500,000)
Retained earnings, 1/1	–0–
Total liabilities and equities	$ 2,870,000

Example: Pushdown Accounting

To illustrate an application of pushdown accounting, we use the Exhibit 2.3 BigNet and Smallport Company example presented previously in this chapter. If Smallport Company applies pushdown accounting, its acquisition-date separately reported balance sheet would appear as presented in Exhibit 2.10:

Note that the values for each asset and liability in Smallport's separate balance sheet above are identical to those reported in BigNet's consolidated acquisition-date balance sheet.

Internal Reporting

Pushdown accounting has several advantages for internal reporting. For example, it simplifies the consolidation process. If the subsidiary enters the acquisition-date fair value allocations into its records, worksheet Entry A (to recognize the allocations originating from the fair-value adjustments) is not needed. Amortizations of the excess fair value allocation (see Chapter 3) would be incorporated in subsequent periods as well.

Despite some simplifications to the consolidation process, pushdown accounting does not address the many issues in preparing consolidated financial statements that appear in subsequent chapters of this text. Therefore, it remains to be seen how many acquired companies will choose to elect pushdown accounting. For newly acquired subsidiaries that expect to issue new debt or eventually undergo an initial public offering, fair values may provide investors with a better understanding of the company.

In summary, pushdown accounting provides a newly acquired subsidiary the option to revalue its assets and liabilities to acquisition-date fair values in its separately reported financial statements. This valuation option may be useful when the parent expects to offer the subsidiary shares to the public following a period of planned improvements. Other benefits from pushdown accounting may arise when the subsidiary plans to issue debt and needs its separate financial statements to incorporate acquisition-date fair values and previously unrecognized intangibles in their standalone financial reports.

Questions

1. What is a business combination?
2. Describe the different types of legal arrangements that can take place to create a business combination.
3. What does the term *consolidated financial statements* mean?
4. Within the consolidation process, what is the purpose of a worksheet?
5. Jones Company obtains all of the common stock of Hudson, Inc., by issuing 50,000 shares of its own stock. Under these circumstances, why might the determination of a fair value for the consideration transferred be difficult?
6. What is the accounting valuation basis for consolidating assets and liabilities in a business combination?
7. How should a parent consolidate its subsidiary's revenues and expenses?
8. Morgan Company acquires all of the outstanding shares of Jennings, Inc., for cash. Morgan transfers consideration more than the fair value of the company's net assets. How should the payment in excess of fair value be accounted for in the consolidation process?
9. Catron Corporation is having liquidity problems, and as a result, it sells all of its outstanding stock to Lambert, Inc., for cash. Because of Catron's problems, Lambert is able to acquire this stock at less than the fair value of the company's net assets. How is this reduction in price accounted for within the consolidation process?

10. Sloane, Inc., issues 25,000 shares of its own common stock in exchange for all of the outstanding shares of Benjamin Company. Benjamin will remain a separately incorporated operation. How does Sloane record the issuance of these shares?
11. To obtain all of the stock of Molly, Inc., Harrison Corporation issued its own common stock. Harrison had to pay $98,000 to lawyers, accountants, and a stock brokerage firm in connection with services rendered during the creation of this business combination. In addition, Harrison paid $56,000 in costs associated with the stock issuance. How will these two costs be recorded?

Problems

LO 2-1

1. Which of the following does not represent a primary motivation for business combinations?
   a. Combinations are often a vehicle to accelerate growth and competitiveness.
   b. Cost savings can be achieved through elimination of duplicate facilities and staff.
   c. Synergies may be available through quick entry for new and existing products into markets.
   d. Larger firms are less likely to fail.

LO 2-2

2. Which of the following is the best theoretical justification for consolidated financial statements?
   a. In form the companies are one entity; in substance they are separate.
   b. In form the companies are separate; in substance they are one entity.
   c. In form and substance the companies are one entity.
   d. In form and substance the companies are separate. (AICPA)

LO 2-3

3. What is a statutory merger?
   a. A merger approved by the Securities and Exchange Commission.
   b. An acquisition involving the purchase of both stock and assets.
   c. A takeover completed within one year of the initial tender offer.
   d. A business combination in which only one company continues to exist as a legal entity.

LO 2-4

4. FASB ASC 805, "Business Combinations," provides principles for allocating the fair value of an acquired business. When the collective fair values of the separately identified assets acquired and liabilities assumed exceed the fair value of the consideration transferred, the difference should be:
   a. Recognized as an ordinary gain from a bargain purchase.
   b. Treated as negative goodwill to be amortized over the period benefited, not to exceed 40 years.
   c. Treated as goodwill and tested for impairment on an annual basis.
   d. Applied pro rata to reduce, but not below zero, the amounts initially assigned to specific noncurrent assets of the acquired firm.

LO 2-8

5. What is the appropriate accounting treatment for the value assigned to in-process research and development acquired in a business combination?
   a. Expense upon acquisition.
   b. Capitalize as an asset.
   c. Expense if there is no alternative use for the assets used in the research and development and technological feasibility has yet to be reached.
   d. Expense until future economic benefits become certain and then capitalize as an asset.

LO 2-8

6. An acquired entity has a long-term operating lease for an office building used for central management. The terms of the lease are very favorable relative to current market rates. However, the lease prohibits subleasing or any other transfer of rights. In its financial statements, the acquiring firm should report the value assigned to the lease contract as
   a. An intangible asset under the contractual-legal criterion.
   b. A part of goodwill.
   c. An intangible asset under the separability criterion.
   d. A building.

LO 2-4

7. When does gain recognition accompany a business combination?
   a. When a bargain purchase occurs.
   b. In a combination created in the middle of a fiscal year.
   c. In an acquisition when the value of all assets and liabilities cannot be determined.
   d. When the amount of a bargain purchase exceeds the value of the applicable noncurrent assets (other than certain exceptions) held by the acquired company.

LO 2-6b

8. According to the acquisition method of accounting for business combinations, costs paid to attorneys and accountants for services in arranging a merger should be
   a. Capitalized as part of the overall fair value acquired in the merger.
   b. Recorded as an expense in the period the merger takes place.

c. Included in recognized goodwill.

d. Written off over a five-year maximum useful life.

LO 2-4

9. When negotiating a business acquisition, buyers sometimes agree to pay extra amounts to sellers in the future if performance metrics are achieved over specified time horizons. How should buyers account for such contingent consideration in recording an acquisition?

a. The amount ultimately paid under the contingent consideration agreement is added to goodwill when and if the performance metrics are met.

b. The fair value of the contingent consideration is expensed immediately at acquisition date.

c. The fair value of the contingent consideration is included in the overall fair value of the consideration transferred, and a liability or additional owners' equity is recognized.

d. The fair value of the contingent consideration is recorded as a reduction of the otherwise determinable fair value of the acquired firm.

LO 2-5

10. An acquired firm's financial records sometimes show goodwill from previous business combinations. How does a parent company account for the preexisting goodwill of its newly acquired subsidiary?

a. The parent tests the preexisting goodwill for impairment before recording the goodwill as part of the acquisition.

b. The parent includes the preexisting goodwill as an identified intangible asset acquired.

c. The parent ignores preexisting subsidiary goodwill and allocates the subsidiary's fair value among the separately identifiable assets acquired and liabilities assumed.

d. Preexisting goodwill is excluded from the identifiable assets acquired unless the subsidiary can demonstrate its continuing value.

LO 2-5

11. On June 1, Cline Co. paid $800,000 cash for all of the issued and outstanding common stock of Renn Corp. The carrying amounts for Renn's assets and liabilities on June 1 follow:

Cash	$150,000
Accounts receivable	180,000
Capitalized software costs	320,000
Goodwill	100,000
Liabilities	(130,000)
Net assets	$620,000

On June 1, Renn's accounts receivable had a fair value of $140,000. Additionally, Renn's in-process research and development was estimated to have a fair value of $200,000. All other items were stated at their fair values. On Cline's June 1 consolidated balance sheet, how much is reported for goodwill?

a. $320,000

b. $120,000

c. $80,000

d. $20,000

Problems 12 and 13 relate to the following:

On May 1, Donovan Company reported the following account balances:

Current assets	$ 90,000
Buildings & equipment (net)	220,000
Total assets	$310,000
Liabilities	$ 60,000
Common stock	150,000
Retained earnings	100,000
Total liabilities and equities	$310,000

On May 1, Beasley paid $400,000 in stock (fair value) for all of the assets and liabilities of Donovan, which will cease to exist as a separate entity. In connection with the merger, Beasley incurred $15,000 in accounts payable for legal and accounting fees.

Beasley also agreed to pay $75,000 to the former owners of Donovan contingent on meeting certain revenue goals during the following year. Beasley estimated the present value of its probability adjusted expected payment for the contingency at $20,000. In determining its offer, Beasley noted the following:

- Donovan holds a building with a fair value $30,000 more than its book value.

- Donovan has developed unpatented technology appraised at $25,000, although is it not recorded in its financial records.
- Donovan has a research and development activity in process with an appraised fair value of $45,000. The project has not yet reached technological feasibility.
- Book values for Donovan's current assets and liabilities approximate fair values.

LO 2-4, 2-5

12. What should Beasley record as total liabilities incurred or assumed in connection with the Donovan merger?
    a. $15,000
    b. $75,000
    c. $95,000
    d. $150,000

LO 2-5, 2-8

13. How much should Beasley record as total assets acquired in the Donovan merger?
    a. $400,000
    b. $420,000
    c. $410,000
    d. $480,000

LO 2-5

14. Prior to being united in a business combination, Atkins, Inc., and Waterson Corporation had the following stockholders' equity figures:

	Atkins	Waterson
Common stock ($1 par value)	$ 180,000	$ 45,000
Additional paid-in capital	90,000	20,000
Retained earnings	300,000	110,000

Atkins issues 51,000 new shares of its common stock valued at $3 per share for all of the outstanding stock of Waterson. Immediately afterward, what are consolidated Additional Paid-In Capital and Retained Earnings, respectively?
a. $104,000 and $300,000
b. $110,000 and $410,000
c. $192,000 and $300,000
d. $212,000 and $410,000

Problems 15 through 18 are based on the following information:

On July 1, TruData Company issues 10,000 shares of its common stock with a $5 par value and a $40 fair value in exchange for all of Webstat Company's outstanding voting shares. Webstat's precombination book and fair values are shown below along with book values for TruData's accounts.

	TruData Book Values	Webstat Book Values	Webstat Fair Values
Revenues (1/1 to 7/1)	$(250,000)	$(130,000)	
Expenses (1/1 to 7/1)	170,000	80,000	
Retained earnings, 1/1	(130,000)	(150,000)	
Cash and receivables	140,000	60,000	$ 60,000
Inventory	190,000	145,000	175,000
Patented technology (net)	230,000	180,000	200,000
Land	400,000	200,000	225,000
Buildings and equipment (net)	100,000	75,000	75,000
Liabilities	(540,000)	(360,000)	(350,000)
Common stock	(300,000)	(70,000)	
Additional paid-in capital	(10,000)	(30,000)	

LO 2-5, 2-9, 2-10

15. On its acquisition-date consolidated balance sheet, what amount should TruData report as goodwill?
    a. –0–
    b. $15,000
    c. $35,000
    d. $100,000

LO 2-5

16. On its acquisition-date consolidated balance sheet, what amount should TruData report as patented technology (net)?
    a. $200,000
    b. $230,000
    c. $410,000
    d. $430,000

LO 2-5, 2-7

17. On its acquisition-date consolidated balance sheet, what amount should TruData report as common stock?
    a. $70,000
    b. $300,000
    c. $350,000
    d. $370,000

LO 2-5, 2-7

18. On its acquisition-date consolidated balance sheet, what amount should TruData report as retained earnings as of July 1?
    a. $130,000
    b. $210,000
    c. $260,000
    d. $510,000

Problems 19 and 20 are based on the following information. The separate condensed balance sheets of Patrick Corporation and its wholly owned subsidiary, Sean Corporation, are as follows:

BALANCE SHEETS
December 31, 2017

	Patrick	*Sean*
Cash	$ 80,000	$ 60,000
Accounts receivable (net)	140,000	25,000
Inventories	90,000	50,000
Plant and equipment (net)	625,000	280,000
Investment in Sean	460,000	
Total assets	$1,395,000	$415,000
Accounts payable	$ 160,000	$ 95,000
Long-term debt	110,000	30,000
Common stock ($10 par)	340,000	50,000
Additional paid-in capital		10,000
Retained earnings	785,000	230,000
Total liabilities and shareholders' equity	$1,395,000	$415,000

Additional Information:

- On December 31, 2017, Patrick acquired 100 percent of Sean's voting stock in exchange for $460,000.
- At the acquisition date, the fair values of Sean's assets and liabilities equaled their carrying amounts, respectively, except that the fair value of certain items in Sean's inventory were $25,000 more than their carrying amounts.

LO 2-4, 2-5

19. In the December 31, 2017, consolidated balance sheet of Patrick and its subsidiary, what amount of total assets should be reported?
    a. $1,375,000
    b. $1,395,000
    c. $1,520,000
    d. $1,980,000

LO 2-4, 2-5

20. In the December 31, 2017, consolidated balance sheet of Patrick and its subsidiary, what amount of total stockholders' equity should be reported?
    a. $1,100,000
    b. $1,125,000

c. $1,150,000

d. $1,355,000

LO 2-8

21. Prycal Co. merges with InterBuy, Inc., and acquires several different categories of intangible assets including trademarks, a customer list, copyrights on artistic materials, agreements to receive royalties on leased intellectual property, and unpatented technology.
    a. Describe the criteria for determining whether an intangible asset acquired in a business combination should be separately recognized apart from goodwill.
    b. For each of the acquired intangibles listed, identify which recognition criteria (separability and legal/contractual) may or may not apply in recognizing the intangible on the acquiring firm's financial statements.

LO 2-6a, 2-6b

22. The following book and fair values were available for Westmont Company as of March 1.

	Book Value	Fair Value
Inventory	$ 630,000	$ 600,000
Land	750,000	990,000
Buildings	1,700,000	2,000,000
Customer relationships	–0–	800,000
Accounts payable	(80,000)	(80,000)
Common stock	(2,000,000)	
Additional paid-in capital	(500,000)	
Retained earnings, 1/1	(360,000)	
Revenues	(420,000)	
Expenses	280,000	

Arturo Company pays $4,000,000 cash and issues 20,000 shares of its $2 par value common stock (fair value of $50 per share) for all of Westmont's common stock in a merger, after which Westmont will cease to exist as a separate entity. Stock issue costs amount to $25,000 and Arturo pays $42,000 for legal fees to complete the transaction. Prepare Arturo's journal entries to record its acquisition of Westmont.

LO 2-6a, 2-6b, 2-8

23. Use the same facts as in problem (22), but assume instead that Arturo pays cash of $4,200,000 to acquire Westmont. No stock is issued. Prepare Arturo's journal entries to record its acquisition of Westmont.

LO 2-4, 2-5, 2-6a, 2-6b, 2-6c

24. Following are preacquisition financial balances for Padre Company and Sol Company as of December 31. Also included are fair values for Sol Company accounts.

	Padre Company Book Values 12/31	Sol Company Book Values 12/31	Sol Company Fair Values 12/31
Cash	$ 400,000	$ 120,000	$ 120,000
Receivables	220,000	300,000	300,000
Inventory	410,000	210,000	260,000
Land	600,000	130,000	110,000
Building and equipment (net)	600,000	270,000	330,000
Franchise agreements	220,000	190,000	220,000
Accounts payable	(300,000)	(120,000)	(120,000)
Accrued expenses	(90,000)	(30,000)	(30,000)
Long-term liabilities	(900,000)	(510,000)	(510,000)
Common stock—$20 par value	(660,000)		
Common stock—$5 par value		(210,000)	
Additional paid-in capital	(70,000)	(90,000)	
Retained earnings, 1/1	(390,000)	(240,000)	
Revenues	(960,000)	(330,000)	
Expenses	920,000	310,000	

Note: Parentheses indicate a credit balance.

On December 31, Padre acquires Sol's outstanding stock by paying $360,000 in cash and issuing 10,000 shares of its own common stock with a fair value of $40 per share. Padre paid legal and accounting fees of $20,000 as well as $5,000 in stock issuance costs.

Determine the value that would be shown in Padre's consolidated financial statements for each of the accounts listed.

Accounts	
Inventory	Revenues
Land	Additional paid-in capital
Buildings and equipment	Expenses
Franchise agreements	Retained earnings, 1/1
Goodwill	Retained earnings, 12/31

LO 2-5, 2-6a, 2-6b, 2-8

25. On May 1, Soriano Co. reported the following account balances along with their estimated fair values:

	Carrying Amount	Fair Value
Receivables	$ 90,000	$ 90,000
Inventory	75,000	75,000
Copyrights	125,000	480,000
Patented technology	825,000	700,000
Total assets	$1,115,000	$1,345,000
Current liabilities	$ 160,000	$ 160,000
Long-term liabilities	645,000	635,000
Common stock	100,000	
Retained earnings	210,000	
Total liabilities and equities	$1,115,000	

On that day, Zambrano paid cash to acquire all of the assets and liabilities of Soriano, which will cease to exist as a separate entity. To facilitate the merger, Zambrano also paid $100,000 to an investment banking firm.

The following information was also available:

- Zambrano further agreed to pay an extra $70,000 to the former owners of Soriano only if they meet certain revenue goals during the next two years. Zambrano estimated the present value of its probability adjusted expected payment for this contingency at $35,000.
- Soriano has a research and development project in process with an appraised value of $200,000. However, the project has not yet reached technological feasibility and the project's assets have no alternative future use.

Prepare Zambrano's journal entries to record the Soriano acquisition assuming its initial cash payment to the former owners was

a. $700,000.

b. $800,000.

LO 2-4, 2-5, 2-6b, 2-7

26. On June 30, 2017, Wisconsin, Inc., issued $300,000 in debt and 15,000 new shares of its $10 par value stock to Badger Company owners in exchange for all of the outstanding shares of that company. Wisconsin shares had a fair value of $40 per share. Prior to the combination, the financial statements for Wisconsin and Badger for the six-month period ending June 30, 2017, were as follows:

	Wisconsin	Badger
Revenues	$ (900,000)	$ (300,000)
Expenses	660,000	200,000
Net income	$ (240,000)	$ (100,000)
Retained earnings, 1/1	$ (800,000)	$ (200,000)
Net income	(240,000)	(100,000)
Dividends declared	90,000	–0–
Retained earnings, 6/30	$ (950,000)	$ (300,000)

(continued)

Cash	$ 80,000	$ 110,000
Receivables and inventory	400,000	170,000
Patented technology (net)	900,000	300,000
Equipment (net)	700,000	600,000
Total assets	$ 2,080,000	$ 1,180,000
Liabilities	$ (500,000)	$ (410,000)
Common stock	(360,000)	(200,000)
Additional paid-in capital	(270,000)	(270,000)
Retained earnings	(950,000)	(300,000)
Total liabilities and equities	$ (2,080,000)	$ (1,180,000)

Wisconsin also paid $30,000 to a broker for arranging the transaction. In addition, Wisconsin paid $40,000 in stock issuance costs. Badger's equipment was actually worth $700,000, but its patented technology was valued at only $280,000.

What are the consolidated balances for the following accounts?

a. **Net income.**

b. **Retained earnings, 1/1/17.**

c. **Patented technology.**

d. **Goodwill.**

e. **Liabilities.**

f. **Common stock.**

g. **Additional paid-in capital.**

LO 2-4, 2-7

27. **On January 1, 2018 Casey Corporation exchanged $3,300,000 cash for 100 percent of the outstanding voting stock of Kennedy Corporation. Casey plans to maintain Kennedy as a wholly owned subsidiary with separate legal status and accounting information systems.**

At the acquisition date, Casey prepared the following fair-value allocation schedule:

Fair value of Kennedy (consideration transferred)		$3,300,000
Carrying amount acquired		2,600,000
Excess fair value		$ 700,000
to buildings (undervalued)	$ 382,000	
to licensing agreements (overvalued)	(108,000)	274,000
to goodwill (indefinite life)		$ 426,000

Immediately after closing the transaction, Casey and Kennedy prepared the following postacquisition balance sheets from their separate financial records.

Accounts	Casey	Kennedy
Cash	$ 457,000	$ 172,500
Accounts receivable	1,655,000	347,000
Inventory	1,310,000	263,500
Investment in Kennedy	3,300,000	–0–
Buildings (net)	6,315,000	2,090,000
Licensing agreements	–0–	3,070,000
Goodwill	347,000	–0–
Total assets	$ 13,384,000	$ 5,943,000
Accounts payable	$ (394,000)	$ (393,000)
Long-term debt	(3,990,000)	(2,950,000)
Common stock	(3,000,000)	(1,000,000)
Additional paid-in capital	–0–	(500,000)
Retained earnings	(6,000,000)	(1,100,000)
Total liabilities and equities	$ (13,384,000)	$ (5,943,000)

Prepare an acquisition-date consolidated balance sheet for Casey Corporation and its subsidiary Kennedy Corporation.

LO 2-4, 2-5, 2-6b, 2-6c, 2-7

eXcel

28. On January 1, 2018, Marshall Company acquired 100 percent of the outstanding common stock of Tucker Company. To acquire these shares, Marshall issued $200,000 in long-term liabilities and 20,000 shares of common stock having a par value of $1 per share but a fair value of $10 per share. Marshall paid $30,000 to accountants, lawyers, and brokers for assistance in the acquisition and another $12,000 in connection with stock issuance costs.

Prior to these transactions, the balance sheets for the two companies were as follows:

	Marshall Company Book Value	Tucker Company Book Value
Cash	$ 60,000	$ 20,000
Receivables	270,000	90,000
Inventory	360,000	140,000
Land	200,000	180,000
Buildings (net)	420,000	220,000
Equipment (net)	160,000	50,000
Accounts payable	(150,000)	(40,000)
Long-term liabilities	(430,000)	(200,000)
Common stock—$1 par value	(110,000)	
Common stock—$20 par value		(120,000)
Additional paid-in capital	(360,000)	–0–
Retained earnings, 1/1/18	(420,000)	(340,000)

Note: Parentheses indicate a credit balance.

In Marshall's appraisal of Tucker, it deemed three accounts to be undervalued on the subsidiary's books: Inventory by $5,000, Land by $20,000, and Buildings by $30,000. Marshall plans to maintain Tucker's separate legal identity and to operate Tucker as a wholly owned subsidiary.

a. Determine the amounts that Marshall Company would report in its postacquisition balance sheet. In preparing the postacquisition balance sheet, any required adjustments to income accounts from the acquisition should be closed to Marshall's retained earnings. Other accounts will also need to be added or adjusted to reflect the journal entries Marshall prepared in recording the acquisition.

b. To verify the answers found in part (*a*), prepare a worksheet to consolidate the balance sheets of these two companies as of January 1, 2018.

LO 2-4, 2-5, 2-7, 2-8

29. Pratt Company acquired all of Spider, Inc.'s outstanding shares on December 31, 2018, for $495,000 cash. Pratt will operate Spider as a wholly owned subsidiary with a separate legal and accounting identity. Although many of Spider's book values approximate fair values, several of its accounts have fair values that differ from book values. In addition, Spider has internally developed assets that remain unrecorded on its books. In deriving the acquisition price, Pratt assessed Spider's fair and book value differences as follows:

	Book Values	Fair Values
Computer software	$ 20,000	$ 70,000
Equipment	40,000	30,000
Client contracts	–0–	100,000
In-process research and development	–0–	40,000
Notes payable	(60,000)	(65,000)

At December 31, 2018, the following financial information is available for consolidation:

	Pratt	Spider
Cash	$ 36,000	$ 18,000
Receivables	116,000	52,000
Inventory	140,000	90,000
Investment in Spider	495,000	–0–
Computer software	210,000	20,000

(*continued*)

Buildings (net)	595,000	130,000
Equipment (net)	308,000	40,000
Client contracts	–0–	–0–
Goodwill	–0–	–0–
Total assets	$ 1,900,000	$ 350,000
Accounts payable	$ (88,000)	$ (25,000)
Notes payable	(510,000)	(60,000)
Common stock	(380,000)	(100,000)
Additional paid-in capital	(170,000)	(25,000)
Retained earnings	(752,000)	(140,000)
Total liabilities and equities	$(1,900,000)	$(350,000)

Prepare a consolidated balance sheet for Pratt and Spider as of December 31, 2018.

LO 2-4, 2-5, 2-6a

30. Allerton Company acquires all of Deluxe Company's assets and liabilities for cash on January 1, 2018, and subsequently formally dissolves Deluxe. At the acquisition date, the following book and fair values were available for the Deluxe Company accounts:

	Book Values	Fair Values
Current assets	$ 60,000	$ 60,000
Building	90,000	50,000
Land	10,000	20,000
Trademark	–0–	30,000
Goodwill	15,000	?
Liabilities	(40,000)	(40,000)
Common stock	(100,000)	
Retained earnings	(35,000)	

Prepare Allerton's entry to record its acquisition of Deluxe in its accounting records assuming the following cash exchange amounts:

1. **$145,000.**
2. **$110,000.**

LO 2-4, 2-5, 2-6a, 2-6b

31. On June 30, 2018, Streeter Company reported the following account balances:

Receivables	$ 83,900	Current liabilities	$ (12,900)
Inventory	70,250	Long-term liabilities	(54,250)
Buildings (net)	78,900	Common stock	(90,000)
Equipment (net)	24,100	Retained earnings	(100,000)
Total assets	$257,150	Total liabilities and equities	$ (257,150)

On June 30, 2018, Princeton Company paid $310,800 cash for all assets and liabilities of Streeter, which will cease to exist as a separate entity. In connection with the acquisition, Princeton paid $15,100 in legal fees. Princeton also agreed to pay $55,600 to the former owners of Streeter contingent on meeting certain revenue goals during 2019. Princeton estimated the present value of its probability adjusted expected payment for the contingency at $17,900.

In determining its offer, Princeton noted the following pertaining to Streeter:

- **It holds a building with a fair value $43,100 more than its book value.**
- **It has developed a customer list appraised at $25,200, although it is not recorded in its financial records.**
- **It has research and development activity in process with an appraised fair value of $36,400. However, the project has not yet reached technological feasibility and the assets used in the activity have no alternative future use.**
- **Book values for the receivables, inventory, equipment, and liabilities approximate fair values.**

Prepare Princeton's accounting entries to record the combination with Streeter.

LO 2-4, 2-5, 2-8, 2-6b

32. SafeData Corporation has the following account balances and respective fair values on June 30:

	Book Values	Fair Values
Receivables	$ 80,000	$ 80,000
Patented technology	100,000	700,000
Customer relationships	–0–	500,000
In-process research and development	–0–	300,000
Liabilities	(400,000)	(400,000)
Common stock	(100,000)	
Additional paid-in capital	(300,000)	
Retained earnings deficit, 1/1	700,000	
Revenues	(300,000)	
Expenses	220,000	

Privacy First, Inc., obtained all of the outstanding shares of SafeData on June 30 by issuing 20,000 shares of common stock having a $1 par value but a $75 fair value. Privacy First incurred $10,000 in stock issuance costs and paid $75,000 to an investment banking firm for its assistance in arranging the combination. In negotiating the final terms of the deal, Privacy First also agrees to pay $100,000 to SafeData's former owners if it achieves certain revenue goals in the next two years. Privacy First estimates the probability adjusted present value of this contingent performance obligation at $30,000.

a. What is the fair value of the consideration transferred in this combination?

b. How should the stock issuance costs appear in Privacy First's postcombination financial statements?

c. How should Privacy First account for the fee paid to the investment bank?

d. How does the issuance of these shares affect the stockholders' equity accounts of Privacy First, the parent?

e. How is the fair value of the consideration transferred in the combination allocated among the assets acquired and the liabilities assumed?

f. What is the effect of SafeData's revenues and expenses on consolidated totals? Why?

g. What is the effect of SafeData's Common Stock and Additional Paid-In Capital balances on consolidated totals?

h. If Privacy First's stock had been worth only $50 per share rather than $75, how would the consolidation of SafeData's assets and liabilities have been affected?

LO 2-4, 2-5, 2-6a, 2-6b, 2-6c

LO 2-7, 2-8

33. On January 1, NewTune Company exchanges 15,000 shares of its common stock for all of the outstanding shares of On-the-Go, Inc. Each of NewTune's shares has a $4 par value and a $50 fair value. The fair value of the stock exchanged in the acquisition was considered equal to On-the-Go's fair value. NewTune also paid $25,000 in stock registration and issuance costs in connection with the merger.

Several of On-the-Go's accounts' fair values differ from their book values on this date:

	Book Values	Fair Values
Receivables	$ 65,000	$ 63,000
Trademarks	95,000	225,000
Record music catalog	60,000	180,000
In-process research and development	–0–	200,000
Notes payable	(50,000)	(45,000)

Precombination book values for the two companies are as follows:

	NewTune	On-the-Go
Cash	$ 60,000	$ 29,000
Receivables	150,000	65,000
Trademarks	400,000	95,000
Record music catalog	840,000	60,000
Equipment (net)	320,000	105,000
Totals	$1,770,000	$354,000

(continued)

Accounts payable	$ (110,000)	$ (34,000)
Notes payable	(370,000)	(50,000)
Common stock	(400,000)	(50,000)
Additional paid-in capital	(30,000)	(30,000)
Retained earnings	(860,000)	(190,000)
Totals	$(1,770,000)	$(354,000)

a. Assume that this combination is a statutory merger so that On-the-Go's accounts will be transferred to the records of NewTune. On-the-Go will be dissolved and will no longer exist as a legal entity. Prepare a postcombination balance sheet for NewTune as of the acquisition date.

b. Assume that no dissolution takes place in connection with this combination. Rather, both companies retain their separate legal identities. Prepare a worksheet to consolidate the two companies as of the combination date.

c. How do the balance sheet accounts compare across parts (*a*) and (*b*)?

LO 2-4, 2-5, 2-6b, 2-6c, 2-7

eXcel

34. On December 31, Pacifica, Inc., acquired 100 percent of the voting stock of Seguros Company. Pacifica will maintain Seguros as a wholly owned subsidiary with its own legal and accounting identity. The consideration transferred to the owner of Seguros included 50,000 newly issued Pacifica common shares ($20 market value, $5 par value) and an agreement to pay an additional $130,000 cash if Seguros meets certain project completion goals by December 31 of the following year. Pacifica estimates a 50 percent probability that Seguros will be successful in meeting these goals and uses a 4 percent discount rate to represent the time value of money.

Immediately prior to the acquisition, the following data for both firms were available:

	Pacifica	Seguros Book Values	Seguros Fair Values
Revenues	$(1,200,000)		
Expenses	875,000		
Net income	$ (325,000)		
Retained earnings, 1/1	$ (950,000)		
Net income	(325,000)		
Dividends declared	90,000		
Retained earnings, 12/31	$(1,185,000)		
Cash	$ 110,000	$ 85,000	$ 85,000
Receivables and inventory	750,000	190,000	180,000
Property, plant, and equipment	1,400,000	450,000	600,000
Trademarks	300,000	160,000	200,000
Total assets	$ 2,560,000	$ 885,000	
Liabilities	$ (500,000)	$(180,000)	$(180,000)
Common stock	(400,000)	(200,000)	
Additional paid-in capital	(475,000)	(70,000)	
Retained earnings	(1,185,000)	(435,000)	
Total liabilities and equities	$(2,560,000)	$(885,000)	

In addition, Pacifica assessed a research and development project under way at Seguros to have a fair value of $100,000. Although not yet recorded on its books, Pacifica paid legal fees of $15,000 in connection with the acquisition and $9,000 in stock issue costs.

Prepare the following:

a. Pacifica's entries to account for the consideration transferred to the former owners of Seguros, the direct combination costs, and the stock issue and registration costs. (Use a 0.961538 present value factor where applicable.)

b. A postacquisition column of accounts for Pacifica.

c. A worksheet to produce a consolidated balance sheet as of the acquisition date.

Appendix 2A Problems

LO 2-9

35. In a pre-2009 business combination, Acme Company acquired all of Brem Company's assets and liabilities for cash. After the combination Acme formally dissolved Brem. At the acquisition date, the following book and fair values were available for the Brem Company accounts:

	Book Values	Fair Values
Current assets	$ 80,000	$ 80,000
Equipment	120,000	180,000
Trademark	–0–	320,000
Liabilities	(55,000)	(55,000)
Common stock	(100,000)	
Retained earnings	(45,000)	

In addition, Acme paid an investment bank $25,000 cash for assistance in arranging the combination.

a. Using the legacy purchase method for pre-2009 business combinations, prepare Acme's entry to record its acquisition of Brem in its accounting records assuming the following cash amounts were paid to the former owners of Brem:

1. $610,000.
2. $425,000.

b. How would these journal entries change if the acquisition occurred post-2009 and therefore Acme applied the acquisition method?

LO 2-9

36. On February 1, Piscina Corporation completed a combination with Swimwear Company. At that date, Swimwear's account balances were as follows:

	Book Values	Fair Values
Inventory	$ 600,000	$ 650,000
Land	450,000	750,000
Buildings	900,000	1,000,000
Unpatented technology	–0–	1,500,000
Common stock ($10 par value)	(750,000)	
Retained earnings, 1/1	(1,100,000)	
Revenues	(600,000)	
Expenses	500,000	

Piscina issued 30,000 shares of its common stock with a par value of $25 and a fair value of $150 per share to the owners of Swimwear for all of their Swimwear shares. Upon completion of the combination, Swimwear Company was formally dissolved.

Prior to 2002, business combinations were accounted for using either purchase or pooling of interests accounting. The two methods often produced substantially different financial statement effects. For the scenario above,

a. What are the respective consolidated values for Swimwear's assets under the pooling method and the purchase method?

b. Under each of the following methods, how would Piscina account for Swimwear's current year, but prior to acquisition, revenues and expenses?

- Pooling of interests method.
- Purchase method.

c. Explain the alternative impact of pooling versus purchase accounting on performance ratios such as return on assets and earnings per share in periods subsequent to the combination.

Appendix 2B Problems

LO 2-10

37. What is push-down accounting?

a. A requirement that a subsidiary must use the same accounting principles as a parent company.

b. Inventory transfers made from a parent company to a subsidiary.

c. A subsidiary's recording of the fair-value allocations as well as subsequent amortization.

d. The adjustments required for consolidation when a parent has applied the equity method of accounting for internal reporting purposes.

LO 2-10

38. On May 1, Burns Corporation acquired 100 percent of the outstanding ownership shares of Quigley Corporation in exchange for $710,000 cash. At the acquisition date, Quigley's book and fair values were as follows:

	Book Values	Fair Values
Cash	$ 95,000	$ 95,000
Receivables	200,000	200,000
Inventory	210,000	260,000
Land	130,000	110,000
Building and equipment (net)	270,000	330,000
Patented technology	-0-	220,000
Total assets	$905,000	$1,215,000
Accounts payable	$120,000	$ 120,000
Long-term liabilities	510,000	510,000
Common stock ($5 par value)	210,000	
Additional paid-in capital	90,000	
Retained earnings	(25,000)	
Total liabilities and stockholders equity	$905,000	

Burns directs Quigley to seek additional financing for expansion through a new long-term debt issue. Consequently, Quigley will issue a set of financial statements separate from that of its new parent to support its request for debt and accompanying regulatory filings. Quigley elects to apply pushdown accounting in order to show recent fair valuations for its assets.

Prepare a separate acquisition-date balance sheet for Quigley Corporation using pushdown accounting.

Develop Your Skills

FASB ASC RESEARCH AND ANALYSIS CASE—CONSIDERATION OR COMPENSATION?

CPA skills

NaviNow Company agrees to pay $20 million in cash to the four former owners of TrafficEye for all of its assets and liabilities. These four owners of TrafficEye developed and patented a technology for real-time monitoring of traffic patterns on the nation's top 200 frequently congested highways. NaviNow plans to combine the new technology with its existing global positioning systems and projects a resulting substantial revenue increase.

As part of the acquisition contract, NaviNow also agrees to pay additional amounts to the former owners upon achievement of certain financial goals. NaviNow will pay $8 million to the four former owners of TrafficEye if revenues from the combined system exceed $100 million over the next three years. NaviNow estimates this contingent payment to have a probability adjusted present value of $4 million.

The four former owners have also been offered employment contracts with NaviNow to help with system integration and performance enhancement issues. The employment contracts are silent as to service periods, have nominal salaries similar to those of equivalent employees, and specify a profit-sharing component over the next three years (if the employees remain with the company) that NaviNow estimates to have a current fair value of $2 million. The four former owners of TrafficEye say they will stay on as employees of NaviNow for at least three years to help achieve the desired financial goals.

Should NaviNow account for the contingent payments promised to the former owners of TrafficEye as consideration transferred in the acquisition or as compensation expense to employees?

ASC RESEARCH CASE—DEFENSIVE INTANGIBLE ASSET

CPA skills

Ahorita Company manufactures wireless transponders for satellite applications. Ahorita has recently acquired Zelltech Company, which is primarily known for its software communications development but also manufactures a specialty transponder under the trade name "Z-Tech" that competes with one of Ahorita's products. Ahorita will now discontinue Z-Tech and projects that its own product line will see a market share increase. Nonetheless, Ahorita's management will maintain the rights to the Z-Tech trade name as a defensive intangible asset to prevent its use by competitors, despite the fact that its highest and best use would be to sell the trade name. Ahorita estimates that the trade name has an internal value of $1.5 million, but if sold would yield $2 million.

Answer the following with supporting citations from the FASB ASC:

a. How does the FASB ASC Glossary define a defensive intangible asset?

b. According to ASC Topic 805, "Business Combinations," what is the measurement principle that an acquirer should follow in recording identifiable assets acquired in a business combination?

c. According to ASC Topic 820, "Fair Value Measurement," what value premise (in-use or in-exchange) should Ahorita assign to the Z-Tech trade name in its consolidated financial statements?

d. According to ASC Topic 350, "General Intangibles Other Than Goodwill," how should Ahorita determine the estimated useful life of its defensive intangible asset?

RESEARCH CASE—CELGENE'S ACQUISITION OF RECEPTOS, INC.

CPA skills

On August 27, 2015, Celgene Corporation acquired all of the outstanding stock of Receptos, Inc., in exchange for $7.6 billion in cash. Referring to Celgene's 2015 financial statements and its July 14, 2015, press release announcing the acquisition, answer the following questions regarding the Receptos acquisition.

1. Why did Celgene acquire Receptos?
2. What accounting method was used, and for what amount, to record the acquisition?
3. What amount did Celgene include in pre-combination service compensation in the total consideration transferred? What support is provided for this treatment in the Accounting Standards Codification (see ASC 805-30-30, paragraphs 9-13)?
4. What allocations did Celgene make to the assets acquired and liabilities assumed in the acquisition? Provide a calculation showing how Celgene determined the amount allocated to goodwill.
5. Describe the nature of the in-process research and development product rights acquired by Celgene in its acquisition of Receptos.
6. How will Celgene account for the in-process research and development product rights acquired in the Receptos combination?

RESEARCH CASE—ARCTIC CAT'S ACQUISITION OF MOTORFIST, LLC.

In February 2015, Arctic Cat, Inc., acquired the assets and liabilities of MotorFist, LLC, a privately owned company based in Idaho Falls, Idaho, in exchange for $9.118 million in cash and contingent consideration. Referring to Arctic Cat's 2015 annual 10-K report, answer the following questions regarding the MotorFist acquisition.

1. Why did Arctic Cat acquire MotorFist?
2. How was the consideration transferred allocated between cash paid and the contingent consideration?
3. Provide a schedule showing Arctic Cat's allocations of the consideration transferred to the identifiable assets acquired and liabilities assumed with the remainder going to goodwill.
4. What is the maximum potential contingent payout (i.e., earnout) to the former owners of MotorFist? Although not explicitly stated in Arctic Cat's fiscal 2015 10-K report (for the year ended March 31, 2015), what may be some possible factors that entered into the determination of the acquisition-date fair value of the contingent consideration?

chapter 3

Consolidations—Subsequent to the Date of Acquisition

In 1996, Berkshire Hathaway, Inc., acquired all of the outstanding stock of Geico, Inc., an insurance company. Although this transaction involved well-known companies, it was not unique; mergers and acquisitions have long been common in the business world.

Berkshire Hathaway's current financial statements indicate that Geico is still a component of this economic entity. However, Geico, Inc., continues as a separate legally incorporated concern long after its acquisition. As discussed in Chapter 2, a parent will often maintain separate legal status for a subsidiary corporation to better utilize its inherent value as a going concern.

For external reporting purposes, maintenance of incorporation creates an ongoing challenge for the accountant. In each subsequent period, consolidation must be simulated anew through the use of a worksheet and consolidation entries. Thus, for many years, the financial data for Berkshire Hathaway and Geico (along with dozens of other subsidiaries) have been brought together periodically to provide figures for the financial statements that represent this business combination.

As also discussed in Chapter 2, the acquisition method governs the way we initially record a business combination. In periods subsequent to acquisition, the fair-value bases (established at the acquisition date) for subsidiary assets acquired and liabilities assumed will be amortized (or tested for possible impairment) for proper income recognition. Additionally, some combinations require accounting for the eventual disposition of contingent consideration, which, as presented later in this chapter, continues to follow a fair-value model.

In the next several sections of this chapter, we present the procedures to prepare consolidated financial statements in the years subsequent to acquisition. We start by analyzing the relation between the parent's internal accounting method for its subsidiary investment and the adjustments required in consolidation. We also examine the specific procedures for amortizing the acquisition-date fair-value adjustments to the subsidiary's assets and liabilities. We then cover testing for goodwill impairment and post-acquisition accounting for contingent consideration. Finally, an appendix presents the alternative goodwill model available as a reporting option for private companies.

Learning Objectives

After studying this chapter, you should be able to:

LO 3-1 Recognize the complexities in preparing consolidated financial reports that emerge from the passage of time.

LO 3-2 Identify and describe the various methods available to a parent company in order to maintain its investment in subsidiary account in its internal records.

LO 3-3 Prepare consolidated financial statements subsequent to acquisition when the parent has applied in its internal records:
a. The equity method.
b. The initial value method.
c. The partial equity method.

LO 3-4 Understand that a parent's internal accounting method for its subsidiary investments has no effect on the resulting consolidated financial statements.

LO 3-5 Discuss the rationale for the goodwill impairment testing approach.

LO 3-6 Describe the procedures for conducting a goodwill impairment test.

LO 3-7 Describe the rationale and procedures for impairment testing for intangible assets other than goodwill.

LO 3-8 Understand the accounting and reporting for contingent consideration subsequent to a business acquisition.

LO 3-9 Appendix: Describe the alternative accounting treatments for goodwill and other intangible assets available for business combinations by private companies.

LO 3-1

Recognize the complexities in preparing consolidated financial reports that emerge from the passage of time.

Consolidation—The Effects Created by the Passage of Time

In Chapter 2, consolidation accounting is analyzed at the date that a combination is created. The present chapter carries this process one step further by examining the consolidation procedures that must be followed in subsequent periods whenever separate incorporation of the subsidiary is maintained.

Despite complexities created by the passage of time, the basic objective of all consolidations remains the same: to combine asset, liability, revenue, expense, and equity accounts of a parent and its subsidiaries. From a mechanical perspective, a worksheet and consolidation entries continue to provide structure for the production of a single set of financial statements for the combined business entity.

Consolidated Net Income Determination

Subsequent to an acquisition, the parent company must report consolidated net income. Consolidated income determination involves first combining the separately recorded revenues and expenses of the parent with those of the subsidiary on a consolidated worksheet. Because of separate record-keeping systems, however, the subsidiary's expenses typically are based on their original book values and not the acquisition-date values the parent must recognize. Consequently, adjustments are made that reflect the amortization of the excess of the parent's consideration transferred over the subsidiary book value. Additionally, the effects of any intra-entity transactions are removed.

The Parent's Choice of Investment Accounting

The time factor introduces other complications into the consolidation process as well. For internal record-keeping purposes, the parent must select and apply an accounting method to monitor the relationship between the two companies. The investment balance recorded by the parent varies over time as a result of the method chosen, as does the income subsequently recognized. These differences affect the periodic consolidation process but not the figures to be reported by the combined entity. Regardless of the amount, the parent's investment account is eliminated (brought to a zero balance) on the worksheet so that the subsidiary's actual assets and liabilities can be consolidated. Likewise, the income figure accrued by the parent is removed each period so that the subsidiary's revenues and expenses can be included when creating an income statement for the combined business entity.

LO 3-2

Identify and describe the various methods available to a parent company in order to maintain its investment in subsidiary account in its internal records.

Investment Accounting by the Acquiring Company

For a parent company's external financial reporting, consolidation of a subsidiary becomes necessary whenever control exists. For internal record-keeping, though, the parent has a choice for monitoring the activities of its subsidiaries. Although several variations occur in practice, three methods have emerged as the most prominent: the equity method, the initial value method,[1] and the partial equity method.

At the acquisition date, each investment accounting method (equity, initial value, and partial equity) begins with an identical value recorded in an investment account. Typically the fair value of the consideration transferred by the parent will serve as the recorded valuation basis on the parent's books.[2]

Subsequent to the acquisition date, the three methods produce different account balances for the parent's investment in subsidiary, income recognized from the subsidiary's activities, and retained earnings accounts. *Importantly, the selection of a particular method does not affect the totals ultimately reported for the combined companies.* However, the parent's

[1] The initial value method is sometimes referred to as the cost method.

[2] In the unusual case of a bargain purchase, the valuation basis for the investment account is the fair value of the net amount of the assets acquired and liabilities assumed.

choice of an internal accounting method does lead to distinct procedures for consolidating the financial information from the separate organizations.

Internal Investment Accounting Alternatives—The Equity Method, Initial Value Method, and Partial Equity Method

The internal reporting philosophy of the acquiring company often determines the accounting method choice for its subsidiary investment. Depending on the measures a company uses to assess the ongoing performances of its subsidiaries, parent companies may choose their own preferred internal reporting method. Regardless of this choice, however, the investment balance will be eliminated in preparing consolidated financial statements for external reporting.

The Equity Method

The equity method embraces full accrual accounting in maintaining the investment account and related income over time. Under the equity method, the acquiring company accrues income when the subsidiary earns it. To match the additional fair value recorded in the combination against income, amortization expense stemming from the original excess fair-value allocations is recognized through periodic adjusting entries. Unrealized gains on intra-entity transactions are deferred; subsidiary dividends serve to reduce the investment balance. As discussed in Chapter 1, the equity method creates a parallel between the parent's investment accounts and changes in the underlying equity of the acquired company.[3]

When the parent has complete ownership, equity method earnings from the subsidiary, combined with the parent's other income sources, create a total income figure reflective of the entire combined business entity. Consequently, the equity method often is referred to as a single-line consolidation. The equity method is especially popular in companies where management periodically (e.g., monthly or quarterly) measures each subsidiary's profitability using accrual-based income figures.

The Initial Value Method

Under the initial value method, the parent recognizes income from its share of any subsidiary dividends when declared. Because little time typically elapses between dividend declaration and cash distribution, the initial value method frequently reflects the cash basis for income recognition. No recognition is given to the income earned by the subsidiary. The investment balance remains on the parent's financial records at the initial fair value assigned at the acquisition date.

The initial value method might be selected because the parent does not require an accrual-based income measure of subsidiary performance. For example, the parent may wish to assess subsidiary performance on its ability to generate cash flows, on revenues generated, or some other nonincome basis. Also, some firms may find the initial value method's ease of application attractive. Because the investment account is eliminated in consolidation, and the actual subsidiary revenues and expenses are eventually combined, firms may avoid the complexity of the equity method unless they need the specific information provided by the equity income measure for internal decision making.

The Partial Equity Method

A third method available to the acquiring company is a partial application of the equity method. Under this approach, the parent recognizes the reported income accruing from the subsidiary. Subsidiary dividends declared reduce the investment balance. However, no other equity adjustments (amortization or deferral of unrealized gains) are recorded. Thus, in many cases, earnings figures on the parent's books approximate consolidated totals but without the effort associated with a full application of the equity method.

[3] In Chapter 1, the equity method was introduced in connection with the external reporting of investments in which the owner held the ability to apply significant influence over the investee (usually by possessing 20 to 50 percent of the company's voting stock). Here, the equity method is utilized for the internal reporting of the parent for investments in which control is maintained. Although the accounting procedures are similar, the reason for using the equity method is different.

EXHIBIT 3.1 Internal Reporting of Investment Accounts by Acquiring Company

Method	Investment Account	Income Account	Advantages
Equity	Continually adjusted to reflect current owner's equity of acquired company.	Income accrued as earned; amortization and other adjustments are recognized.	Acquiring company totals give a true representation of consolidation figures.
Initial value	Remains at acquisition-date value assigned.	Dividends declared recorded as Dividend Income.	It is easy to apply; it often reflects cash flows from the subsidiary.
Partial equity	Adjusted only for accrued income and dividends declared by the acquired company.	Income accrued as earned; no other adjustments recognized.	It usually gives balances approximating consolidation figures, but it is easier to apply than equity method.

Moreover, some parent companies rely on internally designed performance measures (rather than GAAP net income) to evaluate subsidiary management or make resource allocation decisions. For such companies, a full equity method application may be unnecessary for internal purposes. In these cases, the partial equity method, although only approximating the GAAP income measure, may be sufficient for decision making.

Summary of Internal Investment Accounting Methods

Exhibit 3.1 provides a summary of these three internal accounting techniques. Importantly, the method the acquiring company adopts affects only its separate financial records and has no impact on the subsidiary's balances. Regardless of how the parent chooses to account internally for its subsidiary, the selection of a particular method (i.e., initial value, equity, or partial equity) does not affect the amounts ultimately reported on consolidated financial statements to external users.

Because specific worksheet procedures differ based on the investment method utilized by the parent, the consolidation process subsequent to the date of combination will be introduced twice. First, we review consolidations in which the acquiring company uses the equity method. Then we redevelop all procedures when the investment is recorded by one of the alternative methods.

LO 3-3a

Prepare consolidated financial statements subsequent to acquisition when the parent has applied **the equity method** in its internal records.

Subsequent Consolidation—Investment Recorded by the Equity Method

Acquisition Made during the Current Year

As a basis for this illustration, assume that Parrot Company obtains all of the outstanding common stock of Sun Company on January 1, 2017. Parrot acquires this stock for $800,000 in cash.

The book values as well as the appraised fair values of Sun's accounts follow:

	Book Values 1/1/17	Fair Values 1/1/17	Difference
Current assets	$ 320,000	$ 320,000	$ -0-
Trademarks (indefinite life)	200,000	220,000	+ 20,000
Patented technology (10-year remaining life)	320,000	450,000	+130,000
Equipment (5-year remaining life)	180,000	150,000	(30,000)
Liabilities	(420,000)	(420,000)	-0-
Net book value	$ 600,000	$ 720,000	$120,000
Common stock—$40 par value	$ (200,000)		
Additional paid-in capital	(20,000)		
Retained earnings, 1/1/17	(380,000)		

EXHIBIT 3.2
Excess Fair-Value Allocation

PARROT COMPANY
100 Percent Acquisition of Sun Company
Allocation of Acquisition-Date Subsidiary Fair Value
January 1, 2017

Sun Company fair value (consideration transferred by Parrot Company)		$800,000
Book value of Sun Company:		
Common stock	$200,000	
Additional paid-in capital	20,000	
Retained earnings, 1/1/17	380,000	(600,000)
Excess of fair value over book value		200,000
Allocation to specific accounts based on fair values:		
Trademarks	$ 20,000	
Patented technology	130,000	
Equipment (overvalued)	(30,000)	120,000
Excess fair value not identified with specific accounts—goodwill		$ 80,000

Parrot considers the economic life of Sun's trademarks as extending beyond the foreseeable future and thus having an indefinite life. Such assets are not amortized but are subject to periodic impairment testing.[4] For the definite lived assets acquired in the combination (patented technology and equipment), we assume that straight-line amortization and depreciation with no salvage value is appropriate.[5]

Parrot paid $800,000 cash to acquire Sun Company, clear evidence of the fair value of the consideration transferred. As shown in Exhibit 3.2, individual allocations are used to adjust Sun's accounts from their book values to their acquisition-date fair values. Because the total value of these assets and liabilities was only $720,000, goodwill of $80,000 must be recognized for consolidation purposes.

Each of these allocated amounts (other than the $20,000 attributed to trademarks and the $80,000 for goodwill) represents a valuation associated with a definite life. As discussed in Chapter 1, Parrot must amortize each allocation over its expected life. The expense recognition necessitated by this fair-value allocation is calculated in Exhibit 3.3.

Two aspects of this amortization schedule warrant further explanation. First, we use the term *amortization* in a generic sense to include both the amortization of definite-lived intangibles and depreciation of tangible assets. Second, the acquisition-date fair value of Sun's equipment is $30,000 *less* than its book value. Therefore, instead of attributing an additional amount to this asset, the $30,000 allocation actually reflects a fair-value reduction. As such, the amortization shown in Exhibit 3.3 relating to Equipment is not an additional expense but instead is an expense reduction.

EXHIBIT 3.3
Annual Excess Amortization

PARROT COMPANY
100 Percent Acquisition of Sun Company
Excess Amortization Schedule—Allocation of Acquisition-Date Fair Values

Account	Allocation	Remaining Useful Life	Annual Excess Amortizations
Trademarks	$ 20,000	Indefinite	$ -0-
Patented technology	130,000	10 years	13,000
Equipment	(30,000)	5 years	(6,000)
Goodwill	80,000	Indefinite	-0-
			$ 7,000*

*Total excess amortizations will be $7,000 annually for five years until the equipment allocation is fully removed. At the end of each asset's life, future amortizations will change.

[4] In other cases, trademarks can have a definite life and thus would be subject to regular amortization.

[5] Unless otherwise stated, all amortization and depreciation expense computations in this textbook are based on the straight-line method with no salvage value.

Having determined the allocation of the acquisition-date fair value in the previous example as well as the associated amortization, the parent's separate record-keeping for its first year of Sun Company ownership can be constructed. Assume that Sun earns income of $100,000 during the year, declares a $40,000 cash dividend on August 1, and pays the dividend on August 8.

In this first illustration, Parrot has adopted the equity method. Apparently, this company believes that the information derived from using the equity method is useful in its evaluation of Sun.

Application of the Equity Method

	Parrot's Financial Records		
1/1/17	Investment in Sun Company	800,000	
	Cash		800,000
	To record the acquisition of Sun Company.		
8/1/17	Dividend Receivable	40,000	
	Investment in Sun Company		40,000
	To record cash dividend declaration from subsidiary.		
8/8/17	Cash	40,000	
	Dividend Receivable		40,000
	To record receipt of the subsidiary cash dividend.		
12/31/17	Investment in Sun Company	100,000	
	Equity in Subsidiary Earnings		100,000
	To accrue income earned by 100 percent owned subsidiary.		
12/31/17	Equity in Subsidiary Earnings	7,000	
	Investment in Sun Company		7,000
	To recognize amortizations on allocations made in acquisition of subsidiary (see Exhibit 3.3).		

Parrot's application of the equity method, as shown in this series of entries, causes the Investment in Sun Company account balance to rise from $800,000 to $853,000 ($800,000 – $40,000 + $100,000 – $7,000). During the same period the parent recognizes a $93,000 equity income figure (the $100,000 earnings accrual less the $7,000 excess amortization expenses).

The consolidation procedures for Parrot and Sun one year after the date of acquisition are illustrated next. For this purpose, Exhibit 3.4 presents the separate 2017 financial statements for these two companies. Parrot recorded both investment-related accounts (the $853,000 asset balance and the $93,000 income accrual) based on applying the equity method.

Determination of Consolidated Totals

Before becoming immersed in the mechanical aspects of a consolidation, the objective of this process should be understood. As indicated in Chapter 2, in the preparation of consolidated financial reports, the subsidiary's revenue, expense, asset, and liability accounts are added to the parent company balances. Within this procedure, several important guidelines must be followed:

- Sun's assets and liabilities are adjusted to reflect the allocations originating from their acquisition-date fair values.
- Because of the passage of time, the income effects (e.g., amortizations) of these allocations must also be recognized within the consolidation process.
- Any reciprocal or intra-entity[6] accounts must be offset. If, for example, one of the companies owes money to the other, the receivable and the payable balances have no connection with an outside party. Thus, when the companies are viewed as a single consolidated entity, the receivable and the payable represent intra-entity balances that should be eliminated for external reporting purposes.

[6] The FASB Accounting Standards Codification (ASC) uses the term *intra-entity* to describe transfers of assets across business entities affiliated though common stock ownership or other control mechanisms. The phrase indicates that although such transfers occur across separate legal entities, they are nonetheless made within a commonly controlled entity. Prior to the use of the term intra-entity, such amounts were routinely referred to as intercompany balances.

EXHIBIT 3.4 Separate Records—Equity Method Applied

PARROT COMPANY AND SUN COMPANY
Financial Statements
For Year Ending December 31, 2017

	Parrot Company	Sun Company
Income Statement		
Revenues	$ (1,500,000)	$ (400,000)
Cost of goods sold	700,000	232,000
Amortization expense	120,000	32,000
Depreciation expense	80,000	36,000
Equity in subsidiary earnings	(93,000)	–0–
Net income	$ (693,000)	$ (100,000)
Statement of Retained Earnings		
Retained earnings, 1/1/17	$ (840,000)	$ (380,000)
Net income (above)	(693,000)	(100,000)
Dividends declared*	120,000	40,000
Retained earnings, 12/31/17	$ (1,413,000)	$ (440,000)
Balance Sheet		
Current assets	$ 1,040,000	$ 400,000
Investment in Sun Company (at equity)	853,000	–0–
Trademarks	600,000	200,000
Patented technology	370,000	288,000
Equipment (net)	250,000	220,000
Total assets	$ 3,113,000	$ 1,108,000
Liabilities	$ (980,000)	$ (448,000)
Common stock	(600,000)	(200,000)
Additional paid-in capital	(120,000)	(20,000)
Retained earnings, 12/31/17 (above)	(1,413,000)	(440,000)
Total liabilities and equity	$ (3,113,000)	$(1,108,000)

Note: Parentheses indicate a credit balance.
*Dividends declared, whether currently paid or not, provide the appropriate amount to include in a statement of retained earnings. To help keep the number of worksheet rows (i.e., dividends payable and receivable) at a minimum, throughout this text we assume that dividends are declared and paid in the same period.

The consolidation of the two sets of financial information in Exhibit 3.4 is a relatively uncomplicated task and can even be carried out without the use of a worksheet. Understanding the origin of each reported figure is the first step in gaining a knowledge of this process.

- *Revenues* = $1,900,000. The revenues of the parent and the subsidiary are added together.
- *Cost of goods sold* = $932,000. The cost of goods sold of the parent and subsidiary are added together.
- *Amortization expense* = $165,000. The balances of the parent and of the subsidiary are combined along with the $13,000 additional amortization from the recognition of the excess fair value over book value attributed to the subsidiary's patented technology, as shown in Exhibit 3.3.
- *Depreciation expense* = $110,000. The depreciation expenses of the parent and subsidiary are added together along with the $6,000 reduction in equipment depreciation, as indicated in Exhibit 3.3.
- *Equity in subsidiary earnings* = –0–. The investment income recorded by the parent is eliminated and replaced by adding across the subsidiary's revenues and expenses to the consolidated totals.
- *Net income* = $693,000. Consolidated revenues less consolidated expenses.
- *Retained earnings, 1/1/17* = $840,000. The parent figure only. This acquisition-date parent's balance has yet to be affected by any equity method adjustments.

- *Dividends declared* = $120,000. The parent company balance only because the subsidiary's dividends are attributable intra-entity to the parent, not to an outside party.
- *Retained earnings, 12/31/17* = $1,413,000. Consolidated retained earnings as of the beginning of the year plus consolidated net income less consolidated dividends declared.
- *Current assets* = $1,440,000. The parent's book value plus the subsidiary's book value.
- *Investment in Sun Company* = –0–. The asset recorded by the parent is eliminated and replaced by adding the subsidiary's assets and liabilities across to the consolidated totals.
- *Trademarks* = $820,000. The parent's book value plus the subsidiary's book value plus the $20,000 acquisition-date fair-value allocation. Note that the trademark has an indefinite life and therefore is not amortized.
- *Patented technology* = $775,000. The parent's book value plus the subsidiary's book value plus the $130,000 acquisition-date fair-value allocation less current year amortization of $13,000.
- *Equipment* = $446,000. The parent's book value plus the subsidiary's book value less the $30,000 fair-value reduction allocation plus the current year expense reduction of $6,000.
- *Goodwill* = $80,000. The residual allocation shown in Exhibit 3.2. Note that goodwill is considered to have an indefinite life and thus is not amortized.
- *Total assets* = $3,561,000. A vertical summation of consolidated assets.
- *Liabilities* = $1,428,000. The parent's book value plus the subsidiary's book value.
- *Common stock* = $600,000. The parent's book value. Subsidiary shares owned by the parent are treated as if they are no longer outstanding.
- *Additional paid-in capital* = $120,000. The parent's book value. Subsidiary shares owned by the parent are treated as if they are no longer outstanding.
- *Retained earnings, 12/31/17* = $1,413,000. Computed previously.
- *Total liabilities and equities* = $3,561,000. A vertical summation of consolidated liabilities and equities.

Consolidation Worksheet

Although the consolidated figures to be reported can be computed as just shown, accountants normally prefer to use a worksheet. A worksheet provides an organized structure for this process, a benefit that becomes especially important in consolidating complex combinations.

For Parrot and Sun, only five consolidation entries are needed to arrive at the same figures previously derived for this business combination. As discussed in Chapter 2, *worksheet entries are the catalyst for developing totals to be reported by the entity but are not physically recorded in the individual account balances of either company.*

Consolidation Entry S

Common Stock (Sun Company)	200,000	
Additional Paid-In Capital (Sun Company)	20,000	
Retained Earnings, 1/1/17 (Sun Company)	380,000	
Investment in Sun Company		600,000

As shown in Exhibit 3.2, Parrot's $800,000 Investment account balance at January 1, 2017, reflects two components: (1) a $600,000 amount equal to Sun's book value and (2) a $200,000 figure attributed to the acquisition-date difference between the book value and fair value of Sun's assets and liabilities (with a residual allocation made to goodwill). Entry **S** removes the $600,000 component of the Investment in Sun Company account which is then replaced by adding the *book values* of each subsidiary asset and liability across to the consolidated figures. A second worksheet entry (Entry **A**) eliminates the remaining $200,000 portion of the January 1, 2017 Investment in Sun account and replaces it with the specific acquisition-date excess fair over book value allocations along with any goodwill. Importantly, worksheet entries S and A are part of the sequence of worksheet adjustments that bring the investment account to zero.

Entry **S** also removes Sun's stockholders' equity accounts as of the beginning of the year. Because consolidated statements are prepared for the parent company owners, the subsidiary equity accounts are not relevant to the business combination and should be eliminated for consolidation purposes. The elimination is made through this entry because the equity accounts and the $600,000 component of the investment account represent reciprocal balances: Both provide a measure of Sun's book value as of January 1, 2017.

Before moving to the next consolidation entry, a clarification point should be made. In actual practice, worksheet entries are usually identified numerically. However, as in the previous chapter, the label "Entry **S**" used in this example refers to the elimination of Sun's beginning **S**tockholders' Equity. As a reminder of the purpose being served, all worksheet entries are identified in a similar fashion. Thus, throughout this textbook, "Entry **S**" always refers to the removal of the subsidiary's beginning stockholders' equity balances for the year against the book value portion of the investment account.

Consolidation Entry A

Trademarks	20,000	
Patented Technology	130,000	
Goodwill	80,000	
Equipment		30,000
Investment in Sun Company		200,000

Consolidation Entry **A** adjusts the subsidiary balances from their book values to acquisition-date fair values (see Exhibit 3.2) and includes goodwill created by the acquisition. This entry is labeled "Entry **A**" to indicate that it represents the Allocations made in connection with the excess of the subsidiary's fair values over its book values. Sun's accounts are adjusted collectively by the $200,000 excess of Sun's $800,000 acquisition-date fair value over its $600,000 book value.

Consolidation Entry I

Equity in Subsidiary Earnings	93,000	
Investment in Sun Company		93,000

"Entry **I**" (for **I**ncome) removes from the worksheet the subsidiary income recognized by Parrot during the year. For reporting purposes, we must add the subsidiary's individual revenue and expense accounts (and the current excess amortization expenses) to the parent's respective amounts to arrive at consolidated totals. Worksheet entry **I** thus effectively removes the one-line Equity in Subsidiary Earnings which is then replaced with the addition of the subsidiary's separate revenues and expenses (already listed on the worksheet in the subsidiary's balances). The $93,000 figure eliminated here represents the $100,000 income accrual recognized by Parrot, reduced by the $7,000 in excess amortizations. Observe that the entry originally recorded by the parent is simply reversed on the worksheet to remove its impact.

Consolidation Entry D

Investment in Sun Company	40,000	
Dividends Declared		40,000

The dividends declared by the subsidiary during the year also must be eliminated from the consolidated totals. The entire $40,000 dividend goes to the parent, which from the viewpoint of the consolidated entity is simply an intra-entity transfer. The dividend declaration did not affect any outside party. Therefore, "Entry **D**" (for **D**ividends) is designed to offset the impact of this transaction by removing the subsidiary's Dividends Declared account. Because the equity method has been applied, Parrot originally recorded these dividends as a decrease in the Investment in Sun Company account. To eliminate the impact of this reduction, the investment account is increased.

Consolidation Entry E

Amortization Expense	13,000	
Equipment	6,000	
Patented Technology		13,000
Depreciation Expense		6,000

This final worksheet entry recognizes the current year's excess amortization expenses relating to the adjustments of Sun's assets to acquisition-date fair values. Because the equity method amortization was eliminated within Entry **I,** "Entry **E**" (for **E**xpense) now enters on the worksheet the current year expense attributed to each of the specific account allocations (see Exhibit 3.3). Note that we adjust depreciation expense for the tangible asset *equipment* and we adjust amortization expense for the intangible asset *patented technology.* As mentioned earlier, we refer to the adjustments to all expenses resulting from excess acquisition-date fair-value allocations collectively as *excess amortization expenses.*

Thus, the worksheet entries necessary for consolidation when the parent has applied the equity method are as follows:

Entry S—Eliminates the subsidiary's stockholders' equity accounts as of the beginning of the current year along with the equivalent book value component within the parent's investment account.

Entry A—Recognizes the unamortized allocations as of the beginning of the current year associated with the original adjustments to fair value.

Entry I—Eliminates the impact of intra-entity subsidiary income accrued by the parent.

Entry D—Eliminates the impact of intra-entity subsidiary dividends.

Entry E—Recognizes excess amortization expenses for the current period on the allocations from the original adjustments to fair value.

Exhibit 3.5 provides a complete presentation of the December 31, 2017, consolidation worksheet for Parrot Company and Sun Company. The series of entries just described brings together the separate financial statements of these two organizations. Note that the consolidated totals are the same as those computed previously for this combination.

Observe that Parrot separately reports net income of $693,000 as well as ending retained earnings of $1,413,000, figures that are identical to the totals generated for the consolidated entity. However, subsidiary income earned after the date of acquisition is to be *added* to that of the parent. Thus, a question arises in this example as to why the parent company figures alone equal the consolidated balances of both operations.

In reality, Sun's income for this period is contained in both Parrot's reported balances and the consolidated totals. Through the application of the equity method, the current year earnings of the subsidiary have already been accrued by Parrot along with the appropriate amortization expense. *The parent's Equity in Subsidiary Earnings account is, therefore, an accurate representation of Sun's effect on consolidated net income.* If the equity method is employed properly, the worksheet process simply replaces this single $93,000 balance with the specific revenue and expense accounts that it represents. *Consequently, when the parent employs the equity method, its net income and retained earnings mirror consolidated totals.*

Consolidation Subsequent to Year of Acquisition—Equity Method

In many ways, every consolidation of Parrot and Sun prepared after the date of acquisition incorporates the same basic procedures outlined in the previous section. However, the continual financial evolution undergone by the companies prohibits an exact repetition of the consolidation entries demonstrated in Exhibit 3.5.

As a basis for analyzing the procedural changes necessitated by the passage of time, assume that Parrot Company continues to hold its ownership of Sun Company as of December 31, 2020. This date was selected at random; any date subsequent to 2017 would serve equally well to illustrate this process. As an additional factor, assume that Sun now has a $40,000 liability that is payable to Parrot.

EXHIBIT 3.5 Consolidation Worksheet—Equity Method Applied

PARROT COMPANY AND SUN COMPANY
Consolidation Worksheet
For Year Ending December 31, 2017

Investment: Equity Method

Accounts	Parrot Company	Sun Company	Consolidation Entries Debit	Consolidation Entries Credit	Consolidated Totals
Income Statement					
Revenues	(1,500,000)	(400,000)			(1,900,000)
Cost of goods sold	700,000	232,000			932,000
Amortization expense	120,000	32,000	(E) 13,000		165,000
Depreciation expense	80,000	36,000		(E) 6,000	110,000
Equity in subsidiary earnings	(93,000)	–0–	(I) 93,000		–0–
Net income	(693,000)	(100,000)			(693,000)
Statement of Retained Earnings					
Retained earnings, 1/1/17	(840,000)	(380,000)	(S) 380,000		(840,000)
Net income (above)	(693,000)	(100,000)			(693,000)
Dividends declared	120,000	40,000		(D) 40,000	120,000
Retained earnings, 12/31/17	(1,413,000)	(440,000)			(1,413,000)
Balance Sheet					
Current assets	1,040,000	400,000			1,440,000
Investment in Sun Company	853,000	–0–	(D) 40,000	(S) 600,000 (A) 200,000 (I) 93,000	–0–
Trademarks	600,000	200,000	(A) 20,000		820,000
Patented technology	370,000	288,000	(A) 130,000	(E) 13,000	775,000
Equipment (net)	250,000	220,000	(E) 6,000	(A) 30,000	446,000
Goodwill	–0–	–0–	(A) 80,000		80,000
Total assets	3,113,000	1,108,000			3,561,000
Liabilities	(980,000)	(448,000)			(1,428,000)
Common stock	(600,000)	(200,000)	(S) 200,000		(600,000)
Additional paid-in capital	(120,000)	(20,000)	(S) 20,000		(120,000)
Retained earnings, 12/31/17 (above)	(1,413,000)	(440,000)			(1,413,000)
Total liabilities and equities	(3,113,000)	(1,108,000)	982,000	982,000	(3,561,000)

Note: Parentheses indicate a credit balance.
Consolidation entries:
(S) Elimination of Sun's stockholders' equity January 1 balances and the book value portion of the investment account.
(A) Allocation of Sun's acquisition-date excess fair values over book values.
(I) Elimination of parent's equity in subsidiary earnings accrual.
(D) Elimination of intra-entity dividends.
(E) Recognition of current year excess fair-value amortization and depreciation expenses.

For this consolidation, assume that the January 1, 2020, Sun Company's Retained Earnings balance has risen to $600,000. Because that account had a reported total of only $380,000 on January 1, 2017, Sun's book value apparently has increased by $220,000 during the 2017–2019 period. Although knowledge of individual operating figures in the past is not required, Sun's reported totals help to clarify the consolidation procedures.

Year	Sun Company Net Income	Dividends Declared	Increase in Book Value	Ending Retained Earnings
2017	$100,000	$ 40,000	$ 60,000	$ 440,000
2018	140,000	50,000	90,000	530,000
2019	90,000	20,000	70,000	600,000
	$330,000	$110,000	$220,000	

For 2020, the current year, we assume that Sun reports net income of $160,000 and declares and pays cash dividends of $70,000. Because it applies the equity method, Parrot recognizes earnings of $160,000. Furthermore, as shown in Exhibit 3.3, amortization expense of $7,000 applies to 2020 and must also be recorded by the parent. Consequently, Parrot reports an Equity in Subsidiary Earnings balance for the year of $153,000 ($160,000 – $7,000).

Although this income figure can be reconstructed with little difficulty, the current balance in the Investment in Sun Company account is more complicated. Over the years, the initial $800,000 acquisition price has been subjected to adjustments for

1. The annual accrual of Sun's income.
2. The receipt of dividends from Sun.
3. The recognition of annual excess amortization expenses.

Exhibit 3.6 analyzes these changes and shows the components of the Investment in Sun Company account balance as of December 31, 2020.

Following the construction of the Investment in Sun Company account, the consolidation worksheet developed in Exhibit 3.7 should be easier to understand. Current figures for both companies appear in the first two columns. The parent's investment balance and equity income accrual as well as Sun's income and stockholders' equity accounts correspond to the information given previously. Worksheet entries (lettered to agree with the previous illustration) are then utilized to consolidate all balances.

Several steps are necessary to arrive at these reported totals. The subsidiary's assets, liabilities, revenues, and expenses are added to those same accounts of the parent. The unamortized portion of the original acquisition-date fair-value allocations are included along with current excess amortization expenses. The investment and equity income balances are both eliminated as are the subsidiary's stockholders' equity accounts. Intra-entity dividends are removed as are the existing receivable and payable balances between the two companies.

Consolidation Entry S

Once again, this first consolidation entry offsets reciprocal amounts representing the subsidiary's book value as of the beginning of the current year. Sun's January 1, 2020, stockholders'

EXHIBIT 3.6
Investment Account under Equity Method

PARROT COMPANY
Investment in Sun Company Account
As of December 31, 2020
Equity Method Applied

Fair value of consideration transferred at date of acquisition		$ 800,000
Entries recorded in prior years:		
Accrual of Sun Company's income		
2017	$100,000	
2018	140,000	
2019	90,000	330,000
Sun Company—Dividends declared		
2017	$ (40,000)	
2018	(50,000)	
2019	(20,000)	(110,000)
Excess amortization expenses		
2017	$ (7,000)	
2018	(7,000)	
2019	(7,000)	(21,000)
Entries recorded in current year—2020		
Accrual of Sun Company's income	$160,000	
Sun Company—Dividends declared	(70,000)	
Excess amortization expenses	(7,000)	83,000
Investment in Sun Company, 12/31/20		$1,082,000

EXHIBIT 3.7 Consolidation Worksheet Subsequent to Year of Acquisition—Equity Method Applied

PARROT COMPANY AND SUN COMPANY
Consolidation Worksheet
For Year Ending December 31, 2020

Investment: Equity Method

Accounts	Parrot Company	Sun Company	Consolidation Entries Debit	Consolidation Entries Credit	Consolidation Totals
Income Statement					
Revenues	(2,100,000)	(600,000)			(2,700,000)
Cost of goods sold	1,000,000	380,000			1,380,000
Amortization expense	200,000	20,000	(E) 13,000		233,000
Depreciation expense	100,000	40,000		(E) 6,000	134,000
Equity in subsidiary earnings	(153,000)	-0-	(I) 153,000		-0-
Net income	(953,000)	(160,000)			(953,000)
Statement of Retained Earnings					
Retained earnings, 1/1/20	(2,044,000)	(600,000)	(S) 600,000		(2,044,000)
Net income (above)	(953,000)	(160,000)			(953,000)
Dividends declared	420,000	70,000		(D) 70,000	420,000
Retained earnings, 12/31/20	(2,577,000)	(690,000)			(2,577,000)
Balance Sheet					
Current assets	1,705,000	500,000		(P) 40,000	2,165,000
Investment in Sun Company	1,082,000	-0-	(D) 70,000	(S) 820,000	-0-
				(A) 179,000	
				(I) 153,000	
Trademarks	600,000	240,000	(A) 20,000		860,000
Patented technology	540,000	420,000	(A) 91,000	(E) 13,000	1,038,000
Equipment (net)	420,000	210,000	(E) 6,000	(A) 12,000	624,000
Goodwill	-0-	-0-	(A) 80,000		80,000
Total assets	4,347,000	1,370,000			4,767,000
Liabilities	(1,050,000)	(460,000)	(P) 40,000		(1,470,000)
Common stock	(600,000)	(200,000)	(S) 200,000		(600,000)
Additional paid-in capital	(120,000)	(20,000)	(S) 20,000		(120,000)
Retained earnings, 12/31/20 (above)	(2,577,000)	(690,000)			(2,577,000)
Total liabilities and equities	(4,347,000)	(1,370,000)	1,293,000	1,293,000	(4,767,000)

Note: Parentheses indicate a credit balance.
Consolidation entries:
(S) Elimination of Sun's stockholders' equity January 1 balances and the book value portion of the investment account.
(A) Allocation of Sun's acquisition-date excess fair values over book values, unamortized balance as of beginning of year.
(I) Elimination of parent's equity in subsidiary earnings accrual.
(D) Elimination of intra-entity dividends.
(E) Recognition of current year excess fair-value amortization and depreciation expenses.
(P) Elimination of intra-entity receivable/payable.

equity accounts are eliminated against the book value portion of the parent's investment account. Here, though, the amount eliminated is $820,000 rather than the $600,000 shown in Exhibit 3.5 for 2017. Both balances have changed during the 2017–2019 period. Sun's operations caused a $220,000 increase in retained earnings. Parrot's application of the equity method created a parallel effect on its Investment in Sun Company account (the income accrual of $330,000 less dividends collected of $110,000).

Although Sun's Retained Earnings balance is removed in this entry, the income this company earned since the acquisition date is still included in the consolidated figures. Parrot accrues these profits annually through application of the equity method. Thus, elimination of the subsidiary's entire Retained Earnings is necessary; a portion was earned prior to the acquisition and the remainder has already been recorded by the parent.

Entry **S** removes these balances as of the first day of 2020 rather than at the end of the year. The consolidation process is made a bit simpler by segregating the effect of preceding operations from the transactions of the current year. Thus, *all worksheet entries relate specifically to either the previous years (**S** and **A**) or the current period (**I, D, E,** and **P**).*

Consolidation Entry A

In the initial consolidation (2017), fair-value allocations amounting to $200,000 were entered, but these balances have now undergone three years of amortization. As computed in Exhibit 3.8, expenses for these prior years totaled $21,000, leaving a balance of $179,000. Allocation of this amount to the individual accounts is also determined in Exhibit 3.8 and reflected in worksheet Entry **A.** As with Entry **S,** these balances are calculated as of January 1, 2020, and replaced by current year expenses as shown in Entry **E.**

Consolidation Entry I

As before, this entry eliminates the equity income recorded currently by Parrot ($153,000) in connection with its ownership of Sun. The subsidiary's revenue and expense accounts are left intact so they can be included in the consolidated figures.

Consolidation Entry D

This worksheet entry offsets the $70,000 intra-entity dividends (from Sun to Parrot) during the current period.

Consolidation Entry E

Excess amortization expenses relating to acquisition-date fair-value adjustments are individually recorded for the current period.

Before progressing to the final worksheet entry, note the close similarity of these entries with the five entries incorporated in the 2017 consolidation (Exhibit 3.5). Except for the numerical changes created by the passage of time, the entries are identical.

Consolidation Entry P

This last entry (labeled "Entry **P**" because it eliminates an intra-entity **P**ayable) introduces a new element to the consolidation process. As noted earlier, intra-entity reciprocal accounts do not relate to outside parties. Therefore, Sun's $40,000 payable and Parrot's $40,000 receivable must be removed on the worksheet because the companies are being reported as a single entity.

In reviewing Exhibit 3.7, note several aspects of the consolidation process:

- The stockholders' equity accounts of the subsidiary are removed.
- The Investment in Sun Company and the Equity in Subsidiary Earnings are both removed.
- The parent's Retained Earnings balance is not adjusted. Because the parent applies the equity method this account should be correct.
- The acquisition-date fair-value adjustments to the subsidiary's assets are recognized but only after adjustment for prior periods' annual excess amortization expenses.
- Intra-entity balances such as dividends and receivables/payables are offset.

EXHIBIT 3.8
Excess Amortizations Relating to Individual Accounts as of January 1, 2020

		Annual Excess Amortizations			
Accounts	**Original Allocation**	**2017**	**2018**	**2019**	**Balance 1/1/20**
Trademarks	$ 20,000	$ –0–	$ –0–	$ –0–	$ 20,000
Patented technology	130,000	13,000	13,000	13,000	91,000
Equipment	(30,000)	(6,000)	(6,000)	(6,000)	(12,000)
Goodwill	80,000	–0–	–0–	–0–	80,000
	$200,000	$ 7,000	$ 7,000	$ 7,000	$179,000
			$21,000		

LO 3-3b

Prepare consolidated financial statements subsequent to acquisition when the parent has applied **the initial value method** in its internal records.

LO 3-3c

Prepare consolidated financial statements subsequent to acquisition when the parent has applied **the partial equity method** in its internal records.

Subsequent Consolidations—Investment Recorded Using Initial Value or Partial Equity Method

Acquisition Made during the Current Year

As discussed at the beginning of this chapter, the parent company may opt to use the initial value method or the partial equity method for internal record-keeping rather than the equity method. Application of either alternative changes the balances recorded by the parent over time and, thus, the procedures followed in creating consolidations. However, *choosing one of these other approaches does not affect any of the final consolidated figures to be reported.*

When a company utilizes the equity method, it eliminates all reciprocal accounts, assigns unamortized fair-value allocations to specific accounts, and records amortization expense for the current year. Application of either the initial value method or the partial equity method has no effect on this basic process. For this reason, a number of the consolidation entries remain the same regardless of the parent's investment accounting method.

In reality, just three of the parent's accounts actually vary because of the method applied:

- The investment account.
- The income recognized from the subsidiary.
- The parent's retained earnings (in periods after the initial year of the combination).

Only the differences found in these balances affect the consolidation process when another method is applied. Thus, any time after the acquisition date, accounting for these three balances is of special importance.

To illustrate the modifications required by the adoption of an alternative accounting method, the consolidation of Parrot and Sun as of December 31, 2017, is reconstructed. Only one differing factor is introduced: the method by which Parrot accounts for its investment. Exhibit 3.9 presents the 2017 consolidation based on Parrot's use of the initial value method. Exhibit 3.10 demonstrates this same process assuming that the parent applied the partial equity method. Each entry on these worksheets is labeled to correspond with the 2017 consolidation in which the parent used the equity method (Exhibit 3.5). Furthermore, differences with the equity method (both on the parent company records and with the consolidation entries) are highlighted on each of the worksheets.

Initial Value Method Applied—2017 Consolidation

Although the initial value method theoretically stands in marked contrast to the equity method, few reporting differences actually exist. In the year of acquisition, Parrot's income and investment accounts relating to the subsidiary are the only accounts affected.

Under the initial value method, income recognition in 2017 is limited to the $40,000 dividend received by the parent; no equity income accrual is made. At the same time, the investment account retains its $800,000 initial value. Unlike the equity method, no adjustments are recorded in the parent's investment account in connection with the current year operations, subsidiary dividends, or amortization of any fair-value allocations.

After the composition of the dividend income and investment accounts has been established, worksheet entries can be used to produce the consolidated figures found in Exhibit 3.9 as of December 31, 2017.

Consolidation Entry S

As with the previous Entry **S** in Exhibit 3.5, the $600,000 component of the investment account is eliminated against the beginning stockholders' equity account of the subsidiary. Both are equivalent to Sun's net assets at January 1, 2017, and are, therefore, reciprocal balances that must be offset. This entry is not affected by the accounting method in use.

Consolidation Entry A

Sun's $200,000 excess acquisition-date fair value over book value is allocated to Sun's assets and liabilities based on their fair values at the date of acquisition. The $80,000 residual is

EXHIBIT 3.9 Consolidation Worksheet—Initial Value Method Applied

PARROT COMPANY AND SUN COMPANY
Consolidation Worksheet
For Year Ending December 31, 2017

Investment: Initial Value Method

Accounts	Parrot Company	Sun Company	Consolidation Entries Debit	Consolidation Entries Credit	Consolidation Totals
Income Statement					
Revenues	(1,500,000)	(400,000)			(1,900,000)
Cost of goods sold	700,000	232,000			932,000
Amortization expense	120,000	32,000	(E) 13,000		165,000
Depreciation expense	80,000	36,000		(E) 6,000	110,000
Dividend income	(40,000)*	–0–	(I) 40,000*		–0–
Net income	(640,000)	(100,000)			(693,000)
Statement of Retained Earnings					
Retained earnings, 1/1/17	(840,000)	(380,000)	(S) 380,000		(840,000)
Net income (above)	(640,000)	(100,000)			(693,000)
Dividends declared	120,000	40,000		(I) 40,000*	120,000
Retained earnings, 12/31/17	(1,360,000)	(440,000)			(1,413,000)
Balance Sheet					
Current assets	1,040,000	400,000			1,440,000
Investment in Sun Company	800,000*	–0–		(S) 600,000 (A) 200,000	–0–
Trademarks	600,000	200,000	(A) 20,000		820,000
Patented technology	370,000	288,000	(A) 130,000	(E) 13,000	775,000
Equipment (net)	250,000	220,000	(E) 6,000	(A) 30,000	446,000
Goodwill	–0–	–0–	(A) 80,000		80,000
Total assets	3,060,000	1,108,000			3,561,000
Liabilities	(980,000)	(448,000)			(1,428,000)
Common stock	(600,000)	(200,000)	(S) 200,000		(600,000)
Additional paid-in capital	(120,000)	(20,000)	(S) 20,000		(120,000)
Retained earnings, 12/31/17 (above)	(1,360,000)	(440,000)			(1,413,000)
Total liabilities and equities	(3,060,000)	(1,108,000)	889,000	889,000	(3,561,000)

Note: Parentheses indicate a credit balance.
*Boxed items highlight differences with consolidation in Exhibit 3.5.
Consolidation entries:
(S) Elimination of Sun's stockholders' equity January 1 balances and the book value portion of the investment account.
(A) Allocation of Sun's acquisition-date excess fair values over book values.
(I) Elimination of intra-entity dividend income and dividends declared by Sun.
(E) Recognition of current year excess fair-value amortization and depreciation expenses.
Note: Consolidation entry (D) is not needed when the parent applies the initial value method because entry (I) eliminates the intra-entity dividend effects.

attributed to goodwill. This procedure is identical to the corresponding entry in Exhibit 3.5 in which the equity method was applied.

Consolidation Entry I

Under the initial value method, the parent records dividends declared by the subsidiary as income. Entry **I** removes this Dividend Income account along with Sun's Dividends Declared. From a consolidated perspective, these two $40,000 balances represent an intra-entity transfer that had no financial impact outside of the entity. In contrast to the equity method, Parrot has not accrued subsidiary income, nor has amortization been recorded; thus, no further income elimination is needed.

EXHIBIT 3.10 Consolidation Worksheet—Partial Equity Method Applied

PARROT COMPANY AND SUN COMPANY
Consolidation Worksheet
For Year Ending December 31, 2017

Investment: Partial Equity Method

Accounts	Parrot Company	Sun Company	Consolidation Entries Debit	Consolidation Entries Credit	Consolidation Totals
Income Statement					
Revenues	(1,500,000)	(400,000)			(1,900,000)
Cost of goods sold	700,000	232,000			932,000
Amortization expense	120,000	32,000	(E) 13,000		165,000
Depreciation expense	80,000	36,000		(E) 6,000	110,000
Equity in subsidiary earnings	(100,000)*	-0-	(I) 100,000*		-0-
Net income	(700,000)	(100,000)			(693,000)
Statement of Retained Earnings					
Retained earnings, 1/1/17	(840,000)	(380,000)	(S) 380,000		(840,000)
Net income (above)	(700,000)	(100,000)			(693,000)
Dividends declared	120,000	40,000		(D) 40,000	120,000
Retained earnings, 12/31/17	(1,420,000)	(440,000)			(1,413,000)
Balance Sheet					
Current assets	1,040,000	400,000			1,440,000
Investment in Sun Company	860,000*	-0-	(D) 40,000	(S) 600,000 (A) 200,000 (I) 100,000*	-0-
Trademarks	600,000	200,000	(A) 20,000		820,000
Patented technology	370,000	288,000	(A) 130,000	(E) 13,000	775,000
Equipment (net)	250,000	220,000	(E) 6,000	(A) 30,000	446,000
Goodwill	-0-	-0-	(A) 80,000		80,000
Total assets	3,120,000	1,108,000			3,561,000
Liabilities	(980,000)	(448,000)			(1,428,000)
Common stock	(600,000)	(200,000)	(S) 200,000		(600,000)
Additional paid-in capital	(120,000)	(20,000)	(S) 20,000		(120,000)
Retained earnings, 12/31/17 (above)	(1,420,000)	(440,000)			(1,413,000)
Total liabilities and equities	(3,120,000)	(1,108,000)	989,000	989,000	(3,561,000)

Note: Parentheses indicate a credit balance.
*Boxed items highlight differences with consolidation in Exhibit 3.5.
Consolidation entries:
(S) Elimination of Sun's stockholders' equity January 1 balances and the book value portion of the investment account.
(A) Allocation of Sun's acquisition-date excess fair values over book values.
(I) Elimination of parent's equity in subsidiary earnings accrual.
(D) Elimination of intra-entity dividends.
(E) Recognition of current year excess fair-value amortization and depreciation expenses.

Dividend Income	40,000	
Dividends Declared		40,000
To eliminate intra-entity income.		

Consolidation Entry D

When the initial value method is applied, the parent records intra-entity dividends as income. Because these dividends were already removed from the consolidated totals by Entry **I,** no separate Entry **D** is required.

Consolidation Entry E

Regardless of the parent's method of accounting, the reporting entity must recognize excess amortizations for the current year in connection with the original fair-value allocations. Thus, Entry **E** serves to bring the current year expenses into the consolidated financial statements.

Consequently, using the initial value method rather than the equity method changes only Entries **I** and **D** in the year of acquisition. Despite the change in methods, reported figures are still derived by (1) eliminating all reciprocals, (2) allocating the excess portion of the acquisition-date fair values, and (3) recording amortizations on these allocations. As indicated previously, the consolidated totals appearing in Exhibit 3.9 are identical to the figures produced previously in Exhibit 3.5. Although the income and the investment accounts on the parent company's separate statements vary, the consolidated balances are not affected.

One significant difference between the initial value method and equity method does exist: The parent's separate statements do not reflect consolidated income totals when the initial value method is used. Because equity adjustments (such as excess amortizations) are not recorded, neither Parrot's reported net income of $640,000 nor its retained earnings of $1,360,000 provides an accurate portrayal of consolidated figures.

Partial Equity Method Applied—2017 Consolidation

Exhibit 3.10 presents a worksheet to consolidate these two companies for 2017 (the year of acquisition) based on the assumption that Parrot applied the partial equity method. Again, the only changes from previous examples are found in (1) the parent's separate records for this investment and its related income and (2) worksheet Entries **I** and **D.**

As discussed earlier, under the partial equity approach, the parent's record-keeping is limited to two periodic journal entries: the annual accrual of subsidiary income and the recognition of dividends. Hence, within the parent's records, only a few differences exist when the partial equity method is applied rather than the initial value method. The entries recorded by Parrot in connection with Sun's 2017 operations illustrate both of these approaches.

Therefore, by applying the partial equity method, the investment account on the parent's balance sheet rises to $860,000 by the end of 2017. This total is composed of the original $800,000 acquisition-date fair value for Sun adjusted for the $100,000 income recognition and the $40,000 cash dividend. The same $100,000 equity income figure appears within the parent's income statement. These two balances are appropriately found in Parrot's records in Exhibit 3.10.

Because of differences in income recognition and the effects of subsidiary dividends, Entries **I** and **D** again differ on the worksheet. For the partial equity method, the $100,000 equity income is eliminated (Entry **I**) by reversing the parent's entry. Removing this accrual allows the individual revenue and expense accounts of the subsidiary to be reported without double-counting. The $40,000 intra-entity dividend must also be removed (Entry **D**). The Dividends Declared account is simply deleted. However, elimination of the dividend from the

Parrot Company
Initial Value Method 2017

Dividend Receivable	40,000	
Dividend Income......		40,000
Subsidiary dividends declared.		
Cash	40,000	
Dividend Receivable ..		40,000
To record the receipt of the cash dividend.		

Parrot Company
Partial Equity Method 2017

Dividend Receivable	40,000	
Investment in Sun Company		40,000
Subsidiary dividends declared.		
Cash	40,000	
Dividend Receivable ..		40,000
To record the receipt of the cash dividend.		
Investment in Sun Company	100,000	
Equity in Subsidiary Earnings		100,000
Accrual of subsidiary income.		

Investment in Sun Company actually causes an increase because the dividend was recorded by Parrot as a reduction in that account. All other consolidation entries (Entries **S**, **A**, and **E**) are the same for all three methods.

LO 3-4

Understand that a parent's internal accounting method for its subsidiary investments has no effect on the resulting consolidated financial statements.

Comparisons across Internal Investment Methods

Consolidated financial worksheets have now been completed when the parent uses the equity, initial value, and partial equity methods. At this point it is instructive to compare the final consolidated balances in Exhibits 3.5, 3.9, and 3.10. Note the identical final consolidated column balances across the three internal methods of investment accounting. Thus, the parent's internal investment method choice has no effect on the resulting consolidated financial statements.

Consolidation Subsequent to Year of Acquisition—Initial Value and Partial Equity Methods

By again incorporating the December 31, 2020, financial data for Parrot and Sun (presented in Exhibit 3.7), consolidation procedures for the initial value method and the partial equity method are examined for years subsequent to the date of acquisition. *In both cases, establishment of an appropriate beginning retained earnings figure becomes a significant goal of the consolidation.*

Conversion of the Parent's Retained Earnings to a Full-Accrual (Equity) Basis

Consolidated financial statements require a *full accrual-based measurement of both income and retained earnings.* The initial value method, however, recognizes income when the subsidiary declares a dividend thus ignoring when the underlying income was earned. The partial equity method only partially accrues subsidiary income. Thus, neither provides a full accrual-based measure of the subsidiary activities on the parent's income. As a result, over time the parent's retained earnings account fails to show a full accrual-based amount. Therefore, new worksheet adjustments are required to convert the parent's beginning of the year retained earnings balance to a full-accrual basis. These adjustments are made to *beginning of the year retained earnings* because current year earnings are readily converted to full-accrual basis by simply combining current year revenue and expenses. The resulting current year combined income figure is then added to the adjusted beginning of the year retained earnings to arrive at a full-accrual ending retained earnings balance.

This concern was not faced previously when the equity method was adopted. Under that approach, the parent's Retained Earnings account balance already reflects a full-accrual basis so that no adjustment is necessary. In the earlier illustration, the $330,000 income accrual for the 2017–2019 period as well as the $21,000 amortization expense was recognized by the parent in applying the equity method (see Exhibit 3.6). Having been recorded in this manner, these two balances form a permanent part of Parrot's retained earnings and are included automatically in the consolidated total. Consequently, if the equity method is applied, the process is simplified; no worksheet entries are needed to adjust the parent's Retained Earnings account to record subsidiary operations or amortization for past years.

Conversely, if a method other than the equity method is used, a worksheet change must be made to the parent's beginning Retained Earnings account (in every subsequent year) to equate this balance with a full-accrual amount. To quantify this adjustment, the parent's recognized income for these past three years under each method is first determined (Exhibit 3.11). For consolidation purposes, the beginning retained earnings account must then be increased or decreased to create the same effect as the equity method.

EXHIBIT 3.11
Retained Earnings Differences

PARROT COMPANY AND SUN COMPANY
Previous Years—2017–2019

	Equity Method	Initial Value Method	Partial Equity Method
Equity accrual	$330,000	$ –0–	$330,000
Dividend income	–0–	110,000	–0–
Excess amortization expenses	(21,000)	–0–	–0–
Increase in parent's retained earnings	$309,000	$110,000	$330,000

Initial Value Method Applied—Subsequent Consolidation

As shown in Exhibit 3.11, if Parrot applied the initial value method during the 2017–2019 period, it recognizes $199,000 less income than under the equity method ($309,000 – $110,000). Two items cause this difference. First, Parrot has not accrued the $220,000 increase in the subsidiary's book value across the periods prior to the current year. Although the $110,000 in dividends was recorded as income, the parent never recognized the remainder of the $330,000 earned by the subsidiary.[7] Second, no accounting has been made of the $21,000 excess amortization expenses. Thus, the parent's beginning Retained Earnings account is $199,000 ($220,000 – $21,000) below the appropriate consolidated total and must be adjusted.[8]

To simulate the equity method so that the parent's beginning Retained Earnings account reflects a full-accrual basis, this $199,000 increase is recorded through a worksheet entry. The initial value method figures reported by the parent effectively are converted into equity method balances.

Investment in Sun Company	199,000	
Retained Earnings, 1/1/20 (Parrot Company)		199,000
To convert parent's beginning retained earnings from the initial value method to equity method.		

This adjustment is labeled Entry ***C.** The *C* refers to the **c**onversion being made to equity method (full-accrual) totals. The asterisk indicates that this equity simulation relates solely to transactions of prior periods. Thus, *Entry *C should be recorded before the other worksheet entries to align the beginning balances for the year.*

Exhibit 3.12 provides a complete presentation of the consolidation of Parrot and Sun as of December 31, 2020, based on the parent's application of the initial value method. After Entry ***C** has been recorded on the worksheet, the remainder of this consolidation follows the same pattern as previous examples. Sun's stockholders' equity accounts are eliminated (Entry **S**) while the allocations stemming from the $800,000 initial fair value are recorded (Entry **A**) at their unamortized balances as of January 1, 2020 (see Exhibit 3.8). Intra-entity dividend income is removed (Entry **I**) and current year excess amortization expenses are recognized (Entry **E**). To complete this process, the intra-entity receivable and payable of $40,000 are offset (Entry **P**).

In retrospect, the only new element introduced here is the adjustment of the parent's beginning Retained Earnings. For a consolidation produced after the initial year of acquisition, an Entry ***C** is required if the parent has not applied the equity method.

Partial Equity Method Applied—Subsequent Consolidation

Exhibit 3.13 demonstrates the worksheet consolidation of Parrot and Sun as of December 31, 2020, when the investment accounts have been recorded by the parent using the partial equity method. This approach accrues subsidiary income each year but records no other equity adjustments. Therefore, as of December 31, 2020, Parrot's Investment in Sun Company account has a balance of $1,110,000:

[7] Two different calculations are available for determining the $220,000 in nonrecorded income for prior years: (1) subsidiary income less dividends declared and (2) the change in the subsidiary's book value as of the first day of the current year. The second method works only if the subsidiary has had no other equity transactions such as the issuance of new stock or the purchase of treasury shares. Unless otherwise stated, the assumption is made that no such transactions have occurred.

[8] Because neither the income in excess of dividends nor excess amortization is recorded by the parent under the initial value method, its beginning Retained Earnings account is $199,000 less than the $2,044,000 reported under the equity method (Exhibit 3.7). Thus, a $1,845,000 balance is shown in Exhibit 3.12 ($2,044,000 less $199,000). Conversely, if the partial equity method had been applied, Parrot's absence of amortization would cause the Retained Earnings account to be $21,000 higher than the figure derived by the equity method. For this reason, Exhibit 3.13 shows the parent with a beginning Retained Earnings account of $2,065,000 rather than $2,044,000.

Fair value of consideration transferred for Sun Company 1/1/17		$ 800,000
Sun Company's 2017–2019 increase in book value:		
Accrual of Sun Company's income	$330,000	
Sun Company's dividends	(110,000)	220,000
Sun Company's 2020 operations:		
Accrual of Sun Company's income	$160,000	
Sun Company's dividends	(70,000)	90,000
Investment in Sun Company, 12/31/20 (Partial equity method)		$1,110,000

EXHIBIT 3.12 Consolidation Worksheet Subsequent to Year of Acquisition—Initial Value Method Applied

PARROT COMPANY AND SUN COMPANY
Consolidation Worksheet
For Year Ending December 31, 2020

Investment: Initial Value Method

Accounts	Parrot Company	Sun Company	Consolidation Entries Debit	Consolidation Entries Credit	Consolidation Totals
Income Statement					
Revenues	(2,100,000)	(600,000)			(2,700,000)
Cost of goods sold	1,000,000	380,000			1,380,000
Amortization expense	200,000	20,000	(E) 13,000		233,000
Depreciation expense	100,000	40,000		(E) 6,000	134,000
Dividend income	(70,000)*	–0–	(I) 70,000*		–0–
Net income	(870,000)	(160,000)			(953,000)
Statement of Retained Earnings					
Retained earnings, 1/1/20					
Parrot Company	(1,845,000)†*			(*C) 199,000*	(2,044,000)
Sun Company		(600,000)	(S) 600,000		–0–
Net income (above)	(870,000)	(160,000)			(953,000)
Dividends declared	420,000	70,000		(I) 70,000*	420,000
Retained earnings, 12/31/20	(2,295,000)	(690,000)			(2,577,000)
Balance Sheet					
Current assets	1,705,000	500,000		(P) 40,000	2,165,000
Investment in Sun Company	800,000*	–0–	(*C) 199,000	(S) 820,000 (A) 179,000	–0–
Trademarks	600,000	240,000	(A) 20,000		860,000
Patented technology	540,000	420,000	(A) 91,000	(E) 13,000	1,038,000
Equipment (net)	420,000	210,000	(E) 6,000	(A) 12,000	624,000
Goodwill	–0–	–0–	(A) 80,000		80,000
Total assets	4,065,000	1,370,000			4,767,000
Liabilities	(1,050,000)	(460,000)	(P) 40,000		(1,470,000)
Common stock	(600,000)	(200,000)	(S) 200,000		(600,000)
Additional paid-in capital	(120,000)	(20,000)	(S) 20,000		(120,000)
Retained earnings, 12/31/20 (above)	(2,295,000)	(690,000)			(2,577,000)
Total liabilities and equities	(4,065,000)	(1,370,000)	1,339,000	1,339,000	(4,767,000)

Note: Parentheses indicate a credit balance.
*Boxed items highlight differences with consolidation in Exhibit 3.7.
†See footnote 8.
Consolidation entries:
(*C) To convert parent's beginning retained earnings to full accrual basis.
(S) Elimination of Sun's stockholders' equity January 1 balances and the book value portion of investment account.
(A) Allocation of Sun's excess acquisition-date fair value over book value, unamortized balance as of beginning of year.
(I) Elimination of intra-entity dividend income and dividends declared by Sun.
(E) Recognition of current year excess fair-value amortization and depreciation expenses.
(P) Elimination of intra-entity receivable/payable.
Note: Consolidation entry (D) is not needed when the parent applies the initial value method because entry (I) eliminates the intra-entity dividend effects.

EXHIBIT 3.13 Consolidation Worksheet Subsequent to Year of Acquisition—Partial Equity Method Applied

PARROT COMPANY AND SUN COMPANY
Consolidation Worksheet
For Year Ending December 31, 2020

Investment: Partial Equity Method

Accounts	Parrot Company	Sun Company	Consolidation Entries Debit	Consolidation Entries Credit	Consolidation Totals
Income Statement					
Revenues	(2,100,000)	(600,000)			(2,700,000)
Cost of goods sold	1,000,000	380,000			1,380,000
Amortization expense	200,000	20,000	(E) 13,000		233,000
Depreciation expense	100,000	40,000		(E) 6,000	134,000
Equity in subsidiary earnings	(160,000)*	-0-	(I) 160,000*		-0-
Net income	(960,000)	(160,000)			(953,000)
Statement of Retained Earnings					
Retained earnings, 1/1/20					
Parrot Company	(2,065,000)†*		(*C) 21,000*		(2,044,000)
Sun Company		(600,000)	(S) 600,000		-0-
Net income (above)	(960,000)	(160,000)			(953,000)
Dividends declared	420,000	70,000		(D) 70,000*	420,000
Retained earnings, 12/31/20	(2,605,000)	(690,000)			(2,577,000)
Balance Sheet					
Current assets	1,705,000	500,000		(P) 40,000	2,165,000
Investment in Sun Company	1,110,000*	-0-	(D) 70,000	(*C) 21,000*	-0-
				(S) 820,000	
				(A) 179,000	
				(I) 160,000*	
Trademarks	600,000	240,000	(A) 20,000		860,000
Patented technology	540,000	420,000	(A) 91,000	(E) 13,000	1,038,000
Equipment (net)	420,000	210,000	(E) 6,000	(A) 12,000	624,000
Goodwill	-0-	-0-	(A) 80,000		80,000
Total assets	4,375,000	1,370,000			4,767,000
Liabilities	(1,050,000)	(460,000)	(P) 40,000		(1,470,000)
Common stock	(600,000)	(200,000)	(S) 200,000		(600,000)
Additional paid-in capital	(120,000)	(20,000)	(S) 20,000		(120,000)
Retained earnings, 12/31/20 (above)	(2,605,000)	(690,000)			(2,577,000)
Total liabilities and equities	(4,375,000)	(1,370,000)	1,321,000	1,321,000	(4,767,000)

Note: Parentheses indicate a credit balance.
*Boxed items highlight differences with consolidation in Exhibit 3.7.
†See footnote 8.
Consolidation entries:
(*C) To convert parent's beginning retained earnings to full accrual basis.
(S) Elimination of Sun's stockholders' equity January 1 balances and the book value portion of investment account.
(A) Allocation of Sun's excess acquisition-date fair over book value, unamortized balance as of beginning of year.
(I) Elimination of parent's equity in subsidiary earnings accrual.
(D) Elimination of intra-entity dividends.
(E) Recognition of current year excess fair-value amortization and depreciation expenses.
(P) Elimination of intra-entity receivable/payable.

As indicated here and in Exhibit 3.11, Parrot has recognized the yearly equity income accrual but not amortization. When the parent employs the partial equity method, the parent's beginning Retained Earnings account must be adjusted to include this expense. Therefore, Entry ***C** provides the three-year $21,000 amortization total to simulate the equity method and, hence, consolidated totals.

Discussion Question

In consolidation worksheet entry *C, we adjust the parent's *beginning of the year* retained earnings to a full accrual basis. Why don't we adjust to the parent's *end of the year* retained earnings balance on the consolidated worksheet?

Clearly, in a consolidated balance sheet, we wish to report the parent's end-of-period consolidated retained earnings at its full accrual GAAP basis. To accomplish this goal, we utilize the following separate individual components of end-of-period retained earnings available on the worksheet.

Beginning of the year balance (after *C adjustment if parent does not employ equity method)
+ Net income (parent's share of consolidated net income adjusted to full accrual by combining revenues and expenses—including excess acquisition-date fair value amortizations)
− Dividends (parent's dividends)
= End of the year balance

The worksheet provides for the computation of current year full accrual consolidated net income via the income statement section. Dividends are already provided in the retained earnings section of the consolidated worksheet. The only component of the ending balance of retained earnings that requires a special adjustment (*C) is the beginning balance.

How does the consolidation worksheet entry *C differ when the parent uses the initial value method versus the partial equity method? Why is no *C adjustment needed when consolidated statements are prepared for the first fiscal year-end after the business combination?

*Consolidation Entry *C*

Retained Earnings, 1/1/20 (Parrot Company)	21,000	
Investment in Sun Company		21,000
To convert parent's beginning Retained Earnings from partial equity method to equity method by including excess amortizations.		

By recording Entry ***C** on the worksheet, all of the subsidiary's operational results for the 2017–2019 period are included in the consolidation. As shown in Exhibit 3.13, the remainder of the worksheet entries follow the same basic pattern as that illustrated previously for the year of acquisition (Exhibit 3.10).

Summary of Worksheet Procedures

Having three investment methods available to the parent means that three sets of entries must be understood to arrive at reported figures appropriate for a business combination. The process can initially seem to be a confusing overlap of procedures. However, at this point in the coverage, only three worksheet entries actually are affected by the choice of either the equity method, partial equity method, or initial value method: Entries ***C, I,** and **D.** Furthermore, accountants should never get so involved with a worksheet and its entries that they lose sight of the balances that this process is designed to calculate. Exhibit 3.14 provides a summary of the final consolidated totals and how they are calculated. These figures are never affected by the parent's choice of an accounting method.

After the appropriate balance for each account is understood, worksheet entries assist the accountant in deriving these figures. To help clarify the consolidation process required under each of the three accounting methods, Exhibit 3.14 describes the purpose of each worksheet entry: first during the year of acquisition and second for any period following the year of acquisition.

Discussion Question

HOW DOES A COMPANY REALLY DECIDE WHICH INVESTMENT METHOD TO APPLY?

Pilgrim Products, Inc., buys a controlling interest in the common stock of Crestwood Corporation. Shortly after the acquisition, a meeting of Pilgrim's accounting department is convened to discuss the internal reporting procedures required by the ownership of this subsidiary. Each member of the staff has a definite opinion as to whether the equity method, initial value method, or partial equity method should be adopted. To resolve this issue, Pilgrim's chief financial officer outlines several of her concerns about the decision.

> I already understand how each method works. I know the general advantages and disadvantages of all three. I realize, for example, that the equity method provides more detailed information whereas the initial value method is much easier to apply. What I need to know are the factors specific to our situation that should be considered in deciding which method to adopt. I must make a recommendation to the president on this matter, and he will want firm reasons for my favoring a particular approach. I don't want us to select a method and then find out in six months that the information is not adequate for our needs or that the cost of adapting our system to monitor Crestwood outweighs the benefits derived from the data.

What are the factors that Pilgrim's officials should evaluate when making this decision?

EXHIBIT 3.14
Consolidated Totals Subsequent to Acquisition*

Current revenues	Parent revenues are included. Subsidiary revenues are included but only for the period since the acquisition.
Current expenses	Parent expenses are included. Subsidiary expenses are included but only for the period since the acquisition. Amortization expenses of the excess fair-value allocations are included by recognition on the worksheet.
Investment (or dividend) income	Income recognized by parent is eliminated and effectively replaced by the subsidiary's revenues and expenses.
Retained earnings, beginning balance	Parent balance is included. The change in the subsidiary balance since acquisition is included either as a regular accrual by the parent or through a worksheet entry to increase parent balance. Past amortization expenses of the excess fair-value allocations are included either as a part of parent balance or through a worksheet entry.
Assets and liabilities	Parent balances are included. Subsidiary balances are included after adjusting for acquisition-date fair values less amortization to beginning of current period. Intra-entity receivable/payable balances are eliminated.
Goodwill Investment in subsidiary	Original fair-value allocation is included unless reduced by impairment. Asset account recorded by parent is eliminated on the worksheet so that the balance is not included in consolidated figures.
Capital stock and additional paid-in capital	Parent balances only are included although they will have been adjusted at acquisition date if stock was issued.

*The next few chapters discuss the necessity of altering some of these balances for consolidation purposes. Thus, this table is not definitive but is included only to provide a basic overview of the consolidation process as it has been described to this point.

EXHIBIT 3.15 Consolidation Worksheet Entries

Equity Method Applied		Initial Value Method Applied	Partial Equity Method Applied
Any Time during Year of Acquisition			
Entry **S**	Beginning stockholders' equity of subsidiary is eliminated against book value portion of investment account.	Same as equity method.	Same as equity method.
Entry **A**	Excess fair value is allocated to assets and liabilities based on difference in book values and fair values; residual is assigned to goodwill.	Same as equity method.	Same as equity method.
Entry **I**	Equity income accrual (including amortization expense) is eliminated.	Dividend income is eliminated.	Equity income accrual is eliminated.
Entry **D**	Intra-entity dividends declared by subsidiary are eliminated.	No entry—intra-entity dividends are eliminated in Entry **I.**	Same as equity method.
Entry **E**	Current year excess amortization expenses of fair-value allocations are recorded.	Same as equity method.	Same as equity method.
Entry **P**	Intra-entity payable/receivable balances are offset.	Same as equity method.	Same as equity method.
Any Time Following Year of Acquisition			
Entry ***C**	No entry—equity income for prior years has already been recognized along with amortization expenses.	Increase in subsidiary's book value during prior years and excess amortization expenses are recognized (conversion is made to equity method).	Excess amortization expenses for prior years are recognized (conversion is made to equity method).
Entry **S**	Same as initial year.	Same as initial year.	Same as initial year.
Entry **A**	Unamortized excess fair value at beginning of year is allocated to specific accounts and to goodwill.	Same as equity method.	Same as equity method.
Entry **I**	Same as initial year.	Same as initial year.	Same as initial year.
Entry **D**	Same as initial year.	Same as initial year.	Same as initial year.
Entry **E**	Same as initial year.	Same as initial year.	Same as initial year.
Entry **P**	Same as initial year.	Same as initial year.	Same as initial year.

Excess Fair Value Attributable to Subsidiary Long-Term Debt: Post-Acquisition Procedures

In the previous consolidation examples for Parrot and Sun Company, the acquisition-date excess fair values were attributed solely to long-term assets. Similarly, however, the acquisition-date fair value of subsidiary long-term debt may also differ from its carrying amount. Although the long-term debt adjustment to fair value is relatively straightforward, the adjustments to interest expense in periods subsequent to acquisition require additional analysis.

In subsequent periods, the acquisition-date fair value adjustment to long-term debt is amortized to interest expense over the remaining life of the debt. When the acquisition-date fair value of subsidiary long-term debt exceeds its carrying amount on the subsidiary's books, the parent increases the value of the debt reported on its consolidated balance sheet (and vice-versa). Consequently, when the parent reflects the increased value of the subsidiary's long-term debt valuation, it must reduce interest expense recognized on the consolidated income statement over the debt's remaining life. When the long-term debt valuation is decreased, interest expense increases.

Exhibit 3.16 summarizes the worksheet effects when acquisition-date long-term debt's carrying amount differs from its fair value.

EXHIBIT 3.16 Long-Term Debt: Consolidation Worksheet Adjustments

Long-Term Debt Valuation at Acquisition Date	Worksheet Adjustment to Long-Term Debt	Worksheet Adjustment to Interest Expense
Fair value > Carrying amount	Increase long-term debt to adjust to fair value (less previous periods interest amortization)	Debit Long-Term Debt and credit Interest Expense
Fair value < Carrying amount	Decrease long-term debt to adjust to fair value (less previous periods interest amortization)	Debit Interest Expense and credit Long-Term Debt

At first glance, it may seem counterintuitive that when long-term debt is ***increased,*** interest expense is ***decreased.*** Certainly for plant assets like equipment, when we increase their carrying amounts to acquisition-date fair values on the worksheet, we increase the related depreciation expense. Why do we seem to do the opposite for long-term liabilities?

The answer can be seen in the fact that even though the acquisition-date value of the subsidiary's long-term debt exceeds its carrying amount, the acquisition does not affect the subsidiary's contractual obligation for repaying the debt. The ultimate amount of debt to be repaid at maturity remains the same. For example, assume Pax Company acquires Sax Company on January 1, 2017. Exhibit 3.17 provides information about Sax Company's long-term debt:

EXHIBIT 3.17
Acquisition-Date Long-Term Debt Valuation

	Long-Term Debt January 1, 2017	Long-Term Debt Maturity Value January 1, 2022
Fair value	$105,000	$100,000
Carrying amount	100,000	100,000

By acquiring Sax, Pax has taken on $105,000 of fair value debt, but will only have to pay back $100,000 at the debt's maturity date. As shown in Exhibit 3.18, the additional $5,000 excess fair over book value (that will not be repaid) is recognized as a reduction in overall interest expense, similar to amortizing a bond premium. Therefore, when consolidated statements are prepared, interest expense is reduced over the life of the long-term debt.

EXHIBIT 3.18
Worksheet Adjustments for Excess Acquisition-Date Fair Value Attributable to Subsidiary Long-Term Debt

December 31, 2017, Consolidation Worksheet		
Consolidation Entry A		
Investment in Sax Company	5,000	
Long-term debt		5,000
To adjust the subsidiary's long-term debt to acquisition-date fair value.		
Consolidation Entry E		
Long-term debt	1,000	
Interest expense		1,000
To recognize the reduction in current year interest expense		
December 31, 2018, Consolidation Worksheet		
Consolidation Entry A		
Investment in Sax Company	4,000	
Long-term debt		4,000
To adjust the subsidiary's long-term debt to unamortized balance as of the beginning of the year ($5,000 – $1,000 from year 2017).		
Consolidation Entry E		
Long-term debt	1,000	
Interest expense		1,000
To recognize the reduction in current year interest expense		

To complete this example, we assume the sole acquistion-date excess fair value adjustment made by Pax Company is to long-term debt, and straight-line amortization is used for the interest adjustments.

Finally, the carrying amount of a subsidiary's long-term debt may exceed its fair value. In that case, a consolidation entry is required to decrease the long-term debt reported in the consolidated balance sheet. Then, in periods subsequent to acquisition, worksheet entries are also needed to increase the amount of interest expense to be recognized in the consolidated income statement.

LO 3-5

Discuss the rationale for the goodwill impairment testing approach.

Goodwill Impairment

FASB ASC Topic 350, "Intangibles—Goodwill and Other," provides accounting standards for determining, measuring, and reporting goodwill impairment losses. Because goodwill is considered to have an indefinite life, an impairment approach is used rather than amortization. The FASB reasoned that although goodwill can decrease over time, it does not do so in the "rational and systematic" manner that periodic amortization suggests. Only upon recognition of an impairment loss (or partial sale of a subsidiary) will goodwill decline from one period to the next. Goodwill impairment losses are reported as operating items in the consolidated income statement.

The notion of an indefinite life allows many firms to report the original amount of goodwill recognized in a business combination. However, goodwill can become impaired, requiring loss recognition and a reduction in the amount reported in the consolidated balance sheet. Evidence shows that goodwill impairment losses can be substantial. Exhibit 3.19 provides examples of some recent goodwill impairment losses. Unlike amortization, which periodically reduces asset values, impairment must first be revealed before a write-down is justified. Accounting standards therefore require periodic tests for goodwill impairment.

Goodwill impairment tests are performed at the reporting unit level within a combined entity. As discussed next, all assets acquired (including goodwill) and liabilities assumed in a business combination must be assigned to *reporting units* within a consolidated enterprise. The goodwill residing in each reporting unit is then separately subjected to periodic impairment reviews. Current financial reporting standards require, at a minimum, an annual assessment for potential goodwill impairment.

Because impairment testing procedures can be costly, the FASB provides firms the option to first conduct a *qualitative* analysis to assess whether further testing procedures are appropriate. If circumstances indicate a potential decline in the fair value of a reporting unit below its carrying amount, then further tests are required to see if goodwill is the source of the decline. Our coverage of goodwill impairment addresses the following:

- The assignment of acquired goodwill to reporting units.
- The option to conduct an annual qualitative test for potential goodwill impairment.
- Goodwill impairment testing procedures.
- A FASB proposal to simplify goodwill impairment testing.
- Comparison with international accounting standards.

EXHIBIT 3.19
Recent Goodwill Impairments

Microsoft	$5.1 billion
Yahoo!	4.5 billion
Devon Energy	1.9 billion
Rent-a-Center	1.2 billion
Time, Inc.	952 million
J. Crew	676 million
Staples	410 million
The Hershey Company	31 million
Pep Boys	23.9 million

Assigning Goodwill to Reporting Units

Combined companies typically organize themselves into separate *units* along distinct operating lines. Each individual operating unit has responsibility for managing its assets and liabilities to earn profits for the combined entity. These operating units report information about their earnings activities to top management to support decision making. Such operating units are known as *reporting units*.

Following a business combination, the identifiable assets and liabilities acquired are assigned to the firm's reporting units based on where they will be employed. Any amount assigned to goodwill also is assigned to reporting units expected to benefit from the synergies of the combination. Thus, any individual reporting unit where goodwill resides is the appropriate level for goodwill impairment testing.

In practice, firms often assign goodwill to reporting units either at the level of a reporting segment—as described in ASC Topic 280, "Segment Reporting"—or at a lower level within a segment of a combined enterprise. Reporting units may thus include the following:

- A component of an operating segment at a level below that operating segment. Segment management should review and assess performance at this level. Also, the component should be a business in which discrete financial information is available and should differ economically from other components of the operating segment.
- The segments of an enterprise.
- The entire enterprise.

For example, Qorvo, Inc. is a wireless technology firm serving the mobile device, networks infrastructure, and defense and aerospace markets. In its recent annual report Qorvo identified its two business segments, MP and IDP (Mobile Products and Infrastructure and Defense Products), as its reporting units:

> For fiscal 2015, we have determined that our reporting units are MP and IDP for purposes of allocating and testing goodwill. . .Goodwill is allocated to our reporting units based on the expected benefit from the synergies of the business combinations generating the underlying goodwill.

Thus, all goodwill impairment testing is performed at the reporting unit level, rather than collectively at the combined entity level. Separate testing of goodwill within individual reporting units also prevents the masking of goodwill impairment in one reporting unit with contemporaneous increases in the value of goodwill in other reporting units.

LO 3-6

Describe the procedures for conducting a goodwill impairment test.

Qualitative Assessment Option

Because goodwill impairment tests require firms to calculate fair values for their reporting units each year, such a comprehensive measurement exercise can be costly. To help reduce costs, FASB ASC Topic 305 allows an entity the option to first assess qualitative factors to determine whether more rigorous testing for goodwill impairment is needed. The qualitative approach assesses the *likelihood* that a reporting unit's fair value is less than its carrying amount. The more-likely-than-not threshold is defined as having a likelihood of more than 50 percent.

In assessing whether a reporting unit's fair value exceeds its carrying amount, a firm must examine all relevant facts and circumstances, including

- Macroeconomic conditions such as a deterioration in general economic conditions, limitations on accessing capital, fluctuations in foreign exchange rates, or other developments in equity and credit markets.
- Industry and market considerations such as a deterioration in the environment in which an entity operates, an increased competitive environment, a decline (both absolute and relative to its peers) in market-dependent multiples or metrics, a change in the market for an entity's products or services, or a regulatory or political development.
- Cost factors such as increases in raw materials, labor, or other costs that have a negative effect on earnings.
- Overall financial performance such as negative or declining cash flows or a decline in actual or planned revenue or earnings.

- Other relevant entity-specific events such as changes in management, key personnel, strategy, or customers; contemplation of bankruptcy; or litigation.
- Events affecting a reporting unit such as a change in the carrying amount of its net assets, a more-likely-than-not expectation of selling or disposing all, or a portion of, a reporting unit, the testing for recoverability of a significant asset group within a reporting unit, or recognition of a goodwill impairment loss in the financial statements of a subsidiary that is a component of a reporting unit.
- If applicable, a sustained decrease (both absolute and relative to its peers) in share price. (FASB ASC para. 350-20-35-3C)

The underlying rationale for comparing a reporting unit's fair value and carrying amount is as follows. If a reporting unit's fair value is deemed greater than its carrying amount, then its collective net assets are maintaining their value. It then can be argued that a decline in any particular asset (i.e., goodwill) within the reporting unit is also unlikely and no further impairment tests are necessary. On the other hand, if the relevant facts and circumstances listed above suggest that a reporting unit's fair value is likely less than its carrying amount, then more rigorous testing for goodwill impairment is appropriate. Nonetheless, a qualitative assessment of a sufficient fair value for a reporting unit circumvents further goodwill impairment testing.

The FASB ASC (paragraph 350-20-35-28) requires an entity to assess its goodwill for impairment annually for each of its reporting units where goodwill resides. Moreover, more frequent impairment assessment is required if events or circumstances change that make it more likely than not that a reporting unit's fair value has fallen below its carrying amount.

Testing Goodwill for Impairment

Goodwill impairment testing and measurement involves a two-step process.[9] In contrast to the qualitative assessment, Steps 1 and 2 rely on quantitative fair-value measures for reporting units as a whole and for their underlying individual assets and liabilities. If, after performing the qualitative assessment described above, an entity concludes that it is more likely than not that the fair value of a reporting unit is less than its carrying amount, then the entity is required to proceed to the first step of the two-step impairment test.[10]

Step 1: Is the Carrying Amount of a Reporting Unit More Than Its Fair Value?

In the first step of impairment testing, the consolidated entity calculates fair values for each of its reporting units with allocated goodwill. Each reporting unit's fair value is then compared with its carrying amount (*including goodwill*). If an individual reporting unit's fair value exceeds its carrying amount, its goodwill is not considered impaired, and the second step in testing is not performed—goodwill remains at its current carrying amount. However, if the fair value of a reporting unit has fallen below its carrying amount, a potential for goodwill impairment exists. In this case, a second step must be performed to determine whether goodwill has been impaired and to measure the amount of impairment.

Step 2: Is Goodwill's Implied Value Less Than Its Carrying Amount?

If Step 1 indicates potential goodwill impairment, Step 2 then compares the fair value of goodwill to its carrying amount. Because, by definition, goodwill is not separable from other assets, it is not possible to directly observe its fair value. Therefore, an *implied fair value* for goodwill is calculated in a similar manner to the determination of goodwill in a business combination. As stated in the FASB ASC (para. 350-20-35-14):

> The implied fair value of goodwill shall be determined in the same manner as the amount of goodwill recognized in a business combination . . . That is, an entity shall assign the fair value of a reporting unit to all of the assets and liabilities of that unit (including any unrecognized intangible assets) as if the reporting unit had been acquired in a business combination . . .

[9] As discussed later in this chapter, FASB has proposed the elimination of step 2 of the goodwill impairment measurement procedure.

[10] An entity, on the basis of its discretion, may bypass the qualitative assessment for any reporting unit in any period and proceed directly to performing the first step of the impairment test. An entity may resume performing the qualitative assessment in any subsequent period (FASB ASC para. 350-20-35-3B).

The current fair value of the reporting unit is allocated across that unit's identifiable assets and liabilities with any remaining excess considered as the implied value of goodwill.[11] If the implied value of goodwill is less than its carrying amount, impairment has occurred and a loss is recognized. The loss equals the excess of the carrying amount of the reporting unit's goodwill over its implied fair value.[12]

Illustration—Accounting and Reporting for a Goodwill Impairment Loss

To illustrate the testing procedures for goodwill impairment, assume that on January 1, 2017, investors form Newcall Corporation to consolidate the telecommunications operations of DSM, Inc., and VisionTalk Company in a deal valued at $2.2 billion. Newcall organizes each former firm as an operating segment. Additionally, DSM comprises two divisions—DSM Wired and DSM Wireless—that along with VisionTalk are treated as independent reporting units for internal performance evaluation and management reviews. Newcall recognizes $215 million as goodwill at the merger date and allocates this entire amount to its reporting units. That information and each reporting unit's acquisition-date fair values are as follows:

Newcall's Reporting Units	Goodwill	Acquisition-Date Fair Values January 1, 2017
DSM Wired	$22,000,000	$950,000,000
DSM Wireless	155,000,000	748,000,000
VisionTalk	38,000,000	502,000,000

In December 2017, Newcall performs a qualitative analysis for each of its three reporting units to assess potential goodwill impairment. Accordingly, Newcall examines the relevant events and circumstances that may affect the fair values of its reporting units. The analysis reveals that the fair value of each reporting unit likely exceeds its carrying amount except for DSM Wireless. Step 1 of the goodwill impairment test then reveals that DSM Wireless's fair value has fallen to $600 million, well below its current carrying amount. Newcall attributes the decline in value to a failure to realize expected cost-saving synergies with VisionTalk. Then, in Step 2, Newcall compares the implied fair value of the DSM Wireless goodwill to its carrying amount. Newcall derived the implied fair value of goodwill through the following allocation of the December 31, 2017, fair value of DSM Wireless:

DSM Wireless December 31, 2017, fair value		$600,000,000
Fair values of DSM Wireless net assets at December 31, 2017:		
Current assets	$ 50,000,000	
Property	125,000,000	
Equipment	265,000,000	
Subscriber list	140,000,000	
Patented technology	185,000,000	
Current liabilities	(44,000,000)	
Long-term debt	(125,000,000)	
Value assigned to identifiable net assets		$596,000,000
Implied fair value of goodwill		$ 4,000,000
Goodwill carrying amount before impairment		155,000,000
Impairment loss		$151,000,000

Thus, Newcall reports a $151,000,000 goodwill impairment loss as a separate line item in the operating section of its consolidated income statement. Additional disclosures are required describing (1) the facts and circumstances leading to the impairment and (2) the method of determining the fair value of the associated reporting unit (e.g., market prices, comparable business, present value technique, etc.). The reported amounts for the other

[11] This procedure serves only to measure an implied fair value for goodwill. None of the other values allocated to assets and liabilities in the testing comparison are used to adjust their reported amounts.

[12] The loss cannot exceed the carrying amount of goodwill.

assets and liabilities of DSM Wireless remain the same and are not changed based on the goodwill testing procedure.

Reporting Units with Zero or Negative Carrying Amounts

One final issue regarding goodwill impairment testing deserves mentioning. When a reporting unit has a zero or negative carrying amount, the ASC requires a special application of the testing procedure. An exception is needed because a zero or negative carrying amount for a reporting unit accompanied by a positive fair value would always permit an entity to forgo Step 2 of the impairment test even though its underlying goodwill might be impaired. Therefore, in such circumstances, the ASC requires an entity to perform Step 2 of the impairment test when it is more likely than not that a goodwill impairment exists. In judging the likelihood of goodwill impairment, an entity must consider the same factors as in the qualitative assessment for individual reporting units.

Goodwill Impairment Simplified—Proposed Accounting Standards Update (ASU)

In May, 2016, the FASB issued a proposed ASU entitled, "Simplifying the Accounting for Goodwill Impairment."[13] The stated objective of the proposed ASU was "to remove Step 2 from the goodwill impairment test, which includes determining the implied fair value of goodwill and comparing it with the carrying amount of that goodwill." The proposed changes would greatly simplify the accounting procedures previously described. The changes would also save companies the cost involved in determining fair values for each of the assets and liabilities residing in their reporting units. However, the FASB would continue to require a determination of the fair value of its reporting units, should any fail (or elect to forego) the qualitative goodwill impairment assessment.

The FASB's recommendation partially stems from a post-implementation review of accounting for business combinations. That review concluded that current goodwill accounting produces more complexity and costs than the FASB anticipated. Further, the board concluded that eliminating Step 2 would not significantly reduce the usefulness of the goodwill impairment information provided to users of financial statements.

The proposed ASU changes accounting for goodwill impairment as follows:

> . . .an entity would perform its annual, or any interim, goodwill impairment test by comparing the fair value of a reporting unit with its carrying amount. An entity generally would recognize an impairment charge for the amount by which the carrying amount exceeds the reporting unit's fair value. However, that amount should not exceed the carrying amount of goodwill allocated to that reporting unit. An entity would still have the option to perform the qualitative assessment for a reporting unit to determine if the quantitative impairment test is necessary.[14]

Thus, assuming a reporting unit failed (or elected to forego) the qualitative assessment (a likelihood of more than 50 percent that a reporting unit's fair value is less than its carrying amount), a quantitative comparison would be employed to measure the amount of goodwill impairment. For example, assume the following December 31, 2018 values for Quality Road Company's RNT reporting unit:

December 31, 2018	Fair Value	Carrying Amount
RNT reporting unit as a whole	$1,500,000	$1,625,000*
Goodwill	?	148,000

*Reporting unit's assets (including goodwill) – liabilities.

The December 31, 2018 goodwill impairment loss would be measured simply as follows:

RNT reporting unit fair value	$1,500,000
–RNT reporting unit carrying amount	1,625,000
Goodwill impairment loss	$ 125,000

[13] Financial Accounting Standards Board, Exposure Draft: Proposed Accounting Standards Update, Intangibles—Goodwill and Other (Topic 350), "Simplifying the Accounting for Goodwill Impairment," May 12, 2016.

[14] *Ibid.*

By eliminating Step 2 of the impairment test, Quality Road Company would benefit by avoiding costs of determining fair values for the RNT reporting unit's identifiable assets and liabilities. Moreover, no fair values would need to be determined for any unrecorded intangibles of the reporting unit.

The only exception to the previously mentioned impairment measurement occurs when the initially computed goodwill impairment loss exceeds the carrying amount of goodwill. In the earlier example, the RNT reporting unit's goodwill carrying amount is $148,000, sufficient to absorb the $125,000 impairment. However, if the reporting unit's goodwill carrying amount was less than $125,000, the goodwill impairment loss would be limited to the lower carrying amount. Thus, the impairment loss cannot exceed the carrying amount of any particular reporting unit's goodwill.

Another change to goodwill accounting would be the elimination of the differential impairment analysis required for reporting units with zero or negative carrying amounts. According to the proposed ASU, "the same impairment assessment would apply to all reporting units. An entity would be required to disclose the existence of any reporting units with zero or negative carrying amounts and the amount of goodwill allocated to those reporting units."[15] Therefore, if the proposed ASU is ultimately approved, all reporting units would follow an identical model for assessing goodwill impairment.

Comparisons with International Accounting Standards

International Financial Reporting Standards (IFRS) and U.S. GAAP both require goodwill recognition in a business combination when the fair value of the consideration transferred exceeds the net fair values of the assets acquired and liabilities assumed. Subsequent to acquisition, both IFRS and U.S. GAAP require an assessment for goodwill impairment at least annually and more frequently in the presence of indicators of possible impairment. Also for both sets of standards, goodwill impairments, once recognized, are not recoverable. However, differences exist across the two sets of standards in the way goodwill impairment is tested for and recognized. In particular, goodwill allocation, impairment testing, and determination of the impairment loss differ across the two reporting regimes and are discussed below.

Goodwill Allocation

- *U.S. GAAP.* Goodwill acquired in a business combination is allocated to reporting units expected to benefit from the goodwill. Reporting units are operating segments or a business component one level below an operating segment.
- *IFRS.* International Accounting Standard *(IAS) 36* requires goodwill acquired in a business combination to be allocated to cash-generating units or groups of cash-generating units that are expected to benefit from the synergies of the business combination. Cash-generating groups represent the lowest level within the entity at which the goodwill is monitored for internal management purposes and are not to be larger than an operating segment or determined in accordance with *IFRS 8,* "Operating Segments."

Impairment Testing

- *U.S. GAAP.* Firms have the option to perform a qualitative assessment to evaluate possible goodwill impairment based on a greater than 50 percent likelihood that a reporting unit's fair value is less than its carrying amount. If such a likelihood exists, then a two-step testing procedure is performed. In step one, a reporting unit's total fair value is compared to its carrying amount. If the carrying amount exceeds fair value, then a second step comparing goodwill's implied fair value to its carrying amount is performed.
- *IFRS.* A one-step approach compares the fair and carrying amounts of each cash-generating unit with goodwill. If the carrying amount exceeds the fair value of the cash-generating unit, then goodwill (and possibly other assets of the cash-generating unit) is considered impaired.

Determination of the Impairment Loss

- *U.S. GAAP.* In step two, a reporting unit's implied fair value for goodwill is computed as the excess of the reporting unit's fair value over the fair value of its identifiable net assets.

[15] *Ibid.*

If the carrying amount of goodwill is greater than its implied fair value, an impairment loss is recognized for the difference.

- *IFRS.* Any excess carrying amount over fair value for a cash-generating unit is first assigned to reduce goodwill. If goodwill is reduced to zero, then the other assets of the cash-generating unit are reduced pro-rata based on the carrying amounts of the assets.

Finally, the FASB and IASB have agreed to include impairment recognition and reporting as one of their future convergence projects.

LO 3-7

Describe the rationale and procedures for impairment testing for intangible assets other than goodwill.

Amortization and Impairment of Other Intangibles

As discussed in Chapter 2, the acquisition method governs how we initially consolidate the assets acquired and liabilities assumed in a business combination. Subsequent to acquisition, income determination becomes a regular part of the consolidation process. The fair-value bases (established at the acquisition date) for definite-lived subsidiary assets acquired and liabilities assumed will be amortized over their remaining lives for income recognition. For indefinite-lived assets (e.g., goodwill, certain other intangibles), an impairment model is used to assess whether asset write-downs are appropriate.

Current accounting standards suggest categories of intangible assets for possible recognition when one business acquires another. Examples include noncompetition agreements, customer lists, patents, subscriber lists, databases, trademarks, lease agreements, licenses, and many others. All identified intangible assets should be amortized over their economic useful life unless such life is considered *indefinite.* The term *indefinite life* is defined as a life that extends beyond the foreseeable future. A recognized intangible asset with an indefinite life should not be amortized unless and until its life is determined to be finite. Importantly, *indefinite* does not mean "infinite." Also, the useful life of an intangible asset should not be considered indefinite because a precise finite life is not known.

For intangible assets with finite lives, the amortization method should reflect the pattern of decline in the economic usefulness of the asset. If no such pattern is apparent, the straight-line method of amortization should be used. The amount to be amortized should be the value assigned to the intangible asset less any residual value. In most cases, the residual value is presumed to be zero. However, that presumption can be overcome if the acquiring enterprise has a commitment from a third party to purchase the intangible at the end of its useful life or an observable market exists for the intangible asset.

The length of the amortization period for identifiable intangibles (i.e., those not included in goodwill) depends primarily on the assumed economic life of the asset. Factors that should be considered in determining the useful life of an intangible asset include

- Legal, regulatory, or contractual provisions.
- The effects of obsolescence, demand, competition, industry stability, rate of technological change, and expected changes in distribution channels.
- The enterprise's expected use of the intangible asset.
- The level of maintenance expenditure required to obtain the asset's expected future benefits.

Any recognized intangible assets considered to possess indefinite lives are not amortized but instead are assessed for impairment on an annual basis.[16] Similar to goodwill impairment assessment, an entity has the option to first perform qualitative assessments for its indefinite-lived intangibles to see if further quantitative tests are necessary. According to the FASB ASC (350-30-65-3), if an entity elects to perform a qualitative assessment, it examines events and circumstances to determine whether it is more likely than not (that is, a likelihood of more than 50 percent) that an indefinite-lived intangible asset is impaired. Qualitative factors include costs of using the intangible, legal and regulatory factors, industry and market considerations, and other. If the qualitative assessment indicates impairment is unlikely, no additional tests are needed.

[16] An entity has an unconditional option to bypass the qualitative assessment for any indefinite-lived intangible asset in any period and proceed directly to performing the quantitative impairment test.

If the qualitative assessment indicates that impairment is likely, the entity then must perform a quantitative test to determine if a loss has occurred. To test an indefinite-lived intangible asset for impairment, its carrying amount is compared to its fair value. If the fair value is less than the carrying amount, then the intangible asset is considered impaired and an impairment loss is recognized. The asset's carrying amount is reduced accordingly for the excess of its carrying amount over its fair value.

Contingent Consideration

LO 3-8

Understand the accounting and reporting for contingent consideration subsequent to a business acquisition.

Contingency agreements frequently accompany business combinations. In many cases, the target firm asks for consideration based on projections of its future performance. The acquiring firm, however, may not share the projections and, thus, may be unwilling to pay now for uncertain future performance. To close the deal, agreements for the acquirer's future payments to the former owners of the target are common. Alternatively, when the acquirer's stock comprises the consideration transferred, the sellers of the target firm may request a guaranteed minimum market value of the stock for a period of time to ensure a fair price.

Accounting for Contingent Consideration in Business Combinations

As an illustration, assume that Skeptical, Inc., acquires 100 percent of the voting stock of Rosy Pictures Company on January 1, 2017, for the following consideration:

- $550,000 market value of 10,000 shares of its $5-par common stock.
- A contingent payment of $80,000 cash if Rosy Pictures generates cash flows from operations of $20,000 or more in 2017.
- A payment of sufficient shares of Skeptical common stock to ensure a total value of $550,000 if the price per share is less than $55 on January 1, 2018.

Under the acquisition method, each of the three elements of consideration represents a portion of the negotiated fair value of Rosy Pictures and therefore must be included in the recorded value entered on Skeptical's accounting records. For the cash contingency, Skeptical estimates that there is a 30 percent chance that the $80,000 payment will be required. For the stock contingency, Skeptical estimates that there is a 20 percent probability that the 10,000 shares issued will have a market value of $540,000 on January 1, 2018, and an 80 percent probability that the market value of the 10,000 shares will exceed $550,000. Skeptical uses an interest rate of 4 percent to incorporate the time value of money.

To determine the fair values of the contingent consideration, Skeptical computes the present value of the expected payments as follows:

- *Cash contingency* = $80,000 × 30% × [1/(1 + .04)] = $23,077
- *Stock contingency* = $10,000 × 20% × [1/(1 + .04)] = $1,923

Skeptical then records in its accounting records the acquisition of Rosy Pictures as follows:

Investment in Rosy Pictures	575,000	
Common Stock ($5 par)		50,000
Additional Paid-in Capital		500,000
Contingent Performance Obligation		23,077
Additional Paid-in Capital—Contingent Equity Outstanding		1,923
To record acquisition of Rosy Pictures at fair value of consideration transferred including performance and stock contingencies.		

Skeptical will report the contingent cash payment under its liabilities and the contingent stock payment as a component of stockholders' equity. In periods subsequent to acquisition, obligations for contingent consideration that meet the definition of a liability will continue to be measured at fair value with adjustments recognized in income. Those obligations classified as equity are not subsequently remeasured at fair value, consistent with other equity issues (e.g., common stock).

To continue the preceding example, assume that in 2017 Rosy Pictures exceeds the cash flow from operations threshold of $20,000, thus requiring an additional payment of $80,000. Also, Skeptical's stock price had fallen to $54.45 at January 1, 2018. Because the acquisition agreement called for a $550,000 total value at January 1, 2018, Skeptical must issue an additional 101 shares ($5,500 shortfall/$54.45 per share) to the former owners of Rosy Pictures.

Contingent Performance Obligation	23,077	
Loss from Revaluation of Contingent Performance Obligation	56,923	
Cash		80,000
To record contingent cash payment required by original Rosy Pictures acquisition agreement.		
Additional Paid-in Capital—Contingent Equity Outstanding	1,923	
Common Stock		505
Additional Paid-in Capital		1,418
To record contingent stock issue required by original Rosy Pictures acquisition agreement.		

The loss from revaluation of the contingent performance obligation is reported in Skeptical's consolidated income statement as a component of ordinary income. Regarding the additional required stock issue, note that Skeptical's total paid-in capital remains unchanged from the total $551,923 recorded at the acquisition date.

Summary

1. The procedures used to consolidate financial information generated by the separate companies in a business combination are affected by both the passage of time and the method applied by the parent in accounting for the subsidiary. Thus, no single consolidation process that is applicable to all business combinations can be described.
2. The parent might elect to utilize the equity method to account for a subsidiary. As discussed in Chapter 1, the parent accrues income when earned by the subsidiary. The parent records dividend declarations by the subsidiary as reductions in the investment account. The effects of excess fair-value amortizations or any intra-entity transactions also are reflected within the parent's financial records. The equity method provides the parent with accurate information concerning the subsidiary's impact on consolidated totals; however, it is usually somewhat complicated to apply.
3. The initial value method and the partial equity method are two alternatives to the equity method. The initial value method recognizes only the subsidiary's dividends as income while the asset balance remains at the acquisition-date fair value. This approach is simple and typically reflects cash flows between the two companies. Under the partial equity method, the parent accrues the subsidiary's income as earned but does not record adjustments that might be required by excess fair-value amortizations or intra-entity transfers. The partial equity method is easier to apply than the equity method, and, in many cases, the parent's income is a reasonable approximation of the consolidated total.
4. For a consolidation in any subsequent period, all reciprocal balances must be eliminated. Thus, the subsidiary's equity accounts, the parent's investment balance, intra-entity income, dividends, and liabilities are removed. In addition, the remaining unamortized portions of the fair-value allocations are recognized along with excess amortization expenses for the period. If the equity method has not been applied, the parent's beginning Retained Earnings account also must be adjusted for any previous income or excess amortizations that have not yet been recorded.
5. For each subsidiary acquisition, the parent must assign the acquired assets and liabilities (including goodwill) to individual reporting units of the combined entity. The reporting units should be at operating segment level or lower and serve as the basis for future assessments of fair value. Any value assigned to goodwill is not amortized but instead is tested annually for impairment. Firms have the option to perform a qualitative assessment to evaluate whether a reporting unit's fair value more likely than not exceeds its carrying amount. If the assessment shows excess fair value over carrying amount for the reporting unit, a firm can forgo further testing. Otherwise, a two-step test is performed. First, if the fair value of any reporting unit below its carrying amount, then the implied value of the associated goodwill is recomputed. Second, the recomputed implied value of goodwill is compared to its carrying amount. An impairment loss must then be recognized if the carrying amount of goodwill exceeds its implied value.[17]
6. Subsequent to a business combination, any newly recognized subsidiary identifiable intangible assets (i.e., other than goodwill) considered to possess indefinite lives are not amortized but instead are assessed for impairment on an annual basis. Similar to goodwill impairment assessment, an

[17] A proposed FASB Accounting Standards Update would eliminate the second step of the impairment test. Goodwill would simply be the excess of a reporting unit's carrying amount over its fair value (loss not to exceed goodwill's carrying amount).

entity has the option to first perform qualitative assessments for its indefinite-lived intangibles to see if further quantitative tests are necessary. For intangible assets with finite lives, amortization expense is recognized over the intangible asset's useful life. The amortization method should reflect the pattern of decline in the economic usefulness of the asset. If no such pattern is apparent, the straight-line method of amortization should be used.

7. The acquisition-date fair value assigned to a subsidiary can be based, at least in part, on the fair value of any contingent consideration. For contingent obligations that meet the definition of a liability, the obligation is adjusted for changes in fair value over time with corresponding recognition of gains or losses from the revaluation. For contingent obligations classified as equity, no remeasurement to fair value takes place. In either case the initial value recognized in the combination does not change regardless of whether the contingency is eventually paid or not.

Comprehensive Illustration

Problem

(*Estimated Time: 40 to 65 Minutes*) On January 1, 2016, Top Company acquired all of Bottom Company's outstanding common stock for $842,000 in cash. As of that date, one of Bottom's buildings with a 12-year remaining life was undervalued on its financial records by $72,000. Equipment with a 10-year remaining life was undervalued, but only by $10,000. The book values of all of Bottom's other assets and liabilities were equal to their fair values at that time except for an unrecorded licensing agreement with an assessed value of $40,000 and a 20-year remaining useful life. Bottom's book value at the acquisition date was $720,000.

During 2016, Bottom reported net income of $100,000 and declared $30,000 in dividends. Earnings were $120,000 in 2017 with $20,000 in dividends distributed by the subsidiary. As of December 31, 2018, the companies reported the following selected balances, which include all revenues and expenses for the year:

	Top Company December 31, 2018		Bottom Company December 31, 2018	
	Debit	**Credit**	**Debit**	**Credit**
Buildings	$1,540,000		$460,000	
Cash and receivables	50,000		90,000	
Common stock		$ 900,000		$400,000
Dividends declared	70,000		10,000	
Equipment	280,000		200,000	
Cost of goods sold	500,000		120,000	
Depreciation expense	100,000		60,000	
Inventory	280,000		260,000	
Land	330,000		250,000	
Liabilities		480,000		260,000
Retained earnings, 1/1/18		1,360,000		490,000
Revenues		900,000		300,000

Required

a. If Top applies the equity method, what is its investment account balance as of December 31, 2018?

b. If Top applies the initial value method, what is its investment account balance as of December 31, 2018?

c. Regardless of the accounting method in use by Top, what are the consolidated totals as of December 31, 2018, for each of the following accounts?

Buildings	Revenues
Equipment	Net Income
Land	Investment in Bottom
Depreciation Expense	Dividends Declared
Amortization Expense	Cost of Goods Sold

d. Prepare the worksheet entries required on December 31, 2018, to consolidate the financial records of these two companies. Assume that Top applied the equity method to its investment account.

e. How would the worksheet entries in requirement *(d)* be altered if Top has used the initial value method?

Solution

a. To determine the investment balances under the equity method, four items must be determined: the initial value assigned, the income accrual, dividends and amortization of excess acquisition-date fair value over book value. Although the first three are indicated in the problem, amortizations must be calculated separately.

An allocation of Bottom's acquisition-date fair values as well as the related amortization expense follows.

Fair value of consideration transferred by Top Company . .	$ 842,000
Book value of Bottom Company, 1/1/16	(720,000)
Excess fair value over book value.	$ 122,000

Adjustments to specific accounts based on fair values:

		Remaining Life (years)	Annual Amortization
Buildings	$ 72,000	12	$6,000
Equipment	10,000	10	1,000
Licensing agreement	40,000	20	2,000
Totals.	$122,000		$9,000

Thus, if Top adopts the equity method to account for this subsidiary, the Investment in Bottom account shows a December 31, 2018, balance of $1,095,000, computed as follows:

Initial value (fair value of consideration transferred by Top)		$ 842,000
Bottom Company's 2016–2017 increase in book value (income less dividends).		170,000
Excess amortizations for 2016–2017 ($9,000 per year for two years).		(18,000)
Current year recognition (2018):		
Equity income accrual (Bottom's revenues less its expenses) . . .	$120,000	
Excess amortization expenses.	(9,000)	
Dividends from Bottom	(10,000)	101,000
Investment in Bottom Company, 12/31/18		$1,095,000

The $120,000 income accrual and the $9,000 excess amortization expenses indicate that an Equity in Subsidiary Earnings balance of $111,000 appears in Top's income statement for the current period.

b. If Top Company applies the initial value method, the Investment in Bottom Company account permanently retains its original $842,000 balance, and the parent recognizes only the intra-entity dividend of $10,000 as income in 2018.

c.
- The consolidated Buildings account as of December 31, 2018, has a balance of $2,054,000. Although the two book value figures total only $2 million, a $72,000 allocation was made to this account based on fair value at the date of acquisition. Because this amount is being depreciated at the rate of $6,000 per year, the original allocation will have been reduced by $18,000 by the end of 2018, leaving only a $54,000 increase.
- On December 31, 2018, the consolidated Equipment account amounts to $487,000. The book values found in the financial records of Top and Bottom provide a total of $480,000. Once again, the allocation ($10,000) established by the acquisition-date fair value must be included in the consolidated balance after being adjusted for three years of depreciation ($1,000 × 3 years, or $3,000).
- Land has a consolidated total of $580,000. Because the book value and fair value of Bottom's land were in agreement at the date of acquisition, no additional allocation was made to this account. Thus, the book values are simply added together to derive a consolidated figure.
- *Cost of goods sold* = $620,000. The cost of goods sold of the parent and subsidiary are added together.
- *Depreciation expense* = $167,000. The depreciation expenses of the parent and subsidiary are added together along with the $6,000 additional building depreciation and the $1,000 additional equipment depreciation as presented in the fair-value allocation schedule.

- *Amortization expense* = \$2,000. An additional expense of \$2,000 is recognized from the amortization of the licensing agreement acquired in the business combination.
- The Revenues account appears as \$1.2 million in the consolidated income statement. None of the worksheet entries in this example affects the individual balances of either company. Consolidation results merely from the addition of the two book values.
- Net income for this business combination is \$411,000: consolidated expenses of \$789,000 subtracted from revenues of \$1.2 million.
- The parent's Investment in Bottom account is removed entirely on the worksheet so that no balance is reported. For consolidation purposes, this account is always eliminated so that the individual assets and liabilities of the subsidiary can be included.
- Dividends declared for the consolidated entity should be reported as \$70,000, the amount Top distributed. Because Bottom's dividends are entirely intra-entity, they are deleted in arriving at consolidated figures.

d. Consolidation Entries Assuming Equity Method Used by Parent

Entry S

Common Stock (Bottom Company)	400,000	
Retained Earnings, 1/1/18. (Bottom Company)	490,000	
Investment in Bottom Company		890,000

Elimination of subsidiary's beginning stockholders' equity accounts against book value portion of investment account.

Entry A

Buildings	60,000	
Equipment	8,000	
Licensing Agreement	36,000	
Investment in Bottom Company		104,000

To recognize fair-value allocations to the subsidiary's assets in excess of book value. Balances represent original allocations less two years of amortization for the 2016–2017 period.

Entry I

Equity in Subsidiary Earnings	111,000	
Investment in Bottom Company		111,000

To eliminate parent's equity income accrual, balance is computed in requirement (*a*).

Entry D

Investment in Bottom	10,000	
Dividends Declared		10,000

To eliminate intra-entity dividends from the subsidiary to the parent (and recorded as a reduction in the investment account because the equity method is in use).

Entry E

Depreciation Expense	7,000	
Amortization Expense	2,000	
Equipment		1,000
Buildings		6,000
Licensing Agreement		2,000

To recognize excess fair-value depreciation and amortization for 2018.

e. If Top utilizes the initial value method rather than the equity method, three changes are required in the development of consolidation entries:

(1) An Entry *C is required to update the parent's beginning Retained Earnings account as if the equity method had been applied. Both an income accrual as well as excess amortizations for the prior two years must be recognized because these balances were not recorded by the parent.

Entry *C

Investment in Bottom Company	152,000	
Retained Earnings, 1/1/18 (Top Company)		152,000

To convert to the equity method by accruing the net effect of the subsidiary's operations (income less dividends) for the prior two years ($170,000) along with excess amortization expenses ($18,000) for this same period.

(2) An alteration is needed in Entry **I** because, under the initial value method, only dividends are recorded by the parent as income.

Entry I

Dividend Income	10,000	
Dividends Declared		10,000

To eliminate intra-entity dividends recorded by parent as income.

(3) Finally, because the intra-entity dividends have been eliminated in Entry **I,** no separate Entry **D** is needed.

Appendix: Private Company Accounting for Business Combinations

LO 3-9:

Describe the alternative accounting treatments for goodwill and other intangible assets available for business combinations by private companies.

External Reporting Option for Private Company Goodwill Accounting

In January 2014, the Financial Accounting Standards Board (FASB) approved an *Accounting Standards Update* (ASU 2014-02) to Topic 350, "Intangibles—Goodwill and Other, on Accounting for Goodwill." This ASU emerged as a consensus of the FASB's Private Company Council (PCC) and gives private companies an option to apply a simplified alternative to the more complex goodwill accounting model required of public companies. As discussed below, the new standard allows a private company both to amortize goodwill and to apply a simplified impairment test at either the reporting unit or entity level.

The private company standards apply only to businesses that do not meet the definition of a public business entity or a not-for-profit entity. In general, business is a public entity if the Securities and Exchange Commission (or a foreign or other domestic regulatory agency) requires the business to furnish financial statements (ASU 2013-12). In this textbook, our focus is squarely on public business entities. Nonetheless, the goodwill accounting option for private companies provides an interesting alternative that the FASB may someday consider for public entities as well.[18]

The new standard allows a private company to elect to amortize goodwill over a 10-year period.[19] The amortization process effectively treats goodwill as a definite-lived intangible asset. This approach, of course, stands in marked contrast to the goodwill accounting for public companies which treats goodwill as an indefinite-lived asset, prohibits amortization, and requires annual impairment testing for goodwill. In justifying the differential treatment for private companies, the FASB reasoned that, based on research by the PCC, goodwill impairment tests provided

> limited decision-useful information because most users of private company financial statement generally disregard goodwill and goodwill impairment losses in their analysis of a private company's financial condition and operating performance. (ASU 2014-02, Summary)

Equally important, the PCC expressed concerns about the cost and complexity of goodwill impairment tests, especially for private companies. The cost and complexity arise in large part from the efforts required in determining fair values for a company's reporting units and their identifiable assets and liabilities.

In many cases, goodwill amortization will replace the need to periodically assess and, when deemed necessary, write-down goodwill through the recognition of impairment losses. Private companies who elect the alternative goodwill accounting, however, will still be required to test goodwill balances for impairment in some circumstances, although a simplified approach is employed.

[18] In November 2014, the FASB directed its staff to extend its research on goodwill amortization to public companies, focusing on the most appropriate useful life if goodwill were amortized and simplifying the goodwill impairment test.

[19] A less-than-10-year amortization period is available if it can be shown to be appropriate (ASC 350-20-35-63).

The goodwill impairment process is simplified in two respects for private companies. First, if a triggering event occurs (i.e., any event or change in circumstances that may have caused the fair value of the acquired entity—or the reporting unit—to fall below its carrying amount), then the unamortized balance of goodwill must be assessed for impairment.[20] However, to save costs and streamline the process, there is no requirement (as exists for public companies) to remeasure each of the entity's (or reporting unit's) separate assets and liabilities at current fair values to compute a residual implied value for goodwill. The measurement of the goodwill impairment loss simply equals the excess (if any) of the fair value of the acquired entity (or reporting unit) over its total carrying amount. The amount of the impairment loss, however, is limited to the remaining unamortized balance in the goodwill account.

Unlike public companies, a private company also has the option to designate and test goodwill for impairment either at the entity level or the reporting unit level—a policy election made at the adoption of the alternative goodwill method. Thus the accounting for goodwill impairment is simplified by both the ability to assess goodwill at the entity level and the use of a single-step test that compares the fair value of the entity to its carrying amount. Similar to public companies, a private company may skip the qualitative assessment. Unlike public companies, a private company can then go directly to a single-step quantitative impairment test.

External Reporting Option for Private Company Accounting for Other Intangible Assets in a Business Combination

In addition to the private company separate guidance for goodwill, the FASB in December 2014 issued ASU 2014-18, "Accounting for Identifiable Intangible Assets in a Business Combination (a consensus of the Private Company Council)," an amendment of Business Combinations (Topic 805). The new standard allows private companies an option to simplify their accounting by recognizing fewer intangible assets in future business combinations. Private companies can now elect to (1) limit the customer-related intangibles it recognizes separately to those capable of being sold or licensed independently from the other assets of the business, and (2) avoid separate recognition of noncompetition agreements.

By limiting the separate recognition of customer-related intangibles (e.g., customer lists, customer relationships, commodity supply contracts, etc.) and noncompetition agreements, the value of these intangible assets is effectively subsumed into goodwill. As with other private company financial reporting options, the FASB cites cost/benefit considerations.

> By providing an accounting alternative, this Update reduces the cost and complexity associated with the measurement of certain identifiable intangible assets without significantly diminishing decision-useful information to users of private company financial statements (ASU 2014-18, Summary).

A private company may elect this alternative only if it also elects the private company goodwill accounting alternative which includes goodwill amortization—thus ensuring that any non-recognized intangibles subsumed into goodwill are also subject to amortization. Companies that choose the goodwill accounting alternative, however, are not required to elect the intangible assets accounting alternative.

Questions

1. CCES Corporation acquires a controlling interest in Schmaling, Inc. CCES may utilize any one of three methods to internally account for this investment. Describe each of these methods, and indicate their advantages and disadvantages.
2. Maguire Company obtains 100 percent control over Williams Company. Several years after the takeover, consolidated financial statements are being produced. For each of the following accounts, briefly describe the values that should be included in consolidated totals.
   a. Equipment.
   b. Investment in Williams Company.
   c. Dividends Declared.
   d. Goodwill.
   e. Revenues.
   f. Expenses.
   g. Common Stock.
   h. Net Income.
3. When a parent company uses the equity method to account for an investment in a subsidiary, why do both the parent's Net Income and Retained Earnings account balances agree with the consolidated totals?

[20] Distinct from public company requirements, no annual assessment for goodwill impairment is required for private companies.

4. When a parent company uses the equity method to account for investment in a subsidiary, the amortization expense entry recorded during the year is eliminated on a consolidation worksheet as a component of Entry **I.** What is the necessity of removing this amortization?
5. When a parent company applies the initial value method or the partial equity method to an investment, a worksheet adjustment must be made to the parent's beginning Retained Earnings account (Entry *C) in every period after the year of acquisition. What is the necessity for this entry? Why is no similar entry found when the parent utilizes the equity method?
6. Several years ago, Jenkins Company acquired a controlling interest in Lambert Company. Lambert recently borrowed $100,000 from Jenkins. In consolidating the financial records of these two companies, how will this debt be handled?
7. Benns adopts the equity method for its 100 percent investment in Waters. At the end of six years, Benns reports an investment in Waters of $920,000. What figures constitute this balance?
8. One company acquired another in a transaction in which $100,000 of the acquisition price is assigned to goodwill. Several years later, a worksheet is being produced to consolidate these two companies. How is the reported value of the goodwill determined at this date?
9. When should a parent consider recognizing an impairment loss for goodwill associated with a subsidiary? How should the loss be reported in the financial statements?
10. Reimers Company acquires Rollins Corporation on January 1, 2017. As part of the agreement, the parent states that an additional $100,000 payment to the former owners of Rollins will be made in 2018, if Rollins achieves certain income thresholds during the first two years following the acquisition. How should Reimers account for this contingency in its 2017 consolidated financial statements?

Problems

1. A company acquires a subsidiary and will prepare consolidated financial statements for external reporting purposes. For internal reporting purposes, the company has decided to apply the initial value method. Why might the company have made this decision?

LO 3-2

a. It is a relatively easy method to apply.
b. Operating results appearing on the parent's financial records reflect consolidated totals.
c. GAAP now requires the use of this particular method for internal reporting purposes.
d. Consolidation is not required when the parent uses the initial value method.

LO 3-2

2. A company acquires a subsidiary and will prepare consolidated financial statements for external reporting purposes. For internal reporting purposes, the company has decided to apply the equity method. Why might the company have made this decision?
a. It is a relatively easy method to apply.
b. Operating results appearing on the parent's financial records reflect consolidated totals.
c. GAAP now requires the use of this particular method for internal reporting purposes.
d. Consolidation is not required when the parent uses the equity method.

LO 3-4

3. On January 1, 2018, Jay Company acquired all the outstanding ownership shares of Zee Company. In assessing Zee's acquisition-date fair values, Jay concluded that the carrying value of Zee's long-term debt (8-year remaining life) was less than its fair value by $20,000. At December 31, 2018, Zee Company's accounts show interest expense of $12,000 and long-term debt of $250,000. What amounts of interest expense and long-term debt should appear on the December 31, 2018, consolidated financial statements of Jay and its subsidiary Zee?

	Interest expense	*Long-term debt*
a.	$14,500	$270,000
b.	$14,500	$267,500
c.	$9,500	$270,000
d.	$9,500	$267,500

LO 3-5

4. When should a consolidated entity recognize a goodwill impairment loss?
a. If both the fair value of a reporting unit and its associated implied goodwill fall below their respective carrying amounts.
b. Whenever the entity's fair value declines significantly.
c. If the fair value of a reporting unit with goodwill fall below its carrying amount.
d. Annually on a systematic and rational basis.

LO 3-1

5. Paar Corporation bought 100 percent of Kimmel, Inc., on January 1, 2015. On that date, Paar's equipment (10-year remaining life) has a book value of $420,000 but a fair value of $520,000. Kimmel has equipment (10-year remaining life) with a book value of $272,000 but a fair value of $400,000. Paar uses the equity method to record its investment in Kimmel. On December 31, 2017, Paar has equipment with a book value of $294,000 but a fair value of $445,200. Kimmel has equipment with a book value of $190,400 but a fair value of $357,000. What is the consolidated balance for the Equipment account as of December 31, 2017?
   a. $574,000
   b. $802,200
   c. $612,600
   d. $484,400

LO 3-4

6. How would the answer to problem (5) have been affected if the parent had applied the initial value method rather than the equity method?
   a. No effect: The method the parent uses is for internal reporting purposes only and has no impact on consolidated totals.
   b. The consolidated Equipment account would have a higher reported balance.
   c. The consolidated Equipment account would have a lower reported balance.
   d. The balance in the consolidated Equipment account cannot be determined for the initial value method using the information given.

LO 3-5

7. Goodwill recognized in a business combination must be allocated among a firm's identified reporting units. If the fair value of a particular reporting unit with recognized goodwill falls below its carrying amount, which of the following is true?
   a. No goodwill impairment loss is recognized unless the implied value for goodwill exceeds its carrying amount.
   b. A goodwill impairment loss is recognized if the carrying amount for goodwill exceeds its implied value.
   c. A goodwill impairment loss is recognized for the excess of a reporting unit's carrying amount over its fair value, not to exceed the carrying amount of goodwill.
   d. The reporting unit reduces the values assigned to its long-term assets (including any unrecognized intangibles) to reflect its fair value.

LO 3-7

8. If no legal, regulatory, contractual, competitive, economic, or other factors limit the life of an intangible asset, the asset's assigned value is allocated to expense over which of the following?
   a. 20 years.
   b. 20 years with an annual impairment review.
   c. Infinitely.
   d. Indefinitely (no amortization) with an annual impairment review until its life becomes finite.

LO 3-7

9. Dosmann, Inc., bought all outstanding shares of Lizzi Corporation on January 1, 2016, for $700,000 in cash. This portion of the consideration transferred results in a fair-value allocation of $35,000 to equipment and goodwill of $88,000. At the acquisition date, Dosmann also agrees to pay Lizzi's previous owners an additional $110,000 on January 1, 2018, if Lizzi earns a 10 percent return on the fair value of its assets in 2016 and 2017. Lizzi's profits exceed this threshold in both years. Which of the following is true?
   a. The additional $110,000 payment is a reduction in consolidated retained earnings.
   b. The fair value of the expected contingent payment increases goodwill at the acquisition date.
   c. Consolidated goodwill as of January 1, 2018, increases by $110,000.
   d. The $110,000 is recorded as an expense in 2018.

Problems 10, 11, and 12 relate to the following:
On January 1, 2016, Phoenix Co. acquired 100 percent of the outstanding voting shares of Sedona Inc., for $600,000 cash. At January 1, 2016, Sedona's net assets had a total carrying amount of $420,000. Equipment (eight-year remaining life) was undervalued on Sedona's financial records by $80,000. Any remaining excess fair over book value was attributed to a customer list developed by Sedona (four-year remaining life), but not recorded on its books. Phoenix applies the equity method to account for its investment in Sedona. Each year since the acquisition, Sedona has declared a $20,000 dividend. Sedona recorded net income of $70,000 in 2016 and $80,000 in 2017.

Selected account balances from the two companies' individual records were as follows:

	Phoenix	Sedona
2018 Revenues	$498,000	$285,000
2018 Expenses	350,000	195,000
2018 Income from Sedona	55,000	
Retained earnings 12/31/18	250,000	175,000

LO 3-3a

10. What is consolidated net income for Phoenix and Sedona for 2018?
    a. $148,000
    b. $203,000
    c. $228,000
    d. $238,000

LO 3-3a

11. What is Phoenix's consolidated retained earnings balance at December 31, 2018?
    a. $250,000
    b. $290,000
    c. $330,000
    d. $360,000

LO 3-3a

12. On its December 31, 2018, consolidated balance sheet, what amount should Phoenix report for Sedona's customer list?
    a. $10,000
    b. $20,000
    c. $25,000
    d. $50,000

LO 3-7

13. Kaplan Corporation acquired Star, Inc., on January 1, 2017, by issuing 13,000 shares of common stock with a $10 per share par value and a $23 market value. This transaction resulted in recognizing $62,000 of goodwill. Kaplan also agreed to compensate Star's former owners for any difference if Kaplan's stock is worth less than $23 on January 1, 2018. On January 1, 2018, Kaplan issues an additional 3,000 shares to Star's former owners to honor the contingent consideration agreement. Which of the following is true?
    a. The fair value of the number of shares issued for the contingency increases the Goodwill account at January 1, 2018.
    b. The parent's additional paid-in capital from the contingent equity recorded at the acquisition date is reclassified as a regular common stock issue on January 1, 2018.
    c. All of the subsidiary's asset and liability accounts must be revalued for consolidation purposes based on their fair values as of January 1, 2018.
    d. The additional shares are assumed to have been issued on January 1, 2017, so that a retrospective adjustment is required.

LO 3-3, 3-4

14. Herbert, Inc., acquired all of Rambis Company's outstanding stock on January 1, 2017, for $574,000 in cash. Annual excess amortization of $12,000 results from this transaction. On the date of the takeover, Herbert reported retained earnings of $400,000, and Rambis reported a $200,000 balance. Herbert reported internal net income of $40,000 in 2017 and $50,000 in 2018 and declared $10,000 in dividends each year. Rambis reported net income of $20,000 in 2017 and $30,000 in 2018 and declared $5,000 in dividends each year.
    a. Assume that Herbert's internal net income figures above do not include any income from the subsidiary.
       - If the parent uses the equity method, what is the amount reported as consolidated retained earnings on December 31, 2017?
       - Would the amount of consolidated retained earnings change if the parent had applied either the initial value or partial equity method for internal accounting purposes?
    b. Under each of the following situations, what is the Investment in Rambis account balance on Herbert's books on January 1, 2018?
       - The parent uses the equity method.
       - The parent uses the partial equity method.
       - The parent uses the initial value method.

c. Under each of the following situations, what is Entry *C on a 2018 consolidation worksheet?
- The parent uses the equity method.
- The parent uses the partial equity method.
- The parent uses the initial value method.

LO 3-3, 3-4

15. Haynes, Inc., obtained 100 percent of Turner Company's common stock on January 1, 2017, by issuing 9,000 shares of $10 par value common stock. Haynes's shares had a $15 per share fair value. On that date, Turner reported a net book value of $100,000. However, its equipment (with a five-year remaining life) was undervalued by $5,000 in the company's accounting records. Also, Turner had developed a customer list with an assessed value of $30,000, although no value had been recorded on Turner's books. The customer list had an estimated remaining useful life of 10 years.

The following balances come from the individual accounting records of these two companies as of December 31, 2017:

	Haynes	Turner
Revenues	$(600,000)	$(230,000)
Expenses	440,000	120,000
Investment income	Not given	–0–
Dividends declared	80,000	50,000

The following balances come from the individual accounting records of these two companies as of December 31, 2018:

	Haynes	Turner
Revenues	$(700,000)	$(280,000)
Expenses	460,000	150,000
Investment income	Not given	–0–
Dividends declared	90,000	40,000
Equipment	500,000	300,000

a. What balance does Haynes's Investment in Turner account show on December 31, 2018, when the equity method is applied?

b. What is the consolidated net income for the year ending December 31, 2018?

c. What is the consolidated equipment balance as of December 31, 2018? How would this answer be affected by the investment method applied by the parent?

d. If Haynes has applied the initial value method to account for its investment, what adjustment is needed to the beginning of the Retained Earnings account on a December 31, 2018, consolidation worksheet? How would this answer change if the partial equity method had been in use? How would this answer change if the equity method had been in use?

LO 3-6

16. Francisco Inc. acquired 100 percent of the voting shares of Beltran Company on January 1, 2017. In exchange, Francisco paid $450,000 in cash and issued 104,000 shares of its own $1 par value common stock. On this date, Francisco's stock had a fair value of $12 per share. The combination is a statutory merger with Beltran subsequently dissolved as a legal corporation. Beltran's assets and liabilities are assigned to a new reporting unit.

The following reports the fair values for the Beltran reporting unit for January 1, 2017, and December 31, 2018, along with their respective book values on December 31, 2018.

Beltran Reporting Unit	Fair Values 1/1/17	Fair Values 12/31/18	Book Values 12/31/18
Cash	$ 75,000	$ 50,000	$ 50,000
Receivables	193,000	225,000	225,000
Inventory	281,000	305,000	300,000
Patents	525,000	600,000	500,000
Customer relationships	500,000	480,000	450,000
Equipment (net)	295,000	240,000	235,000
Goodwill	?	?	400,000
Accounts payable	(121,000)	(175,000)	(175,000)
Long-term liabilities	(450,000)	(400,000)	(400,000)

a. Prepare Francisco's journal entry to record the assets acquired and the liabilities assumed in the Beltran merger on January 1, 2017.

b. On December 31, 2018, Francisco opts to forgo any goodwill impairment qualitative assessment and estimates that the total fair value of the entire Beltran reporting unit is $1,425,000. What amount of goodwill impairment, if any, should Francisco recognize on its 2018 income statement?

LO 3-6

17. Alomar Co., a consolidated enterprise, conducted an impairment review for each of its reporting units. In its qualitative assessment, one particular reporting unit, Sellers, emerged as a candidate for possible goodwill impairment. Sellers has recognized net assets of $1,094, including goodwill of $755. Seller's fair value is assessed at $1,028 and includes two internally developed unrecognized intangible assets (a patent and a customer list with fair values of $199 and $56, respectively). The following table summarizes current financial information for the Sellers reporting unit:

	Carrying Amounts	Fair Values
Tangible assets, net	$ 84	$ 137
Recognized intangible assets, net	255	326
Goodwill	755	?
Unrecognized intangible assets	0	255
Total	$1,094	$1,028

a. Determine the amount of any goodwill impairment for Alomar's Sellers reporting unit.

b. After recognition of any goodwill impairment loss, what are the reported carrying amounts for the following assets of Alomar's reporting unit Sellers?

- Tangible assets, net.
- Goodwill.
- Patent.
- Customer list.

LO 3-6

18. Destin Company recently acquired several businesses and recognized goodwill in each acquisition. Destin has allocated the resulting goodwill to its three reporting units: Sand Dollar, Salty Dog, and Baytowne. Destin opts to skip the qualitative assessment and therefore performs a quantitative goodwill impairment review annually.

In its current year assessment of goodwill, Destin provides the following individual asset and liability values for each reporting unit:

	Carrying Amounts	Fair Values
Sand Dollar		
Tangible assets	$180,000	$190,000
Trademark	170,000	150,000
Customer list	90,000	100,000
Goodwill	120,000	?
Liabilities	(30,000)	(30,000)
Salty Dog		
Tangible assets	$200,000	$200,000
Unpatented technology	170,000	125,000
Licenses	90,000	100,000
Goodwill	150,000	?
Baytowne		
Tangible assets	$140,000	$150,000
Unpatented technology	–0–	100,000
Copyrights	50,000	80,000
Goodwill	90,000	?

The fair values for each reporting unit (including goodwill) are $510,000 for Sand Dollar, $580,000 for Salty Dog, and $560,000 for Baytowne. To date, Destin has reported no goodwill impairments.

a. How much goodwill impairment should Destin report this year?

b. What changes to the valuations of Destin's tangible assets and identified intangible assets should be reported based on the goodwill impairment tests?

Problems 19 through 21 should be viewed as independent situations. They are based on the following data:

Chapman Company obtains 100 percent of Abernethy Company's stock on January 1, 2017. As of that date, Abernethy has the following trial balance:

	Debit	Credit
Accounts payable		$ 50,000
Accounts receivable	$ 40,000	
Additional paid-in capital		50,000
Buildings (net) (4-year remaining life)	120,000	
Cash and short-term investments	60,000	
Common stock		250,000
Equipment (net) (5-year remaining life)	200,000	
Inventory	90,000	
Land	80,000	
Long-term liabilities (mature 12/31/20)		150,000
Retained earnings, 1/1/17		100,000
Supplies	10,000	
Totals	$600,000	$600,000

During 2017, Abernethy reported net income of $80,000 while declaring and paying dividends of $10,000. During 2018, Abernethy reported net income of $110,000 while declaring and paying dividends of $30,000.

LO 3-3a

19. Assume that Chapman Company acquired Abernethy's common stock for $490,000 in cash. As of January 1, 2017, Abernethy's land had a fair value of $90,000, its buildings were valued at $160,000, and its equipment was appraised at $180,000. Chapman uses the equity method for this investment. Prepare consolidation worksheet entries for December 31, 2017, and December 31, 2018.

LO 3-3b

20. Assume that Chapman Company acquired Abernethy's common stock for $500,000 in cash. Assume that the equipment and long-term liabilities had fair values of $220,000 and $120,000, respectively, on the acquisition date. Chapman uses the initial value method to account for its investment. Prepare consolidation worksheet entries for December 31, 2017, and December 31, 2018.

LO 3-3c

21. Assume that Chapman Company acquired Abernethy's common stock by paying $520,000 in cash. All of Abernethy's accounts are estimated to have a fair value approximately equal to present book values. Chapman uses the partial equity method to account for its investment. Prepare the consolidation worksheet entries for December 31, 2017, and December 31, 2018.

LO 3-3a, 3-3b, 3-4

22. Adams, Inc., acquires Clay Corporation on January 1, 2017, in exchange for $510,000 cash. Immediately after the acquisition, the two companies have the following account balances. Clay's equipment (with a five-year remaining life) is actually worth $440,000. Credit balances are indicated by parentheses.

	Adams	Clay
Current assets	$ 300,000	$ 220,000
Investment in Clay	510,000	–0–
Equipment	600,000	390,000
Liabilities	(200,000)	(160,000)
Common stock	(350,000)	(150,000)
Retained earnings, 1/1/17	(860,000)	(300,000)

In 2017, Clay earns a net income of $55,000 and declares and pays a $5,000 cash dividend. In 2017, Adams reports net income from its own operations (exclusive of any income from Clay) of $125,000 and declares no dividends. At the end of 2018, selected account balances for the two companies are as follows:

	Adams	Clay
Revenues	$(400,000)	$(240,000)
Expenses	290,000	180,000
Investment income	Not given	–0–
Retained earnings, 1/1/18	Not given	(350,000)

(Continued)

(Continued)

	Adams	Clay
Dividends declared	–0–	8,000
Common stock	(350,000)	(150,000)
Current assets	580,000	262,000
Investment in Clay	Not given	–0–
Equipment	520,000	420,000
Liabilities	(152,000)	(130,000)

a. What are the December 31, 2018, Investment Income and Investment in Clay account balances assuming Adams uses the:
- Equity method.
- Initial value method.

b. How does the parent's internal investment accounting method choice affect the amount reported for expenses in its December 31, 2018, consolidated income statement?

c. How does the parent's internal investment accounting method choice affect the amount reported for equipment in its December 31, 2018, consolidated balance sheet?

d. What is Adams's January 1, 2018, Retained Earnings account balance assuming Adams accounts for its investment in Clay using the:
- Equity value method.
- Initial value method.

e. What worksheet adjustment to Adams's January 1, 2018, Retained Earnings account balance is required if Adams accounts for its investment in Clay using the initial value method?

f. Prepare the worksheet entry to eliminate Clay's stockholders' equity.

g. What is consolidated net income for 2018?

LO 3-1, 3-4

23. Following are selected account balances from Penske Company and Stanza Corporation as of December 31, 2018:

	Penske	Stanza
Revenues	$(700,000)	$(400,000)
Cost of goods sold	250,000	100,000
Depreciation expense	150,000	200,000
Investment income	Not given	–0–
Dividends declared	80,000	60,000
Retained earnings, 1/1/18	(600,000)	(200,000)
Current assets	400,000	500,000
Copyrights	900,000	400,000
Royalty agreements	600,000	1,000,000
Investment in Stanza	Not given	–0–
Liabilities	(500,000)	(1,380,000)
Common stock	(600,000) ($20 par)	(200,000) ($10 par)
Additional paid-in capital	(150,000)	(80,000)

On January 1, 2018, Penske acquired all of Stanza's outstanding stock for $680,000 fair value in cash and common stock. Penske also paid $10,000 in stock issuance costs. At the date of acquisition, copyrights (with a six-year remaining life) have a $440,000 book value but a fair value of $560,000.

a. As of December 31, 2018, what is the consolidated copyrights balance?

b. For the year ending December 31, 2018, what is consolidated net income?

c. As of December 31, 2018, what is the consolidated retained earnings balance?

d. As of December 31, 2018, what is the consolidated balance to be reported for goodwill?

LO 3-2, 3-3, 3-4

24. Foxx Corporation acquired all of Greenburg Company's outstanding stock on January 1, 2016, for $600,000 cash. Greenburg's accounting records showed net assets on that date of $470,000, although equipment with a 10-year remaining life was undervalued on the records by $90,000. Any recognized goodwill is considered to have an indefinite life.

Greenburg reports net income in 2016 of $90,000 and $100,000 in 2017. The subsidiary declared dividends of $20,000 in each of these two years.

Account balances for the year ending December 31, 2018, follow. Credit balances are indicated by parentheses.

	Foxx	Greenburg
Revenues	$ (800,000)	$ (600,000)
Cost of goods sold	100,000	150,000
Depreciation expense	300,000	350,000
Investment income	(20,000)	–0–
Net income	$ (420,000)	$ (100,000)
Retained earnings, 1/1/18	$(1,100,000)	$ (320,000)
Net income	(420,000)	(100,000)
Dividends declared	120,000	20,000
Retained earnings, 12/31/18	$(1,400,000)	$ (400,000)
Current assets	$ 300,000	$ 100,000
Investment in subsidiary	600,000	–0–
Equipment (net)	900,000	600,000
Buildings (net)	800,000	400,000
Land	600,000	100,000
Total assets	$ 3,200,000	$ 1,200,000
Liabilities	$ (900,000)	$ (500,000)
Common stock	(900,000)	(300,000)
Retained earnings	(1,400,000)	(400,000)
Total liabilities and equity	$(3,200,000)	$(1,200,000)

a. Determine the December 31, 2018, consolidated balance for each of the following accounts:

Depreciation Expense	Buildings
Dividends Declared	Goodwill
Revenues	Common Stock
Equipment	

b. How does the parent's choice of an accounting method for its investment affect the balances computed in requirement (*a*)?

c. Which method of accounting for this subsidiary is the parent actually using for internal reporting purposes?

d. If the parent company had used a different method of accounting for this investment, how could that method have been identified?

e. What would be Foxx's balance for retained earnings as of January 1, 2018, if each of the following methods had been in use?

- Initial value method.
- Partial equity method.
- Equity method.

LO 3-1, 3-3a, 3-4

25. Allison Corporation acquired all of the outstanding voting stock of Mathias, Inc., on January 1, 2017, in exchange for $5,875,000 in cash. Allison intends to maintain Mathias as a wholly owned subsidiary. Both companies have December 31 fiscal year-ends. At the acquisition date, Mathias's stockholders' equity was $2,000,000 including retained earnings of $1,500,000.

At the acquisition date, Allison prepared the following fair value allocation schedule for its newly acquired subsidiary:

Consideration transferred		$5,875,000
Mathias stockholders' equity		2,000,000
Excess fair over book value		$3,875,000
to unpatented technology (8-year remaining life)	$ 800,000	
to patents (10-year remaining life)	2,500,000	
to increase long-term debt (undervalued, 5-year remaining life)	(100,000)	3,200,000
Goodwill		$ 675,000

Post-acquisition, Allison employs the equity method to account for its investment in Mathias. During the two years following the business combination, Mathias reports the following income and dividends:

	Income	*Dividends*
2017	$480,000	$25,000
2018	960,000	50,000

No asset impairments have occurred since the acquisition date.

Individual financial statements for each company as of December 31, 2018, appear below. Parentheses indicate credit balances. Dividends declared were paid in the same period.

Income Statement	**Allison**	**Mathias**
Sales	(6,400,000)	(3,900,000)
Cost of goods sold	4,500,000	2,500,000
Depreciation expense	875,000	277,000
Amortization expense	430,000	103,000
Interest expense	55,000	60,000
Equity earnings in Mathias	(630,000)	–0–
Net income	(1,170,000)	(960,000)
Statement of Retained Earnings		
Retained earnings 1/1	(5,340,000)	(1,955,000)
Net income (above)	(1,170,000)	(960,000)
Dividends declared	560,000	50,000
Retained earnings 12/31	(5,950,000)	(2,865,000)
Balance Sheet		
Cash	75,000	143,000
Accounts receivable	950,000	225,000
Inventories	1,700,000	785,000
Investment in Mathias	6,580,000	–0–
Equipment (net)	3,700,000	2,052,000
Patents	95,000	–0–
Unpatented technology	2,125,000	1,450,000
Goodwill	425,000	–0–
Total assets	15,650,000	4,655,000
Accounts payable	(500,000)	(90,000)
Long-term debt	(1,000,000)	(1,200,000)
Common stock	(8,200,000)	(500,000)
Retained earnings 12/31	(5,950,000)	(2,865,000)
Total liabilities and equity	(15,650,000)	(4,655,000)

Required:

a. Show how Allison determined its December 31, 2018, Investment in Mathias balance.

b. Prepare a worksheet to determine the consolidated values to be reported on Allison's financial statements.

LO 3-1, 3-3a

26. On January 3, 2016, Persoff Corporation acquired all of the outstanding voting stock of Sea Cliff, Inc., in exchange for $6,000,000 in cash. Persoff elected to exercise control over Sea Cliff as a wholly owned subsidiary with an independent accounting system. Both companies have December 31 fiscal year-ends. At the acquisition date, Sea Cliff's stockholders' equity was $2,500,000 including retained earnings of $1,700,000.

Persoff pursued the acquisition, in part, to utilize Sea Cliff's technology and computer software. These items had fair values that differed from their values on Sea Cliff's books as follows:

Asset	**Book Value**	**Fair Value**	**Remaining Useful Life**
Patented technology	$140,000	$2,240,000	7 years
Computer software	$ 60,000	$1,260,000	12 years

Sea Cliff's remaining identifiable assets and liabilities had acquisition-date book values that closely approximated fair values. Since acquisition, no assets have been impaired. During the next three years, Sea Cliff reported the following income and dividends:

	Net Income	Dividends
2016	$900,000	$150,000
2017	940,000	150,000
2018	975,000	150,000

December 31, 2018, financial statements for each company appear below. Parentheses indicate credit balances. Dividends declared were paid in the same period.

Income Statement	Persoff	Sea Cliff
Revenues	$ (2,720,000)	$(2,250,000)
Cost of goods sold	1,350,000	870,000
Depreciation expense	275,000	380,000
Amortization expense	370,000	25,000
Equity earnings in Sea Cliff	(575,000)	–0–
Net income	$ (1,300,000)	$ (975,000)
Statement of Retained Earnings		
Retained earnings 1/1	$ (7,470,000)	$(3,240,000)
Net income (above)	(1,300,000)	(975,000)
Dividends declared	600,000	150,000
Retained earnings 12/31	$ (8,170,000)	$(4,065,000)
Balance Sheet		
Current assets	$ 490,000	$ 375,000
Investment in Sea Cliff	7,165,000	–0–
Computer software	300,000	45,000
Patented technology	800,000	80,000
Goodwill	100,000	–0–
Equipment	1,835,000	4,500,000
Total assets	$ 10,690,000	$ 5,000,000
Liabilities	$ (520,000)	$ (135,000)
Common stock	(2,000,000)	(800,000)
Retained earnings 12/31	(8,170,000)	(4,065,000)
Total liabilities and equity	$(10,690,000)	$(5,000,000)

a. Construct Persoff's acquisition-date fair-value allocation schedule for its investment in Sea Cliff.

b. Show how Persoff determined its Equity earnings in Sea Cliff balance for the year ended December 31, 2018.

c. Show how Persoff determined its December 31, 2018, Investment in Sea Cliff balance.

d. Prepare a worksheet to determine the consolidated values to be reported on Persoff's financial statements.

LO 3-1, 3-3a

27. On January 1, 2017, Prestige Corporation acquired 100 percent of the voting stock of Stylene Corporation in exchange for $2,030,000 in cash and securities. On the acquisition date, Stylene had the following balance sheet:

Cash	$ 23,000	Accounts payable	$1,050,000
Accounts receivable	97,000		
Inventory	140,000		
Equipment (net)	1,490,000	Common stock	800,000
Trademarks	850,000	Retained earnings	750,000
	$2,600,000		$2,600,000

At the acquisition date, the book values of Stylene's assets and liabilities were generally equivalent to their fair values except for the following assets:

Asset	Book Value	Fair Value	Remaining Useful Life
Equipment	$1,490,000	$1,610,000	8 years
Customer lists	–0–	160,000	4 years
Trademarks	850,000	900,000	Indefinite

During the next two years, Stylene has the following income and dividends in its own separately prepared financial reports to its parent.

	Net Income	Dividends
2017	$175,000	$25,000
2018	375,000	45,000

Dividends are declared and paid in the same period. The December 31, 2018, separate financial statements for each company appear below. Parentheses indicate credit balances.

Income Statement	Prestige	Stylene
Revenues	$ (4,200,000)	$ (2,200,000)
Cost of goods sold	2,300,000	1,550,000
Depreciation expense	495,000	275,000
Amortization expense	105,000	–0–
Equity earnings in Stylene	(320,000)	–0–
Net income	$ (1,620,000)	$ (375,000)
Statement of Retained Earnings		
Retained earnings 1/1	$ (2,900,000)	$ (900,000)
Net income (above)	(1,620,000)	(375,000)
Dividends declared	150,000	45,000
Retained earnings 12/31	$ (4,370,000)	$ (1,230,000)
Balance Sheet		
Cash	$ 430,000	$ 35,000
Accounts receivable	693,000	75,000
Inventory	890,000	420,000
Investment in Stylene	2,400,000	–0–
Equipment	6,000,000	1,400,000
Customer lists	115,000	–0–
Trademarks	2,500,000	850,000
Goodwill	172,000	–0–
Total assets	$ 13,200,000	$ 2,780,000
Accounts payable	$ (330,000)	$ (750,000)
Common stock	(8,500,000)	(800,000)
Retained earnings 12/31	(4,370,000)	(1,230,000)
Total liabilities and equity	$(13,200,000)	$ (2,780,000)

a. Prepare Prestige's acquisition-date fair-value allocation schedule for its investment in Stylene.

b. Show how Prestige determined its December 31, 2018, Investment in Stylene balance.

c. Prepare a worksheet to determine the balances for Prestige's December 31, 2018, consolidated financial statements.

LO 3-1, 3-3a

excel

28. Patrick Corporation acquired 100 percent of O'Brien Company's outstanding common stock on January 1, for $550,000 in cash. O'Brien reported net assets with a carrying amount of $350,000 at that time. Some of O'Brien's assets either were unrecorded (having been internally developed) or had fair values that differed from book values as follows:

	Book Values	Fair Values
Trademarks (indefinite life)	$ 60,000	$160,000
Customer relationships (5-year remaining life)	–0–	75,000
Equipment (10-year remaining life)	342,000	312,000

Any goodwill is considered to have an indefinite life with no impairment charges during the year.

Following are financial statements at the end of the first year for these two companies prepared from their separately maintained accounting systems. O'Brien declared and paid dividends in the same period. Credit balances are indicated by parentheses.

	Patrick	O'Brien
Revenues	$ (1,125,000)	$ (520,000)
Cost of goods sold	300,000	228,000
Depreciation expense	75,000	70,000
Amortization expense	25,000	–0–
Income from O'Brien	(210,000)	–0–
Net Income	$ (935,000)	$ (222,000)
Retained earnings 1/1	$ (700,000)	$ (250,000)
Net Income	(935,000)	(222,000)
Dividends declared	142,000	80,000
Retained earnings 12/31	$ (1,493,000)	$ (392,000)
Cash	$ 185,000	$ 105,000
Receivables	225,000	56,000
Inventory	175,000	135,000
Investment in O'Brien	680,000	–0–
Trademarks	474,000	60,000
Customer relationships	–0–	–0–
Equipment (net)	925,000	272,000
Goodwill	–0–	–0–
Total assets	$ 2,664,000	$ 628,000
Liabilities	$ (771,000)	$ (136,000)
Common stock	(400,000)	(100,000)
Retained earnings 12/31	(1,493,000)	(392,000)
Total liabilities and equity	$ (2,664,000)	$ (628,000)

a. Show how Patrick computed the $210,000 Income of O'Brien balance. Discuss how you determined which accounting method Patrick uses for its investment in O'Brien.

b. Without preparing a worksheet or consolidation entries, determine and explain the totals to be reported for this business combination for the year ending December 31.

c. Verify the totals determined in part (*b*) by producing a consolidation worksheet for Patrick and O'Brien for the year ending December 31.

LO 3-1, 3-3a, 3-3b, 3-4

excel

29. Following are separate financial statements of Michael Company and Aaron Company as of December 31, 2018 (credit balances indicated by parentheses). Michael acquired all of Aaron's outstanding voting stock on January 1, 2014, by issuing 20,000 shares of its own $1 par common stock. On the acquisition date, Michael Company's stock actively traded at $23.50 per share.

	Michael Company 12/31/18	Aaron Company 12/31/18
Revenues	$ (610,000)	$ (370,000)
Cost of goods sold	270,000	140,000
Amortization expense	115,000	80,000
Dividend income	(5,000)	–0–
Net income	$ (230,000)	$ (150,000)
Retained earnings, 1/1/18	$ (880,000)	$ (490,000)
Net income (above)	(230,000)	(150,000)
Dividends declared	90,000	5,000
Retained earnings, 12/31/18	$ (1,020,000)	$ (635,000)
Cash	$ 110,000	$ 15,000
Receivables	380,000	220,000
Inventory	560,000	280,000
Investment in Aaron Company	470,000	–0–
Copyrights	460,000	340,000
Royalty agreements	920,000	380,000
Total assets	$ 2,900,000	$ 1,235,000
Liabilities	$ (780,000)	$ (470,000)
Preferred stock	(300,000)	–0–
Common stock	(500,000)	(100,000)
Additional paid-in capital	(300,000)	(30,000)
Retained earnings, 12/31/18	(1,020,000)	(635,000)
Total liabilities and equity	$ (2,900,000)	$(1,235,000)

On the date of acquisition, Aaron reported retained earnings of $230,000 and a total book value of $360,000. At that time, its royalty agreements were undervalued by $60,000. This intangible was assumed to have a six-year remaining life with no residual value. Additionally, Aaron owned a trademark with a fair value of $50,000 and a 10-year remaining life that was not reflected on its books. Aaron declared and paid dividends in the same period.

a. Using the preceding information, prepare a consolidation worksheet for these two companies as of December 31, 2018.

b. Instead of the initial value method, assume now that Michael applies the equity method to its Investment in Aaron account. What account balances would the parent's individual financial statements then show for the Equity in Subsidiary Earnings, Retained Earnings, and Investment in Aaron accounts?

c. Assuming that Michael applied the equity method to this investment, how would the consolidation entries differ on a December 31, 2018, worksheet?

d. Assuming that Michael applied the equity method to this investment, how would the December 31, 2018, reported consolidated balances differ?

LO 3-1, 3-3, 3-6

eXcel

30. Giant acquired all of Small's common stock on January 1, 2014, in exchange for cash of $770,000. On that day, Small reported common stock of $170,000 and retained earnings of $400,000. At the acquisition date, $90,000 of the fair-value price was attributed to undervalued land while $50,000 was assigned to undervalued equipment having a 10-year remaining life. The $60,000 unallocated portion of the acquisition-date excess fair value over book value was viewed as goodwill. Over the next few years, Giant applied the equity method to the recording of this investment.

Following are individual financial statements for the year ending December 31, 2018. On that date, Small owes Giant $10,000. Small declared and paid dividends in the same period. Credits are indicated by parentheses.

a. How was the $135,000 Equity in Income of Small balance computed?

b. Without preparing a worksheet or consolidation entries, determine and explain the totals to be reported by this business combination for the year ending December 31, 2018.

c. Verify the amounts determined in part (*b*) by producing a consolidation worksheet for Giant and Small for the year ending December 31, 2018.

d. If Giant determined that the entire amount of goodwill from its investment in Small was impaired in 2018, how would the parent's accounts reflect the impairment loss? How would the worksheet process change? What impact does an impairment loss have on consolidated financial statements?

	Giant	Small
Revenues	$(1,175,000)	$ (360,000)
Cost of goods sold	550,000	90,000
Depreciation expense	172,000	130,000
Equity in income of Small	(135,000)	–0–
Net income	$ (588,000)	$ (140,000)
Retained earnings, 1/1/18	$(1,417,000)	$ (620,000)
Net income (above)	(588,000)	(140,000)
Dividends declared	310,000	110,000
Retained earnings, 12/31/18	$(1,695,000)	$ (650,000)
Current assets	$ 398,000	$ 318,000
Investment in Small	995,000	–0–
Land	440,000	165,000
Buildings (net)	304,000	419,000
Equipment (net)	648,000	286,000
Goodwill	–0–	–0–
Total assets	$ 2,785,000	$ 1,188,000
Liabilities	$ (840,000)	$ (368,000)
Common stock	(250,000)	(170,000)
Retained earnings (above)	(1,695,000)	(650,000)
Total liabilities and equity	$(2,785,000)	$(1,188,000

LO 3-1, 3-3a, 3-3b, 3-4

31. On January 1, 2017, Pinnacle Corporation exchanged $3,200,000 cash for 100 percent of the outstanding voting stock of Strata Corporation. On the acquisition date, Strata had the following balance sheet:

Cash	$ 122,000	Accounts payable	$ 375,000
Accounts receivable	283,000	Long-term debt	2,655,000
Inventory	350,000	Common stock	1,500,000
Buildings (net)	1,875,000	Retained earnings	1,100,000
Licensing agreements	3,000,000		$5,630,000
	$5,630,000		

Pinnacle prepared the following fair-value allocation:

Fair value of Strata (consideration transferred)		$3,200,000
Carrying amount acquired		2,600,000
Excess fair value		600,000
to buildings (undervalued)	$300,000	
to licensing agreements (overvalued)	(100,000)	200,000
to goodwill (indefinite life)		$ 400,000

At the acquisition date, Strata's buildings had a 10-year remaining life and its licensing agreements were due to expire in 5 years. At December 31, 2018, Strata's accounts payable included an $85,000 current liability owed to Pinnacle. Strata Corporation continues its separate legal existence as a wholly owned subsidiary of Pinnacle with independent accounting records. Pinnacle employs the initial value method in its internal accounting for its investment in Strata.

The separate financial statements for the two companies for the year ending December 31, 2018, follow. Credit balances are indicated by parentheses.

	Pinnacle	Strata
Sales	$ (7,000,000)	$(3,000,000)
Cost of goods sold	4,650,000	1,700,000
Interest expense	255,000	160,000
Depreciation expense	585,000	350,000
Amortization expense		600,000
Dividend income	(50,000)	
Net income	$ (1,560,000)	$ (190,000)
Retained earnings 1/1/18	$ (5,000,000)	$(1,350,000)
Net income	(1,560,000)	(190,000)
Dividends declared	560,000	50,000
Retained earnings 12/31/18	$ (6,000,000)	$(1,490,000)
Cash	$ 433,000	$ 165,000
Accounts receivable	1,210,000	200,000
Inventory	1,235,000	1,500,000
Investment in Strata	3,200,000	
Buildings (net)	5,572,000	2,040,000
Licensing agreements		1,800,000
Goodwill	350,000	
Total assets	$ 12,000,000	$ 5,705,000
Accounts payable	$ (300,000)	$ (715,000)
Long-term debt	(2,700,000)	(2,000,000)
Common stock	(3,000,000)	(1,500,000)
Retained earnings 12/31/18	(6,000,000)	(1,490,000)
Total liabilities and OE	$(12,000,000)	$(5,705,000)

a. Prepare a worksheet to consolidate the financial information for these two companies.

b. Compute the following amounts that would appear on Pinnacle's 2018 separate (nonconsolidated) financial records if Pinnacle's investment accounting was based on the equity method.
- Subsidiary income.
- Retained earnings, 1/1/18.
- Investment in Strata.

c. What effect does the parent's internal investment accounting method have on its consolidated financial statements?

LO 3-1, 3-3, 3-4

eXcel

32. Following are selected accounts for Mergaronite Company and Hill, Inc., as of December 31, 2018. Several of Mergaronite's accounts have been omitted. Credit balances are indicated by parentheses. Dividends were declared and paid in the same period.

	Mergaronite	Hill
Revenues	$(600,000)	$(250,000)
Cost of goods sold	280,000	100,000
Depreciation expense	120,000	50,000
Investment income	Not given	NA
Retained earnings, 1/1/18	(900,000)	(600,000)
Dividends declared	130,000	40,000
Current assets	200,000	690,000
Land	300,000	90,000
Buildings (net)	500,000	140,000
Equipment (net)	200,000	250,000
Liabilities	(400,000)	(310,000)
Common stock	(300,000)	(40,000)
Additional paid-in capital	(50,000)	(160,000)

Assume that Mergaronite took over Hill on January 1, 2014, by issuing 7,000 shares of common stock having a par value of $10 per share but a fair value of $100 each. On January 1, 2014, Hill's land was undervalued by $20,000, its buildings were overvalued by $30,000, and equipment was undervalued by $60,000. The buildings had a 10-year remaining life; the equipment had a 5-year remaining life. A customer list with an appraised value of $100,000 was developed internally by Hill and was to be written off over a 20-year period.

a. Determine and explain the December 31, 2018, consolidated totals for the following accounts:

Revenues	Amortization Expense	Customer List
Cost of Goods Sold	Buildings	Common Stock
Depreciation Expense	Equipment	Additional Paid-In Capital

b. In requirement (*a*), why can the consolidated totals be determined without knowing which method the parent used to account for the subsidiary?

c. If the parent uses the equity method, what consolidation entries would be used on a 2018 worksheet?

LO 3-3, 3-4, 3-6

excel

33. On January 1, 2018, Brooks Corporation exchanged $1,183,000 fair-value consideration for all of the outstanding voting stock of Chandler, Inc. At the acquisition date, Chandler had a book value equal to $1,105,000. Chandler's individual assets and liabilities had fair values equal to their respective book values except for the patented technology account, which was undervalued by $204,000 with an estimated remaining life of six years. The Chandler acquisition was Brooks's only business combination for the year.

In case expected synergies did not materialize, Brooks Corporation wished to prepare for a potential future spin-off of Chandler, Inc. Therefore, Brooks had Chandler maintain its separate incorporation and independent accounting information system as elements of continuing value.

On December 31, 2018, each company submitted the following financial statements for consolidation. Dividends were declared and paid in the same period. Parentheses indicated credit balances.

	Brooks Corp.	Chandler Inc.
Income Statement		
Revenues	$ (640,000)	$ (587,000)
Cost of goods sold	255,000	203,000
Gain on bargain purchase	(126,000)	–0–
Depreciation and amortization	150,000	151,000
Equity earnings from Chandler	(199,000)	–0–
Net income	$ (560,000)	$ (233,000)
Statement of Retained Earnings		
Retained earnings, 1/1	$(1,835,000)	$ (805,000)
Net income (above)	(560,000)	(233,000)
Dividends declared	100,000	40,000
Retained earnings, 12/31	$(2,295,000)	$ (998,000)
Balance Sheet		
Current assets	$ 343,000	$ 432,000
Investment in Chandler	1,468,000	–0–
Trademarks	134,000	221,000
Patented technology	395,000	410,000
Equipment	693,000	341,000
Total assets	$ 3,033,000	$ 1,404,000
Liabilities	$ (203,000)	$ (106,000)
Common stock	(535,000)	(300,000)
Retained earnings, 12/31	(2,295,000)	(998,000)
Total liabilities and equity	$(3,033,000)	$(1,404,000)

a. Show how Brooks determined the following account balances:
- Gain on bargain purchase.
- Earnings from Chandler.
- Investment in Chandler.

b. Prepare a December 31, 2018, consolidated worksheet for Brooks and Chandler.

LO 3-3a, 3-3b, 3-7

eXcel

34. Branson paid $465,000 cash for all of the outstanding common stock of Wolfpack, Inc., on January 1, 2017. On that date, the subsidiary had a book value of $340,000 (common stock of $200,000 and retained earnings of $140,000), although various unrecorded royalty agreements (10-year remaining life) were assessed at a $100,000 fair value. Any remaining excess fair value was considered goodwill.

In negotiating the acquisition price, Branson also promised to pay Wolfpack's former owners an additional $50,000 if Wolfpack's income exceeded $120,000 total over the first two years after the acquisition. At the acquisition date, Branson estimated the probability-adjusted present value of this contingent consideration at $35,000. On December 31, 2017, based on Wolfpack's earnings to date, Branson increased the value of the contingency to $40,000.

During the subsequent two years, Wolfpack reported the following amounts for income and dividends:

	Net Income	Dividends Declared
2017	$65,000	$25,000
2018	75,000	35,000

In keeping with the original acquisition agreement, on December 31, 2018, Branson paid the additional $50,000 performance fee to Wolfpack's previous owners.

Prepare each of the following:

a. Branson's entry to record the acquisition of the shares of its Wolfpack subsidiary.

b. Branson's entries at the end of 2017 and 2018 to adjust its contingent performance obligation for changes in fair value and the December 31, 2018, payment.

c. Consolidation worksheet entries as of December 31, 2018, assuming that Branson has applied the equity method.

d. Consolidation worksheet entries as of December 31, 2018, assuming that Branson has applied the initial value method.

LO 3-3, 3-8

35. Allen Company acquired 100 percent of Bradford Company's voting stock on January 1, 2014, by issuing 10,000 shares of its $10 par value common stock (having a fair value of $14 per share). As of that date, Bradford had stockholders' equity totaling $105,000. Land shown on Bradford's accounting records was undervalued by $10,000. Equipment (with a five-year remaining life) was undervalued by $5,000. A secret formula developed by Bradford was appraised at $20,000 with an estimated life of 20 years.

Following are the separate financial statements for the two companies for the year ending December 31, 2018. There were no intra-entity payables on that date. Credit balances are indicated by parentheses.

	Allen Company	Bradford Company
Revenues	$ (485,000)	$(190,000)
Cost of goods sold	160,000	70,000
Depreciation expense	130,000	52,000
Subsidiary earnings	(66,000)	–0–
Net income	$ (261,000)	$ (68,000)
Retained earnings, 1/1/18	$ (659,000)	$ (98,000)
Net income (above)	(261,000)	(68,000)
Dividends declared	175,500	40,000
Retained earnings, 12/31/18	$ (744,500)	$(126,000)
Current assets	$ 268,000	$ 75,000
Investment in Bradford Company	216,000	–0–
Land	427,500	58,000
Buildings and equipment (net)	713,000	161,000
Total assets	$ 1,624,500	$ 294,000
Current liabilities	$ (190,000)	$(103,000)
Common stock	(600,000)	(60,000)
Additional paid-in capital	(90,000)	(5,000)
Retained earnings, 12/31/18	(744,500)	(126,000)
Total liabilities and equity	$(1,624,500)	$(294,000)

a. Explain how Allen derived the $66,000 balance in the Subsidiary Earnings account.

b. Prepare a worksheet to consolidate the financial information for these two companies.

LO 3-3a

eXcel

36. Tyler Company acquired all of Jasmine Company's outstanding stock on January 1, 2016, for $206,000 in cash. Jasmine had a book value of only $140,000 on that date. However, equipment (having an eight-year remaining life) was undervalued by $54,400 on Jasmine's financial records. A building with a 20-year remaining life was overvalued by $10,000. Subsequent to the acquisition, Jasmine reported the following:

	Net Income	Dividends Declared
2016	$50,000	$10,000
2017	60,000	40,000
2018	30,000	20,000

In accounting for this investment, Tyler has used the equity method. Selected accounts taken from the financial records of these two companies as of December 31, 2018, follow:

	Tyler Company	Jasmine Company
Revenues—operating	$(310,000)	$(104,000)
Expenses	198,000	74,000
Equipment (net)	320,000	50,000
Buildings (net)	220,000	68,000
Common stock	(290,000)	(50,000)
Retained earnings, 12/31/18	(410,000)	(160,000)

Determine and explain the following account balances as of December 31, 2018:

a. Investment in Jasmine Company (on Tyler's individual financial records).

b. Equity in Subsidiary Earnings (on Tyler's individual financial records).

c. Consolidated Net Income.

d. Consolidated Equipment (net).

e. Consolidated Buildings (net).

f. Consolidated Goodwill (net).

g. Consolidated Common Stock.

h. Consolidated Retained Earnings, 12/31/18.

LO 3-3

eXcel

37. On January 1, 2017, Procise Corporation acquired 100 percent of the outstanding voting stock of GaugeRite Corporation for $1,980,000 cash. On the acquisition date, GaugeRite had the following balance sheet:

Cash	$ 14,000	Accounts payable	$ 120,000
Accounts receivable	100,000	Long-term debt	930,000
Land	700,000	Common stock	1,000,000
Equipment (net)	1,886,000	Retained earnings	650,000
	$2,700,000		$2,700,000

At the acquisition date, the following allocation was prepared:

Fair value of consideration transferred		$1,980,000
Book value acquired		1,650,000
Excess fair value over book value		330,000
To in-process research and development	$44,000	
To equipment (8-year remaining life)	56,000	100,000
To goodwill (indefinite life)		$ 230,000

Although at acquisition date Procise had expected $44,000 in future benefits from GaugeRite's in-process research and development project, by the end of 2017 it was apparent that the research project was a failure with no future economic benefits.

On December 31, 2018, Procise and GaugeRite submitted the following trial balances for consolidation. There were no intra-entity payables on that date.

	Procise	GaugeRite
Sales	$ (3,500,000)	$ (1,000,000)
Cost of goods sold	1,600,000	630,000
Depreciation expense	350,000	130,000
Other operating expenses	190,000	30,000
Subsidiary income	(203,000)	–0–
Net income	$ (1,563,000)	$ (210,000)
Retained earnings 1/1/18	$ (3,000,000)	$ (800,000)
Net income	(1,563,000)	(210,000)
Dividends declared	200,000	25,000
Retained earnings 12/31/18	$ (4,363,000)	$ (985,000)
Cash	$ 228,000	$ 50,000
Accounts receivable	840,000	155,000
Inventory	900,000	580,000
Investment in GaugeRite	2,257,000	–0–
Land	3,500,000	700,000
Equipment (net)	4,785,000	1,700,000
Goodwill	290,000	–0–
Total assets	$ 12,800,000	$ 3,185,000
Accounts payable	$ (193,000)	$ (400,000)
Long-term debt	(3,094,000)	(800,000)
Common stock	(5,150,000)	(1,000,000)
Retained earnings 12/31/18	(4,363,000)	(985,000)
Total liabilities and equities	$(12,800,000)	$ (3,185,000)

a. Show how Procise derived its December 31, 2018, Investment in GaugeRite account balance.

b. Explain the treatment of the acquired in-process research and development.

c. Prepare a consolidated worksheet for Procise and GaugeRite as of December 31, 2018.

LO 3-4a, 3-6

excel

38. On January 1, Prine, Inc., acquired 100 percent of Lydia Company's common stock for a fair value of $120,000,000 in cash and stock. Lydia's assets and liabilities equaled their fair values except for its equipment, which was undervalued by $500,000 and had a 10-year remaining life.

Prine specializes in media distribution and viewed its acquisition of Lydia as a strategic move into content ownership and creation. Prine expected both cost and revenue synergies from controlling Lydia's artistic content (a large library of classic movies) and its sports programming specialty video operation. Accordingly, Prine allocated Lydia's assets and liabilities (including $50,000,000 of goodwill) to a newly formed operating segment appropriately designated as a reporting unit.

The fair values of the reporting unit's identifiable assets and liabilities through the first year of operations were as follows.

	Fair Values	
Account	**1/1**	**12/31**
Cash	$ 215,000	$ 109,000
Receivables (net)	525,000	897,000
Movie library (25-year remaining life)	40,000,000	60,000,000
Broadcast licenses (indefinite life)	15,000,000	20,000,000
Equipment (10-year remaining life)	20,750,000	19,000,000
Current liabilities	(490,000)	(650,000)
Long-term debt	(6,000,000)	(6,250,000)

However, Lydia's assets have taken longer than anticipated to produce the expected synergies with Prine's operations. Accordingly, Prine reviewed events and circumstances and concluded that Lydia's fair value was likely less than its carrying amount. At year-end, Prine reduced its assessment of the Lydia reporting unit's fair value to $110,000,000.

At December 31, Prine and Lydia submitted the following balances for consolidation. There were no intra-entity payables on that date.

	Prine, Inc.	Lydia Co.
Revenues	$ (18,000,000)	$(12,000,000)
Operating expenses	10,350,000	11,800,000
Equity in Lydia earnings	(150,000)	
Dividends declared	300,000	80,000
Retained earnings, 1/1	(52,000,000)	(2,000,000)
Cash	260,000	109,000
Receivables (net)	210,000	897,000
Investment in Lydia	120,070,000	
Broadcast licenses	350,000	14,014,000
Movie library	365,000	45,000,000
Equipment (net)	136,000,000	17,500,000
Current liabilities	(755,000)	(650,000)
Long-term debt	(22,000,000)	(7,250,000)
Common stock	(175,000,000)	(67,500,000)

a. What is the relevant initial test to determine whether goodwill could be impaired?

b. At what amount should Prine record an impairment loss for its Lydia reporting unit for the year?

c. What is consolidated net income for the year?

d. What is the December 31 consolidated balance for goodwill?

e. What is the December 31 consolidated balance for broadcast licenses?

f. Prepare a consolidated worksheet for Prine and Lydia (Prine's trial balance should first be adjusted for any appropriate impairment loss).

Appendix Problems

LO 3-8

39. Briefly discuss the cost savings that may result from a private company electing to amortize goodwill as opposed to annual impairment testing.

LO 3-8

40. Angela Corporation (a private company) acquired all of the outstanding voting stock of Eddy Tech, Inc., on January 1, 2018, in exchange for $9,000,000 in cash. At the acquisition date, Eddy Tech's stockholders' equity was $7,200,000 including retained earnings of $3,000,000.

At the acquisition date, Angela prepared the following fair value allocation schedule for its newly acquired subsidiary:

Consideration transferred		$9,000,000
Eddy's stockholder's equity		7,200,000
Excess fair over book value		$1,800,000
to patented technology (5-year remaining life)	$ 150,000	
to trade names (indefinite remaining life)	500,000	
to equipment (8-year remaining life)	50,000	700,000
Goodwill		$1,100,000

At the end of 2018, Angela and Eddy Tech report the following amounts from their individually maintained account balances, before consideration of their parent-subsidiary relationship. Parentheses indicate a credit balance.

	Angela	Eddy Tech
Sales	(7,850,000)	(2,400,000)
Cost of goods sold	4,200,000	1,300,000
Depreciation expense	425,000	48,000
Amortization expense	250,000	12,000
Other operating expenses	75,000	53,750
Net income	(2,900,000)	(986,250)

Required:

Prepare a 2018 consolidated income statement for Angela and its subsidiary Eddy Tech. Assume that Angela, as a private company, elects to amortize goodwill over a 10-year period.

Develop Your Skills

RESEARCH CASE

CPA skills

Jonas Tech Corporation recently acquired Innovation Plus Company. The combined firm consists of three related businesses that will serve as reporting units. In connection with the acquisition, Jonas requests your help with the following asset valuation and allocation issues. Support your answers with references to FASB ASC as appropriate.

Jonas recognizes several identifiable intangibles from its acquisition of Innovation Plus. It expresses the desire to have these intangible assets written down to zero in the acquisition period.

The price Jonas paid for Innovation Plus indicates that it paid a large amount for goodwill. However, Jonas worries that any future goodwill impairment may send the wrong signal to its investors about the wisdom of the Innovation Plus acquisition. Jonas thus wishes to allocate the combined goodwill of all of its reporting units to one account called *Enterprise Goodwill.* In this way, Jonas hopes to minimize the possibility of goodwill impairment because a decline in goodwill in one business unit could be offset by an increase in the value of goodwill in another business unit.

Required

1. Advise Jonas on the acceptability of its suggested immediate write-off of its identifiable intangibles.
2. Indicate the relevant factors to consider in allocating the value assigned to identifiable intangibles acquired in a business combination to expense over time.
3. Advise Jonas on the acceptability of its suggested treatment of goodwill.
4. Indicate the relevant factors to consider in allocating goodwill across an enterprise's business units.

MICROSOFT IMPAIRMENT ANALYSIS CASE

In 2015 Microsoft Corporation reported a $5.1 billion charge for the impairment of goodwill and a $2.2 billion charge for the impairment of intangible assets in one of its reporting units (segments) in its 10-K annual report. Referring to Microsoft's 2015 financial statements and any other information from the media, address the following:

1. Microsoft's segments serve as its reporting units for assessing goodwill for potential impairments. Which segment suffered a 2015 impairment? Describe the revenue model for this segment.
2. What were the underlying business reasons that required Microsoft to record a goodwill impairment in 2015?
3. How did Microsoft reflect the 2015 goodwill impairment in its income statement and cash flow statement?
4. Describe in your own words the goodwill impairment testing steps performed by Microsoft in 2015 and the consequent loss measurement.

FASB ASC AND IASB RESEARCH CASE

A vice president for operations at Poncho Platforms asks for your help on a financial reporting issue concerning goodwill. Two years ago, the company suffered a goodwill impairment loss for its Chip Integration reporting unit. Since that time, however, the Chip Integration unit has recovered nicely and its current cash flows (and projected cash flows) are at an all-time high. The vice president now asks whether the goodwill loss can be reversed given the reversal of fortunes for the Chip Integration reporting unit.

1. Is impairment of goodwill reversible under U.S. GAAP? How about under IFRS? (Refer to FASB Topic 350, "Intangibles—Goodwill and Other," and *IAS 36,* "Impairment of Assets.")
2. Are goodwill impairment testing procedures the same under IFRS and U.S. GAAP? If not, how is goodwill tested for impairment under IFRS? (Refer to *IAS 36,* "Impairment of Assets.")

EXCEL CASE 1

CPA skills

On January 1, 2017, Innovus, Inc., acquired 100 percent of the common stock of ChipTech Company for $670,000 in cash and other fair-value consideration. ChipTech's fair value was allocated among its net assets as follows:

Fair value of consideration transferred for ChipTech		$670,000
Book value of ChipTech:		
Common stock and Additional Paid-In Capital (APIC)	$130,000	
Retained earnings	370,000	500,000
Excess fair value over book value to		170,000
Trademark (10-year remaining life)	$ 40,000	
Existing technology (5-year remaining life)	80,000	120,000
Goodwill		$ 50,000

The December 31, 2018, trial balances for the parent and subsidiary follow (there were no intra-entity payables on that date):

	Innovus	ChipTech
Revenues	$ (990,000)	$ (210,000)
Cost of goods sold	500,000	90,000
Depreciation expense	100,000	5,000
Amortization expense	55,000	18,000
Dividend income	(40,000)	–0–
Net income	$ (375,000)	$ (97,000)
Retained earnings 1/1/18	$ (1,555,000)	$ (450,000)
Net income	(375,000)	(97,000)
Dividends declared	250,000	40,000
Retained earnings 12/31/18	$ (1,680,000)	$ (507,000)
Current assets	$ 960,000	$ 355,000
Investment in ChipTech	670,000	
Equipment (net)	765,000	225,000
Trademark	235,000	100,000
Existing technology	–0–	45,000
Goodwill	450,000	–0–
Total assets	$ 3,080,000	$ 725,000
Liabilities	$ (780,000)	(88,000)
Common stock	(500,000)	(100,000)
Additional paid-in capital	(120,000)	(30,000)
Retained earnings 12/31/18	(1,680,000)	(507,000)
Total liabilities and equity	$ (3,080,000)	$ (725,000)

Required

a. Using Excel, compute consolidated balances for Innovus and ChipTech. Either use a worksheet approach or compute the balances directly.

b. Prepare a second spreadsheet that shows a 2018 impairment loss for the entire amount of goodwill from the ChipTech acquisition.

EXCEL CASE 2

CPA skills

On January 1, 2017, Hi-Speed.com acquired 100 percent of the common stock of Wi-Free Co. for cash of $730,000. The consideration transferred was allocated among Wi-Free's net assets as follows:

Wi-Free fair value (cash paid by Hi-Speed)		$730,000
Book value of Wi-Free:		
Common stock and additional paid-in capital (APIC)	$130,000	
Retained earnings	370,000	500,000
Excess fair value over book value to		230,000
In-process R&D	$ 75,000	
Computer software (overvalued)	(30,000)	
Internet domain name	120,000	165,000
Goodwill		$ 65,000

At the acquisition date, the computer software had a 4-year remaining life, and the Internet domain name was estimated to have a 10-year remaining life. By the end of 2017, it became clear that the acquired in-process research and development would yield no economic benefits and Hi-Speed.com recognized an impairment loss. At December 31, 2018, Wi-Free's accounts payable included a $30,000 amount owed to Hi-Speed.

The December 31, 2018, trial balances for the parent and subsidiary follow:

	Hi-Speed.com	Wi-Free Co.
Revenues	$ (1,100,000)	$ (325,000)
Cost of goods sold	625,000	122,000
Depreciation expense	140,000	12,000
Amortization expense	50,000	11,000
Equity in subsidiary earnings	(175,500)	–0–
Net income	$ (460,500)	$ (180,000)
Retained earnings 1/1/18	$ (1,552,500)	$ (450,000)
Net income	(460,500)	(180,000)
Dividends declared	250,000	50,000
Retained earnings 12/31/18	$ (1,763,000)	$ (580,000)
Current assets	$ 1,034,000	$ 345,000
Investment in Wi-Free	856,000	–0–
Equipment (net)	713,000	305,000
Computer software	650,000	130,000
Internet domain name	–0–	100,000
Goodwill	–0–	–0–
Total assets	$ 3,253,000	$ 880,000
Liabilities	$ (870,000)	$ (170,000)
Common stock	(500,000)	(110,000)
Additional paid-in capital	(120,000)	(20,000)
Retained earnings 12/31/18	(1,763,000)	(580,000)
Total liabilities and equity	$ (3,253,000)	$ (880,000)

Required

a. Using Excel, prepare calculations showing how Hi-Speed derived the $856,000 amount for its investment in Wi-Free.

b. Using Excel, compute consolidated balances for Hi-Speed and Wi-Free. Either use a worksheet approach or compute the balances directly.

Computer Project

Alternative Investment Methods, Goodwill Impairment, and Consolidated Financial Statements

In this project, you are to provide an analysis of alternative accounting methods for controlling interest investments and subsequent effects on consolidated reporting. The project requires the use of a computer and a spreadsheet software package (e.g., Microsoft Excel, etc.). The use of these tools allows you to assess the sensitivity of alternative accounting methods on consolidated financial reporting without preparing several similar worksheets by hand. Also, by modeling a worksheet process, you can develop a better understanding of accounting for combined reporting entities.

Consolidated Worksheet Preparation

You will be creating and entering formulas to complete four worksheets. The first objective is to demonstrate the effect of different methods of accounting for the investments (equity, initial value, and partial equity) on the parent company's trial balance and on the consolidated worksheet subsequent to acquisition. The second objective is to show the effect on consolidated balances and key financial ratios of recognizing a goodwill impairment loss.

The project requires preparation of the following four separate worksheets:

a. Consolidated information worksheet (follows).
b. Equity method consolidation worksheet.
c. Initial value method consolidation worksheet.
d. Partial equity method consolidation worksheet.

If your spreadsheet package has multiple worksheet capabilities (e.g., Excel), you can use separate worksheets; otherwise, each of the four worksheets can reside in a separate area of a single spreadsheet.

In formulating your solution, each worksheet should link directly to the first worksheet. Also, feel free to create supplemental schedules to enhance the capabilities of your worksheet.

Project Scenario

Pecos Company acquired 100 percent of Suaro's outstanding stock for $1,450,000 cash on January 1, 2017, when Suaro had the following balance sheet:

Assets		**Liabilities and Equity**	
Cash	$ 37,000	Liabilities	$(422,000)
Receivables	82,000		
Inventory	149,000	Common stock	(350,000)
Land	90,000	Retained earnings	(126,000)
Equipment (net)	225,000		
Software	315,000		
Total assets	$898,000	Total liabilities and equity	$(898,000)

At the acquisition date, the fair values of each identifiable asset and liability that differed from book value were as follows:

Land	$ 80,000	
Brand name	60,000	(indefinite life—unrecognized on Suaro's books)
Software	415,000	(2-year estimated remaining useful life)
In-process R&D	300,000	

Additional Information

- Although at acquisition date Pecos expected future benefits from Suaro's in-process research and development (R&D), by the end of 2017 it became clear that the research project was a failure with no future economic benefits.
- During 2017, Suaro earns $75,000 and pays no dividends.
- Selected amounts from Pecos and Suaro's separate financial statements at December 31, 2018, are presented in the consolidated information worksheet. All consolidated worksheets are to be prepared as of December 31, 2018, two years subsequent to acquisition.
- Pecos's January 1, 2018, Retained Earnings balance—before any effect from Suaro's 2017 income—is $(930,000) (credit balance).
- Pecos has 500,000 common shares outstanding for EPS calculations and reported $2,943,100 for consolidated assets at the beginning of the period.

Following is the consolidated information worksheet.

	A	B	C	D
1	**December 31, 2018, trial balances**			
2				
3		**Pecos**	**Suaro**	
4	Revenues	$ (1,052,000)	$ (427,000)	
5	Operating expenses	821,000	262,000	
6	Goodwill impairment loss	?		
7	Income of Suaro	?		
8	Net income	?	$ (165,000)	
9				
10	Retained earnings—Pecos 1/1/18	?		
11	Retained earnings—Suaro 1/1/18		(201,000)	
12	Net income (above)	?	(165,000)	
13	Dividends declared	200,000	35,000	
14	Retained earnings 12/31/18	?	$ (331,000)	
15				
16	Cash	195,000	95,000	
17	Receivables	247,000	143,000	
18	Inventory	415,000	197,000	
19	Investment in Suaro	?		
20				
21				
22				
23	Land	341,000	85,000	
24	Equipment (net)	240,100	100,000	
25	Software		312,000	
26	Other intangibles	145,000		
27	Goodwill			
28	Total assets	?	$ 932,000	
29				
30	Liabilities	(1,537,100)	(251,000)	
31	Common stock	(500,000)	(350,000)	
32	Retained earnings (above)	?	(331,000)	
33	Total liabilities and equity	?	$ (932,000)	
34				
35	Fair-value allocation schedule			
36	Price paid	1,450,000		
37	Book value	476,000		
38	Excess initial value	974,000	Amortizations	
39	to land	(10,000)	2017	2018
40	to brand name	60,000	?	?

(continued)

(continued)

	A	B	C	D
41	to software	100,000	?	?
42	to IPR&D	300,000	?	?
43	to goodwill	524,000	?	?
44				
45	Suaro's RE changes	Income	Dividends	
46	2017	75,000	0	
47	2018	165,000	35,000	

Project Requirements

Complete the four worksheets as follows:

1. Input the **consolidated information worksheet** provided and complete the fair-value allocation schedule by computing the excess amortizations for 2017 and 2018.
2. Using separate worksheets, prepare Pecos's trial balances for each of the indicated accounting methods (equity, initial value, and partial equity). **Use only formulas for the Investment in Suaro, the Income of Suaro, and Retained Earnings accounts.**
3. **Using references to other cells only (either from the consolidated information worksheet or from the separate method sheets), prepare for each of the three consolidation worksheets:**
   - Adjustments and eliminations.
   - Consolidated balances.
4. Calculate and present the effects of a 2018 total goodwill impairment loss on the following ratios for the consolidated entity:
   - Earnings per share (EPS).
   - Return on assets.
   - Return on equity.
   - Debt to equity.

   Your worksheets should have the capability to adjust immediately for the possibility that all acquisition goodwill can be considered impaired in 2018.
5. **Prepare a word-processed report that describes and discusses the following worksheet results:**

   a. The effects of alternative investment accounting methods on the parent's trial balances and the final consolidation figures.

   b. The relation between consolidated retained earnings and the parent's retained earnings under each of the three (equity, initial value, partial equity) investment accounting methods.

   c. The effect on EPS, return on assets, return on equity, and debt-to-equity ratios of the recognition that all acquisition-related goodwill is considered impaired in 2018.

chapter 4

Consolidated Financial Statements and Outside Ownership

Wal-Mart Stores, Inc. (Walmart), in its 2015 consolidated financial statements, includes the accounts of the company and all of its subsidiaries in which a controlling interest is maintained. For those consolidated subsidiaries where Walmart's ownership is less than 100 percent, the outside stockholders' interests are shown as *noncontrolling interests* in the stockholders' equity section of its consolidated balance sheet. On its consolidated income statement, Walmart also allocates a share of the consolidated net income to the noncontrolling interest.

A number of reasons exist for one company to hold less than 100 percent ownership of a subsidiary. The parent might not have had sufficient resources available to obtain all of the outstanding stock. As a second possibility, a few subsidiary stockholders may elect to retain their ownership, perhaps in hope of getting a better price at a later date.

Lack of total ownership is frequently encountered with foreign subsidiaries. The laws of some countries prohibit outsiders from maintaining complete control of domestic business enterprises. In other areas of the world, a parent can seek to establish better relations with a subsidiary's employees, customers, and local government by maintaining some percentage of native ownership.

LO 4-1

Understand that business combinations can occur with less than complete ownership.

Regardless of the reason for owning less than 100 percent, the parent consolidates the financial data of every subsidiary when control is present. As discussed in Chapter 2, *complete ownership is not a prerequisite for consolidation.* A single economic entity is formed whenever one company is able to control the decision-making process of another.

Although most parent companies own 100 percent of their subsidiaries, a significant number, such as Walmart, establish control with a lesser amount of stock. The remaining outside owners are collectively referred to as *a noncontrolling interest,* which replaces the traditional term *minority interest.*[1] The presence of these other stockholders poses a number of reporting questions for the accountant. Whenever less than 100 percent of

[1] The term *minority interest* had been used almost universally to identify the presence of other outside owners. However, current GAAP refers to these outside owners as the noncontrolling interest. Because this term is more descriptive, it is used throughout this textbook.

Learning Objectives

After studying this chapter, you should be able to:

- **LO 4-1** Understand that business combinations can occur with less than complete ownership.
- **LO 4-2** Describe the concepts and valuation principles underlying the acquisition method of accounting for the noncontrolling interest.
- **LO 4-3** Allocate goodwill acquired in a business combination across the controlling and noncontrolling interests.
- **LO 4-4** Demonstrate the computation and allocation of consolidated net income in the presence of a noncontrolling interest.
- **LO 4-5** Identify and calculate the four noncontrolling interest figures that must be included within the consolidation process and prepare a consolidation worksheet in the presence of a noncontrolling interest.
- **LO 4-6** Identify appropriate placements for the components of the noncontrolling interest in consolidated financial statements.
- **LO 4-7** Determine the effect on consolidated financial statements of a control premium paid by the parent.
- **LO 4-8** Understand the impact on consolidated financial statements of a midyear acquisition.
- **LO 4-9** Understand the impact on consolidated financial statements when a step acquisition has taken place.
- **LO 4-10** Record the sale of a subsidiary (or a portion of its shares).

a subsidiary's voting stock is held, how should the subsidiary's accounts be valued within consolidated financial statements? How should the presence of these additional owners be acknowledged?

LO 4-2

Describe the concepts and valuation principles underlying the acquisition method of accounting for the noncontrolling interest.

Consolidated Financial Reporting in the Presence of a Noncontrolling Interest

Noncontrolling Interest Defined

The authoritative accounting literature defines a noncontrolling interest as follows:

> The ownership interests in the subsidiary that are held by owners other than the parent is a noncontrolling interest. The noncontrolling interest in a subsidiary is part of the equity of the consolidated group. (FASB ASC 810-10-45-15)

When a parent company acquires a controlling ownership interest with less than 100 percent of a subsidiary's voting shares, it must account for the noncontrolling shareholders' interest in its consolidated financial statements. The noncontrolling interest represents an additional set of owners who have legal claim to the subsidiary's net assets.

Exhibit 4.1 provides a framework for introducing several fundamental challenges in accounting and reporting for a noncontrolling interest. The issues focus on how the parent, in its consolidated financial statements, should

- Recognize the subsidiary's assets and liabilities.
- Assign values to the subsidiary's assets and liabilities.
- Value and disclose the presence of the other owners.

The acquisition method's solution to these challenges involves both the *economic unit concept* and *fair value.* First, the economic unit concept views the parent and subsidiary companies as a single economic unit for financial reporting purposes. Thus, a controlled company must always be consolidated as a whole regardless of the parent's level of ownership. As shown in Exhibit 4.1, when a parent controls a subsidiary through a 70 percent ownership, the parent must consolidate 100 percent of the subsidiary's (and the parent's) assets and liabilities in order to reflect the single economic unit. The consolidated balance sheet then provides an owners' equity amount for the noncontrolling owners' interest—a recognition that the parent does not own 100 percent of the subsidiary's assets and liabilities.

The acquisition method also captures the subsidiary's acquisition-date fair values as the relevant attribute for reporting the financial effects of the business combination—including the noncontrolling interest. Fair values also provide for managerial accountability to investors and creditors for assessing the success or failure of the combination. In contrast, the parent's assets and liabilities remain at their previous carrying amounts.

Control and Accountability

In acquiring a controlling interest, a parent company becomes responsible for managing all the subsidiary's assets and liabilities even though it may own only a partial interest. If a parent can control the business activities of its subsidiary, it directly follows that the parent

EXHIBIT 4.1
Noncontrolling Interest—Date of Acquisition

PARENT AND 70% OWNED SUBSIDIARY COMPANIES
Consolidated Balance Sheet
Date of Acquisition

Parent's assets (100%)	Parent's liabilities (100%)
Subsidiary's assets (100%)	**Subsidiary's liabilities (100%)**
	Parent company owners' equity
	• 100% of parent's net assets
	• **70% of subsidiary's net assets**
	Noncontrolling owners' interest
	• **30% of subsidiary net assets**

is accountable to its investors and creditors for all of the subsidiary's assets, liabilities, and profits. To provide a complete picture of the acquired subsidiary requires fair-value measurements for both the subsidiary as a whole and its individual assets and liabilities. Thus, for business combinations involving less-than-100 percent ownership, the acquirer recognizes and measures the following at the acquisition date:

- All subsidiary identifiable assets and liabilities at their full fair values.[2]
- Noncontrolling interest at fair value.
- Goodwill or a gain from a bargain purchase.

In concluding that consolidated statements involving a noncontrolling interest should initially show all of the subsidiary's assets and liabilities at their full fair values, the 2005 FASB exposure draft Business Combinations (para. B23.a.) observed:

> The acquirer obtains control of the acquiree at the acquisition date and, therefore, becomes responsible and accountable for all of the acquiree's assets, liabilities, and activities, regardless of the percentage of its ownership in the investee.
>
> . . . an important purpose of financial statements is to provide users with relevant and reliable information about the performance of the entity and the resources under its control. That applies regardless of the extent of the ownership interest a parent holds in a particular subsidiary. The Boards concluded that measurement at fair value enables users to better assess the cash generating abilities of the identifiable net assets acquired in the business combination and the accountability of management for the resources entrusted to it.

To summarize, even though a company acquires less than 100 percent of another firm, financial reporting standards require the parent to include 100 percent of the assets acquired and liabilities assumed. At the acquisition date, the parent measures at fair value both the subsidiary as a whole and its identifiable assets and liabilities. Also, the parent recognizes the noncontrolling interest at its acquisition-date fair value. However, as discussed below, measuring the fair value of the noncontrolling interest presents some special challenges.

Subsidiary Acquisition-Date Fair Value in the Presence of a Noncontrolling Interest

When a parent company acquires a less-than-100 percent controlling interest in another firm, the acquisition method requires a determination of the acquisition-date fair value of the acquired firm for consolidated financial reporting. The total acquired firm fair value in the presence of a partial acquisition is the sum of the following two components at the acquisition date:

- The fair value of the controlling interest.
- The fair value of the noncontrolling interest.

The sum of these two components serves as the starting point for the parent in valuing and reporting the subsidiary acquisition. If the sum exceeds the collective fair values of the identifiable net assets acquired and liabilities assumed, then goodwill is recognized. Conversely, if the collective fair values of the identifiable net assets acquired and liabilities assumed exceed the total fair value, the acquirer recognizes a gain on bargain purchase.

Measurement of the controlling interest fair value remains straightforward in the vast majority of cases—the consideration transferred by the parent typically provides the best evidence of fair value of the acquirer's interest. However, there is no parallel consideration transferred available to value the noncontrolling interest. Therefore, the parent must employ other valuation techniques to estimate the fair value of the noncontrolling interest at the acquisition date.

Usually, a parent can rely on readily available market trading activity to provide a fair valuation for its subsidiary's noncontrolling interest. Market trading prices for the noncontrolling interest shares in the weeks before and after the acquisition provide an objective measure of their fair value. The fair value of these shares then becomes the initial basis for reporting the noncontrolling interest in consolidated financial statements.

[2] As noted in Chapter 2, exceptions to the fair-value measurement principle include deferred taxes, certain employee benefits, indemnification assets, reacquired rights, share-based awards, and assets held for sale.

Discussion Question

The FASB received numerous comment letters during its deliberations prior to adopting the current financial accounting standards on business combinations. Many of these letters addressed the FASB's proposed (and ultimately accepted) use of the economic unit concept as a valuation basis for less-than-100-percent acquisitions. A sampling of these letters includes the following observations:

Bob Laux, Microsoft: Microsoft agrees with the Board that the principles underlying standards should strive to reflect the underlying economics of transactions and events. However, we do not believe the Board's conclusion that recognizing the entire economic value of the acquiree, regardless of the ownership interest in the acquiree at the acquisition date, reflects the underlying economics.

Patricia A. Little, Ford Motor Company: We agree that recognizing 100 percent of the fair value of the acquiree is appropriate. We believe that this is crucial in erasing anomalies which were created when only the incremental ownership acquired was fair valued and the minority interest was reflected at its carryover basis.

Sharilyn Gasaway, Alltel Corporation: One of the underlying principles . . . is that the acquirer should measure and recognize the fair value of the acquiree as a whole. If 100 percent of the ownership interests are acquired, measuring and recognizing 100 percent of the fair value is both appropriate and informative. However, if less than 100 percent of the ownership interests are acquired, recognizing the fair value of 100 percent of the business acquired is not representative of the value actually acquired. In the instance in which certain minority owners retain their ownership interest, recognizing the fair value of the minority interest does not provide sufficient benefit to financial statement users to justify the additional cost incurred to calculate that fair value.

PricewaterhouseCoopers: We agree that the noncontrolling interest should be recorded at its fair value when it is initially recorded in the consolidated financial statements. As such, when control is obtained in a single step, the acquirer would record 100 percent of the fair value of the assets acquired (including goodwill) and liabilities assumed.

Loretta Cangialosi, Pfizer: While we understand the motivation of the FASB to account for all elements of the acquisition transaction at fair value, we are deeply concerned about the practice issues that will result. The heavy reliance on expected value techniques, use of the hypothetical market participants, the lack of observable markets, and the obligation to affix values to "possible" and even "remote" scenarios, among other requirements, will all conspire to create a standard that will likely prove to be nonoperational, unauditable, representationally unfaithful, abuse-prone, costly, and of limited (and perhaps negative) shareholder value.

Do you think the FASB made the correct decision in requiring consolidated financial statements to recognize all of the subsidiary's assets and liabilities at fair value regardless of the percentage ownership acquired by the parent?

Acquirers frequently must pay a premium price per share to garner sufficient shares to ensure a controlling interest. A control premium, however, typically is needed only to acquire sufficient shares to obtain a controlling interest. The remaining (noncontrolling interest) shares no longer provide the added benefit of transferring control to the new owner, and, therefore, may sell at a price less than the shares that yielded control. For example, when Expedia, Inc. acquired its 63 percent controlling interest in Trivago, the fair value of the noncontrolling interest excluded any control premium. In discussing the Trivago acquisition, Expedia's 2015 annual report noted

> The fair value of the 37% noncontrolling interest was estimated to be $344 million at the time of acquisition based on the fair value per share, excluding the control premium. The control premium was derived directly based on the additional consideration paid to certain shareholders in order to obtain control. The additional consideration was determined to be the best estimate to represent the control premium as it was a premium paid only to the controlling shareholders.

Control premiums are properly included in the fair value of the controlling interest, but as the Expedia-Trivago combination demonstrates, they sometimes do not affect the fair values of the remaining subsidiary shares. Therefore, separate independent valuations for the controlling and noncontrolling interests are often needed for measuring the total fair value of the subsidiary.

In the absence of fair value evidence based on market trades, firms must turn to less objective measures of noncontrolling interest fair value. For example, comparable investments may be available to estimate fair value. Alternatively, valuation models based on subsidiary discounted cash flows or residual income projections can be employed to estimate the acquisition-date fair value of the noncontrolling interest. Finally, if a control premium is unlikely, the consideration paid by the parent can be used to imply a fair value for the entire subsidiary. The noncontrolling interest fair value is then simply measured as its percentage of this implied subsidiary total fair value.

Noncontrolling Interest Fair Value as Evidenced by Market Trades

In the majority of cases, direct evidence based on market activity in the outstanding subsidiary shares (not owned by the parent) will provide the best measure of acquisition-date fair value for the noncontrolling interest. For example, assume that Parker Corporation wished to acquire 9,000 of the 10,000 outstanding equity shares of Strong Company and projected substantial synergies from the proposed acquisition. Parker estimated that a 100 percent acquisition was not needed to extract these synergies. Also, Parker projected that financing more than a 90 percent acquisition would be too costly.

Parker then offered all of Strong's shareholders a premium price for up to 90 percent of the outstanding shares.[3] To induce a sufficient number of shareholders to sell, Parker needed to offer $70 per share, even though the shares had been trading in the $59 to $61 range. During the weeks following the acquisition, the 10 percent noncontrolling interest in Strong Company continues to trade in the $59 to $61 range.

In this case, the $70 per share price paid by Parker does not appear representative of the fair value of all the shares of Strong Company. The fact that the noncontrolling interest shares continue to trade around $60 per share indicates a $60,000 fair value for the 1,000 shares not owned by Parker. Therefore, the valuation of the noncontrolling interest is best evidenced by the traded fair value of Strong's shares, not the price paid by Parker.

The $70 share price paid by Parker nonetheless represents a negotiated value for the 9,000 shares. In the absence of any evidence to the contrary, these shares owned by Parker have a fair value of $630,000 incorporating the additional value Parker expects to extract from synergies with Strong. Thus the fair value of Strong is measured as the sum of the respective fair values of the controlling and noncontrolling interests as follows:

Fair value of controlling interest ($70 × 9,000 shares)	$630,000
Fair value of noncontrolling interest ($60 × 1,000 shares).	60,000
Acquisition-date fair value of Strong Company.	$690,000

At the acquisition date, Parker assessed the total fair value of Strong's identifiable net assets at $600,000. Therefore, we compute goodwill as the excess of the acquisition-date fair value of the firm as a whole over the sum of the fair values of the identifiable net assets as follows:

Acquisition-date fair value of Strong Company.	$690,000
Fair value of Strong Company's identifiable net assets	600,000
Goodwill	$ 90,000

[3] A more detailed analysis of the effect of a control premium on consolidated financial reporting is presented later in this chapter.

LO 4-3

Allocate goodwill acquired in a business combination across the controlling and noncontrolling interests.

Allocating Acquired Goodwill to the Controlling and Noncontrolling Interests

To properly report ownership equity in consolidated financial statements, acquisition-date goodwill should be apportioned across the controlling and noncontrolling interests. The parent first allocates goodwill to its controlling interest for the excess of the fair value of the parent's equity interest over its share of the fair value of the identifiable net assets. Any remaining goodwill is then attributed to the noncontrolling interest. As a result, the allocated goodwill will not always be proportional to the percentages owned. Continuing the Parker and Strong example, all of the acquisition goodwill is allocated to the controlling interest as follows:

	Controlling Interest	Noncontrolling Interest	Total
Acquisition-date fair value of Strong Company. . .	$630,000	$60,000	$690,000
Relative fair value of Strong's identifiable net assets (90% and 10% of $600,000)	540,000	60,000	600,000
Goodwill	$ 90,000	$ -0-	$ 90,000

In the unlikely event that the noncontrolling interest's proportionate share of the subsidiary's net asset fair values exceeds its total fair value, such an excess would serve to reduce the goodwill recognized by the parent. For example, if Strong's 10 percent noncontrolling interest had a fair value of $55,000, Strong's total fair value would equal $685,000, and goodwill (all allocated to the controlling interest) would decrease to $85,000. Alternatively, if Strong's 10 percent noncontrolling interest had a fair value of $70,000, Strong's total fair value would equal $700,000. In this case, goodwill would equal $100,000 with $90,000 allocated to the controlling interest and $10,000 allocated to the noncontrolling interest.

Finally, if the total fair value of the acquired firm is less than the collective sum of its identifiable net assets, a *bargain purchase* occurs. In such rare combinations, the parent recognizes the entire gain on bargain purchase in current income. In no case is any amount of the gain allocated to the noncontrolling interest.

Noncontrolling Interest Fair Value Implied by Parent's Consideration Transferred

In other cases, especially when a large percentage of the acquiree's voting stock is purchased, the consideration paid by the parent may be reflective of the acquiree's total fair value. For example, again assume Parker pays $70 per share for 9,000 shares of Strong Company representing a 90 percent equity interest. Also assume that the remaining 1,000 noncontrolling interest shares are not actively traded. If there was no compelling evidence that the $70 acquisition price was not representative of all of Strong's 10,000 shares, then it appears reasonable to estimate the fair value of the 10 percent noncontrolling interest using the price paid by Parker. The total fair value of Strong Company is then estimated at $700,000 and allocated as follows:

Fair value of controlling interest ($70 × 9,000 shares)	$630,000
Fair value of noncontrolling interest ($70 × 1,000 shares).	70,000
Acquisition-date fair value of Strong Company.	$700,000

Note that in this case, because the price per share paid by the parent equals the noncontrolling interest per share fair value, goodwill is recognized proportionately across the two ownership groups. Assuming again that the collective fair value of Strong's identifiable net assets equals $600,000, goodwill is recognized and allocated as follows:

	Controlling Interest	Noncontrolling Interest	Total
Acquisition-date fair value of Strong Company	$630,000	$70,000	$700,000
Relative fair value of Strong's identifiable net assets (90% and 10%)	540,000	60,000	600,000
Goodwill	$ 90,000	$10,000	$100,000

LO 4-4

Demonstrate the computation and allocation of consolidated net income in the presence of a noncontrolling interest.

Allocating Consolidated Net Income to the Parent and Noncontrolling Interest

Consolidated net income measures the results of operations for the combined entity. Reflecting the economic unit concept, consolidated net income includes 100 percent of the parent's net income and 100 percent of the subsidiary's net income, adjusted for excess acquisition-date fair value over book value amortizations. Once consolidated net income is determined, it is then allocated to the parent company and the noncontrolling interests. Because the noncontrolling interests' ownership pertains only to the subsidiary, their share of consolidated net income is limited to a share of the subsidiary's net income adjusted for acquisition-date excess fair-value amortizations.[4]

To illustrate, again assume that Parker acquires 90 percent of Strong Company. Further assume that current year consolidated net income equals $108,000 including $10,000 of annual acquisition-date excess fair-value amortization. If Strong reports revenues of $280,000 and expenses of $160,000 based on its internal book values, then the noncontrolling interest share of Strong's income can be computed as follows:

Noncontrolling Interest in Subsidiary Strong Company Net Income

Strong revenues	$280,000
Strong expenses..	160,000
Strong net income	$120,000
Excess acquisition-date fair-value amortization.......................	10,000
Strong net income adjusted for excess amortization..................	$110,000
Noncontrolling interest percentage................................	10%
Noncontrolling interest share of adjusted subsidiary net income	$ 11,000

The $11,000 noncontrolling interest share of adjusted subsidiary net income is equivalent to the noncontrolling interest share of consolidated net income. This figure is then simply subtracted from the combined entity's consolidated net income to derive the parent's interest in consolidated net income. Thus, the allocation is presented in Parker's consolidated financial statements as follows:

Consolidated Net Income Allocation

Consolidated net income	$108,000
Less: Net income attributable to noncontrolling interest...............	11,000
Net income attributable to parent (controlling interest)................	$ 97,000

Note that the noncontrolling shareholders' portion of consolidated net income is limited to their 10 percent share of the adjusted *subsidiary* income. These shareholders own a 10 percent interest in the subsidiary company, but no ownership in the parent firm.[5]

[4] Adjusting the subsidiary net income for the excess fair-value amortizations recognizes that the noncontrolling interest represents equity in the subsidiary's net assets as remeasured to fair values on the acquisition date.

[5] In this text we assume that the relative ownership percentages of the parent and noncontrolling interest represent an appropriate basis for allocating adjusted subsidiary net income across ownership groups.

LO 4-5

Identify and calculate the four noncontrolling interest figures that must be included within the consolidation process, and prepare a consolidation worksheet in the presence of a noncontrolling interest.

Partial Ownership Consolidations (Acquisition Method)

Having reviewed the basic concepts of accounting for a noncontrolling interest, we now concentrate on the mechanical aspects of the consolidation process when an outside ownership is present. More specifically, we examine consolidations for time periods subsequent to the date of acquisition to analyze the full range of accounting complexities created by a noncontrolling interest. As indicated previously, this discussion centers on the acquisition method as required under generally accepted accounting principles.

The acquisition method focuses on incorporating in the consolidated financial statements 100 percent of the subsidiary's assets and liabilities at their acquisition-date fair values. Note that subsequent to acquisition, changes in current fair values for assets and liabilities are not recognized.[6] Instead, the subsidiary assets acquired and liabilities assumed are reflected in future consolidated financial statements using their acquisition-date fair values net of subsequent excess fair value amortizations (or possibly reduced for impairment).

The presence of a noncontrolling interest does not dramatically alter the consolidation procedures presented in Chapter 3. The unamortized balance of the acquisition-date fair-value allocation must still be computed and included within the consolidated totals. Excess fair-value amortization expenses of these allocations are recognized each year as appropriate. Reciprocal balances are eliminated. Beyond these basic steps, the measurement and recognition of four noncontrolling interest balances add a new dimension to the process of consolidating financial information. The parent company must determine and then enter each of these figures when constructing a worksheet:

- Noncontrolling interest in the subsidiary as of the beginning of the current year.
- Net income attributable to the noncontrolling interest.
- Subsidiary dividends attributable to the noncontrolling interest.
- Noncontrolling interest as of the end of the year (found by combining the three balances above).

Illustration—Partial Acquisition with No Control Premium

To illustrate, assume that King Company acquires 80 percent of Pawn Company's 100,000 outstanding voting shares on January 1, 2017, for \$9.75 per share or a total of \$780,000 cash consideration. Further assume that the 20 percent noncontrolling interest shares traded both before and after the acquisition date at an average of \$9.75 per share. The total fair value of Pawn to be used initially in consolidation is

Consideration transferred by King (\$9.75 × 80,000 shares)	\$780,000
Noncontrolling interest fair value (\$9.75 × 20,000 shares)	195,000
Pawn's acquisition-date fair value	\$975,000

Thus King did not pay a control premium to acquire its share of Pawn—both sets of shares have identical per share fair values.

Exhibit 4.2 presents the book value of Pawn's accounts as well as the fair value of each asset and liability on the acquisition date. Pawn's total fair value is attributed to Pawn's assets and liabilities as shown in Exhibit 4.3. Annual amortization relating to these allocations also is included in this schedule. Although expense figures are computed for only the initial years, some amount of amortization is recognized in each of the 20 years following the acquisition (the life assumed for the patented technology).

Exhibit 4.3 shows first that all identifiable assets acquired and liabilities assumed are adjusted to their full individual fair values at the acquisition date. The noncontrolling

[6] Exceptions common to all firms (whether subject to consolidation or not) include recognizing changing fair values for marketable equity securities and other financial instruments.

EXHIBIT 4.2
Subsidiary Accounts—Date of Acquisition

PAWN COMPANY
Account Balances
January 1, 2017

	Book Value	Fair Value	Difference
Current assets	$ 440,000	$440,000	$ –0–
Trademarks (indefinite life)	260,000	320,000	60,000
Patented technology (20-year remaining life)	480,000	600,000	120,000
Equipment (10-year remaining life)	110,000	100,000	(10,000)
Long-term liabilities (8 years to maturity)	(550,000)	(510,000)	40,000
Net assets	$ 740,000	$950,000	$210,000
Common stock	$(230,000)		
Retained earnings, 1/1/17	(510,000)		

Note: Parentheses indicate a credit balance.

EXHIBIT 4.3 Excess Fair-Value Allocations

KING COMPANY AND 80% OWNED SUBSIDIARY PAWN COMPANY
Fair-Value Allocation and Amortization
January 1, 2017

	Allocation	Remaining Life (years)	Annual Excess Amortizations
Pawn's acquisition-date fair value (100%)	$975,000		
Pawn's acquisition-date book value (100%)	(740,000)		
Fair value in excess of book value	$235,000		
Adjustments (100%) to			
Trademarks	$ 60,000	indefinite	$ –0–
Patented technology	120,000	20	6,000
Equipment	(10,000)	10	(1,000)
Long-term liabilities (8 years to maturity)	40,000	8	5,000
Goodwill	$ 25,000	indefinite	$ –0–
Annual amortizations of excess fair value over book value (initial years)			$ 10,000

Goodwill Allocation to the Controlling and Noncontrolling Interests

	Controlling Interest	Noncontrolling Interest	Total
Fair value at acquisition date	$780,000	$195,000	$975,000
Relative fair value of Pawn's identifiable net assets (80% and 20%)	760,000	190,000	950,000
Goodwill	$ 20,000	$ 5,000	$ 25,000

interest will share proportionately in these fair-value adjustments. Exhibit 4.3 also shows that any excess fair value not attributable to Pawn's identifiable net assets is assigned to goodwill. Because the controlling and noncontrolling interests' acquisition-date fair values are identical at $9.75 per share, the resulting goodwill is allocated proportionately across these ownership interests.

Consolidated financial statements will be produced for the year ending December 31, 2018. This date is arbitrary. Any time period subsequent to 2017 could serve to demonstrate the applicable consolidation procedures. Having already calculated the acquisition-date fair-value allocations and related amortization, the accountant can construct a consolidation of these two companies along the lines demonstrated in Chapter 3. Only the presence of the 20 percent noncontrolling interest alters this process.

To complete the information needed for this combination, assume that Pawn Company reports the following changes in retained earnings since King's acquisition:

Current year (2018)	
Net income	$90,000
Less: Dividends declared	(50,000)
Increase in retained earnings	$40,000
Prior years (only 2017 in this illustration):	
Increase in retained earnings	$70,000

Assuming that King Company applies the equity method, the Investment in Pawn Company account as of December 31, 2018, can be constructed as shown in Exhibit 4.4. Note that the $852,000 balance is computed based on applying King's 80 percent ownership to Pawn's income (less amortization) and dividends. Although 100 percent of the subsidiary's assets, liabilities, revenues, and expenses will be combined in consolidation, the internal accounting for King's investment in Pawn is based on its 80 percent ownership. This technique facilitates worksheet adjustments that allocate various amounts to the noncontrolling interest. Exhibit 4.5 presents the separate financial statements for these two companies as of December 31, 2018, and the year then ended, based on the information provided.

Consolidated Totals

Although the inclusion of a 20 percent outside ownership complicates the consolidation process, the 2018 totals to be reported by this business combination can nonetheless be determined without the use of a worksheet:

- *Revenues* = $1,340,000. The revenues of the parent and the subsidiary are added together. The acquisition method includes the subsidiary's revenues in total although King owns only 80 percent of the stock.
- *Cost of Goods Sold* = $544,000. The parent and subsidiary balances are added together.
- *Depreciation Expense* = $79,000. The parent and subsidiary balances are added together along with the $1,000 reduction in equipment depreciation as indicated in Exhibit 4.3.
- *Amortization Expense* = $181,000. The parent and subsidiary balances are added together along with the $6,000 additional patented technology amortization expense as indicated in Exhibit 4.3.
- *Interest Expense* = $120,000. The parent and subsidiary balances are added along with an additional $5,000. Exhibit 4.3 shows Pawn's long-term debt reduced by $40,000 to fair value. Because the maturity value remains constant, the $40,000 represents a discount amortized to interest expense over the remaining eight-year life of the debt.

EXHIBIT 4.4
Equity Method Investment Balance

KING COMPANY
Investment in Pawn Company
Equity Method
December 31, 2018

Acquisition price for 80% interest		$780,000
Prior year (2017):		
Increase in retained earnings (80% x $70,000)	$56,000	
Excess amortization expenses (80% x $10,000) (Exhibit 4.3)	(8,000)	48,000
Current year (2018):		
Income accrual (80% x $90,000)	72,000	
Excess amortization expense (80% x $10,000) (Exhibit 4.3)	(8,000)	
Equity in subsidiary earnings	64,000*	
Dividends from Pawn (80% x $50,000)	(40,000)	24,000
Balance, 12/31/18		$852,000

*This figure appears in King's 2018 income statement. See Exhibit 4.5.

EXHIBIT 4.5
Separate Financial Records

KING COMPANY AND PAWN COMPANY Separate Financial Statements For December 31, 2018, and the Year Then Ended	King	Pawn
Revenues	$ (910,000)	$ (430,000)
Cost of goods sold	344,000	200,000
Depreciation expense	60,000	20,000
Amortization expense	100,000	75,000
Interest expense	70,000	45,000
Equity in subsidiary earnings (see Exhibit 4.4)	(64,000)	–0–
Net income	$ (400,000)	$ (90,000)
Retained earnings, 1/1/18	$ (860,000)	$ (580,000)
Net income (above)	(400,000)	(90,000)
Dividends declared	60,000	50,000
Retained earnings, 12/31/18	$(1,200,000)	$ (620,000)
Current assets	$ 726,000	$ 445,000
Trademarks	304,000	295,000
Patented technology	880,000	540,000
Equipment (net)	390,000	160,000
Investment in Pawn Company (see Exhibit 4.4)	852,000	–0–
Total assets	$ 3,152,000	$ 1,440,000
Long-term liabilities	$(1,082,000)	$ (590,000)
Common stock	(870,000)	(230,000)
Retained earnings, 12/31/18	(1,200,000)	(620,000)
Total liabilities and equities	$(3,152,000)	$(1,440,000)

Note: Parentheses indicate a credit balance.

- *Equity in Subsidiary Earnings* = –0–. The parent's investment income is replaced with the subsidiary's separate revenues and expenses which are then included in the consolidated totals.
- *Consolidated Net Income* = $416,000. The consolidated entity's total earnings before allocation to the controlling and noncontrolling ownership interests.
- *Net Income Attributable to Noncontrolling Interest* = $16,000. The outside owners are assigned 20 percent of Pawn's reported net income of $90,000 less $10,000 total excess fair-value amortization. The acquisition method shows this amount as an allocation of consolidated net income.
- *Net Income Attributable to King Company* (*Controlling Interest*) = $400,000. The acquisition method shows this amount as an allocation of consolidated net income.
- *Retained Earnings, 1/1* = $860,000. The parent company figure equals the consolidated total because the equity method was applied. If the initial value method or the partial equity method had been used, the parent's balance would require adjustment to include any unrecorded figures.
- *Dividends Declared* = $60,000. Only the parent company balance is reported. Eighty percent of the subsidiary's dividends are distributable to the parent and are thus eliminated. The remaining distribution goes to the outside owners and serves to reduce the noncontrolling interest balance.
- *Retained Earnings,* 12/31 = $1,200,000. The balance is found by adding the controlling interest's share of consolidated net income to the beginning consolidated retained earnings balance and then subtracting the parent's dividends. Because the equity method is utilized, the parent company figure reflects the total for the business combination.
- *Current Assets* = $1,171,000. The parent's and subsidiary's book values are added.

- *Trademarks* = $659,000. The parent's book value is added to the subsidiary's book value plus the $60,000 allocation of the acquisition-date fair value (see Exhibit 4.3).
- *Patented Technology* = $1,528,000. The parent's book value is added to the subsidiary's book value plus the $120,000 excess fair-value allocation less two years' excess amortizations of $6,000 per year (see Exhibit 4.3).
- *Equipment* = $542,000. The parent's book value is added to the subsidiary's book value less the $10,000 acquisition-date fair-value reduction plus two years' expense reductions of $1,000 per year (see Exhibit 4.3).
- *Investment in Pawn Company* = –0–. The balance reported by the parent is eliminated so that the subsidiary's assets and liabilities can be included in the consolidated totals.
- *Goodwill* = $25,000. The total goodwill allocation shown in Exhibit 4.3 is reported.
- *Total Assets* = $3,925,000. This balance is a summation of the consolidated assets.
- *Long-Term Liabilities* = $1,642,000. The parent's book value is added to the subsidiary's book value less the $40,000 acquisition-date fair-value allocation net of two years' amortizations of $5,000 per year (see Exhibit 4.3).
- *Noncontrolling Interest in Subsidiary* = $213,000. The outside ownership is 20 percent of the subsidiary's year-end book value adjusted for any unamortized excess fair value attributed to the noncontrolling interest:

Noncontrolling interest in Pawn at 1/1/18	
20% of $810,000 beginning book value—common stock plus 1/1/18 retained earnings	$162,000
20% of unamortized excess fair-value allocations as of 1/1	45,000
Noncontrolling interest in Pawn 1/1/18	$207,000
Net income attributable to noncontrolling interest (see page 165).	16,000
Dividends distributable to noncontrolling interest (20% of $50,000 total).	(10,000)
Noncontrolling interest in Pawn at 12/31/18.	$213,000

- *Common Stock* = $870,000. Only the parent's balance is reported.
- *Retained Earnings, 12/31* = $1,200,000. Computed on page 165.
- *Total Liabilities and Equities* = $3,925,000. This total is a summation of consolidated liabilities, noncontrolling interest, and equities.

Alternative Calculation of Noncontrolling Interest at December 31, 2018

The acquisition method requires that the noncontrolling interest in the subsidiary's net assets be measured at fair value at the date of acquisition. Subsequent to acquisition, however, the noncontrolling interest value is adjusted for its share of subsidiary net income, excess fair-value amortizations, and dividends. The following schedule demonstrates how the noncontrolling interest's acquisition-date fair value is adjusted to show the ending consolidated balance sheet amount.

Fair value of 20% noncontrolling interest in Pawn at acquisition date . . .		$195,000
20% of $70,000 change in Pawn's 2017 retained earnings	14,000	
20% of excess fair-value amortizations.	(2,000)	12,000
2018 net income allocation [20% × ($90,000 – $10,000)]		16,000
2018 dividends (20% × $50,000)		(10,000)
Noncontrolling interest in Pawn at December 31, 2018.		$213,000

As can be seen in the above schedule, the fair-value principle applies only to the initial noncontrolling interest valuation.

Worksheet Process—Acquisition Method

The consolidated totals for King and Pawn also can be determined by means of a worksheet as shown in Exhibit 4.6. Comparing this example with Exhibit 3.7 in Chapter 3 indicates that the presence of a noncontrolling interest does not create a significant number of changes in the consolidation procedures.

EXHIBIT 4.6 Noncontrolling Interest (No Control Premium) Illustrated

KING COMPANY AND PAWN COMPANY
Consolidation Worksheet
For Year Ending December 31, 2018

Investment: Equity Method **Ownership: 80%**

Accounts	King Company*	Pawn Company*	Consolidation Entries Debit	Consolidation Entries Credit	Noncontrolling Interest	Consolidated Totals
Revenues	(910,000)	(430,000)				(1,340,000)
Cost of goods sold	344,000	200,000				544,000
Depreciation expense	60,000	20,000		(E) 1,000		79,000
Amortization expense	100,000	75,000	(E) 6,000			181,000
Interest expense	70,000	45,000	(E) 5,000			120,000
Equity in Pawn's earnings (see Exhibit 4.4)	(64,000)	–0–	(I) 64,000			–0–
Separate company net income	(400,000)	(90,000)				
Consolidated net income						(416,000)
Net income attributable to noncontrolling interest					(16,000)	16,000
Net income attributable to King Company						(400,000)
Retained earnings, 1/1	(860,000)	(580,000)	(S) 580,000			(860,000)
Net income (above)	(400,000)	(90,000)				(400,000)
Dividends declared	60,000	50,000		(D) 40,000	10,000	60,000
Retained earnings, 12/31	(1,200,000)	(620,000)				(1,200,000)
Current assets	726,000	445,000				1,171,000
Trademarks	304,000	295,000	(A) 60,000			659,000
Patented technology	880,000	540,000	(A) 114,000	(E) 6,000		1,528,000
Equipment (net)	390,000	160,000	(E) 1,000	(A) 9,000		542,000
Investment in Pawn Company (see Exhibit 4.4)	852,000	–0–	(D) 40,000	(S) 648,000 (A) 180,000 (I) 64,000		–0–
Goodwill	–0–	–0–	(A) 25,000			25,000
Total assets	3,152,000	1,440,000				3,925,000
Long-term liabilities	(1,082,000)	(590,000)	(A) 35,000	(E) 5,000		(1,642,000)
Common stock	(870,000)	(230,000)	(S) 230,000			(870,000)
Noncontrolling interest in Pawn, 1/1				(S) 162,000 (A) 45,000	(207,000)	
Noncontrolling interest in Pawn, 12/31					(213,000)	(213,000)
Retained earnings, 12/31	(1,200,000)	(620,000)				(1,200,000)
Total liabilities and equities	(3,152,000)	(1,440,000)	1,160,000	1,160,000		(3,925,000)

*See Exhibit 4.5.
Note: Parentheses indicate a credit balance.
Consolidation entries:
(S) Elimination of subsidiary's stockholders' equity along with recognition of January 1 noncontrolling interest.
(A) Allocation of subsidiary total fair value in excess of book value, unamortized balances as of January 1.
(I) Elimination of intra-entity income (equity accrual less amortization expenses).
(D) Elimination of intra-entity dividends.
(E) Recognition of amortization expenses of fair-value allocations.

The worksheet still includes elimination of the subsidiary's stockholders' equity accounts (Entry **S**) although, as explained next, this entry is expanded to record the beginning noncontrolling interest for the year. The second worksheet entry (Entry **A**) recognizes the excess acquisition-date fair-value allocations at January 1 after one year of amortization with an additional adjustment to the beginning noncontrolling interest. Intra-entity income and dividends are removed also (Entries **I** and **D**) while current-year excess amortization expenses are recognized (Entry **E**). The differences from the Chapter 3 illustrations relate exclusively to the recognition of the three components of the noncontrolling interest. In addition, *a separate Noncontrolling Interest column is added to the worksheet to accumulate these components to form the year-end figure to be reported on the consolidated balance sheet.*

Noncontrolling Interest—Beginning of Year

Under the acquisition method, the noncontrolling interest shares proportionately in the fair values of the subsidiary's identifiable net assets as adjusted for excess fair-value amortizations. On the consolidated worksheet, this total net fair value is represented by two components:

1. Pawn's stockholders' equity accounts (common stock and beginning retained earnings) indicate a January 1, 2018, book value of $810,000.
2. January 1, 2018, acquisition-date fair-value net of previous year's amortizations (in this case 2017 only).

Therefore, the January 1, 2018, balance of the 20 percent outside ownership is computed as follows:

20% x $810,000 subsidiary book value at 1/1/18	$162,000
20% x $225,000* unamortized excess fair-value allocation at 1/1/18	45,000
Noncontrolling interest in Pawn at 1/1/18	$207,000
*Acquisition-date excess fair over book value (Exhibit 4.3)	$235,000
Less: 2017 excess fair over book value amortization	(10,000)
Unamortized excess fair over book value amount at 1/1/18	$225,000

The $207,000 noncontrolling interest balance at 1/1/18 is recognized on the worksheet through Entry **S** ($162,000) and Entry **A** ($45,000):

Consolidation Entry S

Common Stock (Pawn)	230,000	
Retained Earnings, 1/1/18 (Pawn)	580,000	
Investment in Pawn Company (80%)		648,000
Noncontrolling Interest in Pawn Company, 1/1/18 (20%)		162,000

To eliminate beginning stockholders' equity accounts of subsidiary along with book value portion of investment (equal to 80 percent ownership). Noncontrolling interest of 20 percent is also recognized.

Consolidation Entry A

Trademarks	60,000	
Patented Technology	114,000	
Liabilities	35,000	
Goodwill	25,000	
Equipment		9,000
Investment in Pawn Company (80%)		180,000
Noncontrolling Interest in Pawn Company, 1/1/18 (20%)		45,000

To recognize unamortized excess fair value as of January 1, 2018, to Pawn's assets acquired and liabilities assumed in the combination. Also to allocate the unamortized fair value to the noncontrolling interest. Goodwill is attributable proportionately to controlling and noncontrolling interests.

The total $207,000 balance assigned here to the outside owners at the beginning of the year is extended to the Noncontrolling Interest worksheet column (see Exhibit 4.6).

To complete the required worksheet adjustments, Entries **I, D,** and **E** are prepared as follows:

Consolidation Entry I

Equity in Pawn's Earnings	64,000	
Investment in Pawn Company		64,000
To eliminate intra-entity income accrual comprising subsidiary income less excess acquisition-date fair-value amortizations.		

Consolidation Entry D

Investment in Pawn Company	40,000	
Dividends Declared		40,000
To eliminate intra-entity dividends.		

Consolidation Entry E

Amortization Expense	6,000	
Interest Expense	5,000	
Equipment (net)	1,000	
Depreciation Expense		1,000
Patented Technology		6,000
Long-Term Liabilities		5,000
To recognize current year excess fair-value amortizations.		

Noncontrolling Interest—Share of Current Year Consolidated Net Income

Exhibit 4.6 shows the noncontrolling interest's share of current year earnings is $16,000. The amount is based on the subsidiary's $90,000 net income (Pawn Company column) less excess acquisition-date fair-value amortizations. Thus, King assigns $16,000 to the outside owners computed as follows:

Net Income Attributable to Noncontrolling Interest	
Pawn Company net income	$90,000
Excess acquisition-date fair-value amortization	10,000
Net income adjusted for excess amortizations	$80,000
Noncontrolling interest percentage	20%
Net income attributable to noncontrolling interest in Pawn	$16,000

In effect, 100 percent of each subsidiary revenue and expense account (including excess acquisition-date fair-value amortizations) is consolidated with an accompanying 20 percent allocation to the noncontrolling interest. The 80 percent net effect corresponds to King's ownership.

Because $16,000 of consolidated net income accrues to the noncontrolling interest, this amount is added to the $207,000 beginning balance assigned (in Entries **S** and **A**) to these outside owners. The noncontrolling interest increases because the subsidiary generated a profit during the period.

Although we could record this allocation through an additional worksheet entry, the $16,000 is usually shown, as in Exhibit 4.6, by means of a columnar adjustment. The current year accrual is simultaneously entered in the Income Statement section of the consolidated column as an allocation of consolidated net income and in the Noncontrolling Interest column as an increase. This procedure assigns a portion of the combined earnings to the outside owners rather than to the parent company owners.

Noncontrolling Interest—Dividends

The $40,000 dividend to the parent company is eliminated routinely through Entry **D,** but the remainder of Pawn's dividend went to the noncontrolling interest. The impact of the dividend (20 percent of the subsidiary's total) distributable to the other owners must be acknowledged. As shown in Exhibit 4.6, this remaining $10,000 is extended directly into the Noncontrolling Interest column on the worksheet as a reduction. It represents the decrease in the underlying claim of the outside ownership that resulted from the subsidiary's dividend declaration.

Noncontrolling Interest—End of Year

The ending assignment for these other owners is calculated by a summation of

Noncontrolling interest in Pawn beginning of year—credit balance	$207,000
Net income attributable to noncontrolling interest	16,000
Less: Dividends to the outside owners	(10,000)
Noncontrolling interest in Pawn end of year—credit balance	$213,000

The Noncontrolling Interest column on the worksheet in Exhibit 4.6 accumulates these figures. The $213,000 total is then transferred to the balance sheet, where it appears in the consolidated financial statements.

LO 4-6

Identify appropriate placements for the components of the noncontrolling interest in consolidated financial statements.

Consolidated Financial Statements

Having successfully consolidated the information for King and Pawn, the resulting financial statements for these two companies are produced in Exhibit 4.7. These figures are taken from the consolidation worksheet.

Exhibit 4.7 shows first the consolidated income statement. Consolidated net income is computed at the combined entity level as $416,000 and then allocated to the noncontrolling and controlling interests. The statement of changes in owners' equity provides details of the ownership changes for the year for both the controlling and noncontrolling interest shareholders. Finally, note the placement of the noncontrolling interest in the subsidiary's equity squarely in the consolidated owners' equity section.[7]

LO 4-7

Determine the effect on consolidated financial statements of a control premium paid by the parent.

Illustration—Partial Acquisition with Control Premium

To illustrate the valuation implications for an acquisition involving a control premium, again assume that King Company acquires 80 percent of Pawn Company's 100,000 outstanding voting shares on January 1, 2017. We also again assume that Pawn's shares traded before the acquisition date at an average of $9.75 per share. In this scenario, however, we assume that to acquire sufficient shares to gain control King pays $11 per share or a total of $880,000 cash consideration for its 80 percent interest. King thus pays a control premium of $1.25 ($11 – $9.75) per share to acquire Pawn. King anticipates that synergies with Pawn will create additional value for King's shareholders. Finally, following the acquisition, the remaining 20 percent noncontrolling interest shares continue to trade at $9.75.

The total fair value of Pawn to be used initially in consolidation is thus recomputed as follows:

Consideration transferred by King ($11.00 x 80,000 shares)	$ 880,000
Noncontrolling interest fair value ($9.75 x 20,000 shares)	195,000
Pawn's total fair value at January 1, 2017	$1,075,000

[7] If appropriate, each component of other comprehensive income is allocated to the controlling and noncontrolling interests. The statement of changes in owners' equity would also provide an allocation of accumulated other comprehensive income elements across the controlling and noncontrolling interests.

EXHIBIT 4.7
Consolidated Statements with Noncontrolling Interest—Acquisition Method

KING COMPANY AND PAWN COMPANY
Consolidated Financial Statements
Income Statement
Year Ended December 31, 2018

Revenues	$1,340,000
Cost of goods sold	(544,000)
Depreciation expense	(79,000)
Amortization expense	(181,000)
Interest expense	(120,000)
Consolidated net income	$ 416,000
To noncontrolling interest	16,000
To King Company (controlling interest)	$ 400,000

Statement of Changes in Owners' Equity
Year Ended December 31, 2018

	King Company Owners		
	Retained Earnings	**Common Stock**	**Noncontrolling Interest**
Balance, January 1	$ 860,000	$870,000	$207,000
Net income	400,000		16,000
Less: Dividends	(60,000)		(10,000)
Balance, December 31	$1,200,000	$870,000	$213,000

Balance Sheet
At December 31, 2018

Assets	
Current assets	$1,171,000
Trademarks	659,000
Patented technology	1,528,000
Equipment (net)	542,000
Goodwill	25,000
Total assets	$3,925,000
Liabilities	
Long-term liabilities	$1,642,000
Owners' Equity	
Common stock—King Company	870,000
Noncontrolling interest in Pawn	213,000
Retained earnings	1,200,000
Total liabilities and owners' equity	$3,925,000

In keeping with the acquisition method's requirement that identifiable assets acquired and liabilities assumed be adjusted to fair value, King allocates Pawn's total fair value as follows:

Fair value of Pawn at January 1, 2017		$1,075,000
Book value of Pawn at January 1, 2017		(740,000)
Fair value in excess of book value		$ 335,000
Adjustments to		
Trademarks	$ 60,000	
Patented technology	120,000	
Equipment	(10,000)	
Long-term liabilities	40,000	210,000
Goodwill		$ 125,000

Note that the *identifiable* assets acquired and liabilities assumed are again adjusted to their full individual fair values at the acquisition date. Only the amount designated as goodwill is changed to $125,000 from $25,000 in the original fair-value allocation example as shown in Exhibit 4.3. In this case, King allocates $120,000 of the $125,000 total goodwill amount to its own interest as follows:

	Controlling Interest	Noncontrolling Interest	Total
Fair value at acquisition date	$880,000	$195,000	$1,075,000
Relative fair value of Pawn's identifiable net assets (80% and 20%)	760,000	190,000	950,000
Goodwill	$120,000	$ 5,000	$ 125,000

The initial acquisition-date fair value of $195,000 for the noncontrolling interest includes only a $5,000 goodwill allocation from the combination. Because the parent paid an extra $1.25 per share more than the fair value of the noncontrolling interest shares, more goodwill is allocated to the parent.

Next we separate the familiar consolidated worksheet entry **A** into two components labeled **A1** and **A2.** The **A1** worksheet entry allocates the excess acquisition-date fair value to the *identifiable* assets acquired and liabilities assumed (trademarks, patented technology, equipment, and liabilities). Note that the relative ownership percentages of the parent and noncontrolling interest (80 percent and 20 percent) provide the basis for allocating the net $200,000 adjustment to the parent's Investment account ($160,000) and the 1/1/18 balance of the noncontrolling interest ($40,000).

Next, consolidated worksheet entry **A2** provides the recognition and allocation of the goodwill balance taking into account the differing per share prices of the parent's consideration transferred and the noncontrolling interest fair value. Note that the presence of a control premium affects primarily the parents' shares, and thus goodwill is disproportionately (relative to the ownership percentages) allocated to the controlling and noncontrolling interests. Exhibit 4.8 shows the consolidated worksheet for this extension to the King and Pawn example.

Consolidation Entry A1 (see page 171 for excess fair value allocations)

Trademarks	60,000	
Patented Technology	114,000	
Liabilities	35,000	
Equipment		9,000
Investment in Pawn Company (80%)		160,000
Noncontrolling Interest in Pawn 1/1/18 (20%)		40,000

Consolidation Entry A2

Goodwill	125,000	
Investment in Pawn Company		120,000
Noncontrolling Interest in Pawn 1/1/18		5,000

EXHIBIT 4.8 Noncontrolling Interest (Control Premium) Illustrated

KING COMPANY AND PAWN COMPANY
Consolidation Worksheet
For Year Ending December 31, 2018

Investment: Equity Method — *Ownership: 80%*

Accounts	King Company	Pawn Company	Consolidation Entries Debit	Consolidation Entries Credit	Noncontrolling Interest	Consolidated Totals
Revenues	(910,000)	(430,000)				(1,340,000)
Cost of goods sold	344,000	200,000				544,000
Depreciation expense	60,000	20,000		(E) 1,000		79,000
Amortization expense	100,000	75,000	(E) 6,000			181,000
Interest expense	70,000	45,000	(E) 5,000			120,000
Equity in Pawn's earnings	(64,000)	–0–	(I) 64,000			–0–
Separate company net income	(400,000)	(90,000)				
Consolidated net income						(416,000)
Net income attributable to noncontrolling interest					(16,000)	16,000
Net income attributable to King Company						(400,000)
Retained earnings, 1/1	(860,000)	(580,000)	(S) 580,000			(860,000)
Net income (above)	(400,000)	(90,000)				(400,000)
Dividends declared	60,000	50,000		(D) 40,000	10,000	60,000
Retained earnings, 12/31	(1,200,000)	(620,000)				(1,200,000)
Current assets	626,000	445,000				1,071,000
Trademarks	304,000	295,000	(A1) 60,000			659,000
Patented technology	880,000	540,000	(A1) 114,000	(E) 6,000		1,528,000
Equipment (net)	390,000	160,000	(E) 1,000	(A1) 9,000		542,000
Investment in Pawn Company	952,000	–0–	(D) 40,000	(S) 648,000		–0–
				(A1) 160,000		
				(A2) 120,000		
				(I) 64,000		
Goodwill	–0–	–0–	(A2) 125,000			125,000
Total assets	3,152,000	1,440,000				3,925,000
Long-term liabilities	(1,082,000)	(590,000)	(A1) 35,000	(E) 5,000		(1,642,000)
Common stock	(870,000)	(230,000)	(S) 230,000			(870,000)
Noncontrolling interest in Pawn 1/1				(S) 162,000		
				(A1) 40,000		
				(A2) 5,000	(207,000)	
Noncontrolling interest in Pawn 12/31					(213,000)	(213,000)
Retained earnings, 12/31	(1,200,000)	(620,000)				(1,200,000)
Total liabilities and equities	(3,152,000)	(1,440,000)	1,260,000	1,260,000		(3,925,000)

Note: Parentheses indicate a credit balance.
Consolidation entries:
(S) Elimination of subsidiary's stockholders' equity along with recognition of January 1 noncontrolling interest.
(A1) Allocation of subsidiary identifiable net asset fair value in excess of book value, unamortized balances as of January 1.
(A2) Allocation of goodwill to parent and noncontrolling interest.
(I) Elimination of intra-entity income (equity accrual less amortization expenses).
(D) Elimination of intra-entity dividends.
(E) Recognition of amortization expenses of fair-value allocations.

The worksheet calculates the December 31, 2018, noncontrolling balance as follows:

Pawn January 1, 2018: 20% book value	$162,000
January 1, 2018: 20% excess fair-value allocation for Pawn's identifiable net assets ($200,000 × 20%) + $5,000 goodwill allocation	45,000
Noncontrolling interest at January 1, 2018	$207,000
2018 consolidated net income allocation	16,000
Noncontrolling interest share of Pawn dividends	(10,000)
Noncontrolling interest in Pawn, December 31, 2018	$213,000

Note that the $45,000 January 1 excess fair-value allocation to the noncontrolling interest includes the noncontrolling interest's full share of the *identifiable* assets acquired and liabilities assumed in the combination but only $5,000 for goodwill. Because King Company paid a $100,000 control premium (80,000 shares × $1.25), the additional $100,000 is allocated entirely to the controlling interest.

By comparing Exhibits 4.6 and 4.8 we can assess the effect of the separate acquisition-date valuations for the controlling and noncontrolling interests. As seen in the differences across Exhibits 4.6 and 4.8 calculated next, the presence of King's control premium affects the goodwill component in the consolidated financial statements and little else.

	Exhibit 4.6	Exhibit 4.8	Difference
On King's Separate Financial Statements			
Current assets	$ 726,000	$ 626,000	−$100,000
Investment in Pawn	852,000	952,000	+ 100,000
On the Consolidated Balances			
Current assets	1,171,000	1,071,000	− 100,000
Goodwill	25,000	125,000	+ 100,000

Because King paid an additional $100,000 for its 80 percent interest in Pawn, the initial value assigned to the Investment account increases and current assets (i.e., additional cash paid for the acquisition) decreases by $100,000. The extra $100,000 then simply increases goodwill on the consolidated balance sheet. Note that the noncontrolling interest amount remains unchanged at $213,000 across Exhibits 4.6 and 4.8, consistent with the fact that its acquisition-date fair value was left unchanged at $195,000.

Effects Created by Alternative Investment Methods

In the King and Pawn illustrations, the parent uses the equity method and bases all worksheet entries on that approach. As discussed in Chapter 3, had King incorporated the initial value method or the partial equity method, a few specific changes in the consolidation process would be required although the reported figures would be identical.

Initial Value Method

The initial value method ignores two accrual-based adjustments. First, the parent recognizes dividend income rather than an equity income accrual. Thus, the parent does not accrue the percentage of the subsidiary's net income earned in past years in excess of dividends (the increase in subsidiary retained earnings). Second, the parent does not record amortization expense under the initial value method and therefore must include it in the consolidation process if proper totals are to be achieved. Because neither of these figures is recognized in applying the initial value method, an Entry *C is added to the worksheet to convert the previously recorded balances to the equity method. The parent's beginning Retained Earnings is affected by this adjustment as well as the Investment in Subsidiary account. The exact amount is computed as follows.

*Conversion to Equity Method from Initial Value Method (Entry *C)*

Combine:

1. The increase (since acquisition) in the subsidiary's retained earnings during past years (net income less dividends) times the parent's ownership percentage, and
2. The parent's percentage of total amortization expense for these same past years.

The parent's use of the initial value method requires an additional procedural change. Under this method, the parent recognizes income when its subsidiary declares a dividend. Entry **(I)** removes both intra-entity dividend income and subsidiary dividends to the parent. Thus, when the initial value method is used, Entry **D** is unnecessary.

Partial Equity Method

Again, an Entry *C is needed to convert the parent's retained earnings as of January 1 to the equity method. In this case, however, only the amortization expense for the prior years must be included. Recall that under the partial equity method, although the parent accrues its share of reported subsidiary income, it does not recognize any acquisition-date excess fair value amortization expenses.

LO 4-8

Understand the impact on consolidated financial statements of a midyear acquisition.

Revenue and Expense Reporting for Midyear Acquisitions

In virtually all of our previous examples, the parent gains control of the subsidiary on the first day of the fiscal year. How is the consolidation process affected if an acquisition occurs on a midyear (any other than the first day of the fiscal year) date?

When a company gains control at a midyear date, a few obvious changes are needed. The new parent must compute the subsidiary's book value as of that date to determine excess total fair value over book value allocations (e.g., intangibles). Excess amortization expenses as well as any equity accrual and dividend distributions are recognized for a period of less than a year. Finally, because only net income earned by the subsidiary after the acquisition date accrues to the new owners, it is appropriate to include only postacquisition revenues and expenses in consolidated totals.

Consolidating Postacquisition Subsidiary Revenue and Expenses

Following a midyear acquisition, a parent company excludes current-year subsidiary revenue and expense amounts that have accrued prior to the acquisition date from its consolidated totals. For example, when Comcast acquired AT&T Broadband, its December 31 year-end income statement included AT&T Broadband revenues and expenses only subsequent to the acquisition date. Comcast reported $8.1 billion in revenues that year. However, in a pro forma schedule, Comcast noted that had it included AT&T Broadband's revenues from January 1, total revenue for the year would have been $16.8 billion. However, because the $8.7 billion additional revenue ($16.8 billion – $8.1 billion) was not earned by Comcast owners, Comcast excluded this preacquisition revenue from its consolidated total.

To further illustrate the complexities of accounting for a midyear acquisition, assume that Tyler Company acquires 90 percent of Steven Company on July 1, 2018, for $900,000 and prepares the following fair-value allocation schedule:

Steven Company fair value, 7/1/18		$1,000,000
Steven Company book value, 7/1/18		
Common stock	$600,000	
Retained earnings, 7/1/18	200,000	800,000
Excess fair value over book value		$ 200,000
Adjust trademark to fair value (4-year remaining life)		200,000
Goodwill		$ -0-

The affiliates report the following 2018 income statement amounts from their own separate operations:

	Tyler	Steven
Revenues	$450,000	$300,000
Expenses	325,000	150,000
Dividends (declared quarterly)	100,000	20,000

Assuming that all revenues and expenses occurred evenly throughout the year, the December 31, 2018, consolidated income statement appears as follows:

TYLER COMPANY
Consolidated Income Statement
For the Year Ended December 31, 2018

Revenues	$600,000
Expenses	425,000
Consolidated net income	$175,000
To noncontrolling interest	5,000
To Tyler Company (controlling interest)	$170,000

The consolidated income statement components are computed below:

- *Revenues* = $600,000. Combined balances of $750,000 less $150,000 (½ of Steven's revenues).
- *Expenses* = $425,000. Combined balances of $475,000 less $75,000 (½ of Steven's expenses) plus $25,000 excess amortization ($200,000 ÷ 4 years × ½ year).
- *Net Income Attributable to Noncontrolling Interest* = $5,000. 10% × ($150,000 Steven's income − $50,000 excess amortization) × ½ year.

In this example, preacquisition subsidiary revenue and expense accounts are eliminated from the consolidated totals. Note also that by excluding 100 percent of the preacquisition income accounts from consolidation, the noncontrolling interest is viewed as coming into being as of the parent's acquisition date.[8]

A midyear acquisition requires additional adjustments when preparing consolidating worksheets. The balances the subsidiary submits for consolidation typically include results for its entire fiscal period. Thus, in the December 31 financial statements, the book value of the firm acquired on a midyear date is reflected by a January 1 retained earnings balance plus revenues, expenses, and dividends from the beginning of the year to the acquisition date. To effectively eliminate subsidiary book value as of the acquisition date, Consolidation Entry **S** includes these items in addition to the other usual elements of book value (i.e., stock accounts). To illustrate, assuming that both affiliates submit fiscal year financial statements for consolidation, Tyler would make the following 2018 consolidation worksheet entry:

Consolidation Worksheet Entry S

Common Stock—Steven	600,000	
Retained Earnings—Steven (1/1/18)*	135,000	
Revenues	150,000	
Dividends Declared—Steven		10,000
Expenses		75,000
Noncontrolling Interest (7/1/18)		80,000
Investment in Steven		720,000

*To arrive at Steven's January 1 retained earning balance, we use the July 1 balance of $200,000 less income from the first six months of $75,000 (1/2 of $150,000 annual Steven income) plus $10,000 dividends declared.

Through Entry **S**, preacquisition subsidiary revenues, expenses, and dividends are effectively

- Included as part of the subsidiary book value elimination in the year of acquisition.
- Included as components of the beginning value of the noncontrolling interest.
- Excluded from the consolidated income statement and statement of retained earnings.

[8] Current practice provides comparability across fiscal years through pro forma disclosures of various categories of revenue and expense as if the combination had occurred at the beginning of the reporting period. With the advent of modern information systems, separate cutoffs for revenues and expenses are readily available.

Acquisition Following an Equity Method Investment

In many cases, a parent company owns a noncontrolling equity interest in a firm prior to obtaining control. In such cases, as the preceding example demonstrates, the parent consolidates the postacquisition revenues and expenses of its new subsidiary. Because the parent owned an equity investment in the subsidiary prior to the control date, however, the parent reports on its income statement the "equity in earnings of the investee" that accrued up to the date control was obtained. In this case, in the year of acquisition, the consolidated income statement reports both combined revenues and expenses (postacquisition) of the subsidiary and equity method income (preacquisition).

In subsequent years, the need to separate pre- and postacquisition amounts is limited to ensuring that excess amortizations correctly reflect the midyear acquisition date. Finally, if the parent employs the initial value method of accounting for the investment in subsidiary on its books, the conversion to the equity method must also reflect only postacquisition amounts.

Step Acquisitions

LO 4-9

Understand the impact on consolidated financial statements when a step acquisition has taken place.

When Ticketmaster Entertainment Corporation increased its percentage ownership in Front Line Company from 39.4 percent to 82.3 percent, it began consolidating its investment in Front Line. Prior to the acquisition of control through majority ownership, the investment in Front Line was accounted for using the equity method of accounting.

In all previous consolidation illustrations, control over a subsidiary was assumed to have been achieved through a single transaction. Obviously, Ticketmaster's takeover of Front Line shows that a combination also can be the result of a series of stock purchases. These step acquisitions further complicate the consolidation process. The financial information of the separate companies must still be brought together, but varying amounts of consideration have been transferred to former owners at several different dates. How do the initial acquisitions affect this process?

Control Achieved in Steps—Acquisition Method

A **step acquisition** occurs when control is achieved in a series of equity acquisitions, as opposed to a single transaction. As with all business combinations, the acquisition method measures the acquired firm (including the noncontrolling interest) at fair value at the date control is obtained. The acquisition of a controlling interest is considered an important economic, and therefore measurement, event. Consequently, the parent utilizes a single uniform valuation basis for all subsidiary assets acquired and liabilities assumed—fair value at the date control is obtained.

If the parent previously held a noncontrolling interest in the acquired firm, the parent remeasures that interest to fair value and recognizes a gain or loss. For example, when eBay increased its equity ownership from 10 percent to 93 percent, it obtained control over GittiGidiyor, a Turkish online marketplace. To measure the subsidiary's acquisition-date fair value, eBay revalued its previously held 10 percent equity interest to fair value and recognized a $17 million gain. As a result, eBay increased its investment account for both the cash paid for the newly acquired shares and the increase in the fair value of its previously owned shares in GittiGidiyor.

If after obtaining control, the parent increases its ownership interest in the subsidiary, no further remeasurement takes place. The parent simply accounts for the additional subsidiary shares acquired as an equity transaction—consistent with any transactions with other owners, as opposed to outsiders. Next we present an example of consolidated reporting when the parent obtains a controlling interest in a series of steps. Then, we present an example of a parent's post-control acquisition of its subsidiary's shares.

Example: Step Acquisition Resulting in Control—Acquisition Method

To illustrate, assume that Arch Company obtains control of Zion Company through two cash acquisitions. The details of each acquisition are provided in Exhibit 4.9. Assuming that Arch has gained the ability to significantly influence Zion's decision-making process, the first investment, for external reporting purposes, is accounted for by means of the equity method as discussed in Chapter 1. Thus, Arch must determine any allocations and amortization associated with its purchase price (see Exhibit 4.10). A customer base with a 22-year estimated remaining life represented the initial excess payment.

Application of the equity method requires the accrual of investee income by the parent while any dividends from the investee are recorded as a decrease in the Investment account. Arch must also reduce both the income and asset balances in recognition of the annual $2,000 amortization indicated in Exhibit 4.10. Following the information provided in Exhibits 4.9 and 4.10, over the next two years, Arch Company's Investment in Zion account grows to $190,000:

Price paid for 30% investment in Zion—1/1/16	$164,000
Accrual of 2016 equity income ($60,000 × 30%)	18,000
Share of dividends 2016 ($20,000 × 30%)	(6,000)
Amortization for 2016	(2,000)
Accrual of 2017 equity income ($80,000 × 30%)	24,000
Share of dividends 2017 ($20,000 × 30%)	(6,000)
Amortization for 2017	(2,000)
Investment in Zion—1/1/18	$190,000

On January 1, 2018, Arch's ownership is increased to 80 percent by the purchase of another 50 percent of Zion Company's outstanding common stock for $350,000. Although the equity method can still be utilized for internal reporting, this second acquisition necessitates the preparation of consolidated financial statements beginning in 2018. Arch now controls Zion; the two companies are viewed as a single economic entity for external reporting purposes.

Once Arch gains control over Zion on January 1, 2018, the acquisition method focuses exclusively on control-date fair values and considers any previous amounts recorded by the acquirer as irrelevant for future valuations. Thus, in a step acquisition all previous values for the investment, prior to the date control is obtained, are remeasured to fair value on the date control is obtained.

We add the assumption that the $350,000 consideration transferred by Arch in its second acquisition of Zion represents the best available evidence for measuring the fair value of Zion Company at January 1, 2018. Therefore, an estimated fair value of $700,000 ($350,000 ÷ 50%) is assigned to Zion Company as of January 1, 2018, and provides the valuation basis for the assets acquired, the liabilities assumed, and the 20 percent noncontrolling interest.

EXHIBIT 4.9
Consolidation Information for a Step Acquisition

ARCH COMPANY'S ACQUISITIONS OF ZION COMPANY SHARES

	Consideration Transferred	Percentage Acquired	Zion Company (100%) Book Value	Zion Company (100%) Fair Value
January 1, 2016	$164,000	30%	$400,000	$546,667
January 1, 2018	350,000	50	500,000	700,000

Zion Company's Income and Dividends for 2016–2018

	Income	Dividends
2016	$ 60,000	$ 20,000
2017	80,000	20,000
2018	100,000	20,000

EXHIBIT 4.10
Allocation of First Noncontrolling Acquisition

ARCH COMPANY AND ZION COMPANY
Fair Value Allocation and Amortization
January 1, 2016

Fair value of consideration transferred	$ 164,000
Book value equivalent of Arch's ownership ($400,000 × 30%)	(120,000)
Customer base	$ 44,000
Assumed remaining life	22 years
Annual amortization expense	$ 2,000

Exhibit 4.11 shows Arch's allocation of Zion's $700,000 acquisition-date fair value, first to the ownership interests and then to Zion's assets.

Note that the acquisition method views a multiple-step acquisition as essentially the same as a single-step acquisition. In the Arch Company and Zion Company example, once control is evident, the only relevant values in consolidating the accounts of Zion are fair values at January 1, 2018. A new basis of accountability arises for Zion Company on that single date because obtaining control of another firm is considered a significant remeasurement event. Previously owned noncontrolling blocks of stock are consequently revalued to fair value on the date control is obtained.

In revaluing a previous stock ownership in the acquired firm, the acquirer recognizes any resulting gain or loss in income. Therefore, on January 1, 2018, Arch increases the Investment in Zion account to $210,000 (30% × $700,000 fair value) and records the revaluation gain as follows:

Investment in Zion.	20,000	
Gain on Revaluation of Zion		20,000

Fair value of Arch's 30% investment in Zion at 1/1/18 (30% × $700,000).	$210,000
Book value of Arch's 30% investment in Zion at 1/1/18	190,000
Gain on revaluation of Zion to fair value.	$ 20,000

Worksheet Consolidation for a Step Acquisition (Acquisition Method)

To continue the example, the amount in Arch Company's 80 percent Investment in Zion account is updated for 2018:

Investment in Zion (after revaluation on 1/1/18)	$210,000
January 1, 2018—Second acquisition price paid.	350,000
Equity income accrual—2018 (80% × $100,000).	80,000
Amortization of customer base (80% × $10,000).	(8,000)
Share of Zion dividends—2018 (80% × $20,000)	(16,000)
Investment in Zion—12/31/18	$616,000

The worksheet for consolidating Arch Company and Zion Company is shown in Exhibit 4.12. Observe that

- The consolidation worksheet entries are essentially the same as if Arch had acquired its entire 80 percent ownership on January 1, 2018.

EXHIBIT 4.11
Allocation of Acquisition-Date Fair Value

ARCH COMPANY AND ZION COMPANY
Zion Fair Value at Date Control Is Obtained
January 1, 2018

Fair value of Arch's 50% equity acquisition.	$ 350,000
Fair value of 30% equity already owned by Arch	210,000
Fair value of 20% noncontrolling interest	140,000
Total fair value assigned to Zion Company	$ 700,000

Excess Fair over Book Value Allocation and Amortization
January 1, 2018

Zion Company fair value.	$ 700,000
Zion Company book value.	(500,000)
Customer base.	$ 200,000
Assumed remaining life	20 years
Annual amortization expense	$ 10,000

- The noncontrolling interest is allocated 20 percent of the excess fair-value allocation from the customer base.
- The noncontrolling interest is allocated 20 percent of Zion's 2018 income less its share of the excess amortization attributable to the customer base.
- The gain on revaluation of Arch's initial investment in Zion is recognized as income of the current period.

EXHIBIT 4.12 Step Acquisition Illustrated

ARCH COMPANY AND ZION COMPANY
Consolidation Worksheet
For Year Ending December 31, 2018

Investment: Equity Method | ***Ownership: 80%***

Accounts	Arch Company	Zion Company	Consolidation Entries Debit	Consolidation Entries Credit	Noncontrolling Interest	Consolidated Totals
Income Statement						
Revenues	(600,000)	(260,000)				(860,000)
Expenses	425,000	160,000	(E) 10,000			595,000
Equity in subsidiary earnings	(72,000)	–0–	(I) 72,000			–0–
Gain on revaluation of Zion	(20,000)	–0–				(20,000)
Separate company net income	(267,000)	(100,000)				
Consolidated net income						(285,000)
Net income attributable to noncontrolling interest					(18,000)	18,000
Net income attributable to Arch Company						(267,000)
Statement of Retained Earnings						
Retained earnings, 1/1						
Arch Company	(758,000)					(758,000)
Zion Company		(230,000)	(S) 230,000			
Net income (above)	(267,000)	(100,000)				(267,000)
Dividends declared	125,000	20,000		(D) 16,000	4,000	125,000
Retained earnings, 12/31	(900,000)	(310,000)				(900,000)
Balance Sheet						
Current assets	509,000	280,000				789,000
Land	205,000	90,000				295,000
Buildings (net)	646,000	310,000				956,000
Investment in Zion Company	616,000	–0–	(D) 16,000	(A) 160,000 (S) 400,000 (I) 72,000		–0–
Customer base	–0–	–0–	(A) 200,000	(E) 10,000		190,000
Total assets	1,976,000	680,000				2,230,000
Liabilities	(461,000)	(100,000)				(561,000)
Noncontrolling interest in Zion Company, 1/1	–0–	–0–		(S) 100,000 (A) 40,000	(140,000)	
Noncontrolling interest in Zion Company, 12/31	–0–	–0–			(154,000)	(154,000)
Common stock	(355,000)	(200,000)	(S) 200,000			(355,000)
Additional paid-in capital	(260,000)	(70,000)	(S) 70,000			(260,000)
Retained earnings, 12/31 (above)	(900,000)	(310,000)				(900,000)
Total liabilities and equities	(1,976,000)	(680,000)	798,000	798,000		(2,230,000)

Note: Parentheses indicate a credit balance.
Consolidation entries:
(S) Elimination of subsidiary's stockholders' equity along with recognition of 1/1 noncontrolling interest.
(A) Allocation of subsidiary total fair value in excess of book value, unamortized balances as of 1/1.
(I) Elimination of intra-entity income (equity accrual less amortization expenses).
(D) Elimination of intra-entity dividends.
(E) Recognition of amortization expenses on fair-value allocations.

Example: Step Acquisition Resulting after Control Is Obtained

The previous example demonstrates a step acquisition with control achieved with the most recent purchase. Post-control acquisitions by a parent of a subsidiary's stock, however, often continue as well. Recall that the acquisition method measures an acquired firm at its fair value on the date control is obtained.

A parent's subsequent subsidiary stock acquisitions do not affect these initially recognized fair values. For example, when Walmart increased its ownership in Walmart Chile from 75 percent to 100 percent, it did not change the valuation bases of Walmart Chile's assets. The acquisition of the 25 percent noncontrolling interest was treated as an equity transaction with a corresponding adjustment to additional paid-in capital. As the Walmart example shows, once the subsidiary's valuation basis is established as of the date control is obtained, as long as control is maintained, this valuation basis remains the same. Any further purchases (or sales) of the subsidiary's stock are treated as equity transactions.

To illustrate a post-control step acquisition, assume that on January 1, 2017, Amanda Co. obtains 70 percent of Schallman, Inc., for $350,000 cash. We also assume that the $350,000 consideration paid represents the best available evidence for measuring the fair value of the noncontrolling interest. Therefore, Schallman Company's total fair value is assessed at $500,000 ($350,000 ÷ 70%). Because Schallman's net assets' book values equal their collective fair values of $400,000, Amanda recognizes goodwill of $100,000. Then, on January 1, 2018, when Schallman's book value has increased to $420,000, Amanda buys another 20 percent of Schallman for $95,000, bringing its total ownership to 90 percent. Under the acquisition method, the valuation basis for the subsidiary's net assets was established on January 1, 2017, the date Amanda obtained control. Subsequent transactions in the subsidiary's stock (purchases or sales) are now viewed as transactions in the combined entity's own stock. Therefore, when Amanda acquires additional shares post-control, it recognizes the difference between the fair value of the consideration transferred and the underlying subsidiary valuation as an adjustment to Additional Paid-In Capital.

The difference between the $95,000 price and the underlying consolidated subsidiary value is computed as follows:

1/1/18 price paid for 20% interest		$ 95,000
Noncontrolling interest (NCI) acquired:		
Book value (20% of $420,000)	$84,000	
Goodwill (20% of $100,000)	20,000	
Noncontrolling interest book value (20%) 1/1/18		104,000
Additional paid-in capital from 20% NCI acquisition		$ 9,000

Amanda then prepares the following journal entry to record the acquisition of the 20 percent noncontrolling interest:

Investment in Schallman	104,000	
Cash		95,000
Additional Paid-In Capital		9,000

By purchasing 20 percent of Schallman for $95,000, the consolidated entity's owners have acquired a portion of their own firm at a price $9,000 less than consolidated book value. From a worksheet perspective, the $104,000 increase in the investment account simply replaces the 20 percent allocation to the noncontrolling interest. Note that the $95,000 exchanged for the 20 percent interest in Schallman's net assets does not affect consolidated asset valuation. The basis for the reported values in the consolidated financial statements was established on the date control was obtained.

Discussion Question

DOES GAAP UNDERVALUE POST-CONTROL STOCK ACQUISITIONS?

In Berkshire Hathaway's 2012 annual report, Warren Buffett, in discussing the company's post-control step acquisitions of Marmon Holdings, Inc., observed the following:

> Marmon provides an example of a clear and substantial gap existing between book value and intrinsic value. Let me explain the odd origin of this differential.
>
> Last year I told you that we had purchased additional shares in Marmon, raising our ownership to 80% (up from the 64% we acquired in 2008). I also told you that GAAP accounting required us to immediately record the 2011 purchase on our books at far less than what we paid. I've now had a year to think about this weird accounting rule, but I've yet to find an explanation that makes any sense—nor can Charlie or Marc Hamburg, our CFO, come up with one. My confusion increases when I am told that if we hadn't already owned 64%, the 16% we purchased in 2011 would have been entered on our books at our cost.
>
> In 2012 (and in early 2013, retroactive to year end 2012) we acquired an additional 10% of Marmon and the same bizarre accounting treatment was required. The $700 million write-off we immediately incurred had no effect on earnings but did reduce book value and, therefore, 2012's gain in net worth.
>
> The cost of our recent 10% purchase implies a $12.6 billion value for the 90% of Marmon we now own. Our balance-sheet carrying value for the 90%, however, is $8 billion. Charlie and I believe our current purchase represents excellent value. If we are correct, our Marmon holding is worth at least $4.6 billion more than its carrying value.

How would you explain the accounting valuations for the post-control step acquisitions to the Berkshire Hathaway executives? Do you agree or disagree with the GAAP treatment of reporting additional investments in subsidiaries when control has previously been established?

LO 4-10

Record the sale of a subsidiary (or a portion of its shares).

Parent Company Sales of Subsidiary Stock—Acquisition Method

Frequently, a parent company will sell a portion or all of the shares it owns of a subsidiary. For example, when General Electric Company reported the sale of its NBC Universal business, it noted in its financial statements:

> We transferred the assets of the NBCU business and Comcast transferred certain of its assets to a newly formed entity, NBC Universal LLC (NBCU LLC). In connection with the transaction, we received $6,197 million in cash from Comcast and a 49% interest in NBCU LLC. Comcast holds the remaining 51% interest in NBCU LLC. We will account for our investment in NBCU LLC under the equity method. As a result of the transaction, we expect to recognize a small after-tax gain . . .

Importantly, the accounting effect from selling subsidiary shares depends on whether the parent continues to maintain control after the sale. If the sale of the parent's ownership interest results in the loss of control of a subsidiary as in the GE example above, it recognizes any resulting gain or loss in consolidated net income.

If the parent sells some subsidiary shares but retains control, it recognizes no gains or losses on the sale. Under the acquisition method, as long as control remains with the parent, transactions in the stock of the subsidiary are considered to be transactions in the equity of the consolidated entity. Because such transactions are considered to occur with owners, the parent records any difference between proceeds of the sale and carrying amount as additional paid-in capital.

Sale of Subsidiary Shares with Control Maintained

To illustrate, assume Adams Company owns 100 percent of Smith Company's 25,000 voting shares and appropriately carries the investment on its books at January 1, 2018, at $750,000 using the equity method. Assuming Adams sells 5,000 shares to outside interests for $165,000 on January 1, 2018, the transaction is recorded as follows:

Cash	165,000	
Investment in Smith		150,000
Additional Paid-In Capital from Noncontrolling Interest Transaction		15,000
To record sale of 5,000 Smith shares to noncontrolling interest with excess of sale proceeds over carrying amount attributed to additional paid-in capital.		

The $15,000 "gain" on sale of the subsidiary shares is not recognized in income, but is reported as an increase in owners' equity. This equity treatment for the "gain" is consistent with the economic unit notion that as long as control is maintained, payments received from owners of the firm are considered contributions of capital. The ownership group of the consolidated entity specifically includes the noncontrolling interest. Therefore, the above treatment of sales to an ownership group is consistent with accounting for other stock transactions with owners (e.g., treasury stock transactions).

Sale of Subsidiary Shares with Control Lost

The loss of control of a subsidiary is a remeasurement event that can result in gain or loss recognition. The gain or loss is computed as the difference between the sale proceeds and the carrying amount of the shares sold. Using the Adams and Smith example above, assume now that instead of selling 5,000 shares, Adams sells 20,000 of its shares in Smith to outside interests on January 1, 2018, and keeps the remaining 5,000 shares. Assuming sale proceeds of $675,000, we record the transaction as follows:

Cash	675,000	
Investment in Smith		600,000
Gain on Sale of Smith Investment		75,000
To record sale of 20,000 Smith shares, resulting in the loss of control over Smith Company.		

If the former parent retains any of its former subsidiary's shares, the retained investment should be remeasured to fair value on the date control is lost. Any resulting gain or loss from this remeasurement should be recognized in the parent's net income.

In our Adams and Smith example, Adams still retains 5,000 shares of Smith Company (25,000 original investment less 20,000 shares sold). Assuming further that the $675,000 sale price for the 20,000 shares sold represents a reasonable value for the remaining shares of $33.75, Adams's shares now have a fair value of $168,750 ($33.75 × 5,000 shares). Adams would thus record the revaluation of its retained 5,000 shares of Smith as follows:

Investment in Smith	18,750	
Gain on Revaluation of Retained Smith Shares to Fair Value		18,750
To record the revaluation of Smith shares to a $33.75 per share fair value from their previous equity method January 1, 2018, carrying amount of $30.00 per share.		

The above revaluation of retained shares reflects the view that the loss of control of a subsidiary is a significant economic event that changes the fundamental relationship between the former parent and subsidiary. Also, the fair value of the retained investment provides the users of the parent's financial statements with more relevant information about the investment.

Cost-Flow Assumptions

If it sells less than an entire investment, the parent must select an appropriate cost-flow assumption when it has made more than one purchase. In the sale of securities, the use of specific identification based on serial numbers is acceptable, although averaging or FIFO assumptions often are applied. Use of the averaging method is especially appealing because all shares are truly identical, creating little justification for identifying different cost figures with individual shares.

Accounting for Shares That Remain

If Adams sells only a portion of the investment, it also must determine the proper method of accounting for the shares that remain. Three possible scenarios are described below:

1. Adams could have so drastically reduced its interest that the parent no longer controls the subsidiary or even has the ability to significantly influence its decision making. For example, assume that Adams's ownership drops from 80 to 5 percent. In the current period prior to the sale, the 80 percent investment is reported by means of the equity method with the market-value method used for the 5 percent that remains thereafter. Consolidated financial statements are no longer applicable.
2. Adams could still apply significant influence over Smith's operations although it no longer maintains control. A drop in the level of ownership from 80 to 30 percent normally meets this condition. In this case, the parent utilizes the equity method for the entire year. Application is based on 80 percent until the time of sale and then on 30 percent for the remainder of the year. Again, consolidated statements cease to be appropriate because control has been lost.
3. The decrease in ownership could be relatively small so that the parent continues to maintain control over the subsidiary even after the sale. Adams's reduction of its ownership in Smith from 80 to 60 percent is an example of this situation. After the disposal, consolidated financial statements are still required, but the process is based on the *end-of-year ownership percentage.* Because only the retained shares (60 percent in this case) are consolidated, the parent must separately recognize any current year income accruing to it from its terminated interest. Thus, Adams shows earnings on this portion of the investment (a 20 percent interest in Smith for the time during the year that it is held) in the consolidated income statement as a single-line item computed by means of the equity method.

Comparisons with International Accounting Standards

As observed in previous chapters of this text, the accounting and reporting standards for business combinations between U.S. and international standards have largely converged with FASB ASC Topic 805 and *IFRS 3R,* each of which carries the title "Business Combinations" and ASC Topic 810: Consolidation. Each set of standards requires the acquisition method and embraces a fair-value model for the assets acquired and liabilities assumed in a business combination. Both sets of standards treat exchanges between the parent and the noncontrolling interest as equity transactions, unless control is lost. However, as seen below, the accounting for the noncontrolling interest can diverge across the two reporting regimes.

- *U.S. GAAP.* In reporting the noncontrolling interest in consolidated financial statements, U.S. GAAP requires a fair-value measurement attribute, consistent with the overall valuation principles for business combinations. Thus, acquisition-date fair value provides a basis for reporting the noncontrolling interest, which is adjusted for its share of subsidiary income and dividends subsequent to acquisition.

- *IFRS.* In contrast, *IFRS 3R* allows an option for reporting the noncontrolling interest for each business combination. Under IFRS, the noncontrolling interest may be measured either at its acquisition-date fair value, which can include goodwill, or at a proportionate share of the acquiree's identifiable net asset fair value, which excludes goodwill. The IFRS proportionate-share option effectively assumes that any goodwill created through the business combination applies solely to the controlling interest.

Summary

1. A parent company need not acquire 100 percent of a subsidiary's stock to form a business combination. Only control over the decision-making process is necessary, a level that has historically been achieved by obtaining a majority of the voting shares. Ownership of any subsidiary stock that is retained by outside unrelated parties is collectively referred to as a noncontrolling interest.
2. A consolidation takes on an added degree of complexity when a noncontrolling interest is present. The noncontrolling interest represents a group of subsidiary owners and their equity is recognized by the parent in its consolidated financial statements.
3. The valuation principle for the noncontrolling interest is acquisition-date fair value. The fair value of the noncontrolling interest is added to the consideration transferred by the parent to determine the acquisition-date fair value of the subsidiary. This fair value is then allocated to the subsidiary's assets acquired and liabilities assumed based on their individual fair values. At the acquisition date, each of the subsidiary's assets and liabilities is included in consolidation at its individual fair value regardless of the degree of parent ownership. Any remaining excess fair value beyond the total assigned to the identifiable net assets is recognized as goodwill.
4. The fair value of the noncontrolling interest is adjusted over time for subsidiary income (less excess fair-value amortization) and subsidiary dividends.
5. Consolidated goodwill is allocated across the controlling and noncontrolling interests based on the excess of their respective acquisition-date fair values less their percentage share of the identifiable subsidiary net asset fair value. The goodwill allocation, therefore, does not necessarily correspond proportionately to the ownership interest of the parent and the noncontrolling interest.
6. Four noncontrolling interest figures appear in the annual consolidation process. First, a beginning-of-the-year balance in the book value of the subsidiary's net assets is recognized on the worksheet (through Entry **S**) followed by the noncontrolling interest's share of the unamortized excess acquisition-date fair values of the subsidiary's assets and liabilities (including a separate amount for goodwill if appropriate). Next, the noncontrolling interest share of the subsidiary's net income for the period (recorded by a columnar entry) is recognized. Subsidiary dividends to these unrelated owners are entered as a reduction of the noncontrolling interest. The final balance for the year is found as a summation of the Noncontrolling Interest column and is presented on the consolidated balance sheet, within the Stockholders' Equity section.
7. When a midyear business acquisition occurs, consolidated revenues and expenses should not include the subsidiary's current year preacquisition revenues and expenses. Only postacquisition subsidiary revenues and expenses are consolidated.
8. A parent can obtain control of a subsidiary by means of several separate purchases occurring over time, a process often referred to as a step acquisition. Once control is achieved, the acquisition method requires that the parent adjust to fair value all prior investments in the acquired firm and recognize any gain or loss. The fair values of these prior investments, along with the consideration transferred in the current investment that gave the parent control, and the noncontrolling interest fair value all constitute the total fair value of the acquired company.
9. When a parent sells some of its ownership shares of a subsidiary, it must establish an appropriate investment account balance to ensure an accurate accounting. If the equity method has not been used, the parent's investment balance is adjusted to recognize any income or amortization previously omitted. The resulting balance is then compared to the amount received for the stock to arrive at either an adjustment to additional paid-in capital (control maintained) or a gain or loss (control lost). Any shares still held will subsequently be reported through either consolidation, the equity method, or the fair-value method, depending on the influence retained by the parent.

Comprehensive Illustration

Problem

(*Estimated Time: 60 to 75 Minutes*) On January 1, 2014, Father Company acquired an 80 percent interest in Sun Company for $425,000. The acquisition-date fair value of the 20 percent noncontrolling interest's ownership shares was $102,500. Also as of that date, Sun reported total stockholders' equity of $400,000: $100,000 in common stock and $300,000 in retained earnings. In setting the acquisition price, Father appraised four accounts at values different from the balances reported within Sun's financial records.

Buildings (8-year remaining life)	Undervalued by $20,000
Land	Undervalued by $50,000
Equipment (5-year remaining life)	Undervalued by $12,500
Royalty agreement (20-year remaining life)	Not recorded, valued at $30,000

As of December 31, 2018, the trial balances of these two companies are as follows:

	Father Company	Sun Company
Debits		
Current assets	$ 605,000	$ 280,000
Investment in Sun Company	425,000	–0–
Land	200,000	300,000
Buildings (net)	640,000	290,000
Equipment (net)	380,000	160,000
Expenses	550,000	190,000
Dividends declared	90,000	20,000
Total debits	$2,890,000	$1,240,000
Credits		
Liabilities	$ 910,000	$ 300,000
Common stock	480,000	100,000
Retained earnings, 1/1/18	704,000	480,000
Revenues	780,000	360,000
Dividend income	16,000	–0–
Total credits	$2,890,000	$1,240,000

Included in these figures is a $20,000 payable that Sun owes to the parent company. No goodwill impairments have occurred since the Sun Company acquisition.

Required

a. Determine consolidated totals for Father Company and Sun Company for the year 2018.

b. Prepare worksheet entries to consolidate the trial balances of Father Company and Sun Company for the year 2018.

c. Assume instead that the acquisition-date fair value of the noncontrolling interest was $104,500. What balances in the December 31, 2018, consolidated statements would change?

Solution

a. The consolidation of Father Company and Sun Company begins with the allocation of the subsidiary's acquisition-date fair value as shown in Exhibit 4.13. Because this consolidation is taking place after several years, the unamortized balances for the various allocations at the beginning of the current year also should be determined (see Exhibit 4.14).

Next, the parent's method of accounting for its subsidiary should be ascertained. The continuing presence of the original $425,000 acquisition price in the investment account indicates that Father is applying the initial value method. This same determination can be made from the Dividend Income account, which equals 80 percent of the subsidiary's dividends. Thus, Father's accounting records have ignored the increase in Sun's book value as well as the excess amortization expenses for the prior periods of ownership. These amounts have to be added to the parent's January 1, 2018, Retained Earnings account to arrive at the proper consolidated balance.

During the 2014–2017 period of ownership, Sun's Retained Earnings account increased by $180,000 ($480,000 – $300,000). Father's 80 percent interest necessitates an accrual of $144,000

EXHIBIT 4.13 Excess Fair-Value Allocations

FATHER COMPANY AND SUN COMPANY
Acquisition-Date Fair-Value Allocation and Amortization
2014–2017

	Allocation	Remaining Life (years)	Annual Excess Amortization
Acquisition-date fair value	$527,500		
Sun book value (100%)	400,000		
Excess fair value	127,500		
Allocation to specific subsidiary accounts based on fair value:			
Buildings	$ 20,000	8	$ 2,500
Land	50,000	indefinite	–0–
Equipment	12,500	5	2,500
Royalty agreement	30,000	20	1,500
Goodwill	$ 15,000		
Annual excess amortization expenses			$ 6,500

Goodwill Allocation to the Controlling and Noncontrolling Interests

	Controlling Interest	Noncontrolling Interest	Total
Acquisition-date fair value	$425,000	$102,500	$527,500
Relative fair value of Sun's net identifiable assets (80% and 20%)	410,000	102,500	512,500
Goodwill	$ 15,000	$ –0–	$ 15,000

EXHIBIT 4.14 Excess Fair-Value Allocation Balances

FATHER COMPANY AND SUN COMPANY
Unamortized Excess Fair- over Book-Value Allocation
January 1, 2018, Balances

Account	Excess Original Allocation	Excess Amortization 2014–2017	Balance 1/1/18
Buildings	$ 20,000	$10,000	$ 10,000
Land	50,000	–0–	50,000
Equipment	12,500	10,000	2,500
Royalty agreement	30,000	6,000	24,000
Goodwill	15,000	–0–	15,000
Total	$127,500	$26,000	$101,500

($180,000 × 80%) for these years. In addition, the acquisition-date fair-value allocations require the recognition of $20,800 in excess amortization expenses for this same period ($6,500 × 80% × 4 years). Thus, a net increase of $123,200 ($144,000 – $20,800) is needed to adjust the parent's beginning retained earnings balance to reflect the equity method.

Once the adjustment from the initial value method to the equity method is determined, the consolidated figures for 2018 can be calculated:

Current Assets = $865,000. The parent's book value is added to the subsidiary's book value. The $20,000 intra-entity balance is eliminated.

Investment in Sun Company = –0–. The intra-entity ownership is eliminated so that the subsidiary's specific assets and liabilities can be consolidated.

Land = $550,000. The parent's book value is added to the subsidiary's book value plus the $50,000 excess fair-value allocation (see Exhibit 4.13).

Buildings (net) = $937,500. The parent's book value is added to the subsidiary's book value plus the $20,000 fair-value allocation (see Exhibit 4.14) and less five years of amortization (2014 through 2018).

Equipment (net) = $540,000. The parent's book value is added to the subsidiary's book value. The $12,500 fair-value allocation has been completely amortized after five years.

Royalty Agreement = $22,500. The original residual allocation from the acquisition-date fair value is recognized after taking into account five years of amortization (see Exhibit 4.13).

Goodwill = $15,000. Original acquisition-date value assigned.

Liabilities = $1,190,000. The parent's book value is added to the subsidiary's book value. The $20,000 intra-entity balance is eliminated.

Revenues = $1,140,000. The parent's book value is added to the subsidiary's book value.

Expenses = $746,500. The parent's book value is added to the subsidiary's book value plus current year amortization expenses on the fair-value allocations (see Exhibit 4.13).

Consolidated Net Income = $393,500. The combined total of consolidated revenues and expenses.

Net Income Attributable to Noncontrolling Interest = $32,700. The outside owners are assigned a 20 percent share of the subsidiary's net income less excess fair-value amortizations: 20% × ($170,000 – $6,500).

Net Income Attributable to Father Company = $360,800. Consolidated net income less the amount allocated to the noncontrolling interest.

Common Stock = $480,000. Only the parent company's balance is reported.

Retained Earnings, 1/1/18 = $827,200. Only the parent company's balance after a $123,200 increase to convert from the initial value method to the equity method.

Dividends Declared = $90,000. Only parent company dividends are consolidated. Subsidiary dividends distributable to the parent are eliminated; the remainder reduce the Noncontrolling Interest balance.

Retained Earnings 12/31/18 = $1,098,000. The parent's adjusted beginning balance of $827,200, plus $360,800 net income to the controlling interest, less $90,000 dividends declared by Father Company.

Dividend Income = -0-. The intra-entity dividend declarations are eliminated.

Noncontrolling Interest in Subsidiary, 12/31/18 = $162,000.

NCI in Sun's 1/1/18 book value (20% × $580,000)	$116,000
NCI in unamortized excess fair-value allocations (20% × $86,500)	17,300
January 1, 2018, NCI in Sun's fair value	133,300
NCI in Sun's net income [20% × ($360,000 – 196,500)]	32,700
NCI dividend share (20% × $20,000)	(4,000)
Noncontrolling interest in Sun Company, December 31, 2018	$162,000

b. Six worksheet entries are necessary to produce a consolidation worksheet for Father Company and Sun Company.

Entry *C

Investment in Sun Company	123,200	
Retained Earnings, 1/1/18 (parent)		123,200

This increment is required to adjust the parent's Retained Earnings from the initial value method to the equity method.
The amount is $144,000 (80% of the $180,000 increase in the subsidiary's book value during previous years) less $20,800 in excess amortization over this same 4-year period ($6,500 × 80% × 4 years).

Entry S

Common Stock (subsidiary)	100,000	
Retained Earnings, 1/1/18 (subsidiary)	480,000	
Investment in Sun Company (80%)		464,000
Noncontrolling Interest in Sun Company (20%)		116,000

To eliminate beginning stockholders' equity accounts of the subsidiary and recognize the beginning balance book value attributed to the outside owners (20%).

Entry A1 and A2 Combined

Buildings	10,000	
Land	50,000	
Equipment	2,500	
Royalty Agreement	24,000	
Goodwill	15,000	
Investment in Sun Company		84,200
Noncontrolling Interest in Sun Company		17,300

To recognize unamortized excess fair- over book-value allocations as of the first day of the current year (see Exhibit 4.14). All goodwill is attributable to the controlling interest.

Entry I

Dividend Income	16,000	
Dividends Declared		16,000

To eliminate intra-entity dividend declarations recorded by parent (using the initial value method) as income.

Entry E

Depreciation Expense	5,000	
Amortization Expense	1,500	
Buildings		2,500
Equipment		2,500
Royalty Agreement		1,500

To recognize excess amortization expenses for the current year (see Exhibit 4.13).

Entry P

Liabilities	20,000	
Current Assets		20,000

To eliminate the intra-entity receivable and payable.

c. If the acquisition-date fair value of the noncontrolling interest were $104,500, then Sun's fair value would increase by $2,000 to $529,500 and goodwill would increase by the same $2,000 to $17,000. The entire $2,000 increase in goodwill would be allocated to the noncontrolling interest as follows:

	Controlling Interest	Noncontrolling Interest	Total
Acquisition-date fair value	$425,000	$104,500	$529,500
Relative fair value of Sun's identifiable net assets (80% and 20%)	410,000	102,500	512,500
Goodwill	$ 15,000	$ 2,000	$ 17,000

Therefore, the consolidated balance sheet would show goodwill at $17,000 (instead of $15,000) and the noncontrolling interest in Sun Company balance would show $164,000 (instead of $162,000).

Questions

1. What does the term *noncontrolling interest* mean?
2. Atwater Company acquires 80 percent of the outstanding voting stock of Belwood Company. On that date, Belwood possesses a building with a $160,000 book value but a $220,000 fair value. At what value would this building be consolidated?
3. What is a control premium and how does it affect consolidated financial statements?
4. Where should the noncontrolling interest's claims be reported in a set of consolidated financial statements?
5. How is the noncontrolling interest in a subsidiary company calculated as of the end of a reporting period?

6. December 31 consolidated financial statements are being prepared for Allsports Company and its new subsidiary acquired on July 1 of the current year. Should Allsports adjust its consolidated balances for the preacquisition subsidiary revenues and expenses?
7. Tree, Inc., has held a 10 percent interest in the stock of Limb Company for several years. Because of the level of ownership, this investment has been accounted for using the fair-value method. At the beginning of the current year, Tree acquires an additional 70 percent interest, which provides the company with control over Limb. In preparing consolidated financial statements for this business combination, how does Tree account for the previous 10 percent ownership interest?
8. Duke Corporation owns a 70 percent equity interest in Salem Company, a subsidiary corporation. During the current year, a portion of this stock is sold to an outside party. Before recording this transaction, Duke adjusts the book value of its investment account. What is the purpose of this adjustment?
9. In question (8), how would the parent record the sales transaction?
10. In question (8), how would Duke account for the remainder of its investment subsequent to the sale of this partial interest?

Problems

LO 4-1

1. What is a basic premise of the acquisition method regarding accounting for a noncontrolling interest?
   a. Consolidated financial statements should be primarily for the benefit of the parent company's stockholders.
   b. Consolidated financial statements should be produced only if both the parent and the subsidiary are in the same basic industry.
   c. A subsidiary is an indivisible part of a business combination and should be included in its entirety regardless of the degree of ownership.
   d. Consolidated financial statements should not report a noncontrolling interest balance because these outside owners do not hold stock in the parent company.

LO 4-2

2. Mittelstaedt, Inc., buys 60 percent of the outstanding stock of Sherry, Inc. Sherry owns a piece of land that cost $212,000 but had a fair value of $549,000 at the acquisition date. What value should be attributed to this land in a consolidated balance sheet at the date of takeover?
   a. $549,000
   b. $337,000
   c. $127,200
   d. $421,800

LO 4-2

3. Jordan, Inc., holds 75 percent of the outstanding stock of Paxson Corporation. Paxson currently owes Jordan $400,000 for inventory acquired over the past few months. In preparing consolidated financial statements, what amount of this debt should be eliminated?
   a. –0–
   b. $100,000
   c. $300,000
   d. $400,000

LO 4-2

4. On January 1, 2017, Grand Haven, Inc., reports net assets of $760,000 although equipment (with a four-year remaining life) having a book value of $440,000 is worth $500,000 and an unrecorded patent is valued at $45,000. Van Buren Corporation pays $692,000 on that date to acquire an 80 percent equity ownership in Grand Haven. If the patent has a remaining life of nine years, at what amount should the patent be reported on Van Buren's consolidated balance sheet at December 31, 2018?
   a. $28,000
   b. $35,000
   c. $36,000
   d. $40,000

LO 4-6

5. The noncontrolling interest represents an outside ownership in a subsidiary that is not attributable to the parent company. Where in the consolidated balance sheet is this outside ownership interest recognized?
   a. In the liability section.
   b. In a mezzanine section between liabilities and owners' equity.
   c. In the owners' equity section.
   d. The noncontrolling interest is not recognized in the consolidated balance sheet.

LO 4-4

6. On January 1, 2017, Chamberlain Corporation pays $388,000 for a 60 percent ownership in Neville. Annual excess fair-value amortization of $15,000 results from the acquisition. On December 31, 2018, Neville reports revenues of $400,000 and expenses of $300,000 and Chamberlain reports revenues of $700,000 and expenses of $400,000. The parent figures contain no income from the subsidiary. What is consolidated net income attributable to Chamberlain Corporation?
   a. $385,000
   b. $351,000
   c. $366,000
   d. $400,000

Problems 7 and 8 relate to the following:

On January 1, 2016, Pride Corporation purchased 90 percent of the outstanding voting shares of Star, Inc., for $540,000 cash. The acquisition-date fair value of the noncontrolling interest was $60,000. At January 1, 2016, Star's net assets had a total carrying amount of $420,000. Equipment (eight-year remaining life) was undervalued on Star's financial records by $80,000. Any remaining excess fair value over book value was attributed to a customer list developed by Star (four-year remaining life), but not recorded on its books. Star recorded net income of $70,000 in 2016 and $80,000 in 2017. Each year since the acquisition, Star has declared a $20,000 dividend. At January 1, 2018, Pride's retained earnings show a $250,000 balance.

Selected account balances for the two companies from their separate operations were as follows:

	Pride	Star
2018 Revenues	$498,000	$285,000
2018 Expenses	350,000	195,000

LO 4-4

7. What is consolidated net income for 2018?
   a. $194,000
   b. $197,500
   c. $203,000
   d. $238,000

LO 4-4

8. Assuming that Pride, in its internal records, accounts for its investment in Star using the equity method, what amount of retained earnings would Pride report on its January 1, 2018, consolidated balance sheet?
   a. $250,000
   b. $286,000
   c. $315,000
   d. $360,000

LO 4-8

9. James Company acquired 85 percent of Mark-Right Company on April 1. On its December 31 consolidated income statement, how should James account for Mark-Right's revenues and expenses that occurred before April 1?
   a. Include 100 percent of Mark-Right's revenues and expenses and deduct the preacquisition portion as noncontrolling interest in net income.
   b. Exclude 100 percent of the preacquisition revenues and 100 percent of the preacquisition expenses from their respective consolidated totals.
   c. Exclude 15 percent of the preacquisition revenues and 15 percent of the preacquisition expenses from consolidated expenses.
   d. Deduct 15 percent of the net combined revenues and expenses relating to the preacquisition period from consolidated net income.

LO 4-9

10. Amie, Inc., has 100,000 shares of $2 par value stock outstanding. Prairie Corporation acquired 30,000 of Amie's shares on January 1, 2015, for $120,000 when Amie's net assets had a total fair value of $350,000. On July 1, 2018, Prairie bought an additional 60,000 shares of Amie from a single stockholder for $6 per share. Although Amie's shares were selling in the $5 range around July 1, 2018, Prairie forecasted that obtaining control of Amie would produce significant revenue synergies to justify the premium price paid. If Amie's identifiable net assets had a fair value of $500,000 at July 1, 2018, how much goodwill should Prairie report in its postcombination consolidated balance sheet?
    a. $60,000
    b. $90,000
    c. $100,000
    d. $-0-

LO 4-9

11. A parent buys 32 percent of a subsidiary in one year and then buys an additional 40 percent in the next year. In a step acquisition of this type, the original 32 percent acquisition should be
   a. Maintained at its initial value.
   b. Adjusted to its equity method balance at the date of the second acquisition.
   c. Adjusted to fair value at the date of the second acquisition with a resulting gain or loss recorded.
   d. Adjusted to fair value at the date of the second acquisition with a resulting adjustment to additional paid-in capital.

LO 4-4, 4-8

12. On April 1, Pujols, Inc., exchanges $430,000 fair-value consideration for 70 percent of the outstanding stock of Ramirez Corporation. The remaining 30 percent of the outstanding shares continued to trade at a collective fair value of $165,000. Ramirez's identifiable assets and liabilities each had book values that equaled their fair values on April 1 for a net total of $500,000. During the remainder of the year, Ramirez generates revenues of $600,000 and expenses of $360,000 and declared no dividends. On a December 31 consolidated balance sheet, what amount should be reported as noncontrolling interest?
   a. $219,000
   b. $237,000
   c. $234,000
   d. $250,500

LO 4-10

13. McKinley, Inc., owns 100 percent of Jackson Company's 45,000 voting shares. On June 30, McKinley's internal accounting records show a $192,000 equity method adjusted balance for its investment in Jackson. McKinley sells 15,000 of its Jackson shares on the open market for $80,000 on June 30. How should McKinley record the excess of the sale proceeds over its carrying amount for the shares?
   a. Reduce goodwill by $64,000.
   b. Recognize a gain on sale for $16,000.
   c. Increase its additional paid-in capital by $16,000.
   d. Recognize a revaluation gain on its remaining shares of $48,000.

Use the following information for Problems 14 through 16:

West Company acquired 60 percent of Solar Company for $300,000 when Solar's book value was $400,000. The newly comprised 40 percent noncontrolling interest had an assessed fair value of $200,000. Also at the acquisition date, Solar had a trademark (with a 10-year remaining life) that was undervalued in the financial records by $60,000. Also, patented technology (with a 5-year remaining life) was undervalued by $40,000. Two years later, the following figures are reported by these two companies (stockholders' equity accounts have been omitted):

	West Company Book Value	Solar Company Book Value	Solar Company Fair Value
Current assets	$620,000	$300,000	$320,000
Trademarks	260,000	200,000	280,000
Patented technology	410,000	150,000	150,000
Liabilities	(390,000)	(120,000)	(120,000)
Revenues	(900,000)	(400,000)	
Expenses	500,000	300,000	
Investment income	Not given		

LO 4-2

14. What is the consolidated net income before allocation to the controlling and noncontrolling interests?
   a. $400,000
   b. $486,000
   c. $491,600
   d. $500,000

LO 4-4, 4-5

15. Assuming Solar Company has declared no dividends, what are the noncontrolling interest's share of the subsidiary's income and the ending balance of the noncontrolling interest in the subsidiary?
   a. $26,000 and $230,000
   b. $28,800 and $252,000
   c. $34,400 and $240,800
   d. $40,000 and $252,000

LO 4-2

16. What is the consolidated trademarks balance?
    a. $508,000
    b. $514,000
    c. $520,000
    d. $540,000

Use the following information for Problems 17 through 21:

On January 1, Park Corporation and Strand Corporation had condensed balance sheets as follows:

	Park	Strand
Current assets	$ 70,000	$20,000
Noncurrent assets	90,000	40,000
Total assets	$160,000	$60,000
Current liabilities	$ 30,000	$10,000
Long-term debt	50,000	–0–
Stockholders' equity	80,000	50,000
Total liabilities and equities	$160,000	$60,000

On January 2, Park borrowed $60,000 and used the proceeds to obtain 80 percent of the outstanding common shares of Strand. The acquisition price was considered proportionate to Strand's total fair value. The $60,000 debt is payable in 10 equal annual principal payments, plus interest, beginning December 31. The excess fair value of the investment over the underlying book value of the acquired net assets is allocated to inventory (60 percent) and to goodwill (40 percent). On a consolidated balance sheet as of January 2, what should be the amount for each of the following?

LO 4-2

17. Current assets:
    a. $105,000
    b. $102,000
    c. $100,000
    d. $90,000

LO 4-2

18. Noncurrent assets:
    a. $130,000
    b. $134,000
    c. $138,000
    d. $140,000

LO 4-2

19. Current liabilities:
    a. $50,000
    b. $46,000
    c. $40,000
    d. $30,000

LO 4-2

20. Noncurrent liabilities:
    a. $110,000
    b. $104,000
    c. $90,000
    d. $50,000

LO 4-2

21. Stockholders' equity:
    a. $80,000
    b. $90,000
    c. $95,000
    d. $130,000

    (AICPA adapted)

LO 4-4, 4-5

22. On January 1, 2017, Harrison, Inc., acquired 90 percent of Starr Company in exchange for $1,125,000 fair-value consideration. The total fair value of Starr Company was assessed at $1,200,000. Harrison computed annual excess fair-value amortization of $8,000 based on the difference between Starr's total fair value and its underlying book value. The subsidiary reported net

income of $70,000 in 2017 and $90,000 in 2018 with dividend declarations of $30,000 each year. Apart from its investment in Starr, Harrison had net income of $220,000 in 2017 and $260,000 in 2018.

a. What is the consolidated net income in each of these two years?

b. What is the balance of the noncontrolling interest in Starr at December 31, 2018?

LO 4-2, 4-4, 4-5

23. On January 1, 2018, Johnsonville Enterprises, Inc., acquired 80 percent of Stayer Company's outstanding common shares in exchange for $3,000,000 cash. The price paid for the 80 percent ownership interest was proportionately representative of the fair value of all of Stayer's shares.

At acquisition date, Stayer's books showed assets of $4,200,000 and liabilities of $1,600,000. The recorded assets and liabilities had fair values equal to their individual book values except that a building (10-year remaining life) with book value of $195,000 had an appraised fair value of $345,000. Stayer's books showed a $175,500 carrying amount for this building at the end of 2018.

Also, at acquisition date Stayer possessed unrecorded technology processes (zero book value) with an estimated fair value of $1,000,000 and a 20-year remaining life. For 2018 Johnsonville reported net income of $650,000 (before recognition of Stayer's income), and Stayer separately reported earnings of $350,000. During 2018, Johnsonville declared dividends of $85,000 and Stayer declared $50,000 in dividends.

Compute the amounts that Johnsonville Enterprises should report in its December 31, 2018, consolidated financial statements for the following items:

a. Stayer's building (net of accumulated depreciation).

b. Stayer's technology processes (net of accumulated amortization).

c. Net income attributable to the noncontrolling interest.

d. Net income attributable to controlling interest.

e. Noncontrolling interest in Stayer.

LO 4-4, 4-5, 4-7

24. On January 1, Patterson Corporation acquired 80 percent of the 100,000 outstanding voting shares of Soriano, Inc., in exchange for $31.25 per share cash. The remaining 20 percent of Soriano's shares continued to trade for $30 both before and after Patterson's acquisition.

At January 1, Soriano's book and fair values were as follows:

	Book Values	Fair Values	Remaining Life
Current assets	$ 80,000	$ 80,000	
Buildings and equipment	1,250,000	1,000,000	5 years
Trademarks	700,000	900,000	10 years
Patented technology	940,000	2,000,000	4 years
	$2,970,000		
Current liabilities	$ 180,000	$ 180,000	
Long-term notes payable	1,500,000	1,500,000	
Common stock	50,000		
Additional paid-in capital	500,000		
Retained earnings	740,000		
	$2,970,000		

In addition, Patterson assigned a $600,000 value to certain unpatented technologies recently developed by Soriano. These technologies were estimated to have a three-year remaining life.

During the year, Soriano declared a $30,000 dividend for its shareholders. The companies reported the following revenues and expenses from their separate operations for the year ending December 31.

	Patterson	Soriano
Revenues	$3,000,000	$1,400,000
Expenses	1,750,000	600,000

a. What amount should Patterson recognize as the total value of the acquisition in its January 1 consolidated balance sheet?

b. What valuation principle should Patterson use to report each of Soriano's identifiable assets and liabilities in its January 1 consolidated balance sheet?

c. For years subsequent to acquisition, how will Soriano's identifiable assets and liabilities be valued in Patterson's consolidated financial statements?

d. How much goodwill resulted from Patterson's acquisition of Soriano?

e. What is the consolidated net income for the year and what amounts are allocated to the controlling and noncontrolling interests?

f. What is the noncontrolling interest amount reported in the December 31 consolidated balance sheet?

g. Assume instead that, based on its share prices, Soriano's January 1 total fair value was assessed at $2,250,000. How would the reported amounts for Soriano's net assets change on Patterson's acquisition-date consolidated balance sheet?

LO 4-9

25. On January 1, 2017, Palka, Inc., acquired 70 percent of the outstanding shares of Sellinger Company for $1,141,000 in cash. The price paid was proportionate to Sellinger's total fair value, although at the acquisition date, Sellinger had a total book value of $1,380,000. All assets acquired and liabilities assumed had fair values equal to book values except for a patent (six-year remaining life) that was undervalued on Sellinger's accounting records by $240,000. On January 1, 2018, Palka acquired an additional 25 percent common stock equity interest in Sellinger Company for $415,000 in cash. On its internal records, Palka uses the equity method to account for its shares of Sellinger.

During the two years following the acquisition, Sellinger reported the following net income and dividends:

	2017	2018
Net income	$340,000	$440,000
Dividends declared	150,000	180,000

a. Show Palka's journal entry to record its January 1, 2018, acquisition of an additional 25 percent ownership of Sellinger Company shares.

b. Prepare a schedule showing Palka's December 31, 2018, equity method balance for its Investment in Sellinger account.

LO 4-2, 4-7, 4-8

26. Parker, Inc., acquires 70 percent of Sawyer Company for $420,000. The remaining 30 percent of Sawyer's outstanding shares continue to trade at a collective value of $174,000. On the acquisition date, Sawyer has the following accounts:

	Book Value	Fair Value
Current assets	$ 210,000	$ 210,000
Land	170,000	180,000
Buildings	300,000	330,000
Liabilities	(280,000)	(280,000)

The buildings have a 10-year remaining life. In addition, Sawyer holds a patent worth $140,000 that has a five-year remaining life but is not recorded on its financial records. At the end of the year, the two companies report the following balances:

	Parker	Sawyer
Revenues	$(900,000)	$(600,000)
Expenses	600,000	400,000

a. Assume that the acquisition took place on January 1. What figures would appear in a consolidated income statement for this year?

b. Assume that the acquisition took place on April 1. Sawyer's revenues and expenses occurred uniformly throughout the year. What amounts would appear in a consolidated income statement for this year?

LO 4-2, 4-4, 4-5

27. On January 1, Beckman, Inc., acquires 60 percent of the outstanding stock of Calvin for $36,000. Calvin Co. has one recorded asset, a specialized production machine with a book value of $10,000 and no liabilities. The fair value of the machine is $50,000, and the remaining useful life is estimated to be 10 years. Any remaining excess fair value is attributable to an unrecorded process

trade secret with an estimated future life of four years. Calvin's total acquisition-date fair value is $60,000.

At the end of the year, Calvin reports the following in its financial statements:

Revenues	$50,000	Machine	$ 9,000	Common stock	$10,000
Expenses	20,000	Other assets	26,000	Retained earnings	25,000
Net income	$30,000	Total assets	$35,000	Total equity	$35,000
Dividends declared	$ 5,000				

Determine the amounts that Beckman should report in its year-end consolidated financial statements for noncontrolling interest in subsidiary income, noncontrolling interest, Calvin's machine (net of accumulated depreciation), and the process trade secret.

LO 4-1, 4-5, 4-6

28. Plaza, Inc., acquires 80 percent of the outstanding common stock of Stanford Corporation on January 1, 2018, in exchange for $900,000 cash. At the acquisition date, Stanford's total fair value, including the noncontrolling interest, was assessed at $1,125,000. Also at the acquisition date, Stanford's book value was $690,000.

Several individual items on Stanford's financial records had fair values that differed from their book values as follows:

	Book Value	Fair Value
Tradenames (indefinite life)	$ 360,000	$383,000
Property and equipment (net, 8-year remaining life)	290,000	330,000
Patent (14-year remaining life)	132,000	272,000

For internal reporting purposes, Plaza, Inc., employs the equity method to account for this investment. The following account balances are for the year ending December 31, 2018, for both companies.

	Plaza	Stanford
Revenues	$(1,400,000)	$ (825,000)
Cost of goods sold	774,000	395,750
Depreciation expense	328,000	36,250
Amortization expense	–0–	28,000
Equity in income of Stanford	(280,000)	–0–
Net income	$ (578,000)	$ (365,000)
Retained earnings, 1/1/18	$(1,275,000)	$ (530,000)
Net income	(578,000)	(365,000)
Dividends declared	300,000	50,000
Retained earnings, 12/31/18	$(1,553,000)	$ (845,000)
Current assets	$ 860,000	$ 432,250
Investment in Stanford	1,140,000	–0–
Tradenames	240,000	360,000
Property and equipment (net)	1,030,000	253,750
Patents	–0–	104,000
Total assets	$3,270,000	$1,150,000
Accounts payable	$ (142,000)	$ (145,000)
Common stock	(300,000)	(120,000)
Additional paid-in capital	(1,275,000)	(40,000)
Retained earnings (above)	(1,553,000)	(845,000)
Total liabilities and equities	$(3,270,000)	$(1,150,000)

At year-end, there were no intra-entity receivables or payables.

Prepare a worksheet to consolidate the financial statements of Plaza, Inc., and its subsidiary Stanford.

LO 4-3, 4-5, 4-7

29. On January 1, 2016, Parflex Corporation exchanged $344,000 cash for 90 percent of Eagle Corporation's outstanding voting stock. Eagle's acquisition date balance sheet follows:

Cash and receivables	$ 15,000	Liabilities	$ 76,000
Inventory	35,000	Common stock	150,000
Property and equipment (net)	350,000	Retained earnings	174,000
	$400,000		$400,000

On January 1, 2016, Parflex prepared the following fair-value allocation schedule:

Consideration transferred by Parflex	$344,000
10% noncontrolling interest fair value	36,000
Fair value of Eagle	380,000
Book value of Eagle	324,000
Excess fair over book value	56,000
to equipment (undervalued, remaining life of 9 years)	18,000
to goodwill (indefinite life)	$ 38,000

The companies' financial statements for the year ending December 31, 2018, follow:

	Parflex	Eagle
Sales	$ (862,000)	$(366,000)
Cost of goods sold	515,000	209,000
Depreciation expense	191,200	67,000
Equity in Eagle's earnings	(79,200)	–0–
Separate company net income	$ (235,000)	$ (90,000)
Retained earnings 1/1	$ (500,000)	$(278,000)
Net income	(235,000)	(90,000)
Dividends declared	130,000	27,000
Retained earnings 12/31	$ (605,000)	$(341,000)
Cash and receivables	$135,000	$ 82,000
Inventory	255,000	136,000
Investment in Eagle	488,900	–0–
Property and equipment (net)	964,000	328,000
Total assets	$ 1,842,900	$ 546,000
Liabilities	$ (722,900)	(55,000)
Common stock—Parflex	(515,000)	–0–
Common stock—Eagle	–0–	(150,000)
Retained earnings 12/31	(605,000)	(341,000)
Total liabilities and owners' equity	$(1,842,900)	$(546,000)

At year-end, there were no intra-entity receivables or payables.

a. Compute the goodwill allocation to the controlling and noncontrolling interest.

b. Show how Parflex determined its "Investment in Eagle" account balance.

c. Determine the amounts that should appear on Parflex's December 31, 2018, consolidated statement of financial position and its 2018 consolidated income statement.

LO 4-3, 4-5, 4-7

30. On January 1, 2017, Holland Corporation paid $8 per share to a group of Zeeland Corporation shareholders to acquire 60,000 shares of Zeeland's outstanding voting stock, representing a 60 percent ownership interest. The remaining 40,000 shares of Zeeland continued to trade in the market close to its recent average of $6.50 per share both before and after the acquisition by Holland. Zeeland's acquisition date balance sheet follows:

Current assets	$ 14,000	Liabilities	$ 212,000
Property and equipment (net)	268,000	Common stock	100,000
Patents	190,000	Retained earnings	160,000
	$472,000		$472,000

On January 1, 2017, Holland assessed the carrying amount of Zeeland's equipment (5-year remaining life) to be undervalued by $55,000. Holland also determined that Zeeland possessed unrecorded patents (10-year remaining life) worth $285,000. Zeeland's acquisition-date fair values for its current assets and liabilities were equal to their carrying amounts. Any remaining excess of Zeeland's acquisition-date fair value over its book value was attributed to goodwill.

The companies' financial statements for the year ending December 31, 2018, follow:

	Holland	Zeeland
Sales	$ (640,500)	$(428,500)
Cost of goods sold	325,000	200,000
Depreciation expense	80,000	34,000
Amortization expense	14,000	21,000
Other operating expenses	52,000	63,500
Equity in Zeeland earnings	(42,300)	-0-
Separate company net income	$ (211,800)	$(110,000)
Retained earnings 1/1	$ (820,200)	$(296,500)
Net income	(211,800)	(110,000)
Dividends declared	50,000	30,000
Retained earnings 12/31	$ (982,000)	$(376,500)
Current assets	$ 125,000	$ 81,500
Investment in Zeeland	562,500	-0-
Property and equipment (net)	837,000	259,000
Patents	149,000	147,500
Total assets	$ 1,673,500	$ 488,000
Liabilities	$ (371,500)	$ (11,500)
Common stock - Holland	(320,000)	-0-
Common stock - Zeeland	-0-	(100,000)
Retained earnings 12/31	(982,000)	(376,500)
Total liabilities and owners equity	$(1,673,500)	$(488,000)

At year-end, there were no intra-entity receivables or payables.

a. Compute the amount of goodwill recognized in Holland's acquisition of Zeeland and the allocation of goodwill to the controlling and noncontrolling interest.

b. Show how Holland determined its December 31, 2018, Investment in Zeeland account balance.

c. Prepare a worksheet to determine the amounts that should appear on Holland's December 31, 2018, consolidated financial statements.

LO 4-8, 4-9

31. On January 1, 2018, Morey, Inc., exchanged $178,000 for 25 percent of Amsterdam Corporation. Morey appropriately applied the equity method to this investment. At January 1, the book values of Amsterdam's assets and liabilities approximated their fair values.

On June 30, 2018, Morey paid $560,000 for an additional 70 percent of Amsterdam, thus increasing its overall ownership to 95 percent. The price paid for the 70 percent acquisition was proportionate to Amsterdam's total fair value. At June 30, the carrying amounts of Amsterdam's assets and liabilities approximated their fair values. Any remaining excess fair value was attributed to goodwill.

Amsterdam reports the following amounts at December 31, 2018 (credit balances shown in parentheses):

Revenues	$(210,000)
Expenses	140,000
Retained earnings, January 1	(200,000)
Dividends declared, October 1	20,000
Common stock	(500,000)

Amsterdam's revenue and expenses were distributed evenly throughout the year and no changes in Amsterdam's stock have occurred.

Using the acquisition method, compute the following:

a. The acquisition-date fair value of Amsterdam to be included in Morey's June 30 consolidated financial statements.

b. The revaluation gain (or loss) reported by Morey for its 25 percent investment in Amsterdam on June 30.

c. The amount of goodwill recognized by Morey on its December 31 balance sheet (assume no impairments have been recognized).

d. The noncontrolling interest amount reported by Morey on its

- June 30 consolidated balance sheet.
- December 31 consolidated balance sheet.

LO 4-10

32. Posada Company acquired 7,000 of the 10,000 outstanding shares of Sabathia Company on January 1, 2016, for $840,000. The subsidiary's total fair value was assessed at $1,200,000 although its book value on that date was $1,130,000. The $70,000 fair value in excess of Sabathia's book value was assigned to a patent with a five-year remaining life.

On January 1, 2018, Posada reported a $1,085,000 equity method balance in the Investment in Sabathia Company account. On October 1, 2018, Posada sells 1,000 shares of the investment for $191,000. During 2018, Sabathia reported net income of $120,000 and declared dividends of $40,000. These amounts are assumed to have occurred evenly throughout the year.

a. How should Posada report the 2018 income that accrued to the 1,000 shares prior to their sale?

b. What is the effect on Posada's financial statements from this sale of 1,000 shares?

c. How should Posada report in its financial statements the 6,000 shares of Sabathia it continues to hold?

LO 4-5

33. On January 1, 2016, Telconnect acquires 70 percent of Bandmor for $490,000 cash. The remaining 30 percent of Bandmor's shares continued to trade at a total value of $210,000. The new subsidiary reported common stock of $300,000 on that date, with retained earnings of $180,000. A patent was undervalued in the company's financial records by $30,000. This patent had a five-year remaining life. Goodwill of $190,000 was recognized and allocated proportionately to the controlling and noncontrolling interests. Bandmor earns net income and declares cash dividends as follows:

Year	Net Income	Dividends
2016	$ 75,000	$39,000
2017	96,000	44,000
2018	110,000	60,000

On December 31, 2018, Telconnect owes $22,000 to Bandmor.

a. If Telconnect has applied the equity method, what consolidation entries are needed as of December 31, 2018?

b. If Telconnect has applied the initial value method, what Entry *C is needed for a 2018 consolidation?

c. If Telconnect has applied the partial equity method, what Entry *C is needed for a 2018 consolidation?

d. What noncontrolling interest balances will appear in consolidated financial statements for 2018?

LO 4-2, 4-3, 4-5

34. Miller Company acquired an 80 percent interest in Taylor Company on January 1, 2016. Miller paid $664,000 in cash to the owners of Taylor to acquire these shares. In addition, the remaining 20 percent of Taylor shares continued to trade at a total value of $166,000 both before and after Miller's acquisition.

On January 1, 2016, Taylor reported a book value of $600,000 (Common Stock = $300,000; Additional Paid-In Capital = $90,000; Retained Earnings = $210,000). Several of Taylor's buildings that had a remaining life of 20 years were undervalued by a total of $80,000.

During the next three years, Taylor reports income and declares dividends as follows:

Year	Net Income	Dividends
2016	$ 70,000	$10,000
2017	90,000	15,000
2018	100,000	20,000

Determine the appropriate answers for each of the following questions:

a. What amount of excess depreciation expense should be recognized in the consolidated financial statements for the initial years following this acquisition?

b. If a consolidated balance sheet is prepared as of January 1, 2016, what amount of goodwill should be recognized?

c. If a consolidation worksheet is prepared as of January 1, 2016, what Entry S and Entry A should be included?

d. On the separate financial records of the parent company, what amount of investment income would be reported for 2016 under each of the following accounting methods?
- The equity method.
- The partial equity method.
- The initial value method.

e. On the parent company's separate financial records, what would be the December 31, 2018, balance for the Investment in Taylor Company account under each of the following accounting methods?
- The equity method.
- The partial equity method.
- The initial value method.

f. As of December 31, 2017, Miller's Buildings account on its separate records has a balance of $800,000 and Taylor has a similar account with a $300,000 balance. What is the consolidated balance for the Buildings account?

g. What is the balance of consolidated goodwill as of December 31, 2018?

h. Assume that the parent company has been applying the equity method to this investment. On December 31, 2018, the separate financial statements for the two companies present the following information:

	Miller Company	Taylor Company
Common stock	$500,000	$300,000
Additional paid-in capital	280,000	90,000
Retained earnings, 12/31/18	620,000	425,000

What will be the consolidated balance of each of these accounts?

LO 4-1, 4-8

35. Following are several account balances taken from the records of Karson and Reilly as of December 31, 2018. A few asset accounts have been omitted here. All revenues, expenses, and dividend declarations occurred evenly throughout the year. Annual tests have indicated no goodwill impairment.

	Karson	Reilly
Sales	$ (800,000)	$(500,000)
Cost of goods sold	400,000	280,000
Operating expenses	200,000	100,000
Investment income	not given	–0–
Retained earnings, 1/1	(1,400,000)	(700,000)
Dividends declared	80,000	20,000
Trademarks	600,000	200,000
Royalty agreements	700,000	300,000
Licensing agreements	400,000	400,000
Liabilities	(500,000)	(200,000)
Common stock ($10 par value)	(400,000)	(100,000)
Additional paid-in capital	(500,000)	(600,000)

On July 1, 2018, Karson acquired 80 percent of Reilly for $1,330,000 cash consideration. In addition, Karson agreed to pay additional cash to the former owners of Reilly if certain performance measures are achieved after three years. Karson assessed a $30,000 fair value for the contingent performance obligation as of the acquisition date and as of December 31, 2018.

On July 1, 2018, Reilly's assets and liabilities had book values equal to their fair value except for some trademarks (with five-year remaining lives) that were undervalued by $150,000. Karson estimated Reilly's total fair value at $1,700,000 on July 1, 2018.

For the following items, what balances would be reported on Karson's December 31, 2018, consolidated financial statements?

Sales	Consolidated Net Income
Expenses	Retained Earnings, 1/1
Noncontrolling Interest in Subsidiary's Net Income	Trademarks
	Goodwill

LO 4-5

36. Nascent, Inc., acquires 60 percent of Sea-Breeze Corporation for $414,000 cash on January 1, 2015. The remaining 40 percent of the Sea-Breeze shares traded near a total value of $276,000 both before and after the acquisition date. On January 1, 2015, Sea-Breeze had the following assets and liabilities:

	Book Value	Fair Value
Current assets	$150,000	$150,000
Land	200,000	200,000
Buildings (net) (6-year remaining life)	300,000	360,000
Equipment (net) (4-year remaining life)	300,000	280,000
Patent (10-year remaining life)	–0–	100,000
Liabilities	(400,000)	(400,000)

The companies' financial statements for the year ending December 31, 2018, follow:

	Nascent	Sea-Breeze
Revenues	$ (600,000)	$ (300,000)
Operating expenses	410,000	210,000
Investment income	(42,000)	–0–
Net income	$ (232,000)	$ (90,000)
Retained earnings, 1/1/18	$ (700,000)	$ (300,000)
Net income	(232,000)	(90,000)
Dividends declared	92,000	70,000
Retained earnings, 12/31/18	$ (840,000)	$ (320,000)
Current assets	$ 330,000	$ 100,000
Land	220,000	200,000
Buildings (net)	700,000	200,000
Equipment (net)	400,000	500,000
Investment in Sea-Breeze	414,000	–0–
Total assets	$ 2,064,000	$ 1,000,000
Liabilities	$ (500,000)	$ (200,000)
Common stock	(724,000)	(480,000)
Retained earnings, 12/31/18	(840,000)	(320,000)
Total liabilities and equities	$(2,064,000)	$(1,000,000)

Answer the following questions:

a. How can the accountant determine that the parent has applied the initial value method?

b. What is the annual excess amortization initially recognized in connection with this acquisition?

c. If the parent had applied the equity method, what investment income would the parent have recorded in 2018?

d. What amount should the parent report as retained earnings in its January 1, 2018, consolidated balance sheet?

e. What is consolidated net income for 2018 and what amounts are attributable to the controlling and noncontrolling interests?

f. Within consolidated statements at January 1, 2018, what balance is included for the subsidiary's Buildings account?

g. What is the consolidated Buildings reported balance as of December 31, 2018?

LO 4-1, 4-5, 4-7

eXcel

37. On January 1, 2017, Paloma Corporation exchanged $1,710,000 cash for 90 percent of the outstanding voting stock of San Marco Company. The consideration transferred by Paloma provided a reasonable basis for assessing the total January 1, 2017, fair value of San Marco Company. At the acquisition date, San Marco reported the following owners' equity amounts in its balance sheet:

Common stock	$400,000
Additional paid-in capital	60,000
Retained earnings	265,000

In determining its acquisition offer, Paloma noted that the values for San Marco's recorded assets and liabilities approximated their fair values. Paloma also observed that San Marco had developed internally a customer base with an assessed fair value of $800,000 that was not reflected on San Marco's books. Paloma expected both cost and revenue synergies from the combination.

At the acquisition date, Paloma prepared the following fair-value allocation schedule:

Fair value of San Marco Company	$1,900,000
Book value of San Marco Company	725,000
Excess fair value	1,175,000
to customer base (10-year remaining life)	800,000
to goodwill	$ 375,000

At December 31, 2018, the two companies report the following balances:

	Paloma	San Marco
Revenues	$(1,843,000)	$ (675,000)
Cost of goods sold	1,100,000	322,000
Depreciation expense	125,000	120,000
Amortization expense	275,000	11,000
Interest expense	27,500	7,000
Equity in income of San Marco	(121,500)	–0–
Net income	$ (437,000)	$ (215,000)
Retained earnings, 1/1	$(2,625,000)	$ (395,000)
Net income	(437,000)	(215,000)
Dividends declared	350,000	25,000
Retained earnings, 12/31	$(2,712,000)	$ (585,000)
Current assets	$ 1,204,000	$ 430,000
Investment in San Marco	1,854,000	–0–
Buildings and equipment	931,000	863,000
Copyrights	950,000	107,000
Total assets	$ 4,939,000	$ 1,400,000
Accounts payable	$ (485,000)	$ (200,000)
Notes payable	(542,000)	(155,000)
Common stock	(900,000)	(400,000)
Additional paid-in capital	(300,000)	(60,000)
Retained earnings, 12/31	(2,712,000)	(585,000)
Total liabilities and equities	$(4,939,000)	$(1,400,000)

At year-end, there were no intra-entity receivables or payables.

a. Determine the consolidated balances for this business combination as of December 31, 2018.

b. If instead the noncontrolling interest's acquisition-date fair value is assessed at $167,500, what changes would be evident in the consolidated statements?

LO 4-5, 4-6, 4-7

38. The Holtz Corporation acquired 80 percent of the 100,000 outstanding voting shares of Devine, Inc., for $7.20 per share on January 1, 2017. The remaining 20 percent of Devine's shares also traded actively at $7.20 per share before and after Holtz's acquisition. An appraisal made on that date determined that all book values appropriately reflected the fair values of Devine's underlying accounts except that a building with a five-year future life was undervalued by $85,500 and a fully amortized

trademark with an estimated 10-year remaining life had a $64,000 fair value. At the acquisition date, Devine reported common stock of $100,000 and a retained earnings balance of $226,500.

Following are the separate financial statements for the year ending December 31, 2018:

	Holtz Corporation	Devine, Inc.
Sales	$ (641,000)	$(399,000)
Cost of goods sold	198,000	176,000
Operating expenses	273,000	126,000
Dividend income	(16,000)	–0–
Net income	$ (186,000)	$ (97,000)
Retained earnings, 1/1/18	$ (762,000)	$(296,500)
Net income (above)	(186,000)	(97,000)
Dividends declared	70,000	20,000
Retained earnings, 12/31/18	$ (878,000)	$(373,500)
Current assets	$ 121,000	$ 120,500
Investment in Devine, Inc.	576,000	–0–
Buildings and equipment (net)	887,000	335,000
Trademarks	149,000	236,000
Total assets	$ 1,733,000	$ 691,500
Liabilities	$ (535,000)	$(218,000)
Common stock	(320,000)	(100,000)
Retained earnings, 12/31/18 (above)	(878,000)	(373,500)
Total liabilities and equities	$(1,733,000)	$(691,500)

At year-end, there were no intra-entity receivables or payables.

a. Prepare a worksheet to consolidate these two companies as of December 31, 2018.

b. Prepare a 2018 consolidated income statement for Holtz and Devine.

c. If instead the noncontrolling interest shares of Devine had traded for $4.76 surrounding Holtz's acquisition date, what is the impact on goodwill?

LO 4-1, 4-5, 4-6

excel

39. Padre, Inc., buys 80 percent of the outstanding common stock of Sierra Corporation on January 1, 2018, for $802,720 cash. At the acquisition date, Sierra's total fair value, including the noncontrolling interest, was assessed at $1,003,400 although Sierra's book value was only $690,000. Also, several individual items on Sierra's financial records had fair values that differed from their book values as follows:

	Book Value	Fair Value
Land	$ 65,000	$ 290,000
Buildings and equipment (10-year remaining life)	287,000	263,000
Copyright (20-year remaining life)	122,000	216,000
Notes payable (due in 8 years)	(176,000)	(157,600)

For internal reporting purposes, Padre, Inc., employs the equity method to account for this investment. The following account balances are for the year ending December 31, 2018, for both companies.

	Padre	Sierra
Revenues	$(1,394,980)	$ (684,900)
Cost of goods sold	774,000	432,000
Depreciation expense	274,000	11,600
Amortization expense	0	6,100
Interest expense	52,100	9,200
Equity in income of Sierra	(177,120)	–0–
Net income	$ (472,000)	$ (226,000)

(*continued*)

(continued)

	Padre	Sierra
Retained earnings, 1/1/18	$(1,275,000)	$ (530,000)
Net income	(472,000)	(226,000)
Dividends declared	260,000	65,000
Retained earnings, 12/31/18	$(1,487,000)	$ (691,000)
Current assets	$ 856,160	$ 764,700
Investment in Sierra	927,840	–0–
Land	360,000	65,000
Buildings and equipment (net)	909,000	275,400
Copyright	–0–	115,900
Total assets	$ 3,053,000	$ 1,221,000
Accounts payable	$ (275,000)	$ (194,000)
Notes payable	(541,000)	(176,000)
Common stock	(300,000)	(100,000)
Additional paid-in capital	(450,000)	(60,000)
Retained earnings (above)	(1,487,000)	(691,000)
Total liabilities and equities	$(3,053,000)	$(1,221,000)

At year-end, there were no intra-entity receivables or payables.

Prepare a worksheet to consolidate the financial statements of these two companies.

LO 4-1, 4-5

eXcel

40. Adams Corporation acquired 90 percent of the outstanding voting shares of Barstow, Inc., on December 31, 2016. Adams paid a total of $603,000 in cash for these shares. The 10 percent non-controlling interest shares traded on a daily basis at fair value of $67,000 both before and after Adams's acquisition. On December 31, 2016, Barstow had the following account balances:

	Book Value	Fair Value
Current assets	$160,000	$160,000
Land	120,000	150,000
Buildings (10-year remaining life)	220,000	200,000
Equipment (5-year remaining life)	160,000	200,000
Patents (10-year remaining life)	–0–	50,000
Notes payable (due in 5 years)	(200,000)	(180,000)
Common stock	(180,000)	
Retained earnings, 12/31/16	(280,000)	

December 31, 2018, adjusted trial balances for the two companies follow:

	Adams Corporation	Barstow, Inc.
Debits		
Current assets	$ 610,000	$ 250,000
Land	380,000	150,000
Buildings	490,000	250,000
Equipment	873,000	150,000
Investment in Barstow, Inc	702,000	–0–
Cost of goods sold	480,000	90,000
Depreciation expense	100,000	55,000
Interest expense	40,000	15,000
Dividends declared	110,000	70,000
Total debits	$3,785,000	$1,030,000
Credits		
Notes payable	$ 860,000	$ 230,000
Common stock	510,000	180,000
Retained earnings, 1/1/18	1,367,000	340,000
Revenues	940,000	280,000
Investment income	108,000	–0–
Total credits	$3,785,000	$1,030,000

At year-end, there were no intra-entity receivables or payables.

a. Prepare schedules for acquisition-date fair-value allocations and amortizations for Adams's investment in Barstow.

b. Determine Adams's method of accounting for its investment in Barstow. Support your answer with a numerical explanation.

c. Without using a worksheet or consolidation entries, determine the balances to be reported as of December 31, 2018, for this business combination.

d. To verify the figures determined in requirement (*c*), prepare a consolidation worksheet for Adams Corporation and Barstow, Inc., as of December 31, 2018.

LO 4-1, 4-4, 4-8

41. Following are the individual financial statements for Gibson and Davis for the year ending December 31, 2018:

	Gibson	Davis
Sales	$ (600,000)	$ (300,000)
Cost of goods sold	300,000	140,000
Operating expenses	174,000	60,000
Dividend income	(24,000)	–0–
Net income	$ (150,000)	$ (100,000)
Retained earnings, 1/1/18	$ (700,000)	$ (400,000)
Net income	(150,000)	(100,000)
Dividends declared	80,000	40,000
Retained earnings, 12/31/18	$ (770,000)	$ (460,000)
Cash and receivables	$ 248,000	$ 100,000
Inventory	500,000	190,000
Investment in Davis	528,000	–0–
Buildings (net)	524,000	600,000
Equipment (net)	400,000	400,000
Total assets	$ 2,200,000	$ 1,290,000
Liabilities	(800,000)	(490,000)
Common stock	(630,000)	(340,000)
Retained earnings, 12/31/18	(770,000)	(460,000)
Total liabilities and stockholders' equity	$(2,200,000)	$(1,290,000)

Gibson acquired 60 percent of Davis on April 1, 2018, for $528,000. On that date, equipment owned by Davis (with a five-year remaining life) was overvalued by $30,000. Also on that date, the fair value of the 40 percent noncontrolling interest was $352,000. Davis earned income evenly during the year but declared the $40,000 dividend on November 1, 2018.

a. Prepare a consolidated income statement for the year ending December 31, 2018.

b. Determine the consolidated balance for each of the following accounts as of December 31, 2018:

Goodwill	Buildings (net)
Equipment (net)	Dividends Declared
Common Stock	

LO 4-2, 4-3, 4-6, 4-7, 4-8

42. On July 1, 2018, Truman Company acquired a 70 percent interest in Atlanta Company in exchange for consideration of $720,000 in cash and equity securities. The remaining 30 percent of Atlanta's shares traded closely near an average price that totaled $290,000 both before and after Truman's acquisition.

In reviewing its acquisition, Truman assigned a $100,000 fair value to a patent recently developed by Atlanta, even though it was not recorded within the financial records of the subsidiary. This patent is anticipated to have a remaining life of five years.

The following financial information is available for these two companies for 2018. In addition, the subsidiary's income was earned uniformly throughout the year. The subsidiary declared dividends quarterly.

	Truman	Atlanta
Revenues	$ (670,000)	$ (400,000)
Operating expenses	402,000	280,000
Income of subsidiary	(35,000)	–0–
Net income	$ (303,000)	$ (120,000)
Retained earnings, 1/1/18	$ (823,000)	$ (500,000)
Net income (above)	(303,000)	(120,000)
Dividends declared	145,000	80,000
Retained earnings, 12/31/18	$ (981,000)	$ (540,000)
Current assets	$ 481,000	$ 390,000
Investment in Atlanta	727,000	–0–
Land	388,000	200,000
Buildings	701,000	630,000
Total assets	$ 2,297,000	$ 1,220,000
Liabilities	$ (816,000)	$ (360,000)
Common stock	(95,000)	(300,000)
Additional paid-in capital	(405,000)	(20,000)
Retained earnings, 12/31/18	(981,000)	(540,000)
Total liabilities and stockholders' equity	$(2,297,000)	$(1,220,000)

Answer each of the following:

a. How did Truman allocate Atlanta's acquisition-date fair value to the various assets acquired and liabilities assumed in the combination?

b. How did Truman allocate the goodwill from the acquisition across the controlling and noncontrolling interests?

c. How did Truman derive the Investment in Atlanta account balance at the end of 2018?

d. Prepare a worksheet to consolidate the financial statements of these two companies as of December 31, 2018. At year-end, there were no intra-entity receivables or payables.

LO 4-9

43. On January 1, 2017, Allan Company bought a 15 percent interest in Sysinger Company. The acquisition price of $184,500 reflected an assessment that all of Sysinger's accounts were fairly valued within the company's accounting records. During 2017, Sysinger reported net income of $100,000 and declared cash dividends of $30,000. Allan possessed the ability to influence significantly Sysinger's operations and, therefore, accounted for this investment using the equity method.

On January 1, 2018, Allan acquired an additional 80 percent interest in Sysinger and provided the following fair-value assessments of Sysinger's ownership components:

Consideration transferred by Allan for 80% interest	$1,400,000
Fair value of Allan's 15% previous ownership	262,500
Noncontrolling interest's 5% fair value	87,500
Total acquisition-date fair value for Sysinger Company	$1,750,000

Also, as of January 1, 2018, Allan assessed a $400,000 value to an unrecorded customer contract recently negotiated by Sysinger. The customer contract is anticipated to have a remaining life of four years. Sysinger's other assets and liabilities were judged to have fair values equal to their book values. Allan elects to continue applying the equity method to this investment for internal reporting purposes.

At December 31, 2018, the following financial information is available for consolidation:

	Allan Company	Sysinger Company
Revenues	$ (931,000)	$ (380,000)
Operating expenses	615,000	230,000
Equity earnings of Sysinger	(47,500)	–0–
Gain on revaluation of Investment in Sysinger to fair value	(67,500)	–0–
Net income	$ 431,000	$ 150,000

(continued)

(continued)

	Allan Company	Sysinger Company
Retained earnings, January 1	$ (965,000)	$ (600,000)
Net income	(431,000)	(150,000)
Dividends declared	140,000	40,000
Retained earnings, December 31	$(1,256,000)	$ (710,000)
Current assets	$ 288,000	$ 540,000
Investment in Sysinger (equity method)	1,672,000	–0–
Property, plant, and equipment	826,000	590,000
Patented technology	850,000	370,000
Customer contract	–0–	–0–
Total assets	$ 3,636,000	$ 1,500,000
Liabilities	$(1,300,000)	$ (90,000)
Common stock	(900,000)	(500,000)
Additional paid-in capital	(180,000)	(200,000)
Retained earnings, December 31	(1,256,000)	(710,000)
Total liabilities and equities	$(3,636,000)	$(1,500,000)

a. How should Allan allocate Sysinger's total acquisition-date fair value (January 1, 2018) to the assets acquired and liabilities assumed for consolidation purposes?

b. Show how the following amounts on Allan's preconsolidation 2018 statements were derived:

- Equity in earnings of Sysinger.
- Gain on revaluation of Investment in Sysinger to fair value.
- Investment in Sysinger.

c. Prepare a worksheet to consolidate the financial statements of these two companies as of December 31, 2018.

At year-end, there were no intra-entity receivables or payables.

LO 4-9

eXcel

44. On January 1, 2017, Bretz, Inc., acquired 60 percent of the outstanding shares of Keane Company for $573,000 in cash. The price paid was proportionate to Keane's total fair value although at the date of acquisition, Keane had a total book value of $810,000. All assets acquired and liabilities assumed had fair values equal to book values except for a copyright (six-year remaining life) that was undervalued in Keane's accounting records by $120,000. During 2017, Keane reported net income of $150,000 and declared cash dividends of $80,000. On January 1, 2018, Bretz bought an additional 30 percent interest in Keane for $300,000.

The following financial information is for these two companies for 2018. Keane issued no additional capital stock during either 2017 or 2018. Also, at year-end, there were no intra-entity receivables or payables.

	Bretz, Inc.	Keane Company
Revenues	$ (402,000)	$ (300,000)
Operating expenses	200,000	120,000
Equity in Keane earnings	(144,000)	–0–
Net income	$ (346,000)	$ (180,000)
Retained earnings, 1/1	$ (797,000)	$ (500,000)
Net income (above)	(346,000)	(180,000)
Dividends declared	143,000	60,000
Retained earnings, 12/31	$(1,000,000)	$ (620,000)
Current assets	$ 224,000	$ 190,000
Investment in Keane Company	994,500	–0–
Trademarks	106,000	600,000
Copyrights	210,000	300,000
Equipment (net)	380,000	110,000
Total assets	$ 1,914,500	$ 1,200,000

(continued)

(continued)

	Bretz, Inc.	Keane Company
Liabilities	$ (453,000)	$ (200,000)
Common stock	(400,000)	(300,000)
Additional paid-in capital	(60,000)	(80,000)
Additional paid-in capital—step acquisition	(1,500)	–0–
Retained earnings, 12/31	(1,000,000)	(620,000)
Total liabilities and equities	$(1,914,500)	$(1,200,000)

a. Show the journal entry Bretz made to record its January 1, 2018, acquisition of an additional 30 percent of Keane Company shares.

b. Prepare a schedule showing how Bretz determined the Investment in Keane Company balance as of December 31, 2018.

c. Prepare a consolidated worksheet for Bretz, Inc., and Keane Company for December 31, 2018.

Develop Your Skills

ACCOUNTING THEORY RESEARCH CASE

CPA skills

The FASB ASC paragraph 810-10-45-16 states: "The noncontrolling interest shall be reported in the consolidated statement of financial position within equity, separately from the parent's equity. That amount shall be clearly identified and labeled, for example, as noncontrolling interest in subsidiaries."

However, prior to issuing this current reporting requirement, the FASB considered several alternative display formats for the noncontrolling interest. Access the precodification standard, *SFAS 160,* "Noncontrolling Interest in Consolidated Financial Statements," at www.fasb.org to answer the following:

1. What alternative financial statement display formats did the FASB consider for the noncontrolling interest?
2. What criteria did the FASB use to evaluate the desirability of each alternative?
3. In what specific ways did FASB *Concept Statement 6* affect the FASB's evaluation of these alternatives?

RESEARCH CASE: STARBUCKS' STEP ACQUISITIONS OF STARBUCKS COFFEE JAPAN

Since 1995, Starbucks Corporation had owned a 39.5 percent equity interest in Starbucks Coffee Japan, Ltd. ("Starbucks Japan"). Its joint venture partner, Sazaby League of Japan also owned a 39.5 percent equity interest in Starbucks Japan. The remaining 21 percent equity interest was held by public shareholders and option holders.

On October 31, 2014, Starbucks acquired all of Sazaby League's shares of Starbucks Coffee Japan, bringing Starbucks' total ownership to 79 percent. Starbucks paid Sazaby $508.7 million for the additional 39.5 percent ownership. Later in 2014, Starbucks acquired the remaining 21 percent of Starbucks Coffee Japan. Access Starbucks' 2015 10-K annual report and answer the following:

1. What amount did Starbucks estimate for the October 31, 2014, acquisition-date fair value of Starbucks Japan? (*Hint:* include the acquisition-date estimated fair value of the remaining 21 percent noncontrolling interest in Starbucks Japan total fair value.)
2. How did Starbucks allocate the acquisition-date fair value of Starbucks Japan among the assets acquired and liabilities assumed?
3. How does Starbucks explain the three different valuation bases for the following items?
   - Amount paid to Sazaby for 39.5 percent share purchase
   - The fair value of Starbucks' pre-existing 39.5 equity interest
   - The fair value of the 21 percent noncontrolling interest

4. How did Starbucks account for its 39.5 percent ownership interest in Starbucks Japan prior to the acquisition of its controlling interest?
5. Upon acquisition of its controlling interest on October 31, 2014, how did Starbucks account for the change in fair value of its original 39.5 percent ownership interest?
6. Upon acquisition of the 21 percent noncontrolling interest, how did Starbucks account for the difference between the amount paid and the underlying carrying amount of Starbucks Japan?

RESEARCH CASE: COSTCO'S NONCONTROLLING INTERESTS

Costco Wholesale Corporation owns and operates membership warehouses in the United States, Canada, United Kingdom, Mexico, Japan, Australia, and Spain. Costco also engages in retail operations through majority owned subsidiaries in Korea and Taiwan. The outside equity interests (not owned by Costco) in the Korean and Taiwanese subsidiaries are presented collectively as noncontrolling interests in Costco's consolidated financial statements.

Access Costco's 2015 10-K annual report and answer the following:

1. How does Costco present the noncontrolling interest in the following financial statements?
   - Consolidated Balance Sheet
   - Consolidated Income Statement
   - Consolidated Statement of Other Comprehensive Income
   - Consolidated Statement of Cash Flows
2. Explain how Costco's presentations of the noncontrolling interest reflect the acquisition method for consolidated financial reporting as a single economic entity.

BARDEEN ELECTRIC: FASB ASC AND IFRS RESEARCH CASE

On October 18, 2017, Armstrong Auto Corporation ("Armstrong") announced its plan to acquire 80 percent of the outstanding 500,000 shares of Bardeen Electric Corporation's ("Bardeen") common stock in a business combination following regulatory approval. Armstrong will account for the transaction in accordance with ASC 805, "Business Combinations."

On December 1, 2017, Armstrong purchased an 80 percent controlling interest in Bardeen's outstanding voting shares. On this date, Armstrong paid $40 million in cash and issued one million shares of Armstrong common stock to the selling shareholders of Bardeen. Armstrong's share price was $26 on the announcement date and $24 on the acquisition date.

Bardeen's remaining 100,000 shares of common stock had been purchased for $3,000,000 by a small number of original investors. These shares have never been actively traded. Using other valuation techniques (comparable firms, discounted cash flow analysis, etc.), Armstrong estimated the fair value of Bardeen's noncontrolling shares at $16,500,000.

The parties agreed that Armstrong would issue to the selling shareholders an additional one million shares contingent upon the achievement of certain performance goals during the first 24 months following the acquisition. The acquisition-date fair value of the contingent stock issue was estimated at $8 million.

Bardeen has a research and development (R&D) project underway to develop a superconductive electrical/magnetic application. Total costs incurred to date on the project equal $4,400,000. However, Armstrong estimates that the technology has a fair value of $11 million. Armstrong considers this R&D as in-process because it has not yet reached technological feasibility and additional R&D is needed to bring the project to completion. No assets have been recorded in Bardeen's financial records for the R&D costs to date.

Bardeen's other assets and liabilities (at fair values) include the following:

Cash	$ 425,000
Accounts receivable	788,000
Land	3,487,000
Building	16,300,000
Machinery	39,000,000
Patents	7,000,000
Accounts payable	(1,500,000)

Neither the receivables nor payables involve Armstrong.

Answer the following questions citing relevant support from the ASC and IFRS.

1. What is the total consideration transferred by Armstrong to acquire its 80 percent controlling interest in Bardeen?
2. What values should Armstrong assign to identifiable intangible assets as part of the acquisition accounting?
3. What is the acquisition-date value assigned to the 20 percent noncontrolling interest? What are the potential noncontrolling interest valuation alternatives available under IFRS?
4. Under U.S. GAAP, what amount should Armstrong recognize as goodwill from the Bardeen acquisition? What alternative goodwill valuations are allowed under IFRS?

chapter 5

Consolidated Financial Statements—Intra-Entity Asset Transactions

Learning Objectives

After studying this chapter, you should be able to:

LO 5-1 Understand why intra-entity asset transfers create accounting effects within the financial records of affiliated companies that must be eliminated or adjusted in preparing consolidated financial statements.

LO 5-2 Demonstrate the consolidation procedures to eliminate intra-entity sales and purchases balances.

LO 5-3 Explain why consolidated entities defer intra-entity gross profit in ending inventory and the consolidation procedures required to subsequently recognize profits.

LO 5-4 Understand that the consolidation process for inventory transfers is designed to defer the intra-entity gross profit remaining in ending inventory from the year of transfer into the year of disposal or consumption.

LO 5-5 Explain the difference between upstream and downstream intra-entity transfers and how each affects the computation of noncontrolling interest balances.

LO 5-6 Prepare the consolidation entry to defer any gain created by an intra-entity transfer of land from the accounting records of the year of transfer and subsequent years.

LO 5-7 Prepare the consolidation entries to remove the effects of upstream and downstream intra-entity fixed asset transfers across affiliated entities.

Chapter 1 analyzed the deferral and subsequent recognition of gross profits created by inventory transfers between two affiliated companies in connection with equity method accounting. The central theme of that discussion is that intra-entity[1] profits cannot be recognized until the goods are ultimately sold to an unrelated party or consumed in the production process. This same accounting logic applies to transactions between companies within a business combination. Such sales within a single economic entity create neither profits nor losses. In reference to this issue, FASB ASC 810-10-45-1 states,

> As consolidated financial statements are based on the assumption that they represent the financial position and operating results of a single economic entity, such statements shall not include gain or loss on transactions among the entities in the consolidated group. Accordingly, any intra-entity profit or loss on assets remaining within the consolidated group shall be eliminated; the concept usually applied for this purpose is gross profit or loss.

The elimination of the accounting effects created by intra-entity transfers is one of the most significant problems encountered in the consolidation process. Such transfers are especially common in companies organized as a vertically integrated chain of organizations. For example, after acquiring its bottling companies PepsiCo noted,

> we acquired PBG and PAS to create a more fully integrated supply chain and go-to-market business model, improving the effectiveness and efficiency of the distribution of our brands and enhancing our revenue growth.

[1] The FASB *Accounting Standards Codification* (ASC) uses the term *intra-entity* to describe transfers of assets across entities affiliated through common ownership or other control mechanisms. The term indicates that although such transfers occur across separate legal entities, they are nonetheless made within a consolidated entity. In addition to the term *intra-entity,* such transfers are routinely referred to as *intercompany.*

Entities such as Pepsico reduce their costs by developing affiliations in which one operation furnishes products to another. As *Mergers & Acquisitions* observed,

> Downstream acquisitions . . . are aimed at securing critical sources of materials and components, streamlining manufacturing and materials planning, gaining economies of scale, entering new markets, and enhancing overall competitiveness. Manufacturers that combine with suppliers are often able to assert total control over such critical areas as product quality and resource planning.[2]

Intra-entity asset transactions take several forms. In particular, inventory transfers are especially prevalent. However, the sale of land and depreciable assets also can occur between the parties within a combination. This chapter examines the consolidation procedures for each of these different types of intra-entity asset transfers.[3]

LO 5-1

Understand why intra-entity asset transfers create accounting effects within the financial records of affiliated companies that must be eliminated or adjusted in preparing consolidated financial statements.

Intra-Entity Inventory Transfers

As previous chapters discussed, companies that make up a business combination frequently retain their legal identities as separate operating centers and maintain their own record-keeping. Thus, inventory sales between these companies trigger the independent accounting systems of both parties. The seller duly records revenue, and the buyer simultaneously enters the purchase into its accounts. For internal reporting purposes, recording an inventory transfer as a sale/purchase provides vital data to help measure the operational efficiency of each enterprise.[4]

Despite the internal information benefits of accounting for the transaction in this manner, from a consolidated perspective neither a sale nor a purchase has occurred. *An intra-entity transfer is merely the internal movement of inventory, an event that creates no net change in the financial position of the business combination taken as a whole.* Thus, in producing consolidated financial statements, the recorded effects of these transfers are eliminated so that consolidated statements reflect only transactions (and thus profits) with outside parties. Worksheet entries serve this purpose; they adapt the financial information reported by the separate companies to the perspective of the consolidated enterprise. The entire impact of the intra-entity transfer must be identified and then removed. Deleting the effects of the actual transfer is described here first.

LO 5-2

Demonstrate the consolidation procedures to eliminate intra-entity sales and purchases balances.

The Sales and Purchases Accounts

To account for related companies as a single economic entity requires eliminating all intra-entity sales/purchases balances. For example, if Arlington Company makes an $80,000 inventory sale to Zirkin Company, an affiliated party within a business combination, both parties record the transfer in their internal records as a normal sale/purchase. The following consolidation worksheet entry is then necessary to remove the resulting balances from the externally reported figures. Cost of Goods Sold is reduced here under the assumption that the Purchases account usually is closed out prior to the consolidation process.

Consolidation Entry TI		
Sales	80,000	
Cost of Goods Sold (purchases component)		80,000
To eliminate effects of intra-entity transfer of inventory. (Labeled **"TI"** in reference to the transferred inventory.)		

[2] "Acquiring along the Value Chain," *Mergers & Acquisitions*, June-July 1996, p. 8.

[3] In practice, the terms *intra-entity transaction* and *intra-entity transfer* are used interchangeably. Some argue that the use of the term *transaction* should be reserved for activities with entities outside the condolidated group.

[4] For all intra-entity transfers, the two parties involved view the events from different perspectives. Thus, the transfer is both a sale and a purchase, often creating both a receivable and a payable. To indicate the dual nature of such transfers, these accounts are indicated within this text as sales/purchases, receivables/payables, and so on.

In the preparation of consolidated financial statements, the preceding elimination must be made for all intra-entity inventory transfers. The total recorded (intra-entity) sales figure is deleted regardless of whether the transfer was downstream (from parent to subsidiary) or upstream (from subsidiary to parent). Furthermore, any gross profit included in the transfer price does not affect this sales/purchases elimination. Because the entire amount of the transfer occurred between related parties, the total effect must be removed in preparing the consolidated statements.

Intra-Entity Gross Profit—Year of Transfer (Year 1)

Removal of the sale/purchase is often just the first in a series of consolidation entries necessitated by inventory transfers. Despite the previous elimination, gross profits in ending inventory created by such sales can still exist in the accounting records at year-end. These profits initially result when the merchandise is priced at more than historical cost. Actual transfer prices are established in several ways, including the normal sales price of the inventory, sales price less a specified discount, or at a predetermined markup above cost. For example, in past financial statements, Ford Motor Company explained that

> intercompany sales among geographic areas consist primarily of vehicles, parts, and components manufactured by the company and various subsidiaries and sold to different entities within the consolidated group; transfer prices for these transactions are established by agreement between the affected entities.

Regardless of the method used for this pricing decision, gross profits that remain in inventory at year-end as a result of intra-entity sales during the period must be removed in arriving at consolidated figures.

All Inventory Remains at Year-End

LO 5-3

Explain why consolidated entities defer intra-entity gross profit in ending inventory and the consolidation procedures required subsequently to recognize profits.

In the preceding illustration, assume that Arlington acquired or produced this inventory at a cost of $50,000 and then sold it to Zirkin, an affiliated party, at the indicated $80,000 price. From a consolidated perspective, the inventory still has a historical cost of only $50,000. However, Zirkin's records now reflect the inventory at the $80,000 transfer price. In addition, because of the markup, Arlington's records show a $30,000 gross profit from this intra-entity sale. However, because the transaction did not occur with an outside party, recognition of this profit is not appropriate for the combination as a whole.

Thus, although the consolidation entry **TI** shown earlier eliminated the sale/purchase figures, the $30,000 inflation created by the transfer price still exists in two areas of the individual statements:

- Ending inventory remains overstated by $30,000.
- Gross profit is artificially overstated by this same amount.

Correcting the ending inventory requires only reducing the asset. However, correcting gross profit requires a careful analysis of the effect of the intra-entity transfer on the Cost of Goods Sold account. The ending inventory total serves as a negative component within the Cost of Goods Sold computation; it represents the portion of acquired inventory that was not sold. Thus, the $30,000 overstatement of the inventory that is still held incorrectly decreases this expense (the inventory that was sold). *Despite Entry **TI**, the inflated ending inventory figure causes Cost of Goods Sold to be too low and, thus, profits to be too high by $30,000.* For consolidation purposes, we increase Cost of Goods Sold by this amount through a worksheet adjustment that properly removes the gross profit from consolidated net income.

Consequently, if all of the transferred inventory is retained by the business combination at the end of the year, the following worksheet entry also must be included to eliminate the effects of the seller's gross profit that remains within the buyer's ending inventory:

Consolidation Entry G—Year of Transfer (Year 1)		
All Inventory Remains		
Cost of Goods Sold (ending inventory component)	30,000	
Inventory (balance sheet account)		30,000
To remove gross profit in ending inventory created by intra-entity sale.		

Discussion Question

EARNINGS MANAGEMENT

Enron Corporation's 2001 third-quarter 10-Q report disclosed the following activities with LJM2, a nonconsolidated special purpose entity (SPE) that was formed by Enron:

> In June 2000, LJM2 purchased dark fiber optic cable from Enron for a purchase price of $100 million. LJM2 paid Enron $30 million in cash and the balance in an interest-bearing note for $70 million. Enron recognized $67 million in pretax earnings in 2000 related to the asset sale. Pursuant to a marketing agreement with LJM2, Enron was compensated for marketing the fiber to others and providing operation and maintenance services to LJM2 with respect to the fiber. LJM2 sold a portion of the fiber to industry participants for $40 million, which resulted in Enron recognizing agency fee revenue of $20.3 million.

As investigations later discovered, Enron controlled LJM2 in many ways.

The FASB ASC now requires the consolidation of SPEs (as variable interest entities) that are essentially controlled by their primary beneficiary.

By selling goods to SPEs that it controlled but did not consolidate, did Enron overstate its earnings? What effect does consolidation have on the financial reporting for transactions between a firm and its controlled entities?

This entry (labeled **G** for gross profit) reduces the consolidated Inventory account to its original $50,000 historical cost. Furthermore, increasing Cost of Goods Sold by $30,000 effectively removes the intra-entity amount from recognized gross profit. Thus, this worksheet entry resolves both reporting problems created by the transfer price markup.

Only a Portion of Inventory Remains

Obviously, a company does not buy inventory to hold it for an indefinite time. It either uses the acquired items within the company's operations or resells them to unrelated, outside parties. Intra-entity profits ultimately are recognized by subsequently consuming or reselling these goods. Therefore, only the transferred inventory still held at year-end continues to be recorded in the separate statements at a value more than the historical cost. For this reason, *the ending inventory intra-entity gross profit elimination (Entry **G**) is based not on total intra-entity sales but only on the amount of transferred merchandise retained within the business at the end of the year.*

To illustrate, assume that Arlington transferred inventory costing $50,000 to Zirkin, a related company, for $80,000, thus recording a gross profit of $30,000. Assume further that by year-end Zirkin has resold $60,000 of these goods to unrelated parties but retains the other $20,000 (for resale in the following year). From the viewpoint of the consolidated company, it has now completed the revenue recognition process on the $60,000 portion of the intra-entity sale and need not make an adjustment for consolidation purposes.

Nonetheless, any gross profit recorded in connection with the $20,000 in merchandise that remains is still a component within Zirkin's Inventory account. Because the gross profit rate was 37½ percent ($30,000 gross profit/$80,000 transfer price), this retained inventory is stated at a value $7,500 more than its original cost ($20,000 × 37½%). The required reduction (Entry **G**) is not the entire $30,000 shown previously but only the $7,500 intra-entity gross profit that remains in ending inventory.

Consolidation Entry G—Year of Transfer (Year 1) **25% of Inventory Remains (replaces previous entry)**		
Cost of Goods Sold (ending inventory component)	7,500	
Inventory		7,500
To defer the intra-entity gross profit in ending inventory in year of transfer.		

LO 5-4

Understand that the consolidation process for inventory transfers is designed to defer the intra-entity gross profit in ending inventory from the year of transfer into the year of disposal or consumption.

Intra-Entity Gross Profit—Year Following Transfer (Year 2)

Whenever intra-entity profit is present in ending inventory, one further consolidation entry is eventually required. Although Entry **G** removes the gross profit from the *consolidated* inventory balances in the year of transfer, the $7,500 overstatement remains within the separate financial records of the buyer and seller. The effects of this deferred gross profit are carried into their beginning balances in the subsequent year. Hence, a worksheet adjustment is necessary in the period following the transfer. For consolidation purposes, the ending inventory portion of intra-entity gross profit must be adjusted in two successive years (from ending inventory in the year of transfer and from beginning inventory of the next period).

Referring again to Arlington's sale of inventory to Zirkin, the $7,500 intra-entity gross profit is still in Zirkin's Inventory account at the start of the subsequent year. Once again, the overstatement is removed within the consolidation process but this time from the beginning inventory balance (which appears in the financial statements only as a positive component of cost of goods sold). This elimination is termed *Entry *G.* The asterisk indicates that a previous year transfer created the intra-entity gross profits.

Consolidation Entry *G—Year Following Transfer (Year 2)		
Retained Earnings (beginning balance of seller).	7,500	
Cost of Goods Sold (beginning inventory component)		7,500
To remove from retained earnings the gross profit in beginning inventory and to currently recognize the profit through a reduction in cost of goods sold.		

Reducing Cost of Goods Sold (beginning inventory) through this worksheet entry increases the gross profit reported for this second year. For consolidation purposes, the gross profit on the transfer is recognized in the period in which the items are actually sold to outside parties. As shown in the following diagram, Entry **G** initially deferred the $7,500 intra-entity gross profit in the year of transfer. Entry ***G** now increases consolidated net income (by decreasing cost of goods sold) to reflect the sales activity with outside parties in the current year.

In Entry ***G,** removal of the $7,500 from beginning inventory (within Cost of Goods Sold) appropriately increases current net income and should not pose a significant conceptual problem. However, the rationale for decreasing the seller's beginning Retained Earnings deserves further explanation. This reduction removes the intra-entity gross profit in ending inventory

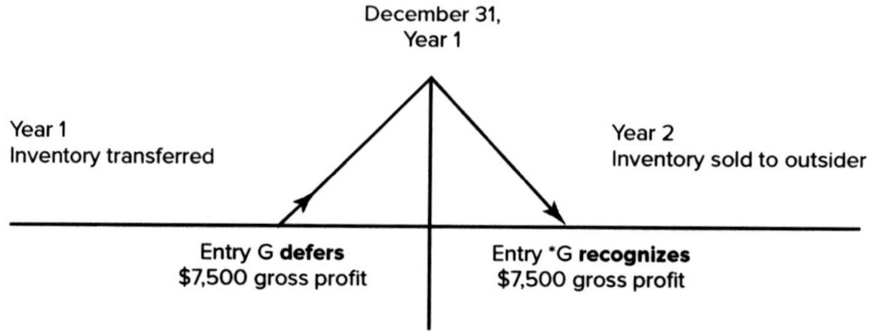

(recognized by the seller in the year of transfer) so that the profit is reported in the period when a sale to an outside party takes place. Despite the consolidation entries in Year 1, the $7,500 gross profit remained on this company's separate books and was closed to Retained Earnings at the end of the period. Recall that consolidation entries are never posted to the individual affiliate's books. Therefore, from a consolidated view, the buyer's Cost of Goods Sold (through the beginning inventory component) and the seller's Retained Earnings accounts as of the beginning of Year 2 contain the intra-entity profit, and must both be reduced in Entry ***G.**[5]

Intra-Entity Beginning Inventory Profit Adjustment—Downstream Sales When Parent Uses Equity Method

The worksheet eliminations for intra-entity sales/purchases (Entry TI) and intra-entity gross profit in ending inventory (Entry G) are both standard, regardless of the circumstances of the consolidation. In contrast, for one specific situation, the consolidation entry to recognize intra-entity beginning inventory gross profit differs from the Entry *G just presented. If (1) the original transfer is downstream (intra-entity sales made by the parent), and (2) the parent applies the equity method for internal accounting purposes, then the **Investment in Subsidiary** account replaces the parent's beginning Retained Earnings in Consolidation Entry *G as follows:

Consolidation Entry *G—Year Following Transfer (Year 2) (replaces previous Entry *G for downstream transfers when the equity method is used)		
Investment in Subsidiary	7,500	
Cost of Goods Sold (beginning inventory component)		7,500
To recognize previously deferred intra-entity downstream inventory gross profit as part of current year net income when the parent uses the equity method.		

Why debit the Investment in Subsidiary (and not the parent's beginning Retained Earnings) account in this situation? When the parent uses the equity method in its internal records, it recognizes beginning inventory gross profits on its books (and defers intra-entity ending inventory gross profits) as part of its equity income accruals. Therefore, both the parent's net income and retained earnings appropriately reflect consolidated balances.

Consolidation Entry I, however, removes the current year equity income accruals from the Investment in Subsidiary account as part of the investment account elimination sequence. With the equity income removed, the beginning inventory intra-entity profit reappears as a credit to the Investment in Subsidiary account's beginning of the year balance. Following our example, Consolidation Entry *G is thus needed to transfer the original $7,500 Year 1 Investment in Subsidiary account credit to a Year 2 earnings credit (through Cost of Goods Sold). Consolidation Entry *G also ensures that the Investment in Subsidiary account is brought to a zero balance on the worksheet.[6]

[5] For upstream intra-entity profit in beginning inventory, the subsidiary's retained earnings remain overstated and must be adjusted through Consolidation Entry ***G.**

[6] An acceptable alternative to recognizing intra-entity inventory profits in the subsidiary's beginning inventory (downstream sale) when the parent uses the equity method (***G**) is as follows:

Equity in Subsidiary Earnings	7,500	
Cost of Goods Sold		7,500

In this case, Consolidation Entry **I** removes the *remaining* amount of the Equity in Subsidiary Earnings against the Investment in Subsidiary account**.** In either alternative adjustment for recognizing intra-entity inventory gross profits in beginning inventory, the final consolidated balances are exactly the same: Equity in Subsidiary Earnings =0, Investment in Subsidiary =0, and Cost of Goods Sold is reduced by $7,500.

EXHIBIT 5.1
Relationship between Gross Profit Rate and Markup on Cost

In determining appropriate amounts of intra-entity profits for deferral and subsequent recognition in consolidated financial reports, two alternative—but mathematically related—profit percentages are often seen. Recalling that Gross Profit = Sales − Cost of Goods Sold, then

$$\textbf{Gross profit rate } (GPR) = \frac{\text{Gross profit}}{\text{Sales}} = \frac{MC}{1 + MC}$$

$$\textbf{Markup on cost } (MC) = \frac{\text{Gross profit}}{\text{Cost of goods sold}} = \frac{GPR}{1 - GPR}$$

Example:	Sales (transfer price)	$1,000
	Cost of goods sold	800
	Gross profit	$ 200

Here the $GPR = (200/1{,}000) = 20\%$ and the $MC = (200/800) = 25\%$. In most intra-entity purchases and sales, the sales (transfer) price is known and therefore the *GPR* is the simplest percentage to use to determine the amount of intra-entity profit.

$$\text{Intra-entity profit} = \text{Transfer price} \times GPR$$

Instead, if the markup on cost is available, it readily converts to a *GPR* by the preceding formula. In this case (0.25/1.25) =20%.

To summarize, for **intra-entity beginning inventory profits resulting from downstream transfers when the parent applies the equity method:**

- The parent's beginning retained earnings reflect the consolidated balance from application of the equity method and need no adjustment.
- The parent's Investment in Subsidiary account as of the beginning of Year 2 contains a credit from the deferral of Year 1 intra-entity downstream profits.
- Worksheet Entry *G debits the Investment account and credits Cost of Goods Sold, effectively recognizing the profit in the year of sale to outsiders.

Finally, various markup percentages determine the dollar values for intra-entity profit deferrals. Exhibit 5.1 shows formulas for both the gross profit rate and markup on cost and the relationship between the two.

LO 5-5

Explain the difference between upstream and downstream intra-entity transfers and how each affects the computation of noncontrolling interest balances.

Intra-Entity Gross Profit—Effect on Noncontrolling Interest

The worksheet entries just described appropriately account for the effects of intra-entity inventory transfers on business combinations. However, one question remains: What impact do these procedures have on the measurement of a noncontrolling interest? In regard to this issue, paragraph 810-10-45-18 of the FASB ASC states,

> The amount of intra-entity profit or loss to be eliminated in accordance with paragraph 810-10-45-1 is not affected by the existence of a noncontrolling interest. The complete elimination of the intra-entity income or loss is consistent with the underlying assumption that consolidated financial statements represent the financial position and operating results of a single economic entity. The elimination of the intra-entity income or loss may be allocated between the parent and noncontrolling interests.

The last sentence indicates that alternative approaches are available in computing the noncontrolling interest's share of a subsidiary's net income. According to this pronouncement, gross profits in inventory resulting from intra-entity transfers *may or may not* affect recognition of outside ownership. Because the amount attributed to a noncontrolling interest reduces consolidated net income, the handling of this issue can affect the reported profitability of a business combination.

To illustrate, assume that Large Company owns 70 percent of the voting stock of Small Company. To avoid extraneous complications, assume that no amortization expense resulted from this acquisition. Assume further that Large reports current net income (from separate operations) of $500,000 while Small earns $100,000. During the current period, intra-entity transfers of $200,000 occur with a total markup of $90,000. At the end of the year, a $40,000 intra-entity gross profit remains within the inventory accounts.

Clearly, the consolidated net income prior to the reduction for the 30 percent noncontrolling interest is $560,000, the two net income balances less the intra-entity gross profit in ending inventory. The problem facing the accountant is the computation of the noncontrolling interest's share of Small's net income. Because of the flexibility allowed by the FASB ASC, this figure may be reported as either $30,000 (30 percent of the $100,000 earnings of the subsidiary) or $18,000 (30 percent of reported net income after that figure is reduced by the $40,000 intra-entity gross profit in ending inventory).

To appropriately measure this noncontrolling interest allocation, the direction of the intra-entity transfer must be considered. If a transfer is downstream (the parent sells inventory to the subsidiary), a logical view would seem to be that the intra-entity gross profit in inventory is that of the parent company. The parent made the original sale; therefore, the gross profit is included in its financial records. Because the subsidiary's net income is unaffected, little justification exists for adjusting the noncontrolling interest to reflect the deferral of the intra-entity gross profit. Consequently, in the example of Large and Small, if the transfers were downstream, the 30 percent noncontrolling interest would be $30,000 based on Small's reported net income of $100,000.

In contrast, when the subsidiary sells inventory to the parent (an upstream transfer), the subsidiary recognizes the entire gross profit in its financial records even though part of the gross profit is deferred from a consolidation perspective. A reasonable conclusion is that because the subsidiary created the gross profit, owners of the noncontrolling interest are entitled to a portion of that profit.

In this textbook, the noncontrolling interest's share of consolidated net income is computed based on the reported net income of the subsidiary after adjusting for intra-entity gross profit in inventories from *upstream* sales. Returning to Large Company and Small Company, if the $40,000 intra-entity gross profit results from an upstream sale from subsidiary to parent, only $60,000 of Small's $100,000 net income should be recognized currently for consolidation purposes. The allocation to the noncontrolling interest is, therefore, reported as $18,000, or 30% of the $60,000 subsidiary net income after adjusting for the intra-entity profit remaining in ending inventory.

Although the noncontrolling interest figure is based here on the subsidiary's reported net income adjusted for the effects of upstream intra-entity transfers, GAAP, as quoted earlier, does not require this treatment. Giving effect to upstream transfers in this calculation but not to downstream transfers is no more than an attempt to select the most logical approach from among acceptable alternatives.[7]

Intra-Entity Inventory Transfers Summarized

To assist in overcoming the complications created by intra-entity transfers, we demonstrate the consolidation process in three different ways:

1. Before proceeding to a numerical example, review the impact of intra-entity transfers on consolidated figures. Ultimately, the accountant must understand how the balances reported by a business combination are derived when intra-entity gross profit in inventory result from either upstream or downstream sales.
2. Next, two different consolidation worksheets are produced: one for downstream transfers and the other for upstream. The various consolidation procedures used in these worksheets are explained and analyzed.
3. Finally, several of the consolidation worksheet entries are shown side by side to illustrate the differences created by the direction of the transfers.

[7] The 100 percent allocation of downstream profits to the parent affects its application of the equity method. As seen later in this chapter, in applying the equity method, the parent removes 100 percent of intra-entity profits resulting from downstream sales from its investment and equity earnings accounts rather than its percentage ownership in the subsidiary.

The Development of Consolidated Totals

A summary of the effects of intra-entity inventory transfers on consolidated totals follows:

Revenues. Parent and subsidiary balances are combined, but all intra-entity transfers are then removed.

Cost of Goods Sold. Parent and subsidiary balances are combined, but all intra-entity transfers are removed. The resulting total is decreased by any intra-entity gross profit in beginning inventory (thus raising net income) and increased by any intra-entity gross profit in ending inventory (reducing net income).

Net Income Attributable to the Noncontrolling Interest. The subsidiary's reported net income is adjusted for any excess acquisition-date fair-value amortizations and the effects of intra-entity gross profits in inventory from upstream transfers (but not downstream transfers) and then multiplied by the percentage of outside ownership.

Retained Earnings at the Beginning of the Year. As discussed in previous chapters, if the equity method is applied, the parent's balance mirrors the consolidated total. When any other method is used, the parent's beginning Retained Earnings must be converted to the equity method by Entry ***C.** Accruals for this purpose must recognize (1) the effects on reported subsidiary net income of intra-entity gross profits in beginning inventory that arose from upstream sales in the prior year, and (2) prior years' excess acquisition-date fair-value amortizations.

Inventory. Parent and subsidiary balances are combined. Any intra-entity gross profit remaining at the end of the current year is removed to adjust the reported balance to historical cost.

Noncontrolling Interest in Subsidiary at End of Year. The final total begins with the noncontrolling interest at the beginning of the year. This figure is based on the subsidiary's book value on that date plus its share of any unamortized acquisition-date excess fair value less its share of gross profits in beginning inventory that arose from upstream sales in the prior year. The beginning balance is updated by adding the portion of the subsidiary's net income assigned to these outside owners (as described above) and subtracting the noncontrolling interest's share of subsidiary dividends.

Intra-Entity Inventory Transfers Illustrated: Parent Uses Equity Method

To examine the various consolidation procedures required by intra-entity inventory transfers, assume that Top Company acquires 80 percent of the voting stock of Bottom Company on January 1, 2017. The parent pays $400,000 and the acquisition-date fair value of the noncontrolling interest is $100,000. Top allocates the entire $50,000 excess fair value over book value to adjust a database owned by Bottom to fair value. The database has an estimated remaining life of 20 years. Top Company applies the equity method to its investment in Bottom.[8]

The subsidiary reports net income of $30,000 in 2017 and $70,000 in 2018, the current year. The subsidiary declares dividends of $20,000 in the first year and $50,000 in the second. After the takeover, intra-entity inventory transfers between the two companies occurred as shown in Exhibit 5.2. A $10,000 intra-entity receivable and payable also exists as of December 31, 2018.

EXHIBIT 5.2
Intra-Entity Transfers

	2017	2018
Transfer prices	$80,000	$100,000
Historical cost	60,000	70,000
Gross profit	$20,000	$ 30,000
Inventory remaining at year-end (at transfer price)	$16,000	$ 20,000
Gross profit percentage	25%	30%
Gross profit remaining in year-end inventory	$ 4,000	$ 6,000

[8] Later in this chapter, we extend the example to when the parent applies the initial value method.

EXHIBIT 5.3
Investment Balances—Equity Method—Downstream Sales

Investment in Bottom Company Analysis 1/1/17 to 12/31/18		
Consideration paid (fair value) 1/1/17		$ 400,000
Bottom Company reported net income for 2017	$30,000	
Database amortization	(2,500)	
Bottom Company adjusted 2017 net income	$27,500	
Top's ownership percentage	80%	
Top's share of Bottom Company's net income	$22,000	
Deferred profit from Top's 2017 downstream sales	(4,000)	
Equity in earnings of Bottom Company, 2017		$ 18,000
Top's share of Bottom Company dividends, 2017 (80%)		(16,000)
Balance 12/31/17		$ 402,000
Bottom Company reported net income for 2018	$70,000	
Database amortization	(2,500)	
Bottom Company adjusted 2018 net income	$67,500	
Top's ownership percentage	80%	
Top's share of Bottom Company's net income	$54,000	
Recognized profit from Top's 2017 downstream sales	4,000	
Deferred profit from Top's 2018 downstream sales	(6,000)	
Equity in earnings of Bottom Company, 2018		$ 52,000
Top's share of Bottom Company dividends, 2018 (80%)		(40,000)
Balance 12/31/18		$ 414,000

The 2018 consolidation of Top and Bottom is presented twice. First, we assume the intra-entity transfers are downstream from parent to subsidiary. Second, consolidated figures are recomputed with the transfers being viewed as upstream. This distinction between upstream and downstream transfer becomes significant when the parent uses the equity method and in the presence of a noncontrolling interest.

Downstream Inventory Transfers: Parent Uses the Equity Method

To understand the consolidation procedures for intra-entity inventory transfers, it's useful first to analyze the parent's internal accounting for the investment. Under the equity method, the parent's investment-related accounts are subjected to (1) income accrual, (2) excess fair over book value amortization, (3) adjustments required by intra-entity gross profit in inventory, and (4) dividends. Exhibit 5.3 shows the changes to the Investment in Bottom Company from the acquisition date until the end of the current year (2018).

Note in particular the computations of Top's equity in earnings of Bottom Company in Exhibit 5.3. First, the calculations for equity method income are identical to those presented in Chapter 4, with the addition of an adjustment for intra-entity profits. Also observe that the $4,000 intra-entity profit deferred in 2017 is subsequently recognized in 2018. Thus, the $4,000 intra-entity profit is not eliminated but simply reallocated across time to the period when it is recognized by the consolidated entity. Next observe that, because the inventory transfers are downstream from parent to subsidiary, 100 percent of the profit deferral and subsequent recognition is allocated to the parent's equity earnings and investment account. As a result, the intra-entity profit reallocation across time affects neither Bottom's net income nor the noncontrolling interest.

Exhibit 5.4 presents the worksheet to consolidate these two companies for the year ending December 31, 2018. Most of the worksheet entries found in Exhibit 5.4 are described and analyzed in previous chapters of this textbook. Thus, we examine only three of these entries in detail along with the computation of the net income attributable to the noncontrolling interest.

First, Consolidation Entry *G adjusts for the intra-entity gross profit carried over in the beginning inventory from the 2017 intra-entity downstream transfers.

EXHIBIT 5.4 Downstream Inventory Transfers

TOP COMPANY AND BOTTOM COMPANY
Consolidation Worksheet
Investment: Equity Method **For Year Ending December 31, 2018** ***Ownership: 80%***

Accounts	Top Company	Bottom Company	Consolidation Entries Debit	Consolidation Entries Credit	Noncontrolling Interest	Consolidated Totals
Income Statement						
Sales	(600,000)	(300,000)	(TI) 100,000			(800,000)
Cost of goods sold	320,000	180,000	(G) 6,000	(*G) 4,000		402,000
				(TI) 100,000		
Operating expenses	170,000	50,000	(E) 2,500			222,500
Equity in earnings of Bottom	(52,000)		(I) 52,000[‡]			–0–
Separate company net income	(162,000)	(70,000)				
Consolidated net income						(175,500)
Net income attributable to noncontrolling interest					(13,500)[†]	13,500
Net income to Top Company						(162,000)
Statement of Retained Earnings						
Retained earnings, 1/1/18						
Top Company	(652,000)					(652,000)
Bottom Company		(310,000)	(S) 310,000			
Net income (above)	(162,000)	(70,000)				(162,000)
Dividends declared	70,000	50,000		(D) 40,000	10,000	70,000
Retained earnings, 12/31/18	(744,000)	(330,000)				(744,000)
Balance Sheet						
Cash and receivables	280,000	120,000		(P) 10,000		390,000
Inventory	220,000	160,000		(G) 6,000		374,000
Investment in Bottom	414,000		(D) 40,000	(I) 52,000		
			(*G) 4,000	(S) 368,000		–0–
				(A) 38,000		
Land	410,000	200,000				610,000
Plant assets (net)	190,000	170,000				360,000
Database			(A) 47,500	(E) 2,500		45,000
Total assets	1,514,000	650,000				1,779,000
Liabilities	(340,000)	(170,000)	(P) 10,000			(500,000)
Noncontrolling interest in Bottom Company, 1/1/18				(S) 92,000		
				(A) 9,500	(101,500)	
Noncontrolling interest in Bottom Company, 12/31/18					(105,000)	(105,000)
Common stock	(430,000)	(150,000)	(S) 150,000			(430,000)
Retained earnings, 12/31/18 (above)	(744,000)	(330,000)				(744,000)
Total liabilities and equities	(1,514,000)	(650,000)	722,000	722,000		(1,779,000)

Note: Parentheses indicate a credit balance.

†Because intra-entity sales are made downstream (by the parent), the subsidiary's adjusted net income is the $70,000 reported less $2,500 excess amortization figure with a 20% allocation to the noncontrolling interest ($13,500).

‡Boxed items highlight differences with upstream transfers examined in Exhibit 5.6.

Consolidation entries:

(*G) Recognition of intra-entity beginning inventory gross profit in current period consolidated net income. Downstream sales are attributed to parent.
(S) Elimination of subsidiary's stockholders' equity accounts along with recognition of the noncontrolling interest as of January 1.
(A) Allocation of excess fair value over subsidiary's book value, unamortized balance as of January 1.
(I) Elimination of intra-entity income remaining after *G elimination.
(D) Elimination of intra-entity dividend.
(E) Recognition of amortization expense for current year on excess fair value allocated to database.
(P) Elimination of intra-entity receivable/payable balances.
(TI) Elimination of intra-entity sales/purchases balances.
(G) Deferral of intra-entity ending inventory gross profit from current period consolidated net income and removal of intra-entity gross profit from ending inventory.

Consolidation Entry *G		
Investment in Bottom	4,000	
Cost of Goods Sold		4,000
To remove 2017 intra-entity gross profit in inventory from seller's beginning balance and recognize the gross profit in 2018 following sales to outsiders. Top uses the equity method and intra-entity sales were downstream.		

The gross profit rate (Exhibit 5.2) on these items was 25 percent ($20,000 gross profit/$80,000 transfer price), indicating an intra-entity profit of $4,000 (25 percent of the remaining $16,000 in inventory). To recognize this gross profit in 2018, Entry ***G** reduces Cost of Goods Sold (or the beginning inventory component of that expense) by that amount. The reduction in Cost of Goods Sold creates an increase in current year net income. From a consolidation perspective, the gross profit is correctly recognized in 2018 when the inventory is sold to an outside party. The debit to the Investment in Bottom account becomes part of the sequence of adjustments to bring that account to a zero balance in consolidation.

Consolidation Entry TI		
Sales.	100,000	
Cost of Goods Sold.		100,000
To eliminate current year intra-entity sales/purchases.		

Entry TI eliminates the intra-entity sales/purchases for 2018. The entire $100,000 transfer recorded by the two parties during the current period is removed to arrive at consolidated figures for the business combination.

Consolidation Entry G		
Cost of Goods Sold.	6,000	
Inventory.		6,000
To defer intra-entity gross profit in ending inventory.		

Entry **G** defers the intra-entity gross profit remaining in ending inventory at the end of 2018. The $20,000 in transferred merchandise (Exhibit 5.2) that Bottom has not yet sold has a gross profit rate of 30 percent ($30,000 gross profit/$100,000 transfer price); thus, the intra-entity gross profit amounts to $6,000. On the worksheet, Entry **G** eliminates this overstatement in the Inventory asset balance as well as the ending inventory (credit) component of Cost of Goods Sold. Because the gross profit must be deferred, the increase in this expense appropriately decreases consolidated net income.

Net Income Attributable to the Noncontrolling Interest

In this first illustration, the intra-entity transfers are downstream. Thus, the deferred intra-entity gross profits are considered to relate solely to the parent company, creating no effect on the subsidiary or the outside ownership. For this reason, the noncontrolling interest's share of consolidated net income is unaffected by the downstream intra-entity profit deferral and subsequent recognition. Therefore, Top allocates $13,500 of Bottom's net income to the noncontrolling interest computed as 20 percent of $67,500 ($70,000 reported net income less $2,500 current year database excess fair-value amortization).

By including these entries along with the other routine worksheet eliminations and adjustments, the accounting information generated by Top and Bottom is brought together into a single set of consolidated financial statements. However, this process does more than simply delete intra-entity transfers; it also affects reported net income. A $4,000 gross profit is removed on the worksheet from 2017 figures and subsequently recognized in 2018 (Entry ***G**). A $6,000 gross profit is deferred in a similar fashion from 2018 (Entry **G**) and subsequently recognized in 2019. However, these changes do not affect the noncontrolling interest because the transfers were downstream.

Special Equity Method Procedures for Deferred Intra-Entity Profits from Downstream Transfers

Exhibit 5.3 presents the parent's equity method investment accounting procedures in the presence of deferred intra-entity gross profits resulting from downstream inventory transfers. This application of the equity method differs from that presented in Chapter 1 for a significant influence (typically 20 to 50 percent ownership) investment. For significant influence investments, an investor company defers intra-entity gross profits in inventory only to the extent of its percentage ownership, regardless of whether the profits resulted from upstream or downstream transfers. In contrast, Exhibit 5.3 shows a 100 percent deferral in 2017, with a subsequent 100 percent recognition in 2018, for intra-entity gross profits resulting from Top's inventory transfers to Bottom, its 80 percent–owned subsidiary.

Why the distinction? When control (rather than just significant influence) exists, 100 percent of all intra-entity gross profits are removed from consolidated net income regardless of the direction of the underlying sale.[9] The 100 percent intra-entity profit deferral on Top's books for downstream sales ensures that none of the deferral will be allocated to the noncontrolling interest. As discussed previously, when the parent is the seller in an intra-entity transfer, little justification exists to allocate a portion of the gross profit deferral to the noncontrolling interest. In contrast, for an upstream sale, the subsidiary recognizes the gross profit on its books. Because the noncontrolling interest owns a portion of the subsidiary (but not of the parent), partial allocation of intra-entity gross profit deferrals and subsequent recognitions to the noncontrolling interest is appropriate when resulting from upstream sales.

Upstream Inventory Transfers: Parent Uses the Equity Method

A different set of consolidation procedures is necessary if the intra-entity transfers are upstream from Bottom to Top. As previously discussed, upstream gross profits are attributed to the subsidiary rather than to the parent company. Therefore, had these transfers been upstream, both the $4,000 beginning inventory gross profit recognition (Entry ***G**) and the $6,000 intra-entity gross profit deferral (Entry **G**) would be considered adjustments to Bottom's reported totals.

In contrast to the downstream example in Exhibit 5.3, Exhibit 5.5 includes the intra-entity profit deferrals and subsequent recognitions in the adjustments to Bottom's net income. Because the inventory transfers are upstream from subsidiary to parent, only 80 percent of the profit deferral and subsequent recognition is allocated to the parent's equity earnings and investment account. As a result, the intra-entity profit reallocation across time affects both the subsidiary's reported net income and the noncontrolling interest. Similar to the previous example, the $4,000 intra-entity profit is not eliminated, but simply reallocated across time to the period when it is recognized by the consolidated entity.

To illustrate the effects of upstream inventory transfers, in Exhibit 5.6, we consolidate the financial statements of Top and Bottom again. *The individual records of the two companies are changed from Exhibit 5.4 to reflect the parent's application of the equity method for upstream sales.* This change creates several important differences between Exhibits 5.4 and 5.6.

[9] When only significant influence is present, purchasing-related decisions are typically made in conjunction with the interests of other outside owners of the investee. Profits are partially deferred because sales are considered to be partially made to the other outside owners. When control is present, decision making usually rests exclusively with the majority owner, providing little basis for objective profit measurement in the presence of intra-entity sales.

EXHIBIT 5.5
Investment Balances—Equity Method—Upstream Sales

Investment in Bottom Company Analysis 1/1/17 to 12/31/18		
Consideration paid (fair value) 1/1/17		$400,000
Bottom Company reported net income for 2017	$30,000	
Database amortization	(2,500)	
Deferred profit from Bottom's 2017 upstream sales	(4,000)	
Bottom Company adjusted 2017 net income	$23,500	
Top's ownership percentage	80%	
Equity in earnings of Bottom Company, 2017		$ 18,800
Top's share of Bottom Company dividends, 2017 (80%)		(16,000)
Balance 12/31/17		$402,800
Bottom Company reported net income for 2018	$70,000	
Database amortization	(2,500)	
Recognized profit from Bottom's 2017 upstream sales	4,000	
Deferred profit from Bottom's 2018 upstream sales	(6,000)	
Bottom Company's adjusted 2018 net income	$65,500	
Top's ownership percentage	80%	
Equity in earnings of Bottom Company, 2018		$ 52,400
Top's share of Bottom Company dividends, 2018 (80%)		(40,000)
Balance 12/31/18		$415,200

Because the intra-entity sales are upstream, the $4,000 beginning intra-entity gross profit (Entry *G) deferral no longer involves a debit to the parent's Investment in Bottom account. Recall that Top and Bottom, as separate legal entities, maintain independent accounting information systems. Thus, when it transferred inventory to Top in 2017, Bottom recorded the transfer as a regular sale even though the counterparty (Top) is a member of the consolidated group. Because $16,000 of these transfers remain in Top's inventory, $4,000 of gross profit (25 percent) is deferred from a consolidated perspective as of January 1, 2018. Also from a consolidated standpoint, Bottom's January 1, 2018, Retained Earnings are overstated by the $4,000 gross profit from the 2017 intra-entity transfers. Thus, Exhibit 5.6 shows a worksheet adjustment that reduces Bottom's January 1, 2018, Retained Earnings balance. Similar to Exhibit 5.4, the credit to Cost of Goods Sold increases consolidated net income to recognize the profit in 2018 from sales to outsiders as follows:

Consolidation Entry *G

Retained earnings—Bottom	4,000	
Cost of Goods Sold		4,000

To remove 2017 intra-entity gross profit in inventory from seller's beginning balance and recognize the gross profit in 2018 following sales to outsiders. Top uses the equity method and intra-entity sales were upstream.

Following this adjustment, Bottom's beginning Retained Earnings on the worksheet becomes $306,000. Reassigning the $4,000 gross profit from 2017 into 2018 dictates the adjustment of the subsidiary's beginning Retained Earnings balance (as the seller of the goods) to $306,000 from the $310,000 found in the company's separate records on the worksheet.

Consolidation Entry **S** eliminates a portion of the parent's investment account and provides the initial noncontrolling interest balance. This worksheet entry also removes the stockholders equity accounts of the subsidiary as of the beginning of the current year. Thus, the

EXHIBIT 5.6 Upstream Inventory Transfers

TOP COMPANY AND BOTTOM COMPANY
Consolidation Worksheet
For Year Ending December 31, 2018

Investment: Equity Method ***Ownership: 80%***

Accounts	Top Company	Bottom Company	Consolidation Entries Debit	Consolidation Entries Credit	Noncontrolling Interest	Consolidated Totals
Income Statement						
Sales	(600,000)	(300,000)	(TI)100,000			(800,000)
Cost of goods sold	320,000	180,000	(G) 6,000	(*G) 4,000 (TI)100,000		402,000
Operating expenses	170,000	50,000	(E) 2,500			222,500
Equity in earnings of Bottom	(52,400)		(I) 52,400‡			
Separate company net income	(162,400)	(70,000)				
Consolidated net income						(175,500)
Net income attributable to noncontrolling interest					(13,100)†	13,100
Net income to Top Company						(162,400)
Statement of Retained Earnings						
Retained earnings, 1/1/18						
Top Company	(652,800)					(652,800)
Bottom Company		(310,000)	(*G) 4,000 (S) 306,000			
Net income (above)	(162,400)	(70,000)				(162,400)
Dividends declared	70,000	50,000		(D) 40,000	10,000	70,000
Retained earnings, 12/31/18	(745,200)	(330,000)				(745,200)
Balance Sheet						
Cash and receivables	280,000	120,000		(P) 10,000		390,000
Inventory	220,000	160,000		(G) 6,000		374,000
Investment in Bottom	415,200		(D) 40,000	(I) 52,400 (S) 364,800 (A) 38,000		–0–
Land	410,000	200,000				610,000
Plant assets (net)	190,000	170,000				360,000
Database			(A) 47,500	(E) 2,500		45,000
Total assets	1,515,200	650,000				1,779,000
Liabilities	(340,000)	(170,000)	(P) 10,000			(500,000)
Noncontrolling interest in Bottom Company, 1/1/18				(S) 91,200 (A) 9,500	(100,700)	
Noncontrolling interest in Bottom Company, 12/31/18					(103,800)	(103,800)
Common stock	(430,000)	(150,000)	(S) 150,000			(430,000)
Retained earnings, 12/31/18 (above)	(745,200)	(330,000)				(745,200)
Total liabilities and equities	(1,515,200)	(650,000)	718,400	718,400		(1,779,000)

Note: Parentheses indicate a credit balance.

†Because intra-entity sales were upstream, the subsidiary's $70,000 net income is decreased for the $6,000 gross profit deferred into next year and increased for $4,000 gross profit deferred from the previous year. After further reduction for $2,500 excess amortization, the resulting $65,500 provides the noncontrolling interest with a $13,100 allocation (20%).

‡Boxed items highlight differences with downstream transfers examined in Exhibit 5.4. Consolidation entries:

(*G) Recognition of intra-entity beginning inventory gross profit in current period consolidated net income. Upstream sales are attributed to the subsidiary.
(S Elimination of adjusted stockholders' equity accounts along with recognition of the noncontrolling interest as of January 1.
(A) Allocation of excess fair value over subsidiary's book value, unamortized balance as of January 1.
(I) Elimination of intra-entity income.
(D) Elimination of intra-entity dividends.
(E) Recognition of amortization expense for current year on database.
(P) Elimination of intra-entity receivable/payable balances.
(TI) Elimination of intra-entity sales/purchases balances.
(G) Deferral of intra-entity ending inventory gross profit from current period consolidated net income and removal of intra-entity gross profit from ending inventory.

above $4,000 reduction in Bottom's January 1, 2018, Retained Earnings to defer the intra-entity gross profit affects Entry **S.** After posting Entry ***G,** only $306,000 remains as the subsidiary's January 1, 2018, Retained Earnings, which along with Bottom's common stock is eliminated as follows:

Consolidation Entry S		
Common Stock—Bottom	150,000	
Retained earnings—Bottom	306,000	
Investment in Bottom		364,800
Noncontrolling Interest		91,200

This combined equity elimination figure ($456,000) above forms the basis for the 20 percent noncontrolling interest ($91,200) and the elimination of the 80 percent parent company investment ($364,800).

In comparing the consolidated totals across Exhibits 5.4 and 5.6, note that consolidated net income, inventory, total assets, and total liabilities and equities are all identical. The sole effect of the direction of the intra-entity inventory transfers (upstream or downstream) resides in the allocation of the temporary income effects of profit deferral and subsequent recognition to the controlling and noncontrolling interests.

Finally, to complete the consolidation, the noncontrolling interest's share of consolidated net income entered on the worksheet is $13,100, computed as follows:

Bottom reported net income, 2018	$70,000
Excess fair-value database amortization ($50,000/20 years)	(2,500)
2017 intra-entity gross profit recognized	4,000
2018 intra-entity gross profit deferred	(6,000)
Bottom 2018 net income adjusted	$65,500
Noncontrolling interest percentage	20%
Net income attributable to the noncontrolling interest, 2018	$13,100

Upstream transfers affect this computation although the downstream sales in the previous example did not. Thus, the noncontrolling interest balance reported previously in the income statement in Exhibit 5.4 differs from the allocation in Exhibit 5.6.

Consolidations—Downstream versus Upstream Transfers

To help clarify the effect of downstream and upstream transfers when the parent uses the equity method, we compare two of the worksheet entries in more detail:

Downstream Transfers

(Exhibit 5.4)

Entry *G

Investment in Bottom	4,000	
Cost of Goods Sold		4,000

To remove 2017 intra-entity gross profit from seller's beginning balance and recognize the gross profit in 2018.

Upstream Transfers

(Exhibit 5.6)

Entry *G

Retained Earnings, 1/1/18—Bottom	4,000	
Cost of Goods Sold		4,000

To remove 2017 intra-entity gross profit from seller's beginning balance and recognize the gross profit in 2018.

Downstream Transfers			Upstream Transfers		
Entry S			**Entry S**		
Common stock—Bottom	150,000		Common stock—Bottom	150,000	
Retained Earnings, 1/1/18—Bottom	310,000		Retaining Earnings, 1/1/18—Bottom (as adjusted)	306,000	
Investment in Bottom (80%)		368,000	Investment in Bottom (80%)		364,800
Noncontrolling interest—1/1/18..... (20%)		92,000	Noncontrolling interest—1/1/18 (20%)		91,200
To remove subsidiary's stockholders' equity accounts and portion of investment balance. Book value at beginning of year is appropriate.			To remove subsidiary's stockholders' equity accounts (as adjusted in Entry *G) and portion of investment balance. Adjusted book value at beginning of year is appropriate.		
Net Income Attributable to the Noncontrolling Interest = $13,500. 20% of Bottom's reported net income less excess database amortization			**Net Income Attributable to the Noncontrolling Interest** = $13,100. 20% of Bottom's net income (after adjustment for intra-entity gross profit in inventory and excess database amortization).		

Effects of Alternative Investment Methods on Consolidation

In Exhibits 5.3 through 5.6 the parent company utilized the equity method. When the parent uses either the initial value or the partial equity method, consolidation procedures normally continue to follow the same patterns analyzed in the previous chapters of this textbook. However, these alternative methods lack the full accrual properties of the equity method. Therefore, an additional worksheet adjustment (***C**) is needed to ensure the consolidated financial statements reflect a full accrual GAAP basis. As was the case previously, the worksheet adjustments depend on whether the intra-entity inventories result from downstream or upstream sales.

Using the same example, we now assume the parent applies the **initial value method.** Given that the subsidiary declares and pays dividends of $20,000 in 2017 and $50,000 in 2018, Top records dividend income of $16,000 ($20,000 × 80%) and $40,000 ($50,000 × 80%) during these two years.

Exhibits 5.7 and 5.8 present the worksheets to consolidate these two companies for the year ending December 31, 2018. As in the previous examples, most of the worksheet entries found in Exhibits 5.7 and 5.8 are described and analyzed in previous chapters of this textbook. Additionally, many of the worksheet entries required by intra-entity sales are identical to those used when the parent applies the equity method. Thus, only Consolidation Entries ***C** and ***G** are examined in detail separately for downstream intra-entity sales (Exhibit 5.7) and upstream intra-entity sales (Exhibit 5.8).

*Downstream Transfers—Consolidation Entries *C and *G: Parent Uses Initial Value Method*

Consolidation Entry ***C** is required in periods subsequent to acquisition whenever the parent does not apply the equity method. This adjustment converts the parent's beginning Retained Earnings to a full-accrual consolidated total. In the current illustration, Top did not accrue its portion of the 2017 increase in Bottom's book value [($30,000 net income less $20,000 in dividends) × 80%, or $8,000] or record the $2,000 amortization expense for this same period.

EXHIBIT 5.7 Downstream Inventory Transfers

TOP COMPANY AND BOTTOM COMPANY
Consolidation Worksheet
For Year Ending December 31, 2018

Investment: Initial Value Method — ***Ownership: 80%***

Accounts	Top Company	Bottom Company	Consolidation Entries Debit	Consolidation Entries Credit	Noncontrolling Interest	Consolidated Totals
Income Statement						
Sales	(600,000)	(300,000)	(TI)100,000			(800,000)
Cost of goods sold	320,000	180,000	(G) 6,000	(*G) 4,000 (TI)100,000		402,000
Operating expenses	170,000	50,000	(E) 2,500			222,500
Dividend income	(40,000)		(I) 40,000			
Separate company net income	(150,000)	(70,000)				
Consolidated net income						(175,500)
Net income attributable to noncontrolling interest					(13,500)†	13,500
Net income to Top Company						(162,000)
Statement of Retained Earnings						
Retained Earnings, 1/1/18						
Top Company	(650,000)		(*G) 4,000	(*C) 6,000		(652,000)
Bottom Company		(310,000)	(S) 310,000‡			
Net income (above)	(150,000)	(70,000)				(162,000)
Dividends declared	70,000	50,000		(I) 40,000	10,000	70,000
Retained earnings, 12/31/18	(730,000)	(330,000)				(744,000)
Balance Sheet						
Cash and receivables	280,000	120,000		(P) 10,000		390,000
Inventory	220,000	160,000		(G) 6,000		374,000
Investment in Bottom	400,000		(*C) 6,000	(S) 368,000 (A) 38,000		–0–
Land	410,000	200,000				610,000
Plant assets (net)	190,000	170,000				360,000
Database	–0–	–0–	(A) 47,500	(E) 2,500		45,000
Total assets	1,500,000	650,000				1,779,000
Liabilities	(340,000)	(170,000)	(P) 10,000			(500,000)
Noncontrolling interest in Bottom Company, 1/1/18				(S) 92,000 (A) 9,500	(101,500)	
Noncontrolling interest in Bottom Company, 12/31/18					105,000	(105,000)
Common stock	(430,000)	(150,000)	(S) 150,000			(430,000)
Retained earnings, 12/31/18 (above)	(730,000)	(330,000)				(744,000)
Total liabilities and equities	(1,500,000)	(650,000)	676,000	676,000		(1,779,000)

Note: Parentheses indicate a credit balance.

†Because intra-entity sales are made downstream (by the parent), the subsidiary's adjusted net income is the $70,000 reported figure less $2,500 excess amortization with a 20% allocation to the noncontrolling interest ($13,500).

‡Boxed items highlight differences with upstream transfers examined in Exhibit 5.8.

Consolidation entries:

(*G) Recognition of intra-entity beginning inventory gross profit in current period consolidated net income. Downstream sales are attributed to the parent.
(*C) Recognition of increase in book value and amortization relating to ownership of subsidiary for year prior to the current year.
(S) Elimination of subsidiary's stockholders' equity accounts along with recognition of the noncontrolling interest as of January 1.
(A) Allocation of subsidiary's fair value in excess of book value, unamortized balance as of January 1.
(I) Elimination of intra-entity dividends recorded by parent as dividend income.
(E) Recognition of amortization expense for current year on database.
(P) Elimination of intra-entity receivable/payable balances.
(TI) Elimination of intra-entity sales/purchases balances.
(G) Deferral of intra-entity ending inventory gross profit from current period consolidated net income and removal of intra-entity gross profit from ending inventory.

EXHIBIT 5.8 Upstream Inventory Transfers

TOP COMPANY AND BOTTOM COMPANY
Consolidation Worksheet
For Year Ending December 31, 2018

Investment: Initial Value Method — ***Ownership: 80%***

Accounts	Top Company	Bottom Company	Consolidation Entries Debit	Consolidation Entries Credit	Noncontrolling Interest	Consolidated Totals
Income Statement						
Sales	(600,000)	(300,000)	(TI)100,000			(800,000)
Cost of goods sold	320,000	180,000	(G) 6,000	(*G) 4,000 (TI)100,000		402,000
Operating expenses	170,000	50,000	(E) 2,500			222,500
Dividend income	(40,000)		(I) 40,000			
Separate company net income	(150,000)	(70,000)				
Consolidated net income						(175,500)
Net income attributable to noncontrolling interest					(13,100)†	13,100
Net income to Top Company						(162,400)
Statement of Retained Earnings						
Retained earnings, 1/1/18						
Top Company	(650,000)			(*C) 2,800		(652,800)
Bottom Company		(310,000)	(*G) 4,000 (S) 306,000‡			
Net income (above)	(150,000)	(70,000)				(162,400)
Dividends declared	70,000	50,000		(I) 40,000	10,000	70,000
Retained earnings, 12/31/18	(730,000)	(330,000)				(745,200)
Balance Sheet						
Cash and receivables	280,000	120,000		(P) 10,000		390,000
Inventory	220,000	160,000		(G) 6,000		374,000
Investment in Bottom	400,000		(*C) 2,800	(S) 364,800 (A) 38,000		-0-
Land	410,000	200,000				610,000
Plant assets (net)	190,000	170,000				360,000
Database	-0-	-0-	(A) 47,500	(E) 2,500		45,000
Total assets	1,500,000	650,000				1,779,000
Liabilities	(340,000)	(170,000)	(P) 10,000			(500,000)
Noncontrolling interest in Bottom Company, 1/1/18				(S) 91,200 (A) 9,500	(100,700)	
Noncontrolling interest in Bottom Company, 12/31/18					(103,800)	(103,800)
Common stock	(430,000)	(150,000)	(S) 150,000			(430,000)
Retained earnings, 12/31/18 (above)	(730,000)	(330,000)				(745,200)
Total liabilities and equities	(1,500,000)	(650,000)	668,800	668,800		(1,779,000)

Note: Parentheses indicate a credit balance.

†Because intra-entity sales were upstream, the subsidiary's $70,000 net income is decreased for the $6,000 gross profit deferred into next year and increased for $4,000 gross profit deferred from the previous year. After further reduction for $2,500 excess amortization, the resulting $65,500 provides the noncontrolling interest with a $13,100 allocation (20%).

‡Boxed items highlight differences with downstream transfers examined in Exhibit 5.7. Consolidation entries:

(*G) Recognition of intra-entity beginning inventory gross profit in current period consolidated net income. Upstream sales are attributed to the subsidiary.
(*C) Recognition of increase in book value and amortization relating to ownership of subsidiary for year prior to the current year.
(S) Elimination of adjusted stockholders' equity accounts along with recognition of the noncontrolling interest as of January 1.
(A) Allocation of subsidiary's fair value in excess of book value, unamortized balance as of January 1.
(I) Elimination of intra-entity dividends recorded by parent as dividend income.
(E) Recognition of amortization expense for current year on fair value allocated to value of database.
(P) Elimination of intra-entity receivable/payable balances. (TI) Elimination of intra-entity sales/purchases balances.
(G) Deferral of intra-entity ending inventory gross profit from current period consolidated net income and removal of intra-entity gross profit from ending inventory.

Discussion Question

WHAT PRICE SHOULD WE CHARGE OURSELVES?

Slagle Corporation is a large manufacturing organization. Over the past several years, it has obtained an important component used in its production process exclusively from Harrison, Inc., a relatively small company in Topeka, Kansas. Harrison charges $90 per unit for this part:

Variable cost per unit	$40
Fixed cost assigned per unit	30
Markup	20
Total price	$90

In hope of reducing manufacturing costs, Slagle purchases all of Harrison's outstanding common stock. This new subsidiary continues to sell merchandise to a number of outside customers as well as to Slagle. Thus, for internal reporting purposes, Slagle views Harrison as a separate profit center.

A controversy has now arisen among company officials about the amount that Harrison should charge Slagle for each component. The administrator in charge of the subsidiary wants to continue the $90 price. He believes this figure best reflects the division's profitability: "If we are to be judged by our profits, why should we be punished for selling to our own parent company? If that occurs, my figures will look better if I forget Slagle as a customer and try to market my goods solely to outsiders."

In contrast, the vice president in charge of Slagle's production wants the price set at variable cost, total cost, or some derivative of these numbers. "We bought Harrison to bring our costs down. It only makes sense to reduce the transfer price; otherwise the benefits of acquiring this subsidiary are not apparent. I pushed the company to buy Harrison; if our operating results are not improved, I will get the blame."

Will the decision about the transfer price affect consolidated net income? Which method would be easiest for the company's accountant to administer? As the company's accountant, what advice would you give to these officials?

Because the parent recognized neither number in its financial records, the worksheet process adjusts the parent's beginning retained earnings by $6,000 as follows:

Consolidation Entry *C		
Investment in Bottom	6,000	
Retained Earnings—Top		6,000
To convert Top's retained earnings to the accrual basis. Intra-entity sales were downstream and therefore do not affect the adjustment.		

The intra-entity inventory transfers do not affect this entry because they were downstream; the gross profits had no impact on the net income recognized by the subsidiary.

Under the initial value method, the parent makes no entries in its internal financial records to adjust for the intra-entity sales. Because in this case the sales are downstream, the parent's January 1, 2018, Retained Earnings will be overstated from a consolidated view by the intra-entity $4,000 gross profit in beginning inventory recognized from its 2017 intra-entity sales.

Consolidation entry ***G** corrects this overstatement and appropriately recognizes (through the credit to Cost of Goods Sold) the profit in the current year as follows:

Consolidation Entry *G		
Retained Earnings—Top	4,000	
Cost of Goods Sold		4,000
To remove 2017 intra-entity gross profit in inventory from seller's beginning balance and recognize the gross profit in 2018 following sales to outsiders. Top uses the initial value method and intra-entity sales were downstream.		

Note that the above entry *G simply reassigns the intra-entity beginning inventory gross profit from downstream transfers to 2018 from 2017.

*Upstream Transfers—Consolidation Entries *C and *G: Parent Uses Initial Value Method*

We now change the example by assuming the intra-entity transfers are upstream from Bottom to Top. In this case, the $4,000 intra-entity gross profit remaining in Top's 2017 ending inventory has been recorded by Bottom as part of its 2017 net income and retained earnings. Because $4,000 of Bottom's 2017 net income is deferred until 2018, the increase in the subsidiary's book value in the previous year is only $6,000 rather than $10,000 ($30,000 net income less $20,000 in dividends) as reported. Consequently, conversion to the equity method (Entry ***C**) requires an increase of just $2,800:

$6,000 net increase (after intra-entity profit deferral) in subsidiary's book value during 2017 × 80%	$4,800
2017 amortization expense (80% × $2,500)	(2,000)
Increase in parent's beginning retained earnings (Entry *C)	$2,800

In applying the initial value method in its financial records, the parent did not recognize the increase in subsidiary book value, excess fair-value amortization, or any effects from intra-entity transfers remaining in inventory. The worksheet process thus adjusts the parent's beginning retained earnings by $2,800 as shown here.

Consolidation Entry *C		
Investment in Bottom	2,800	
Retained Earnings—Top		2,800
To convert Top's retained earnings to the accrual basis. Intra-entity sales were upstream.		

In this case the intra-entity inventory transfers affect Consolidation Entry *C because they were downstream; the gross profits directly affected the net income recognized by the subsidiary.

Using the initial value method, the parent makes no entries in its internal financial records to adjust for the intra-entity sales. Because in this case the sales are upstream, the subsidiary's January 1, 2018, Retained Earnings will be overstated from a consolidated view by the intra-entity gross profit in beginning inventory. Consolidation entry *G corrects this overstatement and appropriately recognizes the profit in the current year as follows:

Consolidation Entry *G		
Retained Earnings—Bottom	4,000	
Cost of Goods Sold		4,000
To remove 2017 intra-entity gross profit in inventory from seller's beginning balance and recognize the gross profit in 2018 following sales to outsiders. Top uses the initial value method and intra-entity sales were upstream.		

Note again how the above entry *G simply reassigns the intra-entity beginning inventory gross profit to 2018 from 2017.

Finally, if the parent had applied the **partial equity method** in its internal records, little would change in the consolidation processes previously described for the equity method. The primary change would involve inclusion of a Consolidation Entry *C. Because the parent would have recorded changes in reported subsidiary book value, the *C adjustment would be computed only for (1) previous years' excess fair over book value amortizations and (2) the immediate past year's intra-entity profit deferral.

LO 5-6

Prepare the consolidation entry to defer any gain created by an intra-entity transfer of land from the accounting records of the year of transfer and subsequent years.

Intra-Entity Land Transfers

Although not as prevalent as inventory transactions, intra-entity sales of other assets occur occasionally. The final two sections of this chapter examine the worksheet procedures that noninventory transfers necessitate. We first analyze land transactions and then discuss the effects created by the intra-entity sale of depreciable assets such as buildings and equipment.

Accounting for Land Transactions

The consolidation procedures necessitated by intra-entity land transfers partially parallel those for intra-entity inventory. As with inventory, the sale of land creates a series of effects on the individual records of the two companies. The worksheet process must then adjust the account balances to reflect the perspective of a single economic entity.

By reviewing the sequence of events occurring in an intra-entity land sale, the similarities to inventory transfers can be ascertained as well as the unique features of this transaction.

1. The original seller of the land reports a gain (losses are rare in intra-entity asset transfers), even though the transaction occurred between related parties. At the same time, the acquiring company capitalizes the inflated transfer price rather than the land's historical cost to the business combination.
2. The gain the seller recorded is closed into Retained Earnings at the end of the year. From a consolidated perspective, this account has been artificially increased by a related party. Thus, both the buyer's Land account and the seller's Retained Earnings account continue to contain the intra-entity gain.
3. The gain on the original transfer is recognized in consolidated net income only when the land is subsequently disposed of to an outside party. Therefore, appropriate consolidation techniques must be designed to eliminate the intra-entity gain each period until the time of resale.

Clearly, two characteristics encountered in inventory transfers also exist in intra-entity land transactions: inflated book values and intra-entity gains subsequently culminated through sales to outside parties. Despite these similarities, significant differences exist. Because of the nature of the transaction, the individual companies do not use sales/purchases accounts when land is transferred. Instead, the seller establishes a separate gain account when it removes the land from its books. And because it's an intra-entity gain, the balance must be eliminated when preparing consolidated statements.

In addition, the subsequent resale of land to an outside party does not always occur in the year immediately following the transfer. Although inventory is normally disposed of within a relatively short time, the buyer often holds land for years if not permanently. Thus, the overvalued Land account can remain on the acquiring company's books indefinitely. As long as the land is retained, the effects of the intra-entity gain (the equivalent of Entry ***G** in inventory transfers) must be eliminated for each subsequent consolidation. By repeating this worksheet entry every year, the consolidated financial statements properly state both the Land and the Retained Earnings accounts.

Eliminating Intra-Entity Gains—Land Transfers

To illustrate these worksheet procedures, assume that Hastings Company and Patrick Company are related parties. On July 1, 2018, Hastings sold land that originally cost $60,000 to Patrick at a $100,000 transfer price. The seller reports a $40,000 gain; the buyer records the land at the $100,000 acquisition price. At the end of this fiscal period, the intra-entity effect of this transaction must be eliminated for consolidation purposes:

Consolidation Entry TL (year of transfer)		
Gain on Sale of Land	40,000	
Land		40,000
To eliminate effects of intra-entity transfer of land. (Labeled **"TL"** in reference to the transferred land.)		

This worksheet entry eliminates the intra-entity gain from the 2018 consolidated statements and returns the land to its recorded value at date of transfer, for consolidated purposes. However, as with the transfer of inventory, the effects created by the original transaction remain in the financial records of the individual companies for as long as the property is held. The gain recorded by Hastings carries through to Retained Earnings while Patrick's Land account retains the inflated transfer price. *Therefore, for every subsequent consolidation until the land is eventually sold, the elimination process must be repeated.* Including the following entry on each subsequent worksheet removes the intra-entity gain from the asset and from the earnings reported by the combination:

Consolidation Entry *GL (every year following transfer)		
Retained Earnings (beginning balance of seller)	40,000	
Land		40,000
To eliminate effects of intra-entity transfer of land made in a previous year. (Labeled **"*GL"** in reference to the gain on a land transfer occurring in a prior year.)		

Note that the reduction in Retained Earnings is changed to an increase in the Investment in Subsidiary account when the original sale is downstream and the parent has applied the equity method. In that specific situation, equity method adjustments have already corrected the timing of the parent's intra-entity gain. Removing the gain has created a reduction in the Investment account that is appropriately allocated to the subsidiary's Land account on the worksheet. Conversely, if sales were upstream, the Retained Earnings of the seller (the subsidiary) continue to be overstated even if the parent applies the equity method.

One final consolidation concern exists in accounting for intra-entity transfers of land. If the property is ever sold to an outside party, the company making the sale records a gain or loss based on its recorded book value. However, this cost figure is actually the internal transfer price. The gain or loss being recognized is incorrect for consolidation purposes; it has not been computed by comparison to the land's historical cost. Again, the separate financial records fail to reflect the transaction from the perspective of the single economic entity.

Therefore, if the company eventually sells the land, it must recognize the gain deferred at the time of the original transfer. Gain recognition is appropriate once the property is sold to outsiders. On the worksheet, the gain is removed one last time from beginning Retained Earnings (or the investment account, if applicable). In this instance, though, the worksheet entry reclassifies the amount as a recognized gain. Thus, the gain recognition is reallocated from the year of transfer into the fiscal period in which the land is sold to the unrelated party.

Returning to the previous illustration, Hastings acquired land for $60,000 and sold it to Patrick, a related party, for $100,000. Consequently, the $40,000 intra-entity gain was eliminated on the consolidation worksheet in the year of transfer as well as in each succeeding period. However, if this land is subsequently sold to an outside party for $115,000, Patrick recognizes only a $15,000 gain. From the viewpoint of the business combination, the land (having been bought for $60,000) was actually sold at a $55,000 gain. To correct the reporting, the following consolidation entry must be made in the year that the property is sold to the unrelated party. This adjustment increases the $15,000 gain recorded by Patrick to the consolidated balance of $55,000:

Consolidation Entry *GL (year of sale to outside party)		
Retained Earnings (Hastings)	40,000	
Gain on Sale of Land		40,000
To remove intra-entity gain from year of transfer so that total profit can be recognized in the current period when land is sold to an outside party.		

As in the accounting for inventory transfers, the entire consolidation process demonstrated here accomplishes two major objectives:

1. It reports historical cost for the transferred land for as long as it remains within the business combination.
2. It defers income recognition until the land is sold to outside parties.

Recognizing the Effect on Noncontrolling Interest—Land Transfers

The preceding discussion of intra-entity land transfers ignores the possible presence of a noncontrolling interest. In constructing financial statements for an economic entity that includes outside ownership, the guidelines already established for inventory transfers remain applicable.

If the original sale was a *downstream* transaction, neither the annual deferral nor the eventual recognition of the intra-entity gain has any effect on the noncontrolling interest. The rationale for this treatment, as previously indicated, is that profits from downstream transfers relate solely to the parent company.

Conversely, if the transfer is made *upstream,* deferral and recognition of gains are attributed to the subsidiary and, hence, to the noncontrolling interest. As with inventory, all noncontrolling interest balances are computed on the reported earnings of the subsidiary after adjustment for any upstream transfers.

To reiterate, the accounting consequences stemming from land transfers are these:

1. In the year of transfer, any intra-entity gain is deferred and the Land account is reduced to historical cost. When an upstream sale creates the gain, the amount also is excluded in calculating the noncontrolling interest's share of the subsidiary's net income for that year.
2. Each year thereafter, the intra-entity gain will be removed from the seller's beginning Retained Earnings. If the transfer was upstream, eliminating this earlier gain directly affects the balances recorded within both Entry ***C** (if conversion to the equity method is required) and Entry **S.** The additional equity accrual (Entry ***C,** if needed) as well as the elimination of beginning Stockholders' Equity (Entry **S**) must be based on the newly adjusted balance in the subsidiary's Retained Earnings. This deferral process also has an impact on the noncontrolling interest's share of the subsidiary's net income, but only in the year of transfer and the eventual year of sale.
3. If the land is ever sold to an outside party, the original gain is recognized and reported in consolidated net income.

Intra-Entity Transfer of Depreciable Assets

LO 5-7

Prepare the consolidation entries to remove the effects of upstream and downstream intra-entity fixed asset transfers across affiliated entities.

Just as related parties can transfer inventory and land, the intra-entity sale of a host of other assets is possible. Equipment, patents, franchises, buildings, and other long-lived assets can be involved. Accounting for such intra-entity transactions resembles that demonstrated for land sales. However, the subsequent calculation of depreciation or amortization provides an added challenge in the development of consolidated financial statements.[10]

[10] To avoid redundancy within this analysis, all further references are made to depreciation expense alone, although this discussion is equally applicable to the amortization of intangible assets and the depletion of wasting assets.

Deferral and Subsequent Recognition of Intra-Entity Gains

When faced with intra-entity sales of depreciable assets, financial reporting objectives remain unchanged: *defer intra-entity gains, re-establish historical cost balances, and recognize appropriate income within the consolidated financial statements.* More specifically, we defer gains created by intra-entity transfers until such time as the subsequent use or resale of the asset consummates the original transaction. For inventory sales, the culminating disposal normally occurs currently or in the year following the transfer. In contrast, transferred land may be kept indefinitely, thus deferring the recognition of the intra-entity profit indefinitely.

When depreciable asset sales occur across firms within a consolidated entity, the accounting effects for both the seller and buyer of the depreciable asset must be analyzed in preparing consolidated financial statements. For example, assume a parent company sells a delivery truck to its subsidiary at a transfer price in excess of the parent's carrying amount for the asset. In recording the sale, the parent recognizes a gain on its books. Clearly, this is an intra-entity gain that must be removed in consolidation.

In the subsidiary's financial records, the purchased truck is recorded at the transfer price and subsequently depreciated. However, because of the parent-subsidiary control relationship, no sale of the truck occurred with an outside entity. Consequently, from a consolidated reporting perspective, the carrying amount of the truck account becomes overstated and further results in overstated depreciation expense and accumulated depreciation. The resulting overstatements of the truck, depreciation expense, and accumulated depreciation must also be removed in consolidation.

However, as the subsidiary uses the truck to generate revenues over time, the decline in the truck's future economic benefit can be viewed as an indirect, gradual sale to outsiders. From a consolidated perspective, as the truck is consumed in producing revenues from outsiders, it becomes gradually "sold" and the intra-entity gain can be gradually recognized. Thus, for depreciable asset transfers, the ultimate recognition of any gain on sale typically occurs over a period of several years.

Because of the long-term nature of depreciable assets, so long as the entity owns the asset, the effects of an intra-entity transfer must be accounted for in preparing the consolidated entity's financial statements. In the year of the intra-entity fixed asset transfer, consolidation procedures to remove the intra-entity gain and its effects on the asset, depreciation expense, and accumulated depreciation are relatively straightforward. First, a worksheet entry eliminates the gain and returns the asset and accumulated depreciation accounts to their pre-transfer amounts. Then, a second worksheet entry accordingly reduces the overstated current year depreciation expense and related accumulated depreciation.

In years subsequent to the intra-entity asset transfer, we observe that the gain on sale recognized by the seller has now been closed to Retained Earnings. The overstated depreciation expense also has been closed to the Retained Earnings of the buyer. Consolidation worksheet entries thus reflect the net effect of the gain on sale and the overstated depreciation on the affiliate's separate accounting records. Below we provide an illustration of the consolidated worksheet entries in the year of the intra-entity transfer followed by the year subsequent to the intra-entity transfer.

Depreciable Asset Intra-Entity Transfers Illustrated

To examine the consolidation procedures required by the intra-entity transfer of a depreciable asset, assume that Able Company sells equipment to Baker Company at the current market value of $90,000. Able originally acquired the equipment for $100,000 several years ago; since that time, it has recorded $40,000 in accumulated depreciation. The transfer is made on January 1, 2017, when the equipment has a 10-year remaining life.[11]

[11] Although this example assumes an intra-entity gain on sale, intra-entity losses may occur as well. If the loss cannot be attributed to an asset impairment, then parallel consolidation procedures to those provided in the example, reflecting a loss, would be appropriate.

Year of Intra-Entity Transfer

The 2017 effects on the separate financial accounts of the two companies can be quickly enumerated:

1. Baker, as the buyer, enters the equipment into its records at the $90,000 transfer price. However, from a consolidated view the asset has not been sold, and therefore the $60,000 book value ($100,000 cost less $40,000 accumulated depreciation) remains appropriate.
2. Able, as the seller, reports a $30,000 gain, although the consolidated entity has not yet sold the asset to outsiders. After preparation of the 12/31/17 consolidated financial statements, Able then closes this gain to its Retained Earnings account.
3. Assuming application of the straight-line depreciation method with no salvage value, Baker records expense of $9,000 at the end of 2017 ($90,000 transfer price/10 years). The proper depreciation expense for consolidation, however, is based on the asset's carrying amount to the consolidated entity at the date of the intra-entity transfer. Consolidated depreciation expense for this asset would thus be $6,000 ($60,000 carrying amount/10 remaining years). This requires a $3,000 consolidated worksheet adjustment to depreciation expense.

To report these events as seen by the consolidated entity, we first acknowledge that an asset write-up cannot be recognized based on an intra-entity transfer. A consolidated worksheet entry must therefore return the asset to its pre-transfer carrying amount based on historical cost. Moreover, both the $30,000 intra-entity gain and the $3,000 overstatement in depreciation expense must be eliminated on the worksheet. The two consolidation entries for 2017 are shown below:

Consolidation Entry TA (year of transfer)[12]

Gain on Sale of Equipment	30,000	
Equipment	10,000	
Accumulated Depreciation		40,000

To remove intra-entity gain and return equipment accounts to balances based on original historical cost. (Labeled **"TA"** in reference to transferred asset.)

Consolidation Entry ED (year of transfer)

Accumulated Depreciation	3,000	
Depreciation Expense		3,000

To eliminate overstatement of depreciation expense caused by inflated transfer price. (Labeled **"ED"** in reference to excess depreciation.) *Entry must be repeated for all 10 years of the equipment's remaining life.*

From the viewpoint of a single consolidated entity, these entries accomplish several objectives:

- Reinstate the asset's historical cost of $100,000.
- Return the January 1, 2017, book value to the appropriate $60,000 figure by recognizing accumulated depreciation of $40,000.
- Eliminate the $30,000 intra-entity gain recorded by Able so the amount does not appear in the consolidated income statement.

[12] If the worksheet uses only one account for a net depreciated asset, this entry would have been

Gain on sale	30,000	
Equipment (net)		30,000

To reduce the $90,000 to original $60,000 book value at date of transfer rather than reinstating original balances.

- Reduce depreciation for the year from $9,000 to $6,000, the appropriate expense based on pre-transfer carrying amount of the asset.
- Although the gain is eliminated, the credit to depreciation expense increases consolidated net income serving as a partial recognition of the gain for 2017.

Over the remaining life of the asset, consolidation entries serve to reallocate the gain from the year of transfer to each of the 10 years following the transfer as the asset is consumed in the production process. Recall that for intra-entity gross profit in ending inventory, the ultimate recognition of the profit deferral was achieved on the consolidated worksheet through a credit to *cost of goods sold.* In a parallel fashion, deferred intra-entity profits on depreciable asset transfers are achieved on the consolidated worksheet through a credit to *depreciation expense.*

In the year of the intra-entity depreciable asset transfer, the preceding consolidation entries **TA** and **ED** are applicable regardless of whether the transfer was upstream or downstream. They are likewise applicable regardless of whether the parent applies the equity method, initial value method, or partial equity method of accounting for its investment. As discussed subsequently, however, in the years following the intra-entity transfer, we make a slight modification to consolidation entry ***TA** for downstream transfers when the equity method is applied.

Years Following the Intra-Entity Transfer

Again, the preceding worksheet entries do not actually remove the effects of the intra-entity transfer from the individual records of these two organizations. Both the intra-entity gain and the excess depreciation expense remain on the separate books and are closed into Retained Earnings of the respective companies at year-end. Similarly, the Equipment account with the related Accumulated Depreciation continues to hold balances based on the transfer price, not historical cost. *Thus, for every subsequent period, the separately reported figures must be adjusted on the worksheet to present the consolidated totals from a single entity's perspective.*

To derive worksheet entries at any future point, the balances in the accounts of the individual companies must be ascertained and compared to the figures appropriate for the consolidated entity. As an illustration, the separate records of Able and Baker two years after the transfer (December 31, 2018) follow. Consolidated totals are calculated based on the original historical cost of $100,000 and accumulated depreciation of $40,000.

Account	Individual Records	Consolidated Perspective	Worksheet Adjustments
Equipment 12/31/18	$90,000	$100,000	$10,000
Accumulated Depreciation 12/31/18	(18,000)	(52,000)*	(34,000)
Depreciation Expense for 2018	9,000	6,000	(3,000)
1/1/18 Retained Earnings effect	(21,000)†	6,000	27,000

Note: Parentheses indicate a credit balance.
*Accumulated depreciation before transfer $(40,000) plus 2 years × $(6,000). †Intra-entity transfer gain ($30,000) less one year's depreciation of $9,000.

Because the intra-entity transfer's effects remain in the separate financial records, the various accounts must be adjusted in each subsequent consolidation. Moreover, the amounts involved must be updated every period because of the continual impact of depreciation recorded by the buyer. Continuing our example, to adjust the individual figures to the consolidated totals derived above, the 2018 worksheet includes the following entries:

Consolidation Entry *TA (year following transfer)		
Equipment	10,000	
Retained Earnings, 1/1/18 (Able)	27,000	
Accumulated Depreciation		37,000
To return the Equipment account to original historical cost and adjust the 1/1/18 balances of Retained Earnings and Accumulated Depreciation.		

Consolidation Entry ED (year following transfer)		
Accumulated Depreciation	3,000	
Depreciation Expense		3,000
To remove excess depreciation expense on the intra-entity transfer price and adjust Accumulated Depreciation to its 12/31/18 consolidated balance.		
Note that the $34,000 increase in 12/31/18 consolidated Accumulated Depreciation results from a $37,000 credit in Entry ***TA** and a $3,000 debit in Entry **ED.**		

We observe that in consolidation entry ***TA,** $27,000 of the original intra-entity gain on sale is removed from Retained Earnings. Then, in consolidation entry **ED,** the $3,000 credit to Depreciation Expense serves to increase consolidated net income by $3,000. Essentially, the remaining intra-entity gain as of the beginning of the year is removed from Retained Earnings and partially recognized as a current year increase in consolidated net income (via the decrease in depreciation expense).[13]

The ***TA** adjustment to the Equipment account remains constant over the life of the asset. However, the ***TA** adjustments to beginning Retained Earnings and Accumulated Depreciation vary with each succeeding consolidation. At December 31, 2017, the individual companies closed out both the intra-entity gain of $30,000 and $9,000 depreciation expense on their books. *Importantly, the $9,000 depreciation expense was overstated by $3,000 from a consolidated perspective.* Therefore, as reflected in Entry ***TA,** the beginning Retained Earnings account for the 2018 consolidation is overstated by a net amount of only $27,000 rather than $30,000. *Over the life of the asset, the intra-entity gain in consolidated retained earnings will be systematically reduced to zero as excess depreciation expense ($3,000) is closed out each year on the books of the company that possesses the asset.* Hence, on subsequent consolidation worksheets, the beginning Retained Earnings account decreases by this amount: $27,000 in 2018, $24,000 in 2019, $21,000 in the following period, and so on. This reduction continues until, at the end of 10 years, the intra-entity gain has been completely recognized in the consolidation process.

Similarly, the change in beginning Accumulated Depreciation varies with each succeeding consolidation. At December 31, 2017, the buyer recorded a $3,000 overstatement of depreciation expense and Accumulated Depreciation. Therefore, as reflected in Entry ***TA,** the Accumulated Depreciation account at the beginning of 2018 is undervalued by a net amount of only $37,000 rather than $40,000.

If this equipment is ever resold to an outside party, the remaining portion of the gain is immediately recognized by the consolidated entity. As in the previous discussion of land, the remaining intra-entity profit existing at the date of resale must be recognized on the consolidated income statement to arrive at the appropriate amount of gain or loss on the sale.

Years Following Downstream Intra-Entity Depreciable Asset Transfers—Parent Uses Equity Method

Consolidation entry ***TA** requires a slight modification when the intra-entity depreciable asset transfer is downstream and the parent uses the equity method. In applying the equity method, the parent adjusts its book income for both the original transfer gain and periodic depreciation expense adjustments. Thus, in downstream intra-entity transfers when the equity method is used, from a consolidated view, the parent's Retained Earnings balance has been already reduced for the gain. Therefore, continuing with the previous example, the following worksheet consolidation entries would be made for a downstream sale assuming that (1) Able is the parent and (2) Able has applied the equity method to account for its investment in Baker.

[13] Alternatively, because the straight line method is used, the depreciation expense adjustment can also be computed as the original gain on sale divided by the remaining life of the transferred asset ($30,000/10 years).

Consolidation Entry *TA (year following transfer)		
Equipment	10,000	
Investment in Baker	27,000	
Accumulated Depreciation		37,000

Consolidation Entry ED (year following transfer)		
Accumulated Depreciation	3,000	
Depreciation Expense		3,000

In Entry ***TA,** note that the Investment in Baker account replaces the parent's Retained Earnings. This temporary increase to the Investment account then effectively allocates the adjustments necessitated by the intra-entity transfer to the appropriate subsidiary Equipment and Accumulated Depreciation accounts.

Effect on Noncontrolling Interest—Depreciable Asset Transfers

Because of the lack of official guidance, no easy answer exists as to the assignment of any income effects created within the consolidation process. Consistent with the previous sections of this chapter, all income is assigned here to the original seller. In Entry ***TA,** for example, the beginning Retained Earnings account of Able (the seller) is reduced. Both the intra-entity gain on the transfer and the excess depreciation expense subsequently recognized are assigned to that party.

Thus, again, downstream sales are assumed to have no effect on any noncontrolling interest values. The parent rather than the subsidiary made the sale. Conversely, the impact on net income created by upstream sales must be considered in computing the balances attributed to these outside owners. Currently, this approach is one of many acceptable alternatives. However, in its future deliberations on consolidation policies and procedures, the FASB could mandate a specific allocation pattern.

Summary

1. The transfer of assets, especially inventory, between the members of a consolidated entity is a common practice. In producing consolidated financial statements, any effects on the separate accounting records created by such transfers must be removed because the transactions did not occur with an outside unrelated party.
2. Inventory transfers are the most prevalent form of intra-entity asset transaction. Despite being only a transfer, one company records a sale while the other reports a purchase. These balances are reciprocals that must be offset on the worksheet in the process of producing consolidated figures.
3. Additional accounting problems result if inventory is transferred at a markup. Any portion of the merchandise still held at year-end is valued at more than historical cost because of the inflation in price. Furthermore, the gross profit that the seller reports on these goods must be deferred from a consolidation perspective. Thus, this gross profit must be removed from the ending Inventory account, a figure that appears as an asset on the balance sheet and as a negative component within cost of goods sold.
4. Intra-entity inventory gross profits in ending inventory also create a consolidation problem in the year following the transfer. Within the separate accounting systems, the seller closes the gross profit to Retained Earnings. The buyer's ending Inventory balance becomes the next period's beginning balance (within Cost of Goods Sold). Therefore, the inflation must be removed again but this time in the subsequent year. The seller's beginning Retained Earnings is decreased to eliminate the intra-entity gross profit while Cost of Goods Sold is reduced to remove the overstatement from the beginning inventory component. However, when the parent applies the equity method and sales are downstream, the parent's Retained Earnings are correctly stated from a consolidated view. Therefore, in this case, the Investment in Subsidiary account is used in the beginning intra-entity inventory profit adjustment, instead of the parent's Retained Earnings. Through this process, the intra-entity profit is deferred from the year of transfer so that recognition can be made at the point of disposal or consumption.

5. The deferral and subsequent recognition of intra-entity gross profits raise a question concerning the measurement of noncontrolling interest balances: Does the change in the period of recognition alter these calculations? Although the issue is currently under debate, no formal answer to this question is yet found in official accounting pronouncements. In this textbook, the deferral of profits from upstream transfers (from subsidiary to parent) is assumed to affect the noncontrolling interest whereas downstream transactions (from parent to subsidiary) do not. When upstream transfers are involved, noncontrolling interest values are based on the gross profit recognized after adjustment for any intra-entity gross profit remaining in inventory.
6. Inventory is not the only asset that can be transferred between the members of a consolidated entity. For example, transfers of land sometimes occur. Again, if the transfer price exceeds original cost, the buyer's records state the asset at an inflated value while the seller recognizes an intra-entity gain. As with inventory, the consolidation process must return the asset's recorded balance to cost while deferring the gain. Repetition of this procedure is necessary in every consolidation for as long as the land remains within the consolidated entity.
7. The consolidation process required by the intra-entity transfer of depreciable assets differs somewhat from that demonstrated for inventory and land. The intra-entity gain created by the transaction must still be deferred along with an adjustment for the asset's overstatement. However, because of subsequent depreciation, these adjustments systematically change from period to period. Additionally, because the excess depreciation is closed annually to Retained Earnings, the overstatement of the equity account resulting from the intra-entity gain is constantly reduced. To produce consolidated figures at any point in time, the remaining overstatement in these figures (as well as in the current depreciation expense) must be determined and removed. Overall, the intra-entity gain is removed from the year of the depreciable asset transfer and subsequently recognized over the remaining life of the asset. Consolidation worksheet entries that serve to reduce depreciation expense become the vehicle for recognizing the annual portion of the intra-entity gain.

Comprehensive Illustration

Problem

(*Estimated Time: 45 to 65 Minutes*) On January 1, 2016, Daisy Company acquired 80 percent of Rose Company for $594,000 in cash. Rose's total book value on that date was $610,000 and the fair value of the noncontrolling interest was $148,500. The newly acquired subsidiary possessed a trademark (10-year remaining life) that, although unrecorded on Rose's accounting records, had a fair value of $75,000. Any remaining excess acquisition-date fair value was attributed to goodwill.

Daisy decided to acquire Rose so that the subsidiary could furnish component parts for the parent's production process. During the ensuing years, Rose sold inventory to Daisy as follows:

Year	Cost to Rose Company	Transfer Price	Gross Profit Rate	Transferred Inventory Still Held at End of Year (at transfer price)
2016	$100,000	$140,000	28.6%	$20,000
2017	100,000	150,000	33.3	30,000
2018	120,000	160,000	25.0	68,000

Any transferred merchandise that Daisy retained at year-end was always put into production during the following period.

On January 1, 2017, Daisy sold Rose several pieces of equipment that had a 10-year remaining life and were being depreciated on the straight-line method with no salvage value. This equipment was transferred at an $80,000 price, although it had an original $100,000 cost to Daisy and a $44,000 book value at the date of exchange.

On January 1, 2018, Daisy sold land to Rose for $50,000, its fair value at that date. The original cost had been only $22,000. By the end of 2018, Rose had made no payment for the land.

The following separate financial statements are for Daisy and Rose as of December 31, 2018. Daisy has applied the equity method to account for this investment.

	Daisy Company	Rose Company
Sales	$ (900,000)	$ (500,000)
Cost of goods sold	598,000	300,000
Operating expenses	210,000	80,000
Gain on sale of land	(28,000)	–0–
Equity in earnings of Rose Company	(60,000)	–0–
Net income	$ (180,000)	$ (120,000)
Retained earnings, 1/1/18	$ (620,000)	$ (430,000)
Net income	(180,000)	(120,000)
Dividends declared	55,000	50,000
Retained earnings, 12/31/18	$ (745,000)	$ (500,000)
Cash and accounts receivable	$ 348,000	$ 410,000
Inventory	430,400	190,000
Investment in Rose Company	737,600	–0–
Land	454,000	280,000
Equipment	270,000	190,000
Accumulated depreciation	(180,000)	(50,000)
Total assets	$ 2,060,000	$ 1,020,000
Liabilities	(715,000)	(120,000)
Common stock	(600,000)	(400,000)
Retained earnings, 12/31/18	(745,000)	(500,000)
Total liabilities and equities	$ (2,060,000)	$(1,020,000)

Required

Answer the following questions:

a. By how much did Rose's book value increase during the period from January 1, 2016, through December 31, 2017?

b. During the initial years after the takeover, what annual amortization expense was recognized in connection with the acquisition-date excess of fair value over book value?

c. What amount of intra-entity gross profit exists within the parent's inventory figures at the beginning and at the end of 2018?

d. Equipment has been transferred between the companies. What amount of additional depreciation is recognized in 2018 because of this transfer?

e. The parent reports Income of Rose Company of $60,000 for 2018. How was this figure calculated?

f. Without using a worksheet, determine consolidated totals.

g. Prepare the December 31, 2018, worksheet entries required by the transfers of inventory, land, and equipment.

Solution

a. The subsidiary's acquisition-date book value is given as $610,000. At the beginning of 2018, the company's common stock and retained earnings total is $830,000 ($400,000 and $430,000, respectively). In the previous years, Rose's book value has apparently increased by $220,000 ($830,000 – $610,000).

b. To determine amortization, an allocation of Daisy's acquisition-date fair value must first be made. The $75,000 allocation needed to show Daisy's equipment at fair value leads to additional annual expense of $7,500 for the initial years of the combination. The $57,500 assigned to goodwill is not subject to amortization.

Acquisition-Date Fair-Value Allocation and Excess Amortization Schedule

Consideration paid by Daisy for 80% of Rose	$ 594,000
Noncontrolling interest (20%) fair value	148,500
Rose's fair value at acquisition date	$ 742,500
Book value of Rose Company	(610,000)
Excess fair value over book value	$ 132,500

		Remaining Life (Years)	Annual Excess Amortizations	Excess Amortizations 2016–2018	Unamortized Balance, 12/31/18
Trademark	$ 75,000	10	$ 7,500	$ 22,500	$52,500
Goodwill	57,500	indefinite	-0-	-0-	57,500
Totals.........	$132,500		$ 7,500	$ 22,500	

c. Of the inventory transferred to Daisy during 2017, $30,000 is still held at the beginning of 2018. This merchandise contains an intra-entity gross profit of $10,000 ($30,000 × 33.3% gross profit rate for that year). At year-end, $17,000 ($68,000 remaining inventory × 25% gross profit rate) remains as intra-entity gross profit in the ending inventory.

d. Additional depreciation for the net addition of 2018 is $3,600. Equipment with a book value of $44,000 was transferred at a price of $80,000. The net of $36,000 to this asset's account balances would be written off over 10 years for an extra $3,600 per year during the consolidation process.

e. According to the separate statements given, the subsidiary reports net income of $120,000. However, in determining the net income allocation between the parent and the noncontrolling interest, this reported figure must be adjusted for the effects of *any upstream transfers.* Because Rose sold the inventory upstream to Daisy, the $10,000 gross profit deferred in requirement (*c*) from 2017 into the current period is attributed to the subsidiary (as the seller). Likewise, the $17,000 intra-entity gross profit at year-end is viewed as a reduction in Rose's net income.

All other transfers are downstream and not considered to have an effect on the subsidiary. Therefore, the Equity in earnings of Rose Company balance can be verified as follows:

Company's reported net income—2018	$120,000
Recognition of 2017 intra-entity gross profit........................	10,000
Deferral of 2018 intra-entity gross profit	(17,000)
Excess amortization expense—2018 (see requirement [*b*])	(7,500)
Recognized subsidiary net income from consolidated perspective	105,500
Parent's ownership percentage..................................	80%
Equity income before downstream transfer effects	$ 84,400
Adjustments attributed to parent's ownership........................	
Deferral of intra-entity gain—land	(28,000)
Removal of excess depreciation (see requirement [*d*])	3,600
Equity in earnings of Rose Company—2018.........................	$ 60,000

f. Each of the 2018 consolidated totals for this business combination can be determined as follows:

Sales = $1,240,000. The parent's balance is added to the subsidiary's balance less the $160,000 in intra-entity transfers for the period.

Cost of Goods Sold = $745,000. The computation begins by adding the parent's balance to the subsidiary's balance less the $160,000 in intra-entity transfers for the period. The $10,000 intra-entity gross profit in inventory from the previous year is deducted to recognize this income currently. Next, the $17,000 ending intra-entity gross profit is added to cost of goods sold to defer the income until a later year when the goods are sold to an outside party.

Operating Expenses =$293,900. The parent's balance is added to the subsidiary's balance. Annual excess fair-value amortization of $7,500 [see requirement (*b*)] is also included. Excess depreciation of $3,600 resulting from the transfer of equipment [see requirement (*e*)] is removed.

Gain on Sale of Land = 0. This amount is eliminated for consolidation purposes because the transaction was intra-entity.

Equity in Earnings of Rose Company = 0. The equity earnings figure is removed and replaced with the subsidiary's actual revenues and expenses in the consolidated financial statements.

Net Income Attributable to Noncontrolling Interest = $21,100. Requirement (*e*) shows the subsidiary's net income from a consolidated perspective as $105,500 after adjustments for intra-entity upstream gains and excess fair-value amortization. Because outsiders hold 20 percent of the subsidiary, a $21,100 allocation ($105,500 × 20%) is made.

Consolidated Net Income = $201,100 computed as Sales less Cost of Goods Sold and Operating Expenses. The consolidated net income is then distributed: $21,100 to the noncontrolling interest and $180,000 to the parent company owners.

Retained Earnings, 1/1/18 = $620,000. The equity method has been applied; therefore, the parent's balance equals the consolidated total.

Dividends Declared = $55,000. Only the parent's dividends are shown in the consolidated statements. Distributions from the subsidiary to the parent are eliminated as intra-entity transfers. Any dividends distributable to the noncontrolling interest reduce the ending balance attributed to these outside owners.

Cash and Accounts Receivable = $708,000. The two balances are added after removal of the $50,000 intra-entity receivable created by the transfer of land.

Inventory = $603,400. The two balances are added after removal of the $17,000 ending intra-entity gross profit [see requirement (*c*)].

Investment in Rose Company = 0. The investment balance is eliminated and replaced with actual assets and liabilities of the subsidiary.

Land = $706,000. The two balances are added. The $28,000 intra-entity gain created by the transfer is removed.

Equipment = $480,000. The two balances are added. Because of the intra-entity transfer, $20,000 must also be included to adjust the $80,000 transfer price to the original $100,000 cost of the asset.

Accumulated Depreciation = $278,800. The balances are combined and adjusted for $52,400 to reinstate the historical balance for the equipment transferred across affiliates ($56,000 written off at date of transfer less $3,600 for the previous year's depreciation on the intra-entity gain). Then, an additional $3,600 is removed for the current year's depreciation on the intra-entity gain.

Trademark = $52,500. The amount from the original $75,000 acquisition-date excess fair-value allocation less three years' amortization at $7,500 per year.

Goodwill = $57,500. The amount from the original allocation of Rose's acquisition-date fair value.

Total Assets = $2,328,600. This figure is a summation of the preceding consolidated assets.

Liabilities = $785,000. The two balances are added after removal of the $50,000 intra-entity payable created by the transfer of land.

Noncontrolling Interest in Subsidiary, 12/31/18 = $198,600. This figure is composed of several different balances:

Rose 20% book value (adjusted for upstream intra-entity profits) at 1/1/18 . .	$164,000
20% of 1/1/18 unamortized excess fair-value allocation for Rose's net identifiable assets and goodwill ($117,500 × 20%)	23,500
Noncontrolling interest at 1/1/18	$187,500
2018 Rose net income allocation	21,100
Noncontrolling interest share of Rose dividends	(10,000)
December 31, 2018, balance	$198,600

Common Stock = $600,000. Only the parent company balance is reported within the consolidated statements.

Retained Earnings, 12/31/18 = $745,000. The retained earnings amount is found by adding the parent's (Daisy) share of consolidated net income to the beginning Retained Earnings balance and then subtracting the parent's dividends. All of these figures have been computed previously.

Total Liabilities and Equities = $2,328,600. This figure is the summation of all consolidated liabilities and equities.

g.

Consolidation Worksheet Entries to Adjust for Intra-Entity Transfers December 31, 2018

Inventory

Entry *G

Retained Earnings, 1/1/18—Subsidiary	10,000	
Cost of Goods Sold		10,000

To remove 2017 intra-entity gross profit from beginning balances of the current year. Because transfers were upstream, retained earnings of the subsidiary (as the original seller) are reduced. Balance is computed in requirement (c).

(continued)

Consolidation Worksheet Entries
to Adjust for Intra-Entity Transfers
December 31, 2018

Entry TI

Sales	160,000	
Cost of Goods Sold		160,000
To eliminate current year intra-entity transfer of inventory.		

Entry G

Cost of Goods Sold	17,000	
Inventory		17,000
To remove 2018 intra-entity gross profit from ending accounts of the current year. Balance is computed in requirement (c).		

Land

Entry TL

Gain on Sale of Land	28,000	
Land		28,000
To eliminate gross profit created on first day of current year by an intra-entity transfer of land.		

Equipment

Entry *TA

Equipment	20,000	
Investment in Rose Company	32,400	
Accumulated Depreciation		52,400
To remove remaining gain (as of January 1, 2018) created by intra-entity transfer of equipment and to adjust equipment and accumulated depreciation to historical cost figures.		

Equipment is increased from the $80,000 transfer price to $100,000 cost.

Accumulated depreciation of $56,000 was eliminated at time of transfer. Excess depreciation of $3,600 per year has been recorded for the prior year ($3,600); thus, the accumulated depreciation is now only $52,400 less than the cost-based figure.

The intra-entity gain on the transfer was $36,000 ($80,000 less $44,000). That figure has now been reduced by one year of excess depreciation ($3,600). Because the parent used the equity method and this transfer was downstream, the adjustment here is to the investment account rather than the parent's beginning Retained Earnings.

Entry ED

Accumulated Depreciation	3,600	
Operating Expenses (depreciation)		3,600
To eliminate the current year overstatement of depreciation created by inflated transfer price.		

Questions

1. Intra-entity transfers between the component companies of a business combination are quite common. Why do these intra-entity transactions occur so frequently?
2. Barker Company owns 80 percent of the outstanding voting stock of Walden Company. During the current year, intra-entity sales amount to $100,000. These transactions were made with a gross profit rate of 40 percent of the transfer price. In consolidating the two companies, what amount of these sales would be eliminated?
3. Padlock Corp. owns 90 percent of Safeco, Inc. During the year, Padlock sold 3,000 locking mechanisms to Safeco for $900,000. By the end of the year, Safeco had sold all but 500 of the locking mechanisms to outside parties. Padlock marks up the cost of its locking mechanisms by 60 percent in computing its sales price to affiliated and nonaffiliated customers. How much intra-entity profit remains in Safeco's inventory at year-end?
4. How are intra-entity inventory gross profits created, and what consolidation entries does the presence of these gross profits necessitate?

5. James, Inc., sells inventory to Matthews Company, a related party, at James's standard gross profit rate. At the current fiscal year-end, Matthews still holds some portion of this inventory. If consolidated financial statements are prepared, why are worksheet entries required in two different fiscal periods?
6. How do intra-entity profits present in any year affect the noncontrolling interest calculations?
7. A worksheet is being developed to consolidate Allegan, Incorporated, and Stark Company. These two organizations have made considerable intra-entity transactions. How would the consolidation process be affected if these transfers were downstream? How would consolidated financial statements be affected if these transfers were upstream?
8. King Company owns a 90 percent interest in the outstanding voting shares of Pawn Company. No excess fair-value amortization resulted from the acquisition. Pawn reports a net income of $110,000 for the current year. Intra-entity sales occur at regular intervals between the two companies. Intra-entity gross profits of $30,000 were present in the beginning inventory balances, whereas $60,000 in similar gross profits were recorded at year-end. What is the noncontrolling interest's share of consolidated net income?
9. When a subsidiary sells inventory to a parent, the intra-entity profit is removed from the subsidiary's net income for consolidation and reduces the income allocation to the noncontrolling interest. Is the profit permanently eliminated from the noncontrolling interest, or is it merely shifted from one period to the next? Explain.
10. The consolidation process applicable when intra-entity land transfers have occurred differs somewhat from that used for intra-entity inventory sales. What differences should be noted?
11. A subsidiary sells land to the parent company at a significant gain. The parent holds the land for two years and then sells it to an outside party, also for a gain. How does the business combination account for these events?
12. Why does an intra-entity sale of a depreciable asset (such as equipment or a building) require subsequent adjustments to depreciation expense within the consolidation process?
13. If a seller makes an intra-entity sale of a depreciable asset at a price above book value, the seller's beginning Retained Earnings is reduced when preparing each subsequent consolidation. Why does the amount of the adjustment change from year to year?

Problems

LO 5-1

1. What is the primary reason we defer financial statement recognition of gross profits on intra-entity sales for goods that remain within the consolidated entity at year-end?
   a. Revenues and COGS must be recognized for all intra-entity sales regardless of whether the sales are upstream or downstream.
   b. Intra-entity sales result in gross profit overstatements regardless of amounts remaining in ending inventory.
   c. Gross profits must be deferred indefinitely because sales among affiliates always remain in the consolidated group.
   d. When intra-entity sales remain in ending inventory, control of the goods has not changed.

LO 5-3

2. James Corporation owns 80 percent of Carl Corporation's common stock. During October, Carl sold merchandise to James for $250,000. At December 31, 40 percent of this merchandise remains in James's inventory. Gross profit percentages were 20 percent for James and 30 percent for Carl. The amount of intra-entity gross profit in inventory at December 31 that should be eliminated in the consolidation process is
   a. $24,000
   b. $30,000
   c. $20,000
   d. $75,000

LO 5-5

3. In computing the noncontrolling interest's share of consolidated net income, how should the subsidiary's net income be adjusted for intra-entity transfers?
   a. The subsidiary's reported net income is adjusted for the impact of upstream transfers prior to computing the noncontrolling interest's allocation.
   b. The subsidiary's reported net income is adjusted for the impact of all transfers prior to computing the noncontrolling interest's allocation.
   c. The subsidiary's reported net income is not adjusted for the impact of transfers prior to computing the noncontrolling interest's allocation.
   d. The subsidiary's reported net income is adjusted for the impact of downstream transfers prior to computing the noncontrolling interest's allocation.

LO 5-2, 5-3

4. Parkette, Inc., acquired a 60 percent interest in Skybox Company several years ago. During 2017, Skybox sold inventory costing $160,000 to Parkette for $200,000. A total of 18 percent of this inventory was not sold to outsiders until 2018. During 2018, Skybox sold inventory costing $297,500 to Parkette for $350,000. A total of 30 percent of this inventory was not sold to outsiders until 2019. In 2018, Parkette reported cost of goods sold of $607,500 while Skybox reported $450,000. What is the consolidated cost of goods sold in 2018?
   a. $698,950
   b. $720,000
   c. $1,066,050
   d. $716,050

LO 5-2, 5-3

5. Top Company holds 90 percent of Bottom Company's common stock. In the current year, Top reports sales of $800,000 and cost of goods sold of $600,000. For this same period, Bottom has sales of $300,000 and cost of goods sold of $180,000. During the current year, Top sold merchandise to Bottom for $100,000. The subsidiary still possesses 40 percent of this inventory at the current year-end. Top had established the transfer price based on its normal gross profit rate. What are the consolidated sales and cost of goods sold?
   a. $1,000,000 and $690,000
   b. $1,000,000 and $705,000
   c. $1,000,000 and $740,000
   d. $970,000 and $696,000

LO 5-2, 5-3, 5-5

6. Use the same information as in problem (5) except assume that the transfers were from Bottom Company to Top Company. What are the consolidated sales and cost of goods sold?
   a. $1,000,000 and $720,000
   b. $1,000,000 and $755,000
   c. $1,000,000 and $696,000
   d. $970,000 and $712,000

LO 5-3, 5-4, 5-5

7. Angela, Inc., holds a 90 percent interest in Corby Company. During 2017, Corby sold inventory costing $77,000 to Angela for $110,000. Of this inventory, $40,000 worth was not sold to outsiders until 2018. During 2018, Corby sold inventory costing $72,000 to Angela for $120,000. A total of $50,000 of this inventory was not sold to outsiders until 2019. In 2018, Angela reported separate net income of $150,000 while Corby's net income was $90,000 after excess amortizations. What is the noncontrolling interest in the 2018 income of the subsidiary?
   a. $8,000
   b. $8,200
   c. $9,000
   d. $9,800

LO 5-7

8. Dunn Corporation owns 100 percent of Grey Corporation's common stock. On January 2, 2017, Dunn sold to Grey $40,000 of machinery with a carrying amount of $30,000. Grey is depreciating the acquired machinery over a five-year remaining life by the straight-line method. The net adjustments to compute 2017 and 2018 consolidated net income would be an increase (decrease) of

	2017	2018
a.	$(8,000)	$2,000
b.	$(8,000)	–0–
c.	$(10,000)	$2,000
d.	$(10,000)	–0–

(AICPA adapted)

LO 5-7

9. Thomson Corporation owns 70 percent of the outstanding stock of Stayer, Incorporated. On January 1, 2016, Thomson acquired a building with a 10-year life for $460,000. Thomson depreciated the building on the straight-line basis assuming no salvage value. On January 1, 2018, Thomson sold this building to Stayer for $430,400. At that time, the building had a remaining life of eight years but still no expected salvage value. In preparing financial statements for 2018, how does this transfer affect the computation of consolidated net income?
   a. Net income is reduced by $62,400.
   b. Net income is reduced by $59,440.
   c. Net income is reduced by $70,200.
   d. Net income is reduced by $54,600.

Use the following data for Problems 10–15:

On January 1, Jarel acquired 80 percent of the outstanding voting stock of Suarez for $260,000 cash consideration. The remaining 20 percent of Suarez had an acquisition-date fair value of $65,000. On January 1, Suarez possessed equipment (five-year remaining life) that was undervalued on its books by $25,000. Suarez also had developed several secret formulas that Jarel assessed at $50,000. These formulas, although not recorded on Suarez's financial records, were estimated to have a 20-year future life.

As of December 31, the financial statements appeared as follows:

	Jarel	Suarez
Revenues	$ (300,000)	$(200,000)
Cost of goods sold	140,000	80,000
Expenses	20,000	10,000
Net income	$ (140,000)	$(110,000)
Retained earnings, 1/1	$ (300,000)	$(150,000)
Net income	(140,000)	(110,000)
Dividends declared	–0–	–0–
Retained earnings, 12/31	$ (440,000)	$(260,000)
Cash and receivables	$ 210,000	$ 90,000
Inventory	150,000	110,000
Investment in Suarez	260,000	–0–
Equipment (net)	440,000	300,000
Total assets	$ 1,060,000	$ 500,000
Liabilities	$ (420,000)	$(140,000)
Common stock	(200,000)	(100,000)
Retained earnings, 12/31	(440,000)	(260,000)
Total liabilities and equities	$(1,060,000)	$(500,000)

Included in the above statements, Jarel sold inventory costing $80,000 to Suarez for $100,000. Of these goods, Suarez still owns 60 percent on December 31.

LO 5-2

10. What is the total of consolidated revenues?
    a. $500,000
    b. $460,000
    c. $420,000
    d. $400,000

LO 5-2, 5-3

11. What is the total of consolidated cost of goods sold?
    a. $140,000
    b. $152,000
    c. $132,000
    d. $145,000

LO 3-1 (Chapter 3)

12. What is the total of consolidated expenses?
    a. $30,000
    b. $36,000
    c. $37,500
    d. $39,000

LO 5-5

13. What is the consolidated total of noncontrolling interest appearing on the balance sheet?
    a. $85,500
    b. $83,100
    c. $87,000
    d. $70,500

LO 5-7

14. What is the consolidated total for equipment (net) at December 31?
    a. $735,000.
    b. $740,000.
    c. $760,000.
    d. $765,000.

LO 5-3

15. What is the consolidated total for inventory at December 31?
    a. $240,000
    b. $248,000
    c. $250,000
    d. $260,000

LO 5-2, 5-3, 5-5

16. Following are several figures reported for Allister and Barone as of December 31, 2018:

	Allister	Barone
Inventory	$ 500,000	$300,000
Sales	1,000,000	800,000
Investment income	not given	
Cost of goods sold	500,000	400,000
Operating expenses	230,000	300,000

Allister acquired 90 percent of Barone in January 2017. In allocating the newly acquired subsidiary's fair value at the acquisition date, Allister noted that Barone had developed a customer list worth $78,000 that was unrecorded on its accounting records and had a 4-year remaining life. Any remaining excess fair value over Barone's book value was attributed to goodwill. During 2018, Barone sells inventory costing $130,000 to Allister for $180,000. Of this amount, 10 percent remains unsold in Allister's warehouse at year-end.

Determine balances for the following items that would appear on Allister's consolidated financial statements for 2018:

Inventory
Sales
Cost of Goods Sold
Operating Expenses
Net Income Attributable to Noncontrolling Interest

LO 5-3, 5-4, 5-5

17. On January 1, 2017, Corgan Company acquired 80 percent of the outstanding voting stock of Smashing, Inc., for a total of $980,000 in cash and other consideration. At the acquisition date, Smashing had common stock of $700,000, retained earnings of $250,000, and a noncontrolling interest fair value of $245,000. Corgan attributed the excess of fair value over Smashing's book value to various covenants with a 20-year remaining life. Corgan uses the equity method to account for its investment in Smashing.

During the next two years, Smashing reported the following:

	Net Income	Dividends Declared	Inventory Purchases from Corgan
2017	$150,000	$35,000	$100,000
2018	130,000	45,000	120,000

Corgan sells inventory to Smashing using a 60 percent markup on cost. At the end of 2017 and 2018, 40 percent of the current year purchases remain in Smashing's inventory.

a. Compute the equity method balance in Corgan's Investment in Smashing, Inc., account as of December 31, 2018.

b. Prepare the worksheet adjustments for the December 31, 2018, consolidation of Corgan and Smashing.

LO 5-1, 5-3, 5-4, 5-5, 5-6, 5-7

18. Placid Lake Corporation acquired 80 percent of the outstanding voting stock of Scenic, Inc., on January 1, 2017, when Scenic had a net book value of $400,000. Any excess fair value was assigned to intangible assets and amortized at a rate of $5,000 per year.

Placid Lake's 2018 net income before consideration of its relationship with Scenic (and before adjustments for intra-entity sales) was $300,000. Scenic reported net income of $110,000. Placid Lake declared $100,000 in dividends during this period; Scenic paid $40,000. At the end of 2018, selected figures from the two companies' balance sheets were as follows:

	Placid Lake	Scenic
Inventory	$140,000	$ 90,000
Land	600,000	200,000
Equipment (net)	400,000	300,000

During 2017, intra-entity sales of $90,000 (original cost of $54,000) were made. Only 20 percent of this inventory was still held within the consolidated entity at the end of 2017. In 2018, $120,000 in intra-entity sales were made with an original cost of $66,000. Of this merchandise, 30 percent had not been resold to outside parties by the end of the year.

Each of the following questions should be considered as an independent situation for the year 2018.

a. What is consolidated net income for Placid Lake and its subsidiary?

b. If the intra-entity sales were upstream, how would consolidated net income be allocated to the controlling and noncontrolling interest?

c. If the intra-entity sales were downstream, how would consolidated net income be allocated to the controlling and noncontrolling interest?

d. What is the consolidated balance in the ending Inventory account?

e. Assume that no intra-entity inventory sales occurred between Placid Lake and Scenic. Instead, in 2017, Scenic sold land costing $30,000 to Placid Lake for $50,000. On the 2018 consolidated balance sheet, what value should be reported for land?

f. Assume that no intra-entity inventory or land sales occurred between Placid Lake and Scenic. Instead, on January 1, 2017, Scenic sold equipment (that originally cost $100,000 but had a $60,000 book value on that date) to Placid Lake for $80,000. At the time of sale, the equipment had a remaining useful life of five years. What worksheet entries are made for a December 31, 2018, consolidation of these two companies to eliminate the impact of the intra-entity transfer? For 2018, what is the noncontrolling interest's share of Scenic's net income?

LO 5-2, 5-3, 5-4, 5-5

19. On January 1, 2017, Doone Corporation acquired 60 percent of the outstanding voting stock of Rockne Company for $300,000 consideration. At the acquisition date, the fair value of the 40 percent noncontrolling interest was $200,000 and Rockne's assets and liabilities had a collective net fair value of $500,000. Doone uses the equity method in its internal records to account for its investment in Rockne. Rockne reports net income of $160,000 in 2018. Since being acquired, Rockne has regularly supplied inventory to Doone at 25 percent more than cost. Sales to Doone amounted to $250,000 in 2017 and $300,000 in 2018. Approximately 30 percent of the inventory purchased during any one year is not used until the following year.

a. What is the noncontrolling interest's share of Rockne's 2018 income?

b. Prepare Doone's 2018 consolidation entries required by the intra-entity inventory transfers.

LO 5-3, 5-4, 5-5, 5-7

20. Protrade Corporation acquired 80 percent of the outstanding voting stock of Seacraft Company on January 1, 2017, for $612,000 in cash and other consideration. At the acquisition date, Protrade assessed Seacraft's identifiable assets and liabilities at a collective net fair value of $765,000 and the fair value of the 20 percent noncontrolling interest was $153,000. No excess fair value over book value amortization accompanied the acquisition.

The following selected account balances are from the individual financial records of these two companies as of December 31, 2018:

	Protrade	Seacraft
Sales	$880,000	$600,000
Cost of goods sold	410,000	317,000
Operating expenses	174,000	129,000
Retained earnings, 1/1/18	980,000	420,000
Inventory	370,000	144,000
Buildings (net)	382,000	181,000
Investment income	Not given	–0–

Each of the following problems is an independent situation:

a. Assume that Protrade sells Seacraft inventory at a markup equal to 60 percent of cost. Intra-entity transfers were $114,000 in 2017 and $134,000 in 2018. Of this inventory, Seacraft retained and then sold $52,000 of the 2017 transfers in 2018 and held $66,000 of the 2018 transfers until 2019.

Determine balances for the following items that would appear on consolidated financial statements for 2018:

Cost of Goods Sold
Inventory
Net Income Attributable to Noncontrolling Interest

b. Assume that Seacraft sells inventory to Protrade at a markup equal to 60 percent of cost. Intra-entity transfers were $74,000 in 2017 and $104,000 in 2018. Of this inventory, $45,000 of the 2017 transfers were retained and then sold by Protrade in 2018, whereas $59,000 of the 2018 transfers were held until 2019.

Determine balances for the following items that would appear on consolidated financial statements for 2018:

Cost of Goods Sold
Inventory
Net Income Attributable to Noncontrolling Interest

c. Protrade sells Seacraft a building on January 1, 2017, for $128,000, although its book value was only $74,000 on this date. The building had a five-year remaining life and was to be depreciated using the straight-line method with no salvage value.

Determine balances for the following items that would appear on consolidated financial statements for 2018:

Buildings (net)
Operating Expenses
Net Income Attributable to Noncontrolling Interest

LO 5-3, 5-4, 5-5

21. Akron, Inc., owns all outstanding stock of Toledo Corporation. Amortization expense of $15,000 per year for patented technology resulted from the original acquisition. For 2018, the companies had the following account balances:

	Akron	Toledo
Sales	$1,100,000	$600,000
Cost of goods sold	500,000	400,000
Operating expenses	400,000	220,000
Investment income	Not given	–0–
Dividends declared	80,000	30,000

Intra-entity sales of $320,000 occurred during 2017 and again in 2018. This merchandise cost $240,000 each year. Of the total transfers, $70,000 was still held on December 31, 2017, with $50,000 unsold on December 31, 2018.

a. For consolidation purposes, does the direction of the transfers (upstream or downstream) affect the balances to be reported here?

b. Prepare a consolidated income statement for the year ending December 31, 2018.

LO 5-7

22. On January 1, 2017, QuickPort Company acquired 90 percent of the outstanding voting stock of NetSpeed, Inc., for $810,000 in cash and stock options. At the acquisition date, NetSpeed had common stock of $800,000 and Retained Earnings of $40,000. The acquisition-date fair value of the 10 percent noncontrolling interest was $90,000. QuickPort attributed the $60,000 excess of NetSpeed's fair value over book value to a database with a five-year remaining life.

During the next two years, NetSpeed reported the following:

	Net Income	Dividends Declared
2017	$ 80,000	$8,000
2018	115,000	8,000

On July 1, 2017, QuickPort sold communication equipment to NetSpeed for $42,000. The equipment originally cost $48,000 and had accumulated depreciation of $9,000 and an estimated remaining life of three years at the date of the intra-entity transfer.

a. Compute the equity method balance in QuickPort's Investment in NetSpeed, Inc., account as of December 31, 2018.

b. Prepare the worksheet adjustments for the December 31, 2018, consolidation of QuickPort and NetSpeed.

LO 5-7

23. Padre holds 100 percent of the outstanding shares of Sonora. On January 1, 2016, Padre transferred equipment to Sonora for $95,000. The equipment had cost $130,000 originally but had a $50,000 book value and five-year remaining life at the date of transfer. Depreciation expense is computed according to the straight-line method with no salvage value.

Consolidated financial statements for 2018 currently are being prepared. What worksheet entries are needed in connection with the consolidation of this asset? Assume that the parent applies the partial equity method.

LO 5-7

24. On January 1, 2018, Ackerman sold equipment to Brannigan (a wholly owned subsidiary) for $200,000 in cash. The equipment had originally cost $180,000 but had a book value of only $110,000 when transferred. On that date, the equipment had a five-year remaining life. Depreciation expense is computed using the straight-line method.

Ackerman reported $300,000 in net income in 2018 (not including any investment income) while Brannigan reported $98,000. Ackerman attributed any excess acquisition-date fair value to Brannigan's unpatented technology, which was amortized at a rate of $4,000 per year.

a. What is consolidated net income for 2018?

b. What is the parent's share of consolidated net income for 2018 if Ackerman owns only 90 percent of Brannigan?

c. What is the parent's share of consolidated net income for 2018 if Ackerman owns only 90 percent of Brannigan and the equipment transfer was upstream?

d. What is the consolidated net income for 2019 if Ackerman reports $320,000 (does not include investment income) and Brannigan $108,000 in income? Assume that Brannigan is a wholly owned subsidiary and the equipment transfer was downstream.

LO 5-2, 5-3, 5-4, 5-7

25. Allison Corporation acquired 90 percent of Bretton on January 1, 2016. Of Bretton's total acquisition-date fair value, $60,000 was allocated to undervalued equipment (with a 10-year remaining life) and $80,000 was attributed to franchises (to be written off over a 20-year period).

Since the takeover, Bretton has transferred inventory to its parent as follows:

Year	Cost	Transfer Price	Remaining at Year-End
2016	$45,000	$90,000	$30,000 (at transfer price)
2017	48,000	80,000	35,000 (at transfer price)
2018	69,000	92,000	50,000 (at transfer price)

On January 1, 2017, Allison sold Bretton a building for $50,000 that had originally cost $70,000 but had only a $30,000 book value at the date of transfer. The building is estimated to have a five-year remaining life (straight-line depreciation is used with no salvage value).

Selected figures from the December 31, 2018, trial balances of these two companies are as follows:

	Allison	Bretton
Sales	$700,000	$400,000
Cost of goods sold	440,000	220,000
Operating expenses	120,000	80,000
Investment income	Not given	–0–
Inventory	210,000	90,000
Equipment (net)	140,000	110,000
Buildings (net)	350,000	190,000

Determine consolidated totals for each of these account balances.

LO 5-3, 5-4, 5-5, 5-7

26. On January 1, 2018, Sledge had common stock of $120,000 and retained earnings of $260,000. During that year, Sledge reported sales of $130,000, cost of goods sold of $70,000, and operating expenses of $40,000.

On January 1, 2016, Percy, Inc., acquired 80 percent of Sledge's outstanding voting stock. At that date, $60,000 of the acquisition-date fair value was assigned to unrecorded contracts (with a 20-year life) and $20,000 to an undervalued building (with a 10-year remaining life).

In 2017, Sledge sold inventory costing $9,000 to Percy for $15,000. Of this merchandise, Percy continued to hold $5,000 at year-end. During 2018, Sledge transferred inventory costing $11,000 to Percy for $20,000. Percy still held half of these items at year-end.

On January 1, 2017, Percy sold equipment to Sledge for $12,000. This asset originally cost $16,000 but had a January 1, 2017, book value of $9,000. At the time of transfer, the equipment's remaining life was estimated to be five years.

Percy has properly applied the equity method to the investment in Sledge.

a. Prepare worksheet entries to consolidate these two companies as of December 31, 2018.

b. Compute the net income attributable to the noncontrolling interest for 2018.

LO 5-1, 5-2, 5-3, 5-4, 5-5, 5-7

27. Pitino acquired 90 percent of Brey's outstanding shares on January 1, 2016, in exchange for $342,000 in cash. The subsidiary's stockholders' equity accounts totaled $326,000 and the noncontrolling interest had a fair value of $38,000 on that day. However, a building (with a nine-year remaining life) in Brey's accounting records was undervalued by $18,000. Pitino assigned the rest of the excess fair value over book value to Brey's patented technology (six-year remaining life).

Brey reported net income from its own operations of $64,000 in 2016 and $80,000 in 2017. Brey declared dividends of $19,000 in 2016 and $23,000 in 2017.

Brey sells inventory to Pitino as follows:

Year	Cost to Brey	Transfer Price to Pitino	Inventory Remaining at Year-End (at transfer price)
2016	$69,000	$115,000	$25,000
2017	81,000	135,000	37,500
2018	92,800	160,000	50,000

At December 31, 2018, Pitino owes Brey $16,000 for inventory acquired during the period.

The following separate account balances are for these two companies for December 31, 2018, and the year then ended. Credits are indicated by parentheses.

	Pitino	Brey
Sales revenues	$ (862,000)	$(366,000)
Cost of goods sold	515,000	209,000
Expenses	185,400	67,000
Equity in earnings of Brey	(68,400)	–0–
Net income	$ (230,000)	$ (90,000)
Retained earnings, 1/1/18	$ (488,000)	$(278,000)
Net income (above)	(230,000)	(90,000)
Dividends declared	136,000	27,000
Retained earnings, 12/31/18	$ (582,000)	$(341,000)
Cash and receivables	$ 146,000	$ 98,000
Inventory	255,000	136,000
Investment in Brey	450,000	–0–
Land, buildings, and equipment (net)	964,000	328,000
Total assets	$ 1,815,000	$ 562,000
Liabilities	$ (718,000)	$ (71,000)
Common stock	(515,000)	(150,000)
Retained earnings, 12/31/18	(582,000)	(341,000)
Total liabilities and equities	$(1,815,000)	$(562,000)

Answer each of the following questions:

a. What was the annual amortization resulting from the acquisition-date fair-value allocations?

b. Were the intra-entity transfers upstream or downstream?

c. What intra-entity gross profit in inventory existed as of January 1, 2018?

d. What intra-entity gross profit in inventory existed as of December 31, 2018?

e. What amounts make up the $68,400 Equity Earnings of Brey account balance for 2018?

f. What is the net income attributable to the noncontrolling interest for 2018?

g. What amounts make up the $450,000 Investment in Brey account balance as of December 31, 2018?

h. Prepare the 2018 worksheet entry to eliminate the subsidiary's beginning owners' equity balances.

i. Without preparing a worksheet or consolidation entries, determine the consolidation balances for these two companies.

LO 5-2, 5-3, 5-4

28. ProForm acquired 70 percent of ClipRite on June 30, 2017, for $910,000 in cash. Based on ClipRite's acquisition-date fair value, an unrecorded intangible of $400,000 was recognized and is being amortized at the rate of $10,000 per year. No goodwill was recognized in the acquisition.

The noncontrolling interest fair value was assessed at $390,000 at the acquisition date. The 2018 financial statements are as follows:

	ProForm	ClipRite
Sales	$ (800,000)	$ (600,000)
Cost of goods sold	535,000	400,000
Operating expenses	100,000	100,000
Dividend income	(35,000)	–0–
Net income	$ (200,000)	$ (100,000)
Retained earnings, 1/1/18	$ (1,300,000)	$ (850,000)
Net income	(200,000)	(100,000)
Dividends declared	100,000	50,000
Retained earnings, 12/31/18	$ (1,400,000)	$ (900,000)
Cash and receivables	$ 400,000	$ 300,000
Inventory	290,000	700,000
Investment in ClipRite	910,000	–0–
Fixed assets	1,000,000	600,000
Accumulated depreciation	(300,000)	(200,000)
Totals	$ 2,300,000	$ 1,400,000
Liabilities	$ (600,000)	$ (400,000)
Common stock	(300,000)	(100,000)
Retained earnings, 12/31/18	(1,400,000)	(900,000)
Totals	$ (2,300,000)	$(1,400,000)

ProForm sold ClipRite inventory costing $72,000 during the last six months of 2017 for $120,000. At year-end, 30 percent remained. ProForm sells ClipRite inventory costing $200,000 during 2018 for $250,000. At year-end, 10 percent is left. With these facts, determine the consolidated balances for the following:

Sales
Cost of Goods Sold
Operating Expenses
Dividend Income
Net Income Attributable to Noncontrolling Interest
Inventory
Noncontrolling Interest in Subsidiary, 12/31/18

LO 5-2, 5-3, 5-4, 5-5

29. Compute the balances in problem (28) again, assuming that all intra-entity transfers were made from ClipRite to ProForm.

LO 5-1, 5-2, 5-3, 5-4, 5-5, 5-6, 5-7

30. Following are financial statements for Moore Company and Kirby Company for 2018:

	Moore	Kirby
Sales	$ (800,000)	$ (600,000)
Cost of goods sold	500,000	400,000
Operating and interest expenses	100,000	160,000
Net income	$ (200,000)	$ (40,000)
Retained earnings, 1/1/18	$ (990,000)	$ (550,000)
Net income	(200,000)	(40,000)
Dividends declared	130,000	–0–
Retained earnings, 12/31/18	$(1,060,000)	$ (590,000)

(continued)

	Moore	Kirby
Cash and receivables	$ 217,000	$ 180,000
Inventory	224,000	160,000
Investment in Kirby	657,000	–0–
Equipment (net)	600,000	420,000
Buildings	1,000,000	650,000
Accumulated depreciation—buildings	(100,000)	(200,000)
Other assets	200,000	100,000
Total assets	$ 2,798,000	$ 1,310,000
Liabilities	$(1,138,000)	$ (570,000)
Common stock	(600,000)	(150,000)
Retained earnings, 12/31/18	(1,060,000)	(590,000)
Total liabilities and equity	$(2,798,000)	$(1,310,000)

- Moore purchased 90 percent of Kirby on January 1, 2017, for $657,000 in cash. On that date, the 10 percent noncontrolling interest was assessed to have a $73,000 fair value. Also at the acquisition date, Kirby held equipment (four-year remaining life) undervalued in its financial records by $20,000 and interest-bearing liabilities (five-year remaining life) overvalued by $40,000. The rest of the excess fair over book value was assigned to previously unrecognized brand names and amortized over a 10-year life.
- During 2017 Kirby reported a net income of $80,000 and declared no dividends.
- Each year Kirby sells Moore inventory at a 20 percent gross profit rate. Intra-entity sales were $145,000 in 2017 and $160,000 in 2018. On January 1, 2018, 30 percent of the 2017 transfers were still on hand, and on December 31, 2018, 40 percent of the 2018 transfers remained.
- Moore sold Kirby a building on January 2, 2017. It had cost Moore $100,000 but had $90,000 in accumulated depreciation at the time of this transfer. The price was $25,000 in cash. At that time, the building had a five-year remaining life.

Determine all consolidated balances either computationally or by using a worksheet.

LO 5-2, 5-3, 5-4, 5-5

eXcel

31. On January 1, 2017, McIlroy, Inc., acquired a 60 percent interest in the common stock of Stinson, Inc., for $372,000. Stinson's book value on that date consisted of common stock of $100,000 and retained earnings of $220,000. Also, the acquisition-date fair value of the 40 percent noncontrolling interest was $248,000. The subsidiary held patents (with a 10-year remaining life) that were undervalued within the company's accounting records by $70,000 and an unrecorded customer list (15-year remaining life) assessed at a $45,000 fair value. Any remaining excess acquisition-date fair value was assigned to goodwill. Since acquisition, McIlroy has applied the equity method to its Investment in Stinson account and no goodwill impairment has occurred. At year end, there are no intra-entity payables or receivables.

Intra-entity inventory sales between the two companies have been made as follows:

Year	Cost to McIlroy	Transfer Price to Stinson	Ending Balance (at transfer price)
2017	$120,000	$150,000	$50,000
2018	112,000	160,000	40,000

The individual financial statements for these two companies as of December 31, 2018, and the year then ended follow:

	McIlroy, Inc.	Stinson, Inc.
Sales	$ (700,000)	$(335,000)
Cost of goods sold	460,000	205,000
Operating expenses	188,000	70,000
Equity in earnings in Stinson	(28,000)	–0–
Net income	$ (80,000)	$ (60,000)

	McIlroy, Inc.	Stinson, Inc.
Retained earnings, 1/1/18	$ (695,000)	$ (280,000)
Net income	(80,000)	(60,000)
Dividends declared	45,000	15,000
Retained earnings, 12/31/18	$ (730,000)	$ (325,000)
Cash and receivables	$ 248,000	$ 148,000
Inventory	233,000	129,000
Investment in Stinson	411,000	–0–
Buildings (net)	308,000	202,000
Equipment (net)	220,000	86,000
Patents (net)	–0–	20,000
Total assets	$ 1,420,000	$ 585,000
Liabilities	$ (390,000)	$ (160,000)
Common stock	(300,000)	(100,000)
Retained earnings, 12/31/18	(730,000)	(325,000)
Total liabilities and equities	$(1,420,000)	$ (585,000)

a. Show how McIlroy determined the $411,000 Investment in Stinson account balance. Assume that McIlroy defers 100 percent of downstream intra-entity profits against its share of Stinson's income.

b. Prepare a consolidated worksheet to determine appropriate balances for external financial reporting as of December 31, 2018.

LO 5-2, 5-3, 5-4, 5-5

excel

32. On January 1, 2016, Plymouth Corporation acquired 80 percent of the outstanding voting stock of Sander Company in exchange for $1,200,000 cash. At that time, although Sander's book value was $925,000, Plymouth assessed Sander's total business fair value at $1,500,000. Since that time, Sander has neither issued nor reacquired any shares of its own stock.

The book values of Sander's individual assets and liabilities approximated their acquisition-date fair values except for the patent account, which was undervalued by $350,000. The undervalued patents had a five-year remaining life at the acquisition date. Any remaining excess fair value was attributed to goodwill. No goodwill impairments have occurred.

Sander regularly sells inventory to Plymouth. Below are details of the intra-entity inventory sales for the past three years:

Year	Intra-Entity Sales	Intra-Entity Ending Inventory at Transfer Price	Gross Profit Rate on Intra-Entity Inventory Transfers
2016	$125,000	$ 80,000	25%
2017	220,000	125,000	28
2018	300,000	160,000	25

Separate financial statements for these two companies as of December 31, 2018, follow:

	Plymouth	Sander
Revenues	$(1,740,000)	$ (950,000)
Cost of goods sold	820,000	500,000
Depreciation expense	104,000	85,000
Amortization expense	220,000	120,000
Interest expense	20,000	15,000
Equity in earnings of Sander	(124,000)	–0–
Net income	$ (700,000)	$ (230,000)

(continued)

	Plymouth	Sander
Retained earnings 1/1/18	$(2,800,000)	$ (345,000)
Net income	(700,000)	(230,000)
Dividends declared	200,000	25,000
Retained earnings, 12/31/18	$(3,300,000)	$ (550,000)
Cash	$ 535,000	$ 115,000
Accounts receivable	575,000	215,000
Inventory	990,000	800,000
Investment in Sander	1,420,000	–0–
Buildings and equipment	1,025,000	863,000
Patents	950,000	107,000
Total assets	$ 5,495,000	$ 2,100,000
Accounts payable	$ (450,000)	$ (200,000)
Notes payable	(545,000)	(450,000)
Common stock	(900,000)	(800,000)
Additional paid-in capital	(300,000)	(100,000)
Retained earnings, 12/31/18	(3,300,000)	(550,000)
Total liabilities and stockholders' equity	$(5,495,000)	$(2,100,000)

a. Prepare a schedule that calculates the Equity in Earnings of Sander account balance.

b. Prepare a worksheet to arrive at consolidated figures for external reporting purposes. At year-end, there are no intra-entity payables or receivables.

LO 5-2, 5-3, 5-4, 5-5, 5-7

33. On January 1, 2016, Monica Company acquired 70 percent of Young Company's outstanding common stock for $665,000. The fair value of the noncontrolling interest at the acquisition date was $285,000. Young reported stockholders' equity accounts on that date as follows:

Common stock—$10 par value	$300,000
Additional paid-in capital.	90,000
Retained earnings.	410,000

In establishing the acquisition value, Monica appraised Young's assets and ascertained that the accounting records undervalued a building (with a five-year remaining life) by $50,000. Any remaining excess acquisition-date fair value was allocated to a franchise agreement to be amortized over 10 years.

During the subsequent years, Young sold Monica inventory at a 30 percent gross profit rate. Monica consistently resold this merchandise in the year of acquisition or in the period immediately following. Transfers for the three years after this business combination was created amounted to the following:

Year	Transfer Price	Inventory Remaining at Year-End (at transfer price)
2016	$60,000	$10,000
2017	80,000	12,000
2018	90,000	18,000

In addition, Monica sold Young several pieces of fully depreciated equipment on January 1, 2017, for $36,000. The equipment had originally cost Monica $50,000. Young plans to depreciate these assets over a six-year period.

In 2018, Young earns a net income of $160,000 and declares and pays $50,000 in cash dividends. These figures increase the subsidiary's Retained Earnings to a $740,000 balance at the end of 2018. During this same year, Monica reported dividend income of $35,000 and an investment account containing the initial value balance of $665,000. No changes in Young's common stock accounts have occurred since Monica's acquisition.

Prepare the 2018 consolidation worksheet entries for Monica and Young. In addition, compute the net income attributable to the noncontrolling interest for 2018.

LO 5-2, 5-3, 5-4, 5-5, 5-7

34. Assume the same basic information as presented in problem (33) except that Monica employs the equity method of accounting. Hence, it reports $102,740 investment income for 2018 with an Investment account balance of $826,220. Under these circumstances, prepare the worksheet entries required for the consolidation of Monica Company and Young Company.

LO 5-1, 5-2, 5-3, 5-4, 5-5, 5-6, 5-7

eXcel

35. The individual financial statements for Gibson Company and Keller Company for the year ending December 31, 2018, follow. Gibson acquired a 60 percent interest in Keller on January 1, 2017, in exchange for various considerations totaling $570,000. At the acquisition date, the fair value of the noncontrolling interest was $380,000 and Keller's book value was $850,000. Keller had developed internally a customer list that was not recorded on its books but had an acquisition-date fair value of $100,000. This intangible asset is being amortized over 20 years.

Gibson sold Keller land with a book value of $60,000 on January 2, 2017, for $100,000. Keller still holds this land at the end of the current year.

Keller regularly transfers inventory to Gibson. In 2017, it shipped inventory costing $100,000 to Gibson at a price of $150,000. During 2018, intra-entity shipments totaled $200,000, although the original cost to Keller was only $140,000. In each of these years, 20 percent of the merchandise was not resold to outside parties until the period following the transfer. Gibson owes Keller $40,000 at the end of 2018.

	Gibson Company	Keller Company
Sales	$ (800,000)	$ (500,000)
Cost of goods sold	500,000	300,000
Operating expenses	100,000	60,000
Equity in earnings of Keller	(84,000)	–0–
Net income	$ (284,000)	$ (140,000)
Retained earnings, 1/1/18	$(1,116,000)	$ (620,000)
Net income (above)	(284,000)	(140,000)
Dividends declared	115,000	60,000
Retained earnings, 12/31/18	$(1,285,000)	$ (700,000)
Cash	$ 177,000	$ 90,000
Accounts receivable	356,000	410,000
Inventory	440,000	320,000
Investment in Keller	726,000	–0–
Land	180,000	390,000
Buildings and equipment (net)	496,000	300,000
Total assets	$ 2,375,000	$ 1,510,000
Liabilities	$ (480,000)	$ (400,000)
Common stock	(610,000)	(320,000)
Additional paid-in capital	–0–	(90,000)
Retained earnings, 12/31/18	(1,285,000)	(700,000)
Total liabilities and equities	$(2,375,000)	$(1,510,000)

a. Prepare a worksheet to consolidate the separate 2018 financial statements for Gibson and Keller.

b. How would the consolidation entries in requirement (*a*) have differed if Gibson had sold a building with a $60,000 book value (cost of $140,000) to Keller for $100,000 instead of land, as the problem reports? Assume that the building had a 10-year remaining life at the date of transfer.

LO 5-2, 5-3, 5-4, 5-6

36. On January 1, 2017, Panther, Inc., issued securities with a total fair value of $577,000 for 100 percent of Stark Corporation's outstanding ownership shares. Stark has long supplied inventory to Panther. The companies expect to achieve synergies with production scheduling and product development with this combination.

Although Stark's book value at the acquisition date was $300,000, the fair value of its trademarks was assessed to be $45,000 more than their carrying amounts. Additionally, Stark's patented technology was undervalued in its accounting records by $232,000. The trademarks were considered to have indefinite lives, and the estimated remaining life of the patented technology was eight years.

In 2017, Stark sold Panther inventory costing $75,000 for $125,000. As of December 31, 2017, Panther had resold 74 percent of this inventory. In 2018, Panther bought from Stark $140,000 of inventory that had an original cost of $70,000. At the end of 2018, Panther held $38,000 (transfer price) of inventory acquired from Stark, all from its 2018 purchases.

During 2018, Panther sold Stark a parcel of land for $88,000 and recorded a gain of $16,000 on the sale. Stark still owes Panther $62,000 (current liability) related to the land sale.

At the end of 2018, Panther and Stark prepared the following statements in preparation for consolidation.

	Panther, Inc.	Stark Corporation
Revenues	$ (710,000)	$ (360,000)
Cost of goods sold	305,000	189,000
Other operating expenses	167,000	81,000
Gain on sale of land	(16,000)	–0–
Equity in Stark's earnings	(39,000)	–0–
Net income	$ (293,000)	$ (90,000)
Retained earnings, 1/1/18	$ (367,000)	$ (292,000)
Net income	(293,000)	(90,000)
Dividends declared	80,000	25,000
Retained earnings, 12/31/18	$ (580,000)	$(357,000)
Cash and receivables	$ 102,000	$ 154,000
Inventory	311,000	110,000
Investment in Stark	691,000	–0–
Trademarks	–0–	58,000
Land, buildings, and equip. (net)	638,000	280,000
Patented technology	–0–	125,000
Total assets	$ 1,742,000	$ 727,000
Liabilities	$ (462,000)	$ (220,000)
Common stock	(400,000)	(100,000)
Additional paid-in capital	(300,000)	(50,000)
Retained earnings, 12/31/18	(580,000)	(357,000)
Total liabilities and equity	$(1,742,000)	$ (727,000)

a. Show how Panther computed its $39,000 equity in Stark's earnings balance.

b. Prepare a 2018 consolidated worksheet for Panther and Stark.

Develop Your Skills

EXCEL CASE

CPA skills

On January 1, 2017, James Company purchased 100 percent of the outstanding voting stock of Nolan, Inc., for $1,000,000 in cash and other consideration. At the purchase date, Nolan had common stock of $500,000 and retained earnings of $185,000. James attributed the excess of acquisition-date fair value over Nolan's book value to a trade name with an estimated 25-year remaining useful life. James uses the equity method to account for its investment in Nolan.

During the next two years, Nolan reported the following:

	Income	Dividends Declared	Inventory Transfers to James at Transfer Price
2017	$78,000	$25,000	$190,000
2018	85,000	27,000	210,000

Nolan sells inventory to James after a markup based on a gross profit rate. At the end of 2017 and 2018, 30 percent of the current year purchases remain in James's inventory.

Required

Create an Excel spreadsheet that computes the following:

1. Equity method balance in James' Investment in Nolan, Inc., account as of December 31, 2018.
2. Worksheet adjustments for the December 31, 2018, consolidation of James and Nolan.

Formulate your solution so that Nolan's gross profit rate on sales to James is treated as a variable.

ANALYSIS AND RESEARCH CASE: ACCOUNTING INFORMATION AND SALARY NEGOTIATIONS

CPA skills

Hamilton Hawks Players' Association and Mr. Sideline, the CEO and majority owner of Hamilton Hawks Soccer, Inc, ask your help in resolving a salary dispute. Mr. Sideline presents the following income statement to the players' representatives.

HAMILTON HAWKS SOCCER, INC.
Income Statement

Ticket revenues		$ 3,500,000
Stadium rent expense	$2,500,000	
Ticket expense	30,000	
Promotion expense	80,000	
Player salaries	700,000	
Staff salaries and miscellaneous	265,000	3,575,000
Net income (loss)		$ (75,000)

The players contend that their salaries are below market and a raise is warranted. Mr. Sideline argues that the Hamilton Hawks really lose money and, until ticket revenues increase, a salary hike is out of the question.

As a result of your inquiry, you discover that Hamilton Hawks Soccer Company owns 85 percent of the voting stock in Hawks Stadium, Inc. This venue is specifically designed for soccer and is where the Hawks play their entire home game schedule. However, Mr. Sideline does not wish to consider the profits of Hawks Stadium in the negotiations with the players. He claims that "the stadium is really a separate business entity that was purchased separately from the team and therefore does not concern the players. On top of that, we allocate all the ticket revenues to the team's income statement."

The Hawks Stadium income statement appears as follows:

HAWKS STADIUM, INC.
Income Statement

Stadium rent revenue	$2,500,000	
Concession revenue	875,000	
Parking revenue	95,000	$3,470,000
Cost of goods sold	270,000	
Depreciation expense	90,000	
Grounds maintenance expense	410,000	
Staff salaries and miscellaneous	200,000	970,000
Net income (loss)		$2,500,000

Required

1. What advice would you provide the negotiating parties regarding the issue of considering the Hawks Stadium income statement in their discussions? What authoritative literature could you cite in supporting your advice?
2. What other pertinent information would you need to provide a specific recommendation regarding players' salaries?

chapter 6

Variable Interest Entities, Intra-Entity Debt, Consolidated Cash Flows, and Other Issues

The consolidation of financial information can be a highly complex process often encompassing a number of practical challenges. This chapter examines the procedures required by several additional issues:

- Variable interest entities.
- Intra-entity debt.
- Subsidiary preferred stock.
- The consolidated statement of cash flows.
- Computation of consolidated earnings per share.
- Subsidiary stock transactions.

Variable interest entities emerged over the past two decades as a new type of business structure that provided effective control of one firm by another without overt ownership. In response to the evolving nature of control relationships among firms, the FASB expanded its definition of control beyond the long-standing criterion of a majority voting interest to include control exercised through variable interests. This topic and some of the more traditional advanced business combination subjects listed above provide for further exploration of the complexities faced by the financial reporting community in providing relevant and reliable information to users of consolidated financial reports.

Learning Objectives

After studying this chapter, you should be able to:

LO 6-1 Describe a variable interest entity, a primary beneficiary, and the factors used to decide when a variable interest entity is subject to consolidation.

LO 6-2 Demonstrate the process to consolidate a primary beneficiary with a variable interest entity.

LO 6-3 Demonstrate the consolidation procedures to eliminate all intra-entity debt accounts and recognize any associated gain or loss created whenever one company acquires an affiliate's debt instrument from an outside party.

LO 6-4 Understand that subsidiary preferred stock not owned by the parent is a component of the noncontrolling interest and is initially measured at acquisition-date fair value.

LO 6-5 Prepare a consolidated statement of cash flows.

LO 6-6 Compute basic and diluted earnings per share for a business combination.

LO 6-7 Demonstrate the accounting effects of subsidiary stock transactions on the parent's financial records and consolidated financial statements.

Consolidation of Variable Interest Entities

Several decades ago, many firms began establishing separate business structures to help finance their operations at favorable rates. These structures became commonly known as *special purpose entities* (SPEs), *special purpose vehicles,* or *off-balance-sheet structures*. In this text, we refer to all such entities collectively as *variable interest entities,* or VIEs. Many firms routinely included their VIEs in their consolidated financial reports. However, others sought to avoid consolidation.

VIEs can help accomplish legitimate business purposes. Nonetheless, their use was widely criticized in the aftermath of Enron Corporation's 2001 collapse. Because many firms avoided consolidation and used VIEs for off-balance sheet financing, such entities were often characterized as

LO 6-1

Describe a variable interest entity, a primary beneficiary, and the factors used to decide when a variable interest entity is subject to consolidation.

vehicles to hide debt and mislead investors. Other critics observed that firms with variable interests recorded questionable profits on sales to their VIEs that were not arm's-length transactions.[1] The FASB ASC "Variable Interest Entities" sections within the "Consolidations" Topic were issued in response to such financial reporting abuses.

What Is a VIE?

A VIE can take the form of a trust, partnership, joint venture, or corporation although sometimes it has neither independent management nor employees. Most are established for valid business purposes, and transactions involving VIEs have become widespread. Common examples of VIE activities include transfers of financial assets, leasing, hedging financial instruments, research and development, and other arrangements. An enterprise often creates a VIE to accomplish a well-defined and limited business activity and to provide low-cost financing.

Low-cost financing of asset purchases is frequently a main benefit available through VIEs. Rather than engaging in the transaction directly, a business enterprise may establish a VIE to purchase and finance an asset acquisition. The VIE then leases the asset back to the business enterprise that established the VIE. This strategy saves the business enterprise money because the VIE is often eligible for a lower interest rate. This advantage is achieved for several reasons. First, the VIE typically operates with a very limited set of assets—in many cases just one asset. By isolating an asset in a VIE, the asset's risk is isolated from the business enterprise's overall risk. Thus the VIE creditors remain protected by the specific collateral in the asset. Second, the governing documents can strictly limit the actions of a VIE. These limits further protect lenders by preventing the VIE from engaging in any activities not specified in its agreements. As a major public accounting firm noted,

> The borrower/transferor gains access to a source of funds less expensive than would otherwise be available. This advantage derives from isolating the assets in an entity prohibited from undertaking any other business activity or taking on any additional debt, thereby creating a better security interest in the assets for the lender/investor.[2]

Because governing agreements limit activities and decision making in most VIEs, ownership of a VIE's common stock typically does not provide control of the VIE. In fact, the enterprise that created the VIE may own very little, if any, of the VIE's voting stock. Prior to current consolidation requirements for VIEs, many enterprises left such entities unconsolidated in their financial reports because technically they did not own a majority of the entity's voting stock. In utilizing the VIE as a conduit to provide financing, the related assets and debt were effectively removed from the enterprise's balance sheet.

In general, the party that primarily benefits (or risks losses) from the economic activities of the VIE and has the power to direct the VIE's activities is deemed to have a controlling financial interest in the VIE. We use the term **primary beneficiary** to designate the party with such financial control. The primary beneficiary (most often a business) typically exercises its financial control through governance documents or other contractual agreements that provide it with decision-making authority over the VIE. Once identified, the primary beneficiary must consolidate in its financial statements the VIE's assets, liabilities, revenues, expenses, and noncontrolling interest.

Characteristics of Variable Interest Entities

Similar to most business entities, VIEs generally have assets, liabilities, and investors with equity interests. Unlike most businesses, because a VIE's activities and decision-making can be strictly limited, the role of the equity investors can be fairly minor. The VIE may have been created specifically by the primary beneficiary to provide it with low-cost financing.

[1] In its 2001 fourth quarter 10-Q, Enron recorded earnings restatements of more than $400 million related to its failure to properly consolidate several of its SPEs (e.g., Chewco and LJM2). Enron also admitted an improper omission of $700 million of its SPE's debt. Within a month of the restatements, Enron filed for bankruptcy.

[2] KPMG, "Defining Issues: New Accounting for SPEs," March 1, 2002.

Thus, the equity investors may serve simply as a technical requirement to allow the VIE to function as a legal entity. Because they bear relatively low economic risk, equity investors may be provided only a small rate of return.

The small equity investments in a VIE normally are insufficient to induce lenders to provide financing for the VIE. As a result, another party (e.g., the primary beneficiary) must contribute substantial resources—often loans and/or guarantees—to enable the VIE to secure additional financing needed to accomplish its purpose. For example, the primary beneficiary may guarantee the VIE's debt, thus assuming the risk of default. Other contractual arrangements may limit returns to equity holders while participation rights provide increased profit potential and risks to the primary beneficiary. Risks and rewards such as these cause the primary beneficiary's economic interest to vary depending on the created entity's success—hence the term **variable interest entity**. In contrast to a traditional entity, a VIE's risks and rewards frequently are distributed not according to stock ownership but according to other variable interests. Exhibit 6.1 describes variable interests further and provides several examples.

Variable interests increase a firm's risk as the resources it provides (or guarantees) to the VIE increase. With increased risks come incentives to restrict the VIE's decision making. In fact, a firm with variable interests will regularly limit the equity investors' power through the VIE's governance documents. As noted by GAAP literature,

> If the total equity investment at risk is not sufficient to permit the legal entity to finance its activities, the parties providing the necessary additional subordinated financial support most likely will not permit an equity investor to make decisions that may be counter to their interests. (FASB ASC 810-10-05-13)

Although the equity investors are technically the owners of the VIE, in reality they may retain little of the traditional responsibilities, risks, and benefits of ownership. In fact, the equity investors sometimes cede financial control of the VIE to those with variable interests in exchange for a guaranteed rate of return. Alternatively, equity ownership is also a variable interest and a minority equity holder may be the primary beneficiary and end up consolidating the VIE.

Consolidation of Variable Interest Entities

Prior to current financial reporting standards, assets, liabilities, and results of operations for VIEs and other entities frequently were not consolidated with those of the firm that controlled the entity. These firms invoked a reliance on voting interests, as opposed to

EXHIBIT 6.1
Examples of Variable Interests

Variable interests in a variable interest entity are contractual, ownership, or other pecuniary interests in an entity that change with changes in the entity's net asset value. Variable interests absorb portions of a variable interest entity's expected losses if they occur or receive portions of the entity's expected residual returns if they occur.

The following are some examples of variable interests and the related potential losses or returns:

Variable interests	Potential losses or returns
• Participation rights.	• Entitles holder to residual profits.
• Asset purchase options.	• Entitles holder to benefit from increases in asset fair values.
• Guarantees of debt.	• If a VIE cannot repay liabilities, honoring a debt guarantee will produce a loss.
• Subordinated debt instruments.	• If a VIE's cash flow is insufficient to repay all senior debt, subordinated debt may be required to absorb the loss.
• Lease residual value guarantees.	• If leased asset declines below the residual value, honoring the guarantee will produce a loss.
• Common stock	• Entitles holder to residual profits, losses, and dividends.

variable interests, to indicate a lack of a controlling financial interest. As legacy FASB standard *FIN 46R*[3] observed,

> An enterprise's consolidated financial statements include subsidiaries in which the enterprise has a controlling financial interest. That requirement usually has been applied to subsidiaries in which an enterprise has a majority voting interest, but in many circumstances, the enterprise's consolidated financial statements do not include variable interest entities with which it has similar relationships. The voting interest approach is not effective in identifying controlling financial interests in entities that are not controllable through voting interests or in which the equity investors do not bear residual economic risk. (Summary, page 2)

Thus, a business enterprise is required to consolidate the assets and liabilities of a variable interest entity if it can exercise financial control through its role as a primary beneficiary. Variable interests often serve as the vehicle for a controlling financial interest, even in the absence of any equity investment whatsoever.

Business enterprises must first determine if they have a controlling financial interest in any affiliated entity by applying the variable interest model. Each enterprise involved with a VIE must evaluate whether it possesses a controlling financial interest and thus qualifies as the primary beneficiary of the VIE's activities. The VIE's primary beneficiary is then required to include the assets, liabilities, and results of the activities of the VIE in its consolidated financial statements. If the affiliated entity is not a VIE, then a voting interest model is utilized to assess whether financial control exists.

As noted by General Electric Company in its 2015 annual report:

> Our financial statements consolidate all of our affiliates – entities in which we have a controlling financial interest, most often because we hold a majority voting interest. To determine if we hold a controlling financial interest in an entity, we first evaluate if we are required to apply the variable interest entity (VIE) model to the entity, otherwise, the entity is evaluated under the voting interest model.
>
> Where we hold current or potential rights that give us the power to direct the activities of a VIE that most significantly impact the VIE's economic performance, combined with a variable interest that gives us the right to receive potentially significant benefits or the obligation to absorb potentially significant losses, we have a controlling financial interest in that VIE.

Identification of a Variable Interest Entity

An entity qualifies as a VIE if either of the following conditions exists:

- The total equity at risk is not sufficient to permit the entity to finance its activities without additional subordinated financial support provided by any parties, including equity holders. In most cases, if equity at risk is less than 10 percent of total assets, the risk is deemed insufficient.[4]
- The equity investors in the VIE, as a group, lack any one of the following three characteristics of a controlling financial interest:
  1. The power, through voting rights or similar rights, to direct the activities of an entity that most significantly impact the entity's economic performance.
  2. The obligation to absorb the expected losses of the entity (e.g., the primary beneficiary may guarantee a return to the equity investors).
  3. The right to receive the expected residual returns of the entity (e.g., the investors' return may be capped by the entity's governing documents or other arrangements with variable interest holders).

Identification of the Primary Beneficiary of the VIE

Once it is established that a firm has a relationship with a VIE, the firm must determine whether it qualifies as the VIE's primary beneficiary. An enterprise with a variable interest

[3] FASB *Interpretation No. 46R (FIN 46R)*, "Consolidation of Variable Interest Entities," December 2003.

[4] Alternatively, a 10 percent or higher equity interest may also be insufficient. According to GAAP, "Some entities may require an equity investment greater than 10 percent of their assets to finance their activities, especially if they engage in high-risk activities, hold high-risk assets, or have exposure to risks that are not reflected in the reported amounts of the entities' assets or liabilities." [FASB ASC (para. 810-10-25-46)]

that provides it with a controlling financial interest in a variable interest entity is the primary beneficiary and will have both of the following characteristics:

- The power to direct the activities of a variable interest entity that most significantly impact the entity's economic performance.
- The obligation to absorb losses of the entity that could potentially be significant to the variable interest entity or the right to receive benefits from the entity that could potentially be significant to the variable interest entity.

Note that these characteristics mirror those that the equity investors often lack in a VIE. Instead, the primary beneficiary will absorb a significant share of the VIE's losses or receive a significant share of the VIE's residual returns or both. The fact that the primary beneficiary may own no voting shares whatsoever becomes inconsequential because such shares do not effectively give the equity investors power to exercise control. Thus, a careful examination of the VIE's governing documents, contractual arrangements among parties involved, and who bears the risk is necessary to determine whether a reporting entity possesses control over a VIE.

The magnitude of the effect of consolidating an enterprise's VIEs can be large. For example, Walt Disney Company consolidates its international theme parks as variable interest entities. In its 2015 annual report, Disney states the following:

> The Company enters into relationships or investments with other entities that may be a variable interest entity (VIE). A VIE is consolidated in the financial statements if the Company has the power to direct activities that most significantly impact the economic performance of the VIE and has the obligation to absorb losses or the right to receive benefits from the VIE that could potentially be significant to the VIE (as defined by ASC 810-10-25-38). Disneyland Paris, HKDL and Shanghai Disney Resort (collectively the International Theme Parks) are VIEs.

As a result of the 2015 consolidation of these VIEs, Disney's total assets increased by $3.98 billion while its total debt increased by $955 million.

Example of a Primary Beneficiary and Consolidated Variable Interest Entity

Assume that Twin Peaks Electric Company seeks to acquire a generating plant for a negotiated price of $400 million from Ace Electric Company. Twin Peaks wishes to expand its market share and expects to be able to sell the electricity generated by the plant acquisition at a profit to its owners.

In reviewing financing alternatives, Twin Peaks observed that its general credit rating allowed for a 4 percent annual interest rate on a debt issue. Twin Peaks also explored the establishment of a separate legal entity whose sole purpose would be to own the electric generating plant and lease it back to Twin Peaks. Because the separate entity would isolate the electric generating plant from Twin Peaks's other risky assets and liabilities and provide specific collateral, an interest rate of 3 percent on the debt is available, producing before-tax savings of $4 million per year. To obtain the lower interest rate, however, Twin Peaks must guarantee the separate entity's debt. Twin Peaks must also maintain certain of its own predefined financial ratios and restrict the amount of additional debt it can assume.

To take advantage of the lower interest rate, on January 1, 2017, Twin Peaks establishes Power Finance Co., an entity designed solely to own, finance, and lease the electric generating plant to Twin Peaks.[5] The documents governing the new entity specify the following:

- The sole purpose of Power Finance is to purchase the Ace electric generating plant, provide equity and debt financing, and lease the plant to Twin Peaks.
- An outside investor will provide $16 million in exchange for a 100 percent nonvoting equity interest in Power Finance.
- Power Finance will issue debt in exchange for $384 million. Because the $16 million equity investment by itself is insufficient to attract low-interest debt financing, Twin Peaks will guarantee the debt.

[5] This arrangement is similar to a "synthetic lease" commonly used in utility companies. Synthetic leases also can have tax advantages because the sponsoring firm accounts for them as capital leases for tax purposes.

- Twin Peaks will lease the electric generating plant from Power Finance in exchange for payments of $12 million per year based on a 3 percent fixed interest rate for both the debt and equity investors for an initial lease term of five years.
- At the end of the 5-year lease term (or any extension), Twin Peaks must do one of the following:
  - Renew the lease for five years subject to the approval of the equity investor.
  - Purchase the electric generating plant for $400 million.
  - Sell the electric generating plant to an independent third party. If the proceeds of the sale are insufficient to repay the equity investor, Twin Peaks must make a payment of $16 million to the equity investor.

Once the purchase of the electric generating plant is complete and the equity and debt are issued, Power Finance Company reports the following balance sheet:

POWER FINANCE COMPANY
Balance Sheet
January 1, 2017

Electric Generating Plant	$400M	Long-Term Debt.	$384M
		Owners' Equity.	16M
Total Assets	$400M	Total Liabilities and OE.	$400M

Exhibit 6.2 shows the relationships between Twin Peaks, Power Finance, the electric generating plant, and the parties financing the asset purchase.

In evaluating whether Twin Peaks Electric Company must consolidate Power Finance Company, two conditions must be met. First, Power Finance must qualify as a VIE by either (1) an inability to secure financing without additional subordinated support or (2) a lack of either the risk of losses or entitlement to residual returns (or both). Second, Twin Peaks must qualify as the primary beneficiary of Power Finance.

In assessing the first condition, several factors point to VIE status for Power Finance. Its owners' equity comprises only 4 percent of total assets, far short of the 10 percent benchmark. Moreover, Twin Peaks guarantees Power Finance's debt, suggesting insufficient equity to finance its operations without additional support. Finally, the equity investor appears to bear

EXHIBIT 6.2
Variable Interest Entity to Facilitate Financing

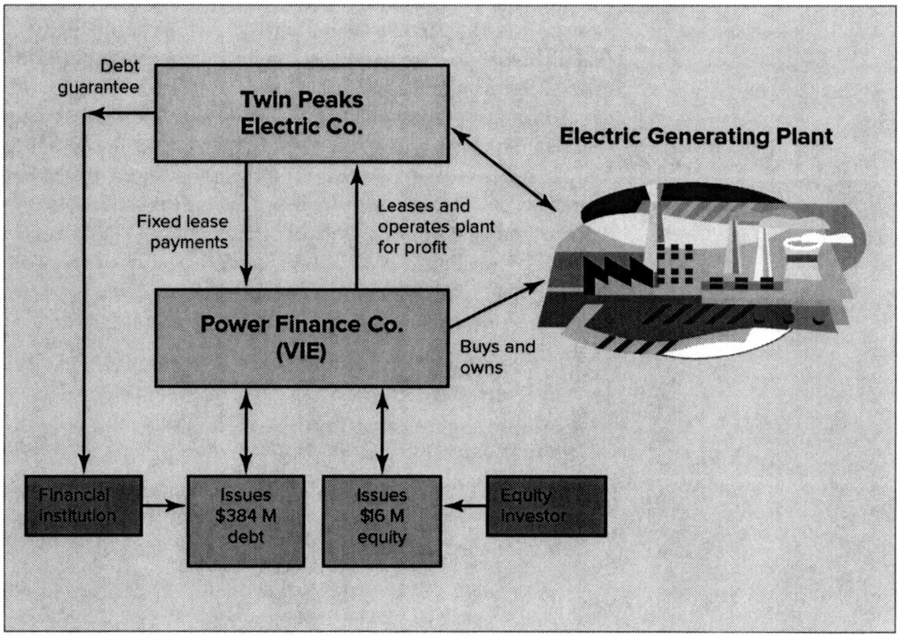

almost no risk with respect to the operations of the Ace electric plant. These characteristics indicate that Power Finance qualifies as a VIE.

In evaluating the second condition for consolidation, an assessment is made to determine whether Twin Peaks qualifies as Power Finance's primary beneficiary. Clearly, Twin Peaks has the power to direct Power Finance's activities. But to qualify for consolidation, Twin Peaks must also have the obligation to absorb losses or the right to receive returns from Power Finance—either of which could potentially be significant to Power Finance. But what possible losses or returns would accrue to Twin Peaks? What are Twin Peaks's variable interests that rise and fall with the fortunes of Power Finance?

As stated in the VIE agreement, Twin Peaks will pay a fixed fee to lease the electric generating plant. It will then operate the plant and sell the electric power in its markets. If the business plan is successful, Twin Peaks will enjoy residual profits from operating while Power Finance's equity investors receive the fixed fee. On the other hand, if prices for electricity fall, Twin Peaks may generate revenues insufficient to cover its lease payments while Power Finance's equity investors are protected from this risk. Moreover, if the plant's fair value increases significantly, Twin Peaks can exercise its option to purchase the plant at a fixed price and either resell it or keep it for its own future use. Alternatively, if Twin Peaks were to sell the plant at a loss, it must pay the equity investors all of their initial investment, furthering the loss to Twin Peaks. Each of these elements points to Twin Peaks as the primary beneficiary of its VIE through variable interests. As the primary beneficiary, Twin Peaks must consolidate the assets, liabilities, and results of operations of Power Finance with its own.

Procedures to Consolidate Variable Interest Entities

As Power Finance's balance sheet exemplifies, VIEs typically possess only a few assets and liabilities. Also, their business activities usually are strictly limited. Thus, the actual procedures to consolidate VIEs are relatively uncomplicated.

Initial Measurement Issues

Just as in business combinations accomplished through voting interests, the financial reporting principles for consolidating variable interest entities require asset, liability, and noncontrolling interest valuations. These valuations initially, and with few exceptions, are based on fair values.

Recall that the acquisition method requires an allocation of the acquired business fair value based on the underlying fair values of its assets and liabilities. The fair-value principle applies to consolidating VIEs in the same manner as business combinations accomplished through voting interests. If the total business fair value of the VIE exceeds the collective fair values of its net assets, goodwill is recognized.[6] Conversely, if the collective fair values of the net assets exceed the total business fair value, then the primary beneficiary recognizes a gain on bargain purchase.

In the previous example, assuming that the debt and noncontrolling interests are stated at fair values, Twin Peaks simply includes in its consolidated balance sheet the Electric Generating Plant at $400 million, the Long-Term Debt at $384 million, and a noncontrolling interest of $16 million.

Consolidation of VIEs Subsequent to Initial Measurement

After the initial measurement, consolidations of VIEs with their primary beneficiaries should follow the same process as if the entity were consolidated based on voting interests. Importantly, all intra-entity transactions between the primary beneficiary and the VIE (including fees, expenses, other sources of income or loss, and intra-entity inventory purchases) must be eliminated in consolidation. Finally, the VIE's income must be allocated among the parties involved (i.e., equity holders and the primary beneficiary). For a VIE, contractual arrangements, as opposed to ownership percentages, typically specify the distribution of its income.

[6] The FASB ASC Glossary defines a business as an integrated set of activities and assets that is capable of being conducted and managed for the purpose of providing a return in the form of dividends, lower costs, or other economic benefits directly to investors or other owners, members, or participants. Alternatively, if the activities of the VIE are so restricted that it does not qualify as a business, the excess fair value is recognized as an acquisition loss, as opposed to goodwill.

Therefore, a close examination of these contractual arrangements is needed to determine the appropriate allocation of VIE income to its equity owners and those holding variable interests.

LO 6-2

Demonstrate the process to consolidate a primary beneficiary with a variable interest entity.

Consolidation of a Primary Beneficiary and VIE Illustrated

The next example considers (1) the issues that arise when a primary beneficiary obtains control through variable interests of an existing business, and (2) financial reporting for a VIE in periods subsequent to obtaining control.

Assume that on January 1, 2018, Prescott Corporation provides a $2,200,000 loan to Valente, Inc., a business entity. The loan is due on January 1, 2023. Until receiving the loan from Prescott, Valente had been unable to secure from the debt market the financing needed to continue its operations.

As part of the loan agreement, Valente agrees to provide the following to Prescott during the next five years:

- 5 percent annual interest (market rate) on the loan from Prescott.
- Decision-making power over Valente's operating and financing activities.
- 100 percent participation rights to all of Valente's profits less a $7,000 guaranteed annual dividend to Valente's common shareholders.

At the end of the five-year agreement Prescott has the option of either acquiring ownership of Valente, Inc., for $500,000 or extending the original agreement for an additional five years.

As a result of the agreement, Valente is a variable interest entity and Prescott is its primary beneficiary. Upon consummation of the variable interest agreement, Prescott's and Valente's balance sheets appears below:

January 1, 2018	Prescott	Valente
Cash	$ 85,000	$ 2,308,000
Accounts receivable	133,000	145,000
Loan receivable from Valente	2,200,000	–0–
Patented technology	–0–	9,000
Equipment (net)	2,458,000	900,000
Total assets	$ 4,876,000	$ 3,362,000
Accounts payable	$ (408,000)	$(1,144,000)
Long-term debt	(954,000)	(2,200,000)
Common stock	(2,500,000)	(10,000)
Retained earnings, 1/1/18	(1,014,000)	(8,000)
Total liabilities and equity	$(4,876,000)	$(3,362,000)

At January 1, 2018, Prescott estimated the fair value of Valente's common stock at $143,000. The $125,000 difference between the fair value of the common stock and Valente's book value ($143,000 - $18,000) was attributed entirely to the patented technology with a five-year estimated remaining life.

Exhibit 6.3 shows the consolidation worksheet for Prescott (the primary beneficiary) and Valente (the variable interest entity) at January 1, 2018, the date Prescott obtained financial control over Valente.

Observe that in Exhibit 6.3

- Consolidation Entry **S** eliminates the VIE's owners' equity account balances and recognizes the 100 percent equity ownership as a noncontrolling interest.
- Consolidation Entry **P** eliminates the intra-entity Long-Term Debt and Loan Receivable from Valente.
- Consolidation Entry **A** allocates the excess fair over book value to Patented Technology with a corresponding increase in the noncontrolling interest.
- The noncontrolling interest appears in the consolidated balance sheet at its acquisition-date fair value of $143,000.

EXHIBIT 6.3 Acquisition-Date Consolidation Worksheet—Primary Beneficiary and VIE

PRESCOTT AND VALENTE COMPANY
Consolidation Worksheet
At January 1, 2018

Balance Sheet	Prescott	Valente	Consolidation Entries		Noncontrolling Interest	Consolidated Balance Sheet
Cash	85,000	2,308,000				2,393,000
Accounts receivable	133,000	145,000				278,000
Loan receivable from Valente	2,200,000			(P)2,200,000		–0–
Patented technology		9,000	(A) 125,000			134,000
Equipment (net)	2,458,000	900,000				3,358,000
Total assets	4,876,000	3,362,000				6,163,000
Accounts payable	(408,000)	(1,144,000)				(1,552,000)
Long-term debt	(954,000)	(2,200,000)	(P)2,200,000			(954,000)
Common stock—Prescott	(2,500,000)					(2,500,000)
Common stock—Valente		(10,000)	(S) 10,000			
Retained earnings—Prescott	(1,014,000)					(1,014,000)
Retained earning—Valente		(8,000)	(S) 8,000			
Noncontrolling interest				(S) 18,000 (A) 125,000	(143,000)	(143,000)
Total liabilities and equity	(4,876,000)	(3,362,000)	2,343,000	2,343,000		(6,163,000)

Consolidation of VIEs Subsequent to Initial Measurement

Following the first year of operations, Exhibit 6.4 shows the consolidation worksheet for December 31, 2018, at the end of the first year in which Prescott obtained control of the variable interest entity. At the end of the year, Valente paid the guaranteed $7,000 dividend to its equity holders.

The following worksheet entries, as seen in Exhibit 6.4, are used to consolidate the financial statements of Prescott Corporation and its VIE, Valente, as of December 31, 2018:

Consolidation Entry S

Retained earnings—Valente 1/1/18	8,000	
Common stock—Valente.	10,000	
Noncontrolling interest		18,000

To eliminate the beginning stockholders' equity of the VIE and recognize the 100 percent equity ownership of the noncontrolling interest.

Consolidation Entry P

Long-term debt	2,200,000	
Loan receivable from Valente		2,200,000

To eliminate the long-term receivable and debt representing Prescott's initial investment in Valente.

Consolidation Entry IE

Interest income	110,000	
Interest expense.		110,000

To eliminate the intra-entity interest related to the loan from Prescott to Valente.

Consolidation Entry A		
Patented technology	125,000	
Noncontrolling interest		125,000
To allocate the excess fair value to patented technology and credit the noncontrolling interest as part of their fair valuation as of the date Prescott obtained control.		

Consolidation Entry E		
Other operating expenses	25,000	
Patented technology		25,000
To amortize the excess fair value allocation to unpatented technology over its five-year remaining life.		

EXHIBIT 6.4 Consolidation Worksheet for Primary Beneficiary and VIE (Post-Control)

PRESCOTT AND VALENTE COMPANY
Consolidation Worksheet
For the year ended, December 31, 2018

Income Statement	**Prescott**	**Valente**	**Consolidation Entries**		**Noncontrolling Interest**	**Consolidated**
Sales	(623,000)	(400,000)				(1,023,000)
Cost of goods sold	230,000	190,000				420,000
Other operating expenses	155,000	55,000	(E) 25,000			235,000
Interest income	(110,000)		(IE) 110,000			–0–
Interest expense		110,000		(IE) 110,000		–0–
Net income	(348,000)	(45,000)				
Consolidated net income						(368,000)
to noncontrolling interest					(7,000)	7,000
to controlling interest						(361,000)
Statement of Retained Earnings						
Retained earnings, 1/1	(1,014,000)	(8,000)	(S) 8,000			(1,014,000)
Net income	(348,000)	(45,000)				(361,000)
Dividends declared	50,000	7,000			7,000	50,000
Retained earnings, 12/31	(1,312,000)	(46,000)				(1,325,000)
Balance Sheet						
Cash	214,000	131,800				345,800
Accounts receivable	258,000	181,000				439,000
Loan receivable from Valente	2,200,000			(P)2,200,000		–0–
Patented technology		7,200	(A) 125,000	(E) 25,000		107,200
Equipment (net)	2,328,000	2,050,000				4,378,000
Total assets	5,000,000	2,370,000				5,270,000
Accounts payable	(434,000)	(114,000)				(548,000)
Long-term debt	(754,000)	(2,200,000)	(P) 2,200,000			(754,000)
Common stock	(2,500,000)	(10,000)	(S) 10,000			(2,500,000)
Retained earnings, 12/31	(1,312,000)	(46,000)				(1,325,000)
				(A) 125,000		
				(S) 18,000	(143,000)	
Noncontrolling interest					(143,000)	(143,000)
Total liabilities and equities	(5,000,000)	(2,370,000)	2,478,000	2,478,000		(5,270,000)

In Exhibit 6.4, we observe that the noncontrolling interest (NCI) column for a VIE differs from a consolidation resulting from voting interest control. For a VIE, contractual arrangements, as opposed to ownership percentages, typically specify the distribution of its income. In Exhibit 6.4, the only income allocation to the NCI is the $7,000 annual dividend guaranteed through the variable interest arrangement. Because of its profit participation rights, Prescott simply receives the remainder of the consolidated net income beyond the $7,000 provided to Valente's equity holders, i.e., the NCI of the consolidated entity.

Also note that the NCI amount recognized after one year did not change from the consolidated balance sheet as of the date control was obtained. The NCI did not change because its entire fixed income share was distributed to the equity holders as a dividend.

Overall, as shown by Exhibit 6.4, consolidation of a VIE with its primary beneficiary follows a similar process as if the entity were consolidated based on voting interests. Importantly, all intra-entity transactions between the primary beneficiary and the VIE (including fees, expenses, other sources of income or loss, and intra-entity transfers) must be eliminated in consolidation. Because VIEs typically have noncontrolling interests, an appropriate allocation of the VIE's net income requires a close examination of the underlying contractual arrangements between the primary beneficiary and other holders of variable interests.

Other Variable Interest Entity Disclosure Requirements

VIE disclosure requirements are designed to provide users of financial statements with more transparent information about an enterprise's involvement in a VIE. The enhanced disclosures are required for any enterprise that holds a variable interest in a VIE.

Included among the enhanced disclosures are requirements to show:

- The VIE's nature, purpose, size, and activities.
- The significant judgments and assumptions made by an enterprise in determining whether it must consolidate a VIE and/or disclose information about its involvement in a VIE.
- The nature of restrictions on a consolidated VIE's assets and on the settlement of its liabilities reported by an enterprise in its statement of financial position, including the carrying amounts of such assets and liabilities.
- The nature of, and changes in, the risks associated with an enterprise's involvement with the VIE.
- How an enterprise's involvement with the VIE affects the enterprise's financial position, financial performance, and cash flows.

Comparisons with International Accounting Standards

Under both U.S. GAAP and IFRS, a controlling financial interest is the critical concept in assessing whether an entity should be consolidated by a reporting enterprise. Nonetheless, the FASB and IASB so far have employed different criteria to determine the existence of control. IFRS employs a single consolidation model for all entities regardless of whether control is evidenced by voting interests or variable interests. In contrast, U.S. GAAP employs separate models for assessing control for variable interest entities and voting interest entities. As a result, current reporting standards differ across jurisdictions for enterprises seeking to determine whether to consolidate another entity. While the FASB continues its deliberations on consolidation policies and procedures, the IASB has issued two updated standards in this area.

The International Accounting Standards Board *IFRS 10*, "Consolidated Financial Statements" and *IFRS 12*, "Disclosure of Interests in Other Entities" cover situations where financial control exists either through a majority voting share or other means. These standards define control to encompass all possible ways (voting power, contractual power, decision-making rights, etc.) in which one entity can exercise power over another. In particular, the criteria for assessing control are

- Power over an investee—does the reporting entity have the current ability to direct activities that significantly affect another entity's returns?

- Exposure to, or rights to, variable returns from involvement with another entity
- Linkage between power and returns—does the investor have the ability to affect its returns through its power?

These criteria recognize one entity can control another through its power to direct its operating and financing activities. For example, even with less than majority ownership, voting interests can provide an enterprise control if the nonowned shares are diffusely held and lack arrangements to act in a coordinated manner. Control can also be achieved through obtaining decision-making rights that relate to the relevant activities of an investee. Importantly, such decision-making rights can extend beyond merely voting rights. By establishing a broad concept of control as opposed to a bright line rule (e.g., consolidate if an entity has majority voting rights or the majority of risks and rewards), the IASB seeks to avoid standards that create structuring opportunities to achieve a particular accounting outcome.[7]

IFRS 12 provides for enhanced disclosures about the relationship between a parent and the entities it controls. These disclosures focus on helping investors understand first why a parent controls (or does not control) another entity and the claims of the noncontrolling interest. Second, the disclosures are designed to help investors evaluate the risks assumed by the parent.[8]

LO 6-3

Demonstrate the consolidation procedures to eliminate all intra-entity debt accounts and recognize any associated gain or loss created whenever one company acquires an affiliate's debt instrument from an outside party.

Intra-Entity Debt Transactions

The previous chapter explored the consolidation procedures required by the intra-entity transfer of inventory, land, and depreciable assets. In preparing consolidated financial statements, all resulting gains were deferred until either the asset was sold to an outside party or consumed through use. Deferral was necessary because these gains, although legitimately recognized by the individual companies, were based on activities of the consolidated entity with itself. The separate financial information of each company was adjusted on the worksheet to be consistent with treating the related companies as a single economic concern.

This same objective applies in consolidating all other intra-entity activities: The financial statements must represent the business combination as one enterprise rather than as a group of independent organizations. Consequently, in designing consolidation procedures for intra-entity transactions, we first isolate the effects recorded by the individual companies. After analyzing the impact of each action, worksheet entries recast these events from the vantage point of the business combination. Although this process involves a number of nuances and complexities, the desire for reporting financial information solely from the perspective of the consolidated entity remains constant.

We introduced the intra-entity sales of inventory, land, and depreciable assets together (in Chapter 5) because these transfers result in similar consolidation procedures. In each case, one of the affiliated companies recognizes a gain prior to the time the consolidated entity is entitled to recognize it. The worksheet entries required by these transactions simply realign the separate financial information to agree with the viewpoint of the business combination. The gain is removed and the inflated asset value is reduced to historical cost.

The next section of this chapter examines the intra-entity acquisition of bonds and notes. Although accounting for the related companies as a single economic entity continues to be the central goal, the consolidation procedures applied to intra-entity debt transactions stand in marked contrast to the process utilized in Chapter 5 for asset transfers.

Before delving into this topic, note that *direct* loans used to transfer funds between affiliated companies create no unique consolidation problems. Regardless of whether bonds or notes generate such amounts, the resulting receivable/payable balances are necessarily identical. Because no money is owed to or from an outside party, these reciprocal accounts must

[7] Patrick Finnegan, Board Member of the IASB. "At Long-Last–A Single Model for Consolidation," IFRS Foundation, May 2011 perspectives.

[8] Ibid.

be eliminated in each subsequent consolidation. A worksheet entry simply offsets the two corresponding balances. Furthermore, the interest revenue/expense accounts associated with direct loans also agree and are removed in the same fashion.

Acquisition of Affiliate's Debt from an Outside Party

The difficulties encountered in consolidating intra-entity liabilities relate to a specific type of transaction: the purchase of an affiliate's debt instrument from an outside third party. For example, a subsidiary may have issued bonds in the past that continue to be traded in the open market. If the parent then purchases all or a portion of these outstanding subsidiary bonds in the open market, from a consolidated view, the combined entity (parent and subsidiary) has reacquired its own bonds. Nonetheless, because the companies maintain independent accounting systems, the parent records an Investment in Bonds account as well as periodic interest income. The subsidiary shows the bonds as still outstanding and records periodic interest expense.

Although the individual companies continue to carry both the debt and the investment on their individual financial records, *from a consolidation viewpoint this liability is effectively retired as of the debt reacquisition date.* From that date forward, the debt is no longer owed to a party outside the business combination. Subsequent interest payments are simply intra-entity cash transfers. To create consolidated statements, worksheet entries must be developed to adjust the various balances to report the debt's effective retirement.

Acquiring an affiliate's bond or note from an unrelated party poses no significant consolidation problems if the purchase price equals the corresponding carrying amount of the liability. Reciprocal balances within the individual records would always be identical in value and easily offset in each subsequent consolidation.

Realistically, though, such reciprocity rarely occurs when a debt instrument is purchased from a third party. A variety of economic factors typically produce a difference between the price paid for the investment and the carrying amount of the obligation. The debt is originally sold under market conditions at a particular time. Any premium or discount associated with this issuance is then amortized over the life of the bond, creating a continuous adjustment to its carrying amount. The acquisition of this instrument at a later date is made at a price influenced by current economic conditions, prevailing interest rates, and myriad other financial and market factors.

Therefore, the cost paid to purchase the debt could be either more or less than the carrying amount of the liability currently found within the issuing company's financial records. *To the business combination, this difference is a gain or loss because the acquisition effectively retires the bond; the debt is no longer owed to an outside party.* For external reporting purposes, this gain or loss must be recognized immediately by the consolidated entity.

Accounting for Intra-Entity Debt Transactions—Individual Financial Records

The following accounting problems emerge in consolidating intra-entity debt transactions:

1. Intra-entity investments in debt securities and related debt accounts must be eliminated in consolidation despite their differing balances.
2. Intra-entity interest revenue/expense (as well as any interest receivable/payable accounts) must be removed although these balances also fail to agree in amount.
3. The amortization process for discounts and premiums causes continual changes in each of the preceding accounts.
4. The business combination must recognize the gain or loss on the effective retirement of the debt, even though it is not recognized within the financial records of either company.

To illustrate, assume that Alpha Company possesses an 80 percent interest in the outstanding voting stock of Omega Company. On January 1, 2015, Omega issued $1 million in 10-year bonds paying cash interest of 9 percent annually. Because of market conditions prevailing on that date, Omega sold the debt for $938,555 to yield an effective interest rate of 10 percent per year. Shortly thereafter, the interest rate began to fall, and by January 1, 2017, Omega made the decision to retire this debt prematurely and refinance it at a currently lower rate. To carry out this plan, Alpha purchased all of these bonds in the open market on January 1, 2017, for $1,057,466. This price was based on an effective yield of 8 percent, which is assumed to be in line with the interest rates at the time.

Many reasons could exist for having Alpha, rather than Omega, reacquire this debt. For example, company cash levels at that date could necessitate Alpha's role as the purchasing agent. Also, contractual limitations could prohibit Omega from repurchasing its own bonds.

In accounting for this business combination, Omega Company's bonds have been effectively retired. Thus, the difference between the $1,057,466 payment and the January 1, 2017, carrying amount of the liability must be recognized in the consolidated statements as a gain or loss. The carrying amount for the debt on that date depends on the amortization process. Exhibit 6.5 shows the bond amortization schedule for January 1, 2015, through December 31, 2018.[9]

As seen in Exhibit 6.5, the carrying amount of Omega Company's bonds has increased to $946,651 as of December 31, 2016, the date immediately before the day that Alpha Company acquired the bonds.

Because Alpha paid $110,815 in excess of the recorded liability ($1,057,466 – $946,651), the consolidated entity must recognize a loss of this amount. After the loss has been acknowledged, the bond is considered to be retired and no further reporting is necessary by the *business combination* after January 1, 2017.

Despite the simplicity of this approach for consolidation, neither company separately accounts for the event in this manner. Omega retains the $1 million debt balance within its separate financial records and amortizes the remaining discount each year. Annual cash interest payments of $90,000 (9 percent) continue to be made. At the same time, Alpha records the investment at the historical cost of $1,057,466, an amount that also requires periodic amortization. Furthermore, as the owner of these bonds, Alpha receives the $90,000 interest payments made by Omega.

To organize the accountant's approach to this consolidation, we analyze the subsequent financial records for each company. Omega records only two journal entries during 2017 assuming that interest is paid each December 31:

	Omega Company's Financial Records		
12/31/17	Interest Expense	90,000	
	Cash		90,000
	To record payment of annual cash interest on $1 million, 9 percent bonds payable.		
12/31/17	Interest Expense	4,665	
	Discount on Bonds Payable		4,665
	To adjust interest expense to effective rate based on original yield rate of 10 percent ($946,651 carrying amount for 2017 × 10% = $94,665). Carrying amount increases to $951,316.		

EXHIBIT 6.5
Omega Company Bond Issue Amortization Schedule

Date	Face Value	Unamortized Discount	Carrying Amount	Effective Interest	Cash Interest	Discount Amortized
1/1/15	$1,000,000	$61,445	$938,555			
12/31/15	1,000,000	57,590	942,410	$93,855	$90,000	$3,855
12/31/16	1,000,000	53,349	946,651	94,241	90,000	4,241
12/31/17	1,000,000	48,684	951,316	94,665	90,000	4,665
12/31/18	1,000,000	43,552	956,448	95,132	90,000	5,132

[9] The effective rate method of amortization is demonstrated here because this approach is theoretically preferable. However, the straight-line method can be applied if the resulting balances are not materially different from the figures computed using the effective rate method.

Concurrently, Alpha journalizes entries to record its ownership of this investment:

	Alpha Company's Financial Records		
1/1/17	Investment in Omega Company Bonds	1,057,466	
	Cash		1,057,466
	To record acquisition of $1,000,000 in Omega Company bonds paying 9 percent cash interest, acquired to yield an effective rate of 8 percent.		
12/31/17	Cash	90,000	
	Interest Income		90,000
	To record receipt of cash interest from Omega Company bonds ($1,000,000 × 9%).		
12/31/17	Interest Income	5,403	
	Investment in Omega Company Bonds		5,403
	To reduce $90,000 interest income to effective rate based on original yield rate of 8 percent ($1,057,466 carrying amount for 2017 × 8% = $84,597). Carrying amount decreases to $1,052,063.		

Even a brief review of these entries indicates that the reciprocal accounts to be eliminated within the consolidation process do not agree in amount. You can see the dollar amounts appearing in each set of financial records in Exhibit 6.6. Despite the presence of these recorded balances, none of the four intra-entity accounts (the bond liability, investment, interest expense, and interest revenue) appear in the consolidated financial statements. *The only figure that the business combination reports is the $110,815 loss created by the effective extinguishment of this debt.*

Effects on Consolidation Process

As previous discussions indicated, consolidation procedures convert information generated by the individual accounting systems to the perspective of a single economic entity. A worksheet entry is therefore required on December 31, 2017, to eliminate the intra-entity balances shown in Exhibit 6.6 and to recognize the loss resulting from the effective retirement. Mechanically, the differences in the liability and investment balances as well as the interest expense and interest income accounts stem from the $110,815 difference between the purchase price of the investment and the carrying amount of the liability. Recognition of this loss, in effect, bridges the gap between the divergent figures.

Consolidation Entry B (December 31, 2017)		
Bonds Payable	1,000,000	
Interest Income	84,597	
Loss on Retirement of Bonds	110,815	
Discount on Bond Payable		48,684
Investment in Omega Company Bonds		1,052,063
Interest Expense		94,665
To eliminate intra-entity bonds and related interest accounts and to recognize loss on effective retirement. (Labeled "**B**" in reference to bonds.)		

The preceding entry successfully transforms the separate financial reporting of Alpha and Omega to that appropriate for the business combination. The objective of the consolidation process has been met: The statements present the bonds as having been retired on January 1, 2017. The debt and the corresponding investment are eliminated along with both interest accounts. Only the loss now appears on the worksheet to be reported within the consolidated financial statements.

EXHIBIT 6.6

ALPHA COMPANY AND OMEGA COMPANY
Effects of Intra-Entity Debt Transaction 2017

	Omega Company Reported Debt	Alpha Company Investment
2017 interest expense*	$ 94,665	$ –0–
2017 interest income†	–0–	(84,597)
Bonds payable	(1,000,000)	–0–
Discount on bonds payable*	48,684	–0–
Investment in bonds, 12/31/17†	–0–	1,052,063
Loss on retirement	–0–	–0–

Note: Parentheses indicate a credit balance.
*Company total is adjusted for 2017 amortization of $4,665 (see journal entry).
†Adjusted for 2017 amortization of $5,403 (see journal entry).

Assignment of Retirement Gain or Loss

An issue in accounting for intra-entity debt repurchases concerns the assignment of any retirement gains or losses. Should the $110,815 loss just reported be attributed to Alpha or to Omega? From a practical perspective, this assignment affects only the consolidated net income allocation to the controlling and noncontrolling interests. In the absence of FASB guidance on the assignment of retirement gain or loss, all income effects in this textbook relating to intra-entity debt transactions are assigned solely to the parent company. Such treatment is consistent with the perspective that the parent company ultimately controls the repurchase decision.

Intra-Entity Debt Transactions—Years Subsequent to Effective Retirement

Even though the preceding Entry **B** correctly eliminates Omega's bonds in the year of retirement for consolidation purposes, the debt remains within the financial accounts of both companies until maturity. Therefore, in each succeeding time period, all balances must again be consolidated so that the liability is always reported as having been extinguished on January 1, 2017. Unfortunately, a simple repetition of Entry **B** is not possible. Developing the appropriate worksheet entry is complicated by the amortization process that produces continual change in the various account balances. Thus, as a preliminary step in each subsequent consolidation, current carrying amounts, as reported by the two parties, must be identified.

To illustrate, the 2018 journal entries for Alpha and Omega follow. Exhibit 6.7 shows the resulting account balances as of the end of that year.

EXHIBIT 6.7

ALPHA COMPANY AND OMEGA COMPANY
Effects of Intra-Entity Debt Transactions 2018

	Omega Company Reported Debt	Alpha Company Investment
2018 interest expense*	$ 95,132	$ –0–
2018 interest income†	–0–	(84,165)
Bonds payable	(1,000,000)	–0–
Discount on bonds payable*	43,552	–0–
Investment in bonds, 12/31/18†	–0–	1,046,228
Income effect within retained earnings, 1/1/18‡	94,665	(84,597)

Note: Parentheses indicate a credit balance.
*Company total is adjusted for 2018 amortization of $5,132 (see journal entry).
†Adjusted for 2018 amortization of $5,835 (see journal entry).
‡The balance shown for the Retained Earnings account of each company represents the 2017 reported interest figures.

Discussion Question

WHO LOST THIS $300,000?

Several years ago, Penston Company purchased 90 percent of the outstanding shares of Swansan Corporation. Penston made the acquisition because Swansan produced a vital component used in Penston's manufacturing process. Penston wanted to ensure an adequate supply of this item at a reasonable price. The former owner, James Swansan, retained the remaining 10 percent of Swansan's stock and agreed to continue managing this organization. He was given responsibility for the subsidiary's daily manufacturing operations but not for any financial decisions.

Swansan's takeover has proven to be a successful undertaking for Penston. The subsidiary has managed to supply all of the parent's inventory needs and distribute a variety of items to outside customers.

At a recent meeting, Penston's president and the company's chief financial officer began discussing Swansan's debt position. The subsidiary had a debt-to-equity ratio that seemed unreasonably high considering the significant amount of cash flows being generated by both companies. Payment of the interest expense, especially on the subsidiary's outstanding bonds, was a major cost, one that the corporate officials hoped to reduce. However, the bond indenture specified that Swansan could retire this debt prior to maturity only by paying 107 percent of face value.

This premium was considered prohibitive. Thus, to avoid contractual problems, Penston acquired a large portion of Swansan's liability in the open market for 101 percent of face value. Penston's purchase created an effective loss of $300,000 on the debt, the excess of the price over the carrying amount of the debt, as reported on Swansan's books.

Company accountants currently are computing the noncontrolling interest's share of consolidated net income to be reported for the current year. They are unsure about the impact of this $300,000 loss. The subsidiary's debt was retired, but officials of the parent company made the decision. Who lost this $300,000?

Omega Company's Financial Records—December 31, 2018		
Interest Expense	90,000	
Cash		90,000
To record payment of annual cash interest on $1 million, 9 percent bonds payable.		
Interest Expense	5,132	
Discount on Bonds Payable		5,132
To adjust interest expense to effective rate based on an original yield rate of 10 percent ($951,316 carrying amount for 2018 × 10% = $95,132). Carrying amount increases to $956,448.		

Alpha Company's Financial Records—December 31, 2018		
Cash	90,000	
Interest Income		90,000
To record receipt of cash interest from Omega Company bonds.		
Interest Income	5,835	
Investment in Omega Company Bonds		5,835
To reduce $90,000 interest income to effective rate based on an original yield rate of 8 percent ($1,052,063 carrying amount for 2018 × 8% = $84,165). Carrying amount decreases to $1,046,228.		

After assembling the information in Exhibit 6.7, the necessary December 31, 2018, consolidation entry is prepared. We first assume that the parent applies either the initial value or the partial equity method to its Investment in Omega account. We then show this final consolidation entry assuming the parent applies the equity method.

Parent Applies the Initial Value or Partial Equity Method

To recognize the January 1, 2017, effective retirement on the December 31, 2018, consolidated financial statements, the individual affiliate's balances for the intra-entity bonds and interest income and expense must be removed. Because neither the initial value nor the partial equity method recognizes the retirement loss, the parent's retained earnings will fail to reflect the prior year effective retirement loss. However, retained earnings will reflect past interest income and expense to the extent of any discount or premium amortization.[10] A worksheet adjustment therefore reduces Alpha's January 1, 2018, retained earnings by $110,815 to reflect the original loss net of the prior year's discount and premium amortizations.

Consolidation Entry *B, When Parent Uses the Initial Value or Partial Equity Method (December 31, 2018)

Bonds Payable	1,000,000	
Interest Income	84,165	
Retained Earnings—Alpha	100,747	
Discount on Bond Payable		43,552
Investment in Omega Company Bonds		1,046,228
Interest Expense		95,132

To eliminate intra-entity bond and related interest accounts and to adjust Alpha's Retained Earnings from $10,068 (currently recorded net debit balance) to $110,815. (Labeled "*B" in reference to prior year bond transaction.)

Analysis of this latest consolidation entry should emphasize several important factors:

1. The individual account balances change during the present fiscal period so that the current consolidation entry differs from Entry **B.** These alterations are a result of the amortization process. To ensure the accuracy of the worksheet entry, the adjusted balances are isolated in Exhibit 6.7.
2. As indicated previously, all income effects arising from intra-entity debt transactions are assigned to the parent company. For this reason, the adjustment to beginning Retained Earnings in Entry ***B** is attributed to Alpha, as is the $10,967 increase in current income ($95,132 interest expense elimination less the $84,165 interest revenue elimination).[11] Consequently, the noncontrolling interest balances are not altered by Entry ***B.**
3. The 2018 reduction to beginning Retained Earnings in Entry ***B** ($100,747) does not agree with the original $110,815 retirement loss. The individual companies have recorded a net deficit balance of $10,068 (the amount by which previous interest expense exceeds interest revenue) at the start of 2018. To achieve the proper consolidated total, an adjustment of only $100,747 is required ($110,815 – $10,068).

Retained earnings balance—consolidation perspective (loss on retirement of debt)		$110,815
Individual retained earnings balances, 1/1/18:		
Omega Company (interest expense—2017)	$94,665	
Alpha Company (interest income—2017)	(84,597)	10,068
Adjustment to consolidated retained earnings, 1/1/18		$100,747

Note: Parentheses indicate a credit balance

[10] If there is no discount or premium amortization, interest revenue will simply offset interest expense, leaving no net effect on retained earnings.

[11] Had the effects of the retirement been attributed solely to the original issuer of the bonds, the $10,967 addition to current income would have been assigned to Omega (the subsidiary), thus creating a change in the noncontrolling interest computations.

The periodic amortization of both the bond payable discount and the premium on the investment impacts the interest expense and revenue recorded by the two companies. As this schedule shows, these two interest accounts do not offset exactly; a $10,068 net residual amount remains in Retained Earnings after the first year. Because this balance continues to increase each year, the subsequent consolidation adjustments to record the loss decrease to $100,747 in 2018 and constantly lesser thereafter. *Over the life of the bond, the amortization process gradually brings the totals in the individual Retained Earnings accounts into agreement with the consolidated balance.*

Parent Applies the Equity Method

Entry ***B** as shown is appropriate for consolidations in which the parent has applied either the initial value or the partial equity method. However, a deviation is required if the parent uses the equity method for internal reporting purposes. Properly applying the equity method ensures that the parent's income and, hence, its retained earnings are correctly stated prior to consolidation. Alpha would have already recognized the loss in accounting for this investment. Consequently, when the parent applies the equity method, no adjustment to Retained Earnings is needed. In this one case, the $100,747 debit in Entry ***B** is made to the Investment in Omega Company (instead of Retained Earnings) because the loss has become a component of that account.

Consolidation Entry *B, When Parent Uses the Equity Method (December 31, 2018)		
Bonds Payable	1,000,000	
Interest Income	84,165	
Investment in Omega	100,747	
Discount on Bond Payable		43,552
Investment in Omega Company Bonds		1,046,228
Interest Expense		95,132
To eliminate intra-entity bond and related interest accounts and to adjust the Investment in Omega from $10,068 (currently recorded net debit balance) to $110,815. (Labeled "***B**" in reference to prior year bond transaction.)		

The Entry *B debit to the Investment in Omega account then serves as part of the investment account elimination sequence.

LO 6-4

Understand that subsidiary preferred stock not owned by the parent is a component of the noncontrolling interest and is initially measured at acquisition-date fair value.

Subsidiary Preferred Stock

Although both small and large corporations routinely issue preferred shares, their presence within a subsidiary's equity structure adds a new dimension to the consolidation process. What accounting should be made of a subsidiary's preferred stock and the parent's payments that are made to acquire these shares?

Recall that preferred shares, although typically nonvoting, possess other "preferences" over common shares such as a cumulative dividend preference or participation rights. Some preferred shares even offer limited voting rights. Regardless, preferred shares are part of the subsidiary's stockholders' equity and are treated as such in consolidated financial reports.

The existence of subsidiary preferred shares does little to complicate the consolidation process. The acquisition method measures all business acquisitions (whether 100 percent or less than 100 percent acquired) at their full fair values. In accounting for the acquisition of a subsidiary with preferred stock, the essential process of determining the acquisition-date business fair value of the subsidiary remains intact. Any preferred shares not owned by the parent simply become a component of the noncontrolling interest and are included in the subsidiary business fair-value calculation. The acquisition-date fair value for any subsidiary common and/or preferred shares owned by outsiders becomes the basis for the noncontrolling interest valuation in the parent's consolidated financial reports.

To illustrate, assume that on January 1, 2017, High Company acquires control over Low Company by purchasing 80 percent of its outstanding common stock and 60 percent of its non-voting, cumulative, preferred stock. Low owns land undervalued in its records by $100,000, but all other assets and liabilities have fair values equal to their book values. High paid $1 million for the common shares and $62,400 for the preferred shares. On the acquisition date, the 20 percent noncontrolling interest in the common shares had a fair value of $250,000 and the 40 percent preferred stock noncontrolling interest had a fair value of $41,600.

Low's capital structure immediately prior to the acquisition is shown below:

Common stock, $20 par value (20,000 shares outstanding).	$ 400,000
Preferred stock, 6% cumulative with a par value of $100 (1,000 shares outstanding)	100,000
Additional paid-in capital	200,000
Retained earnings	516,000
Total stockholders' equity (book value).	$1,216,000

Exhibit 6.8 shows High's calculation of the acquisition-date fair value of Low and the allocation of the difference between the fair and book values to land and goodwill.

As seen in Exhibit 6.8, the subsidiary's ownership structure (i.e., comprising both preferred and common shares) does not affect the fair-value principle for determining the basis for consolidating the subsidiary. Moreover, the acquisition method follows the same procedure for calculating business fair value regardless of the various preferences the preferred shares may possess. Any cumulative or participating preferences (or other rights) attributed to the preferred shares are assumed to be captured by the acquisition-date fair value of the shares and thus automatically incorporated into the subsidiary's valuation basis for consolidation.

By utilizing the information above, we next construct a basic worksheet entry as of January 1, 2017 (the acquisition date). In the presence of both common and preferred subsidiary shares, combining the customary consolidation entries S and A avoids an unnecessary allocation of the subsidiary's retained earnings across these equity shares. The combined consolidation entry also recognizes the allocations made to the undervalued land and goodwill. No other consolidation entries are needed because no time has passed since the acquisition took place.

Consolidation Entries S and A (combined)		
Common Stock (Low)	400,000	
Preferred Stock (Low)	100,000	
Additional Paid-In Capital (Low)	200,000	
Retained Earnings (Low)	516,000	
Land	100,000	
Goodwill	38,000	
Investment in Low's Common Stock		1,000,000
Investment in Low's Preferred Stock		62,400
Noncontrolling Interest		291,600
To eliminate the subsidiary's common and preferred shares, recognize the fair values of the subsidiary's assets, and recognize the outside ownership.		

The above combined consolidation entry recognizes the noncontrolling interest as the total of acquisition-date fair values of $250,000 for the common stock and $41,600 for the preferred shares. Consistent with previous consolidation illustrations throughout the text, the entire subsidiary's stockholders' equity section is eliminated along with the parent's investment accounts—in this case for both the common and preferred shares.

Allocation of Subsidiary Income

The final factor influencing a consolidation that includes subsidiary preferred shares is the allocation of the company's income between the two types of stock. A division must be made for every period subsequent to the takeover (1) to compute the noncontrolling interest's share and

EXHIBIT 6.8

LOW COMPANY
Acquisition-Date Fair Value
January 1, 2017

Consideration transferred for 80% interest in Low's common stock	$1,000,000
Consideration transferred for 60% interest in Low's preferred stock	62,400
Noncontrolling interest in Low's common stock (20%)	250,000
Noncontrolling interest in Low's preferred stock (40%)	41,600
Total fair value of Low on 1/1/17	$1,354,000

HIGH'S ACQUISITION OF LOW
Excess Fair Value Over Book Value Allocation
January 1, 2017

Low Company business fair value		$1,354,000
Low Company book value		1,216,000
Excess acquisition-date fair value over book value		$ 138,000
Assigned to land	$100,000	
Assigned to goodwill	38,000	138,000
		$ -0-

(2) for the parent's own recognition purposes. For a cumulative nonparticipating preferred stock such as the one presently being examined, only the specified annual dividend is attributed to the preferred stock with all remaining income assigned to common stock. Consequently, if we assume that Low reports earnings of $100,000 in 2017 while declaring and paying the annual $6,000 dividend on its preferred stock, we allocate income for consolidation purposes as follows:

	Income
Subsidiary total	$100,000
Preferred stock (6% dividend × $100,000 par value of the stock)	$ 6,000
Common stock (residual amount)	94,000

During 2017, High Company, as the parent, is entitled to $3,600 in dividends ($6,000 × 60%) from Low's preferred stock because of its 60 percent ownership. In addition, High holds 80 percent of Low's common stock so that another $75,200 of the income ($94,000 × 80%) is attributed to the parent. The noncontrolling interest in consolidated net income can be calculated in a similar fashion:

		Percentage Outside Ownership	Noncontrolling Interest
Preferred stock dividend	$ 6,000	40%	$ 2,400
Income attributed to common stock	94,000	20	18,800
Noncontrolling interest in consolidated net income			$21,200

LO 6-5

Prepare a consolidated statement of cash flows.

Consolidated Statement of Cash Flows

Current accounting standards require that companies include a statement of cash flows among their consolidated financial reports. The main purpose of the statement of cash flows is to provide information about the entity's cash receipts and cash payments during a period. The statement is also designed to show why an entity's net income is different from its operating cash flows. For a consolidated entity, the cash flows relate to the entire business combination including the parent and all of its subsidiaries.

The statement of cash flows allocates the consolidated entity's overall change in cash during a period to three separate categories:

1. Cash flows from operating activities.
2. Cash flows from investing activities.
3. Cash flows from financing activities.

The cash flows from operating activities can be shown using either the indirect method or the direct method. The indirect method begins with consolidated net income and then adds and subtracts various items to adjust the accrual number to a cash flow amount. The direct method examines cash flows directly from distinct sources that typically include revenues, purchases of inventory, and cash payments of other expenses. However, firms using the direct method must also supplement the statement with the calculation of cash flows from operating activities using the indirect method.

The consolidated statement of cash flows is not prepared from the individual cash flow statements of the separate companies. Instead, the consolidated income statements and balance sheets are first brought together on the worksheet. The cash flows statement is then based on the resulting consolidated figures. Thus, this statement is not actually produced by a consolidation worksheet, but is created from numbers generated by the process. Because special accounting procedures are needed in the period when the parent acquires a subsidiary, we first discuss preparation of the consolidated statement of cash flows for periods in which an acquisition takes place, followed by statement preparation in periods subsequent to acquisition.

Acquisition Period Statement of Cash Flows

If a business combination occurs during a particular reporting period, the consolidated cash flow statement must properly reflect several considerations. For many business combinations, the following issues frequently are present:

Business Acquisitions in Exchange for Cash

Cash purchases of businesses are an investing activity. The *net cash outflow* (cash paid less subsidiary cash acquired) is reported as the amount paid in a business acquisition.[12]

Operating Cash Flow Adjustments

Keeping in mind that the focus is on the consolidated entity's cash flows (not just the parent's), consolidated net income is the starting point for the indirect calculation of consolidated operating cash flows. Recall that consolidated net income includes only postacquisition subsidiary revenues and expenses. Therefore, the adjustment to the accrual-based income number must also reflect only postacquisition amounts for the subsidiary. One important category of adjustments to consolidated net income to arrive at cash flows from operations involves changes in current operating accounts (e.g., accounts receivable, accounts payable, etc.).

For example, an increase in an accounts receivable balance typically indicates that a firm's accrual-based sales exceed the actual cash collections for sales during a period. Therefore, in computing operating cash flows, the increase in accounts receivable are deducted from the sales amount (direct method) or the net income (indirect method). However, when an acquisition takes place, the change in accounts receivable will often include amounts from the newly acquired subsidiary. Because the consolidated entity recognizes only postacquisition subsidiary revenues, such acquired receivables do not reflect sales that have been made by the consolidated entity. Therefore any subsidiary acquisition-date current operating account balances must be removed before calculating the change in accounts receivable.

[12] For acquisitions that do not involve cash, or only partially involve cash, the details of the acquisitions should be provided in a supplemental disclosure to the statement of cash flows for "significant noncash investing and financing activities."

In fact, any changes in operating balance sheet accounts (accounts receivable, inventory, accounts payable, etc.) must be computed net of the amounts acquired in the combination. Use of the direct method of presenting operating cash flows also reports the separate computations of cash collected from customers and cash paid for inventory net of acquisition-date balances of newly acquired businesses.

Excess Fair-Value Amortizations

Any adjustments arising from the subsidiary's revenues or expenses (e.g., depreciation, amortization) must reflect only postacquisition amounts. Closing the subsidiary's books at the date of acquisition facilitates the determination of the appropriate current year postacquisition subsidiary effects on the consolidated entity's cash flows.

Subsidiary Dividends Paid

The cash outflow from subsidiary dividends only leaves the consolidated entity when paid to the noncontrolling interest. Thus dividends paid by a subsidiary to its parent do not appear as financing outflows. However, subsidiary dividends paid to the noncontrolling interest are a component of cash outflows from financing activities.

Intra-Entity Transfers

A significant volume of transfers between affiliated companies comprising a business combination often occurs. The resulting effects of intra-entity activities are eliminated in the preparation of consolidated statements. Likewise, the consolidated statement of cash flows does not include the impact of these transfers. Intra-entity sales and purchases do not change the amount of cash held by the business combination when viewed as a whole. Because the statement of cash flows is derived from the consolidated balance sheet and income statement, the impact of all transfers is already removed. Therefore, the proper presentation of cash flows requires no special adjustments for intra-entity transfers. The worksheet entries produce correct balances for the consolidated statement of cash flows.

Consolidated Statement of Cash Flows Illustration

Assume that on July 1, 2017, Pinto Company acquires 90 percent of Salida Company's outstanding stock for $774,000 in cash. At the acquisition date, the 10 percent noncontrolling interest has a fair value of $86,000. Exhibit 6.9 shows book and fair values of Salida's assets and liabilities and Pinto's acquisition-date fair-value allocation schedule.

At the end of 2017, the following comparative balance sheets and consolidated income statement are available:

PINTO COMPANY AND SUBSIDIARY SALIDA COMPANY
Comparative Balance Sheets

	Pinto Co. January 1, 2017	Consolidated December 31, 2017
Cash	$ 170,000	$ 431,000
Accounts receivable (net)	118,000	319,000
Inventory	310,000	395,000
Land	250,000	370,000
Buildings (net)	350,000	426,000
Equipment (net)	1,145,000	1,380,000
Database	–0–	49,000
Total assets	$2,343,000	$3,370,000
Accounts payable	$50,000	$ 45,000
Long-term liabilities	18,000	522,000
Common stock	1,500,000	1,500,000
Noncontrolling interest	–0–	98,250
Retained earnings	775,000	1,204,750
Total liabilities and equities	$2,343,000	$3,370,000

EXHIBIT 6.9

SALIDA COMPANY
Book and Fair Values
July 1, 2017

Account	Book Value	Fair Value
Cash	$ 35,000	$ 35,000
Accounts receivable	145,000	145,000
Inventory	90,000	90,000
Land	100,000	120,000
Buildings	136,000	136,000
Equipment	259,000	299,000
Database	–0–	50,000
Accounts payable	(15,000)	(15,000)
Net book value	$750,000	$860,000

PINTO'S ACQUISITION OF SALIDA
Excess Fair Value over Book Value Allocation
July 1, 2017

Consideration transferred by Pinto		$774,000
Noncontrolling interest fair value		86,000
Salida's total fair value		$860,000
Salida's book value		750,000
Excess fair over book value		$110,000
To land	$ 20,000	
To equipment (5-year remaining life)	40,000	
To database (25-year remaining life)	50,000	110,000
		$ –0–

PINTO COMPANY AND SUBSIDIARY SALIDA COMPANY
Consolidated Income Statement (partial presentation)
For the Year Ended December 31, 2017

Revenues		$1,255,000
Cost of goods sold	$600,000	
Depreciation	124,000	
Database amortization	1,000	
Interest and other expenses	35,500	760,500
Consolidated net income		$ 494,500

Additional Information for 2017

- The consolidated income statement totals include Salida's postacquisition revenues and expenses.
- During the year, Pinto paid $50,000 in dividends. On August 1, Salida paid a $25,000 dividend.
- During the year, Pinto issued $504,000 in long-term debt at par value.
- No asset purchases or dispositions occurred during the year other than Pinto's acquisition of Salida.

In preparing the consolidated statement of cash flows, note that each adjustment derives from the consolidated income statement or changes from Pinto's January 1, 2017, balance sheet to the consolidated balance sheet at December 31, 2017.

Depreciation and Amortization

These expenses do not represent current operating cash outflows and thus are added back to convert accrual basis income to cash provided by operating activities.

Increases in Accounts Receivable, Inventory, and Accounts Payable (net of acquisition)

Changes in balance sheet accounts affecting operating cash flows must take into account amounts acquired in business acquisitions. In this case, note that the changes in Accounts Receivable, Inventory, and Accounts Payable are computed as follows:

	Accounts Receivable	Inventory	Accounts Payable
Pinto's balance, 1/1/17	$118,000	$310,000	$50,000
Increase from Salida acquisition	145,000	90,000	15,000
Adjusted beginning balance	263,000	400,000	65,000
Consolidated balance, 12/31/17	319,000	395,000	45,000
Operating cash flow adjustment	$ 56,000	$ 5,000	$20,000

Acquisition of Salida Company

The Investing Activities section of the cash flow statement shows increases and decreases in assets purchased or sold involving cash. The cash outflow from the acquisition of Salida Company is determined as follows:

Cash paid for 90% interest in Salida	$774,000
Cash acquired	(35,000)
Net cash paid for Salida investment	$739,000

Note here that although Pinto acquires only 90 percent of Salida, 100 percent of Salida's cash is offset against the cash consideration paid in the acquisition in determining the investing cash outflow. Ownership divisions between the noncontrolling and controlling interests do not affect reporting for the entity's investing cash flows.

Issue of Long-Term Debt

Pinto Company's issuance of long-term debt represents a cash inflow from financing activities.

Dividends

The dividends paid to Pinto Company owners ($50,000) combined with the dividends paid to the noncontrolling interest ($2,500) represent cash outflows from financing activities.

Based on the consolidated totals from the comparative balance sheets and the consolidated income statement, the following consolidated statement of cash flows is then prepared. Pinto chooses to use the indirect method of reporting cash flows from operating activities.

PINTO COMPANY AND SUBSIDIARY SALIDA COMPANY
Consolidated Statement of Cash Flows (partial presentation)
For the Year Ended December 31, 2017

Consolidated net income		$ 494,500
Depreciation expense	$ 124,000	
Amortization expense	1,000	
Increase in accounts receivable (net of acquisition effects)	(56,000)	
Decrease in inventory (net of acquisition effects)	5,000	
Decrease in accounts payable (net of acquisition effects)	(20,000)	54,000
Net cash provided by operating activities		$ 548,500
Purchase of Salida Company (net of cash acquired)		
Net cash used in investing activities	$(739,000)	(739,000)
Issue long-term debt	$ 504,000	
Dividends	(52,500)	
Net cash provided by financing activities		451,500
Increase in Cash, 1/1/17 to 12/31/17		**$261,000**

Statement of Cash Flows in Periods Subsequent to Acquisition

Preparing a consolidated statement of cash flows during periods of no acquisition is relatively uncomplicated. As before, consolidated net income is the starting point for the indirect calculation of consolidated operating cash flows. If the operating accounts (e.g., accounts receivable, accounts payable, etc.) do not include amounts acquired in a business combination, then no further special adjustments are required. Because the consolidation process eliminates intra-entity balances, preparation of the operating activity section of the statement of cash flows typically proceeds in a straightforward manner using the already available consolidated income statement and balance sheet amounts. Finally, subsidiary dividends paid to the noncontrolling interest are shown as a component of cash outflows from financing activities.

LO 6-6

Compute basic and diluted earnings per share for a business combination.

Consolidated Earnings per Share

The consolidation process affects one other intermediate accounting topic, the computation of earnings per share (EPS). Publicly held companies must disclose EPS each period.

The following steps calculate such figures:

- Determine basic EPS by dividing the parent's share of consolidated net income (after reduction for preferred stock dividends) by the weighted-average number of common stock shares outstanding for the period. If the reporting entity has no dilutive options, warrants, or other convertible items, only basic EPS is presented on the face of the income statement. However, diluted EPS also must be presented if any dilutive convertibles are present.
- Compute diluted EPS by combining the effects of *any dilutive securities* with basic earnings per share. Stock options, stock warrants, convertible debt, and convertible preferred stock often qualify as dilutive securities.[13]

In most instances, the computation of EPS for a business combination follows the same general pattern. Consolidated net income attributable to the parent company owners along with the number of outstanding parent shares provides the basis for calculating basic EPS. Any convertibles, warrants, or options for the parent's stock that can possibly dilute the reported figure must be included as described earlier in determining diluted EPS.

However, a problem arises if warrants, options, or convertibles that can dilute the subsidiary's earnings are outstanding. Although the parent company is not directly affected, the potential impact of these items on its share of consolidated net income must be given weight in computing diluted EPS for the consolidated income statement. Because of possible conversion, the subsidiary earnings figure included in consolidated net income is not necessarily applicable to the diluted EPS computation. *Thus, the accountant must separately determine the parent's share of subsidiary income that should be used in deriving diluted EPS.*

Finally, the focus is on earnings per share for the parent company stockholders, even in the presence of a noncontrolling interest. As stated in FASB ASC (para. 260-10-45-11A):

> For purposes of computing EPS in consolidated financial statements (both basic and diluted), if one or more less-than-wholly-owned subsidiaries are included in the consolidated group, income from continuing operations and net income shall exclude the income attributable to the noncontrolling interest in subsidiaries.

Thus, consolidated income attributable to the parent's interest forms the basis for the numerator in all EPS calculations for consolidated financial reporting.

[13] Complete coverage of the EPS computation can be found in virtually any intermediate accounting textbook. To adequately understand this process, a number of complex procedures must be mastered, including these:

- Calculation of the weighted-average number of common shares outstanding.
- Understanding the method of including stock rights, convertible debt, and convertible preferred stock within the computation of diluted EPS.

Earnings per Share Illustration

Assume Big Corporation has 100,000 shares of its common stock outstanding during the current year. The company also has issued 20,000 shares of nonvoting preferred stock, paying an annual cumulative preferred dividend of $5 per share ($100,000 total). Each of these preferred shares is convertible into two shares of Big's common stock.

Assume also that Big owns 90 percent of Little's common stock and 60 percent of its preferred stock (which pays $12,000 in preferred dividends per year). Annual amortization is $26,000, attributable to various intangibles. Big is preparing its EPS computations for 2017. During the year, Big reported separate income of $600,000 and Little earned $100,000. A simplified consolidation of the figures for the year indicates consolidated net income attributable to Big of $663,000:

Big's separate income for 2017		$600,000
Little's separate income for 2017	$100,000	
Amortization expense resulting from original fair-value allocation	(26,000)	
Little's income after excess fair-value amortization		74,000
Consolidated net income		$674,000
Noncontrolling interest in Little—common stock (10% × $62,000 [$74,000 income less $12,000 preferred stock dividends])	$ (6,200)	
Noncontrolling interest in Little—preferred stock (40% of dividends)	(4,800)	
Net income attributable to the noncontrolling interest		(11,000)
Net income attributable to Big (parent)		$663,000

Little has 20,000 shares of common stock and 4,000 shares of preferred stock outstanding. The preferred shares pay a $3 per year dividend, and each can be converted into two shares of common stock (or 8,000 shares in total). Because Big owns only 60 percent of Little's preferred stock, a $4,800 dividend is distributed each year to the outside owners (40 percent of the $12,000 total payment).

Assume finally that the subsidiary also has $200,000 in convertible bonds outstanding that were originally issued at face value. This debt has both a cash and an effective interest rate of 10 percent ($20,000 per year) and can be converted by the owners into 9,000 shares of Little's common stock. Big owns none of these bonds. Little's tax rate is 30 percent.

To better visualize these factors, the convertible items are scheduled as follows:

Company	Item	Interest or Dividend	Conversion	Big Owns
Big	Preferred stock	$100,000/year	40,000 shares	Not applicable
Little	Preferred stock	12,000/year	8,000 shares	60%
Little	Bonds	14,000/year*	9,000 shares	–0–

*Interest on the bonds is shown net of the 30 percent tax effect ($20,000 interest less $6,000 tax savings). No tax is computed for the preferred shares because distributed dividends do not create a tax impact.

Because the subsidiary has convertible items that can affect the company's outstanding shares and net income, Little's diluted earnings per share must be derived *before* Big's diluted EPS can be determined. As shown in Exhibit 6.10, Little's diluted EPS are $2.38. Two aspects of this schedule should be noted:

- The individual impact of the convertibles ($1.50 for the preferred stock and $1.56 for the bonds) did not raise the EPS figures above the $3.10 basic EPS. Thus, neither the preferred stock nor the bonds are antidilutive, and both are properly included in these computations.
- Absent the presence of the subsidiary's convertible bonds and preferred stock, the parent's share of consolidated net income would form the basis for computing EPS.

EXHIBIT 6.10
Subsidiary's Diluted Earnings per Share

LITTLE COMPANY
Basic and Diluted Earnings per Common Share
For Year Ending December 31, 2017

	Earnings		Shares	
Little's income after amortization . .	$74,000		20,000	
Preferred stock dividends	(12,000)			
Basic EPS	$62,000		20,000	$3.10 ($62,000/20,000)
Effect of possible preferred stock conversion:				
Dividends saved	$12,000	New shares	8,000	$1.50 impact (12,000/8,000)
Effect of possible bond conversion:				
Interest saved (net of taxes).	$14,000		9,000	$ 1.56 impact (14,000/9,000)
Diluted EPS.	$88,000		37,000	$ 2.38 (rounded)

As shown in Exhibit 6.10, Little's income is $88,000 for diluted EPS. The issue then becomes how much of this amount should be included in computing the parent's diluted EPS. This allocation is based on the percentage of shares controlled by the parent. Note that if the subsidiary's preferred stock and bonds are converted into common shares, Big's ownership falls from 90 to 62 percent. For diluted EPS, 37,000 shares are appropriate. Big's 62 percent ownership (22,800/37,000) is the basis for allocating the subsidiary's $88,000 income to the parent.

Supporting Calculations for Diluted Earnings per Share

	Little Company Shares	Big's Percentage	Big's Ownership
Common stock	20,000	90%	18,000
Possible new shares—preferred stock	8,000	60	4,800
Possible new shares—bonds	9,000	–0–	–0–
Total	37,000		22,800

Big's ownership (diluted): 22,800/37,000 = 62% (rounded)
Income assigned to Big (diluted earnings per share computation): $88,000 × 62% = $54,560

We can now determine Big Company's EPS. Only $54,560 of subsidiary income is appropriate for computing diluted EPS. Because separate income figures are utilized, Exhibit 6.11 (page 289) shows separate basic and diluted EPS calculations. Consequently, Big Company reports basic EPS of $5.63 and diluted earnings per share of $4.68.

LO 6-7

Demonstrate the accounting effects of subsidiary stock transactions on the parent's financial records and consolidated financial statements.

Subsidiary Stock Transactions

A note to the financial statements of Gerber Products Company disclosed a transaction carried out by one of the organization's subsidiaries: "The Company's wholly owned Mexican subsidiary sold previously unissued shares of common stock to Grupo Coral, S.A., a Mexican food company, at a price in excess of the shares' net book value." The note added that Gerber had increased consolidated Additional Paid-In Capital by $432,000 as a result of this stock sale.

As this illustration shows, subsidiary stock transactions can alter the level of parent ownership. A subsidiary, for example, can decide to sell previously unissued stock to raise needed capital. Although the parent company can acquire a portion or even all of these new shares,

EXHIBIT 6.11

BIG COMPANY AND CONSOLIDATED SUBSIDIARY
Basic Earnings per Common Share
For Year Ending December 31, 2017

	Earnings		Shares	
Consolidated net income (to Big) . .	$663,000			
Big's shares outstanding			100,000	
Preferred stock dividends (Big)	(100,000)			
Basic EPS	$563,000		100,000	$5.63

Diluted Earnings per Common Share
For Year Ending December 31, 2017

	Earnings		Shares	
Computed below	$654,560*			
Big's shares outstanding			100,000	
Preferred stock dividends (Big)	(100,000)			
Effect of possible preferred stock (Big) conversion:				
Dividends saved	100,000	New shares	40,000	$2.50 impact (100,000/40,000)
Diluted EPS	$654,560		140,000	$4.68 (rounded)

*Net income computation:

Big's separate income	$600,000	
Portion of Little's income assigned to diluted earnings per share calculation	54,560	(computed in supporting calculations)
Earnings of the business combination applicable to diluted earnings per share	$654,560	

such issues frequently are marketed entirely to outsiders. A subsidiary could also be legally forced to sell additional shares of its stock. As an example, companies holding control over foreign subsidiaries occasionally encounter this problem because of laws in the individual localities. Regulations requiring a certain percentage of local ownership as a prerequisite for operating within a country can mandate issuance of new shares. Of course, changes in the level of parent ownership do not result solely from stock sales: A subsidiary also can repurchase its own stock. The acquisition, as well as the possible retirement, of such treasury shares serves as a means of reducing the percentage of outside ownership.

Changes in Subsidiary Value—Stock Transactions

When a subsidiary subsequently buys or sells its own stock, a nonoperational increase or decrease occurs in the company's fair and book value. Because the transaction need not involve the parent, the parent's investment account does not automatically reflect the effect of this change. However, the parent's percentage ownership of the subsidiary may change. *Thus, a separate adjustment must be recorded to maintain reciprocity between the subsidiary's stockholders' equity accounts and the parent's investment balance.* The accountant measures the impact the stock transaction has on the parent to ensure that this effect is appropriately recorded in the parent's investment account and then reflected in the consolidation process.

An overall perspective of accounting for subsidiary stock transactions follows from the fundamental notion that the parent establishes the subsidiary's valuation basis at fair value as of the acquisition date. Over time, the parent adjusts this initial fair value for subsidiary income less excess amortization and subsidiary dividends. If the subsidiary issues (or buys) any of its own stock subsequent to acquisition, the effect on the parent will depend on whether the price received (or paid) is greater or less than the per share subsidiary adjusted fair value at that point in time.

An example demonstrates the mechanics of this issue. Assume that on January 1, 2017, Giant Company acquires in the open market 60,000 of Small Company's outstanding 80,000 shares and prepares the following fair-value allocation schedule:

Consideration transferred by Giant	$480,000	
Noncontrolling interest fair value	160,000	
Small Company acquisition-date fair value		$640,000
Small Company acquisition-date book value		
Common stock (80,000 shares outstanding)	$ 80,000	
Additional paid-in capital	200,000	
Retained earnings, 1/1/17	260,000	540,000
Excess fair value assigned to trademark (10-year remaining life)		$100,000

Assuming Small reports earnings of $50,000 in 2017 and pays no dividends, Giant prepares the following routine consolidation entries for the December 31, 2017, worksheet. Giant uses the equity method to account for its 75 percent interest in Small.

December 31, 2017, Consolidation Worksheet Entries

Consolidation Entry S		
Common Stock (Small Company)	80,000	
Additional Paid-In Capital (Small Company)	200,000	
Retained Earnings, 1/1/17 (Small Company)	260,000	
Investment in Small Compan'y (75%)		405,000
Noncontrolling Interest in Small Company (25%)		135,000
To eliminate subsidiary's stockholders' equity accounts and recognize noncontrolling interest beginning balance in Small's book value.		

Consolidation Entry A		
Trademark	100,000	
Investment in Small Company (75%)		75,000
Noncontrolling Interest in Small Company (25%)		25,000
To recognize the excess acquisition-date fair value assigned to Small's trademark with allocations to the controlling and noncontrolling interest.		

Consolidation Entry I		
Equity in Small's Earnings	30,000	
Investment in Small Company		30,000
To eliminate Giant's equity in Small's earnings (75% x [$50,000 less $10,000 trademark excess amortization]).		

Consolidation Entry E		
Amortization Expense	10,000	
Trademark		10,000
To recognize the excess trademark amortization ($100,000 ÷ 10 years).		

We now introduce a subsidiary stock transaction to demonstrate the effect created on the consolidation process. Assume that on January 1, 2018, Giant announces plans for expansion of Small's operations. To help finance the expansion, Small sells 20,000 previously unissued shares of its common stock to outside parties for $10 per share. After the stock issue, Small's book value is as follows:

Common stock ($1.00 par value with 100,000 shares issued and outstanding)	$100,000
Additional paid-in capital	380,000
Retained earnings, 1/1/18	310,000
Total stockholders' equity, 1/1/18	$790,000

Note that the common stock and additional paid-in capital balances reflect increases from the new stock issue. Retained earnings have also increased from Small's $50,000 income in 2017 (no dividends). Although Small's book value is now $790,000, its valuation for the consolidated entity is derived from its acquisition-date fair value as adjusted through time as follows:

Consideration transferred	$480,000
Noncontrolling interest acquisition-date fair value	160,000
2017 Small income less excess amortization	40,000
Adjusted subsidiary value, 1/1/18	$680,000
Stock issue proceeds ($10 × 20,000 shares)	200,000
Subsidiary valuation basis, 1/1/18	$880,000

Because of Small's stock issue, Giant no longer possesses a 75 percent interest. Instead, the parent now holds 60 percent (60,000 shares of a total of 100,000 shares) of Small Company. The effect on the parent's ownership can be computed as follows:

Small's valuation basis, 1/1/18 (above)	$880,000
Giant's post-issue ownership (60,000 shares ÷ 100,000 shares)	60%
Giant's post, stock issue ownership balance	$528,000
Giant's equity-adjusted investment account ($480,000 + [75% × $40,000])	510,000
Required adjustment—increase in Giant's additional paid-in capital	$ 18,000

Independent of any action by the parent company, the assigned fair-value equivalency of this investment has risen from $510,000 to $528,000. Small's ability to sell shares of stock at more than the per share consolidated subsidiary value ($680,000 ÷ 80,000 shares = $8.50 per share) created an increased value for the parent. Therefore, Giant records the $18,000 increment as an adjustment to both its investment account (because the underlying value of the subsidiary has increased) and additional paid-in capital:

Giant Company's Financial Records—January 1, 2018		
Investment in Small Company	18,000	
Additional Paid-In Capital (Giant Company)		18,000
To recognize change in equity of business combination created by Small Company issuing 20,000 additional shares of common stock at above the previously assigned fair value.		

Note that the parent reports a change in stockholders' equity (i.e., Additional Paid-In Capital) for effects from subsidiary stock transactions. GAAP literature states that

> [c]hanges in a parent's ownership interest while the parent retains its controlling financial interest in its subsidiary shall be accounted for as equity transactions (investments by owners and distributions to owners acting in their capacity as owners). Therefore, no gain or loss shall be recognized in consolidated net income or comprehensive income. The carrying amount of the noncontrolling interest shall be adjusted to reflect the change in its ownership interest in the subsidiary. Any difference between the fair value of the consideration received or paid and the amount by which the noncontrolling interest is adjusted shall be recognized in equity attributable to the parent. [FASB ASC (para. 810-10-45-23)]

Consistent with this view, this textbook treats the effects from subsidiary stock transactions on the consolidated entity as adjustments to Additional Paid-In Capital.

After the change in the parent's records has been made, the consolidation process can proceed in a normal fashion. Assuming Small reports earnings of $85,000 in 2018 and pays no dividends, Giant prepares the following routine consolidation entries for the December 31, 2018, worksheet. *Although the investment and subsidiary equity accounts are removed here, the change recorded earlier in Giant's Additional Paid-In Capital remains within the consolidated figures.*

December 31, 2018, Consolidation Worksheet Entries

Consolidation Entry S		
Common Stock (Small Company)	100,000	
Additional Paid-In Capital (Small Company)	380,000	
Retained Earnings (Small Company)	310,000	
Investment in Small Company (60%)		474,000
Noncontrolling Interest in Small Company (40%)		316,000
To eliminate subsidiary's stockholders' equity accounts and recognize noncontrolling interest book value beginning balance. Small's capital accounts have been updated to reflect the issuance of 20,000 shares of $1 par value common stock at $10 per share.		

Consolidation Entry A		
Trademark	90,000	
Investment in Small Company (60%)		54,000
Noncontrolling Interest in Small Company (40%)		36,000
To recognize the unamortized excess acquisition-date fair value assigned to Small's trademark as of the beginning of the period with allocations to the controlling and noncontrolling interests' adjusted ownership percentages.		

Consolidation Entry I		
Equity in Small's Earnings	45,000	
Investment in Small Company		45,000
To eliminate Giant's equity in Small's earnings (60% × [$85,000 – $10,000 trademark excess amortization]).		

Consolidation Entry E		
Amortization Expense	10,000	
Trademark		10,000
To recognize the excess trademark amortization ($100,000 ÷ 10 years).		

The noncontrolling interest now stands at 40 percent ownership. Because these 40 percent owners will share in the profits generated by the subsidiary's trademark, they are allocated a 40 percent share to their overall equity balance in the consolidated financial statements. The noncontrolling interest is also assigned 40 percent of the excess fair-value trademark amortization.

Subsidiary Stock Transactions—Illustrated

No single example can demonstrate the many possible variations that different types of subsidiary stock transactions could create. To provide a working knowledge of this process, we analyze four additional cases briefly, each based on the following scenario:

Assume that Antioch Company acquires 90 percent of the common stock of Westminster Company on January 1, 2017, in exchange for $1,350,000 cash. The acquisition-date fair value of the 10 percent noncontrolling interest is $150,000. At that date, Westminster has the following stockholders' equity accounts:

Common stock—100,000 shares outstanding	$ 200,000
Additional paid-in capital	450,000
Retained earnings, 1/1/17	750,000
Total stockholders' equity	$1,400,000

The $100,000 excess acquisition-date fair over book value was allocated to a customer list with a five-year remaining life. In 2017, Westminster reports $190,000 in earnings and declares a $30,000 dividend. Antioch accrues its share of Westminster's income (less excess fair-value amortization related to the customer list) through application of the equity method. Antioch's equity method balance for its investment in Westminster is computed as follows:

Consideration transferred for 90% of Westminster	$1,350,000
Equity earnings of Westminster (90% × [$190,000 – $20,000 excess amortization])	153,000
Dividends from Westminster (90% × $30,000)	(27,000)
Equity method balance, 12/31/17	$1,476,000

View each of the following cases as an independent situation.

Case 1

Assume that on January 1, 2018, Westminster Company sells 25,000 shares of previously unissued common stock to outside parties for $14.40 per share. This stock issue changes both the parent's percentage interest in the subsidiary and the subsidiary's consolidated valuation basis. The parent's percentage ownership declines to 72 percent (90,000 shares ÷ 125,000 total shares). The subsidiary's valuation basis for consolidation becomes:

Consideration transferred	$1,350,000
Noncontrolling interest acquisition-date fair value	150,000
2017 Westminster income less excess amortization	170,000
Westminster dividends	(30,000)
Stock issue proceeds ($14.40 × 25,000 shares)	360,000
Subsidiary valuation basis, 1/1/18	$2,000,000

Next, the effect on the parent's ownership can be computed as follows:

Westminster's valuation basis, 1/1/18 (above)	$2,000,000
Antioch's post, stock issue ownership (90,000 shares ÷ 125,000 shares)	72%
Antioch's post, stock issue ownership balance	$1,440,000
Antioch's pre, stock issue equity-adjusted investment account (above)	1,476,000
Required adjustment—decrease in Antioch's additional paid-in capital	$ 36,000

To reflect this effect of the stock issue change on its valuation of the subsidiary, the parent makes the following journal entry on its financial records.

Antioch Company's Financial Records		
Additional Paid-In Capital (Antioch Company)	36,000	
Investment in Westminster Company		36,000
To recognize change in equity of business combination created by issuance of 25,000 additional shares of Westminster's common stock.		

Case 2

Assume that on January 1, 2018, Westminster issues 20,000 new shares of common stock for $16 per share. Of this total, Antioch acquires 18,000 shares to maintain its 90 percent level of ownership. Antioch pays a total of $288,000 (18,000 shares × $16) for this additional stock. Outside parties buy the remaining shares.

Under these circumstances, the stock transaction alters the consolidated valuation basis of the subsidiary but not the percentage owned by the parent. Thus, only the subsidiary value must be updated prior to determining the necessity of an equity revaluation:

Consideration transferred	$1,350,000
Noncontrolling interest acquisition-date fair value	150,000
2017 Westminster income less excess amortization	170,000
Westminster dividends	(30,000)
Stock issue proceeds ($16 × 20,000 shares)	320,000
Subsidiary valuation basis 1/1/18	$1,960,000

The effect on the parent's ownership is computed as follows:

Westminster's valuation basis 1/1/18 (above)		$1,960,000
Antioch's post, stock issue ownership (108,000 shares ÷ 120,000 shares)		90%
Antioch's post, stock issue ownership balance		$1,764,000
Antioch's equity-adjusted investment account before stock purchase	$1,476,000	
Additional payment for 18,000 shares of Westminster	288,000	1,764,000
Required adjustment		$ –0–

This case requires no adjustment because Antioch's underlying interest remains aligned with the subsidiary's consolidated valuation basis. Any purchase of new stock by the parent in the same ratio as previous ownership does not affect consolidated Additional Paid-In Capital. The transaction creates no proportionate increase or decrease.

Case 3

Assume that instead of issuing new stock, on January 1, 2018, Westminster reacquires all 10,000 shares owned by the noncontrolling interest. It pays $16 per share for this treasury stock.

This illustration presents another type of subsidiary stock transaction: the acquisition of treasury stock. In this case the effect on the parent can be computed by reference to the amount of noncontrolling interest that must be reduced to zero in the consolidated financial statements.

Noncontrolling interest (NCI) acquisition-date fair value	$150,000
NCI share of 2017 Westminster income less excess amortization ($170,000 × 10%)	17,000
NCI share of Westminster dividends ($30,000 × 10%)	(3,000)
Noncontrolling interest valuation basis at 1/1/18	$164,000
Treasury stock purchase ($16 × 10,000 shares)	(160,000)
Required adjustment—increase in Antioch's additional paid-in capital	$ 4,000

The consolidated entity paid $160,000 to reduce a $164,000 owners' equity interest (the noncontrolling interest) to zero, thus increasing its own equity by $4,000. As usual, the increase in equity is attributed to additional paid-in capital and is recorded on the parent's records.

Antioch Company's Financial Records		
Investment in Westminster Company	4,000	
Additional Paid-In Capital (Antioch Company)		4,000
To recognize change in equity of business combination created by acquisition of 10,000 treasury shares by Westminster.		

This third illustration represents a newly introduced subsidiary stock transaction, the purchase of treasury stock. Therefore, display of consolidation Entries **S** and **A** are also presented. These entries demonstrate the worksheet eliminations required when the subsidiary holds treasury shares:

Consolidation Entry S		
Common Stock (Westminster Company)	200,000	
Additional Paid-In Capital (Westminster Company)	450,000	
Retained Earnings, 1/1/18 (Westminster Company)	910,000	
Treasury Stock		160,000
Investment in Westminster Company		1,400,000
To eliminate equity accounts of Westminster Company.		

Consolidation Entry A		
Customer List	80,000	
Investment in Westminster Company		80,000
To recognize the beginning-of-year unamortized excess acquisition-date fair value allocated to the customer list.		

Note first the absence of a noncontrolling interest entry. Also note that the sum of the credits to the Investment in Westminster account is $1,480,000, which is the pretreasury stock purchase equity method balance of $1,476,000 plus the $4,000 addition from the acquisition of the noncontrolling interest.

Case 4

Assume that on January 1, 2018, Westminster issues a 10 percent stock dividend (10,000 new shares) to its owners when the stock's fair value is $15 per share.

This final case illustrates another example of a subsidiary stock transaction producing no effect on the parent's records. Stock dividends, whether large or small, capitalize a portion of the issuing company's retained earnings without altering total book value. Shareholders recognize the receipt of a stock dividend as a change in the per share value rather than as an adjustment to the investment balance. Because neither party perceives a net effect, the consolidation process proceeds in a routine fashion. Therefore, a subsidiary stock dividend requires no special treatment prior to development of a worksheet.

Consideration transferred	$1,350,000
Noncontrolling interest acquisition-date fair value	150,000
2017 Westminster income less excess amortization	170,000
Westminster dividends	(30,000)
Subsidiary valuation basis, 1/1/18	$1,640,000
Antioch's ownership (adjusted for 10% stock dividend 99,000 ÷ 110,000 shares)	90%
Antioch's post, stock dividend ownership interest	$1,476,000
Antioch's equity-adjusted investment account	1,476,000
Adjustment required by stock dividend	$ –0–

The consolidation Entries **S** and **A** made just after the stock dividend follow. The $1,404,000 component of the investment account is offset against the stockholders' equity of the subsidiary. Although the stock dividend did not affect the parent's investment, the equity accounts of the subsidiary have been realigned in recognition of the $150,000 stock dividend (10,000 shares of $2 par value stock valued at $15 per share):

Consolidation Entry S		
Common Stock (Westminster Company)	220,000	
Additional Paid-In Capital (Westminster Company)	580,000	
Retained Earnings, 1/1/18 (Westminster Company)	760,000	
Investment in Westminster Company (90%)		1,404,000
Noncontrolling Interest (10%)		156,000

Consolidation Entry A		
Customer List	80,000	
Investment in Westminster Company		72,000
Noncontrolling Interest		8,000
To recognize the beginning-of-year unamortized excess fair value attributable to the customer list.		

Note here that the sum of the credits to the Investment in Westminster account is $1,476,000, which equals the pre–stock dividend equity method balance.

Summary

1. Variable interest entities (VIEs) typically take the form of a trust, partnership, joint venture, or corporation. In most cases, a sponsoring firm creates these entities to engage in a limited and well-defined set of business activities. Control of VIEs, by design, often does not rest with their equity holders. Instead, control is exercised through contractual arrangements with the sponsoring firm that becomes the entity's "primary beneficiary." These contracts can take the form of leases, participation rights, guarantees, or other residual interests. Through contracting, the primary beneficiary bears a significant portion of the risks and receives a significant portion of the rewards of the entity, often without owning any voting shares. Current accounting standards require a business that has a controlling financial interest in a VIE to consolidate the financial statements of the VIE with its own.
2. In periods after the primary beneficiary gains control over a VIE, consolidation procedures follow a similar process as if the entity were controlled by voting interests. All intra-entity transactions between the primary beneficiary and the VIE must be eliminated in consolidation. The consolidated net income distribution to the noncontrolling interest, however, must be based on the contractual agreement with the primary beneficiary, rather than voting interests.
3. If one member of a business combination acquires an affiliate's debt instrument (e.g., a bond or note) from an outside party, the purchase price usually differs from the carrying amount of the liability. Thus, a gain or loss has been incurred from the perspective of the business combination. However, both the debt and investment remain in the individual financial accounts of the two companies, but the gain or loss goes unrecorded. The consolidation process must adjust all balances to reflect the effective retirement of the debt.
4. Following a related party's acquisition of a company's debt, Interest Income and Expense are recognized. Because these accounts result from intra-entity transactions, they also must be removed in every subsequent consolidation along with the debt and investment figures. Retained Earnings also requires adjustment in each year after the purchase to record the impact of the gain or loss.
5. Amortization of intra-entity debt/investment balances often is necessary because of discounts and/or premiums. Consequently, the Interest Income and Interest Expense figures reported by the two parties will not agree. The closing of these two accounts into Retained Earnings each year gradually reduces the consolidation adjustment that must be made to this equity account.
6. When acquired, many subsidiaries have preferred stock outstanding as well as common stock. The existence of subsidiary preferred shares does little to complicate the consolidation process. The acquisition method values all business acquisitions at their full fair values. If a subsidiary has preferred stock, the essential process of determining its acquisition-date business fair value remains

intact. Any preferred shares not owned by the parent simply become a component of the noncontrolling interest and are included in the acquisition-date measure of subsidiary fair value.

7. Every business combination must prepare a statement of cash flows. This statement is not created by consolidating the individual cash flows of the separate companies. Instead, both a consolidated income statement and balance sheet are produced, and the cash flows statement is developed from these figures. Dividends paid to the noncontrolling interest are listed as a financing activity.
8. For most business combinations, the determination of earnings per share (EPS) follows the normal pattern presented in intermediate accounting textbooks. However, if the subsidiary has potentially dilutive items outstanding (stock warrants, convertible preferred stock, convertible bonds, etc.), a different process must be followed. The subsidiary's own diluted EPS is computed as a preliminary procedure. The parent and the outside owners then allocate the earnings used in each of these calculations based on the ownership levels of the subsidiary's shares and the dilutive items. The determination of the EPS figures to be reported for the business combination is based on the portion of consolidated net income assigned to the parent.
9. After the combination is created, a subsidiary may enter into stock transactions such as issuing additional shares or acquiring treasury stock. Such actions normally create a proportional increase or decrease in the subsidiary's equity when compared with the parent's investment. The change is measured and then reflected in the consolidated statements through the Additional Paid-In Capital account. To achieve the appropriate accounting, the parent adjusts the Investment in Subsidiary account as well as its own Additional Paid-In Capital. Because the worksheet does not eliminate this equity balance, the required increase or decrease carries over to the consolidated figures.

Comprehensive Illustration

Problem: Consolidated Statement of Cash Flows and Earnings per Share

(*Estimated Time: 35 to 45 Minutes*) Pop, Inc., acquires 90 percent of the 20,000 shares of Son Company's outstanding common stock on December 31, 2016. Of the acquisition-date fair value, it allocates $80,000 to trademarks, a figure amortized at the rate of $2,000 per year. Comparative consolidated balance sheets for 2018 and 2017 are as follows:

	2018	2017
Cash	$ 210,000	$ 130,000
Accounts receivable	350,000	220,000
Inventory	320,000	278,000
Land, buildings, and equipment (net)	1,090,000	1,120,000
Trademarks	78,000	80,000
Total assets	$2,048,000	$1,828,000
Accounts payable	$ 290,000	$ 296,000
Long-term liabilities	650,000	550,000
Noncontrolling interest	37,800	34,000
Preferred stock (10% cumulative)	100,000	100,000
Common stock (26,000 shares outstanding)	520,000	520,000
Retained earnings, 12/31	450,200	328,000
Total liabilities and stockholders' equity	$2,048,000	$1,828,000

Additional Information for 2018

- Consolidated net income (after adjustments for all intra-entity items) was $178,000.
- Consolidated depreciation and amortization equaled $52,000.

- On April 10, Son sold a building with a $40,000 book value, receiving cash of $50,000. Later that month, Pop borrowed $100,000 from a local bank and purchased equipment for $60,000. These transactions were all with outside parties.
- During the year, Pop declared and paid $40,000 dividends on its common stock and $10,000 on its preferred stock, and Son declared and paid a $20,000 dividend on its common stock.
- Son has long-term convertible debt of $180,000 outstanding included in consolidated liabilities. It recognized interest expense of $16,000 (net of taxes) on this debt during the year. This debt can be exchanged for 10,000 shares of the subsidiary's common stock. Pop owns none of this debt.
- Son recorded $60,000 net income from its own operations. Noncontrolling interest in consolidated net income was $5,800.
- Pop recorded $4,000 in profits on sales of goods to Son. These goods remain in Son's warehouse at December 31.
- Pop applies the equity method to account for its investment in Son. On its own books, Pop recognized $48,200 equity in earnings from Son [90% × ($60,000 less $2,000 amortization) and $4,000 intra-entity gross profit in inventory from its sales to Son].

Required

a. Prepare a consolidated statement of cash flows for Pop, Inc., and Son Company for the year ending December 31, 2018. Use the indirect method for determining the amount of cash provided from operations.[14]

b. Compute basic earnings per share and diluted earnings per share for Pop, Inc.

Solution

a. Consolidated Statement of Cash Flows

The problem specifies that the indirect method should be used in preparing the consolidated statement of cash flows. Therefore, all items that do not represent cash flows from operations must be removed from the $178,000 consolidated net income. For example, both the depreciation and amortization are eliminated (noncash items) as well as the gain on the sale of the building (a nonoperational item). In addition, each of the changes in consolidated Accounts Receivable, Inventory, and Accounts Payable produces a noncash impact on net income. The increase in Accounts Receivable, for example, indicates that the sales figure for the period was larger than the amount of cash collected so that adjustment is required in producing this statement.

From the information given, several nonoperational changes in cash can be determined: the bank loan, the acquisition of equipment, the sale of a building, the dividend paid by Son to the noncontrolling interest, and the dividend paid by the parent. Each of these transactions is included in the consolidated statement of cash flows shown in Exhibit 6.12, which explains the $80,000 increase in cash experienced by the entity during 2018.

b. Earnings per Share

The subsidiary's convertible debt has a potentially dilutive effect on earnings per share. Therefore, diluted EPS cannot be determined for the business combination directly from consolidated net income. First, the diluted EPS figure must be calculated for the subsidiary. This information then is used in the computations made by the consolidated entity.

Diluted EPS of $2.47 for the subsidiary is determined as follows:

Son Company—Diluted Earnings per Share

	Earnings		Shares	
As reported less excess amortization . . .	$58,000		20,000	$2.90
Effect of possible debt conversion:				
Interest saved (net of taxes).	16,000	New shares	10,000	$1.60 impact (16,000/10,000)
Diluted EPS.	$74,000		30,000	$2.47 (rounded)

The parent owns none of the convertible debt included in computing diluted EPS. Pop holds only 18,000 (90 percent of the outstanding common stock) of the 30,000 shares used in this EPS calculation.

[14] Prior to attempting this problem, a review of an intermediate accounting textbook might be useful to obtain a complete overview of the production of a statement of cash flows.

EXHIBIT 6.12

POP, INC., AND SON COMPANY
Consolidated Statement of Cash Flows
Year Ending December 31, 2018

Cash flows from operating activities		
Consolidated net income		$178,000
Adjustments to reconcile consolidated net income to net cash provided by operating activities:		
Depreciation and amortization	$ 52,000	
Gain on sale of building	(10,000)	
Increase in accounts receivable	(130,000)	
Increase in inventory	(42,000)	
Decrease in accounts payable	(6,000)	(136,000)
Net cash provided from operations		$ 42,000
Cash flows from investing activities		
Purchase of equipment	$ (60,000)	
Sale of building	50,000	
Net cash used in investing activities		(10,000)
Cash flows from financing activities		
Payment of cash dividends—Pop	$ (50,000)	
Payment of cash dividend to noncontrolling owners of Son	(2,000)	
Borrowed from bank	100,000	
Net cash provided by financing activities		48,000
Net increase in cash		$ 80,000
Cash, January 1, 2018		130,000
Cash, December 31, 2018		$210,000

Consequently, in determining diluted EPS for the parent company, only $44,400 of the subsidiary's income is applicable:

$$\$74{,}000 \times 18{,}000/30{,}000 = \$44{,}400$$

Exhibit 6.13 reveals basic EPS of $6.24 and diluted EPS of $5.94. Because the subsidiary's earnings figure is included separately in the computation of diluted EPS, the parent's individual income must be identified in the same manner. Thus, the effect of the equity income and intra-entity (downstream) transactions are taken into account in arriving at the parent's separate earnings.

EXHIBIT 6.13

POP, INC., AND SON COMPANY
Earnings per Share
Year Ending December 31, 2018

	Earnings	Shares	
	Basic Earnings per Share		
Pop's share of consolidated net income	$172,200		
Preferred dividend declared by Pop	(10,000)		
Basic EPS	162,200	26,000	$6.24 (rounded)
	Diluted Earnings per Share		
Pop's share of consolidated net income	$172,200		
Remove equity income	(48,200)		
Remove intra-entity gross profit	(4,000)		
Preferred stock dividend	(10,000)		
Common shares outstanding (Pop, Inc.)		26,000	
Common stock income—Pop (for EPS computations)	$110,000		
Income of Son (for diluted EPS)	44,400		
Diluted EPS	$154,400	26,000	$5.94 (rounded)

Questions

1. What is a variable interest entity (VIE)?
2. What are variable interests in an entity and how might they provide financial control over an entity?
3. When is a firm required to consolidate the financial statements of a VIE with its own financial statements?
4. A parent company acquires from a third party bonds that had been issued originally by one of its subsidiaries. What accounting problems are created by this purchase?
5. In question (4), why is the consolidation process simpler if the bonds had been acquired directly from the subsidiary than from a third party?
6. When a company acquires an affiliated company's debt instruments from a third party, how is the gain or loss on extinguishment of the debt calculated? When should this balance be recognized?
7. Several years ago, Bennett, Inc., bought a portion of the outstanding bonds of Smith Corporation, a subsidiary organization. The acquisition was made from an outside party. In the current year, how should these intra-entity bonds be accounted for within the consolidation process?
8. One company purchases the outstanding debt instruments of an affiliated company on the open market. This transaction creates a gain that is appropriately recognized in the consolidated financial statements of that year. Thereafter, a worksheet adjustment is required to correct the beginning balance of consolidated Retained Earnings (or the parent's Investment in Subsidiary account when the equity method is employed). Why is the amount of this adjustment reduced from year to year?
9. A parent acquires the outstanding bonds of a subsidiary company directly from an outside third party. For consolidation purposes, this transaction creates a gain of $45,000. Should this gain be allocated to the parent or the subsidiary? Why?
10. Perkins Company acquires 90 percent of the outstanding common stock of the Butterfly Corporation as well as 55 percent of its preferred stock. How should these preferred shares be accounted for within the consolidation process?
11. The income statement and the balance sheet are produced using a worksheet, but a consolidated statement of cash flows is not. What process is followed in preparing a consolidated statement of cash flows?
12. How do noncontrolling interest balances affect the consolidated statement of cash flows?
13. In many cases, EPS is computed based on the parent's portion of consolidated net income and parent company shares and convertibles. However, a different process must be used for some business combinations. When is this alternative approach required?
14. A subsidiary has (1) a convertible preferred stock and (2) a convertible bond. How are these items factored into the computation of earnings per share for the parent company?
15. Why might a subsidiary decide to issue new shares of common stock to parties outside the business combination?
16. Washburn Company owns 75 percent of Metcalf Company's outstanding common stock. During the current year, Metcalf issues additional shares to outside parties at a price more than its per share consolidated value. How does this transaction affect the business combination? How is this impact recorded within the consolidated statements?
17. Assume the same information as in question (16) except that Metcalf issues a 10 percent stock dividend instead of selling new shares of stock. How does this transaction affect the business combination?

Problems

LO 6-1

1. An enterprise that holds a variable interest in a variable interest entity (VIE) is required to consolidate the assets, liabilities, revenues, expenses, and noncontrolling interest of that entity if:
   a. The VIE has issued no voting stock.
   b. The variable interest held by the enterprise involves a lease.
   c. The enterprise has a controlling financial interest in the VIE.
   d. Other equity interests in the VIE have the obligation to absorb the expected losses of the VIE.

LO 6-2

2. Prairie Corporation is a primary beneficiary for Vintage Company, a variable interest entity. When Prairie obtained financial control over Vintage, any excess fair value over Prairie's book value was attributed solely to goodwill. Prairie owns 15 percent of Vintage Company's common stock and participation rights that entitle it to an additional 40 percent of Vintage's net income. In the current year Prairie reports $400,000 of net income before consideration of its investment in Vintage.

Vintage Company reports net income of $100,000. What amount of consolidated net income is attributable to the noncontrolling interest?

a. $15,000
b. $45,000
c. $60,000
d. $85,000

LO 6-3

3. A parent company buys bonds on the open market that had been previously issued by its subsidiary. The price paid by the parent is less than the carrying amount of the bonds on the subsidiary's records. How should the parent report the difference between the price paid and the carrying amount of the bonds on its consolidated financial statements?
   a. As a loss on retirement of the bonds.
   b. As a gain on retirement of the bonds.
   c. As an increase to interest expense over the remaining life of the bonds.
   d. Because the bonds now represent intra-entity debt, the difference is not reported.

LO 6-3

4. A subsidiary has a debt outstanding that was originally issued at a discount. At the beginning of the current year, the parent company acquired the debt at a slight premium from outside parties. Which of the following statements is true?
   a. Whether the balances agree or not, both the subsequent interest income and interest expense should be reported in a consolidated income statement.
   b. The interest income and interest expense will agree in amount and should be offset for consolidation purposes.
   c. In computing any noncontrolling interest allocation, the interest income should be included but not the interest expense.
   d. Although subsequent interest income and interest expense will not agree in amount, both balances should be eliminated for consolidation purposes.

LO 6-4

5. The parent company acquires all of a subsidiary's common stock but only 70 percent of its preferred shares. This preferred stock pays a 7 percent annual cumulative dividend. No dividends are in arrears at the current time. How is the noncontrolling interest's share of the subsidiary's income computed?
   a. As 30 percent of the subsidiary's preferred dividend.
   b. No allocation is made because the dividends have been paid.
   c. As 30 percent of the subsidiary's income after all dividends have been subtracted.
   d. Income is assigned to the preferred stock based on total par value and 30 percent of that amount is allocated to the noncontrolling interest.

LO 6-5

6. Aceton Corporation owns 80 percent of the outstanding stock of Voctax, Inc. During the current year, Voctax made $140,000 in sales to Aceton. How does this transfer affect the consolidated statement of cash flows?
   a. The transaction should be included if payment has been made.
   b. Only 80 percent of the transfers should be included because the subsidiary made the sales.
   c. Because the transfers were from a subsidiary organization, the cash flows are reported as investing activities.
   d. Because of the intra-entity nature of the transfers, the amount is not reported in the consolidated cash flow statement.

Problems 7 and 8 are based on the following information.

Comparative consolidated balance sheet data for Iverson, Inc., and its 80 percent–owned subsidiary Oakley Co. follow:

	2018	2017
Cash	$ 7,000	$ 20,000
Accounts receivable (net)	55,000	38,000
Merchandise inventory	85,000	45,000
Buildings and equipment (net)	95,000	105,000
Trademark	85,000	100,000
Totals	$327,000	$308,000

(continued)

(continued)

	2018	2017
Accounts payable	$ 75,000	$ 63,000
Notes payable, long-term	–0–	25,000
Noncontrolling interest	39,000	35,000
Common stock, $10 par	200,000	200,000
Retained earnings (deficit)	13,000	(15,000)
Totals	$327,000	$308,000

Additional Information for Fiscal Year 2018

- Iverson and Oakley's consolidated net income was $45,000.
- Oakley paid $5,000 in dividends during the year. Iverson paid $12,000 in dividends.
- Oakley sold $11,000 worth of merchandise to Iverson during the year.
- There were no purchases or sales of long-term assets during the year.

In the 2018 consolidated statement of cash flows for Iverson Company:

LO 6-5

7. Net cash flows from operating activities were
   a. $12,000
   b. $20,000
   c. $24,000
   d. $25,000

LO 6-5

8. Net cash flows from financing activities were
   a. $(25,000)
   b. $(37,000)
   c. $(38,000)
   d. $(42,000)

LO 6-6

9. Bensman Corporation is computing EPS. One of its subsidiaries has stock warrants outstanding. How do these convertible items affect Bensman's EPS computation?
   a. No effect is created because the stock warrants were for the subsidiary company's shares.
   b. The stock warrants are not included in the computation unless they are antidilutive.
   c. The effect of the stock warrants must be computed in deriving the amount of subsidiary income to be included in making the diluted EPS calculation.
   d. The stock warrants are included only in basic EPS but never in diluted EPS.

LO 6-7

10. Arcola, Inc., acquires all 40,000 shares of Tuscola Company for $725,000. A year later, when Arcola's equity adjusted balance in its investment in Tuscola equals $800,000, Tuscola issues an additional 10,000 shares to outside investors for $25 per share. Which of the following best describes the effect of Tuscola's stock issue on Arcola's investment account?
    a. No effect because the shares were all sold to outside parties.
    b. The investment account is reduced because Arcola now owns a smaller percentage of Tuscola.
    c. The investment account is increased because Arcola's share of Tuscola's value has increased.
    d. No effect because Arcola maintains control over Tuscola despite the new stock issue.

LO 6-3

11. Dane, Inc., owns Carlton Corporation. For the current year, Dane reports net income (without consideration of its investment in Carlton) of $185,000 and the subsidiary reports $105,000. The parent had a bond payable outstanding on January 1, with a carrying amount of $209,000. The subsidiary acquired the bond on that date for $196,000. During the current year, Dane reported interest expense of $18,000 while Carlton reported interest income of $19,000, both related to the intra-entity bond payable. What is consolidated net income?
    a. $289,000
    b. $291,000
    c. $302,000
    d. $304,000

LO 6-6

12. Mattoon, Inc., owns 80 percent of Effingham Company. For the current year, this combined entity reported consolidated net income of $500,000. Of this amount $465,000 was attributable to Mattoon's controlling interest while the remaining $35,000 was attributable to the noncontrolling interest. Mattoon has 100,000 shares of common stock outstanding and Effingham has 25,000 shares outstanding.

Neither company has issued preferred shares or has any convertible securities outstanding. On the face of the consolidated income statement, how much should be reported as Mattoon's earnings per share?

a. $5.00

b. $4.65

c. $4.00

d. $3.88

LO 6-3

13. Aaron Company's books show current earnings of $430,000 and $46,000 in cash dividends. Zeese Company earns $164,000 in net income and declares $11,500 in dividends. Aaron has held a 70 percent interest in Zeese for several years, an investment with an acquisition-date excess fair over book value attributable solely to goodwill. Aaron uses the initial value method to account for these shares and includes dividend income in its internal earnings reports.

On January 1 of the current year, Zeese acquired in the open market $64,400 of Aaron's 8 percent bonds. The bonds had originally been issued several years ago at 92, reflecting a 10 percent effective interest rate. On the date of purchase, the carrying amount of the bonds payable was $60,200. Zeese paid $56,000 based on a 12 percent effective interest rate over the remaining life of the bonds.

What is consolidated net income for this year?

a. $598,900

b. $589,450

c. $438,050

d. $590,850

LO 6-3

14. Redfield Company reports current earnings of $420,000 while declaring $52,000 in cash dividends. Snedeker Company earns $147,000 in net income and declares $13,000 in dividends. Redfield has held a 70 percent interest in Snedeker for several years, an investment with an acquisition-date excess fair over book value attributable solely to goodwill. Redfield uses the initial value method to account for these shares.

On January 1 of the current year, Snedeker acquired in the open market $51,600 of Redfield's 8 percent bonds. The bonds had originally been issued several years ago at 92, reflecting a 10 percent effective interest rate. On the date of purchase, the carrying amount of the bonds payable was $50,400. Snedeker paid $49,200 based on a 12 percent effective interest rate over the remaining life of the bonds.

What is the noncontrolling interest's share of consolidated net income?

a. $40,200

b. $44,100

c. $40,560

d. $44,460

LO 6-3

15. Pesto Company possesses 80 percent of Salerno Company's outstanding voting stock. Pesto uses the initial value method to account for this investment. On January 1, 2014, Pesto sold 9 percent bonds payable with a $10 million face value (maturing in 20 years) on the open market at a premium of $600,000. On January 1, 2017, Salerno acquired 40 percent of these same bonds from an outside party at 96.6 percent of face value. Both companies use the straight-line method of amortization. For a 2018 consolidation, what adjustment should be made to Pesto's beginning Retained Earnings as a result of this bond acquisition?

a. $320,000 increase

b. $326,000 increase

c. $331,000 increase

d. $340,000 increase

LO 6-4

16. On January 1, Tesco Company spent a total of $4,384,000 to acquire control over Blondel Company. This price was based on paying $424,000 for 20 percent of Blondel's preferred stock and $3,960,000 for 90 percent of its outstanding common stock. At the acquisition date, the fair value of the 10 percent noncontrolling interest in Blondel's common stock was $440,000. The fair value of the 80 percent of Blondel's preferred shares not owned by Tesco was $1,696,000. Blondel's stockholders' equity accounts at January 1 were as follows:

Preferred stock—9%, $100 par value, cumulative and participating; 10,000 shares outstanding	$ 1,000,000
Common stock—$50 par value; 40,000 shares outstanding	2,000,000
Retained earnings	3,000,000
Total stockholders' equity	$ 6,000,000

Tesco believes that all of Blondel's accounts approximate their fair values within the company's financial statements. What amount of consolidated goodwill should be recognized?

a. $ 300,000
b. $ 316,000
c. $ 364,000
d. $ 520,000

LO 6-4

17. On January 1, Coldwater Company has a net book value of $2,174,000 as follows:

2,000 shares of preferred stock; par value $100 per share; cumulative, nonparticipating, nonvoting; call value $108 per share . . .	$ 200,000
34,500 shares of common stock; par value $40 per share. . .	1,380,000
Retained earnings . . .	594,000
Total . . .	$2,174,000

Westmont Company acquires all outstanding preferred shares for $214,000 and 60 percent of the common stock for $1,253,280. The acquisition-date fair value of the noncontrolling interest in Coldwater's common stock was $835,520. Westmont believed that one of Coldwater's buildings, with a 12-year remaining life, was undervalued by $63,600 on the company's financial records.

What amount of consolidated goodwill would be recognized from this acquisition?

a. $61,600
b. $65,200
c. $60,400
d. $59,200

LO 6-5

18. Premier Company owns 90 percent of the voting shares of Stanton, Inc. Premier reports sales of $480,000 during the current year and Stanton reports $264,000. Stanton sold inventory costing $28,800 to Premier (upstream) during the year for $57,600. Of this amount, 25 percent is still in ending inventory at year-end. Total receivables on the consolidated balance sheet were $81,800 at the first of the year and $119,100 at year-end. No intra-entity debt existed at the beginning or ending of the year. Using the direct method, what is the consolidated amount of cash collected by the business combination from its customers?

a. $706,700
b. $649,100
c. $686,400
d. $744,000

LO 6-7

19. Aaron owns 100 percent of the 12,000 shares of Veritable, Inc. The Investment in Veritable account has a balance of $588,000, corresponding to the subsidiary's unamortized acquisition-date fair value of $49 per share. Veritable issues 3,000 new shares to the public for $50 per share. How does this transaction affect the Investment in Veritable account?

a. It is not affected because the shares were sold to outside parties.
b. It should be increased by $2,400.
c. It should be increased by $3,000.
d. It should be decreased by $117,600.

Problems 20 through 22 are based on the following information.
Neill Company purchases 80 percent of the common stock of Stamford Company on January 1, 2017, when Stamford has the following stockholders' equity accounts:

Common stock—40,000 shares outstanding . . .	$100,000
Additional paid-in capital . . .	75,000
Retained earnings, 1/1/17 . . .	540,000
Total stockholders' equity . . .	$715,000

To acquire this interest in Stamford, Neill pays a total of $592,000. The acquisition-date fair value of the 20 percent noncontrolling interest was $148,000. Any excess fair value was allocated to goodwill, which has not experienced any impairment.

On January 1, 2018, Stamford reports retained earnings of $620,000. Neill has accrued the increase in Stamford's retained earnings through application of the equity method.

View the following problems as independent situations:

LO 6-7

20. On January 1, 2018, Stamford issues 10,000 additional shares of common stock for $25 per share. Neill acquires 8,000 of these shares. How will this transaction affect the parent company's Additional Paid-In Capital account?
    a. Has no effect on it.
    b. Increases it by $20,500.
    c. Increases it by $36,400.
    d. Increases it by $82,300.

LO 6-7

21. On January 1, 2018, Stamford issues 10,000 additional shares of common stock for $15 per share. Neill does not acquire any of this newly issued stock. How does this transaction affect the parent company's Additional Paid-In Capital account?
    a. Has no effect on it.
    b. Increases it by $44,000.
    c. Decreases it by $35,200.
    d. Decreases it by $55,000.

LO 6-7

22. On January 1, 2018, Stamford reacquires 8,000 of the outstanding shares of its own common stock for $24 per share. None of these shares belonged to Neill. How does this transaction affect the parent company's Additional Paid-In Capital account?
    a. Has no effect on it.
    b. Decreases it by $55,000.
    c. Decreases it by $35,000.
    d. Decreases it by $28,000.

LO 6-2

23. Hillsborough Country Outfitters, Inc., entered into an agreement for HCO Media LLC to exclusively conduct Hillsborough's e-commerce initiatives through a jointly owned (50 percent each) Internet site known as HCO.com. HCO Media receives 2 percent of all sales revenue generated through the site up to a maximum of $500,000 per year. Both Hillsborough and HCO Media pay 50 percent of the costs to maintain the Internet site. However, if HCO Media's fees are insufficient to cover its 50 percent share of the costs, Hillsborough absorbs the loss.

    Assuming that HCO Media qualifies as a VIE, should Hillsborough consolidate HCO Media LLC?

LO 6-2

24. The following describes a set of arrangements between TecPC Company and a variable interest entity (VIE) as of December 31, 2017. TecPC agrees to design and construct a new research and development (R&D) facility. The VIE's sole purpose is to finance and own the R&D facility and lease it to TecPC Company after construction is completed. Payments under the operating lease are expected to begin in the first quarter of 2019.

    The VIE has financing commitments sufficient for the construction project from equity and debt participants (investors) of $4 million and $42 million, respectively. TecPC, in its role as the VIE's construction agent, is responsible for completing construction by December 31, 2018. TecPC has guaranteed a portion of the VIE's obligations during the construction and post-construction periods.

    TecPC agrees to lease the R&D facility for five years with multiple extension options. The lease is a variable rate obligation indexed to a three-month market rate. As market interest rates increase or decrease, the payments under this operating lease also increase or decrease, sufficient to provide a return to the investors. If all extension options are exercised, the total lease term is 35 years.

    At the end of the first five-year lease term or any extension, TecPC may choose one of the following:

    - Renew the lease at fair value subject to investor approval.
    - Purchase the facility at its original construction cost.
    - Sell the facility on the VIE's behalf to an independent third party. If TecPC sells the project and the proceeds from the sale are insufficient to repay the investors their original cost, TecPC may be required to pay the VIE up to 85 percent of the project's cost.

    a. What is the purpose of reporting consolidated statements for a company and the entities that it controls?
    b. When should a VIE's financial statements be consolidated with those of another company?

c. Identify the risks of ownership of the R&D facility that (1) TecPC has effectively shifted to the VIE's owners and (2) remain with TecPC.

d. What characteristics of a primary beneficiary does TecPC possess?

LO 6-2

25. On December 31, 2017, PanTech Company invests $20,000 in SoftPlus, a variable interest entity. In contractual agreements completed on that date, PanTech established itself as the primary beneficiary of SoftPlus. Previously, PanTech had no equity interest in SoftPlus. Immediately after PanTech's investment, SoftPlus presents the following balance sheet:

Cash	$ 20,000	Long-term debt	$120,000
Marketing software	140,000	Noncontrolling interest	60,000
Computer equipment	40,000	PanTech equity interest	20,000
Total assets	$200,000	Total liabilities and equity	$200,000

Each of the above amounts represents an assessed fair value at December 31, 2017, except for the marketing software. Accordingly the December 31 fair value of SoftPlus is assessed at $80,000.

a. If the marketing software was undervalued by $20,000, what amounts for SoftPlus would appear in PanTech's December 31, 2017, consolidated financial statements?

b. If the marketing software was overvalued by $20,000, what amounts for SoftPlus would appear in PanTech's December 31, 2017, consolidated financial statements?

LO 6-2

excel

26. On January 1, 2018, Access IT Company exchanged $1,000,000 for 40 percent of the outstanding voting stock of Net Connect. Especially attractive to Access IT was a research project underway at Net Connect that would enhance both the speed and quantity of client-accessible data. Although not recorded in Net Connect's financial records, the fair value of the research project was considered to be $1,960,000.

In contractual agreements with the sole owner of the remaining 60 percent of Net Connect, Access IT was granted (1) various decision-making rights over Net Connect's operating decisions and (2) special service purchase provisions at below-market rates. As a result of these contractual agreements, Access IT established itself as the primary beneficiary of Net Connect. Immediately after the purchase, Access IT and Net Connect presented the following balance sheets:

	Access IT	Net Connect
Cash	$ 61,000	$ 41,000
Investment in Net Connect	1,000,000	
Capitalized software	981,000	156,000
Computer equipment	1,066,000	56,000
Communications equipment	916,000	336,000
Patent		191,000
Total assets	$ 4,024,000	$ 780,000
Long-term debt	(941,000)	(616,000)
Common stock—Access IT	(2,660,000)	
Common stock—Net Connect		(41,000)
Retained earnings	(423,000)	(123,000)
Total liabilities and equity	$(4,024,000)	$(780,000)

Each of the above amounts represents a fair value at January 1, 2018. The fair value of the 60 percent of Net Connect shares not owned by Access IT was $1,500,000.

Prepare an acquisition-date consolidation worksheet for Access IT and its variable interest entity.

LO 6-2

27. On January 1, 2018, Primair Corporation loaned Vista Company $300,000 and agreed to guarantee all of Vista's long-term debt in exchange for (1) decision-making authority over all of Vista's activities and (2) an annual cash payment of 25 percent of Vista's revenues. As a result of the agreement, Primair is the primary beneficiary of Vista (a variable interest entity). Primair's loan to Vista stipulated a 7 percent (market) rate of interest to be paid annually.

On January 1, 2018, Primair estimated that the fair value of Vista's equity shares equaled $150,000 while Vista's book value was $55,000. Any excess fair over book value at that date was attributed to Vista's trademark with an indefinite life. Because Primair owns no equity in Vista, all of the acquisition-date excess fair over book value is allocated to the non-controlling interest.

Vista paid Primair 25 percent of its 2018 revenues at the end of the year. On December 31, 2018, Primair and Vista submitted the following statements for consolidation. Parentheses indicate credit balances.

	Primair	Vista
Revenues	(839,500)	(188,000)
Cost of good sold	612,000	75,000
Other operating expenses	78,000	25,000
Interest income	(21,000)	–0–
Interest expense	–0–	21,000
Net income	(170,500)	(67,000)
Retained earnings, 1/1	(1,555,000)	(40,000)
Net income	(170,500)	(67,000)
Dividends declared	250,000	–0–
Retained earnings, 12/31	(1,475,500)	(107,000)
Current assets	460,500	50,000
Loan receivable from Vista	300,000	
Equipment (net)	794,000	525,000
Trademark	–0–	45,000
Total assets	1,554,500	620,000
Current liabilities	(29,000)	(18,000)
Long-term debt	–0–	(180,000)
Loan payable to Primair		(300,000)
Common stock	(50,000)	(15,000)
Retained earnings, 12/31	(1,475,500)	(107,000)
Total liabilities and equity	(1,554,500)	(620,000)

In computing the amount of Vista's net income attributable to the non-controlling interest,

- Vista's net income should be reduced by the 25% revenue allocation to Primair.
- Interest expense paid to Primair is not excluded from Vista's net income because it is a contractual distribution of Vista's net income to Primair.

Prepare the December 31, 2018, consolidation worksheet for Primair and Vista.

LO 6-3

28. Cairns owns 75 percent of the voting stock of Hamilton, Inc. The parent's interest was acquired several years ago on the date that the subsidiary was formed. Consequently, no goodwill or other allocation was recorded in connection with the acquisition. Cairns uses the equity method in its internal records to account for its investment in Hamilton.

    On January 1, 2014, Hamilton sold $1,000,000 in 10-year bonds to the public at 105. The bonds had a cash interest rate of 9 percent payable every December 31. Cairns acquired 40 percent of these bonds at 96 percent of face value on January 1, 2016. Both companies utilize the straight-line method of amortization. Prepare the consolidation worksheet entries to recognize the effects of the intra-entity bonds at each of the following dates.

    a. December 31, 2016
    b. December 31, 2017
    c. December 31, 2018

LO 6-3

29. Highlight, Inc., owns all outstanding stock of Kiort Corporation. The two companies report the following balances for the year ending December 31, 2017:

	Highlight	Kiort
Revenues and interest income	$(670,000)	$(390,000)
Operating and interest expense	540,000	221,000
Other gains and losses	(120,000)	(32,000)
Net income	$(250,000)	$(201,000)

On January 1, 2017, Highlight acquired on the open market bonds for $108,000 originally issued by Kiort. This investment had an effective rate of 8 percent. The bonds had a face value of $100,000 and a cash interest rate of 9 percent. At the date of acquisition, these bonds were shown as liabilities by Kiort with a carrying amount of $84,000 (based on an effective rate of 11 percent). Determine the balances that should appear on a consolidated income statement for 2017.

LO 6-3

30. Several years ago Brant, Inc., sold $900,000 in bonds to the public. Annual cash interest of 9 percent ($81,000) was to be paid on this debt. The bonds were issued at a discount to yield 12 percent. At the beginning of 2016, Zack Corporation (a wholly owned subsidiary of Brant) purchased $180,000 of these bonds on the open market for $201,000, a price based on an effective interest rate of 7 percent. The bond liability had a carrying amount on that date of $760,000. Assume Brant uses the equity method to account internally for its investment in Zack.
    a. What consolidation entry would be required for these bonds on December 31, 2016?
    b. What consolidation entry would be required for these bonds on December 31, 2018?

LO 6-3

31. Opus, Incorporated, owns 90 percent of Bloom Company. On December 31, 2017, Opus acquires half of Bloom's $500,000 outstanding bonds. These bonds had been sold on the open market on January 1, 2015, at a 12 percent effective rate. The bonds pay a cash interest rate of 10 percent every December 31 and are scheduled to come due on December 31, 2025. Bloom issued this debt originally for $435,763. Opus paid $283,550 for this investment, indicating an 8 percent effective yield.
    a. Assuming that both parties use the effective rate method, what gain or loss from the retirement of this debt should be reported on the consolidated income statement for 2017?
    b. Assuming that both parties use the effective rate method, what balances should appear in the Investment in Bloom Bonds account on Opus's records and the Bonds Payable account of Bloom as of December 31, 2018?
    c. Assuming that both parties use the straight-line method, what consolidation entry would be required on December 31, 2018, because of these bonds? Assume that the parent is not applying the equity method.

LO 6-4

32. Hepner Corporation has the following stockholders' equity accounts:

Preferred stock (6% cumulative dividend)	$500,000
Common stock	750,000
Additional paid-in capital	300,000
Retained earnings..............................	950,000

The preferred stock is participating. Wasatch Corporation buys 80 percent of this common stock for $1,600,000 and 70 percent of the preferred stock for $630,000. The acquisition-date fair value of the noncontrolling interest in the common shares was $400,000 and was $270,000 for the preferred shares. All of the subsidiary's assets and liabilities are viewed as having fair values equal to their book values. What amount is attributed to goodwill on the date of acquisition?

LO 6-4

33. Smith, Inc., has the following stockholders' equity accounts as of January 1, 2018:

Preferred stock—$100 par, nonvoting and nonparticipating, 8% cumulative dividend	$2,000,000
Common stock—$20 par value	4,000,000
Retained earnings............................	10,000,000

Haried Company purchases all of Smith's common stock on January 1, 2018, for $14,040,000. The preferred stock remains in the hands of outside parties. Any excess acquisition-date fair value will be assigned to franchise contracts with a 40-year remaining life.

During 2018, Smith reports earning $450,000 in net income and declares $360,000 in cash dividends. Haried applies the equity method to this investment.
    a. What is the noncontrolling interest's share of consolidated net income for this period?
    b. What is the balance in the Investment in Smith account as of December 31, 2018?
    c. What consolidation entries are needed for 2018?

LO 6-4

34. Through the payment of $10,468,000 in cash, Drexel Company acquires voting control over Young Company. This price is paid for 60 percent of the subsidiary's 100,000 outstanding common shares ($40 par value) as well as all 10,000 shares of 8 percent, cumulative, $100 par value preferred stock. Of the total payment, $3.1 million is attributed to the fully participating preferred stock with the remainder paid for the common. This acquisition is carried out on January 1, 2018, when

Young reports retained earnings of $10 million and a total book value of $15 million. The acquisition-date fair value of the noncontrolling interest in Young's common stock was $4,912,000. On this same date, a building owned by Young (with a 5-year remaining life) is undervalued in the financial records by $200,000, while equipment with a 10-year remaining life is overvalued by $100,000. Any further excess acquisition-date fair value is assigned to a brand name with a 20-year remaining life.

During 2018, Young reports net income of $900,000 while declaring $400,000 in cash dividends. Drexel uses the initial value method to account for both of these investments.

Prepare appropriate consolidation entries for 2018.

LO 6-5

35. The following information has been taken from the consolidation worksheet of Peak and its 90 percent–owned subsidiary, Valley:
    - Peak reports a $12,000 gain on the sale of a building. The building had a book value of $32,000 but was sold for $44,000 cash.
    - Intra-entity inventory transfers of $129,000 occurred during the current period.
    - Valley declared and paid a $30,000 dividend during the year with $27,000 of this amount going to Peak.
    - Amortization of an intangible asset recognized by Peak's worksheet was $16,000 for the current period.
    - Consolidated accounts payable decreased by $11,000 during the year.

    Indicate how to reflect each of these events on a consolidated statement of cash flows.

LO 6-5

36. Alford Company and its 80 percent–owned subsidiary, Knight, have the following income statements for 2018:

	Alford	Knight
Revenues	$(500,000)	$(230,000)
Cost of goods sold	300,000	140,000
Depreciation and amortization	40,000	10,000
Other expenses	20,000	20,000
Gain on sale of equipment	(30,000)	–0–
Equity in earnings of Knight	(36,200)	–0–
Net income	$(206,200)	$ (60,000)

Additional Information for 2018

- Intra-entity inventory transfers during the year amounted to $90,000. All intra-entity transfers were downstream from Alford to Knight.
- Intra-entity gross profits in inventory at January 1 were $6,000, but at December 31 they are $9,000.
- Annual excess amortization expense resulting from the acquisition is $11,000.
- Knight paid dividends totaling $20,000.
- The noncontrolling interest's share of the subsidiary's income is $9,800.
- During the year, consolidated inventory rose by $11,000 while accounts receivable and accounts payable declined by $8,000 and $6,000, respectively.

Using either the direct or indirect method, compute net cash flows from operating activities during the period for the business combination.

LO 6-6

37. Porter Corporation owns all 30,000 shares of the common stock of Street, Inc. Porter has 60,000 shares of its own common stock outstanding. During the current year, Porter earns net income (without any consideration of its investment in Street) of $150,000 while Street reports $130,000. Annual amortization of $10,000 is recognized each year on the consolidation worksheet based on acquisition-date fair-value allocations. Both companies have convertible bonds outstanding. During the current year, bond-related interest expense (net of taxes) is $32,000 for Porter and $24,000 for Street. Porter's bonds can be converted into 8,000 shares of common stock; Street's bonds can be converted into 10,000 shares. Porter owns none of these bonds. What are the earnings per share amounts that Porter should report in its current year consolidated income statement?

LO 6-6

38. Primus, Inc., owns all outstanding stock of Sonston, Inc. For the current year, Primus reports net income (exclusive of any investment income) of $600,000. Primus has 100,000 shares of common

stock outstanding. Sonston reports net income of $200,000 for the period with 40,000 shares of common stock outstanding. Sonston also has 10,000 stock warrants outstanding that allow the holder to acquire shares at $10 per share. The value of this stock was $20 per share throughout the year. Primus owns 2,000 of these warrants. What amount should Primus report for diluted earnings per share?

LO 6-6

39. Garfun, Inc., owns all of the stock of Simon, Inc. For 2018, Garfun reports income (exclusive of any investment income) of $480,000. Garfun has 80,000 shares of common stock outstanding. It also has 5,000 shares of preferred stock outstanding that pay a dividend of $15,000 per year. Simon reports net income of $290,000 for the period with 80,000 shares of common stock outstanding. Simon also has a liability for 10,000 of $100 bonds that pay annual interest of $8 per bond. Each of these bonds can be converted into three shares of common stock. Garfun owns none of these bonds. Assume a tax rate of 30 percent. What amount should Garfun report as diluted earnings per share?

LO 6-6

40. The following separate income statements are for Burks Company and its 80 percent–owned subsidiary, Foreman Company:

	Burks	Foreman
Revenues	$(430,000)	$(330,000)
Expenses	280,000	240,000
Gain on sale of equipment	–0–	(30,000)
Equity earnings of subsidiary	(64,000)	–0–
Net income	$(214,000)	$(120,000)
Outstanding common shares	65,000	40,000

Additional Information

- Amortization expense resulting from Foreman's excess acquisition-date fair value is $40,000 per year.
- Burks has convertible preferred stock outstanding. Each of these 8,000 shares is paid a dividend of $4 per year. Each share can be converted into four shares of common stock.
- Stock warrants to buy 20,000 shares of Foreman are also outstanding. For $15, each warrant can be converted into a share of Foreman's common stock. The fair value of this stock is $20 throughout the year. Burks owns none of these warrants.
- Foreman has convertible bonds payable that paid interest of $45,000 (after taxes) during the year. These bonds can be exchanged for 10,000 shares of common stock. Burks holds 10 percent of these bonds, which it bought at book value directly from Foreman.

Compute basic and diluted EPS for Burks Company.

LO 6-7

41. DeMilo, Inc., owns 100 percent of the 40,000 outstanding shares of Ricardo, Inc. DeMilo currently carries the Investment in Ricardo account at $490,000 using the equity method.

Ricardo issues 10,000 new shares to the public for $15.75 per share. How does this transaction affect the Investment in Ricardo account that appears on DeMilo's financial records?

LO 6-7

excel

42. Albuquerque, Inc., acquired 16,000 shares of Marmon Company several years ago for $600,000. At the acquisition date, Marmon reported a book value of $710,000, and Albuquerque assessed the fair value of the noncontrolling interest at $150,000. Any excess of acquisition-date fair value over book value was assigned to broadcast licenses with indefinite lives. Since the acquisition date and until this point, Marmon has issued no additional shares. No impairment has been recognized for the broadcast licenses.

At the present time, Marmon reports $800,000 as total stockholders' equity, which is broken down as follows:

Common stock ($10 par value)	$200,000
Additional paid-in capital	230,000
Retained earnings	370,000
Total	$800,000

View the following as independent situations:

a. Marmon sells 5,000 shares of previously unissued common stock to the public for $47 per share. Albuquerque purchased none of this stock. What journal entry should Albuquerque make to recognize the impact of this stock transaction?

b. Marmon sells 4,000 shares of previously unissued common stock to the public for $33 per share. Albuquerque purchased none of this stock. What journal entry should Albuquerque make to recognize the impact of this stock transaction?

LO 6-7

43. On January 1, 2016, Aronsen Company acquired 90 percent of Siedel Company's outstanding shares. Siedel had a net book value on that date of $480,000: common stock ($10 par value) of $200,000 and retained earnings of $280,000.

Aronsen paid $584,100 for this investment. The acquisition-date fair value of the 10 percent noncontrolling interest was $64,900. The excess fair value over book value associated with the acquisition was used to increase land by $89,000 and to recognize copyrights (16-year remaining life) at $80,000. Subsequent to the acquisition, Aronsen applied the initial value method to its investment account.

In the 2016–2017 period, the subsidiary's retained earnings increased by $100,000. During 2018, Siedel earned income of $80,000 while declaring $20,000 in dividends. Also, at the beginning of 2018, Siedel issued 4,000 new shares of common stock for $38 per share to finance the expansion of its corporate facilities. Aronsen purchased none of these additional shares and therefore recorded no entry. Prepare the appropriate 2018 consolidation entries for these two companies.

LO 6-3

44. Pavin acquires all of Stabler's outstanding shares on January 1, 2015, for $460,000 in cash. Of this amount, $30,000 was attributed to equipment with a 10-year remaining life and $40,000 was assigned to trademarks expensed over a 20-year period. Pavin applies the partial equity method so that income is accrued each period based solely on the earnings reported by the subsidiary.

On January 1, 2018, Pavin reports $300,000 in bonds outstanding with a carrying amount of $282,000. Stabler purchases half of these bonds on the open market for $145,500.

During 2018, Pavin begins to sell merchandise to Stabler. During that year, inventory costing $80,000 was transferred at a price of $100,000. All but $10,000 (at sales price) of these goods were resold to outside parties by year-end. Stabler still owes $33,000 for inventory shipped from Pavin during December.

The following financial figures are for the two companies for the year ending December 31, 2018. Dividends were both declared and paid during the current year. Prepare a worksheet to produce consolidated balances. (Credits are indicated by parentheses.)

	Pavin	Stabler
Revenues	$ (740,000)	$(505,000)
Cost of goods sold	455,000	240,000
Expenses	125,000	158,500
Interest expense—bonds	36,000	–0–
Interest income—bond investment	–0–	(16,500)
Loss on extinguishment of bonds	–0–	–0–
Equity in Stabler's income	(123,000)	–0–
Net income	$ (247,000)	$(123,000)
Retained earnings, 1/1/18	$ (345,000)	$(361,000)
Net income (above)	(247,000)	(123,000)
Dividends declared	155,000	61,000
Retained earnings, 12/31/18	$ (437,000)	$(423,000)
Cash and receivables	$ 217,000	$ 35,000
Inventory	175,000	87,000
Investment in Stabler	613,000	–0–
Investment in Pavin bonds	–0–	147,000
Land, buildings, and equipment (net)	245,000	541,000
Trademarks	–0–	–0–
Total assets	$ 1,250,000	$ 810,000
Accounts payable	$ (225,000)	$(167,000)
Bonds payable	(300,000)	(100,000)
Discount on bonds	12,000	–0–
Common stock	(300,000)	(120,000)
Retained earnings (above)	(437,000)	(423,000)
Total liabilities and stockholders' equity	$(1,250,000)	$(810,000)

LO 6-3

excel

45. Fred, Inc., and Herman Corporation formed a business combination on January 1, 2016, when Fred acquired a 60 percent interest in Herman's common stock for $312,000 in cash. The book value of Herman's assets and liabilities on that day totaled $300,000 and the fair value of the noncontrolling interest was $208,000. Patents being held by Herman (with a 12-year remaining life) were undervalued by $90,000 within the company's financial records and a customer list (10-year life) worth $130,000 was also recognized as part of the acquisition-date fair value.

Intra-entity inventory transfers occur regularly between the two companies. Merchandise carried over from one year to the next is always sold in the subsequent period.

Year	Original Cost to Herman	Transfer Price to Fred	Ending Balance at Transfer Price
2016	$80,000	$100,000	$20,000
2017	100,000	125,000	40,000
2018	90,000	120,000	30,000

Fred had not paid for half of the 2018 inventory transfers by year-end.

On January 1, 2017, Fred sold $15,000 in land to Herman for $22,000. Herman is still holding this land.

On January 1, 2018, Herman acquired $20,000 (face value) of Fred's bonds in the open market. These bonds had an 8 percent cash interest rate. On the date of repurchase, the liability was shown within Fred's records at $21,386, indicating an effective yield of 6 percent. Herman's acquisition price was $18,732 based on an effective interest rate of 10 percent.

Herman indicated earning a net income of $25,000 within its 2018 financial statements. The subsidiary also reported a beginning Retained Earnings balance of $300,000, dividends of $4,000, and common stock of $100,000. Herman has not issued any additional common stock since its takeover. The parent company has applied the equity method to record its investment in Herman.

a. Prepare consolidation worksheet adjustments for 2018.

b. Calculate the amount of consolidated net income attributable to the noncontrolling interest for 2018. In addition, determine the ending 2018 balance for noncontrolling interest in the consolidated balance sheet.

c. Determine the consolidation worksheet adjustments needed in 2019 in connection with the intra-entity bonds.

LO 6-3, 6-4

46. On January 1, 2017, Mona, Inc., acquired 80 percent of Lisa Company's common stock as well as 60 percent of its preferred shares. Mona paid $65,000 in cash for the preferred stock, with a call value of 110 percent of the $50 per share par value. The remaining 40 percent of the preferred shares traded at a $34,000 fair value. Mona paid $552,800 for the common stock. At the acquisition date, the noncontrolling interest in the common stock had a fair value of $138,200. The excess fair value over Lisa's book value was attributed to franchise contracts of $40,000. This intangible asset is being amortized over a 40-year period. Lisa pays all preferred stock dividends (a total of $8,000 per year) on an annual basis. During 2017, Lisa's book value increased by $50,000.

On January 2, 2017, Mona acquired one-half of Lisa's outstanding bonds payable to reduce the business combination's debt position. Lisa's bonds had a face value of $100,000 and paid cash interest of 10 percent per year. These bonds had been issued to the public to yield 14 percent. Interest is paid each December 31. On January 2, 2017, these bonds had a total $88,350 carrying amount. Mona paid $53,310, indicating an effective interest rate of 8 percent.

On January 3, 2017, Mona sold Lisa fixed assets that had originally cost $100,000 but had accumulated depreciation of $60,000 when transferred. The transfer was made at a price of $120,000. These assets were estimated to have a remaining useful life of 10 years.

The individual financial statements for these two companies for the year ending December 31, 2018, are as follows:

	Mona, Inc.	**Lisa Company**
Sales and other revenues	$ (500,000)	$ (200,000)
Expenses	220,000	120,000
Dividend income—Lisa common stock	(8,000)	–0–
Dividend income—Lisa preferred stock	(4,800)	–0–
Net income	$ (292,800)	$ (80,000)
Retained earnings, 1/1/18	$ (700,000)	$ (500,000)
Net income (above)	(292,800)	(80,000)
Dividends declared—common stock	92,800	10,000
Dividends declared—preferred stock	–0–	8,000
Retained earnings, 12/31/18	$ (900,000)	$ (562,000)
Current assets	$ 130,419	$ 500,000
Investment in Lisa—common stock	552,800	–0–
Investment in Lisa—preferred stock	65,000	–0–
Investment in Lisa—bonds	51,781	–0–
Fixed assets	1,100,000	800,000
Accumulated depreciation	(300,000)	(200,000)
Total assets	$ 1,600,000	$ 1,100,000
Accounts payable	$ (400,000)	$ (144,580)
Bonds payable	–0–	(100,000)
Discount on bonds payable	–0–	6,580
Common stock	(300,000)	(200,000)
Preferred stock	–0–	(100,000)
Retained earnings, 12/31/18	(900,000)	(562,000)
Total liabilities and equities	$(1,600,000)	$(1,100,000)

a. What consolidation worksheet adjustments would have been required as of January 1, 2017, to eliminate the subsidiary's common and preferred stocks?

b. What consolidation worksheet adjustments would have been required as of December 31, 2017, to account for Mona's purchase of Lisa's bonds?

c. What consolidation worksheet adjustments would have been required as of December 31, 2017, to account for the intra-entity sale of fixed assets?

d. Assume that consolidated financial statements are being prepared for the year ending December 31, 2018. Calculate the consolidated balance for each of the following accounts:

Franchises

Fixed Assets

Accumulated Depreciation

Expenses

LO 6-5

47. Bolero Company holds 80 percent of the common stock of Rivera, Inc., and 40 percent of this subsidiary's convertible bonds. The following consolidated financial statements are for 2017 and 2018:

Bolero Company and Consolidated Subsidiary Rivera

	2017	**2018**
Revenues	$ (900,000)	$(1,030,000)
Cost of goods sold	610,000	650,000
Depreciation and amortization	100,000	120,000
Gain on sale of building	–0–	(30,000)
Interest expense	40,000	40,000
Consolidated net income	(150,000)	(250,000)
to noncontrolling interest	19,000	21,000
to parent company	$ (131,000)	$ (229,000)

(continued)

(continued)

Bolero Company and Consolidated Subsidiary Rivera	2017	2018
Retained earnings, 1/1	$ (310,000)	$ (381,000)
Net income	(131,000)	(229,000)
Dividends declared	60,000	110,000
Retained earnings, 12/31	$ (381,000)	$ (500,000)
Cash	$ 90,000	$ 180,000
Accounts receivable	170,000	150,000
Inventory	210,000	360,000
Buildings and equipment (net)	650,000	710,000
Databases	170,000	155,000
Total assets	$ 1,290,000	$ 1,555,000
Accounts payable	$ (160,000)	$ (110,000)
Bonds payable	(410,000)	(520,000)
Noncontrolling interest in Rivera	(42,000)	(61,000)
Common stock	(110,000)	(140,000)
Additional paid-in capital	(187,000)	(224,000)
Retained earnings	(381,000)	(500,000)
Total liabilities and equities	$(1,290,000)	$(1,555,000)

Additional Information for 2018

- The parent issued bonds during the year for cash.
- Amortization of databases amounts to $15,000 per year.
- The parent sold a building with a cost of $80,000 but a $40,000 book value for cash on May 11.
- The subsidiary purchased equipment on July 23 for $205,000 in cash.
- Late in November, the parent issued stock for cash.
- During the year, the subsidiary paid dividends of $10,000. Both parent and subsidiary pay dividends in the same year as declared.

Prepare a consolidated statement of cash flows for this business combination for the year ending December 31, 2018. (Use indirect method.)

LO 6-6

excel

48. Following are separate income statements for Austin, Inc., and its 80 percent–owned subsidiary, Rio Grande Corporation as well as a consolidated statement for the business combination as a whole.

	Austin	Rio Grande	Consolidated
Revenues	$(700,000)	$(500,000)	$(1,200,000)
Cost of goods sold	400,000	300,000	700,000
Operating expenses	100,000	70,000	195,000
Equity in earnings of Rio Grande	(84,000)		
Individual company net income	$(284,000)	$(130,000)	
Consolidated net income			$ (305,000)
Noncontrolling interest in consolidated net income			(21,000)
Consolidated net income attributable to Austin			$ (284,000)

Additional Information

- Annual excess fair over book value amortization of $25,000 resulted from the acquisition.
- The parent applies the equity method to this investment.

- Austin has 50,000 shares of common stock and 10,000 shares of preferred stock outstanding. Owners of the preferred stock are paid an annual dividend of $40,000, and each share can be exchanged for two shares of common stock.
- Rio Grande has 30,000 shares of common stock outstanding. The company also has 5,000 stock warrants outstanding. For $10, each warrant can be converted into a share of Rio Grande's common stock. Austin holds half of these warrants. The price of Rio Grande's common stock was $20 per share throughout the year.
- Rio Grande also has convertible bonds, none of which Austin owned. During the current year, total interest expense (net of taxes) was $22,000. These bonds can be exchanged for 10,000 shares of the subsidiary's common stock.

Determine Austin's basic and diluted EPS.

LO 6-6

excel

49. On January 1, Paisley, Inc., paid $560,000 for all of Skyler Corporation's outstanding stock. This cash payment was based on a price of $180 per share for Skyler's $100 par value preferred stock and $38 per share for its $20 par value common stock. The preferred shares are voting, cumulative, and fully participating. At the acquisition date, the book values of Skyler's accounts equaled their fair values. Any excess fair value is assigned to an intangible asset and will be amortized over a 10-year period.

During the year, Skyler sold inventory costing $60,000 to Paisley for $90,000. All but $18,000 (measured at transfer price) of this merchandise has been resold to outsiders by the end of the year. At the end of the year, Paisley continues to owe Skyler for the last shipment of inventory priced at $28,000.

Also, on January 2 Paisley sold Skyler equipment for $20,000 although it had a carrying amount of only $12,000 (original cost of $30,000). Both companies depreciate such property according to the straight-line method with no salvage value. The remaining life at this date was four years.

The following financial statements are for each company for the year ending December 31. Determine consolidated financial totals for this business combination.

	Paisley, Inc.	Skyler Corporation
Sales	$ (800,000)	$(400,000)
Cost of goods sold	528,000	260,000
Expenses	180,000	130,000
Gain on sale of equipment	(8,000)	–0–
Net income	$ (100,000)	$ (10,000)
Retained earnings, 1/1	$ (400,000)	$(150,000)
Net income	(100,000)	(10,000)
Dividends declared	60,000	–0–
Retained earnings, 12/31	$ (440,000)	$(160,000)
Cash	$ 30,000	$ 40,000
Accounts receivable	300,000	100,000
Inventory	260,000	180,000
Investment in Skyler Corporation	560,000	–0–
Land, buildings, and equipment	680,000	500,000
Accumulated depreciation	(180,000)	(90,000)
Total assets	$ 1,650,000	$ 730,000
Accounts payable	$ (140,000)	$ (90,000)
Long-term liabilities	(240,000)	(180,000)
Preferred stock	–0–	(100,000)
Common stock	(620,000)	(200,000)
Additional paid-in capital	(210,000)	–0–
Retained earnings, 12/31	(440,000)	(160,000)
Total liabilities and equity	$(1,650,000)	$(730,000)

LO 6-5

50. On June 30, 2018, Plaster, Inc., paid $916,000 for 80 percent of Stucco Company's outstanding stock. Plaster assessed the acquisition-date fair value of the 20 percent noncontrolling interest at $229,000. At acquisition date, Stucco reported the following book values for its assets and liabilities:

Cash	$ 60,000
Accounts receivable	127,000
Inventory	203,000
Land	65,000
Buildings	175,000
Equipment	300,000
Accounts payable	(35,000)

On June 30, Plaster allocated the excess acquisition-date fair value over book value to Stucco's assets as follows:

Equipment (3-year remaining life)	$ 75,000
Database (10-year remaining life)	175,000

At the end of 2018, the following comparative (2017 and 2018) balance sheets and consolidated income statement were available:

	Plaster, Inc. December 31, 2017	Consolidated December 31, 2018
Cash	$ 43,000	$ 242,850
Accounts receivable (net)	362,000	485,400
Inventory	415,000	720,000
Land	300,000	365,000
Buildings (net)	245,000	370,000
Equipment (net)	1,800,000	2,037,500
Database	–0–	166,250
Total assets	$3,165,000	$4,387,000
Accounts payable	$ 80,000	$ 107,000
Long-term liabilities	400,000	1,200,000
Common stock	1,800,000	1,800,000
Noncontrolling interest	–0–	255,500
Retained earnings	885,000	1,024,500
Total liabilities and equities	$3,165,000	$4,387,000

PLASTER, INC., AND SUBSIDIARY STUCCO COMPANY
Consolidated Income Statement
For the Year Ended December 31, 2018

Revenues		$1,217,500
Cost of goods sold	$737,500	
Depreciation	187,500	
Database amortization	8,750	
Interest and other expenses	9,750	943,500
Consolidated net income		$ 274,000

Additional Information for 2018

- On December 1, Stucco paid a $40,000 dividend. During the year, Plaster paid $100,000 in dividends.
- During the year, Plaster issued $800,000 in long-term debt at par.
- Plaster reported no asset purchases or dispositions other than the acquisition of Stucco.

Prepare a 2018 consolidated statement of cash flows for Plaster and Stucco. Use the indirect method of reporting cash flows from operating activities.

Develop Your Skills

EXCEL CASE: INTRA-ENTITY BONDS

Place Company owns a majority voting interest in Sassano, Inc. On January 1, 2016, Place issued $1,000,000 of 11 percent 10-year bonds at $943,497.77 to yield 12 percent. On January 1, 2018, Sassano purchased all of these bonds in the open market at a price of $904,024.59 with an effective yield of 13 percent.

Required

Using an Excel spreadsheet, do the following:

1. Prepare amortization schedules for the Place Company bonds payable and the Investment in Place Bonds for Sassano, Inc.
2. Using the values from the amortization schedules, compute the worksheet adjustment for a December 31, 2018, consolidation of Place and Sassano to reflect the effective retirement of the Place bonds. Formulate your solution to be able to accommodate various yield rates (and therefore prices) on the repurchase of the bonds.

Hints

Present value of $1 = 1/(1 + r)n$
Present value of an annuity of $1 = (1 - 1/[1 + r]n)/r$
Where r = effective yield and n = years remaining to maturity

RESEARCH CASE: STATEMENT OF CASH FLOWS

Download Pfizer's 2015 annual report (search Pfizer Investor Relations). Locate the firm's consolidated statement of cash flows and answer the following:

- Does the firm employ the direct or indirect method of accounting for operating cash flows?
- Why does the firm account for the changes in balances in operating accounts (e.g., accounts receivable, inventory, accounts payable) in determining operating cash flows as net of acquisitions and divestitures?
- Describe the accounting for cash paid for business acquisitions in the statement of cash flows.
- Describe the accounting for any noncontrolling subsidiary interest and any other business combination–related items in the consolidated statement of cash flows.

FINANCIAL REPORTING RESEARCH AND ANALYSIS CASE

The FASB ASC Subtopic "Variable Interest Entities" affects thousands of business enterprises that now, as primary beneficiaries, consolidate entities that qualify as controlled VIEs. Retrieve the annual reports of one or more of the following companies (or any others you may find) that consolidate VIEs:

- The Walt Disney Company.
- General Electric.
- Allegheny Energy.

Required

Write a brief report that describes

1. The reasons for consolidation of the company's VIE(s).
2. The effect of the consolidation of the VIE(s) on the company's financial statements.

chapter 8

Segment and Interim Reporting

As one of the largest companies in the United States, The Walt Disney Company reported consolidated revenues of $52.5 billion in 2015. The Walt Disney Company is well known as a filmmaker and operator of theme parks, but it is perhaps less well known as the owner of the ESPN and ABC television networks. How much of the company's consolidated revenues did these different lines of business generate? Knowing this could be very useful to potential investors as opportunities for future growth and profitability in these different industries could differ significantly.

To comply with U.S. GAAP, Disney disaggregated its 2015 consolidated operating revenues and reported that the company's revenues were generated from five different operating segments: Approximately $23.3 billion came from Media Networks, $16.2 billion from Parks and Resorts, $7.4 billion from Studio Entertainment, $4.5 billion from Consumer Products, and $1.2 billion from Interactive. Additional information disclosed by Disney indicated that $40.3 billion of consolidated revenues were generated in the United States and Canada, $6.5 billion in Europe, $4.0 billion in Asia Pacific, and $1.7 billion in Latin America and other parts of the world. Such information, describing the various components of Disney's operations (both by line of business and by geographic area), can often be more useful to an analyst than the single sales figure reported in the consolidated income statement. "All investors like segment reporting—separate financials for each division—because it enables them to analyze how well each part of a corporation is doing."[1]

In its 2015 Annual Report, the Boeing Company reported net earnings of $5,176 million for the year ended December 31, 2015. This information was not made available to the public until early in 2016 after the company had closed the books and prepared audited financial statements for the prior year. To provide more timely information on which investors could base their decisions about the company throughout the year, Boeing published separate interim reports for each of the first three quarters of 2015. Net earnings declined from $1,336 million in the first quarter to $1,110 million in the second quarter, then rose to $1,704 million in the third quarter, and then decreased to $1,026 million in the fourth quarter. Information about the results of operations for time intervals of less than one year can be very useful to an analyst.

The first part of this chapter examines the specific requirements for disaggregating financial statement information as required by authoritative accounting literature. Companies must disclose specific items of information for each reportable operating segment and provide additional enterprisewide

Learning Objectives

After studying this chapter, you should be able to:

LO 8-1 Understand how an enterprise determines its operating segments and the factors that influence this determination.

LO 8-2 Apply the three tests that are used to determine which operating segments are of significant size to warrant separate disclosure.

LO 8-3 List the basic disclosure requirements for operating segments.

LO 8-4 Determine when and what types of information must be disclosed for geographic areas.

LO 8-5 Apply the criterion for determining when disclosure of a major customer is required.

LO 8-6 Understand and apply procedures used in interim financial reports to treat an interim period as an integral part of the annual period.

LO 8-7 List the minimum disclosure requirements for interim financial reports.

[1] Robert A. Parker, "How Do You Play the New Annual Report Game?" *Communication World,* September 1990, p. 26.

disclosures. The second part of the chapter concentrates on the special rules required to be applied in preparing interim reports. All publicly traded companies in the United States are required to prepare interim reports on a quarterly basis.

LO 8-1

Understand how an enterprise determines its operating segments and the factors that influence this determination.

Segment Reporting

According to FASB *Accounting Standards Codification®* (ASC) Topic 280, "Segment Reporting," the objective of segment reporting is to provide information about the different business activities in which an enterprise engages and the different economic environments in which it operates to help users of financial statements

- Better understand the enterprise's performance.
- Better assess its prospects for future net cash flows.
- Make more informed judgments about the enterprise as a whole.

The Management Approach

To achieve this objective, U.S. GAAP follows a management approach for determining segments. The management approach is based on the way that management disaggregates the enterprise for making operating decisions. These disaggregated components are *operating segments,* which will be evident from the enterprise's organization structure. More specifically, an operating segment is a component of an enterprise if

- It engages in business activities from which it recognizes revenues and incurs expenses.
- The chief operating decision maker regularly reviews its operating results to assess performance and make resource allocation decisions.
- Its discrete financial information is available.

An organizational unit can be an operating segment even if all of its revenues or expenses result from transactions with other segments as might be the case in a vertically integrated company. However, not all parts of a company are necessarily included in an operating segment. For example, a research and development unit that incurs expenses but does not recognize revenues would not be an operating segment. Similarly, corporate headquarters might not recognize revenues or might recognize revenues that are only incidental to the enterprise's activities and therefore would not be considered an operating segment.

For many companies, only one set of organizational units qualifies as operating segments. In some companies, however, business activities are disaggregated in more than one way and the chief operating decision maker uses multiple sets of reports. For example, a company might generate reports by geographic region *and* by product line. In those cases, two additional criteria must be considered to identify operating segments:

1. An operating segment has a segment manager who is directly accountable to the chief operating decision maker for its financial performance. If more than one set of organizational units exist but segment managers are held responsible for only one set, that set constitutes the operating segments.
2. If segment managers exist for two or more overlapping sets of organizational units (as in a matrix form of organization), the nature of the business activities must be considered, and the organizational units based on products and services constitute the operating segments. For example, if certain managers are responsible for different product lines and other managers are responsible for different geographic areas, the enterprise components based on products would constitute the operating segments.

LO 8-2

Apply the three tests that are used to determine which operating segments are of significant size to warrant separate disclosure.

Determination of Reportable Operating Segments

After a company has identified its operating segments based on its internal reporting system, management must decide which segments to report separately. Generally, information must be reported separately for each operating segment that meets one or more quantitative thresholds. *However, if two or more operating segments have essentially the same business activities in essentially the same economic environments, information for those individual segments may be combined.* For example, a retail chain may have five stores, each of which meets the definition of an operating segment, but each store is essentially the same as the others. In that case, the benefit to be derived from separately reporting each operating segment would not justify the cost of disclosure. In determining whether business activities and environments are similar, management must consider these aggregation criteria:

1. The nature of the products and services provided by each operating segment.
2. The nature of the production process.
3. The type or class of customer.
4. The distribution methods.
5. If applicable, the nature of the regulatory environment.

Segments must be similar in each and every one of these areas to be combined. However, aggregation of similar segments is not required.

Quantitative Thresholds

After determining whether any segments are to be combined, management next must decide which of its operating segments are significant enough to justify separate disclosure. The FASB established three tests for identifying operating segments for which separate disclosure is required:

1. A revenue test.
2. A profit or loss test.
3. An asset test.

An operating segment needs to satisfy only one of these tests to be considered of significant size to necessitate separate disclosure.

To apply these three tests, a segment's revenues, profit or loss, and assets (before any intra-entity eliminations) must be determined. Additionally, general corporate (nontraceable) revenues and expenses are not considered in conducting these tests because corporate headquarters is not a separate unit for segment reporting. Authoritative literature does not stipulate a specific measure of profit or loss, such as operating profit or income before taxes, to be used in applying these tests. Instead, the profit measure used by the chief operating decision maker in evaluating operating segments is to be used. An operating segment is considered to be significant if it meets any one of the following tests:

1. *Revenue test.* Segment revenues, both external and intersegment, are 10 percent or more of the combined revenue, internal and external, of all reported operating segments.
2. *Profit or loss test.* Segment profit or loss is 10 percent or more of the larger (in absolute terms) of the combined reported profit of all profitable segments or the combined reported loss of all segments incurring a loss.
3. *Asset test.* Segment assets are 10 percent or more of the combined assets of all operating segments.

Application of the revenue and asset tests appears to pose few challenges. In contrast, the profit or loss test is more complicated and warrants illustration. For this purpose, assume that Durham Company has five separate operating segments with the following profits or losses:

Durham Company Segments—Profits and Losses

Soft drinks	$1,700,000
Wine	(600,000)
Food products	240,000
Paper packaging	880,000
Recreation parks	(130,000)
Net operating profit	$2,090,000

Three of these industry segments (soft drinks, food products, and paper packaging) report profits that total $2,820,000. The two remaining segments have losses of $730,000 for the year.

Profits		Losses	
Soft drinks	$ 1,700,000	Wine	$ 600,000
Food products	240,000	Recreation parks	130,000
Paper packaging	880,000		
Total	$ 2,820,000	Total	$ 730,000

Consequently, $2,820,000 serves as the basis for the profit or loss test because that amount is larger in absolute terms than $730,000. Based on the 10 percent threshold, any operating segment with either a profit *or loss* of more than $282,000 (10% × $2,820,000) is considered material and, thus, must be disclosed separately. According to this one test, the soft drinks and paper packaging segments (with operating profits of $1.7 million and $880,000, respectively) are both judged to be reportable, as is the wine segment, despite having a loss of $600,000.

Operating segments that do not meet any of the quantitative thresholds may be combined to produce a reportable segment if they share *a majority* of the aggregation criteria listed earlier. Durham Company's food products and recreation parks operating segments do not meet any of the aggregation criteria. Operating segments that are not individually significant and that cannot be aggregated with other segments are combined and disclosed in an *All Other* category. The sources of the revenues included in the All Other category must be disclosed.

Testing Procedures—Complete Illustration

To provide a comprehensive example of all three of these testing procedures, assume that Atkinson Company is a large business combination comprising six operating segments: automotive, furniture, textbook, motion picture, appliance, and finance. Complete information about each of these segments, as reported internally to the chief operating decision maker, appears in Exhibit 8.1.

The Revenue Test

In applying the revenue test to Atkinson Company's operating segments, the combined revenue of all segments must be determined:

Operating Segment	Total Revenues
Automotive	$ 41.6*
Furniture	9.0
Textbook	6.8
Motion picture	22.8
Appliance	5.3
Finance	12.3
Combined total	$ 97.8

*All figures are in millions.

Because these six segments have total revenues of $97.8 million, that amount is used in applying the revenue test. Based on the 10 percent significance level, any segment with revenues of more than $9.78 million qualifies for required disclosure. Accordingly, the automotive, motion picture, and finance segments have satisfied this particular criterion. Atkinson must present appropriate disaggregated information for each of these three operating segments within its financial statements.

EXHIBIT 8.1 Reportable Segment Testing

ATKINSON COMPANY	Automotive	Furniture	Textbook	Motion Picture	Appliance	Finance
Revenues:						
Sales to outsiders	$32.6*	$6.9	$ 6.6	$22.2	$3.1	$ -0-
Intersegment transfers	6.6	1.2	-0-	-0-	1.9	-0-
Interest revenue—outsiders.	2.4	0.9	0.2	0.6	0.3	8.7
Interest revenue—intersegment loans	-0-	-0-	-0-	-0-	-0-	3.6
Total revenues	$41.6	$9.0	$6.8	$22.8	$5.3	$12.3
Expenses:						
Operating expenses—outsiders	$14.7	$3.3	$7.2	$21.0	$3.4	$ 1.8
Operating expenses—intersegment transfers	4.8	1.0	-0-	-0-	0.8	0.8
Depreciation and amortization	2.4	0.3	0.1	3.0	0.2	0.5
Interest expense	2.1	1.0	2.2	4.6	-0-	6.1
Income taxes	6.6	1.4	(1.5)	(3.1)	0.4	0.1
Total expenses.	$30.6	$7.0	$ 8.0	$25.5	$4.8	$ 9.3
Profit (loss).	$11.0	$2.0	$(1.2)	$ (2.7)	$0.5	$ 3.0
Assets:						
Tangible.	$ 9.6	$1.1	$ 0.8	$10.9	$0.9	$ 9.2
Intangible.	1.8	0.2	0.7	3.6	0.1	-0-
Intersegment loans	-0-	-0-	-0-	-0-	-0-	5.4
Total assets.	$11.4	$1.3	$ 1.5	$14.5	$1.0	$14.6

*All figures are in millions.

The Profit or Loss Test

Subtracting segment expenses from total segment revenues determines the profit or loss of each operating segment. Common costs are not required to be allocated to individual segments to determine segment profit or loss if this is not normally done for internal purposes. For example, an enterprise that accounts for pension expense only on a consolidated basis is not required to allocate pension expense to each operating segment. Any allocations of common costs that are made must be done on a reasonable basis. Moreover, segment profit or loss does not have to be calculated in accordance with generally accepted accounting principles if the measure reported internally is calculated on another basis. To assist the readers of financial statements in understanding segment disclosures, any differences in the basis of measurement between segment and consolidated amounts must be disclosed.

Each operating segment's profit or loss is calculated as follows:

Operating Segment	Total Revenues	Total Expenses	Profit	Loss
Automotive	$41.6*	$30.6	$11.0	$-0-
Furniture	9.0	7.0	2.0	-0-
Textbook.	6.8	8.0	-0-	1.2
Motion picture.	22.8	25.5	-0-	2.7
Appliance	5.3	4.8	0.5	-0-
Finance	12.3	9.3	3.0	-0-
Totals	$97.8	$85.2	$16.5	$ 3.9

*All figures are in millions.

The $16.5 million in total profit is larger in an absolute sense than the $3.9 million in losses. Therefore, this larger balance is the basis for the second quantitative test. As a result of the 10 percent criterion, either a profit or loss of $1.65 million or more qualifies a segment for disaggregation. According to the profit or loss totals just calculated, Atkinson Company's automotive, furniture, motion picture, and finance segments are large enough to warrant separate disclosure.

The Asset Test

The final test is based on the operating segments' combined total assets:

Operating Segment	Assets
Automotive	$11.4*
Furniture	1.3
Textbook	1.5
Motion picture	14.5
Appliance	1.0
Finance	14.6
Combined total	$44.3

*All figures are in millions.

Because 10 percent of the combined total equals $4.43 million, any segment holding at least that amount of assets is viewed as a reportable segment. Consequently, according to this final significance test, the automotive, motion picture, and finance segments are all considered of sufficient size to require disaggregation. The three remaining segments do not have sufficient assets to pass this particular test.

Summary of Test Results

A summary of all three significance tests as applied to Atkinson Company follows:

Operating Segments	Revenue Test	Profit or Loss Test	Asset Test
Automotive	✓	✓	✓
Furniture		✓	
Textbook			
Motion picture	✓	✓	✓
Appliance			
Finance	✓	✓	✓

Four of this company's operating segments meet at least one of the quantitative thresholds (automotive, furniture, motion picture, and finance) and therefore are separately reportable. Because neither the textbook nor the appliance segment has met any of these three tests, disaggregated information describing their *individual* operations is not required. However, the financial data accumulated from these two nonsignificant segments still have to be presented. The amounts for these two segments can be combined and disclosed as aggregate amounts in an All Other category with appropriate disclosure of the source of revenues.

Other Guidelines

Additional guidelines apply to the disclosure of operating segment information. These rules are designed to ensure that the disaggregated data are consistent from year to year and relevant to the needs of financial statement users. For example, any operating segment that has been reportable in the past and is judged by management to be of continuing significance should be disclosed separately in the current financial statements regardless of the outcome of the testing process. This ensures the ongoing usefulness of segment information, especially for comparison purposes.

In a similar manner, if an operating segment newly qualifies for disclosure in the current year, prior period segment data presented for comparative purposes must be restated to reflect the newly reportable segment as a separate segment. Again, the comparability of information has high priority in setting the standards for disclosure.

Another issue concerns the number of operating segments that should be disclosed. To enhance the value of the disaggregated information, a substantial portion of a company's operations should be presented individually. A sufficient number of segments is presumed to be included only if the combined segment sales to unaffiliated customers are at least 75 percent of total company consolidated sales made to outsiders. If this lower limit is not achieved, additional segments must be disclosed separately despite their failure to satisfy even one of the three quantitative thresholds.

As an illustration, assume that Brendan Corporation identified seven operating segments that generated revenues as follows (in millions):

Operating Segments	Sales to Unaffiliated Customers	Intersegment Transfers	Segment Revenues (and percentage of total)	
Housewares	$ 5.5	$ 1.6	$ 7.1	9.3%
Toys	6.2	–0–	6.2	8.1
Pottery	3.4	7.9	11.3	14.8 ✓
Lumber.	6.6	10.4	17.0	22.3 ✓
Lawn mowers	7.2	–0–	7.2	9.4
Appliances.	2.1	6.2	8.3	10.9 ✓
Construction	19.2	–0–	19.2	25.2 ✓
Totals	$50.2	$26.1	$76.3	100

Based on the 10 percent revenue test, four of these segments are reportable (because each has total revenues of more than $7.63 million): pottery, lumber, appliances, and construction. Assuming that none of the other segments qualifies as significant in either of the two remaining tests, disclosure of disaggregated data is required for only these four segments. However, the 75 percent rule has not been met; the reportable segments generate just 62.4 percent of the company's total sales to unrelated parties (in millions):

Reportable Segments	Sales to Unaffiliated Customers
Pottery	$ 3.4
Lumber.	6.6
Appliances.	2.1
Construction	19.2
Total	$31.3

Information being disaggregated: $31.3 million/$50.2 million = 62.4%

To satisfy the 75 percent requirement, Brendan Corporation must also include the lawn mowers segment within the disaggregated data. With the addition of this nonsignificant segment, sales of $38.5 million ($31.3 + $7.2) to outside parties now are disclosed. This amounts to 76.7 percent of the company total ($38.5 million/$50.2 million). The two remaining segments—housewares and toys—could still be included separately within the disaggregated data; disclosure is not prohibited. However, information for these two segments probably would be combined and reported as aggregate amounts in an All Other category.

One final aspect of these reporting requirements should be mentioned. Some companies might be organized in such a fashion that a relatively large number of operating segments exist. The authoritative guidance suggests that there could be a practical limit to the number of operating segments that should be reported separately. Beyond that limit, the information becomes too detailed to be useful. Although a maximum number is not prescribed, FASB

EXHIBIT 8.2 Flowchart for Determining Reportable Operating Segments

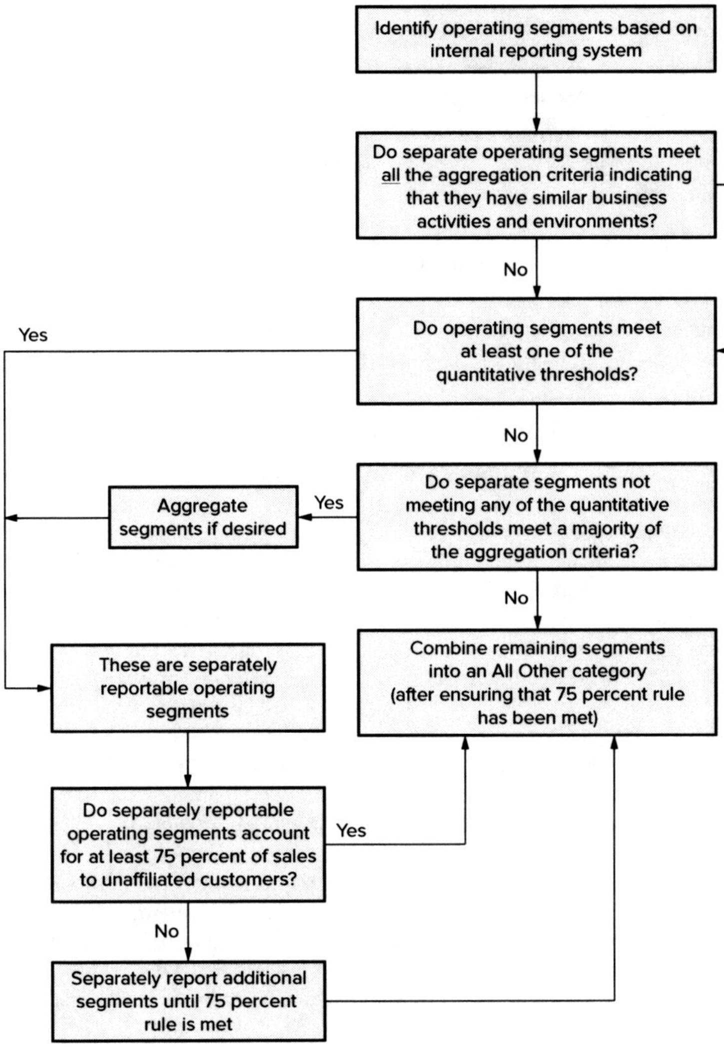

ASC 280-10-50-18 suggests that 10 separately reported segments might be the practical limit. Exhibit 8.2 provides a flowchart summarizing the procedures for determining separately reportable operating segments.

LO 8-3

List the basic disclosure requirements for operating segments.

Information to Be Disclosed by Reportable Operating Segments

A significant amount of information is required to be disclosed for each operating segment:

1. *General information* about the operating segment:
   - Factors used to identify reportable operating segments.
   - Types of products and services from which each operating segment reported derives its revenues.

2. *Segment profit or loss* and each of the following if it is regularly provided to or included in the measure of segment profit or loss reviewed by the chief operating decision maker:
   - Revenues from external customers.
   - Revenues from transactions with other operating segments.
   - Interest revenue and interest expense (reported separately); net interest revenue may be reported for finance segments if this measure is used internally for evaluation.
   - Depreciation, depletion, and amortization expenses.
   - Unusual items.
   - Equity in the net income of investees accounted for by the equity method.
   - Income tax expense or benefit.
   - Other significant noncash items included in segment profit or loss.
3. *Total segment assets* and the following related items:
   - Investment in equity method affiliates.
   - Expenditures for additions to long-lived assets.

The measure of segment profit or loss and segment assets disclosed must be the same as the measure reported to the chief operating decision maker for the purpose of assessing performance and allocating resources to segments. If, for example, the chief operating decision maker evaluates segment performance on the basis of earnings before interest, taxes, depreciation, and amortization (EBITDA), then EBITDA must be disclosed for each reportable segment. In that case, interest revenue and interest expense; income tax expense or benefit; and depreciation, depletion, and amortization need not be disclosed by segment, unless these amounts are reported to the chief operating decision maker in addition to EBITDA.

Authoritative guidance does not specifically require cash flow information to be reported for each operating segment because this information often is not generated by segment for internal reporting purposes. The requirement to disclose significant noncash items other than depreciation is an attempt to provide information that might enhance users' ability to estimate cash flow from operations.

Immaterial items need not be disclosed. For example, some segments do not have material amounts of interest revenue and expense, and therefore disclosure of these items of information is not necessary. In addition, if the internal financial reporting system does not generate information for an item on a segment basis, that item need not be disclosed. This is consistent with the rationale that segment reporting should create as little additional cost to an enterprise as possible.

To demonstrate how the operating segment information might be disclosed, we return to the Atkinson Company example earlier in this chapter. Application of the quantitative threshold tests resulted in four separately reportable segments (automotive, furniture, motion picture, and finance). The nonsignificant operating segments (textbook and appliance) are combined in an All Other category. Exhibit 8.3 shows the operating segment disclosures included in Atkinson's financial statements. Depreciation and amortization, interest, and income taxes are disclosed for each segment because these expenses are included in the measure of segment profit or loss reported to the chief operating decision maker.

In addition to the information in Exhibit 8.1, data on other significant noncash items, and expenditures for long-lived segment assets were gathered for each operating segment to comply with the disclosure requirements. Only the automotive segment has other significant noncash items, and none of the segments have equity method investments. Atkinson had no unusual items during the year.

To determine whether a sufficient number of segments is reported separately, the ratio of combined sales to unaffiliated customers for the separately reported operating segments must be compared with total company sales made to outsiders. The combined amount of revenues

EXHIBIT 8.3 Operating Segment Disclosures

ATKINSON COMPANY					
	Operating Segment				
	Automotive	Furniture	Motion Picture	Finance	All Other
Segment profit (loss)	**$11.0***	**$2.0**	**$(2.7)**	**$ 3.0**	**$(0.7)**
Revenues from external customers	32.6*	6.9	22.2	—	9.7
Intersegment revenues	6.6	1.2	-0-	—	1.9
Interest revenue	2.4	0.9	0.6	—	0.5
Interest expense	2.1	1.0	4.6	—	2.2
Net interest revenue	—	—	—	6.2	—
Depreciation and amortization	2.4	0.3	3.0	0.5	0.3
Other significant noncash items:					
Cost in excess of billings on long-term contracts	0.8	-0-	-0-	-0-	-0-
Income tax expense (benefit)	6.6	1.4	(3.1)	0.1	(1.1)
Segment assets	**11.4**	**1.3**	**14.5**	**14.6**	**2.5**
Expenditures for long-lived segment assets	3.5	0.4	3.7	1.7	1.3

*All figures are in millions.

from external customers disclosed for the automotive, furniture, motion picture, and finance segments is $61.7 million. Total revenues from external customers are $71.4 million:

$$\$61.7 \text{ million}/\$71.4 \text{ million} = 86.4\%$$

Because 86.4 percent exceeds the lower limit of 75 percent, Atkinson's level of disaggregation is adequate.

Reconciliations to Consolidated Totals

As noted earlier, segment information is to be provided as the company's internal reporting system prepares it even if not based on GAAP. Preparing segment information in accordance with authoritative accounting literature used at the consolidated level is difficult in some cases because some GAAP is not intended to apply at the segment level. Examples are accounting for (1) inventory on a LIFO basis when inventory pools include items in more than one segment, (2) companywide pension plans, and (3) litigation obligations. Accordingly, allocation of these items to individual operating segments is not required.

However, the total of the reportable segments' revenues must be reconciled to consolidated revenues, the total of the reportable segments' profit or loss must be reconciled to consolidated income before tax, and the total of the reportable segments' assets must be reconciled to consolidated total assets. To carry out this reconciliation, adjustments and eliminations that have been made to prepare consolidated financial statements in compliance with GAAP must be identified. Examples are the elimination of intersegment revenues and an adjustment for companywide pension expense.

In addition, in reconciling the total of segments' revenues, profit or loss, and assets to the consolidated totals, the aggregate amount of revenues, profit or loss, and assets from immaterial operating segments must be disclosed. The company also must disclose assets, revenues, expenses, gains, losses, interest expense, and depreciation, depletion, and amortization expense for components of the enterprise that are not operating segments. This includes, for example, assets and expenses associated with corporate headquarters. See Exhibit 8.4 for an example of how Atkinson might present these reconciliations.

Atkinson Company must make four types of adjustments in reconciling segment results with consolidated totals. The first type of adjustment is to eliminate intra-entity revenues, profit or loss, and assets that are not included in consolidated totals. The elimination of intersegment revenues includes intersegment transfers amounting to $9.7 million plus $3.6 million of intersegment interest revenue generated by the finance segment (total $13.3 million).

EXHIBIT 8.4
Reconciliation of Segment Results to Consolidated Totals

ATKINSON COMPANY	
Revenues:	
Total segment revenues	$97.8*
Elimination of intersegment revenues	(13.3)
Total consolidated revenues	$84.5
Profit or loss:	
Total segment profit or loss	$12.6
Total segment income taxes	3.9
Total segment profit before income taxes	$16.5
Elimination of intersegment profits	(5.9)
Unallocated amounts:	
Litigation settlement received	3.6
Other corporate expenses	(2.7)
Adjustment to pension expense in consolidation	(0.8)
Consolidated income before income taxes	$10.7
Assets:	
Total for reported segments	$44.3
Elimination of intersegment loans	(5.4)
Other corporate assets	5.8
Total consolidated assets	$44.7

*All figures are in millions.

Likewise, intersegment loans made by the finance segment must be eliminated to reconcile to total consolidated assets. The second adjustment adds total segment income taxes back to total segment profit to be able to reconcile to income before tax for the company as a whole. The third type of adjustment relates to corporate items that have not been allocated to the operating segments, including a litigation settlement received by the company, and corporate headquarters expenses and assets. The fourth adjustment reconciles differences in segment accounting practices from accounting practices used in the consolidated financial statements. The only adjustment of this nature that Atkinson made relates to the accounting for pension expense. Individual operating segments measure pension expense based on cash payments made to the pension plan. Because GAAP requires measuring pension expense on an accrual basis, an adjustment for the amount of pension expense to be recognized in the consolidated statements is necessary.

Explanation of Measurement

In addition to the operating segment disclosures and reconciliation of segment results to consolidated totals, companies also must explain the measurement of segment profit or loss and segment assets, including a description of any differences in measuring (1) segment profit or loss and consolidated income before tax, (2) segment assets and consolidated assets, and (3) segment profit or loss and segment assets. An example of this last item would be the allocation of depreciation expense to segments in determining segment profit or loss even though the related depreciable assets are not included in segment assets. The basis of accounting for intersegment transactions also must be described.

Examples of Operating Segment Disclosures

A majority of companies are organized along product and/or service lines. Exhibit 8.5 shows operating segment disclosures for Fluor Corporation. Fluor provides a reconciliation of total segment profit to consolidated earnings before taxes in its segment disclosures. Because Fluor measures segment profit on a before-tax basis, it does not report income tax expense or

EXHIBIT 8.5 Operating Segment Disclosures in Fluor Corporation's 2014 Annual Report

15. Operations by Business Segment and Geographical Area

The company provides professional services in the fields of engineering, procurement, construction, fabrication and modularization, commissioning and maintenance, as well as project management, on a global basis and serves a diverse set of industries worldwide. The five principal business segments are: Oil & Gas, Industrial & Infrastructure, Government, Global Services and Power, as discussed further below.

Operating Information by Segment

	Year Ended December 31,		
(in millions)	**2014**	**2013**	**2012**
External revenue			
Oil & Gas	**$ 11,368.9**	$11,519.8	$ 9,513.9
Industrial & Infrastructure	**6,061.7**	11,081.7	13,237.8
Government	**2,511.9**	2,749.1	3,304.7
Global Services	**585.0**	611.8	679.6
Power	**1,004.1**	1,389.2	841.1
Total external revenue	**$21,531.60**	$27,351.6	$27,577.1
Segment profit (loss)			
Oil & Gas	**$ 673.4**	$ 441.1	$ 334.7
Industrial & Infrastructure	**391.2**	476.0	176.5
Government	**92.7**	161.4	149.7
Global Services	**73.8**	119.7	125.4
Power	**31.3**	11.7	(16.9)
Total segment profit	**$ 1,262.4**	$ 1,209.9	$ 769.4
Depreciation and amortization of fixed assets			
Oil & Gas	**$ —**	$ —	$ —
Industrial & Infrastructure	**2.6**	1.5	2.4
Government	**5.4**	9.5	12.9
Global Services	**111.8**	117.7	124.6
Power	**1.6**	1.1	0.9
Corporate and other	**70.3**	76.5	69.0
Total depreciation and amortization of fixed assets	**$ 191.7**	$ 206.3	$ 210.4
Capital expenditures			
Oil & Gas	**$ —**	$ —	$ —
Industrial & Infrastructure	**8.3**	2.9	0.5
Government	**2.2**	4.1	5.7
Global Services	**224.0**	145.3	184.5
Power	**2.1**	1.3	3.6
Corporate and other	**88.1**	134.9	60.4
Total capital expenditures	**$ 324.7**	$ 288.5	$ 209.8
Total assets			
Oil & Gas	**$ 1,708.2**	$ 1,643.8	
Industrial & Infrastructure	**871.9**	909.7	
Government	**540.1**	580.6	
Global Services	**795.3**	758.9	
Power	**178.6**	154.9	
Corporate and other	**4,100.3**	4,276.0	
Total assets	**$ 8,194.4**	$ 8,323.9	

The reportable segments follow the same accounting policies as those described in Major Accounting Policies. Management evaluates a segment's performance based upon segment profit. The company incurs cost and expenses and holds certain assets at the corporate level which relate to its business as a whole. Certain of these amounts have been charged to the company's business segments by various methods, largely on the basis of usage. Total assets not allocated to segments and held in "Corporate and other" primarily include cash, marketable securities, income-tax related assets, pension assets, deferred compensation trust assets and corporate property, plant, and equipment.

(continued)

EXHIBIT 8.5 (Continued)

Reconciliation of Segment Information to Consolidated Amounts

	Year Ended December 31,		
(in millions)	**2014**	**2013**	**2012**
Total segment profit	**$1,262.4**	$1,209.9	$769.4
Corporate general and administrative expense	**(182.7)**	(175.1)	(151.0)
Interest expense, net	**(11.4)**	(12.5)	(0.5)
Earnings attributable to noncontrolling interests	**136.6**	155.3	115.6
Earnings before taxes	**$1,204.9**	$1,177.6	$733.5

benefit by operating segment. A significant amount of corporate general and administrative expense is not allocated to individual operating segments. Likewise, net interest expense and noncontrolling interests are treated as corporate level items, and the company thus does not disclose these amounts by operating segment.

Some companies, such as McDonald's, Coca-Cola, and Nike, are organized geographically and define operating segments as regions of the world. McDonald's has four operating segments: United States; Europe; Asia, Pacific, Middle East, Africa (APMEA); and Other Countries and Corporate. Some companies report a combination of products or services and international segments. Walmart has three operating segments: Walmart U.S., Walmart International, and Sam's Club. PepsiCo has six reportable segments: Frito-Lay North America (FLNA); Quaker Foods North America (QFNA); Latin America Foods (LAF); PepsiCo Americas Beverages (PAB); Pepsico Europe; and Pepsico Asia, Middle East, and Africa (AMEA). The nature of these companies' segmentation provides considerable insight into the way upper management views and evaluates the various parts of the consolidated enterprise.

Entitywide Information

Information about Products and Services

The authoritative literature recognizes that some enterprises are not organized along product or service lines. For example, some enterprises are organized geographically. Moreover, some enterprises may have only one operating segment yet provide a range of different products and services. To provide some comparability between enterprises, FASB ASC 280-10-50-40 requires *disclosure of revenues derived from transactions with external customers from each product or service* if operating segments have not been determined based on differences in products or services. An enterprise with only one operating segment also must disclose revenues from external customers on the basis of product or service. However, providing this information is not required if impracticable; that is, the information is not available and the cost to develop it would be excessive.

Lowe's Companies, Inc., operates in only one segment; nevertheless, it reported "sales by product category," as required in its 2014 annual report. See Exhibit 8.6 for that information.

LO 8-4

Determine when and what types of information must be disclosed for geographic areas.

Information about Geographic Areas

For those companies with international activities, two items of information—revenues from external customers and long-lived assets—must be reported (1) for the *domestic country* and (2) for *all foreign countries in total* in which the enterprise derives revenues or holds assets. In addition, if revenues from external customers attributed to an *individual foreign country* are material, the specific country and amount of revenues must be disclosed separately as

EXHIBIT 8.6 Sales by Product Category in Lowe's Companies, Inc., 2014 Annual Report

	Sales by Product Category					
	2014		2013*		2012*	
(Dollars in millions)	Total Sales	%	Total Sales	%	Total Sales	%
Kitchen & Appliances	$ 8,007	14%	$ 7,527	14%	$ 6,973	14%
Lumber & Building Materials	6,884	12	6,596	12	6,276	12
Tools & Hardware	6,263	11	5,873	11	5,633	11
Fashion Fixtures	5,591	10	5,271	10	4,964	10
Rough Plumbing & Electrical	4,928	9	4,423	9	4,356	9
Lawn & Garden	4,639	8	4,423	8	4,340	9
Seasonal Living	3,717	7	3,615	7	3,433	7
Paint	3,614	6	3,471	7	3,306	6
Home Fashions, Storage & Cleaning	3,263	6	3,176	6	3,050	6
Flooring	3,219	6	3,066	6	2,864	6
Millwork	3,135	6	2,926	5	2,793	5
Outdoor Power Equipment	2,339	4	2,224	4	2,046	4
Other	624	1	565	1	487	1
Totals	**$56,223**	**100%**	**$53,417**	**100%**	**$50,521**	**100%**

* Certain prior period amounts have been reclassified to conform to current product category classifications.

must a material amount of long-lived assets located in an individual foreign country. Even if the company has only one operating segment and therefore does not otherwise provide segment information, it must report geographic area information.

Thus, U.S.-based companies are required to disclose the amount of revenues generated and long-lived assets held in (1) the United States, (2) all other countries in total, and (3) each material foreign country. Requiring disclosure at the individual country level is a significant change from previous accounting standards, which required disclosures according to groups of countries in the same region of the world (such as Asia-Pacific). Current U.S. GAAP does not preclude companies from continuing to provide information by region, and for consistency purposes many companies continue to do so even if they determine no single foreign country to be material. The reporting requirement was changed from geographic regions to individual countries because reporting information about individual countries has two benefits. First, it reduces the burden on financial statement preparers because most companies likely have material operations in only a few countries, perhaps only their country of domicile. Second, and more important, country-specific information is easier to interpret and therefore more useful. Individual countries within a region of the world often experience very different rates of economic growth and economic conditions. Disclosures by individual country rather than groups of countries provide investors and other financial statement readers better information for assessing the risk level associated with a company's foreign operations.

Although a 10 percent threshold was considered for determining when a country is material, ultimately the FASB decided to leave this to management's judgment. In determining materiality, management should apply the concept that an item is material if its omission could change a user's decision about the enterprise as a whole. U.S. GAAP does not provide more specific guidance on this issue.

Considerable variation exists with respect to how companies apply the materiality rule for determining separately reportable countries. For example, International Business Machines Corporation (IBM) provides disclosures only for those countries with 10 percent or more of revenues or net plant, property, and equipment. Exhibit 8.7 contains the geographic area information included in IBM's 2014 Annual Report. With respect to revenue, only the United States and Japan meet the company's materiality threshold of 10 percent. As a result, the location of more than 50 percent of IBM's revenues is not disclosed. Only the United States meets the 10 percent threshold for net plant, property, and equipment.

Discussion Question

HOW DOES A COMPANY DETERMINE WHETHER A FOREIGN COUNTRY IS MATERIAL?

Segment reporting can provide useful information for investors and competitors. Segment disclosures could result in competitive harm for the company making the disclosures. By analyzing segment information, potential competitors can identify and concentrate on the more successful areas of a disclosing company's business. Indeed, the FASB recognized competitive harm as an issue of concern for companies disclosing segment information. In developing the current segment reporting guidelines, the FASB considered but ultimately decided not to provide companies an exemption from providing segment information if they believed that doing so would result in competitive harm. The FASB believed that such an exemption would be inappropriate because it would provide a means for broad noncompliance with the standard.

The previous segment reporting standard required geographic segments with 10 percent or more of total firm revenues, operating profit, or identifiable assets to be reported separately. In contrast, the current guidelines require disclosures to be provided by country when revenues or long-lived assets in an individual country are material. However, U.S. GAAP does not specify what is material for this purpose but leaves this to management judgment. Some commentators have expressed a concern that firms might use high materiality thresholds to avoid making individual country disclosures, perhaps to avoid potential competitive harm. Anecdotally, the very different levels of disclosure provided in 2014 by IBM and DuPont shown in Exhibits 8.7 and 8.8, respectively, show that companies define materiality differently.

What factors might a company consider in determining whether an individual foreign country is material to its operations? Should U.S. GAAP require a percentage test to determine when an individual country is material?

EXHIBIT 8.7
IBM's Geographic Area Disclosures

INTERNATIONAL BUSINESS MACHINES CORPORATION
GEOGRAPHIC INFORMATION

The following provides information for those countries that are 10 percent or more of the specific category.

Revenue*			
($ in millions)			
For the year ended December 31:	**2014**	**2013**	**2012**
United States	**$ 32,021**	$33,427	$ 34,653
Japan	**8,382**	9,070	10,696
Other countries.	**52,390**	55,871	57,525
Total IBM consolidated revenue . . .	**$ 92,793**	$98,368	$102,874
Plant and Other Property—Net			
($ in millions).			
At December 31:	**2014**	**2013**	**2012**
United States	**$ 4,388**	$ 6,723	$ 6,555
Other countries.	**5,690**	6,257	6,299
Total.	**$ 10,078**	$12,979	$ 12,854

*Revenues are attributed to countries based on the location of the client. There is a difference between the sum of the individual amounts and the "total" amounts reported by IBM for 2013, apparently due to rounding.

Also using a 10 percent materiality threshold, Hewlett Packard (HP) stated in Note 2 of its 2014 annual report: "For each of the fiscal years of 2014, 2013 and 2012, other than the U.S., no country represented more than 10% of HP net revenue." As a result, for 2014, HP reported $38,805 million in net revenue in the United States and $72,649 million in net revenue from Other Countries, with no disclosure of net revenue in any individual foreign country.

In contrast, Exhibit 8.8 provides the net sales by geographic area disclosures made by E.I. du Pont de Nemours and Company in its 2014 Annual Report. In providing this information, DuPont defines materiality at 2 percent. DuPont provided disclosures for 10 individual countries (including the United States) that comprised 73 percent of the company's total net sales in 2014.

For export sales, companies must choose whether to attribute the sales revenue to the country in which the selling entity is located or to the country in which the customer is located, and the basis for identifying the location of sales must be disclosed. Both IBM and DuPont provide a footnote to the geographic information that indicates revenue is attributed to the country in which the customer (client) is located. In contrast, in Note 25 of its 2014 annual report, Ford Motor Company indicates that revenues are attributed to the "countries where our major subsidiaries are domiciled."

LO 8-5

Apply the criterion for determining when disclosure of a major customer is required.

Information about Major Customers

FASB ASC 280-10-50-42 requires one final but important disclosure. A reporting entity must indicate its reliance on any major external customer. *Presentation of this information is required whenever 10 percent or more of a company's consolidated revenues is derived from a single external customer.* The existence of all major customers must be disclosed along with the related amount of revenues and the identity of the operating segment generating the revenues. Interestingly enough, the company need not reveal the customer's identity.

EXHIBIT 8.8
DuPont's Geographic Information, Net Sales

E. I. DU PONT DE NEMOURS AND COMPANY

	Geographic Information		
		Net Sales*	
(Dollars in millions)	**2014**	**2013**	**2012**
United States	**$13,081**	$13,763	$13,284
Canada	**$ 973**	$ 1,025	$ 921
EMEA‡			
France	**776**	749	765
Germany	**1,510**	1,502	1,557
Italy	**750**	728	764
Africa	**568**	597	361
Other	**4,879**	4,803	4,493
Total EMEA	**$ 8,483**	$ 8,379	$ 8,040
Asia Pacific			
China	**2,835**	2,720	2,666
India	**787**	740	745
Japan	**1,218**	1,292	1,577
Other	**2,863**	3,023	3,039
Total Asia Pacific	**$ 7,703**	$ 7,775	$ 8,027
Latin America			
Brazil	**2,328**	2,565	2,363
Mexico	**1,088**	1,070	1,044
Other	**1,067**	1,157	1,133
Total Latin America	**4,483**	$ 4,792	$ 4,540
Total	**$34,723**	$35,734	$34,812

* Net sales, based on the location of the customer, are generally presented for locations with greater than two percent of total net sales.
‡ Europe, Middle East, and Africa (EMEA).

The 2014 Annual Report of toy manufacturer Hasbro, Inc., provides an example of how this information is disclosed. Although not required to do so, Hasbro has elected to disclose the names of its major customers. In Note 18, Segment Reporting, Hasbro discloses:

> Sales to the Company's three largest customers, Wal-Mart Stores, Inc., Toys 'R' Us, Inc. and Target Corporation, amounted to 16%, 9% and 8%, respectively, of consolidated net revenues during 2014, 16%, 10% and 9%, respectively, of consolidated net revenues during 2013, and 17%, 11% and 10%, respectively, of consolidated net revenues during 2012. These sales were primarily within the U.S. and Canada segment.

The authoritative literature requires major customer disclosures even if a company operates in only one segment and therefore does not provide segment information. Also, to avoid any confusion, a group of entities under common control is considered to be a single customer, and federal, state, local, and foreign governments are each considered to be a single customer.

International Financial Reporting Standard 8—Operating Segments

IFRS 8, "Operating Segments," became effective for annual periods beginning on or after January 1, 2009, and substantially converges IFRS with U.S. GAAP. *IFRS 8* requires disclosures to be provided for separately reportable operating segments as well as certain enterprise-wide disclosures. Paragraph 1 establishes the "core principle" of *IFRS 8* to be the following:

> An entity shall disclose information to enable users of its financial statements to evaluate the nature and financial effects of the business activities in which it engages and the economic environments in which it operates.

The major differences between *IFRS 8* and U.S. GAAP are:

1. *IFRS 8* requires disclosure of total assets and total liabilities by operating segment, but only if such information is provided to the chief operating decision maker. U.S. GAAP requires disclosure of segment assets in general and is silent with respect to the disclosure of liabilities, even if this information is provided to the chief operating decision maker.
2. *IFRS 8* indicates that intangible assets are to be included in providing disclosure of long-lived assets attributable to geographic segments. In contrast, U.S. GAAP does not define what is intended to be included in long-lived assets. However, FASB ASC 280-10-55-23 indicates long-lived assets "implies hard assets that cannot be readily removed, which would exclude intangibles." Many U.S. companies define long-lived assets as property, plant, and equipment only, which is inconsistent with *IFRS 8.*
3. When a company has a matrix form of organization, *IFRS 8* indicates operating segments are to be determined based on the core principle of the standard. As a result, operating segments can be based on either products and services or geographic areas. U.S. GAAP stipulates that in a matrix form of organization, segments must be based on products and services, not geographic areas.

LO 8-6

Understand and apply procedures used in interim financial reports to treat an interim period as an integral part of the annual period.

Interim Reporting

To give investors and creditors more timely information than an annual report provides, companies publish financial information for periods of less than one year. The SEC requires publicly traded companies in the United States to provide financial statements on a quarterly basis. Unlike annual financial statements, financial statements included in quarterly reports filed with the SEC need not be audited. This allows companies to disseminate the information to investors and creditors as quickly as possible. FASB ASC Topic 270, "Interim Reporting," provides guidance to companies as to how to prepare interim statements.

Some inherent problems are associated with determining the results of operations for time periods of less than one year, especially with regard to expenses that do not occur evenly throughout the year. Two approaches can be followed in preparing interim reports: (1) Treat the interim period as a **discrete** accounting period, standing on its own, or (2) treat it as an **integral** portion of a longer period. Considering the annual bonus a company pays to key employees in December of each year illustrates the distinction between these two approaches. Under the *discrete* period approach, the company reports the entire bonus as an expense in December, reducing fourth quarter income only. Under the *integral* part of an annual period approach, a company accrues a portion of the bonus to be paid in December as an expense in each of the first three quarters of the year. Application of the integral approach requires estimating the annual bonus early in the year and developing a method for allocating the bonus to the four quarters of the year. The advantage of this approach is that there is less volatility in quarterly earnings as irregularly occurring costs are spread over the entire year.

FASB ASC 270 requires companies to treat interim periods as integral parts of an annual period rather than as discrete accounting periods in their own right. Generally speaking, companies should prepare interim financial statements following the same accounting principles and practices they use in preparing annual statements. However, deviation from this general rule is necessary for several items so that the interim statements better reflect the expected annual amounts. Special rules related to revenues, inventory and cost of goods sold, other costs and expenses, income taxes, accounting changes, and seasonal items are discussed in turn in the following sections.

Revenues

Companies should recognize revenues in interim periods the same way they recognize revenues on an annual basis. For example, revenues from a long-term construction contract that includes performance obligations that are satisfied by a company over time should be recognized in interim periods on the same basis as such revenues are recognized for the full year. Moreover, a company should recognize projected losses on long-term construction contracts to their full extent in the interim period in which it becomes apparent that a loss will arise.

Inventory and Cost of Goods Sold

Interim period accounting for inventory and cost of goods sold requires several modifications to procedures used on an annual basis. The modifications relate to (1) a LIFO liquidation, (2) application of the lower-of-cost-or-net realizable value rule, and (3) standard costing.

1. *LIFO liquidation:* Companies using the last-in, first-out (LIFO) cost-flow assumption to value inventory experience a LIFO liquidation at the end of an interim period when the number of units of inventory sold exceeds the number of units added to inventory during the period. When prices are rising, matching beginning inventory cost (carried at low LIFO amounts) against the current period sales revenue results in an unusually high amount of gross profit. If the company expects to replace by year-end the units of beginning inventory sold, there is no LIFO liquidation on an annual basis. In that case, gross profit for the interim period should not reflect the temporary LIFO liquidation, and inventory reported on the interim balance sheet should include the expected cost to replace the beginning inventory sold.

To illustrate, assume that Liquid Products Company began the first quarter with 100 units of inventory that cost $10 per unit. During the first quarter, it purchased 200 units at a cost of $15 per unit, and sold 240 units at $20 per unit. During the first quarter, the company experienced a liquidation of 40 units of beginning inventory. It calculates gross profit as follows:

Sales (240 units @ $20)		$4,800
Cost of goods sold:		
200 units @ $15	$3,000	
40 units @ $10 (LIFO historical cost)	400	3,400
Gross profit		$1,400

However, during the second quarter, the company expects to replace the units of beginning inventory sold at a cost of $17 per unit and that inventory at year-end will be at least 100 units. Therefore, it calculates gross profit for the first quarter as follows:

Sales (240 units @ $20)		$4,800
Cost of goods sold:		
200 units @ $15	$3,000	
40 units @ $17 (replacement cost)	680	3,680
Gross profit		$1,120

The journal entry to record cost of goods sold in the first quarter is:

Cost of Goods Sold	3,680	
Inventory		3,400
Excess of Replacement Cost over Historical Cost of LIFO Liquidation		280
To record cost of goods sold with a historical cost of $3,400 and an excess of replacement cost over historical cost for beginning inventory liquidated of $280 [($17 – $10) × 40 units].		

Thus, ending inventory is still reported at the original LIFO cost. The LIFO liquidation account will be removed in the second quarter when new goods are purchased.

2. *Lower-of-cost-or-net realizable value:* If at the end of an interim period, the net realizable value of inventory is less than its cost, the company normally should write down inventory and recognize a loss. However, if the company expects the net realizable value to recover above the inventory's original cost by year-end, it should not write down inventory and recognize a loss at the interim balance sheet date. Instead, it should continue to carry inventory at cost.

3. *Standard costing:* A company should not reflect in interim financial statements planned price, volume, or capacity variances arising from the use of a standard cost system that are expected to be absorbed by the end of the annual period. However, it should report unplanned variances at the end of the interim period in the same fashion as it would in the annual financial statements.

Other Costs and Expenses

A company should charge costs and expenses not directly matched with revenues to income in the interim period in which they occur unless they can be identified with activities or benefits of other interim periods. In that case, the cost should be allocated among interim periods on a reasonable basis through the use of accruals and deferrals. For example, assume that a company required to prepare quarterly financial statements pays annual property taxes of $100,000 on April 10. One-fourth of the estimated property tax should be accrued as expense in the first quarter of the year. When it makes the payment, it should apply one-fourth against the accrued property tax payable from the previous quarter and charge one-fourth to second-quarter income. The company should defer one-half of the payment as a prepaid expense to be allocated to the third and fourth quarters of the year. The following journal entries demonstrate the procedures for ensuring that the company recognizes one-fourth of the annual payment as expense in each quarter of the year.

March 31

Property Tax Expense	25,000	
Accrued Property Tax Payable		25,000
To accrue one-fourth of the estimated annual property tax as expense for the quarter ended March 31.		

April 10

Accrued Property Tax Payable	25,000	
Property Tax Expense	25,000	
Prepaid Property Tax (Current Asset)	50,000	
Cash		100,000
To record the payment of the annual property tax, recognize one-fourth as property tax expense for the quarter ending June 30, and defer one-half as a prepaid expense.		

September 30

Property Tax Expense	25,000	
Prepaid Property Tax		25,000
To record property tax expense for the quarter ended September 30.		

December 31

Property Tax Expense	25,000	
Prepaid Property Tax		25,000
To record property tax expense for the quarter ended December 31.		

Other items requiring similar treatment include annual major repairs and advertising. In addition, a number of adjustments such as bad debt expense, executive bonuses, and quantity discounts based on annual sales volume that are normally made at year-end actually relate to the entire year. To the extent that the company can estimate annual amounts, it should make adjustments at the end of each interim period so that the interim periods bear a reasonable portion of the expected annual amount.

Income Taxes

Companies should compute income tax related to ordinary income at an estimated *annual* effective tax rate. At the end of each interim period, a company makes its best estimate of the effective tax rate for the entire year. The effective tax rate reflects anticipated tax credits, foreign tax rates, and tax planning activities for the year. It then applies this rate to the pretax ordinary income earned to date during the year, resulting in the cumulative income tax expense to recognize to date. The difference between the cumulative income tax recognized to date and income tax recognized in earlier interim periods is the amount of income tax expense recognized in the current interim period.

Assume that Viertel Company estimated its effective annual tax rate at 42 percent in the first quarter of 2017. Pretax income for the first quarter was $500,000. At the end of the second quarter of 2017, the company expects its effective annual tax rate will be only 40 percent because of the planned usage of foreign tax credits. Pretax income in the second quarter of 2017 is also $500,000. No items require net-of-tax presentation in either quarter. The income tax expense recognized in each of the first two quarters of 2017 is determined as follows:

First Quarter	
Pretax income for first quarter of 2017	$500,000
Estimated annual income tax rate	42%
Income tax expense	$210,000

Second Quarter		
Pretax income for first quarter of 2017	$500,000	
Pretax income for second quarter of 2017	500,000	
Year-to-date income statement		$1,000,000
Estimated annual income tax rate		40%
Year-to-date income tax expense		$ 400,000
Income tax expense recognized in first quarter		210,000
Income tax expense recognized in second quarter		$ 190,000

The same process is followed for the third and fourth quarters of the year.

Discontinued operations should be reported in net income on a *net of tax* basis in the interim period in which a business component is discontinued or classified as held-for-sale. The income tax on an interim period discontinued operation is calculated at the margin as the difference between income tax on income including discontinued operations and income tax on income excluding discontinued operations.

Change in Accounting Principle

Current accounting guidelines require retrospective application of a new accounting principle to prior periods' financial statements. *Retrospective application* means that comparative financial statements will be restated as if the new accounting principle had always been used. Whether an accounting change occurs in the first or in a subsequent interim period has no bearing on the manner in which the change is reflected in the interim financial statements. Changes in accounting principle, regardless of when the accounting change is made, are handled as follows (according to FASB ASC 250-10-45-5):

a. The cumulative effect of the change to the new accounting principle on periods prior to those presented is reflected in the carrying amounts of assets and liabilities as of the beginning of the first period presented.

b. An offsetting adjustment, if any, is made to the opening balance of retained earnings (or other appropriate components of equity or net assets in the statement of financial position) for that period.

c. Financial statements for each individual prior period are adjusted to reflect the period-specific effects of applying the new accounting principle.

When the accounting change takes place in other than the first interim period, current guidelines require information for the interim periods prior to the change to be reported by retrospectively applying the new accounting principle to those prechange interim periods. If retrospective application is impracticable, the accounting change is not allowed to be made in an interim period but may be made at the beginning of the next fiscal year. Situations in which the retrospective application of a new accounting principle to prechange interim periods is not feasible should be rare.

Illustration of Accounting Change Made in Other Than First Interim Period

Modal Company began operations on January 1, 2016. The company's interim income statements as originally reported under the LIFO inventory valuation method follow:

	2016				2017
	1stQ	**2ndQ**	**3rdQ**	**4thQ**	**1stQ**
Sales	$2,000	$2,000	$2,000	$2,000	$2,200
Cost of goods sold (LIFO)	900	950	1,000	1,000	1,050
Operating expenses	500	500	500	500	600
Income before income taxes	$ 600	$ 550	$ 500	$ 500	$ 550
Income taxes (40%)	240	220	200	200	220
Net income	$ 360	$ 330	$ 300	$ 300	$ 330

Modal has 500 shares of common stock outstanding. The company's interim report for the first quarter of 2017 included the following information:

	Three Months Ended March 31	
	2016	2017
Net income	$ 360	$ 330
Net income per common share.	$0.72	$0.66

In June 2017, Modal adopts the FIFO method of inventory valuation for both financial reporting and tax purposes. Retrospective application of the FIFO method to previous quarters results in the following amounts of cost of goods sold:

	2016				2017
	1stQ	2ndQ	3rdQ	4thQ	1stQ
Cost of goods sold (FIFO).	$800	$850	$1,000	$900	$950

Retrospective application of the FIFO method results in the following restatements of income:

	2016				2017
	1stQ	2ndQ	3rdQ	4thQ	1stQ
Sales.	$2,000	$2,000	$2,000	$2,000	$2,200
Cost of goods sold (FIFO).	800	850	1,000	900	950
Operating expenses	500	500	500	500	600
Income before income taxes. . . .	$ 700	$ 650	$ 500	$ 600	$ 650
Income taxes (40%)	280	260	200	240	260
Net income	$ 420	$ 390	$ 300	$ 360	$ 390

Sales for the second quarter of 2017 are $2,400, cost of goods sold under the FIFO method is $1,000, and operating expenses are $600. Income before income taxes in the second quarter of 2017 is $800, income taxes are $320, and net income is $480.

To prepare interim statements for the second quarter of 2017 in accordance with U.S. GAAP, net income as originally reported in the first and second quarters of 2016, as well as in the first quarter of 2017, is restated to reflect the change to FIFO. The manner in which the accounting change is reflected in the second quarter of 2017, with year-to-date information, and comparative information for similar periods in 2016 follow:

	Three Months Ended June 30		Six Months Ended June 30	
	2016	2017	2016	2017
Net income	$390	$480	$810	$870
Net income per common share.	0.78	0.96	1.62	1.74

Seasonal Items

The sales volume of some companies experiences significant seasonal variation. Summer sports equipment manufacturers, for example, are likely to have a significant upward spike in sales during the second quarter of the year. To avoid the risk that investors and creditors will be misled into believing that second-quarter earnings indicate earnings for the entire year, FASB ASC 270-10-45 requires companies to disclose the seasonal nature of their business operations. In addition, such companies should consider supplementing their interim reports with reports on the 12-month period ended at the interim date for both the current and preceding years. An excerpt from the seasonality disclosure provided by Callaway Golf Company in its Form 10-Q for the quarter ended June 30, 2015, is shown here:

> **Seasonality.** In most of the regions where the Company does business, the game of golf is played primarily on a seasonal basis. Weather conditions generally restrict golf from being played year-round, except in a few regions, with many of the Company's on-course customers closing for the cold weather months. The Company's business is therefore subject to seasonal fluctuations. . . The Company's fourth-quarter sales are generally less than the other quarters due to the end of the golf season in many of the Company's key regions.

LO 8-7

List the minimum disclosure requirements for interim financial reports.

Minimum Disclosures in Interim Reports

Many companies provide summary financial statements and notes in their interim reports that contain less information than is included in the annual financial statements. Authoritative accounting literature requires companies to provide the following minimum information in their interim reports:

- Sales or gross revenues, provision for income taxes, and net income.
- Earnings per share.
- Seasonal revenues and expenses.
- Significant changes in estimates or provisions for income taxes.
- Disposal of a component of the business and unusual or infrequently occurring items.
- Contingent items.
- Changes in accounting principles or estimates.
- Significant changes in financial position.

Authoritative guidelines also encourage, but do not require, companies to publish balance sheet and cash flow information in interim reports. If they do not include this information, companies must disclose significant changes since the last period in cash and cash equivalents, net working capital, long-term liabilities, and stockholders' equity.

Companies that provide interim reports on a quarterly basis are not required to publish a fourth-quarter report because this coincides with the end of the annual period. When a company does not provide a separate fourth-quarter report, it should disclose special accounting items occurring in the fourth quarter in the notes to financial statements in the annual report. These items include unusual and infrequently occurring items, disposals of a component of the business, and the aggregate effect of year-end adjustments that are material to the results of the fourth quarter.

The SEC requires companies to include selected quarterly financial data in their annual report to shareholders. Southwest Airlines Co. provided quarterly data in its 2014 annual report as shown in Exhibit 8.9.

EXHIBIT 8.9
Quarterly Financial Data from Southwest Airlines Co.'s 2014 Annual Report

QUARTERLY FINANCIAL DATA (Unaudited)

	Three Months Ended			
(in millions, except per share amounts)	March 31	June 30	Sept. 30	Dec. 31
2014				
Operating revenues	$4,166	$5,011	$4,800	$4,628
Operating income	215	775	614	621
Income before income taxes.	244	746	525	302
Net income	152	465	329	190
Net income per share, basic	0.22	0.67	0.48	0.28
Net income per share, diluted.	0.22	0.67	0.48	0.28

Segment Information in Interim Reports

The management approach to determining operating segments results in readily available information for disclosure because, by definition, management already collects this data. Because the information is available on a timely basis, segment disclosures also must be included in interim reports. U.S. GAAP requires that the following information be included in interim reports for each operating segment:

- Revenues from external customers.
- Intersegment revenues.
- Segment profit or loss.
- Total assets, if there has been a material change from the last annual report.

In addition, an enterprise must reconcile total segments' profit or loss to the company's total income before taxes and disclose any change from the last annual report in the basis for measuring segment profit or loss. Requiring only a few items of information in interim reports is a compromise between users' desire to have the same information as is provided in annual financial statements and preparers' cost in reporting the information. There is no requirement to provide information about geographic areas or major customers in interim reports.

International Accounting Standard 34—Interim Financial Reporting

In contrast to U.S. GAAP, which does not require the presentation of financial statements *per se* in an interim report, *IAS 34,* "Interim Financial Reporting," provides guidance with respect to the form and content of interim financial statements, and the recognition and measurement principles to be followed in preparing them.[2] *IAS 34* requires the following minimum components in an interim report:

- A condensed statement of financial position (balance sheet).
- A condensed statement of comprehensive income, presented as:
  a. A condensed single statement of net income and comprehensive income, or
  b. Separate condensed statements of net income and comprehensive income.
- A condensed statement of changes in equity.
- A condensed statement of cash flows.
- Selected explanatory notes.

Unlike U.S. GAAP, *IAS 34* requires each interim period to be treated as a discrete period in determining the amounts to be recognized. Thus, expenses that are incurred in one quarter are recognized in full in that quarter, even though the expenditure benefits the entire year. In addition, there is no accrual in earlier quarters for expenses expected to be incurred in a later quarter of the year. The only exception to this rule is the accrual of income tax expense at the end of each interim period.

Summary

1. The consolidation of information from varied operations into a set of consolidated financial statements tends to camouflage the characteristics of the individual components. FASB ASC 280, "Segment Reporting," requires enterprises to follow a management approach in providing disaggregated information by operating segment.
2. The management approach to disaggregating information bases operating segments on a company's organization structure and internal reporting system. The management approach should enhance the usefulness of segment information because it highlights the risks and opportunities that management

[2] Note that the IASB has no jurisdictional authority to require the preparation of interim reports; it simply provides requirements (through *IAS 34*) for how those reports should be prepared. *IAS 34* must be followed in those jurisdictions that require the use of IFRS and require the preparation of interim reports.

believes are important and allows the analyst to see the company through management's eyes. This approach also has the advantage of reducing the cost of providing segment information because that information already is being produced for internal use.

3. Once operating segments have been identified, a company must determine which segments are of significant magnitude to warrant separate disclosure. Three quantitative threshold tests (revenue, profit or loss, and asset) are used to identify reportable segments. A segment need satisfy only one of these tests to be considered of sufficient size to necessitate disclosure. Each test is based on identifying segments that meet a 10 percent minimum of the related combined total. The profit and loss test has a 10 percent criterion based on the higher (in an absolute sense) of the total profit from all segments with profits or the total loss from all segments with losses.
4. Companies must report several information types for each reportable operating segment, including selected revenues, profit or loss, selected expenses, assets, capital expenditures, and equity method investment and income. Companies must report revenues from external customers separately from intersegment revenues. In addition, the types of products and services from which each segment derives its revenues must be disclosed.
5. A set of parameters determines the number of segments an enterprise reports. As a minimum, the separately disclosed units must generate at least 75 percent of the total sales made to unaffiliated parties. For an upper limit, authoritative literature suggests that the disclosure of more than 10 operating segments reduces the usefulness of the information.
6. Companies must reconcile the total of all segments' revenues, profit or loss, and assets to the consolidated totals. The major reconciliation adjustments relate to intra-entity revenues, profit or loss, and assets eliminated in consolidation; revenues, profit or loss, and assets that have not been allocated to individual operating segments; and differences in accounting methods used by segments and in preparing consolidated financial statements.
7. U.S. GAAP requires several entitywide disclosures. If an enterprise does not define operating segments internally on a product line basis or has only one operating segment, disclosure of revenues derived from each product or service is required.
8. In addition, companies must report revenues from external customers and long-lived assets for the domestic country, for each foreign country that generates a material amount of revenues or holds assets, and for all foreign countries in total. Current guidelines do not provide any threshold tests for determining when operations in a foreign country are material. Instead, determining materiality is left to management's judgment.
9. Authoritative accounting literature requires disclosure of one other type of information. The reporting entity must indicate the existence of major customers when 10 percent or more of consolidated revenues are derived from a single unaffiliated party. However, the identity of the major customer need not be disclosed.
10. To converge with U.S. GAAP, the IASB issued *IFRS 8*, "Operating Segments." The major differences between IFRS and U.S. GAAP are that *IFRS 8* (1) requires the disclosure of liabilities by operating segment if this information is reported to the chief operating decision maker, (2) requires the inclusion of intangible assets in the disclosure of long-lived assets by geographic area, and (3) allows companies with matrix organizations to define operating segments on the basis of either products and services or geographic areas.
11. For interim reporting purposes, U.S. GAAP requires time intervals of less than one year to be treated as an integral part of the annual period.
12. Costs and expenses not directly matched with revenues should be charged to income in the interim period in which they occur unless they can be identified with activities or benefits of other interim periods. In that case, the cost should be allocated among interim periods on a reasonable basis by using accruals and deferrals. Items related to the whole year but recorded as an adjustment only at year-end should be estimated and accrued in each interim period of the year.
13. Companies determine interim period income tax expense by applying the estimated annual effective income tax rate to year-to-date pretax ordinary income, resulting in the cumulative income tax expense to be recognized to date. The cumulative income tax to be recognized to date less income tax recognized in earlier interim periods is the amount of income tax expense recognized in the current interim period.
14. When an accounting change is made in other than the first interim period, information for the prechange interim periods should be reported based on retrospective application of the new accounting principle to those periods. An accounting change may be made only at the beginning of a fiscal year if retrospective application of the new accounting principle to prechange interim periods is not practicable.

15. The minimum information to disclose in interim reports includes sales, income taxes, net income, earnings per share, seasonal revenues and expenses, and significant changes in financial position. Publication of balance sheet and cash flow information in interim reports is not required. However, if this information is not included, any significant changes since the last period in cash and cash equivalents, net working capital, long-term liabilities, and stockholders' equity must be disclosed.
16. Certain segment information items need to be disclosed in interim reports. Specifically, companies must disclose revenues from outside customers, intersegment revenues, and segment profit or loss in interim reports for each operating segment. In addition, companies must report total assets by segment if a material change occurred since the last annual report.
17. Unlike U.S. GAAP, the IASB's *IAS 34,* "Interim Financial Reporting," requires the presentation of condensed financial statements in an interim report. Also, each interim period should be treated as a discrete period rather than as an integral part of an annual period in determining amounts to be recognized. The exception to this rule is the accrual of income tax expense to determine net income for each interim period.

Comprehensive Illustration

(Estimated Time: 25 to 40 Minutes) Battey Corporation manufactures several products: natural fibers, synthetic fibers, leather, plastics, and wood. It is organized into five operating divisions based on these different products. The company has a number of subsidiaries that perform operations throughout the world. At the end of 2017 as part of the internal reporting process, Battey reported the revenues, profits, and assets (in millions) to the chief operating decision maker:

Problem

Revenues by Operating Segment	United States	Canada	Mexico	France	Italy	Brazil
Natural fibers:						
Sales to external customers	$1,739	$-0-	$342	$606	$-0-	$1,171
Intersegment sales	-0-	-0-	-0-	-0-	-0-	146
Synthetic fibers:						
Sales to external customers	290	116	-0-	-0-	-0-	37
Intersegment sales	12	5	-0-	-0-	-0-	-0-
Leather:						
Sales to external customers	230	-0-	57	-0-	278	55
Intersegment sales	22	-0-	9	-0-	34	9
Plastics:						
Sales to external customers	748	286	-0-	83	92	528
Intersegment sales	21	12	-0-	-0-	-0-	72
Wood:						
Sales to external customers	116	22	-0-	-0-	-0-	149
Intersegment sales	17	3	-0-	-0-	-0-	28

Operating Profit or Loss by Operating Segment	United States	Canada	Mexico	France	Italy	Brazil
Natural fibers	$ 526	$-0-	$ 92	$146	$-0-	$ 404
Synthetic fibers	21	8	-0-	-0-	-0-	10
Leather	70	-0-	27	-0-	94	24
Plastics	182	74	-0-	18	24	68
Wood	18	5	-0-	-0-	-0-	37

Assets by Operating Segment	United States	Canada	Mexico	France	Italy	Brazil
Natural fibers	$1,005	$-0-	$223	$296	$-0-	$ 817
Synthetic fibers	163	50	-0-	-0-	-0-	74
Leather	146	-0-	41	-0-	150	38
Plastics	425	173	-0-	54	58	327
Wood	66	19	-0-	-0-	-0-	143

Required

a. Determine the operating segments that should be reported separately in Battey's 2017 financial statements.

b. Determine the countries for which Battey should report revenues separately in its 2017 financial statements. Assume that Battey has elected to define a material country as one in which sales to external customers are 10 percent or more of consolidated sales.

c. Determine the volume of revenues that a single customer must generate to necessitate disclosure of a major customer.

Solution

a. Battey Corporation determines its reportable operating segments by following a three-step process. First, it identifies operating segments. Second, it examines aggregation criteria to determine whether any operating segments may be combined. Third, it determines reportable operating segments by applying the three quantitative threshold tests.

Identification of Operating Segments Battey's internal reporting system provides information to the chief operating decision maker by operating division and by country. Either of these components conceivably could be identified as operating segments for segment reporting purposes. However, U.S. GAAP stipulates that, in this situation, the components based on products and services constitute the operating segments. Thus, the five operating divisions are identified as Battey's operating segments.

Aggregation Criteria Aggregation criteria are examined next to determine whether any operating segments can be combined. Management determines that the economic characteristics of the natural fibers and synthetic fibers operating divisions are very similar. In addition, they are considerably similar with regard to the nature of the product, production process, customers, and distribution methods. Because each aggregation criterion is met, Battey elects to combine these two segments into a single fibers category.

Quantitative Threshold Tests Determining Battey's reportable operating segments depends on the three materiality tests described in this chapter. The revenue test can be performed directly from the information provided. Any operating segment with total revenues (including intersegment sales) equal to 10 percent or more of combined revenue (internal and external) must be reported separately:

Revenue Test (in millions)

Operating Segments	Total Revenues (Including Intersegment)	
Fibers	$4,464	60.8%
Leather	694	9.5
Plastics	1,842	25.1
Wood	335	4.6
Total combined revenues	$7,335	100.0%

Reportable segments are fibers and plastics.

The profit or loss test is performed next. Battey must separately report any operating segment with profit or loss equal to 10 percent or more of the larger, in absolute amount, of combined segment profit (for those segments with a profit) or combined segment loss (for those segments with a loss). Because each of Battey's operating segments generated a profit in 2015, this test can be applied by determining the total combined profit:

Profit or Loss Test (in millions)

Operating Segments	Total Profit or Loss	
Fibers	$1,207	65.3%
Leather	215	11.6
Plastics	366	19.8
Wood	60	3.3
Total combined segment profit	$1,848	100.0%

Reportable segments are fibers, leather, and plastics.

Finally, Battey performs the asset test:

Asset Test (in millions)

Operating Segments	**Total Assets**	
Fibers	$2,628	61.6%
Leather	375	8.8
Plastics	1,037	24.3
Wood	228	5.3
Total combined segment assets	$4,268	100.0%

Reportable segments are fibers and plastics.

Based on these three tests, data about the fibers, leather, and plastics operating segments must be reported separately. Information on the immaterial wood segment need not be reported. However, the revenues, profit, and assets of this segment are included in reconciliations to consolidated totals.

b. Battey must report sales to external customers for the U.S., for each individual foreign country in which the company generates a material amount of revenues, and for all foreign countries in total. Authoritative accounting literature does not provide quantitative tests for determining when a foreign country is material but leaves this to management's judgment. Battey has decided to define *materiality* as sales to external customers equal to 10 percent or more of consolidated revenues.

Revenue Test (in millions)

Country	**Sales to External Customers**	
United States	$3,123	45.0%
Canada	424	6.1
Mexico	399	5.8
France	689	9.9
Italy	370	5.3
Brazil	1,940	27.9
Total consolidated revenues	$6,945	100.0%

Using this criterion, Battey reports results for the United States and Brazil separately and combines the remaining countries into an All Other category. Alternatively, if Battey had established a materiality threshold of 5 percent, it would report separately each of the foreign countries in which it generates revenues. Again, determination of materiality is left to management's judgment.

c. The significance test for disclosure of a major customer is 10 percent of consolidated revenues. Battey must report the existence of any major customer from which it generated $694.5 million or more in revenues during 2017.

Questions

1. How does the consolidation process tend to disguise information needed to analyze the financial operations of a diversified organization?
2. What is disaggregated financial information?
3. According to the FASB, what is the major objective of segment reporting?
4. The management approach requires a firm to define segments on the basis of its internal organizational structure. What are the advantages in defining segments on this basis?
5. What is an operating segment?
6. How should a company determine operating segments when it organizes business activities in more than one way and the chief operating decision maker uses multiple sets of reports?
7. Describe the three tests to identify reportable operating segments.

8. What information must an enterprise provide for each of its separately reportable operating segments?
9. Under what conditions must an enterprise provide information about products and services?
10. Under what conditions must an enterprise provide information about geographic areas?
11. What information must an enterprise report by geographic area?
12. To satisfy geographic area disclosure requirements, what are the minimum and maximum numbers of countries for which information should be reported separately?
13. Under what conditions should a company disclose the amount of sales from a major customer?
14. What are the major differences between U.S. GAAP and *IFRS 8* with respect to the disclosures that are required to be provided for each separately reportable operating segment?
15. Why are publicly traded companies in the United States required to prepare interim reports on a quarterly basis?
16. What approach are companies required to follow in preparing interim financial statements?
17. How should a company handle a LIFO liquidation in an interim period when the liquidated inventory is expected to be replaced by year-end?
18. How does a company determine the amount of income tax expense to report in an interim period?
19. What procedures must companies follow to account for a change in accounting principle made in other than the first interim period of the year?
20. What minimum information must an enterprise provide in an interim report?
21. What type of segment information must companies provide in interim financial statements?
22. How would an annual bonus paid at year-end be treated under *IAS 34* and how does this treatment differ from what is required under U.S. GAAP?

Problems

LO 8-1

1. Which of the following does U.S. GAAP *not* consider to be an objective of segment reporting?
   a. It helps users better understand the enterprise's performance.
   b. It helps users better assess the enterprise's prospects for future cash flows.
   c. It helps users make more informed judgments about the enterprise as a whole.
   d. It helps users make comparisons between a segment of one enterprise and a similar segment of another enterprise.

LO 8-3

2. Under current U.S. accounting guidelines, which of the following items of information is a company *not* required to disclose, even if it were material in amount?
   a. Revenues generated from sales of its consumer products line of goods.
   b. Revenues generated by its Japanese subsidiary.
   c. Revenues generated from export sales.
   d. Revenues generated from sales to Walmart.

LO 8-3

3. Which of the following operating segment disclosures is *not* required under current U.S. accounting guidelines?
   a. Liabilities
   b. Interest expense
   c. Intersegment sales
   d. Unusual items

LO 8-2

4. In determining whether a particular operating segment is of significant size to warrant disclosure, which of the following is true?
   a. Three tests are applied, and all three must be met.
   b. Four tests are applied, and only one must be met.
   c. Three tests are applied, and only one must be met.
   d. Four tests are applied, and all four must be met.

LO 8-1, 8-3, 8-4

5. Which of the following statements is *not* true under U.S. GAAP?
   a. Operating segments can be determined by looking at a company's organization chart.
   b. Companies must combine individual foreign countries into geographic areas to comply with the geographic area disclosure requirements.

c. Companies that define their operating segments by product lines must provide revenue and asset information for the domestic country, for all foreign countries in total, and for each material foreign country.

d. Companies must disclose total assets, investment in equity method affiliates, and total expenditures for long-lived assets by operating segment.

LO 8-1

6. Which of the following is *not* necessarily true for an operating segment?

a. An operating segment earns revenues and incurs expenses.

b. The chief operating decision maker regularly reviews an operating segment to assess performance and make resource allocation decisions.

c. Discrete financial information generated by the internal accounting system is available for an operating segment.

d. An operating segment regularly generates a profit from its normal ongoing operations.

LO 8-2

7. Which of the following is a criterion for determining whether an operating segment is separately reportable?

a. Segment liabilities are 10 percent or more of consolidated liabilities.

b. Segment profit or loss is 10 percent or more of consolidated net income.

c. Segment assets are 10 percent or more of combined segment assets.

d. Segment revenues from external sales are 5 percent or more of combined segment revenues from external sales.

LO 8-1, 8-3, 8-4, 8-5

8. Which of the following statements concerning U.S. GAAP is true?

a. Does not require segment information to be reported in accordance with generally accepted accounting principles.

b. Does not require a reconciliation of segment assets to consolidated assets.

c. Requires geographic area information to be disclosed in interim financial statements.

d. Requires disclosure of a major customer's identity.

LO 8-3

9. Plume Company has a paper products operating segment. Which of the following items does it *not* have to report for this segment?

a. Interest expense.

b. Research and development expense.

c. Depreciation and amortization expense.

d. Interest income.

LO 8-4

10. Which of the following items is required to be disclosed by geographic area?

a. Total assets.

b. Revenues from external customers.

c. Profit or loss.

d. Capital expenditures.

LO 8-4

11. For a U.S.-based company, which of the following would be an acceptable presentation of countries for providing information by geographic area?

a. United States, Mexico, Japan, Spain, All Other Countries.

b. United States, Canada and Mexico, Germany, Italy.

c. Europe, Asia, Africa.

d. Canada, Germany, France, All Other Countries.

LO 8-4

12. What information about revenues by geographic area should a company present?

a. Disclose separately the amount of sales to unaffiliated customers and the amount of intra-entity sales between geographic areas.

b. Disclose as a combined amount sales to unaffiliated customers and intra-entity sales between geographic areas.

c. Disclose separately the amount of sales to unaffiliated customers but not the amount of intra-entity sales between geographic areas.

d. No disclosure of revenues from foreign operations need be reported.

LO 8-5

13. Which of the following information items with regard to a major customer must be disclosed?

a. The identity of the major customer.

b. The percentage of total sales derived from the major customer.

c. The operating segment making sales to the major customer.

d. The geographic area in which sales to the major customer are made.

LO 8-6

14. Which of the following statements is true for a company that has managers responsible for product and service lines of business and managers responsible for geographic areas (matrix form of organization)?

a. Under U.S. GAAP, the company must base operating segments on geographic areas.

b. Under IFRS, the company must base operating segments on product and service lines of business.

c. Under U.S. GAAP, the company may choose to define operating segments on the basis of either products and services or geographic areas.

d. Under IFRS, the company must refer to the core principle of *IFRS 8* to determine operating segments.

LO 8-6

15. In considering interim financial reporting, how does current U.S. GAAP require that such reporting be viewed?

a. As a special type of reporting that need not follow generally accepted accounting principles.

b. As useful only if activity is evenly spread throughout the year making estimates unnecessary.

c. As reporting for a basic accounting period.

d. As reporting for an integral part of an annual period.

LO 8-6

16. How should material seasonal variations in revenue be reflected in interim financial statements?

a. The seasonal nature should be disclosed, and the interim report should be supplemented with a report on the 12-month period ended at the interim date for both the current and preceding years.

b. The seasonal nature should be disclosed, but no attempt should be made to reflect the effect of past seasonality on financial statements.

c. The seasonal nature should be reflected by providing pro forma financial statements for the current interim period.

d. No attempt should be made to reflect seasonality in interim financial statements.

LO 8-6

17. For interim financial reporting, a gain from the sale of land occurring in the second quarter should be

a. Recognized ratably over the last three quarters.

b. Recognized ratably over all four quarters, with the first quarter being restated.

c. Recognized in the second quarter.

d. Disclosed by footnote only in the second quarter.

LO 8-7

18. Which of the following items must be disclosed in interim reports?

a. Total assets.

b. Total liabilities.

c. Cash flow from operating activities.

d. Gross revenues.

LO 8-7

19. Which of the following items is *not* required to be reported in interim financial statements for each material operating segment?

a. Revenues from external customers.

b. Intersegment revenues.

c. Segment assets.

d. Segment profit or loss.

LO 8-6

20. Niceville Company pays property taxes of $100,000 in the second quarter of the year. Which of the following statements is true with respect to the recognition of property tax expense in interim financial statements?

a. Under U.S. GAAP, the company would report property tax expense of $100,000 in the second quarter of the year.

b. Under IFRS, the company would report property tax expense of $100,000 in the second quarter of the year.

c. Under U.S. GAAP, the company would report property tax expense of $33,333 in each of the second, third, and fourth quarters of the year.

d. Under IFRS, the company would report property tax expense of $25,000 in the first quarter of the year.

LO 8-2

21. Livro Company has three operating segments with the following information:

	Books	Calendars	Bags
Sales to outsiders	$12,000	$9,000	$8,000
Intersegment transfers	1,000	500	1,500

In addition, corporate headquarters generates revenues of $2,000.

What is the minimum amount of revenue that each of these segments must generate to be considered separately reportable?

a. $2,900
b. $3,200
c. $3,300
d. $3,400

LO 8-5

22. Nottage Company has four separate operating segments:

	East	West	North	South
Sales to outsiders	$188,000	$126,000	$65,000	$43,000
Intersegment transfers	16,000	6,000	13,000	8,000

What revenue amount must one customer generate before it must be identified as a major customer?

a. $39,600
b. $42,200
c. $46,500
d. $49,200

LO 8-2

23. Howard Corporation has six different operating segments reporting the following operating profit and loss figures:

A	$ 80,000 profit	D	$440,000 loss
B	140,000 loss	E	50,000 profit
C	100,000 profit	F	170,000 profit

With respect to the profit or loss test, which of the following statements is *not* true?

a. A is a reportable segment based on this one test.
b. C is not a reportable segment based on this one test.
c. E is not a reportable segment based on this one test.
d. F is a reportable segment based on this one test.

LO 8-2

24. Hyams Corp. engages solely in manufacturing operations. The following data pertain to the operating segments for the current year:

Operating Segment	Total Revenues	Profit (Loss)	Assets at 12/31
U	$13,000,000	$2,000,000	$15,000,000
V	9,500,000	1,200,000	11,000,000
W	5,500,000	(1,000,000)	3,000,000
X	3,000,000	600,000	7,500,000
Y	2,000,000	400,000	4,500,000
Z	2,000,000	300,000	2,000,000
Total	$35,000,000	$3,500,000	$43,000,000

In its segment information for the current year, how many reportable segments does Hyams have?

a. Three
b. Four
c. Five
d. Six

LO 8-2

25. What is the minimum number of operating segments that must be separately reported?
    a. Ten.
    b. Segments with at least 75 percent of revenues as measured by the revenue test.
    c. At least 75 percent of the segments must be separately reported.
    d. Segments with at least 75 percent of the revenues generated from outside parties.

LO 8-2

26. Chambers Company has seven operating segments but only four (One, Two, Three, and Four) are of significant size to warrant separate disclosure. As a whole, the segments generated revenues of $1,010,000 ($780,000 + $230,000) from sales to outside customers. In addition, the segments had $300,000 in intersegment sales ($250,000 + $50,000).

	Outside Sales	Intersegment Sales
One	$270,000	$110,000
Two	200,000	70,000
Three	160,000	40,000
Four	150,000	30,000
Totals	$780,000	$250,000
Five	$100,000	$ 20,000
Six	80,000	10,000
Seven	50,000	20,000
Totals	$230,000	$ 50,000

Which of the following statements is true?

a. A sufficient number of segments is being reported because those segments have $1,030,000 in total sales of a total of $1,310,000 for the company as a whole.
b. Not enough segments are being reported because those segments have $780,000 in outside sales of a total of $1,010,000 for the company as a whole.
c. Not enough segments are being reported because those segments have $1,030,000 in total revenues of a total of $1,310,000 for the company as a whole.
d. A sufficient number of segments is being reported because those segments have $780,000 in outside sales of a total of $1,010,000 for the company as a whole.

LO 8-6

27. Baton Company estimates that the amounts for total depreciation expense for the year ending December 31 will be $120,000 and for year-end bonuses to employees will be $200,000. What total amount of expense relating to these two items should Baton report in its quarterly income statement for the three months ended March 31?
    a. $0
    b. $30,000
    c. $50,000
    d. $80,000

LO 8-6

28. Rouge Company's $250,000 net income for the quarter ended September 30 included the following after-tax items:
    - A $20,000 cumulative effect loss resulting from a change in inventory valuation method made on September 1.
    - $0 of the $60,000 annual property taxes paid on February 1.

    For the quarter ended September 30, the amount of net income that Rouge should report is
    a. $235,000
    b. $250,000
    c. $255,000
    d. $270,000

LO 8-6

29. In March of the current year, Mooney Company estimated its year-end executive bonuses to be $800,000. The executive bonus paid in the previous year was $950,000. What amount of bonus expense, if any, should Mooney recognize in determining net income for the first quarter of the current calendar year?
    a. –0–
    b. $200,000
    c. $237,500
    d. $800,000

Use the following information for Problems 30 and 31.

On March 15, Calloway, Inc., paid property taxes of $480,000 for the calendar year.

LO 8-6

30. How much of this expense should Calloway's income statement reflect for the quarter ending March 31?
    a. -0-
    b. $40,000
    c. $120,000
    d. $480,000

LO 8-6

31. The journal entry at March 15 to record the payment of property taxes would include which of the following?
    a. A debit to Property Tax Expense of $480,000.
    b. A credit to Cash of $120,000.
    c. A debit to Prepaid Property Taxes of $360,000.
    d. A credit to Prepaid Property Taxes of $40,000.

Use the following information for Problems 32 and 33.

Tristan, Inc., uses the LIFO cost-flow assumption to value inventory. It began the current year with 2,000 units of inventory carried at LIFO cost of $20 per unit. During the first quarter, it purchased 8,000 units at an average cost of $40 per unit and sold 9,500 units at $60 per unit.

LO 8-6

32. Assume the company does not expect to replace the units of beginning inventory sold; it plans to reduce inventory by year-end to 500 units. What amount of cost of goods sold should be recorded for the quarter ended March 31?
    a. $335,000
    b. $350,000
    c. $380,000
    d. $387,500

LO 8-6

33. Assume the company expects to replace the units of beginning inventory sold in April at a cost of $45 per unit and expects inventory at year-end to be between 2,100 and 2,500 units. What amount of cost of goods sold should be recorded for the quarter ended March 31?
    a. $335,000
    b. $350,000
    c. $380,000
    d. $387,500

LO 8-2

34. Vehicle Corporation is organized into four operating segments. The internal reporting system generated the following segment information:

	Revenues from Outsiders	Intersegment Transfers	Operating Expenses
Autos	$4,000,000	$100,000	$3,600,000
Trucks	3,500,000	200,000	4,000,000
SUVs	2,600,000	-0-	2,000,000
Motorcycles	900,000	50,000	1,020,000

The company incurred additional operating expenses (of a general nature) of $1,200,000.

Perform the profit or loss test to determine which of these segments is separately reportable.

LO 8-2

35. Ecru Company has identified five industry segments: plastics, metals, lumber, paper, and finance. It appropriately consolidated each of these segments in producing its annual financial statements. Information describing each segment (in thousands) follows:

	Plastics	Metals	Lumber	Paper	Finance
Sales to outside parties	$6,694	$2,354	$ 711	$422	$-0-
Intersegment transfers	148	173	138	150	-0-
Interest income from outside parties	-0-	34	21	-0-	42

(continued)

(continued)

	Plastics	Metals	Lumber	Paper	Finance
Interest income from intersegment loans	–0–	–0–	–0–	–0–	201
Operating expenses	4,214	1,762	1,066	654	31
Interest expense	76	31	66	28	102
Tangible assets	1,501	3,196	524	771	179
Intangible assets	87	403	–0–	63	–0–
Intersegment loans (debt)	–0–	–0–	–0–	–0–	706

Ecru does not allocate its $1,460,000 in common expenses to the various segments.

Perform testing procedures to determine Ecru's reportable operating segments.

LO 8-2, 8-5

36. Following is financial information describing the six operating segments that make up Fairfield, Inc. (in thousands):

	Segments					
	Red	Blue	Green	Pink	Black	White
Sales to outside parties	$1,811	$812	$514	$309	$121	$99
Intersegment revenues	16	91	109	–0–	16	302
Salary expense	614	379	402	312	317	62
Rent expense	139	166	81	92	42	31
Interest expense	65	59	82	49	14	5
Income tax expense (savings)	141	87	61	(86)	(64)	–0–

Consider the following questions independently. None of the six segments has a primarily financial nature.

a. What minimum revenue amount must any one segment generate to be of significant size to require disaggregated disclosure?

b. If only Red, Blue, and Green necessitate separate disclosure, is Fairfield disclosing disaggregated data for enough segments?

c. What volume of revenues must a single customer generate to necessitate disclosing the existence of a major customer?

d. If each of these six segments has a profit or loss (in thousands) as follows, which warrants separate disclosure?

Red	$1,074	Pink	$(94)
Blue	449	Black	(222)
Green	140	White	308

LO 8-2

37. Mason Company has prepared consolidated financial statements for the current year and is now gathering information in connection with the following five operating segments it has identified.

Determine the reportable segments by performing each applicable test. Also describe the procedure utilized to ensure that a sufficient number of segments are being separately disclosed. (Figures are in thousands.)

	Company Total	Books	Computers	Maps	Travel	Finance
Sales to outside parties	$ 1,547	$ 121	$ 696	$ 416	$ 314	$ –0–
Intersegment sales	421	24	240	39	118	–0–
Interest income—external	97	60	–0–	–0–	–0–	37
Interest income—intersegment loans	147	–0–	–0–	–0–	–0–	147
Assets	3,398	206	1,378	248	326	1,240
Operating expenses	1,460	115	818	304	190	33

(continued)

(continued)

	Company Total	Books	Computers	Maps	Travel	Finance
Expenses—intersegment sales	198	70	51	31	46	–0–
Interest expense—external	107	–0–	–0–	–0–	–0–	107
Interest expense—intersegment loans	147	21	71	38	17	–0–
Income tax expense (savings)	21	12	(41)	27	31	(8)
General corporate expenses	55					
Unallocated operating costs	80					

LO 8-4

38. **Taft Corporation operates primarily in the United States. However, a few years ago it opened a plant in Spain to produce merchandise to sell there. This foreign operation has been so successful that during the past 24 months the company started a manufacturing plant in Italy and another in Greece. Financial information for each of these facilities follows:**

	Spain	Italy	Greece
Sales	$175,000	$600,000	$450,000
Intersegment transfers	–0–	100,000	60,000
Operating expenses	172,000	206,000	190,000
Interest expense	16,000	29,000	19,000
Income taxes	67,000	19,000	34,000
Long-lived assets	91,000	150,000	100,000

The company's domestic (U.S.) operations reported the following information for the current year:

Sales to unaffiliated customers	$ 4,500,000
Intersegment transfers	427,000
Operating expenses	2,410,000
Interest expense	136,000
Income taxes	819,000
Long-lived assets	2,200,000

Taft has adopted the following criteria for determining the materiality of an individual foreign country: (1) Sales to unaffiliated customers within a country are 10 percent or more of consolidated sales or (2) long-lived assets within a country are 10 percent or more of consolidated long-lived assets.

Apply Taft's materiality tests to identify the countries to report separately with respect to (a) revenues and (b) long-lived assets.

LO 8-6

39. **Noventis Corporation prepared the following estimates for the four quarters of the current year:**

	First Quarter	Second Quarter	Third Quarter	Fourth Quarter
Sales	$1,300,000	$1,560,000	$1,820,000	$2,080,000
Cost of goods sold	430,000	510,000	580,000	630,000
Administrative costs	310,000	185,000	190,000	200,000
Advertising costs	–0–	100,000	–0–	–0–
Executive bonuses	–0–	–0–	–0–	76,000
Provision for bad debts	–0–	–0–	–0–	64,000
Annual maintenance costs	72,000	–0–	–0–	–0–

Additional Information

- **First-quarter administrative costs include the $160,000 annual insurance premium.**
- **Advertising costs paid in the second quarter relate to television advertisements that will be broadcast throughout the entire year.**

- No special items affect income during the year.
- Noventis estimates an effective income tax rate for the year of 40 percent.

a. Assuming that actual results do *not* vary from the estimates provided, determine the amount of net income to be reported each quarter of the current year.

b. Assume that actual results do *not* vary from the estimates provided except for that in the third quarter, the estimated annual effective income tax rate is revised downward to 38 percent. Determine the amount of net income to be reported each quarter of the current year.

LO 8-6

40. Cambi Company began operations on January 1, 2016. In the second quarter of 2017, it adopted the FIFO method of inventory valuation. In the past, it used the LIFO method. The company's interim income statements as originally reported under the LIFO method follow:

	2016				2017
	1stQ	2ndQ	3rdQ	4thQ	1stQ
Sales.	$10,000	$12,000	$14,000	$16,000	$18,000
Cost of goods sold (LIFO)	4,000	5,000	5,800	7,000	8,500
Operating expenses . . .	2,000	2,200	2,600	3,000	3,200
Income before income taxes.	$ 4,000	$ 4,800	$ 5,600	$ 6,000	$ 6,300
Income taxes (40%)	1,600	1,920	2,240	2,400	2,520
Net income	$ 2,400	$ 2,880	$ 3,360	$ 3,600	$ 3,780

If the FIFO method had been used since the company began operations, cost of goods sold in each of the previous quarters would have been as follows:

	2016				2017
	1stQ	2ndQ	3rdQ	4thQ	1stQ
Cost of goods sold (FIFO). .	$ 3,800	$ 4,600	$ 5,200	$ 6,000	$ 7,400

Sales for the second quarter of 2017 are $20,000, cost of goods sold under the FIFO method is $9,000, and operating expenses are $3,400. The effective tax rate remains 40 percent. Cambi Company has 1,000 shares of common stock outstanding.

Prepare a schedule showing the calculation of net income and earnings per share that Cambi reports for the three-month period and the six-month period ended June 30, 2017.

LO 8-6

41. The following information for Dorado Corporation relates to the three-month period ending September 30.

	Units	Price per Unit
Sales.	425,000	$36
Beginning inventory	35,000	18
Purchases	400,000	24
Ending inventory	10,000	?

Dorado expects to purchase 150,000 units of inventory in the fourth quarter of the current calendar year at a cost of $25 per unit, and to have on hand 40,000 units of inventory at year-end. Dorado uses the last-in, first-out (LIFO) method to account for inventory costs.

Determine the cost of goods sold and gross profit amounts Dorado should record for the three months ending September 30. Prepare journal entries to reflect these amounts.

Develop Your Skills

RESEARCH CASE 1—SEGMENT REPORTING

CPA skills

Many companies make annual reports available on their corporate web page, often under an Investors tab. Annual reports also can be accessed through the SEC's EDGAR system at www.sec.gov (under Filings, click Company Filings Search, type in Company Name, and under Filing Type, search for 10-K).

Access the most recent annual report for a company with which you are familiar to complete the following requirements.

Required

Prepare a one-page report describing your findings for the following:

1. The company's reported operating segments and whether they are based on product lines, geographic areas, or some other basis.
2. The importance of each operating segment for the company as a whole in terms of revenues, income, and assets.
3. Whether the company provides any enterprisewide disclosures in addition to disclosures related to its operating segments.
4. Whether the company provides disclosures about major customers.

RESEARCH CASE 2—INTERIM REPORTING

CPA skills

Many companies make quarterly reports available on their corporate web page. Quarterly reports also can be accessed through the SEC's EDGAR system at www.sec.gov (under Filings, click Company Filings Search, type in Company Name, and under Filing Type, search for 10-Q).

Access the most recent quarterly report for a company with which you are familiar to complete the following requirements.

Required

Prepare a one-page report describing your findings for the following:

1. Whether the company provides the minimum disclosures required for interim reports.
2. Any disclosures the company provides that exceed the minimum disclosures required.
3. The various year-to-year comparisons that can be made using the disclosures provided in the quarterly report.

RESEARCH CASE 3—OPERATING SEGMENTS

CPA skills

Many companies make annual reports available on their corporate Internet home page. Annual reports also can be accessed through the SEC's EDGAR system at www.sec.gov (under Filings, click Company Filings Search, type in Company Name, and under Filing Type, search for 10-K). Access the most recent annual report for each of the following companies to complete the requirements:

Abbott Laboratories
Eaton
General Electric
United Technologies

Required

Prepare a one-page report summarizing your findings for the following:

1. The two most important operating segments in terms of percentage of total revenues.
2. The two operating segments with the largest growth in revenues.
3. The two most profitable operating segments in terms of profit margin.

RESEARCH CASE 4—COMPARABILITY OF GEOGRAPHIC AREA INFORMATION

CPA skills

Many companies make annual reports available on their corporate Internet home page. Annual reports also can be accessed through the SEC's EDGAR system at www.sec.gov (under Filings, click Company Filings Search, type in Company Name, and under Filing Type, search for 10-K). Access the most recent annual report for each of the following companies:

Bristol-Myers Squibb
Eli Lilly
Merck
Pfizer

Required

Prepare a one-page report describing the extent to which direct comparisons can be made of the geographic area information provided by these companies.

EVALUATION CASE—OPERATING SEGMENT DISCLOSURES

CPA skills

Corcoran Heavy Industries Company (CHIC) is organized into four divisions, each of which operates in a different industry. The types of customer served and the method used to distribute products differ across all four of these industries. In addition, each division must comply with its own unique set of industry regulations related to issues such as safety and recyclability of materials.

Operating profit before depreciation and amortization is the measure of profit regularly used by the chief operating decision maker for evaluating the performance of each of these divisions. In addition, information for each division on capital expenditures and depreciation and amortization is routinely provided by corporate headquarters to the chief operating decision maker. A summary of the information provided to the chief operating decision maker at the end of the current year is as follows:

	Division				
($ in thousands)	Automobiles	Trucks	Helicopters	Ships	Total
Sales to outside parties	**$4,007,304**	**$3,796,432**	**$1,411,235**	**$1,003,809**	**$10,218,780**
Intersegment sales	644,243	307,982	—	—	952,225
Total sales	$ 4,651,547	$ 4,104,414	$ 1,411,235	$ 1,003,809	$ 11,171,005
Operating expenses—external	3,480,666	3,147,086	1,004,464	958,743	8,590,959
Operating expense—internal	289,589	500,798	57,893	103,945	952,225
Operating profit before depreciation and amortization	$ 881,292	$ 456,530	$ 348,878	$ (58,879)	$ 1,627,821
Depreciation and amortization	180,345	170,976	97,638	58,617	507,576
Interest expense					130,655
Income before tax					$ 989,590
Income taxes					376,044
Profit (loss)					$ 613,546
Segment assets	**$3,987,776**	**$3,209,078**	**$1,587,006**	**$1,209,970**	**$ 9,993,830**
Corporate headquarters assets					1,008,988
Total assets					$ 11,002,818
Capital expenditures	$ 349,776	$ 365,543	$ 276,655	$ 23,695	$ 1,015,669

In compiling notes to the financial statements, CHIC's accountants prepared the following Note to comply with the operating segment disclosure requirements of ASC Topic 280, "Segment Reporting."

Note X. Operating Segments

($ in thousands)	Automobiles	Trucks	Other
Revenues	$4,651,547	$4,104,414	$2,415,044
Segment Profit (Loss)	$ 881,292	$ 456,530	$ 289,999
Assets	$3,987,776	$3,209,078	$2,796,976

Required

1. Prepare a report for CHIC's management evaluating whether the operating segments disclosures prepared by CHIC's accountants comply with ASC 280.
2. Prepare a revised operating segments note to comply with ASC 280. CHIC does not have any unusual or extraordinary items, significant noncash items other than depreciation and amortization, or equity method affiliates.

ACCOUNTING STANDARDS CASE 1—SEGMENT REPORTING

CPA skills

Nuland International Corporation recently acquired 40 percent of Scott Trading Company and appropriately accounts for this investment under the equity method. Nuland's corporate controller is in the process of determining the company's operating segments for purposes of preparing financial statements for the current year. He has determined that the investment in Scott meets the definition of an operating segment (i.e., Scott earns revenues and incurs expenses, Nuland's chief operating officer regularly reviews Scott's operating results, and Scott provides Nuland with a complete set of financial statements). However, because Nuland does not control Scott, the controller is not sure whether the investment in Scott can be considered a separate operating segment.

Required

Search current U.S. authoritative accounting literature to determine whether an equity method investment can be treated as an operating segment for financial reporting purposes. If so, explain the conditions under which this would be possible. Identify the source of guidance for answering this question.

ACCOUNTING STANDARDS CASE 2—INTERIM REPORTING

CPA skills

Caplan Pharma, Inc., recently was sued by a competitor for possible infringement of the competitor's patent on a top-selling flu vaccine. The plaintiff is suing for damages of $15 million. Caplan's CFO has discussed the case with legal counsel, who believes it is possible that Caplan will not be able to successfully defend the lawsuit. The CFO knows that current U.S. accounting guidelines require that contingencies (such as lawsuits) must be disclosed in the annual report when a loss is possible. However, she is unsure whether this rule must be applied in the preparation of interim financial statements. She also knows that disclosure is necessary only if the amount is material, but she is unsure whether materiality should be assessed in relation to results for the interim period or for the entire year.

Required

Search current U.S. accounting standards to determine whether contingencies are required to be disclosed in interim reports, and, if so, how materiality is to be determined. Identify the source of guidance for answering these questions.

ANALYSIS CASE 1—WALMART INTERIM AND SEGMENT REPORTING

CPA skills

The following information was extracted from quarterly reports for Wal-Mart Stores, Inc. (amounts in millions):

	Three Months Ended April 30		Three Months Ended July 31		Three Months Ended October 31	
Segment Operating Income	**2014**	**2013**	**2014**	**2013**	**2014**	**2013**
Walmart U.S.	$4,975	$5,197	$5,252	$5,383	$4,932	$4,991
Walmart International.	1,202	1,163	1,489	1,379	1,430	1,379
Sam's Club	479	490	494	518	493	440

The following information was extracted from the notes to the financial statements in the Wal-Mart Stores, Inc., Annual Report (for the fiscal year ended January 31, 2015, amounts in millions):

14 Segments Fiscal Year Ended January 31, 2015

	Walmart U.S.	Walmart International	Sam's Club	Corporate and Support	Consolidated
Net sales	$288,049	$136,160	$58,020	—	$482,229
Operating income (loss).	21,336	6,171	1,976	(2,336)	27,147
Total assets.	101,381	80,505	13,995	7,825	203,706

16 Quarterly Financial Data (Unaudited) (amounts in millions except per share data)

	Fiscal Year Ended January 31, 2015			
	Q1	Q2	Q3	Q4
Net sales	$114,167	$119,336	$118,076	$130,650
Cost of sales	86,714	90,010	89,247	99,115
Income from continuing operations	3,711	4,089	3,826	5,188

Required

1. Assess the seasonal nature of Walmart's sales and income for the company as a whole and by operating segment.
2. Assess Walmart's profitability by quarter and by operating segment.

ANALYSIS CASE 2—COCA-COLA OPERATING SEGMENT INFORMATION

CPA *skills*

The Coca-Cola Company is organized geographically and defines reportable operating segments as regions of the world. The following information was extracted from Note 19 Operating Segments in the Coca-Cola Company 2014 Annual Report:

Information about our Company's operations by operating segment for the years ended December 31, 2014, 2013, and 2012, is as follows (in millions):

	Eurasia & Africa	Europe	Latin America	North America	Asia Pacific	Bottling Investments	Corporate	Eliminations	Consolidated
2014									
Net operating revenues:									
Third party	$2,730	$4,844	$4,597	$21,462	$5,257	$6,972	$ 136	$ —	$45,998
Intersegment	—	692	60	17	489	67	—	(1,325)	—
Total net revenues	2,730	5,536	4,657	21,479	5,746	7,039	136	(1,325)	45,998
Operating income (loss)	1,084	2,852	2,316	2,447	2,448	9	(1,448)	—	9,708
Interest income	—	—	—	—	—	—	594	—	594
Interest expense	—	—	—	—	—	—	483	—	483
Depreciation and amortization	47	75	56	1,195	96	315	192	—	1,976
Equity income (loss)—net	35	31	10	(16)	12	691	6	—	769
Income (loss) before income taxes	1,125	2,892	2,319	1,633	2,464	715	(1,823)	—	9,325
Identifiable operating assets	1,298	3,358	2,426	33,066	1,793	6,975	29,482	—	78,398
Investments	1,081	90	757	48	157	8,781	2,711	—	13,625
Capital expenditures	30	54	55	1,293	76	628	270	—	2,406
2013									
Net operating revenues:									
Third party	$2,763	$4,645	$4,748	$21,574	$5,372	$7,598	$ 154	$ —	$46,854
Intersegment	—	689	191	16	497	78	—	(1,471)	—
Total net revenues	2,763	5,334	4,939	21,590	5,869	7,676	154	(1,471)	46,854
Operating income (loss)	1,087	2,859	2,908	2,432	2,478	115	(1,651)	—	10,228
Interest income	—	—	—	—	—	—	534	—	534
Interest expense	—	—	—	—	—	—	463	—	463
Depreciation and amortization	42	86	58	1,192	130	335	134	—	1,977
Equity income (loss)—net	22	24	13	2	19	524	(2)	—	602
Income (loss) before income taxes	1,109	2,923	2,920	2,434	2,494	679	(1,082)	—	11,477
Identifiable operating assets	1,273	3,713	2,918	33,964	1,922	7,011	27,742	—	78,543
Investments	1,157	106	545	49	143	9,424	88	—	11,512
Capital expenditures	40	34	63	1,374	117	643	279	—	2,550
2012									
Net operating revenues:									
Third party	$2,697	$4,481	$4,560	$21,665	$5,680	$8,807	$ 127	$ —	$48,017
Intersegment	—	642	271	15	628	88	—	(1,644)	—
Total net revenues	2,697	5,123	4,831	21,680	6,308	8,895	127	(1,644)	48,017
Operating income (loss)	1,078	2,960	2,879	2,597	2,516	140	(1,391)	—	10,779
Interest income	—	—	—	—	—	—	471	—	471
Interest expense	—	—	—	—	—	—	397	—	397
Depreciation and amortization	33	100	70	1,083	119	406	171	—	1,982
Equity income (loss)—net	20	45	4	13	2	732	3	—	819
Income (loss) before income taxes	1,101	3,015	2,882	2,624	2,523	904	(1,240)	—	11,809
Identifiable operating assets	1,299	2,976	2,759	34,114	2,163	9,648	22,767	—	75,726
Investments	1,155	271	539	39	127	8,253	64	—	10,448
Capital expenditures	51	30	88	1,447	107	867	190	—	2,780

Required

1. Calculate the following measures for each of Coca-Cola's operating segments (excluding Bottling Investments and Corporate):

   Percentage of total net revenues, 2013 and 2014.

   Percentage change in total net revenues, 2012 to 2013 and 2013 to 2014.

   Operating income as a percentage of total net revenues (profit margin), 2013 and 2014.
2. Determine whether you believe Coca-Cola should attempt to expand its operations in a particular region of the world to increase operating revenues and operating income.
3. List any additional information you would like to have to conduct your analysis.

CPSIA information can be obtained
at www.ICGtesting.com
Printed in the USA
FFOW02n0005230717
37941FF

MGH0000079024